The BiblioPlan Companion, Year Three: A Text for

EARLY MODERN HISTORY

U.S. and World History from 1600 – 1850

with Missionary Highlights and U.S. Geography

VOLUME TWO

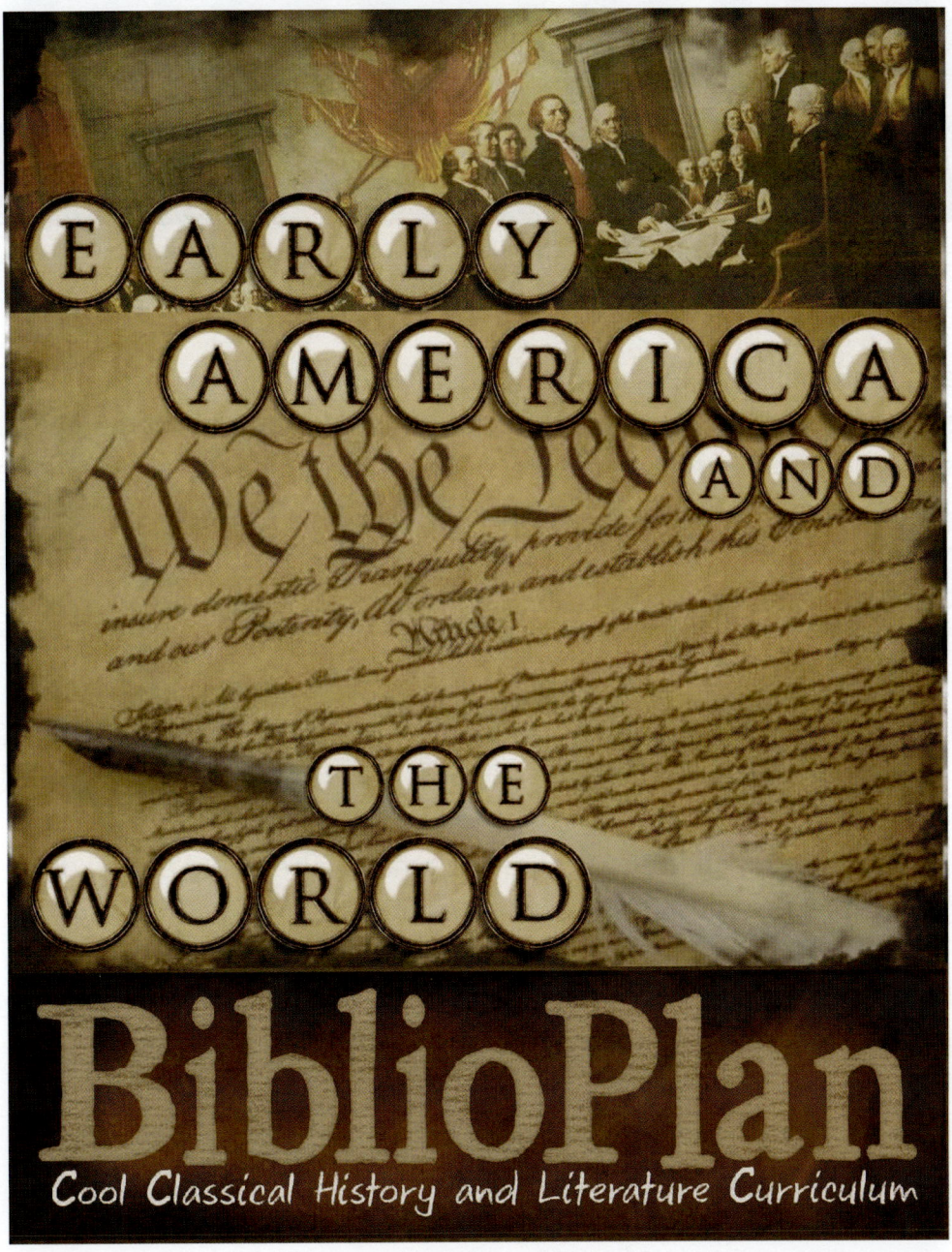

by Rob and Julia Nalle

Copyright ©2014, Rob and Julia Nalle. All rights reserved.
Printed in the USA.

Published in Palmyra, Virginia by BiblioPlan for Families.

ISBN 978-1-942405-00-9

BIBLIOPLAN COPYRIGHT POLICY

All of the text, reading lists, explanations, directions, schedules, questions, maps and other content contained in these pages are copyrighted materials owned by BiblioPlan for Families. Please DO NOT reproduce any of these materials on websites or e-mail.

Families who purchase these materials may make as many copies of the Cool History assignments, Maps, Timelines or Coloring Books as they need for use WITHIN THEIR FAMILY ONLY.

Co-ops and schools MAY NOT photocopy, e-mail or reproduce ANY of BiblioPlan's materials.

Co-ops and schools who wish to use BiblioPlan's materials should e-mail us at contactus@biblioplan.net for bulk purchasing options.

Please see BiblioPlan's website at www.biblioplan.net or email contactus@biblioplan.net to let us know how we may best serve your family, co-op or school.

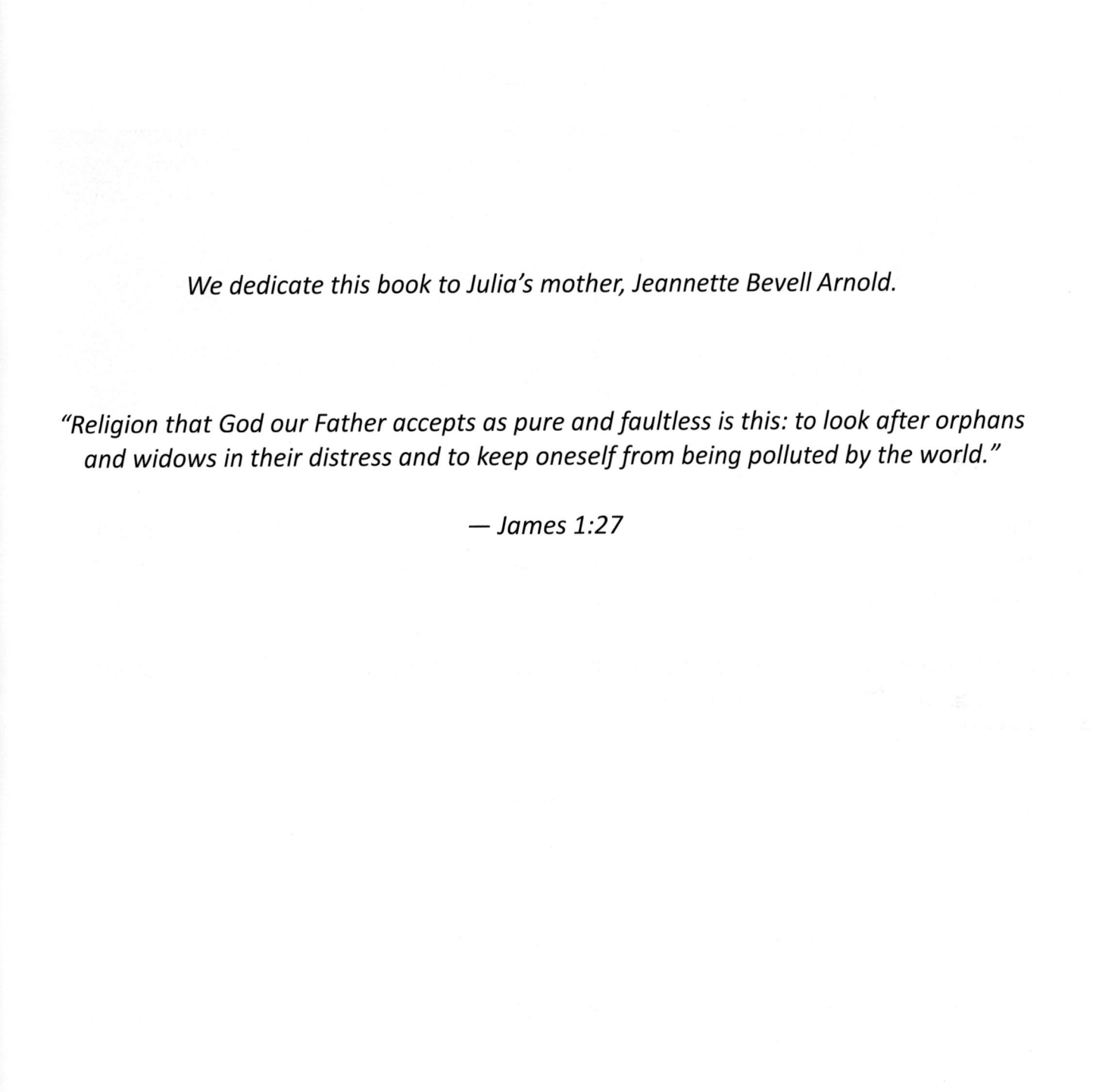

We dedicate this book to Julia's mother, Jeannette Bevell Arnold.

"Religion that God our Father accepts as pure and faultless is this: to look after orphans and widows in their distress and to keep oneself from being polluted by the world."

— James 1:27

Table of Contents for Volume Two

WHAT HAS GONE BEFORE: A Brief Review of Medieval History from the Fall of Rome Through the Age of Discovery Vol. 1	**CHAPTER 19:** The Great Awakening, Part Two; the French and Indian War 445
CHAPTER 1: The Spanish Empire in the New World Vol. 1	**CHAPTER 20:** The Seven Years' War; Catherine the Great 471
CHAPTER 2: The Scottish Reformation; the Dutch Revolt Vol. 1	**CHAPTER 21:** The Declaration of Independence 496
CHAPTER 3: The Union of the Crowns; Jamestown, Part One Vol. 1	**CHAPTER 22:** The American Revolutionary War 524
CHAPTER 4: Jamestown, Part Two Vol. 1	**CHAPTER 23:** The Constitution of the United States of America 551
CHAPTER 5: New France; the Iroquois Confederacy Vol. 1	**CHAPTER 24:** Australia and New Zealand 577
CHAPTER 6: Puritans and Separatists; Plymouth Colony Vol. 1	**CHAPTER 25:** The French Revolution 602
CHAPTER 7: New Netherland; the Thirty Years' War Vol. 1	**CHAPTER 26:** The Whiskey Rebellion; Napoleon's Rise 627
CHAPTER 8: The Puritan Migration; the English Civil War Vol. 1	**CHAPTER 27:** The First Party System; the Louisiana Purchase 652
CHAPTER 9: Church and State in New England; the Peace of Westphalia Vol. 1	**CHAPTER 28:** The War of 1812; Napoleon's Fall 679
CHAPTER 10: More English Colonies; the Restoration of the Monarchy Vol. 1	**CHAPTER 29:** The Congress of Vienna; More Atlantic Revolutions 707
CHAPTER 11: Bacon's Rebellion; King Philip's War Vol. 1	**CHAPTER 30:** The Indian Removal Act; the Industrial Revolution 734
CHAPTER 12: Freedom of Religion for the Middle Colonies; the Glorious Revolution Vol. 1	**CHAPTER 31:** The British Empire in India and China 760
CHAPTER 13: China; the Covenanter Martyrs Vol. 1	**CHAPTER 32:** The Abolitionist Movement; the Boers in South Africa 786
CHAPTER 14: Japan; the Salem Witch Trials Vol. 1	**CHAPTER 33:** The Mexican War of Independence; the Mexican-American War 813
CHAPTER 15: India; the Golden Age of Piracy Vol. 1	**CHAPTER 34:** California; the Second Great Awakening 838
CHAPTER 16: The Ottoman Empire; Slavery in the Colonies Vol. 1	**IMAGE CREDITS** 863
CHAPTER 17: Russia; More French Explorers Vol. 1	**BIBLIOGRAPHY** 865
CHAPTER 18: The Rise of Prussia; the Great Awakening, Part One Vol. 1	**INDEX** 878

CHAPTER 19: The Great Awakening, Part Two; the French and Indian War

U.S. HISTORY FOCUS, PART ONE

Founding Georgia

The last of the original Thirteen Colonies, Georgia, was the special project of James Oglethorpe.

> BRILLIANT BRITONS: James Edward Oglethorpe (1696 – 1785)
>
> James Oglethorpe was a Member of Parliament with a zeal for reforming British law, especially laws that punished poor Britons who couldn't pay their debts. The Britain of Oglethorpe's day was extremely hard on debtors: for failing to pay the smallest of debts, courts often sent debtors to notoriously miserable debtors' prisons like Fleet Prison, Marshalsea or the Clink. Because being imprisoned made it even more difficult to earn money, few inmates ever left debtors' prison without help from outside.
>
> Oglethorpe belonged to the **Country Party**, a group of reform-minded politicians who wanted to right a number of wrongs in Britain:
>
> - They wanted Britain's prisons to focus on reforming their inmates, not on punishing them mercilessly.
>
> - They wanted to reform Britain's corrupt government, which so often favored the rich over the poor.
>
> - They wanted their government to help poor Britons overcome their desperate circumstances.
>
> - They wanted more Britons to have the dignity that came with landownership. Country Party men hated the indignity that came with being crowded into a large, industrialized city. They wanted Britons to work their own land, rather than flocking to cities to find anonymous, menial jobs.

Portrait of James Oglethorpe

Robert Castell (d. 1729)

Part of James Oglethorpe's zeal for reform sprang from his friendship with Robert Castell, a gifted architect/author with a regrettable habit of spending more than he earned. Castell hoped to pay off his debts by selling a work he wrote on classical architecture; but unfortunately, the cost of printing the work only added to his debts. In 1728, six years after Oglethorpe won election to Parliament, a judge sent Castell to London's Fleet Prison for failing to pay his debts.

Like most British prisons of its day, the Fleet was a for-profit business operated by corrupt wardens— greedy prison bosses who aimed not to reform their inmates, but to squeeze as much money out of them as possible. Despite its inmates' debts, the Fleet demanded payment for room, board (food) and special privileges; and if they couldn't pay, then their wardens sent them to live in the filthiest cells with the sickest inmates. When Robert Castell couldn't afford any special privileges, his warden placed him with a cellmate who was

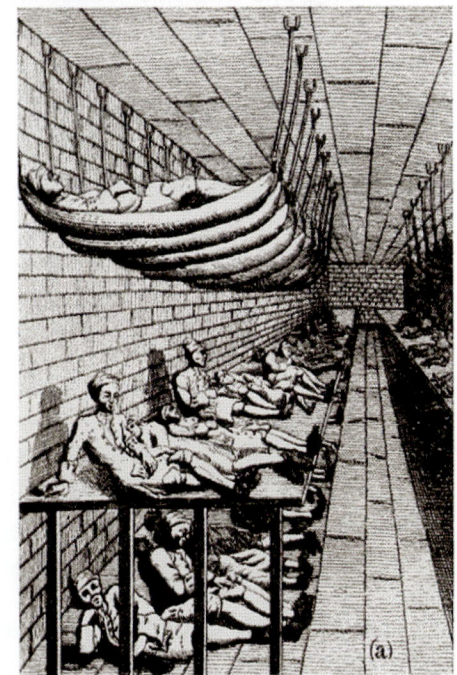
Illustration of Marshalsea Prison's sick ward

dying of smallpox. Thus for the crime of falling behind on his bills, a fine young man who should have enjoyed a long, successful career as an architect instead died of smallpox.

FASCINATING FACTS: Charles Dickens' Personal Experience with Marshalsea Prison

Marshalsea Prison in the early 1700s

The life of English author Charles Dickens (1812 – 1870)— author of *Great Expectations*, *A Tale of Two Cities* and other classics— was forever changed by his experience with England's cruel prison system. When Charles was 12 years old, a judge sent his father to Marshalsea for failing to pay a small debt he owed a local baker. For several months in 1824, one of London's ugliest prisons served as Dickens' family home.

Like the Fleet, Marshalsea was a for-profit business that demanded rent from its inmates. To earn this rent, Charles' parents stopped sending him to school, and instead sent him to work in a shoe polish factory. There the 12-year-old Charles spent ten hours per day, six days per week wrapping jars in colorful paper and pasting labels on them. The six shillings Charles earned each week helped persuade the warden not to send his family to Marshalsea's worst cells.

Unlike most debtors' stories, the Dickens family's had a happy ending. After a few months in Marshalsea, one of Charles' father's relatives died, leaving him an inheritance that allowed him to pay off his debts and free his family. Even so, Charles' close scrape with poverty gave him a lifelong understanding of the problems of the poor— an understanding that appeared in *Oliver Twist*, *David Copperfield* and other Dickens novels.

The Charter of Georgia

James Oglethorpe's strategy for righting wrongs like the ones Robert Castell suffered was an idealistic one: instead of sending debtors to prison, Oglethorpe wanted to help them work off their debts. Oglethorpe's plan was to build a special new colony for the "worthy poor"— hardworking citizens whose poverty was no fault of their own, and who only needed new opportunities to get back on their feet.

In 1730, Oglethorpe and his Country Party allies asked King George II for permission to build such a colony south of the Carolinas. George II's answer was the Charter of Georgia, issued in 1732.

ILLUMINATING EXCERPTS from King George II's Charter of Georgia (1732)

- "Whereas we are credibly informed, that many of our poor subjects are, through misfortunes and want of employment, reduced to great necessity… and if they had means to defray their charges of passage… they would be glad to settle in any of our provinces in America where by cultivating the lands, at present waste and desolate, they might not only gain a comfortable subsistence for themselves and families, but also strengthen our colonies and increase the trade, navigation and wealth of these our realms."

- "And whereas our provinces in North America, have been frequently ravaged by Indian enemies… And whereas we think it highly becoming our crown and royal dignity, to protect all our loving subjects, be they ever so distant from us; to extend our fatherly compassion even to the meanest and most unfortunate of our people, and to relieve the wants of our above mentioned poor subjects; and that it will be highly conducive for accomplishing those ends, that a regular colony of the said poor people be settled and established in the southern territories of Carolina."

In other words, Georgia began as a social experiment with three goals: (1) providing opportunities for the worthy poor; (2) boosting British trade; and (3) defending the Carolinas' southern border. Because Georgia began as a social experiment to benefit the poor, its leaders and citizens agreed to abide by unusual rules:

- **Georgia was to have no large cities teeming with masses of demeaned poor**. Instead, Georgia was to have only towns and villages where small landowners could live with dignity. Each townsman was to receive two plots of land: a 60' x 90' plot in town for his house, and 50 acres in the countryside for his farm. Each villager was to receive one plot of 50 acres to contain both house and farm.

- **Georgia was to have no large landowners, and no absentee landlords**. Each man was to work his own farm, or have his hired servant work it for him; and no man could divide his farm for sale, nor combine it with other farms to make a larger farm, without special permission from Georgia's trustees (caretakers).

- **Georgia was to have no slaves**. Slave labor ran counter to Oglethorpe's vision, which was for small landowners to work their own farms. There was also the danger that slaves who ran away from Georgia might join Britain's enemies, either the Spanish or the natives.

- **Georgians were not to trade with the natives without a license**. The idea was to labor for oneself, not to exploit the labor of others through trade.

- **Georgia was to have no rum;** for drunkenness was one of the main difficulties that kept the poor in poverty.

In late 1732, Oglethorpe landed at Charles Town, South Carolina accompanied by his first 100 or so colonists. Then in 1733, Oglethorpe laid out Georgia's first British town, Savannah, on a bluff about 15 miles from the mouth of the Savannah River. By agreement, Georgia's early colonists worked on the colony's defenses for one year before starting work on their own farms.

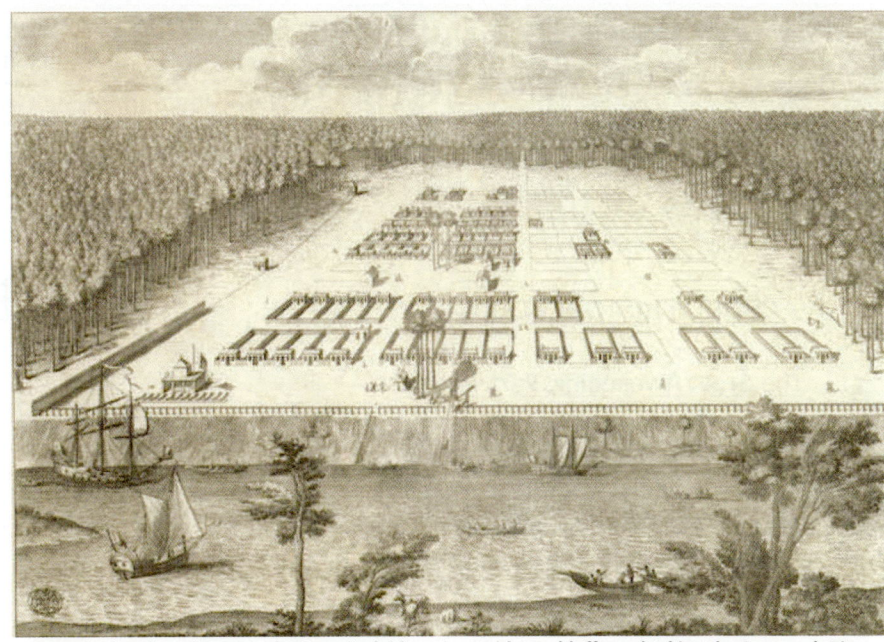
An early drawing of Savannah, Georgia, laid out in a grid on a bluff overlooking the Savannah River

The End of the Experiment
Sadly, Oglethorpe's idealistic social experiment lasted only a few years before difficulties began to tear it down. As early as 1738, Georgia colonists were already complaining that:

1. Georgia couldn't succeed without slave labor— not when other colonies nearby used slaves so freely. Aided by cheap slave labor, South Carolinians could sell crops and timber for far lower prices than Georgians could.
2. Georgia's ban on trade with the natives blocked Georgians from entering profitable businesses.
3. Georgia's strict landownership laws meant that Georgians couldn't sell their land easily— and therefore couldn't use their land as collateral for the loans they needed to do business.

Goaded by such complaints, Georgia gradually relaxed its strict laws. Oglethorpe's social experiment essentially ended in 1752— the year the 21-year Charter of Georgia expired, and Georgia became a regular Crown colony. By that time, Georgia's laws were much like the other southern colonies'.

REFRESHING REVIEWS: The Thirteen Colonies and Their Origins

Colony[1]	Founding Date	English / British Founders
Virginia	1607	The Virginia Company of London under King James I
Massachusetts	1620 – 1630	Pilgrims at Plymouth (1620), Puritans at Massachusetts Bay (1630)
New Hampshire	1623	Captain John Mason
Maryland	1634	Cecilius Calvert, Lord Baltimore under King Charles I
Connecticut	1634 – 1636	Thomas Hooker and others
Rhode Island	1636	Roger Williams
North Carolina	1663	The Lords Proprietor of Carolina under King Charles II
South Carolina	1663	
New York	1664	James, Duke of York[2]
New Jersey	1664	George Carteret and John Berkeley under James, Duke of York[2,3]
Pennsylvania	1682	William Penn
Delaware	1704	William Penn[2,3] (1704 was the year when Delaware's legislature broke away from Pennsylvania's)
Georgia	1732	James Oglethorpe under King George II

[1] Neither Maine nor Vermont was among the original Thirteen Colonies. After the French and Indian War, New York and New Hampshire battled over the territory that is now Vermont; Vermont declared independence from both during the Revolutionary War, and joined the Union in 1791 as the 14th state. Massachusetts governed the District of Maine until Maine joined the Union in 1820 as the 23rd state.
[2] Parts of New York, New Jersey and Delaware began as the Dutch colony of New Netherland.
[3] Parts of Delaware and New Jersey began as the Swedish colony of New Sweden.

CHURCH HISTORY FOCUS

The Great Awakening, Part Two

James Oglethorpe's social experiment in Georgia attracted the interest of three more heroes of the Great Awakening: Count Nicolaus Zinzendorf, John Wesley and Charles Wesley.

GIANTS OF THE FAITH: Count Nicolaus Zinzendorf (1700 – 1760), Leader of the Moravian Revival

REFRESHING REMINDERS from Chapter 7:
- The Moravian Brethren were an early Protestant church that developed in the Czech-speaking kingdoms of Moravia, Bohemia and Silesia under the ministry of Jan Hus (1369 – 1415, see Year Two).

- In a 1618 act of defiance called the Defenestration of Prague, a band of Moravian Brethren heaved two of the Holy Roman Emperor's Catholic officials out of a high window in Prague, Bohemia— thus launching the Bohemian Revolt, the first phase of the terrible Thirty Years' War.

- After the emperor crushed the Bohemian Revolt, he banished the few surviving Moravian Brethren from all Habsburg lands. However, a tiny remnant of Moravian Brethren managed to hold onto their homes by worshipping in secret.

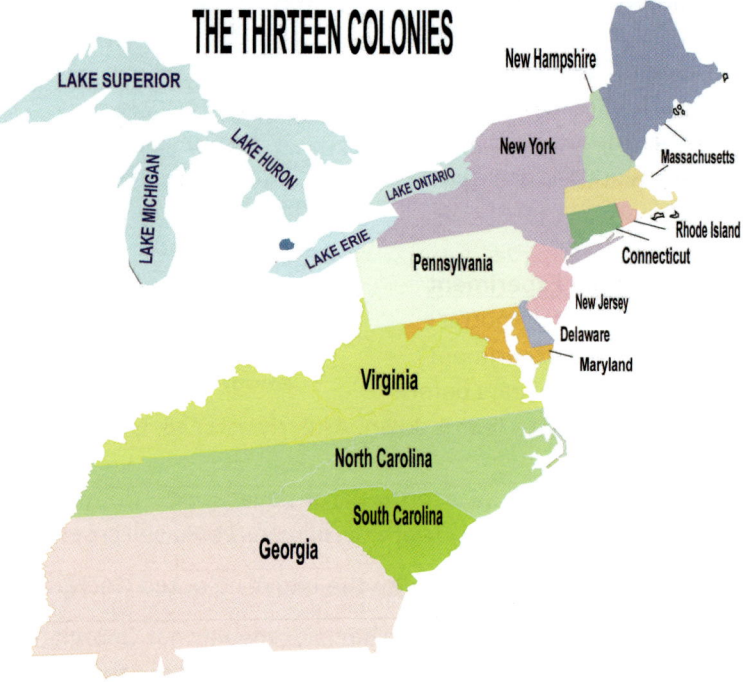
THE THIRTEEN COLONIES

> DEFINITION: The **Pietists** of the late 1600s and early 1700s were mostly German-speaking Lutherans who believed that the Lutheran church needed revival as badly as the Puritan church did. Pietists longed to revive their struggling church by focusing on the fruits of the Holy Spirit: "love, joy, peace, patience, kindness, goodness, faithfulness, gentleness and self-control" (Galatians 5:22-23).

Count Zinzendorf was a wealthy Pietist from Saxony, a part of the Holy Roman Empire that bordered Moravia. Like other Pietists, Zinzendorf longed to revive his Lutheran Church; but ironically, the church Zinzendorf ended up reviving was the Moravian Brethren.

In 1722, a wandering Moravian-born carpenter named Christian David asked Zinzendorf to help him ease the suffering of the few Moravian Brethren who still lived under the Habsburgs. David's plan was to lead a Moravian exodus— a migration of Moravian Brethren from the Habsburg kingdoms to Saxony, where they would be free to worship as they chose. With Zinzendorf's permission, David started work on the settlement of *Herrnhut*— German for "Lord's Cap"— atop a hill on Zinzendorf's Saxony estate. Over the next few years, David made several trips back and forth to Moravia, inviting more and more persecuted Moravian believers to come and share the haven of religious freedom he was building at Herrnhut.

Count Zinzendorf

Unfortunately, Herrnhut had a problem. By the 1720s, the Moravian Brethren had been living underground for a century, long enough to develop different beliefs. Therefore instead of becoming a harmonious community of like-minded believers, Herrnhut became a chaotic community of constant religious arguments.

The Moravian Pentecost (August 12 – 13, 1727)

Into the midst of this chaos strode the Pietist Count Zinzendorf. Determined to bring peace to Herrnhut, Zinzendorf started leading Bible studies with believers on all sides of every argument. Zinzendorf's studies focused on the Acts of the Apostles and the epistles of Paul— books that describe how the Christians of the early church lived together in peace and love, sacrificing themselves for one another. Under Zinzendorf's patient coaxing, the Moravian Brethren of Herrnhut confessed that they had failed to love one another. They also committed themselves to spend more time praying and studying their Bibles, and less time arguing.

On the evening of August 12, 1727, Count Zinzendorf called all 300 or so of Herrnhut's Moravian Brethren together for an all-night prayer vigil; and that night, the Holy Spirit descended on their church in a profound way. Like the Christians who first received the Holy Spirit at Pentecost (Acts 2), the Moravian Brethren felt God's presence that night as they had never felt it before, and prayed as they had never prayed before. According to Zinzendorf, the Moravian Pentecost brought "a Spirit of whom we had hitherto not had any experience or knowledge. Hitherto we [Zinzendorf and a few allies] had been the leaders and helpers. Now the Holy Spirit Himself took full control of everything and everybody."

Figurative image of Zinzendorf preaching to people of all nations

Guided by the Holy Spirit, the Moravian Brethren became well-known for three Godly qualities:

1. **A commitment to prayer.** Soon after the Moravian Pentecost, the Moravian Brethren started arranging their schedules so that at least three of them would be praying at all times, day and night. This was the beginning of a continuous prayer vigil that was to go on unbroken for over 100 years.

2. **A deep, abiding faith.** Moravian Brethren grew so confident in God's grace, goodness and providence that they never despaired, even when calamity struck.

3. **A commitment to sharing their faith around the world.** Long before most other churches, the Moravian Brethren sent out missionaries in all directions— including the direction of Georgia, where the first Moravians arrived in 1735 – 1736.

GIANTS OF THE FAITH: John Wesley (1703 – 1791) and Charles Wesley (1707 – 1788), Founders of Methodism

Aboard ship with the first Moravian missionaries to Georgia were two members of the Holy Club, the Oxford University club to which George Whitefield also belonged (see Chapter 18). John and Charles Wesley were both going to Georgia at James Oglethorpe's request: John was to minister in the new town of Savannah, while Charles was to add duties as Oglethorpe's secretary to his duties as a minister.

Although both Wesleys had been ministers for years before sailing for Georgia, both had a strong feeling that something was missing from the Anglican faith they had learned at Oxford. That feeling grew even stronger when they met the Moravian Brethren, whose deep, warm faith impressed everyone they met.

John Wesley preaching the Word

ILLUMINATING EXCERPTS from John Wesley's Journal

John Wesley was particularly impressed with the Moravians' faith when he attended one of their worship services aboard ship during a storm, as he recorded in his personal journal:

"In the midst of the Psalm wherewith their service began, the sea broke over, split the mainsail in pieces, covered the ship and poured in between the decks, as if the great deep had already swallowed us up. A terrible screaming began among the English... [but] the Germans calmly sung on. I asked one of them afterwards: 'Were you not afraid?' He answered, 'I thank God, no.' I asked: 'But were not your women and children afraid?' He replied mildly: 'No, our women and children are not afraid to die.'"

The Aldersgate Experience (May 24, 1738)

Perhaps because they were so uncertain about their faith, the Wesleys struggled in Georgia— so badly that within about two years, both returned to England in failure. Deeply depressed, and still uncertain what he believed, John sought help from the Moravian Brethren whose faith he had admired aboard ship. The Moravians offered John the advice of Martin Luther: to place his hope for salvation in Christ alone, not in any good works of his own. John finally understood this advice on May 24, 1738, the evening of his **Aldersgate Experience**:

"In the evening, I went very unwillingly to a society in Aldersgate Street, where one was reading Luther's preface to the Epistle to the Romans. About a quarter before nine, while he was describing the change which God works in the heart through faith in Christ, I felt my heart strangely warmed. I felt I did trust in Christ, Christ alone for salvation, and an assurance was given me that he had taken away my sins, even mine, and saved me from the law of sin and death."

Boosted by the confident faith he gained at Aldersgate, John began to preach with more conviction. After George Whitefield preached his first open-air sermon at Bristol in 1739, he invited John to preach in the open air as well; and soon John's ministry was growing as fast as Whitefield's. Like Whitefield, John Wesley went on to preach tens of thousands of sermons, and to log a fantastic number of miles as a traveling preacher— perhaps as many as 4,000 miles per year. However, Wesley and Whitefield had two important differences:

1. Unlike Whitefield, Wesley was an organizer as well as a preacher. John Wesley trained lay ministers to shepherd his converts; organized his converts into districts; set supervisors over each district; and did all the other things large church organizations do for individual churches. Although both Wesleys agonized over leaving the Anglican Church, they disagreed with their Anglican bishops so often that in the end, John formed a separate church: the Methodist Church.

2. Unlike Whitefield, who remained a strict Calvinist all his life, John Wesley leaned toward Arminianism (see Chapter 9). Where Whitefield emphasized God's sovereignty, Wesley emphasized perfecting oneself through holiness and good works, as reflected in his motto:

Charles Wesley

> "Do all the good you can, by all the means you can, in all the ways you can, in all the places you can, at all the times you can, to all the people you can, as long as ever you can."

Charles Wesley's conversion experience came three days before John's, on May 21, 1738. Where John was known for preaching sermons, Charles was better known for writing hymns. Many of the Christian church's gladdest, most honored hymns came from the pen of Charles Wesley, including all of these:

Arise My Soul Arise	And Can It Be that I Should Gain	Christ the Lord is Risen Today
Come Thou Long-Expected Jesus	Hark! The Herald Angels Sing	Jesus, Lover of My Soul
Love Divine, All Loves Excelling	O for a Thousand Tongues to Sing	Rejoice, the Lord is King

GIANTS OF THE FAITH: Susanna Wesley (1669 – 1742), "Mother of Methodism"

The Wesley brothers' father, Samuel Wesley, was an Anglican minister who was often away on church business, leaving his wife Susanna Wesley to raise and educate their children almost by herself.

During one long absence in 1711, Samuel Wesley assigned a curate named Inman to lead his church for him. Unfortunately, Inman turned out to be such a poor preacher that no one learned anything from him. Determined to provide good Christian teaching for her children, Susanna found a way to fill the gap herself: every Sunday after church, Susanna chose a sermon from her husband's library and read it to her children at a family service of her own.

When other church members heard about Susanna's skillfully-read sermons, they wanted to hear them too. Soon Susanna's services were drawing about 200 people each week, far more than Inman's. Enraged at being outdone by a woman, Inman wrote Samuel Wesley that his wife's preaching would surely cause a scandal in their church, and asked him to put a stop to it.

The first suggestion Samuel wrote to his wife was that some man should read the sermons for her. Susanna replied that there wasn't a single man in their church who could read a sermon without

Susanna Wesley

ruining it. When Inman continued to complain, Samuel finally wrote Susanna that he "desired" her to stop preaching. This time, Susanna responded with a long defense of all the good her services were doing in their church, closing her letter with this plea:

"If after all this you think fit to dissolve this assembly do not tell me you *desire* me to do it, for that will not satisfy my conscience; but send your positive command in such full and express terms as may absolve me from all guilt and punishment for neglecting this opportunity for doing good when you and I shall appear before the great and awful tribunal of our Lord Jesus Christ."

Like the Wesley brothers, the Moravian Brethren left Georgia within a few years, but for a different reason: because they were pacifists who refused to serve in the militia when the War of Jenkins' Ear began.

WORLD HISTORY FOCUS

REFRESHING REMINDERS: Four Major Wars in Europe and North America

European War	Dates	Corresponding American War(s)
1. War of the Grand Alliance	1688 – 1697	King William's War
2. War of the Spanish Succession	1701 – 1714	Queen Anne's War
3. War of the Austrian Succession	1739 – 1748	War of Jenkins' Ear / King George's War
4. Seven Years' War	1754 – 1763	French and Indian War

War Number Three, North and South American Theater: The War of Jenkins' Ear (1739 – 1748)

Opponents in North and South America: Britain versus Spain and France

Ended with the: Treaty of Aix-la-Chapelle (1748)

DEFINITION: The *Asiento* was a special trade monopoly granted by the Crown of Spain. The trading company that held the *Asiento* had exclusive permission to sell slaves to Spain's colonies in the Americas.

British Slave Traders in Spain's Colonies

Among the provisions in the Treaty of Utrecht, the treaty that ended the War of the Spanish Succession in 1714, was one in which Spain transferred the *Asiento* to Britain. Ordinarily, Spain allowed only Spanish or Portuguese traders to sell slaves at its American ports; but in the Treaty of Utrecht, Spain granted that profitable privilege to British traders. Over the next 25 years, Britain's South Sea Company would sell more than 30,000 African slaves at Spanish ports in the Americas.

However, the *Asiento* wasn't an unlimited monopoly; for the law set limits on the amounts of goods British traders could legally sell in Spain's colonies. To enforce those limits, Spanish coast guard captains took to boarding incoming British trade vessels and inspecting their holds before allowing them to land. Given the long history of hatred between Spanish and British sailors, these inspections were a recipe for disaster.

Robert Jenkins' Ear

Disaster struck in April 1731, when Spanish captain Julio Fandiño attacked the defenseless trade vessel of a British master mariner named Robert Jenkins. According to the British side of the story, Fandiño bullied Jenkins mercilessly, tying him to a mast while the coast guard searched his hold for smuggled goods. Even though Fandiño didn't find any evidence of smuggling, he still wanted to send a message to all British smugglers. Therefore Fandiño drew his cutlass, sliced off Jenkins' ear and handed it to him with a harsh warning— arrogantly adding that if King George had been aboard, then he would have sliced off the king's ear as well.

Years later, in 1738, Jenkins appeared before Britain's House of Commons to share his tale of brutal mistreatment at Spanish hands. By this time, trouble between Spanish and British ships had become so widespread that Parliament needed only a small push to drive it over the edge toward war. Goaded in part by the horrifying story of Jenkins' ear, Britain declared war on Spain in October 1739.

The War Begins

British Royal Navy Admiral Edward Vernon began the War of Jenkins' Ear with attacks on Spanish ports along the coasts of Central and South America—ports

Robert Jenkins, the wigless man at center left, shows his severed ear to British Prime Minister

where the Spanish Treasure Fleets still loaded their holds with American silver and gold every year. Vernon's first victory came at Portobello, a small Spanish port in what is now Panama.

INSPIRING ODES: "Rule, Britannia"

When patriotic Britons back home learned that Admiral Vernon had captured tiny, little-defended Portobello, they celebrated this minor victory as gladly as if they had won the war. British hearts swelled with pride as they imagined their great empire overspreading not only North America, but also Central America, South America and the West Indies.

Partly to celebrate Vernon's victory at Portobello, composer Thomas Arne and lyricist  James Thomson collaborated on a patriotic song titled "Rule, Brittania." Thomson's theme was that Britain's unstoppable mastery of the high seas had always saved her from tyrants like the ones who ruled Spain, and always would. Over the years, the chorus of Arne's tune became so well-known that great composers like Handel, Beethoven and Wagner all borrowed it for works of their own.

Britons' premature celebrations came to an abrupt end about 1-1/2 years after Portobello, when they learned that their proud navy had suffered one of its worst defeats ever. Admiral Vernon's plan for capturing the Spanish port of Cartagena de Indias— now Cartagena, Colombia— was to land several thousand marines equipped with long siege ladders for scaling the fortress's walls. When Vernon's marines landed, though, they found that the Spanish had dug deep trenches just outside their walls— which meant that Vernon's siege ladders were too short. With no way to climb, Vernon's marines could do little except stand helplessly while Cartagena's defenders tore them apart.

After the battle, an outbreak of yellow fever helped bring the total British dead at the disastrous Battle of Cartagena de Indias to somewhere near 10,000, with many thousands more sick or wounded.

OTHER INTERESTING FACTS about the War of Jenkins' Ear

British marines landing at the Battle of Cartagena de Indias

- Lawrence Washington, elder half-brother to George Washington, served under Admiral Edward Vernon at the terrible Battle of Cartagena de Indias. Even though the battle ended in disaster, and Lawrence nearly died of yellow fever, he remained so loyal to Vernon that he later renamed his Virginia estate "Mount Vernon."

- Georgia founder James Oglethorpe laid siege to St. Augustine, Spanish Florida in 1740, but failed to capture the fortress. A Spanish counter-invasion in 1742 failed as well.

- After a couple of years, the War of Jenkins' Ear merged into King George's War and the War of the Austrian Succession (see Chapter 18). Although these wars caused immeasurable suffering, little colonial territory changed hands in any permanent way.

BIBULOUS BEVERAGES: Grog

Admiral Edward Vernon was also well-known for changing the recipe for grog, the much-beloved alcoholic drink the British Royal Navy served its sailors twice each day.

Grog was the navy's answer to the problem of storing fresh water for its sailors to drink on long voyages. Because fresh water tended to go stagnant and foul-tasting when stored for more than a few days, the navy found a way to sweeten its water: by mixing in a bit of rum. Diluted at the rate of ½-pint of rum to 1 quart of water, grog contained enough alcohol to keep sailors happy, but not enough to cause problems with drunkenness. By regulation, British Royal Navy sailors received their carefully-measured ration of grog every day for more than two centuries, from 1756 – 1970.

Admiral Vernon's contribution to the grog recipe was to add citrus juices like lime and lemon, thus sweetening it even further. Soon after Vernon started adding citrus to his grog, navy doctors noticed that Vernon's sailors stayed healthier than other commanders' on long voyages. In 1747, inspired by Vernon's success, navy Doctor James Lind conducted an experiment which proved that citrus fruits were the perfect cure for scurvy.

Other interesting facts:
- Almost two centuries after Dr. Lind's experiment, doctors discovered why citrus cures scurvy: because it is rich in vitamin C.
- The name <u>grog</u> may be an abbreviation of <u>grog</u>ram, the type of fabric Vernon preferred for his coats.

MUSICAL MASTERS: Joseph Haydn (1732 – 1809)

Joseph Haydn was an Austrian-born musical prodigy from a family of music lovers. Recognizing that Joseph would have few musical opportunities in Rohrau, the small village of his birth, his parents sent him to live with a relative in the Danube River town of Hainburg at age six. At Hainburg, Joseph's beautiful singing impressed a recruiter for the famous Vienna Boys' Choir, which invited him to join at age eight. After moving to Vienna, Haydn never lived with his parents again.

Where Handel was known for hot-headedness, Haydn was known for his sense of humor. For example:

- The 17-year-old Haydn lost his place in the Vienna Boys' Choir partly because he prankishly cut off the pigtails of the boy who stood in front of him.

- Haydn's well-known *Surprise Symphony* first lulled audiences to sleep with quiet tones, and then shocked them awake with raucous ones.

1792 portrait of Joseph Haydn

- As longtime court composer to a country-living Austrian noble named Nikolaus Esterhazy, Haydn often had to stay in the country longer than he liked. In a symphony titled *The Farewell*, Hadyn found a clever way to chide his employer for keeping his orchestra too long: near the end, Haydn's players left the stage one by one, snuffing out their music-stand candles as they went, until only two remained.

Other interesting facts:

- Hadyn's best-known composition is probably the tune for Germany's national anthem, "Song of Germany."

- Haydn was already a well-established, successful composer when he met two younger Austrian composers: his personal friend Wolfgang Mozart, and his student Ludwig van Beethoven.

- The childless Haydn's nickname, "Papa Haydn," had three meanings: (1) it recalled his fatherly treatment of his musicians; (2) it recalled his place as a founding father among Classical-era composers; and (3) among later, Romantic-era composers, it mocked him as a stodgy composer of dull, dated music.

U.S. GEOGRAPHY FOCUS

The Ohio River

The Ohio River is the longest river in the eastern United States, and the Mississippi River's largest tributary by volume. The Ohio forms at Pittsburgh, Pennsylvania, where two major rivers—the Allegheny and the Monongahela— flow together at Point State Park. From there, the Ohio winds generally southwestward for nearly 1,000 miles before joining the Mississippi River at Fort Defiance State Park in Cairo, Illinois. Along the way, the Ohio forms a border for five U.S. states: Ohio, Indiana and Illinois to the north, and West Virginia and Kentucky to the south.

In addition to Pittsburgh, the Ohio passes through several other well-known cities, including: (1) Huntington, West Virginia; (2) Cincinnati, Ohio; (3) Evansville, Indiana; and (4) Louisville, Kentucky.

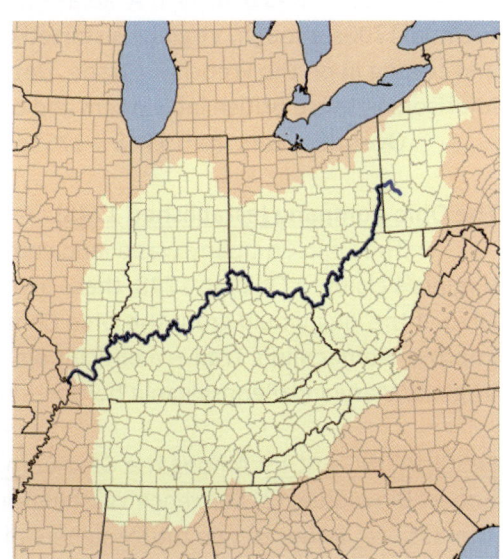
The Ohio River in blue with its watershed in yellow

DEFINITION: The **Ohio Country** was the region between the Ohio River and Lake Erie. In addition to what is now Ohio, the Ohio Country included parts of what are now western Pennsylvania and eastern Indiana.

U.S. HISTORY FOCUS, PART TWO

War Number Four, North American Theater: The French and Indian War (1754 – 1763)

Opponents in North America: Great Britain, the Iroquois Confederacy and other tribes versus France, the Wabanaki Confederacy, the Shawnee and other tribes

Ended with the: Treaty of Paris (1763)

SUCCINCT SUMMARIES: The French and Indian War was the war in which France lost Canada to Great Britain. After the war, the only territories that remained to France in all of North America were St. Pierre and Miquelon, two tiny islands near Newfoundland— islands that Britain allowed France to keep so that French fishermen would have a place to land and dry their fish.

Crossing the Appalachians

The French and Indian War began as a contest to see who would control the Ohio Country, Britain or France.

1. Britain laid two early claims to Ohio: one that dated back to 1606, the year King James I chartered the Virginia Company (see Chapter 3); and another that dated all the way back to explorer John Cabot in 1497.

2. France's claim was much more recent, dating only to La Salle's mission down the Mississippi River in 1682 – 1683. Even though England's claim was older, the French considered their claim stronger— because La Salle explored Ohio in person, while Britain's explorers never came anywhere near Ohio.

The Appalachian Mountains in brown

For more than a century, the Appalachians formed a strong natural barrier between British and French: the British held the territory east of the mountains, while the French held the territory west. When the two rivals clashed, it was usually in Acadia— where both sides tried to settle, and no mountains separated them. In the mid-1700s, though, Virginians started crossing the Appalachians into the Ohio Country, spying out the land and cutting in on the French fur trade. Determined to hold their side of the Appalachians, the French started imprisoning these British interlopers and confiscating their goods.

Over the years from 1748 – 1753, both sides took more forceful steps to claim Ohio.

The Ohio Company (established 1748)

The Ohio Company was a land company formed by a group of wealthy Virginia investors to press Virginia's claim to Ohio. In 1748, these investors approached King George II with a business plan for settling Ohio. If the king would grant the Ohio Company a large tract of Ohio land to sell, then the company would improve **Nemacolin's Trail**— a difficult old Native American trail that crossed the Appalachians near the Virginia/Maryland/Pennsylvania border— thus making it easier for settlers to reach Ohio.

FASCINATING FACTS: Among the Ohio Company's investors were powerful Virginians like (1) Acting Governor Robert Dinwiddie; (2) Lawrence Washington, elder half-brother to George Washington; and (3) former Governor Thomas Lee, father to two future signers of the Declaration of Independence named Richard Henry Lee and Francis Lightfoot Lee.

In the following year, 1749, King George II granted the Ohio Company 200,000 acres of Ohio Country land, with a promise of 300,000 more if the company could accomplish two goals: (1) settling at least 100 families in Ohio within seven years, and (2) building at least one strong fort to defend Ohio against the French.

French Forts in Ohio (1753 – 1760)

The French longed to connect their old colonies in Canada with their newer ones along the Mississippi River and the Gulf of Mexico; and the best route to the Mississippi lay across the Ohio Country and down the Ohio River. To secure this route, the French planned a string of forts across the Ohio Country. Beginning in 1753, the French built: (1) Fort Presque Isle on the southeastern shore of Lake Erie; (2) Fort Le Boeuf on French Creek, which led to the Allegheny River; and (3) Fort Machault on the Allegheny, which led to the Ohio.

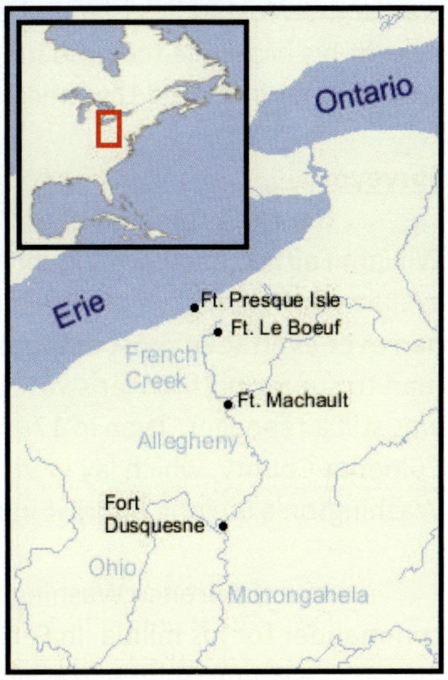

When Acting Virginia Governor Robert Dinwiddie learned that the French were building forts in the Ohio Country, he penned an official letter with these words of warning to the French:

"The lands upon the River Ohio, in the western parts of the Colony of Virginia, are so notoriously known to be the property of the Crown of Great Britain that it is a matter of equal concern and surprise to me, to hear that a body of French forces are erecting fortresses and making settlements upon that river... I must desire you to acquaint me by whose authority and instructions you have lately marched from Canada with an armed force, and invaded the King of Great Britain's territories... it becomes my duty to require your peaceable departure."

To deliver his letter, Dinwiddie chose a 21-year-old Virginia militia officer named George Washington.

AMAZING AMERICANS: George Washington (February 22, 1732 – December 14, 1799)

George Washington came from an old Virginia family. The first Washington in Virginia, George's great-grandfather John Washington, emigrated from England in 1656. John went on to command Virginia's militia in the Susquehannock War of 1675 – 1676 (see Chapter 11). From John's day through George's, the wealthy Washingtons accumulated several thousand acres of Virginia land— mostly on the Northern Neck, the part of Virginia between the Potomac and Rappahannock rivers.

Although George received little formal education, he received an excellent practical education from three forceful men— one a farmer, one a soldier and one a land agent.

Farmer

From his farmer father Augustine Washington, George learned that farming was the most respectable profession of all. George loved farming all his life, and often wished that he could spend more time at it. Sadly, Augustine Washington died in 1743, when George was only 11.

Portrait of George Washington at age 25

Soldier

After Augustine's death, the man who influenced George most was his elder half-brother Lawrence— a respected military man who, after serving under Admiral Vernon in the War of Jenkins' Ear, won appointment as commander of Virginia's militia. From Lawrence, George learned soldierly virtues like toughness, discipline, bravery and loyalty, along with a calm confidence that helped George inspire loyalty in others.

Sadly, Lawrence Washington suffered from tuberculosis. The only overseas journey George ever took was to the West Indies island of Barbados, where he went with Lawrence in 1751 to see if the tropical air might benefit his brother's tortured lungs. Sadly, Barbados failed to help, leaving Lawrence to die in 1752 at age 34. George later inherited Lawrence's Potomac River estate, Mount Vernon, from Lawrence's wife Anne.

Surveyor

George's third major influence also came through Lawrence— for Lawrence's wife Anne was daughter to William Fairfax, northern Virginia's biggest land agent. William's elder brother Thomas, Lord Fairfax tasked William with managing and selling the millions of acres he owned in Virginia. At the time, though, no white man had ever even seen most of those acres, let alone surveyed them. In need of some strong, trustworthy young man to survey his brother's vast property, William Fairfax sent George on his first surveying expeditions when he was still a teenager. Then in 1749, Fairfax helped George win a high-paying job as chief surveyor for the new Culpeper County, which lay in Virginia's Piedmont region just west of the Northern Neck. Thus began George Washington's lifelong interest in exploring the American frontier.

After Lawrence Washington's death, Acting Virginia Governor Robert Dinwiddie needed a new commander for his militia. In February 1753, Dinwiddie divided his militia into four districts, and placed the tall, impressive young George Washington in command of one— just in time for Washington to deliver the governor's letter to those unwelcome French forts in the Ohio Country.

A Brief Timeline of the French and Indian War

1753, December 12: George Washington delivers Governor Dinwiddie's letter of warning to the French commander at Ft. Le Boeuf, Ohio.

1753, December 16: Washington sets out for Virginia with the French commander's reply, which includes this politely veiled threat: "As to the summons you send me to retire, I do not think myself obliged to obey it."

George Washington in the Virginia Regiment uniform he wore during the French and Indian War

FASCINATING FACTS: "The Journal of Major George Washington" (published February 1754)

After Washington returned from his mission to Ohio, Governor Dinwiddie encouraged him to publish his mission report in a short work titled "The Journal of Major George Washington." Readers on both sides of the Atlantic eagerly devoured exciting tales from Washington's journey, including two in which he nearly died:

1. While Washington and his companion Christopher Gist were trudging through deep snow on their way home from Fort Le Boeuf, a French-allied native suddenly fired a musket at them from a distance of "not 15 steps"— and yet somehow missed. After that, the two men raced to put the Allegheny River between themselves and their enemies, in case the French should send another attacker who wouldn't miss.

2. Upon reaching the Allegheny, Washington and Gist found it rushing with broken, unsteady ice— impossible to cross without a raft. Because the two men had only one "poor hatchet" between them, they needed a full day to build a crude raft. The next day, they managed to pole their raft only about halfway across the river

before shifting ice trapped them, and nearly capsized them. When Washington tried to free the raft with his pole, the river tore at the pole with such force that it dragged both pole and Washington into the freezing water. Fortunately, the two men managed to make their way to an island in the river, where they spent one of the coldest, most miserable nights either would ever spend. Gist suffered frostbite in all of his fingers and some of his toes. Despite his dunking, though, the future Father of his Country somehow emerged unscathed. In the end, that night's severe cold turned out to be a blessing in disguise— for the next morning, the two men found the river frozen enough to cross on foot.

Washington's journal revealed him to be a man of intelligence, bravery and incredible toughness— a fitting military hero for rugged, frontier-loving colonials.

Early 1754: Governor Dinwiddie sends about 40 Virginians to build a fort at the Forks of the Ohio, the point where the Allegheny and Monongahela flow together to form the Ohio. Washington and others have noted that a strong fort at the Forks could control trade throughout the Ohio Country.

1754, March: Dinwiddie orders Washington back to Ohio to help complete his new fort at the Forks.

1754, April 16: Before Washington can reach the Forks, a small French army seizes the fort there, driving off Dinwiddie's small band of Virginians without firing a shot.

Portrait of Governor Robert Dinwiddie

A LOOK AHEAD: After finishing the fort the Virginians started, the French will name it Fort Duquesne in honor of their new governor.

1754, April - May: On his way to Ohio, Washington learns that Virginia has surrendered the Forks to the French. Meanwhile, the French at the Forks send out a small expedition to warn Washington away from the Forks, commanded by an officer named Joseph de Jumonville.

1754, May 28 – The Battle of Jumonville Glen: George Washington and his native allies strike the first deadly blows of the French and Indian War.

FASCINATING FACTS: The Battle of Jumonville Glen

Before Washington departed Virginia for the Forks of the Ohio, Governor Dinwiddie gave him this guidance for any encounters he might have with the French:

"You are to act on the defensive, but in case any attempts are made to obstruct the works or interrupt our settlements by any persons whatsoever, you are to restrain all such offenders; and in case of resistance to make prisoners of or kill and destroy them."

National Park Service artist's concept of the scene just before the Battle of Jumonville Glen

In seizing the Forks, the French had certainly "obstructed the works"; so now, Dinwiddie's orders authorized Washington to "kill and destroy" the French if necessary.

Necessary or not, on May 28, 1754, Washington and his native allies silently surrounded de Jumonville's small expedition before any of the French knew their enemies were upon them. Exactly who fired the first shot is uncertain; but when the shooting stopped 15 minutes later, about 10 Frenchmen lay dead, and about 25 were Washington's prisoners. French commander Joseph de Jumonville lay among the dead.

Other interesting facts:
- In a letter to his younger brother, Washington wrote this description of his first serious battle: "I can with truth assure you, I heard bullets whistle and believe me, there was something charming in the sound."

1754, June: Expecting trouble after Jumonville Glen, Washington and his men build tiny Fort Necessity— which is no more than a leaky shack surrounded by a low wooden palisade— on a high plain near what is now Farmington, PA.

1754, July 3 – The Battle of Fort Necessity: A French force about twice the size of Washington's arrives at Fort Necessity. After a rain-soaked battle, the French allow Washington and his defeated Virginians to evacuate Fort Necessity— leaving the Ohio Country entirely in French hands, for the moment.

Modern-day replica of Washington's hastily-built Fort Necessity

INTERESTING IDEAS: When Governor Dinwiddie asked his fellow colonial governors to help him drive the French out of Ohio, they raised these two serious objections:

1. Some of the governors couldn't help noticing that Dinwiddie owned stock in the Ohio Company— which meant that their troops would be fighting not only to save Virginia, but also to fatten Dinwiddie's wallet.
2. Pennsylvania's governor believed that his own colony, not Virginia, had the strongest claim to Ohio.

For these reasons among others, Virginia received little help from her sister colonies early in the war.

1755, February: British Major General Edward Braddock arrives in the colonies to take command of the war effort, accompanied by two full regiments of regular army and their officers— more than 2,000 red-coated British troops. Braddock's arrival brings major changes to the French and Indian War, including these two:

1. The presence of British regular army officers means that many colonial militia officers, including George Washington, lose their command ranks.
2. Now that the Crown is involved, Virginia's sister colonies become more willing to join her war effort.

1755, February - May: Braddock plans simultaneous assaults on four French targets for the coming summer: (1) Fort Duquesne at the Forks of the Ohio; (2) Fort Niagara on Lake Ontario; (3) Fort St. Frederick on Lake Champlain; and (4) Fort Beausejour on the Isthmus of Chignecto— the thin strip of land that connects Nova Scotia to mainland Canada.

REFRESHING REMINDERS from Chapter 18: When Queen Anne's War ended in 1713, France ceded the southern part of what is now Nova Scotia to Britain. However, the northern part of Nova Scotia, Cape Breton Island, remained in French hands— as did the rest of Acadia, the parts that are now New Brunswick and Prince Edward Island.

1755, June: Britain wins its only real victory of the year at Fort Beausejour, thus capturing most of Acadia. To strengthen its hold on Acadia, Britain begins expelling the French-speaking Acadians from their homeland.

FASCINATING FACTS: The Expulsion of the Acadians (1755 – 1764)

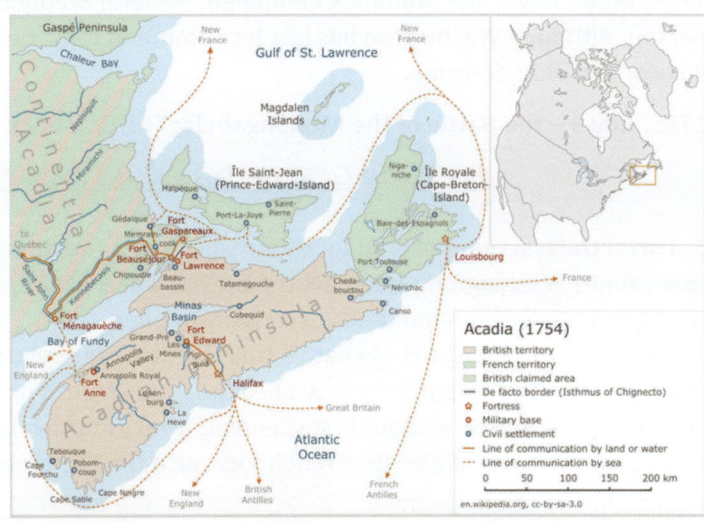

From the British capture of southern Nova Scotia in 1713 through the British victory at For Beausejour in 1755, Nova Scotia was at best a mixed blessing for the British— mainly because Nova Scotia's people, the Acadians, refused to switch loyalties. Despite the British takeover, most Acadians were determined to remain as French and Catholic as ever. Between Queen Anne's War and the French and Indian War, the Acadians and their native allies, the Micmac people, launched two troublesome rebellions against British authority: Father Rale's War (1722 – 1725) and Father Le Loutre's War (1749 – 1755).

For decades, Britain tried to control the Acadians by asking them to swear oaths of unconditional loyalty to the British Crown. Much to Britons' frustration, most Acadians refused to swear these unconditional oaths. Instead, they swore conditional oaths— oaths in which they promised to abide by British law, but only so long as Britain never asked them to take up arms against France. Such oaths convinced Britons that Acadians' true loyalties still lay with France, and always would. Furthermore, Britons feared that Nova Scotia would never be truly British so long as Acadians retained their French language, religion and culture— especially with Britain and France so often at war.

After their 1755 victory at Fort Beausejour, the British decided that the best way to strengthen their hold on Acadia was to expel these disloyal Acadians. At the time, the Acadian population stood somewhere near 12,000 – 18,000— a large number, but no larger than some armies Britain had moved.

British troops loading Acadians aboard ships for their journeys into exile

The British spent the remaining years of the French and Indian war deporting as many Acadians as possible from places like Grand-Pre and Annapolis Royal, the former Port Royal. Some Acadians the British deported south to the Thirteen Colonies; while others it deported all the way back to France. In the process, most Acadians lost everything they owned— including their homes, which the British burned; their land, which the British confiscated; and their money, which they spent to cover the high costs of relocating. Except for a small remnant that survived by going into hiding, the Acadian people disappeared from Acadia forever.

Other interesting facts:
- American author Henry Wadsworth Longfellow retold the story of the Expulsion of the Acadians in an epic poem titled *Evangeline, a Tale of Acadie*. Longfellow's Evangeline is a young Acadian who becomes

> separated from her beloved fiancé Gabriel during the expulsion, and wanders in search of him for decades. By the time Evangeline finally finds Gabriel, she is an old woman, and he is so sick that he dies in her arms.

1755, May - July – The Braddock Campaign: General Braddock leads the campaign against Fort Duquesne in person. Although Washington has lost his command rank, he gladly accompanies the honored Braddock as his advisor and aide-de-camp.

1755, July 9 – the Battle of the Monongahela: The Braddock Campaign ends in disaster for the British.

> FASCINATING FAILURES: Two Keys to the Failure of the Braddock Campaign
>
> **1. Travel Delays:** General Braddock's mission across the Appalachians was quite large— about 2,100 troops, many times Washington's numbers the previous year. To supply so many troops, Braddock needed a long train of wagons loaded with hundreds of tons of supplies.
>
> Unfortunately, the old native trail that led over the Appalachians wasn't wide enough for large wagons, nor solid enough to keep Braddock's heavy cannon from sinking into the roadbed. Therefore Braddock couldn't attack Fort Duquesne without first spending weeks improving the road. Washington chafed at this delay, worrying that it would give the French too much time to prepare their defense.

> A LOOK AHEAD: The road Braddock improves on this campaign, Braddock's Road, will later become part of the National Road— the first road ever funded by the U.S. government. Part of modern-day U.S. Route 40 follows the same route Braddock followed over the Appalachians.

General Braddock struck down at the Battle of Monongahela

> **2. Braddock's Inexperience with Wilderness Fighting:** When Braddock finally reached the Monongahela Valley, he divided his army into two sections: (1) a fast-moving, 1,300-man "flying column" that moved ahead to surprise Fort Duquesne; and (2) a slower-moving, 800-man supply column that stayed behind with his wagons. Braddock's flying column crossed the Monongahela about 9 miles southeast of Fort Duquesne on the morning of July 9, 1755, confident of capturing the fort before the day was out.
>
> Meanwhile, the French and their native allies took aggressive action. Instead of waiting for Braddock to surround Fort Duquesne, the French dispatched an army of some 300 French troops and 600 natives— about two-thirds the size of Braddock's flying column— to block Braddock's river crossing.
>
> Finding Braddock already across, the French commander fell back on a different plan, ordering his troops to hide behind trees and rocks and lie in ambush. Because Braddock deployed too few advance scouts, he had no idea what ambush might await him. When Braddock's flying column moved between the French and their native allies, they immediately opened fire on the startled British.
>
> Here Braddock made his greatest mistake: instead of allowing his troops to take cover, Braddock ordered them to reform their lines and advance. Having learned to fight on the open battlefields of Europe, Braddock believed in the power of large infantry columns with all his heart; and on those battlefields, such columns were indeed mighty. In the wilderness, though, a tightly-packed column of red-coated soldiers made a perfect target for woods-crafty enemies firing from the cover of rocks and trees.
>
> Near the end of a long, deadly battle that killed or wounded about three-fourths of Braddock's flying

column, Braddock went down with a bullet in his lung, leaving George Washington to command the British retreat. As for Washington, he emerged from his third serious battle without one bullet wound— although he did suffer two horses shot beneath him, and would later find four bullet holes in his uniform.

The honored Braddock died four days later. As the expedition's chaplain lay wounded, Washington personally conducted Braddock's funeral. For the rest of this life, Washington never went anywhere without a fine officer's sash that he received as a gift from General Braddock just before he died.

1756 - 1757: For two years after Braddock's defeat, French Major General Louis-Joseph de Montcalm defeats the British at every turn. During this time, Washington commands Virginia's defense, but leads no more attacks.

1758 – The Advent of William Pitt: When a brilliant Member of Parliament named William Pitt takes control of Britain's military strategy, the tide of war begins to turn in Britain's favor.

1758, July – The Battle of Carillon: William Pitt's powerful new strategy suffers a setback when a small French army fights off a far larger British one at Fort Carillon, the future Fort Ticonderoga.

BRILLIANT BATTLES: The Battle of Carillon (July 8, 1758)

Like General Braddock, Member of Parliament William Pitt planned to attack Canada by every route available. One route lay up the Hudson Valley, across Lake Champlain, and then down the Richelieu River to the St. Lawrence River.

A LOOK BEHIND: This was the same route that Samuel de Champlain followed in reverse when he explored Lake Champlain back in 1609 (see Chapter 5).

New France's main defense along this route was Fort Carillon, a star-shaped fort built near the southern end of Lake Champlain in 1755. Fort Carillon's strengths were that (1) it was almost completely surrounded by rivers and lakes, and (2) its only approach over land was both narrow and heavily fortified. However, Fort Carillon also suffered one rather glaring weakness: across the water from the fort stood a high, undefended hill from which enemy cannon could easily bombard it.

As the campaign season of 1758 approached, the competent General Montcalm reinforced Fort Carillon with about 3,600 French and native troops. The less-competent British commander, General Abercrombie, attacked with far more troops, about 16,000.

General Montcalm's troops celebrating victory at the Battle of Carillon

Unfortunately for the British, Abercrombie didn't understand siege warfare. Instead of seizing the hill and bombarding the fort with his cannon, Abercrombie ordered a reckless frontal assault that crammed thousands of British troops into the fort's one narrow approach, where they became easy targets for the French. With Abercrombie making things easy for them, the French mowed down terrible British casualties— some 1,000 dead, and another 1,500 wounded— within just a few hours.

1758, July – The Siege of Louisbourg: Three weeks after its disaster at Fort Carillon, a more competent British commander wins a major victory at Louisburg, an important French fortress on Cape Breton Island. Holding Louisbourg gives Britain two advantages: (1) it firms Britain's grip on Acadia; and (2) it allows British ships to sail into the Gulf of St. Lawrence without fear that French ships based at Louisbourg will attack them from the rear.

1758, August – The Battle of Fort Frontenac: British troops diverted from the disaster at Fort Carillon redeem themselves by capturing Fort Frontenac, which lies where Lake Ontario drains into the St. Lawrence River. With the British in control of Fort Frontenac, French settlements to the south and west are cut off from Quebec City.

1758, September - November – The Forbes Expedition: British Brigadier General John Forbes finally captures Fort Duquesne on the Forks of the Ohio, but not before the French blow it up. George Washington commands the troops who finally enter Fort Duquesne's burned-out husk.

> A LOOK AHEAD: Later, the British will replace Fort Duquesne with the new and improved Fort Pitt, named for successful war strategist William Pitt. The city in which Fort Pitt stands, Pittsburgh, will also be named for Pitt.

1758, October – The Treaty of Easton: Native American chiefs from several Ohio Country tribes, including some who had been allies of the French, agree to become allies of the British. In exchange, the British promise not to build any more new settlements west of the Appalachians. Abandoned by most of his allies, General Montcalm retreats to two of his last strongholds: Quebec City and Montreal.

> TWO LOOKS AHEAD:
> - Britain's promise to build no more new settlements west of the Appalachians will provoke great anger in the Thirteen Colonies, where many believe that claiming the Ohio Country was the whole point of fighting the French and Indian War. This grievance will become a cause of the American Revolutionary War.
> - The year 1759 will be the *Annus Mirabilis* of the Seven Years' War, a "miraculous year" in which British forces win great victories around the world. One of these victories will come at Quebec City.

1759, June: An expedition commanded by British General James Wolfe sails up the St. Lawrence River and lays siege to the all-important Quebec City.

1759, July – The Battle of Ticonderoga: The British easily capture Fort Carillon, the fort where Montcalm embarrassed them so badly a year before. Afterward, the British rename their prize Fort Ticonderoga.

1759, September 13 – The Battle of the Plains of Abraham: After a months-long siege, the British finally capture Quebec City in battle on the Plains of Abraham, a high plateau just outside the city. Sadly, three French bullets pierce General Wolfe. As he lies dying on the Plains of Abraham, Wolfe gives thanks for his great victory with these last words: "Now, God be praised, I die contented." The French commander, General Montcalm, dies of his wounds the next day.

British General James Wolfe dying on the Plains of Abraham

1760, August – The Siege of Montreal: The British capture one of New France's last strongholds, the important trading post of Montreal.

1760, September: The Governor of New France surrenders Canada to Britain. Although the Seven Years' War will continue elsewhere, the French and Indian War in the colonies is essentially over.

SUCCINCT SUMMARIES: Some Results of the French and Indian War

- In the 1763 Treaty of Paris, negotiated at the end of the Seven Years' War, France formally ceded all of North America east of the Mississippi River to Britain— except New Orleans, which it had secretly ceded to Spain the year before.

- When New France surrendered, about 80,000 French Catholic Canadians suddenly became British subjects for the first time. Instead of expelling these Canadians as it had expelled the Acadians, Britain tried something different: it allowed the Canadians to (1) continue their Catholic worship, (2) keep their property, and even (3) keep their French laws— subject to the British Crown, of course. Thanks to these concessions, Canadian culture went on to become a unique blend of French and British cultures.

- The French and Indian War cost Britain a mountain of war debt. Because King George III and his Parliament found it easier to tax the colonies than the homeland, they tried to erase some of that debt by taxing the colonies. The colonists' anger over these high, unfair taxes was to become another cause of the American Revolutionary War.

FASCINATING FACTS: Burying the Hatchet

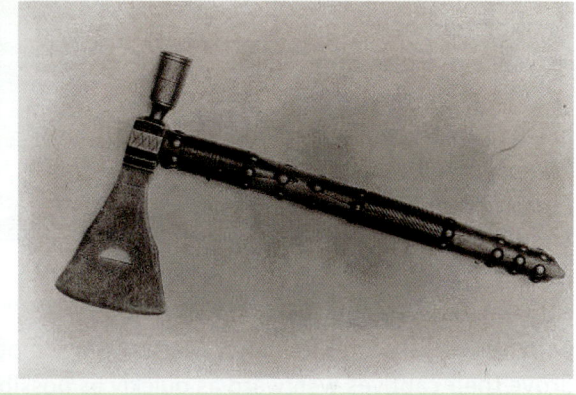

When warring Native American tribes were ready to make peace, they sometimes formalized their treaties with a hatchet-burying ceremony— a solemn rite in which they symbolically put away forever the weapons they had used to wage war.

One early hatchet-burying ceremony was the one the Great Peacemaker and Hiawatha held when they united the Five Nations of the Iroquois Confederacy (see Chapter 5). According to Haudenosaunee tradition, the Five Nations buried their hatchets beneath the very Tree of Great Peace where their Great Council of 50 sachems held its meetings. Also according to tradition, some peace-loving spirit sent an underground river to carry the buried hatchets away, thus barring the Iroquois from fighting among themselves ever again.

After the French surrendered in 1760, the British Governor of Nova Scotia invited the Acadians' Micmac allies to bury the hatchet with him. In a solemn ceremony held in 1761, four Micmac chiefs buried the hatchet with the British at Halifax, Nova Scotia.

A LOOK AHEAD: Despite their chiefs' hatchet-burying, some of the Micmac will fight on for another 20 years.

Raids, Massacres and Kidnappings

The French and Indian War wasn't all big battles; it was also small raids, massacres and kidnappings. Because the British outnumbered the French so badly— only about 80,000 French colonists lived in North America at the time, compared to 1.5 million or more British colonists— the French relied on their Native American allies far more than the British did. The natives' main mode of fighting was to raid and terrorize British settlements all along the frontier.

Early in the war, a Shawnee raid captured a 12-year-old Irish-born colonist named Mary Jemison.

ILLUMINATING EXCERPTS from *A Narrative of the Life of Mrs. Mary Jemison* by James Seaver (published 1824)

Mary Jemison was an Irish girl born aboard a ship bound for Philadelphia in 1743. Finding themselves too poor to buy a farm in the settled parts of Pennsylvania, Mary's parents Thomas and Jane Jemison joined other poor immigrants in scratching out new farms on Pennsylvania's western frontier. In the ten years after their arrival in Pennsylvania, Thomas and Jane Jemison built a prosperous farm near what is now Gettysburg, complete with a "mansion" Mary described as a "little paradise."

Unfortunately, the Jemisons' little paradise lay dangerously close to the Ohio Country, where the French and Indian War was soon to begin. The first rumblings of war reached the Jemisons in 1752, when they began to hear of "Indian barbarities inflicted on the whites." The following year, Mary heard that

> "many murders were committed; and many captives were exposed to meet death in its most frightful form, by having their bodies stuck full of pine splinters, which were immediately set on fire, while their tormentors, exulting in their distress, would rejoice at their agony!"

In 1754, Thomas Jemison's brother John died fighting for George Washington at the Battle of Fort Necessity (see above). Despite his brother's fate— coupled with a devastating defeat which left the whole frontier open to attack— Thomas Jemison made the fateful decision to remain on his farm for at least one more season.

In the spring of 1755, a war party of six Shawnee and four Frenchmen descended upon the Jemison farm and shot one of Thomas' neighbors to death. Finding Thomas unarmed, the party kidnapped him at gunpoint, along

Illustration of General Montcalm trying to stop his native allies from massacring innocents

with his wife Jane, his daughter Mary and three other Jemison children. Anxious to evade pursuit, the war party drove their captives westward as quickly as possible. When the little ones cried, the Shawnee whipped them; and when they begged for water, the Shawnee gave them urine to drink.

Two days later, the Shawnee learned that some of the Jemisons' neighbors were still tracking them, hoping to rescue their friends. Alarmed at this news, the Shawnee adopted a strategy that would end all thoughts of rescue. On the evening of the second day, as Jane Jemison watched the Shawnee strip off Mary's hard shoes and replace them with soft leather moccasins, Jane understood why: because young Mary was going to walk on with the Shawnee, and the rest of the family was not. Before the Shawnee led Mary away, Jane shared these last instructions with her 12-year-old daughter:

> "Alas, my dear! My heart bleeds at the thoughts of what awaits you; but, if you leave us, remember my child your own name, and the name of your father and mother. Be careful and not forget your English tongue. If you shall have an opportunity to get away from the Indians, don't try to escape; for if you do they will find and destroy you. Don't forget, my little daughter, the prayers that I have learned you— say them often; be a good child, and God will bless you. May God bless you my child, and make you comfortable and happy."

The next evening, Mary watched the Shawnee dry several human scalps at their campfire, scraping them clean of dead flesh so that rot wouldn't set in. Because Jane Jemison's hair was red, Mary had no trouble recognizing her beloved mother's scalp among the rest. Later, Mary learned that the Shawnee had mutilated her family's remains in unspeakable ways; and that when her neighbors found those remains lying in the woods, they gave up the chase and went home.

Several days after the massacre of her family, Mary and her captors reached Fort Duquesne. There, the Shawnee either sold or gave Mary to a pair of Seneca women, who led her miles down the Ohio River to their summer village. Upon reaching their village, the two women threw away Mary's torn clothing, scrubbed her clean and dressed her in fine new clothes, as if for some ceremony. Minutes later, Mary found herself surrounded by sobbing, wailing women mourning over some lost Seneca warrior they had loved. Mary had become a captive in the Mourning Wars, the wars some tribes fought to replace dead relatives (see Chapter 5).

Illustration of Mary Jemison being re-dressed in Seneca garb

Later, Mary learned more about the Mourning Wars. According to Mary, Seneca warriors did their best to bring home at least one prize for every warrior they lost in battle— either a prisoner or an enemy scalp. If they brought home a prisoner, then the dead warrior's family had a choice: they could either (1) take out their anger on the prisoner, torturing him to gain satisfaction for his people's crimes, or (2) adopt the prisoner as a replacement for their lost loved one. Fortunately for Mary, her two Seneca women chose adoption.

From the moment of her adoption, Mary Jemison lived as a full-fledged member of the Seneca family, with the same privileges and duties as any other member. Mary shared the familial love of several adoptive Seneca brothers and sisters. Although she was always careful to honor her mother's last request— her promises to remember her family, language and prayers— Mary came to think of herself as a Seneca, not a colonist.

When the French and Indian War ended several years later, Mary had an excellent chance to return to the colonies; for the British offered a reward for the return of any prisoner, and one Seneca chief was eager to claim Mary's reward. When the chief came for her, though, Mary ran away as fast as her still-young legs would carry her; and in the end, the chief left without her. The adult Mary went on to wed two Seneca husbands, and bore several Seneca children.

Decades of living among the Seneca gave the adult Mary unique insights into the Seneca people, and Native American peoples in general. Despite the murders of her family members, Mary no longer believed that all natives were savages:

"Notwithstanding all that has been said against the Indians, in consequence of their cruelties to their enemies— cruelties that I have witnessed, and had abundant proof of— it is a fact that they are naturally kind, tender and peaceable towards their friends, and strictly honest; and that those cruelties have been practiced only upon their enemies, according to their idea of justice."

In other words, Mary came to understand that native peoples tortured and killed not because all natives were savage devils, but because their sense of justice demanded severe punishment for crimes. Mary also came to admire the natives' simple way of life:

"If peace ever dwelt with men, it was in former times, in the recesses from war, amongst what are now termed barbarians. The moral character of the Indians was... uncontaminated. Their fidelity was perfect...; they were strictly honest; they despised deception and falsehood; and chastity was held in high veneration, and a violation of it was considered sacrilege. They were temperate in their desires, moderate in their passions, and candid and honorable in the expression of their sentiments on every subject of importance.

One of the complications that destroyed that simple way of life, Mary said, was the natives' unbreakable addiction to the alcohol Europeans brought among them:

"... not even the love of life will restrain an Indian from sipping the poison that he knows will destroy him. The voice of nature, the rebukes of reason, the advice of parents, the expostulations of friends, and the numerous instances of sudden death, are all insufficient to reclaim an Indian, who has once experienced the exhilarating and inebriating effects of spirits, from seeking his grave in the bottom of his bottle!"

NOTED NOVELS: *The Last of the Mohicans: A Narrative of 1757* by James Fennimore Cooper (Published 1826)

The Last of the Mohicans is a work of historical fiction set in upstate New York during the French and Indian War. It is the second of five novels in *The Leatherstocking Tales*, a series that follows the adventures of hero Natty Bumppo— also known as Leatherstocking, Deerslayer and Hawkeye— over the years from about 1740 – 1800.

Cooper's long, complicated tale begins with a small column of British soldiers escorting two young sisters to Fort William Henry, where their father is in command. For a guide, the British have chosen a Huron named Magua whom they believe to be their friend. Unknown to the British, Magua is actually a traitor who bears a deadly grudge against them; for Magua believes that the British have ruined his people's lives by introducing them to alcohol.

Along the way to the fort, the treacherous Magua leads the British column directly into a Huron ambush. Leatherstocking and two Mohican friends arrive just in time to save a few British, including the two sisters. When the Huron give chase, though, the fugitives have to separate, and the Huron end up recapturing the sisters. Leatherstocking and his friends spend the rest of the novel trying to rescue the sisters.

Cover illustration from a German children's edition of *The Leatherstocking Tales*

FASCINATING FACTS: Cajuns

Although the British didn't deport any Acadians directly to New Orleans, several thousand deported Acadians eventually found their way to New Orleans. Because France had ceded New Orleans to Catholic Spain, Catholic Acadians felt more comfortable in New Orleans than in the mostly-Protestant Thirteen Colonies. Modern-day New Orleans' French language, culture and religion descend directly from the expelled Acadians who moved there during and after the French and Indian War.

Over time, the name "Acadian" gradually shortened in speakers' mouths to "Cajun."

FASCINATING FACTS: Cajun Wedding Traditions

- **Jumping the Broom**: In its early years, Cajun country had too few Catholic priests to cover such a wide area— which meant that young couples often had to wait a long time before a priest arrived to conduct their weddings. To ease the waiting, some Cajun couples held "broomstick weddings"— unofficial ceremonies in which they symbolically marked their union by jumping over a broomstick together. In Cajun eyes, a broomstick wedding was good enough to last until the circuit-riding priest came around for the official ceremony.

- The traditional food served at most Cajun wedding receptions is **gumbo** – chicken, shrimp and/or sausage cooked in spicy broth and served over rice.

- Guests at Cajun wedding receptions often buy dances with the bride or groom by pinning gifts of money onto their clothes.
- If a younger brother or sister marries before the elder, then the elder must dance with a mop dressed as a bride or groom.
- Cajun newlyweds often awaken to the noise of **charivari**— a custom in which their friends beat on pots and pans outside newlyweds' homes, raising a terrible ruckus in hopes of being invited inside for food and drink. These unruly, unwelcome guests often refuse to leave until the wee hours of the next morning.

A bowl of Cajun gumbo

FASCINATING FACTS: Egg Pocking

Egg pocking is an Eastertime custom some Cajuns take quite seriously. The game itself is simple: two contestants strike two hard-boiled Easter eggs together, and the one whose egg breaks first loses. The complications lie in the details: some Cajuns prepare for months beforehand, testing and experimenting to produce the best possible eggs and techniques. Some place their faith in certain chicken feed recipes, swearing that certain feeds produce the toughest eggshells. Others boil their eggs slowly and carefully, lining their boiling pots with cloth to keep the eggs from striking the sides of the pot. Still others add coffee grounds to the water, believing that this toughens eggshells. Others yet restrict their eggs so that they boil point-side down, believing that this forces the air pocket inside the egg to the small end. Some even switch out chicken eggs for duck, guinea or other fowl— although others consider this cheating.

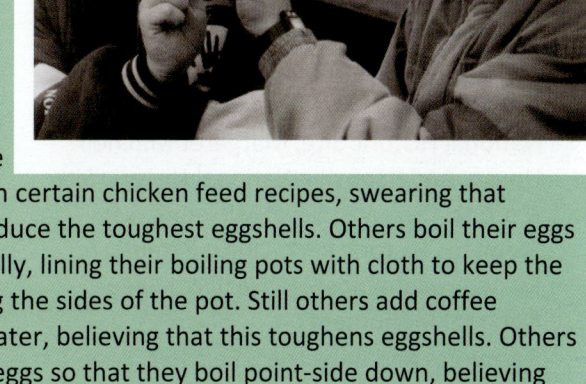

Easter eggs dyed red to symbolize the blood of Christ

FASCINATING FACTS: Vision Quests and Medicine Shields

Many Native American tribes sent their young men on **vision quests**, coming-of-age trials in which they sought spiritual names or spirit guides. While each tribe followed a different tradition, the common thread was that each young man spent several days away from the care of his people, supplied with no food, water or protection. The stress of this time apart hopefully brought on a vision that he could share with a holy man, who could then help him interpret his vision.

This vision became the emblem of the young man's life, a symbol to paint on his **medicine shield** and the walls of his tepee. Some Native Americans carried these medicine shields for life— not for protection in battle, but for protection against spiritual menaces. When the warrior died, his family buried his shield with him so that he could continue to carry its protection even in the afterlife.

U.S. STATE FOCUS

Georgia

FASCINATING FACTS about Georgia:

- State Capital: Atlanta
- State Abbreviation: GA
- Statehood: Georgia became the 4th US state on January 2, 1788.
- Area: About 59,000 square miles (Ranks 24th in size)
- Bordering States: South Carolina, North Carolina, Tennessee, Alabama, Florida
- Meaning of Name: Georgia's name honors King George II of England.
- State Nickname: "Peach State"
- State Bird: Brown Thrasher
- State Tree: Southern Live Oak (Evergreen Oak)
- State Flower: Cherokee Rose
- State Song: "Georgia on My Mind" by Stuart Gorrell and Hoagy Carmichael
- State Motto: "Wisdom, justice, moderation"
- Historic Places to Visit: Martin Luther King Jr. National Historic Site, Margaret Mitchell House, Andersonville National Historic Site, National Civil War Naval Museum, A.H. Stephens Historic Park, Uncle Remus Museum, John Ross House, Ocmulgee National Monument
- Resources and Industries: Peaches, peanuts, carpet, lumber, turpentine, aerospace, manufacturing

Atlanta house where author Margaret Mitchell wrote "Gone With the Wind"

State Flag: Georgia's flag has two sections: (1) A field divided into three wide, horizontal stripes, red-white-red; and (2) a canton (corner emblem) with Georgia's state seal in gold, surrounded by 13 white stars that represent the original 13 U.S. states, all on a blue background. Georgia's state seal depicts 3 pillars that represent the three branches of government—executive, legislative and judicial— supporting an arch that represents the Constitution. An American soldier of the Revolutionary War stands by with sword in hand, ready to defend the Constitution.

CHAPTER 20: The Seven Years' War; Catherine the Great

WORLD HISTORY FOCUS

REFRESHING REMINDERS: Four Major Wars in Europe and North America

European War	Dates	Corresponding American War(s)
1. War of the Grand Alliance	1688 – 1697	King William's War
2. War of the Spanish Succession	1701 – 1714	Queen Anne's War
3. War of the Austrian Succession	1739 – 1748	War of Jenkins' Ear / King George's War
4. Seven Years' War	1754 – 1763	French and Indian War

War Number Four, European Theater: The Seven Years' War (1756 – 1763)

Opponents in Europe: Prussia, Britain and others versus Austria, France, Russia, Sweden and others

Ended with the: Treaties of Paris and Hubertusburg (1763)

The French and Indian War (see Chapter 19) was only one theater of the Seven Years' War, a far larger war fought in theaters around the globe:

- In the West Indies, Britain invaded French-held islands like Guadeloupe, Dominica and Martinique.
- In India and the East Indies, Britain and France struggled for control of colonies and trade routes.
- In Western Europe, France invaded British-allied Hanover, and tried to invade Britain as well.
- In Central and Eastern Europe, Frederick the Great of Prussia continued his territory war against Maria Theresa of Austria. Instead of adding to Prussia's territory, though, Frederick very nearly lost Prussia itself.

REFRESHING REMINDERS from Chapter 18:
- The War of the Austrian Succession arose because the most powerful royal in Central Europe— Holy Roman Emperor Charles VI, who was also Archduke of Austria, King of Hungary and King of Bohemia— fathered only daughters, no sons. Within weeks after Charles' bright, capable daughter Maria Theresa inherited his thrones in 1740, male rivals converged from all sides to claim territories from Austria's supposedly weak female ruler.

- Maria Theresa's most aggressive rival was Frederick the Great of Prussia, who seized Silesia— a valuable sub-kingdom of Bohemia— in 1741. By capturing Silesia and holding it throughout the War of the Austrian Succession, Frederick the Great won Prussia a place on the list of Europe's great powers.

Empress Maria Theresa of Austria

The Diplomatic Revolution of 1756

DEFINITION: The **Diplomatic Revolution of 1756** was a dramatic reversal of European alliances just before the Seven Years' War.

Maria Theresa never forgave Frederick the Great for stealing Silesia from her, and never stopped plotting to regain her lost territory. The Empress-Queen spent the eight years between the War of the Austrian Succession and the Seven Years' War building up Austria— centralizing its government, boosting its tax revenue and doubling its armies— so that when the time came to retake Silesia from Prussia, Austria would be ready.

Maria Theresa also spent those eight years reconsidering her alliances. In the previous war, Austria's alliance with Britain had brought her a great deal of money, but very few troops; Britain's strength had always been its navy, not its army. Furthermore, in the negotiations that ended that war, the British had done nothing to help Austria reclaim Silesia— which made Maria Theresa doubt that they would help her reclaim Silesia now.

In search of allies who shared her hatred of Prussia and Frederick the Great, Maria Theresa reached out in two directions:

- To the west, Maria Theresa approached Austria's old enemy, the hated rival that had done so much damage to the Austrian cause in the Thirty Years' War: France. At the time, King Louis XV of France was enjoying the company of a beautiful, clever mistress called Madame Pompadour. Frederick the Great had made the mistake of publicly criticizing Pompadour, deriding her as the unworthy leader of a "petticoat dynasty" at the effeminate French court in Versailles. By cultivating a relationship with the influential Madame Pompadour— and by promising France a corner of the Netherlands that Austria controlled— Maria Theresa finally coaxed France into joining her alliance against Prussia.

Madame Pompadour, influential mistress to King Louis XV of France

- To the east, Maria Theresa approached Empress Elizabeth of Russia, daughter to Peter the Great (see Chapter 17). Partly because Elizabeth, too, personally disliked Frederick the Great— he had once criticized her as "too fat and too [Eastern] Orthodox"— Empress Elizabeth agreed to join Maria Theresa's band of angry women aligned against Frederick.

Austria's new alliance with France was particularly alarming to Austria's old ally Britain, for two reasons:

1. Because Britain was already fighting the French and Indian War in North America, and didn't want Austria joining the war on France's side.
2. Because Britain's special relationship with the Electorate of Hanover, home to Britain's royal House of Hanover, required Britain to defend Hanover; and Britain's small army couldn't possibly defend Hanover against the combined might of France and Austria.

Fortunately for Britain, Prussia was perfectly placed to defend Hanover; and with Maria Theresa preparing to invade, Prussia needed allies as badly as Britain did. Therefore Britain and Prussia formed a counter-alliance, and British gold flowed to defend Prussia and Hanover against Austria, France and Russia.

Preemptive War

Instead of waiting for his enemies' hammers to strike him, Frederick struck first. In late August 1756, Frederick led more than 60,000 Prussian troops into Silesia's western neighbor, Austrian-allied Saxony, on a mission to seize the Saxon capital city of Dresden. Frederick planned to use Saxony's resources to help capture his next target: Bohemia. By controlling Saxony and Bohemia, Frederick hoped to establish a buffer zone between the realm he wanted to protect, Silesia, and Maria Theresa's realms of Austria and Hungary.

INTERESTING IDEAS: Historians are of two minds about the order in which the alliances of the Diplomatic Revolution formed, and their effect on the outbreak of the Seven Years' War:

1. Some say that when Prussia invaded Saxony, Austria and France had yet to complete their alliance— and that they might never have completed it if Frederick hadn't recklessly attacked Saxony first. According to this view, Frederick's needless attack on Saxony launched an ugly war that otherwise might never have happened.

2. Others say that whether or not the alliance between Austria and France was complete on paper, it was complete in reality— and that if Frederick hadn't acted when he did to save himself, then his enemies might have destroyed him the following year.

The Battle of Lobositz (October 1, 1756)

The only real resistance Frederick met in Saxony came at Pirna, a fortified town on the Elbe River about ten miles southeast of Dresden. When Frederick attacked Dresden, about 18,000 surprised Saxon troops sealed themselves inside Pirna, hoping to hold Frederick off until reinforcements from Austria could arrive.

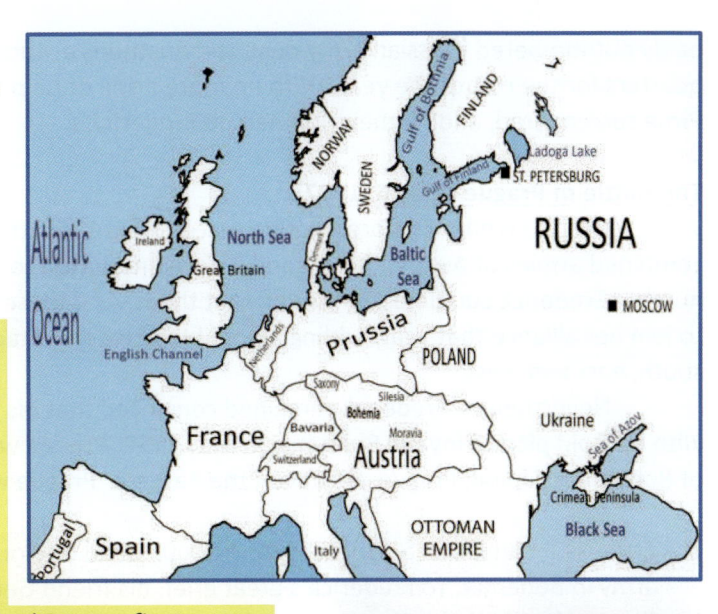

Portrait of Frederick the Great

Scene from the Battle of Lobositz

While Frederick was busy coaxing the Saxons inside Pirna to surrender, Maria Theresa dispatched about 35,000 – 45,000 Austrian troops to attack Frederick's rear. The Austrians knew that if they could join forces with the besieged Saxons inside Pirna, then they would easily outnumber whatever force Frederick could set against them— for in order to control all of Saxony, Frederick had been forced to divide his army.

True to form, though, the aggressive Frederick didn't dawdle outside Pirna, waiting for his enemy's next move. Instead, Frederick left behind enough troops at Pirna to maintain his siege, and then marched out with the rest of his army to meet the Austrians. 40 miles south of Pirna, near what is now Lovosice, Czech Republic, a badly outnumbered Prussian army dealt the Austrians a stunning defeat that sent them scurrying into winter quarters for the rest of the year. With no more hope of help from Austria that year, the 18,000 Saxons inside Pirna surrendered, adding their numbers to Frederick's.

The Battle of Prague (May 6, 1757)

Despite Frederick's preemptive successes in 1756, the dawn of 1757 was a dark time for Prussia. The combined armies of Austria, Russia and France amounted to some 400,000 troops, four times the largest number Frederick could hope to set against them. As if these weren't enough, Maria Theresa convinced Sweden to join her alliance that year, adding a possible northern attack to the ones Prussia already expected from the south, east and west.

Nevertheless, Frederick remained convinced that his best defense was a good offense; so he went ahead with his bold plan to invade Bohemia. In May 1757, Prussia won a second surprising victory over Austria just east of Bohemia's capital, Prague. However, the Battle of Prague was no great victory for Prussia, for two reasons:

1. Because it came at a terrible cost of 14,000+ dead or wounded, more than one-fifth of Frederick's entire army in Bohemia. To Frederick's great grief, his friend General Schwerin— the honored hero who had saved the day for him in his first battle as king, the Battle of Mollwitz (see Chapter 18)— lay among the dead.

2. Because at battle's end, some 40,000 Austrian troops managed to retreat safely inside Prague's walls, forcing Frederick to lay siege to the city— even as a second Austrian army as large as the first approached from the east.

The Battle of Kolin (June 18, 1757)

Sandwiched as he was between two large armies, Frederick had little choice but to divide his own army. Detaching about 20,000 troops to maintain the Siege of Prague, Frederick led another 30,000 or so to face the new threat to his east. Unfortunately for Frederick, this new threat consisted of at least 44,000, and perhaps as many as 65,000, fresh Austrian troops— all led by the cleverest general Frederick had yet faced, Marshal Leopold von Daun.

Nor were superior numbers von Daun's only advantages. Von Daun calculated that Frederick would want to attack him as quickly as possible— for Frederick must fear that if he didn't return to Prague quickly, then the Austrians inside Prague might emerge to attack him from the rear. Therefore instead of rushing to meet Frederick, von Daun

Scene from the Battle of Kolin

prepared a strong defensive position atop a range of hills near what is now Kolin, Czech Republic, about 30 miles east of Prague, and waited for Frederick to come to him. While Frederick was nervously hastening eastward, von Daun was calmly arranging his cannon to cover every possible approach to the hills in a deadly crossfire. These careful preparations meant that in order to attack Von Daun, Frederick would have to drive his foot-weary infantrymen uphill against rested enemies who far outnumbered them, all under withering cannon fire.

Under the combined weight of so many disadvantages, not even Frederick the Great could stand. Early in the Battle of Kolin, it seemed that Frederick might work his magic yet again; but after several hours of battle, his stalwart Prussian infantry finally collapsed. By battle's end, another 14,000 irreplaceable Prussian troops lay dead or wounded, leaving Frederick with no choice but to retreat— not only from Kolin, but also from Prague. After this first serious defeat of his long military career, the beaten Frederick the Great gave up on capturing Bohemia, and retreated back toward Saxony.

Later that year, the armies Frederick had left behind to defend his homeland suffered more defeats:

- In the east, a huge Russian army defeated a far smaller Prussian one at the Battle of Gross-Jägersdorf, near what is now Kaliningrad, Russia.
- In the north, a Swedish army fought to expand Swedish Pomerania, the territory Sweden held around the important Baltic Sea port of Stralsund.
- In the west, the French invaded and occupied Hanover, the ally Britain had hired Prussia to defend.

Not for nothing, though, was Frederick called great. Later that year, Frederick rescued Prussia from what seemed like certain destruction with two stunning victories:

1. The Battle of Rossbach (November 5, 1757)

Among the many threats Prussia faced in late 1757, the most immediate was the French Marshal Charles de Rohan, Prince of Soubise. Soubise spent that summer guiding some 60,000 French and German troops in the direction of Leipzig, Saxony. As he advanced, he boasted that his splendid army would defeat Frederick's easily, and that he expected to spend the coming winter resting comfortably inside Prussia's capital, Berlin. Nor did Soubise's boast seem overly bold; for with enemies threatening on all sides, the largest army Frederick could set against Soubise numbered just 22,000, hardly more than one-third his enemy's numbers.

Soubise and Frederick spent about a month maneuvering around one another in Saxony, each waiting for the other to make a mistake. Soubise's mistake came on a patch of hilly ground near Rossbach, Saxony (now Braunsbedra, Germany), about 20 miles west of Leipzig. The unevenness of the terrain around Rossbach meant that the two armies sometimes couldn't see one another, even though they watched from the highest belfries in the area. Frederick turned this blindness into an advantage.

Sometime after noon on November 5, 1757, Frederick noticed Soubise executing a clumsy move to his own southeast, trying to get around the Prussians' left flank. Pretending fear, Frederick retreated eastward— but only until his army moved behind a large hill, out of Soubise's sight. Once his army was safely hidden behind the hill, Frederick turned it sharply southward, preparing his troops to attack Soubise anywhere along his line of approach. So silently and efficiently did Frederick's Prussians maneuver that when Soubise approached Frederick's hill, he had no idea that Frederick's whole army was waiting for him just beyond its crest.

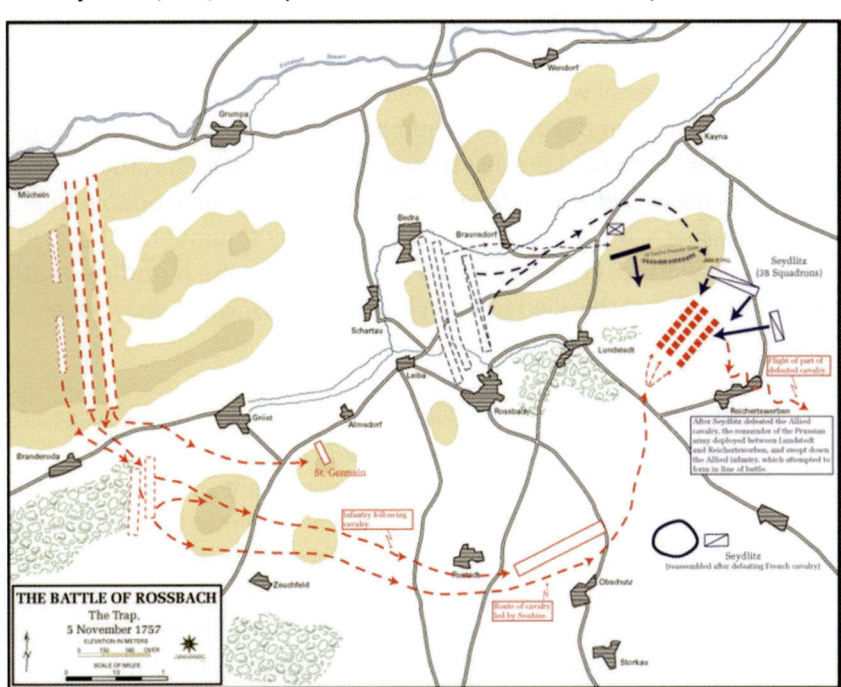

Maneuvers at the Battle of Rossbach: Frederick in blue, Soubise in red

The moment Soubise came into range, Frederick's artillery crested the hill and opened fire. Meanwhile, Frederick's cavalry crested a hilltop farther east and charged down on Soubise's exposed, completely defenseless right flank. So swift and terrifying was Prussia's charge that Soubise's troops instantly fled, the men in front trampling the men in the rear in their haste to escape. In a little over an hour, Frederick's Prussians killed or wounded 5,000 of Soubise's troops, and captured 5,000 more— versus just over 500 casualties on the Prussian side. Prussia's victory was so swift and complete that according to Frederick, most of his infantrymen never even had time to unshoulder their muskets.

Scene from the Battle of Rossbach

2. The Battle of Leuthen (December 5, 1757)

A second grave threat awaited Frederick more than 200 miles to the east, at the Silesian capital city of Breslau (now Wroclaw, Poland). Between the battles of Kolin and Rossbach, Austrian commanders Charles of Lorraine and Marshal von Daun invaded Silesia with a combined total of some 80,000 troops, more than enough to seize Breslau from the badly outnumbered army Frederick had left behind to defend it. Frederick calculated that if the Austrians held Breslau through the coming winter, then Silesia was as good as lost.

On his way east to retake Breslau, Frederick managed to gather some 30,000 – 36,000 troops— more than at Rossbach, but still less than half his enemy's numbers. About 30 miles west of Breslau, near what is now Prochowice, Poland, Frederick took a moment to inspire his officers with a now-famous speech called the **Parchwitz Address**, which may have included words like these:

> "Against all the rules of military science I am going to engage an army nearly three times greater than my own. I fully recognize the dangers attached to this enterprise, but in my present situation I must conquer or die. If we go under, all is lost. We must either beat the enemy, or all together make for ourselves graves before his batteries. This I mean and thus will I act. Bear in mind, gentlemen, that you are Prussians; we shall be fighting for our glory, the preservation of our homes, and for our wives and children. Those who think as I do can rest assured that if they are killed, then I will look after their families. If anybody prefers to take his leave, he can have it now, but he will cease to have any claim on my benevolence."

Frederick the Great

Frederick's enemies awaited him about 10 miles west of Breslau, stretched out along a four-mile-long battlefront that ran through Leuthen, Silesia (now Lutynia, Poland). As always, Frederick studied the battlefield, searching for an opportunity to attack his enemy's little-defended flanks. Frederick noted that his enemies had anchored their northern flank in swampy ground, rendering attack from that direction all but impossible. However, he also noted that no such obstacle guarded his enemy's southern flank. Furthermore, there was a conveniently-placed line of hills that might hide his army as it maneuvered around that southern flank, much as his hill had hidden him at Rossbach.

To conceal his maneuvers, Frederick needed to distract his enemies. Therefore his first move was to send part of his army north, miles from where the main attack would fall. While this diversionary force noisily blasted away in the north, Frederick's main army silently disappeared behind his range of hills and stole around to the south. Frederick's troops were so disciplined that tens of thousands of them somehow managed to reach the Austrians' southern flank completely undetected.

After issuing careful instructions to his eager troops, Frederick unleashed a firestorm of destruction on his enemies' utterly defenseless southern flank. In 5-1/2 hours of battle, the Prussians killed or wounded about 10,000 Austrians, and captured 12,000 more. In recapturing Silesia, Frederick also captured the troops Austria had sent to defend it, another 17,000 men. However, this victory was far costlier the one at Rossbach; for at battle's end, more than 6,000 irreplaceable Prussian troops lay dead or wounded.

Prussia Near Collapse (1758 – 1762)

Through the remaining years of the Seven Years' War, Frederick was forced to follow the less aggressive strategy of defending the territory he had, rather than seizing territory he didn't have— partly because his enemies outnumbered him so badly, and partly because the first three years of war had cost him his best officers and troops. Frederick wrote in 1759:

> "I would fear nothing if I still had ten battalions of the quality of 1757. But this cruel war has killed off our finest soldiers, and the ones we have left do not even measure up to the worst of our troops at the outset."

As the war dragged on, the strain of it reached beyond Prussia's armies, and began to drag down Prussia itself. Except for the gold Prussia's ally Britain provided, all of the tremendous resources needed to fight this long, terrible war— all of the food, shelter and fuel; all of the horses and fodder; all of the weapons, gunpowder and ammunition; and especially all of the brave young men— had to come from tiny Prussia, whose population measured a fraction of any one of its enemies'. The unbearable strain of providing so many resources for so long led to hunger, cold, sickness, grief and every other sort of suffering imaginable. Frederick wrote of Prussia's plight in 1759:

> "A damned soul in hell is in no more abominable situation than this in which I find myself."

The Miracles of the House of Brandenburg

Twice, the strain of the Seven Years' War grew so great that Frederick feared Prussia would soon fall; but each time, miracles intervened to save Prussia.

1. The Battle of Kunersdorf (August 12, 1759):

In the summer of 1759, an allied Russian-Austrian army nearly 60,000 strong drew dangerously close to Berlin. Desperate to save his capital, Frederick led about 50,000 Prussians out to meet his enemies at Kunersdorf, Prussia (now Kunowice, Poland), a village near the east bank of the Oder River about 50 miles east of Berlin.

Frederick being chased by Russian Cossack troops at the Battle of Kunersdorf

Frederick's situation before the Battle of Kunersdorf was much like his situation before the Battle of Kolin: he was threatened on all sides, and needed to defeat this new threat quickly so that he could face other threats. In his desperation, Frederick pushed his troops too hard, spending them so recklessly that when his beaten army scattered at battle's end, tens of thousands of Prussians— perhaps more than 25,000— were either dead, wounded, captured or missing.

What alarmed Frederick most about this devastating loss was that it left him with too few troops to defend Berlin. Certain that his enemies would now take advantage of his weakness by seizing Berlin, Frederick wrote in despair after the Battle of Kunersdorf:

"At the moment in which I report all this, everyone is on the run; I am no more master of my troops... I do not have any more resources, and— frankly confessed— I believe that everything is lost. I will not survive the doom of my fatherland. Farewell forever!"

FASCINATING FACTS: The First Miracle of the House of Brandenburg

To Frederick's astonishment and delight, a quarrel among his enemies prevented them from seizing Berlin when they had the chance. The allied Russian-Austrian army that defeated Frederick at Kunersdorf had contained more than 40,000 Russians, and fewer than 20,000 Austrians. All by itself, the Russian side had suffered losses nearly as high as Prussia's— perhaps more than 20,000 dead, wounded or missing, all in a single battle. Austria, on the other hand, came through the battle relatively unscathed. Partly because their losses were so uneven, the allies quarreled after the battle. The Austrian commander, Frederick's old nemesis von Daun, wanted to press the allies' advantage right away; but the Russian commander refused, insisting that he needed the coming winter to rest and rebuild his army. Thus the alliance dissolved for the moment, with Russians and Austrians retreating in different directions— giving Frederick the crucial time he needed to rebuild Prussia's decimated army.

In a letter to his brother Henry Louis dated September 1, 1759, Frederick referred to this fortuitous Russian-Austrian quarrel as the **Miracle of the House of Brandenburg**.

2. The Siege of Kolberg (August – December 1761): By 1761, Prussia was down to just one port on the Baltic Sea, one last pipeline for receiving supplies from overseas: Kolberg (now Kołobrzeg, Poland), about 120 miles west of Gdansk. Russia had already laid siege to Kolberg twice, once in 1759 and again in 1760. Both times, Prussia had managed to fight Russia off. In December 1761, though, Prussia finally surrendered Kolberg to an allied Russian-Swedish army after a four-month siege.

The fall of Kolberg was the last in a long string of defeats that

The fall of the Prussian fortress at Kolberg

left Prussia more desperate than ever. With no more supplies coming in from Kolberg, and with his enemies closing in on all sides, Frederick had every reason to fear that Prussia would soon fall.

FASCINATING FACTS: The Second Miracle of the House of Brandenburg

In his despair near the end of the Seven Years' War, Frederick the Great considered several schemes for saving Prussia:

- One scheme was to propose an alliance with Austria's deadly enemy to the south, the Ottoman Empire; but the Ottomans weren't interested.

- A second was to negotiate with his enemies for peace; but Frederick's enemies, sensing that Prussia was near collapse, refused to negotiate away territory that they might soon win on the battlefield.

- Frederick also considered abdicating Prussia's throne, handing it down to his nephew in the hope that his enemies might leave some part of Prussia in some Hohenzollern's hands.

- Failing all of these, Frederick even considered taking poison so that he wouldn't live to witness the demise of his beloved fatherland.

To Frederick's great relief, all of these schemes became unnecessary on January 5, 1762, the day a second Miracle of the House of Brandenburg rescued Prussia a second time. On that day, Maria Theresa's faithful ally Elizabeth of Russia died, leaving her throne to her nephew Peter III of Russia.

Emperor Peter III was Empress Elizabeth's opposite. Having been born and raised in Germany, Peter was a great admirer of Frederick the Great, and detested his aunt's war on Prussia. Therefore when Peter took his aunt's place, he immediately withdrew Russia from its alliance with Austria, and formed a new alliance with Prussia. To the bewilderment of his generals, Peter restored hard-won Kolberg to Prussia, along with a great deal of territory in East Prussia— all territories for which tens of thousands of Russian troops had sacrificed their lives. Peter even went so far as to commit Russian troops to Prussia's defense, setting them against their former allies in Austria.

German-born Russian Emperor Peter III

The Treaty of Hubertusburg (1763)

Russia's abrupt change of alliances dramatically reversed the course of the Seven Years' War. Soon after Russia dropped out of Maria Theresa's anti-Prussian alliance, Sweden dropped out as well, leaving Austria with no more allies in the east. Meanwhile Austria's western ally, France, had already lost the French and Indian War to Britain, and was growing weary of its back-and-forth war in Hanover.

These abandonments left Maria Theresa standing all alone against one of the most terrifying foes imaginable: a revitalized, vengeful Frederick the Great. When the spring of 1762 arrived, Frederick emerged from winter quarters and, with a string of victories, quickly reclaimed most of the territory he had lost to Austria— including Silesia, the valuable prize that had started all the bloodshed. Weakened though Frederick was, Maria Theresa could see no hope of defeating this greatest of generals without allies; so she finally, reluctantly gave up on Silesia, and entered negotiations for peace.

SUCCINCT SUMMARIES: The Seven Years' War in Central and Eastern Europe ended with the **Treaty of Hubertusburg**, signed by Austria, Prussia and Saxony in 1763. Ironically, not one of these countries gained any territory in exchange for the seven years of terrible war it had just endured. All sides had to satisfy themselves with the territories they held before the war.

REFRESHING REMINDERS: The Seven Years' War had far greater territorial consequences in North America, where Austria's ally France lost all of Canada to Britain.

MUSICAL MASTERS: Wolfgang Amadeus Mozart (1756 – 1791)

The Austrian musical prodigy Wolfgang Amadeus Mozart started practicing on several instruments, both keyboards and strings, at age four. By age six, he was already performing for Empress-Queen Maria Theresa of Austria; and at age eleven, he composed his first opera. During his too-short lifetime, this prolific genius would compose over six hundred works— more than 200 hours of music. Papa Haydn once remarked to Mozart's proud father: "I tell you before God, and as an honest man, your son is the greatest composer known to me by person and repute; he has taste, and what is more, the greatest skill in composition."

Mozart's best-known works include:

- *The Marriage of Figaro* (debuted 1786), a comic opera composed as a sequel to the well-known *Barber of Seville*.

Portrait of Mozart as a child prodigy

- *Don Giovanni* (debuted 1789), another comic opera based on the legend of the romantic Don Juan.

- *The Magic Flute* (debuted 1791), a comical-magical *singspiel*— in other words, part opera and part dramatic play.

- *Requiem Mass in D minor*, an anonymously-commissioned death mass that was not quite finished when Mozart died in 1791. According to legend, the ailing Mozart believed that whoever commissioned *Requiem* knew that Mozart was soon to die, and actually commissioned it for Mozart himself.

Unfortunately, Mozart struggled with a bad habit of spending more than he earned. Despite successes that brought in a great deal of money, Mozart suffered grievous money problems throughout his adult life. When Mozart died of some unknown illness at age 35, his wife Constanze couldn't afford a tombstone for her illustrious husband; so his remains went to a common pauper's grave.

Posthumous portrait of Mozart

Russia under Peter III and Catherine the Great

To no one's surprise, few Russians rejoiced to see their new emperor freely giving away valuable territories which their beloved sons had purchased with their lives. Peter III's foolish generosity to Frederick the Great was the main reason for Peter's early demise, and for the rise of Russia's next empress: his wife Catherine.

ILLUMINATING LISTS: Emperors of All the Russias from Peter the Great through Catherine the Great

Tsar/Emperor	Reign	Tsar/Emperor	Reign
Peter I the Great	1682 – 1725	Catherine I (Peter I's wife)	1725 – 1727
Peter II (Peter I's grandson)	1727 – 1730	Anna (Ivan V's daughter)	1730 – 1740
Ivan VI (Ivan V's great-grandson)	1740 – 1741	Elizabeth (Peter I's daughter)	1741 – 1762
Peter III (Elizabeth's nephew)	1762 – 1762	Catherine II the Great	1762 – 1796

REFRESHING REMINDERS from Chapter 17: Near the end of his reign, Peter the Great changed his title from "Tsar of Russia" to "Emperor of All Russia."

INTERESTING INDIVIDUALS: Empress Catherine II of Russia, a.k.a. Catherine the Great (1729 – 1796)

Ironically, the second Emperor of All Russia to bear the honored title "Great" wasn't even Russian-born. The future Catherine the Great was born in Stettin, Prussia as Princess Sophia Augusta Fredericka von Anhalt. Her father was a German prince, and her mother a princess of German and Swedish descent. For the sake of winning Russian hearts, though, Sophia was willing to make herself as Russian as anyone could wish.

Becoming Russian, Becoming Orthodox

When Sophia was not quite 15, her mother received a long business letter full of important news about Sophia's future. For years, Sophia had known that Empress Elizabeth of Russia was considering her as a bride for the heir to Russia's throne, the future Emperor Peter III. Although Sophia hadn't read her mother's letter, she felt certain that it contained an invitation to Russia.

Both of Sophia's parents were wary of accepting this invitation. Sophia's father, a devout Lutheran, didn't want his beloved daughter converting to Russian Orthodoxy; while her mother worried that Russia was an unstable country full of mean drunks and assassins. Sophia, though, was less Lutheran than her father, and less fearful than her mother. With a bit of coaxing, Sophia convinced her parents that this was the opportunity of a lifetime, her only chance to wear one of the greatest crowns in the world. Before departing Germany for Russia in 1744, Sophia made up her mind to do whatever was necessary— to learn any language, adopt any customs and profess any religion she had to— for the sake of wearing Russia's crown.

Portrait of Princess Sophia at age 15 or 16

Sophia's determination to become Russian was so strong that it nearly killed her. When Sophia reached Moscow, the Russian court assigned her three instructors: one for Russian language, one for the Russian Orthodox faith and one for Russian dance. Determined to make swift progress in her language lessons, Sophia took to rising in the middle of the night to practice them. Having no experience of Russia's cold climate, she didn't bother putting on shoes and extra robes for these late-night sessions. Thirteen days after her arrival, her lack of caution brought on high fever and terrible pain in her side— symptoms of pleurisy, an inflammation of the lining around the lungs. Sophia's doctors wanted to bleed her; but her mother, who was convinced that bloodletting had killed her brother, wouldn't hear of it. Finally, Empress Elizabeth took the decision out of Sophia's mother's hands. On Elizabeth's orders, doctors bled Sophia again and again, up to four times per day. Whether or not bloodletting actually helped, the infection in Sophia's lungs finally burst, allowing her to recover.

Dangerous though Sophia's illness was, it aided her campaign to win Russian hearts. Once when Sophia seemed near death, her mother asked her if she would like to see a Lutheran priest. Sick though she was, Sophia still understood how important the Orthodox faith was to her new Russian friends; so she replied that an Orthodox priest would make her happier. After that, no one doubted the sincerity of her Orthodox faith. Sophia's illness also helped teach her Russian politics— for by feigning sleep while visitors chatted in her sickroom, she overheard whispered secrets that she never would have learned otherwise.

Before Sophia could be betrothed to Peter, she needed to be confirmed in the Orthodox faith. It was at her confirmation ceremony that she received her new, more Russian-sounding name: Ekaterina, or Catherine.

INTERESTING IDEAS: The reason Sophia couldn't use her given name was because that name belonged to one of Russia's more notorious villains: Sophia Alexeievna, elder sister to Peter the Great (see Chapter 17). In light of Sophia's many misdeeds— murdering Peter's uncles, the Streltsy Uprising and so on— Empress Elizabeth sought a more respectable name for her heir's wife; so she chose "Catherine" in honor of Peter's beloved wife.

Problems with Peter III

Catherine's betrothed, too, hailed from Germany. The future Peter III was born in 1728 to the Duke of Holstein, Germany, and raised there through the age of 14; and because of these German roots, Peter always considered himself a German. However, Peter also had Russian roots through his mother Anna Petrovna, daughter to Peter the Great.

Catherine first met Peter in 1739, when his only official rank was Heir to the Duke of Holstein. At the time, Catherine found Peter "good-looking, well-mannered and courteous." However, she also heard rumors "that he already had a great inclination for drink"— even though he was only 11 years old at the time.

Between this first meeting and the next one in 1744, Peter's rank improved mightily: (1) in 1739, he inherited his father's place as Duke of Holstein; and (2) in 1742, his royal aunt Empress Elizabeth officially named him heir to Russia's throne. Despite Peter's much-loftier rank at this second meeting, Catherine found less to admire about him; for while he was still "quite good-looking," he was also "small and infantile, talking of nothing but soldiers and toys... he spent his time in his room playing soldiers with his valets, flunkeys, his dwarfs, and his gentlemen-in-waiting."

Later in 1744, Peter lost even his good looks— for a bad case of smallpox marred his face with deep, permanent pockmarks, leaving him "horrid to look at" in Catherine's eyes. Nor was Peter overly fond of Catherine; for before their wedding, he admitted to her that he preferred other women. Nevertheless, for the sakes of both their dynasties, the two went through with their wedding on August 21, 1745.

After the wedding, the royal couple's relationship went from bad to worse. Because neither loved the other, both sought love in other relationships. Peter enjoyed a string of mistresses, and often threatened to replace Catherine with one of them. For her part, Catherine entertained a string of handsome lovers. If Catherine's memoirs are true, then there is every reason to doubt that Peter was the true father of her first child, the future Emperor Paul I of Russia. As for her other two children, Peter certainly fathered neither.

Catherine around the time of her wedding

Peter's Problems with the Russian People

As bad as Peter's problems with Catherine were, his problems with the Russian people were worse— for unlike Catherine, Peter made not the slightest effort to win Russian hearts. From the beginning, Peter sneered at Russia's language, customs, and religion— leaving no doubt that in his mind, Germany was superior to Russia in all three. As Duke of Holstein, Peter insisted on wearing his German military uniform at all state functions, making it clear that he considered the German military superior as well. Peter even wore his German uniform when he led drills with the Russian army, leaving Russian troops to wonder where his true loyalties lay. Peter's childish delight with all things German caused even greater resentment after 1756, when Russia joined the Seven Years' War against German-speaking Prussia (see above).

The deeper the Russian people's resentment for Peter grew, the more Catherine feared for her safety. Her first fear was that Peter might make good his threat to divorce her and send her to a nunnery. Failing that, Catherine calculated, she had just two options:

1. She could remain at Peter's side— in which case she would certainly share the same miserable doom that was sure to befall Peter.
2. She could break with Peter— in which case she might hope that the Russian people wouldn't blame her for her husband's mistakes.

As Catherine saw her dilemma in the days leading up to Empress Elizabeth's death:

> "… it was a matter of either perishing with— or because of— him; or else of saving myself, the children and perhaps the state from the wreckage to which the [wretched] moral and physical qualities of this prince were leading us."

Overthrowing Peter III

On the Orthodox Christmas Day of January 5, 1762, Empress Elizabeth died, and her heir took his place as Peter III, Emperor of All Russia. Far from mourning his aunt's passing, Peter welcomed it as his chance to do what he had been waiting to do for years: remake Russia in Germany's image. To the Russian people's horror, Peter showed not the slightest respect for their time-honored customs, nor for the painful sacrifices their war against Prussia had cost them:

- Peter ordered new uniforms for the Russian army, modeling them after the uniforms of Prussia— the very country Russia had been battling for the last six years.

- Peter seized church properties that had long been set aside to provide incomes for Orthodox priests, making them government properties instead— leaving Russia's beloved priests with no way to support themselves.

Peter III's Prussian friend Frederick the Great stepping over Russian corpses at the Seven Years' War Battle of Zorndorf, which cost the Russians some 18,000 dead or wounded

- Worst of all, Peter made peace with Prussia— freely handing back all of the territory that Russia had captured from Prussia in the Seven Years' War, as if the tens of thousands of Russian lives sacrificed to win that territory meant nothing to him.

With these rapid changes, Peter foolishly declared war on all three of Russia's most powerful institutions: the army, the Orthodox Church and the Russian people.

Catherine, on the other hand, behaved as the Russian people expected their emperor to behave. During the six weeks of mourning the Orthodox Church prescribed after Elizabeth's passing, thousands of Russians saw Catherine beside the late Empress' bier, respectfully mourning Elizabeth as Peter never did. Catherine's proper dignity won her the Russian people's love and respect, even as they lost all respect for their new emperor.

The Russian people's smoldering resentment against Peter burst into full flame in June 1762, at a celebration Peter held to honor his new alliance with Prussia— an alliance everyone but Peter loathed. During this uncomfortable celebration, someone proposed a toast to the royal family's health. Catherine— who understood Russian customs well enough to know that it was improper to toast one's own health— remained respectfully seated. Seeing this, Peter— who cared nothing for Russian customs, and who loved alcohol as much as he loved Prussia— openly mocked Catherine for keeping her seat. Peter's mockery backfired on him; for the Russian people honored Catherine's quiet dignity, and despised Peter for abusing her.

The shame of this incident so angered Peter that he finally ordered Catherine's arrest. Although Peter withdrew this order before his police could act on it, Catherine heard all about it, and understood what it meant: that if she didn't do something soon, then she might find herself locked inside some nunnery or prison— or worse, dead.

To avoid all of these unpleasant possibilities, Catherine made secret arrangements with several powerful army officers, most of whom were more than eager to help her dispense with Peter III. On the morning of June 28, 1762, Catherine's officers gathered some 20,000 Russian troops for a revolution designed to force Peter off his throne, and set Catherine in his place. Given the hatred these troops already bore Peter, Catherine had no trouble winning their loyalty with two promises: (1) that she would defend the Russian Orthodox Church, which Peter had carelessly undermined; and (2) that she would defend glorious Russia, which Peter had foolishly deprived of the Prussian territory it had fought so hard to win.

In light of the way Peter III had spent his life so far— constantly rehearsing for war, first with toy soldiers in his room, and then with live troops on the parade ground— Catherine might have expected him to at least try to resist her. Instead, Peter meekly surrendered without a fight. Even Peter's supposed friend Frederick the Great mocked the easy way Peter signed his abdication, "like a child who is sent to bed." The whole affair passed without bloodshed: Catherine became Empress of All Russia, and Peter became her prisoner.

The new Empress Catherine on horseback, wearing the uniform of one of the army units that helped her overthrow Peter III

Remarkably, the former emperor who had only lately owned everything imaginable now asked Catherine for just four items in prison: "his mistress, his dog, his negro and his violin."

FASCINATING FATES: The Fate of Emperor Peter III

Only about a week after the coup that set her on Russia's throne, Catherine received news that may or may not have surprised her: her husband Peter was dead. The official cause of death, announced by Catherine and defended in letters to her friends, was a brain hemorrhage brought on by a colic, which in turn was brought on by the fright of losing his throne. Being satisfied with this medical explanation, Catherine never ordered any criminal investigation, nor punished anyone for Peter's death.

Because Peter's death was so convenient for Catherine, even loyal supporters doubted her official story. From Catherine's day through present day, historians have wondered: Did Catherine order Peter's murder? Or did one of her officers surmise that she would welcome news of Peter's death, and take Peter's murder upon himself? Did one of Catherine's lovers murder Peter, perhaps so that Catherine would be free to marry? Or did Peter perhaps decide that his new life as a prisoner wasn't worth living, and commit suicide?

ANOTHER FASCINATING FATE: Two years after Peter III's death, another competitor for Catherine's throne met a sudden, violent end. Ivan VI of Russia was a great-grandson of Ivan V, the weak-minded elder brother of Peter the Great who shared Peter's throne for a time (see Chapter 17). The infant Ivan VI had served as Emperor briefly back in 1740 – 1741, before a coup set Empress Elizabeth on the throne. Since then, jailers had held this poor young man in the cruelest isolation imaginable, denying him family, friends and even an education so that he could never claim Russia's throne.

In 1764, one of Catherine's enemies tried to free Ivan VI so that he could challenge her. This scheme failed when, on Catherine's orders, Ivan's jailers killed him to prevent his escape. Thus Catherine may have had the blood of not one, but two former Russian emperors on her hands.

The Russian Enlightenment

Catherine went on to reign in Russia for 31 years, earning the title "Great" for all she accomplished. One great task of Catherine's reign was to finish the difficult work begun under Ivan the Terrible and Peter the Great— the work of bringing backward Russia up to speed with the fast-advancing West. To accomplish this **Russian Enlightenment**, Catherine:

- Built as many schools as Russia could afford, modeling them after English, Prussian and other European schools. Among Catherine's new schools was the **Smolny Institute**— the first academy where the daughters of Russian nobles could learn not only etiquette and dance, but also philosophy, math and science.

- Built a new Imperial Academy of the Arts, a school where budding Russian talents could study art and architecture. During Catherine's reign, her architects helped transform St. Petersburg from a plain city of wood into a beautiful city of stone.

- Built more and better hospitals, sometimes importing Western doctors to train Russian ones.

- Wrote the *Nakaz*, a guide for reforming Russia's backward legal code. Among other things, Catherine's *Nakaz* stressed the common law principle of equal punishment for equal crimes; and it also discouraged cruel and unusual punishments such as torture and the death penalty.

The Smolny Institute

- Gradually brought the Russian Orthodox Church under government control— partly because traditional church courts were incompatible with common law. Ironically, the Russian people made relatively little fuss about Catherine's interference with Orthodox traditions, even though this was one of the very crimes for which they had condemned Peter III.

For advice on these reforms, Catherine corresponded with the most enlightened philosophers of her day— especially the French author Voltaire (see Chapter 25), with whom she exchanged letters for more than 15 years. However, Catherine was careful not to carry Voltaire's ideas too far; for unlike Voltaire, Catherine never stopped believing that absolute monarchy was the best form of government for Russia. Catherine explanation for this difference with Voltaire appears in the *Nakaz*:

"[Russia's vast size] requires an absolute power to be vested in that person who rules over it... Every other form of government whatsoever would not only have been prejudicial to Russia, but would even have proved its entire ruin." <u>In other words</u>: *Russia was simply too big to be governed effectively by squabbling parliaments like the ones the West favored.*

Expanding Russia

A second great task of Catherine's reign was to expand Russia's territory. Under Catherine, Russia added another 200,000-odd square miles to its already-vast territory, mainly in two directions:

1. To the south, Catherine captured New Russia— a region that included southern Ukraine, the Crimean Peninsula and other territories around the Black Sea— from Russia's old enemies, the Ottoman Empire and the Crimean Khanate. Like Ivan the Terrible and Peter the Great, Catherine dreamed that her **Russo-Turkish Wars** might capture Constantinople from the Ottomans; but they never did.
2. To the west, Catherine used diplomacy backed by threats of force to seize great chunks of territory from her weakest neighbor, Poland. Over the course of three **Partitions of Poland**— one each in 1772, 1793 and 1795— Russia, Prussia and Austria gradually divided Poland's territory between them until there was none left. About two-thirds of Poland's former territory went to Russia, leaving Prussia and Austria to divide the other one-third.

Catherine the Great at work on the *Nakaz*

A LOOK AHEAD: Although Poland officially ceased to exist near the end of Catherine's reign, the Polish people remained separate, proud and independent-minded. Poland will reappear in 1918, when the Polish people will declare independence from Russia and Germany at the close of World War I.

LASTING LEGENDS: Potemkin Villages

DEFINITION: A **Potemkin village** is a false village made of shell buildings with no interiors, built to fool passersby into believing that a region is prosperous when it really isn't.

In 1787, Catherine the Great led a large group of courtiers and foreign ambassadors on a rare diplomatic tour of New Russia, the region Russia conquered in the Russo-Turkish War of 1768 – 1774. The main goal of Catherine's expedition was to convince her allies how profitable her first Russo-Turkish War had been, so that they would be more willing to support her in her second Russo-Turkish War.

News of Catherine's tour came as an unpleasant surprise to her friend Gregory Potemkin, Governor of New Russia. To Potemkin had fallen the unenviable task of rebuilding a region devastated by years of ugly warfare. In his eagerness to please Catherine, Potemkin had exaggerated how well the rebuilding was going. To Potemkin's horror, Catherine was so pleased with his glowing reports of thriving villages filled with cheerful, contented villagers that she was coming to see this fantastic progress in person.

According to legend, Potemkin found a clever way out of this sticky situation. At several points along Ukraine's Dnieper River— points where Catherine was scheduled to pass by on her royal barge, but not stop to visit— Potemkin hastily erected false villages filled with shell buildings, populating them with peasants paid to wave cheerfully as Catherine passed. After Catherine's slow-moving barge floated past each false village, Potemkin's men tore the village down, loaded it onto horse-drawn carts and raced to rebuild it farther downriver. If the legend is true, then Catherine and her diplomats had no idea that they were seeing the same false buildings, smiling peasants and herds of livestock each time they floated past a Potemkin village.

FASCINATING FACTS: Russian Ballet

In 1740, professional dancers in St. Petersburg, Russia opened the first Russian ballet company, with the goal of entertaining the royal court of Empress Elizabeth. Empress Catherine the Great, too, was a great supporter of Russian ballet. Under their empresses' patronage, Russian dancers developed a style so beautiful and unique that for the first time, Western artists longed to learn from Russian ones, instead of the other way around. Russia's best-known ballet company, the *Bolshoi* or Grand Ballet, appeared in 1776.

The best-known work of Russian ballet is one American audiences still flock to see every Christmas: *The Nutcracker*, a tale of Christmas toys and candy magically coming to life. In 1891, French choreographer Marius Petipa commissioned Russian composer Peter Tchaikovsky to create music for a ballet based on "The Nutcracker and the Mouse King"— a short fantasy written by German Romantic author E. T. Hoffman, and adapted for children by French author Alexander Dumas. Over the years, Tchaikovsky's magical music gradually boosted *The Nutcracker* to its lofty place as one of the most-performed operas of all time.

Russian ballet dancers performing the Nutcracker

FASCINATING FACTS: Russian Birch Bark Manuscripts

When Native Americans looked at the large sheets of bark they pulled off birch trees, they saw canoe skins (see Chapter 5); but when the Russians looked at this bark, they saw paper and canvas:

- Centuries before the first Russian paper mill, Russians used sheets of birch bark to write everything from personal letters to official documents. Even after paper mills, Russian prisoners exiled to Siberia wrote their letters home on Siberian birch bark, which was far easier to find in Siberia than paper.

- Some Russian artists still prefer to paint on birch bark— partly because the contours of the bark make their paintings three-dimensional, much as *impasto* made Rembrandt's canvas art three-dimensional.

Letter written in Old Russian on birch bark

FASCINATING FACTS: Lozhki

Lozhki are decorated wooden spoons that early Russian folk musicians adopted as rhythm instruments because they could afford no better. At first, poor musicians simply clacked two or more spoons together to make a sound like castanets. Later musicians developed more refined techniques. In time, skilled percussionists developed lozhki music into a unique Russian art form.

Lozhki set

U.S. HISTORY FOCUS

Settling Kentucky

The Loyal Company of Virginia

The Ohio Company (see Chapter 19) wasn't the only investment company interested in the land west of the Appalachians. While the Ohio Company pursued the territory north of the Ohio River, the Loyal Company of Virginia pursued the territory south of the Ohio. In 1748, the same year the Ohio Company received its charter, the Governor's Council of Virginia granted the Loyal Company permission "… to take up and survey Eight Hundred Thousand Acres of Land in one or more Surveys, beginning on the Bounds between this Colony and North Carolina, and running to the Westward and to the North…"

FASCINATING FACTS: Among the Loyal Company's investors were prominent Virginians like (1) Peter Jefferson, father to Thomas Jefferson; and (2) John Lewis and Thomas Meriwether, grandfathers to Jefferson's explorer friend Meriwether Lewis (see Chapter 27).

U.S. National Park Service photo of Cumberland Gap

Two years later, in 1750, Loyal Company investor Thomas Walker became one of the first Virginians to pass through Cumberland Gap.

DEFINITION: **Cumberland Gap** is a mountain pass that breaks through the Appalachian Mountains near the corner where modern-day Virginia, Kentucky and Tennessee meet. As the best pass through the southern Appalachians, Cumberland Gap became the main route for Kentucky-bound settlers traveling from southern Virginia and North Carolina.

Unfortunately for both companies, the end of the French and Indian War brought royal interference which wiped out both of their claims, at least for the moment.

DEFINITION: The **Royal Proclamation of 1763** was a royal decree issued by King George III at the end of the French and Indian War. For the sake of peace with the natives, the Royal Proclamation included a provision that stopped the heart of every colonist who had been hoping to move west. "Until our further pleasure be known," the king reserved for the natives any lands "beyond the Heads or Sources of any of the Rivers which fall into the Atlantic Ocean from the West and North West."

In other words, King George ceded to the natives all territory west of the Appalachians, excepting only (1) the Province of Quebec and (2) the far northern, fur-trading territory of the Hudson's Bay Company. Furthermore, the Royal Proclamation ordered every colonist who already lived west of the Appalachians to move back east, on "Pain of our Displeasure."

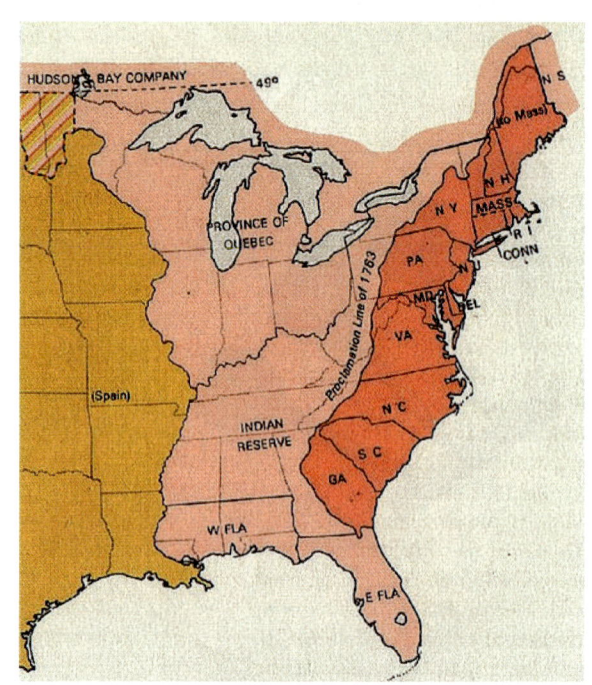

Eastern North America as divided under the Royal Proclamation

The Treaty of Fort Stanwix (1768)

To no one's surprise, the Royal Proclamation of 1763 was highly unpopular with the people of the Thirteen Colonies— many of whom felt that claiming the land west of the Appalachians had been the whole point of the French and Indian War. With more colonists than ever eager to move west, both land companies pressed the Crown to buy back the territory covered in their charters. To accomplish this, Britain negotiated treaties with two native peoples:

1. In the 1768 **Treaty of Fort Stanwix**, the Iroquois Confederacy sold its claim to most of the territory that now belongs to Kentucky and West Virginia— in exchange for a combination of money and goods worth more than 10,000 British pounds, the largest price paid in any treaty so far.

2. In a separate treaty that same year, the Iroquois Confederacy's largest southern rivals, the Cherokee people, relinquished their claims to some of that same territory.

Unfortunately, neither treaty mentioned several other peoples who also claimed that territory— including the powerful Shawnee people. Therefore when longhunters like Daniel Boone started wandering into Kentucky, the Shawnee fought to defend their hunting grounds.

AMAZING AMERICANS: Daniel Boone (1734 – 1820)

Daniel Boone was the 6th of 11 children born to Squire Boone, a Quaker who fled from England to Pennsylvania in 1713 to escape religious persecution. Thirty years later, Squire Boone ironically found himself facing persecution from the Quakers— for when his eldest son married a non-Quaker, and Squire refused to criticize his son for this obvious sin, the Quakers expelled both from their fellowship. The Quakers' strict dealings with his family so disillusioned Daniel that after the Boone family moved to North Carolina— which it did around 1750— Daniel rarely darkened the door of any church, Quaker or otherwise.

Daniel Boone was 20 years old in 1754, the year the French and Indian War broke out. Boone first crossed the Appalachians in 1755, as a wagon driver for the ill-fated Braddock Campaign. Like George Washington, Daniel Boone survived the disastrous Battle of the Monongahela, and returned to defend his North Carolina home later that year.

The following year, Boone married his sweetheart Rebecca Bryan. Daniel and Rebecca's remarkable marriage was to last more than 56 years, and produce 10 children.

Unfinished portrait of Daniel Boone

Longhunters

Back in North Carolina, Boone earned most of his living as a hunter. Daniel and his brother Squire, Jr. were among the first **longhunters**—skilled woodsmen from western North Carolina and Virginia who spent several months each year hunting the unsettled lands farther west, collecting furs to sell back home. Between the French and Indian War and the Revolutionary War, the Boone brothers became legendary woodsmen, doughty survivors with wilderness skills to match any native's. No matter how far from home Daniel Boone wandered, he was never lost, rarely went hungry and only occasionally missed a mark with his long, heavy rifle.

Exploring Kentucky (1767 – 1771)

The more colonists settled in North Carolina, the farther west longhunters had to travel in search of game. Around 1767, Daniel Boone's travels started carrying him beyond the Appalachians, into the eastern fringes of what are now Tennessee and Kentucky.

In May 1769, Boone set out on a long hunt with John Stewart— a hunting companion from his French and Indian War days who had already passed through Cumberland Gap, and wanted to share the matchless abundance of Kentucky's game with his friend. In his brief autobiography, embellished by interviewer John Filson, Boone describes the vast, unspoiled wonder of Kentucky as he and Stewart first saw it:

> "We found everywhere abundance of wild beasts of all sorts, through this vast forest. The buffaloes were more frequent than I have seen cattle in the settlements, browsing on the leaves of the cane, or cropping the herbage on those extensive plains— fearless, because ignorant, of the violence of man… Nature was here a series of wonders, and a fund of delight. Here she displayed her ingenuity and industry in a variety of flowers and fruits, beautifully colored, elegantly shaped, and charmingly flavored; and we were diverted with innumerable animals presenting themselves perpetually to our view…"

That December, though, came Boone's first encounter with the biggest drawback of settling in Kentucky: the hostile Shawnee who were determined to defend it. Having been left out of the Treaty of Fort Stanwix, the Shawnee regarded all British hunters in Kentucky as illegal poachers. When the Shawnee saw how many furs Boone and Stewart had amassed, they confiscated the entire cache, and took the two longhunters prisoner.

Fortunately, the freedom-loving Shawnee made poor jailers, as Boone was to prove more than once. After about a week, the Shawnee tired of watching their prisoners so closely, allowing Boone to take advantage of their exhaustion:

> "… in the dead of night, as we lay in a thick cane-brake by a large fire, when sleep had locked up their senses, my situation not disposing me for rest, I touched my companion, and gently awoke him. We improved this favorable opportunity, and departed, leaving them to take their rest…"

Meanwhile, Daniel's brother Squire Jr. was making his way through Cumberland Gap with extra gunpowder, shot and other necessities. Despite having little idea where in all of Kentucky his brother might be, this incomparable woodsman somehow found Daniel and replenished his dwindling supplies before winter set in. With help from Squire, Daniel was able to explore Kentucky for nearly two years, learning more about the lay of this abundant new land than any other white man in the world.

Squire Boone, Jr. searching the trackless wilderness of Kentucky for his brother Daniel

Before he returned to North Carolina in the spring of 1771, Daniel Boone decided that possessing Kentucky was worth any risk.

FASCINATING FATES: During the spring of 1770, John Stewart left the Boones' camp for a short hunting trip and never came back. Daniel never knew his friend's fate until five years later, when Stewart's remains turned up inside a hollow tree. Apparently, the Shawnee had caught up to Stewart and shot him; he had crawled inside the tree to hide from his attackers, and wound up dying there.

The Boone Expedition (1773)

Boone spent the next two years sharing the wonder of Kentucky with his North Carolina neighbors, drumming up support for what he hoped to do next: establish a permanent settlement in Kentucky. By 1773, Boone had sold everything he owned back east, and was ready to move west.

In September 1773, Daniel and Rebecca Boone led about five other families on a pioneering journey toward Cumberland Gap. As the Boone Expedition approached the Gap, though, a band of natives fell upon its rear, killing six settlers and scattering the expedition's cattle. To the Boones' grief, their eldest son James lay among the dead. Boone had hoped that the few scattered natives he had met in Kentucky so far wouldn't dare attack such a large, well-armed expedition. Instead, the natives appeared to be gearing up for all-out war.

Lord Dunmore's War (1774)

The attack on the Boone Expedition turned out to be an early battle of Lord Dunmore's War, a struggle for West Virginia and Kentucky fought mainly in 1774. The Boone expedition was not the only expedition into this territory; for after the Treaty of Fort Stanwix, settlers encroached on Shawnee hunting grounds at every Appalachian mountain pass. The more settlers appeared, the angrier the Shawnee grew— until finally, the Shawnee allied with the Cherokee and others to drive out these unwanted intruders.

In this second war of his career, Daniel Boone served as both guide and soldier. In June 1774, Boone volunteered to rescue a party of Virginia surveyors at the falls of the Ohio— hundreds of miles away on the far side of Kentucky, where no one else could have hoped to find them. Boone's unbelievable sense of direction carried him unerringly across some 800 miles of trackless wilderness in just 62 days. Partly in honor of this achievement, Boone won promotion as captain in charge of defending the Clinch River Valley, the Boone family's temporary home just south of Cumberland Gap.

Lord Dunmore's War reached its climax at the October 10, 1774 Battle of Point Pleasant, fought along the Ohio River near what is now Point Pleasant, West Virginia. After a bloody battle that killed dozens on both sides, the Shawnee reluctantly relinquished their claims to West Virginia and Kentucky— for the moment.

The Transylvania Purchase (1775)

With the Shawnee temporarily shoved aside by Lord Dunmore's War, the race was on to see who could settle Kentucky first. In early 1775, a North Carolina investor named Richard Henderson hired Daniel Boone to travel through southern Kentucky and northern Tennessee, inviting every Cherokee he met to a hurried meeting. In the **Treaty of Sycamore Shoals**, negotiated on the banks of the Watauga River in what is now northeast Tennessee, Henderson purchased from the Cherokee all territory between the Kentucky and Cumberland Rivers— an enormous swath that covered about half of what is now Kentucky, along with part of northern Tennessee. In exchange for this vast territory, called the **Transylvania Purchase**, Henderson paid the Cherokee the princely sum of 10,000 British pounds— nearly as much as the Crown had paid the Iroquois in the Treaty of Fort Stanwix.

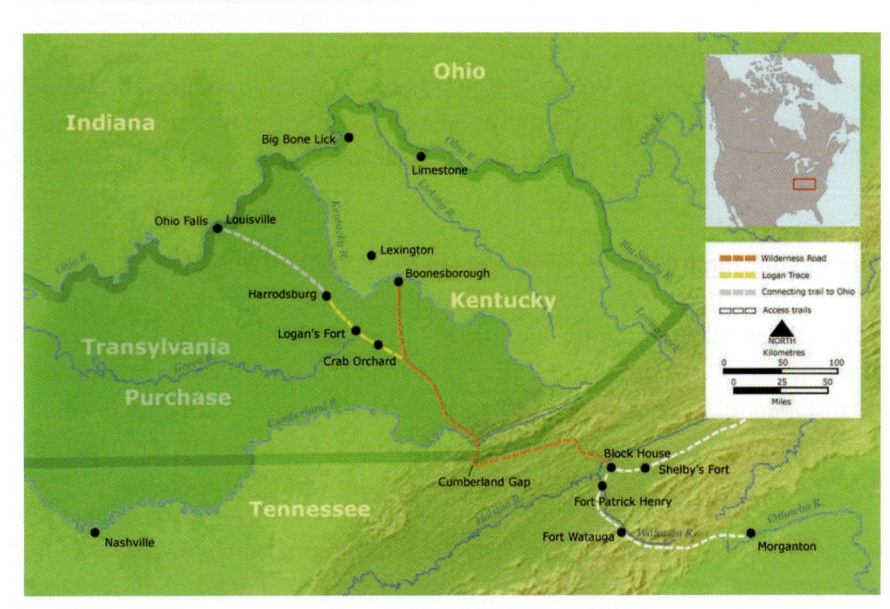

> INTERESTING IDEAS: Exotic and sinister though the name "Transylvania Purchase" may sound, its meaning was simple: *Transylvania* is Latin for "land across the forest."

As the Cherokee signed the Treaty of Sycamore Shoals, one of them took Daniel Boone by the hand and uttered these prophetic words: "Brother, we have given you a fine land, but I believe you will have much trouble in settling it."

Founding Boonesborough (April 1, 1775)

Next, Henderson hired Boone to lead a trailblazing expedition through Cumberland Gap and across central Kentucky, all the way to the Transylvania Purchase's northern boundary on the Kentucky River. At a convenient location near a salt lick on that river's south bank, Boone established his first permanent settlement in Kentucky: Boonesborough.

DEFINITION: After a bit of widening, the trail Daniel Boone blazed became the **Wilderness Road**, the only road into Kentucky from the south for many years. Unfortunately, the Wilderness Road suffered from two major inconveniences: (1) it was too steep for wagons, and (2) its many hills and turns provided the Shawnee with countless hiding places from which to ambush unwary travelers.

Daniel Boone guiding settlers to Boonesborough along the Wilderness Road

The first traveler who fell prey to ambush on the Wilderness Road was Daniel Boone himself. Before Boone and his 30-odd trailblazing axmen even reached the site of Boonesborough for the first time, a band of natives fell upon them as they slept, killing two. Three days later, a second attack killed two more. Some of Boone's attackers were Shawnee who were still fighting Lord Dunmore's War; while others were Cherokee who disliked the Treaty of Sycamore Shoals.

The Revolutionary War in Kentucky (1775 – 1783)

Less than three weeks after Boonesborough's founding on April 1, 1775, a shot fired in Concord, Massachusetts rendered the situation in Kentucky even more dangerous (see Chapter 21). When the Revolutionary War broke out between Britain and her Thirteen Colonies, the Shawnee and their allies abandoned all thought of abiding by their treaties, and instead focused on driving Boone and his fellow settlers out of Kentucky— reasoning that British attacks in the east might draw settlers away from the west. From their stronghold in Quebec, the British encouraged these Shawnee attacks, and kept the Shawnee supplied.

Daniel Boone fought the entire Revolutionary War in Kentucky, risking his neck in numerous, unspeakably bloody battles that scarred his memory for the rest of his life. Two of these cost Boone more family members: his brother Edward died in battle in 1780, and his son Israel in 1782.

Rescuing Jemima Boone (1776)

Soon after Boonesborough's founding, Daniel Boone's wife Rebecca and daughter Jemima became the first white women to stand on the banks of the Kentucky River. In moving his family to Boonesborough, Boone took a risk that would lead to the most heroic episode of his life.

One Sunday afternoon in July 1776, 14-year-old Jemima Boone and two of her girlfriends were idly floating on the Kentucky River when their canoe hit a snag on the north bank. As the three girls tried to free their canoe, a band of Shawnee leapt out of the woods, seized them and started dragging them northward through the woods, racing to put some distance between themselves and Boonesborough before anyone discovered that the girls were missing.

When Jemima didn't return in time to milk the cows, her father went looking for her, and found her canoe still stuck on the river's edge. Without even going back to don his moccasins, Daniel started tracking the Shawnee through the woods, following them alone for hours before more Boonesborough men caught up with him and joined the chase. Fortunately, the Shawnee fashioned shoes for the barefoot Jemima out of scraps of cloth torn from her long skirt. This mistake allowed Jemima to leave behind a trail of threads for her father to follow— until the Shawnee caught her at it, and threatened to kill her if she didn't stop.

Jemima Boone taken captive by the Shawnee

Thanks to their hours-long head start and the uncertainties of the trail, the Shawnee stayed ahead of the Boonesborough men for two days and nights. On the third morning, though, Daniel Boone made the Shawnee wish they had found someone else's daughter to kidnap. Silently sneaking into rifle range, Boone and his men took careful aim and opened fire on the breakfasting Shawnee, killing two and sending the rest scurrying for cover. Beyond torn skirts, none of the young women was any the worse for wear.

INTERESTING IDEAS: Daniel Boone's dramatic rescue of his daughter Jemima was one inspiration behind James Fennimore Cooper's *Last of the Mohicans*, in which the heroic Leatherstocking— also inspired partly by Boone— desperately tries to rescue two young sisters from their Huron captors.

FASCINATING FACTS: Moccasins

Like other longhunters, Daniel Boone found Native American-style leather moccasins the perfect footwear for moving through the woods—comfortable, versatile, easy to make and hard to track.

- **Tanning**— the process of transforming raw deer, elk or other hides into leather soft enough for clothing— involves soaking rawhide in a tanning solution. The key ingredient in most Native American tanning solutions was the brain of the animal from which they harvested the hide. Tanning also involves stretching, rubbing, drying and re-soaking the hide until it grows soft and supple.

- Each Native American people produced moccasins in its own unique pattern and style. Experienced trackers could guess a quarry's tribe based on his moccasin print: northern peoples made heavier, boot-like moccasins; while southern peoples made lighter, sandal-like ones. Some peoples also decorated their moccasins with beads, braids, ribbons or bits of metal.

A Prisoner, Again (1778)

In February 1778, Boone was outside Boonesborough on a salt-making expedition when a party of about 100 Shawnee took him by surprise, capturing him and 27 others. This time, Boone had to treat the Shawnee as friends for months before they trusted him enough to drop their guard.

That June, Boone's captors led him to a Shawnee village in what is now Chillicothe, Ohio. There Boone found some 450 warriors, the largest native army he had ever seen, preparing to march on Boonesborough. Desperate to save his family, Boone slipped away under cover of darkness and raced to Boonesborough on foot— covering 160 miles of pathless wilderness in just four days, taking only one meal to sustain him in all that time. Under Boone's skilled leadership, Boonesborough managed to survive a 12-day siege against overwhelming odds.

As the Revolutionary War drew to a close, Boone recalled in his autobiography all that settling Kentucky had cost him:

> "Two darling sons, and a brother, have I lost by savage hands, which have also taken from me forty valuable horses, and abundance of cattle. Many dark and sleepless nights have I been a companion for owls, separated from the cheerful society of men, scorched by the summer's sun, and pinched by the winter's cold, an instrument ordained to settle the wilderness. But now the scene is changed: Peace crowns the sylvan shade…"

An older Daniel Boone

A LOOK AHEAD: During the Revolutionary War, the state of Virginia will declare Colonel Henderson's Transylvania Purchase illegal, thereby reasserting Virginia's right to govern Kentucky. Kentucky will remain part of Virginia until 1792, when the United States Congress will admit Kentucky as the 15th state.

FASCINATING FACTS: Brown Bess Muskets versus Rifles

The most common weapon of the French and Indian and Revolutionary wars was a British-made musket soldiers affectionately called the **Brown Bess**. Although the Brown Bess was a fearsome weapon when fired by massed ranks of infantry, it was also notoriously inaccurate— mainly because of its smooth 0.75" bore. Because the Brown Bess's bore was usually caked with gunpowder residue, it required a bullet smaller than its bore, often less than .70". After hurtling down the Brown Bess's grimy bore, crashing from side to side as they went, bullets might fly out in any of several directions.

Flintlock mechanism from a Brown Bess musket

As a result, the Brown Bess was highly inaccurate beyond a range of about 50 yards, and far more effective at half that distance.

Longhunters like Daniel Boone preferred a far more accurate weapon, one that was only beginning to come into wide use in the mid-1700s: the **rifle**, named for its rifled bore. Machined inside the rifle's bore were helical grooves which set bullets spinning as they flew down

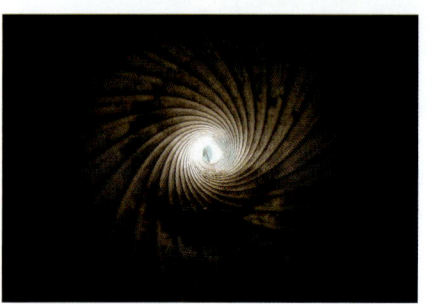

Rifling inside the barrel of a modern-day gun

the barrel, giving them an angular momentum that helped them fly far, straight and true— much as a bicycle rides straighter when its wheels are spinning.

FASCINATING FACTS:
- Although rifle marksmen like Daniel Boone could easily hit targets as small as squirrels, they didn't like the damage large bullets did to small prey. Instead of shooting the squirrel itself, they often shot the tree directly beneath the squirrel, and let the resulting explosion of wood chips kill the squirrel for them.
- The most celebrated American rifleman of the Revolutionary War was General Daniel Morgan, whose well-trained troops fired with devastating accuracy in battles all the way from Saratoga, NY to South Carolina (see Chapter 22).

U.S. STATE FOCUS

Kentucky

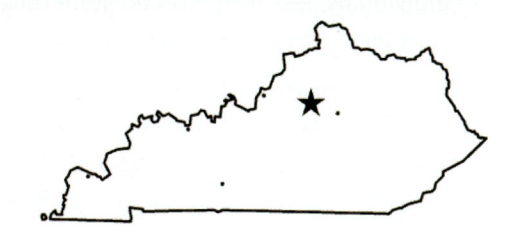

FASCINATING FACTS about Kentucky:

- State Capital: Frankfort
- State Abbreviation: KY
- Statehood: Kentucky became the 15th US state on June 1, 1792.
- Area: About 40,000 square miles (Ranks 37th in size)
- Bordering States: Virginia, West Virginia, Ohio, Indiana, Illinois, Missouri, Tennessee
- Meaning of Name: Uncertain; may have come from any of several different native words.
- State Nickname: "Bluegrass State"
- State Bird: Cardinal
- State Tree: Tulip Poplar
- State Flower: Goldenrod
- State Song: "My Old Kentucky Home" by Stephen Foster
- State Motto: "United we stand, divided we fall"
- Historic Places to Visit: Henry Clay Home, Fort Boonesborough Site, President Zachary Taylor House, Shakertown
- Resources and Industries: Horse racing and breeding, bourbon whiskey, grass seed, tobacco, farming, manufacturing

Churchill Downs, home of the Kentucky Derby thoroughbred horse race, in 1901

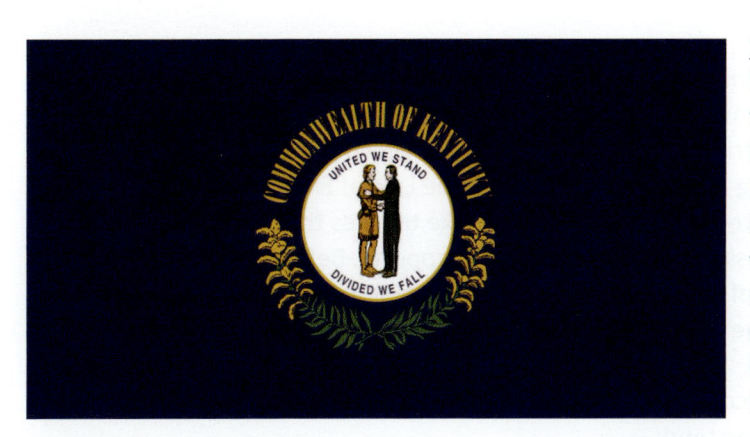

State Flag: Kentucky's state seal centered on a blue field. The seal depicts two Kentuckians, one a frontiersman and the other a statesman, shaking hands; the frontiersman may represent Daniel Boone, while the statesman may represent longtime Kentucky Senator Henry Clay. Encircling the two men is Kentucky's motto, "United we stand, divided we fall." Above the seal is written in gold letters "Commonwealth of Kentucky"; and beneath the seal are wrapped two sprigs of Kentucky's state flower, goldenrod.

CHAPTER 21: The Declaration of Independence

U.S. HISTORY FOCUS

The Age of Enlightenment, Part One

> DEFINITIONS:
> - The **Age of Enlightenment** was an era when Western philosophers like Locke, Montesquieu, Rousseau and Voltaire taught Westerners new ways of thinking about government, religion and science. The learned philosophers of the Enlightenment cared less for the Divine Right of Kings, and more for the rights of individuals; less for enforced state religion, and more for freedom of religion; less for science based on religious dogma, and more for science based on the Baconian Method (see Chapter 3).
> - The **Atlantic Revolutions** were rebellions against royal authority that sprang up on both sides of the Atlantic during the Age of Enlightenment— first in the Thirteen Colonies (1775 – 1783); then in France (1789 – 1799); then in the West Indies and South America (around 1791 – 1833). Many of these revolutions' leaders used Enlightenment philosophy to explain and justify their wars of independence.

> BRILLIANT BRITONS: John Locke (1632 – 1704)
>
> John Locke was an ingenious philosopher-author who lived through two English revolutions against two tyrannical Stuart kings— first the English Civil War, in which Oliver Cromwell overthrew and beheaded King Charles I; and then the Glorious Revolution, in which William of Orange overthrew and banished King James II. Although Locke was born too late to take part in the first revolution, his ideas helped inspire the second.
>
> In 1689, the year of the Glorious Revolution, Locke published an essay that was to have a profound effect on a third, much later revolution: the American Revolution. Many of the ideas in founding documents like the Declaration of Independence, the U.S. Constitution and the Bill of Rights descend either directly or indirectly from Locke's greatest essay, his *Second Treatise on Government*. Founding Father Thomas Jefferson was so grateful for Locke's influence that he included him on his list of the three greatest men who ever lived— a list that also included Sir Francis Bacon (see Chapter 3) and Sir Isaac Newton (see Chapter 11).

Locke's Second Treatise on Government

John Locke's *Second Treatise on Government* is a 55,000-word essay on "The Original, Extent and End of Civil Government"— in other words, on how governments came to be and what their true purposes are.

Locke's essay begins at the beginning, describing the **state of nature** in which people lived before there were governments. Locke does not teach what King James I taught in his "True Law of Free Monarchies"— that God created a few men to be kings, and all others to obey kings. Rather, Locke teaches that God created all men equal, with equal rights to enjoy the God-given blessings of life, liberty and property. Before there were governments, Locke says, all men lived in "a state of perfect freedom to order their actions, and dispose of their possessions and persons as they think fit, within the bounds of the law of nature, without asking leave or depending upon the will of any other man."

Nor was this state of nature lawless; for according to Locke, there exists a natural law of goodness, fairness and justice that all reasonable people understand:

> "The state of nature has a law of nature to govern it, which obliges every one: and reason, which is that law, teaches all mankind, who will but consult it, that being all equal and independent, no one ought to harm another in his life, health, liberty, or possessions…"

The problem, Locke says, is that while everyone understands the natural law, not everyone obeys it. When all men are free, then selfish men are free to take away the God-given rights of others— unless unselfish men band together to stop them. According to Locke, the purpose of governments is to fill three needs that the natural law doesn't fill:

1. **The need for "settled, known law."** Because the natural law is unwritten, people often disagree over exactly what it says. Good governments help avoid disagreements by writing bodies of settled law that everyone can know in advance.

2. **The need for "a known and indifferent judge."** People are often too selfish to judge fairly in cases involving themselves, their friends or their families. Therefore governments provide good judges— fair, impartial guardians of the law who (a) never take sides, and (b) always decide similar cases the same way.

3. **The need for "power to back and support the sentence when right, and to give it due execution."** Because some people will always flout the law, governments provide an executive with the authority and power to punish lawbreakers.

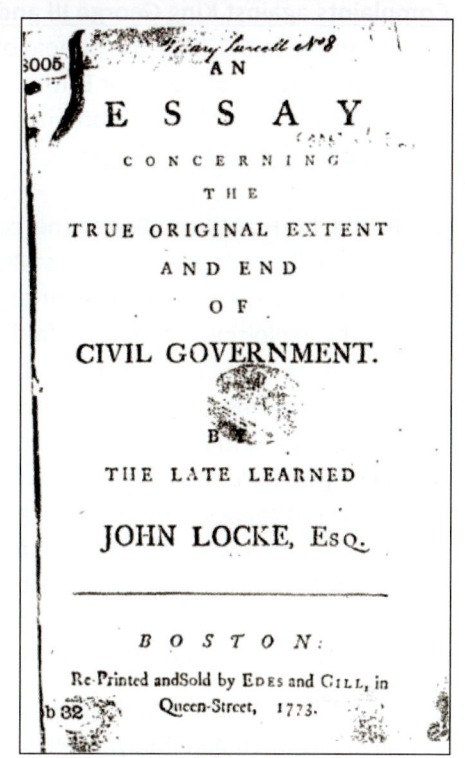

Edition of Locke's *Second Treatise on Government* published in the Colonies in 1773

A LOOK AHEAD: Locke's three purposes of government correspond precisely with the three branches of government outlined in the U.S. Constitution: (1) a legislative branch to write the law; (2) a judicial branch to adjudge the law; and (3) an executive branch to enforce the law.

From all this political philosophy, Locke derives these four principles, among others:

1. **The main purpose of any good government is to protect its people's God-given rights to life, liberty and property.** <u>In Locke's words</u>: "The great and chief end… of men's… putting themselves under government, is the preservation of their property. To which in the state of nature there are many things wanting."

2. **The authority to govern comes not from the government, but from the people; good government is by consent of the governed.** <u>In Locke's words</u>: "Men being… by nature all free, equal, and independent, no one can be put out of this estate, and subjected to the political power of another, without his own consent."

3. **Good governments exist only to benefit the people, never to enslave them.** <u>In Locke's words</u>: "[The government's] power, in the utmost bounds of it, is limited to the public good of the society. It is a power that hath no other end but preservation, and therefore can never have a right to destroy, enslave, or… impoverish the subjects."

4. **If any government turns tyrannical, and starts taking away the God-given rights it is designed to protect, then the people have a right to overthrow that government.** <u>In Locke's words</u>: "But if a long train of abuses, prevarications and artifices, all tending the same way, make the design visible to the people, and they cannot but feel what they lie under, and see whither they are going [i.e. toward tyranny], it is not to be wondered that they should then rouse themselves, and endeavor to put the rule into such hands which may secure to them the ends for which government was at first erected."

The Road to Independence

Complaints against King George III and Parliament

In the mid-1700s, the people of the Thirteen Colonies began to complain about their British government more than usual. Most of the colonists' complaints fell into one of three categories:

1. **British Mercantilism:** British mercantilism was a set of trade policies designed to boost Britain's wealth at other countries' expense. One way British traders grew wealthy was by exploiting— that is, unfairly using to their advantage— the people of the Thirteen Colonies. By controlling when, where and how colonists bought and sold goods, British mercantilists could force colonists to pay higher prices for goods imported from overseas. They could also force colonists to sell goods produced in the Colonies for lower prices. These manipulations taught the colonists how British mercantilists really looked at them— not as fellow citizens with the same rights as all Britons, but rather as second-class citizens to be exploited.

Members of the Committee of Five consult on the Declaration of Independence

2. **Violations of Colonists' Rights as Englishmen:** Ever since the Glorious Revolution and the 1689 Bill of Rights, all Englishmen had enjoyed certain basic human rights— including (1) the right to elect representatives to Parliament; (2) the right to be tried by juries of their peers; and (3) the right to live in peace without unreasonable harassment from public officials. Rough treatment from British officials taught the colonists that they were in danger of losing these rights.

3. **Taxation without Representation:** The end of the French and Indian War/Seven Years' War left the British government with a mountain of war debt, which required higher taxes. Because Britons always complained when Parliament raised taxes on the homeland, Parliament decided to raise taxes on the Thirteen Colonies instead. Colonists were used to the taxes their colonial governments levied. However, they drew the line at extra taxes levied directly by Parliament— a distant legislature that included not a single elected representative from the Thirteen Colonies.

In time, the colonists' long list of complaints against King George III and his Parliament began to look like the "long train of abuses" that John Locke described in his *Second Treatise on Government*. After enduring these abuses for decades, some patriotic colonists decided that it was time to take Locke's advice— to cast off their abusive government, and replace it with a new one that would "secure to them the ends for which government was at first erected."

ILLUMINATING LISTS: Some British Laws and Policies Patriotic Colonists Despised

Navigation Acts (1651 – 1849)	Molasses Act (1733)	Writs of Assistance (1760)
Royal Proclamation of 1763	Sugar Act (1764)	Admiralty Courts (1764, 1767)
Quartering Acts (1765, 1774)	Stamp Act (1765)	Declaratory Act (1766)
Townshend Acts (1767)	Tea Act (1773)	Intolerable Acts (1774)

A Brief Timeline of the American Revolution

1651: During the run-up to the First Anglo-Dutch War, Parliament passes its first Navigation Act.

FASCINATING FACTS: The Navigation Acts

The Navigation Acts were trade restrictions designed to give British traders advantages over Dutch and colonial ones. One such restriction required all foreign goods bound for the Colonies to go first to Britain, where they were unloaded, measured and taxed— a time-consuming process that not only raised these goods' prices, but also made perishable goods less fresh. Parliament insisted that even goods produced on the Colonies' side of the Atlantic— goods like molasses from the Spanish, French and Dutch West Indies— must first cross the Atlantic all the way to Britain, and then cross back again before they could be sold in the Colonies. Thus the Navigation Acts took away every possible advantage colonial traders might have had over homeland traders.

The Navigation Acts taught the colonists that in their mercantilist Parliament's view, the Thirteen Colonies had just one purpose: to enrich the British homeland.

1733: Parliament uses the Molasses Act to manipulate colonial rum distillers into buying overpriced molasses.

FASCINATING FACTS: The Molasses Act

The Molasses Act levied a 6-penny tax on every gallon of foreign molasses imported to the Colonies. The point of this tax was not to raise revenue for Britain. Rather, it was to boost the price of foreign molasses, thus forcing colonial rum distillers to buy the molasses Britain wanted them to buy: molasses from the British West Indies. By raising molasses prices, Britain hoped to accomplish two goals:

1. It hoped to boost the British West Indies' struggling economies.
2. It hoped to raise the price of colonial-made rum— hopefully high enough to drive colonial rum distillers out of business, to the great benefit of rum distillers in the British homeland.

Cutting West Indies sugar cane to process into molasses

Unfortunately for Britain, colonial rum distillers found a way around the Molasses Act: instead of buying British molasses, they started smuggling in foreign molasses. If any British customs official dared object, then smugglers either (1) bribed him into overlooking taxable cargo, or (2) threatened him with serious bodily harm. In the rare event that a colonial court tried a smuggler for these crimes, a jury of sympathetic colonists was sure to return the verdict "Not guilty."

The Molasses Act helped create a generation of New England trader/smugglers with decades of experience at evading British ships and defying British law.

INTERESTING IDEAS: The reason British mercantilists favored the British West Indies was because they approved of what those colonists were doing: exploiting slaves to produce molasses, something the homeland couldn't do for itself. Mercantilists did not, however, approve of what New Englanders were doing: distilling molasses into rum, a profitable business that the homeland preferred to do for itself.

1760: King George II dies, and his 22-year-old grandson takes his place as King George III. George II's death means that writs of assistance issued in his name will soon expire, and must be renewed.

DEFINITION: In colonial law, a **writ of assistance** was a long-term search warrant designed to help British customs officials find evidence against smugglers who defied the Molasses Act. Writs of assistance gave customs officials the power to search any home or business in the Colonies, with or without the owner's permission.

AMAZING AMERICANS: James Otis (1725 – 1783)

James Otis was a Boston attorney who argued strenuously against renewing British customs officials' writs of assistance. Otis' long, impassioned speech before the Massachusetts Superior Court in 1761 included these words:

"A man's house is his castle; and whilst he is quiet, he is as well guarded as a prince in his castle. This writ, if it should be declared legal, would totally annihilate this privilege. Custom-house officers may enter our houses when they please; we are commanded to permit their entry. Their menial servants may enter, may break locks, bars, and everything in their way; and whether they break through malice or revenge, no man, no court may inquire."

Despite Otis' persuasive speech, the court stubbornly renewed the writs of assistance anyway. Another Boston attorney, John Adams, later said of Otis' speech:

"… the child "Independence" was then and there born, [for] every man of an immense crowded audience appeared to me to go away as I did, ready to take arms against writs of assistance."

Portrait of King George III in his coronation robes

1763 – The Royal Proclamation of 1763: At the end of the French and Indian War, King George III tries to ensure peace between colonist and native by promising that no more colonists will settle west of the Appalachians. Most colonists believe that winning the Ohio Country has been the whole point of fighting this war. Now that they have won Ohio, though, their new king is stubbornly forbidding them to settle there (see Chapters 19 – 20).

1764: Parliament further angers the colonists with two new hated acts: the Sugar Act and the Currency Act.

FASCINATING FACTS: The Sugar Act and Admiralty Courts

After the French and Indian War, Parliament really needed the money that the Molasses Act had been failing to collect for 30 years. Therefore Parliament settled on a compromise. To benefit the colonists, the new Sugar Act cut the tax on molasses in half. To benefit Parliament, the new law included tough measures to make sure the colonists actually paid the tax— including the creation of a special admiralty court.

Under the Sugar Act, accused smugglers were no longer to be tried in the Thirteen Colonies by juries of sympathetic colonists. Instead, the government would ship the accused to Halifax, Nova Scotia at the accuseds' expense, where they would appear before a new **admiralty court** specially designed to punish smugglers. In the place of a jury, the admiralty court had a single, highly biased British Royal Navy officer as a judge— one of the very officers whom New England smugglers had been evading and embarrassing for so long. These judges had extra incentive to convict smugglers— for every conviction allowed them to claim 5% of the smuggler's cargo.

Admiralty courts attacked one of the colonists' basic rights as Englishmen— the right to trial by a jury of their peers.

1764: In another impassioned speech against British abuses, Boston attorney James Otis uses the phrase "Taxation without representation is tyranny!" Otis' phrase will become a favorite catchphrase, and a main principle behind the American Revolution.

1765, March: Parliament passes a new and even more hated tax law called the Stamp Act.

FASCINATING FACTS: The Stamp Act

The Stamp Act was yet another hated tax on the Colonies, this time on printed documents. The law required nearly all printed materials— everything from attorney's licenses to college diplomas to newspapers to playing cards— to have an official British stamp in the proper amount. The tax ranged anywhere from a half-penny for a half-page leaflet to a hefty ten pounds for an attorney's license.

At more than 13,000 words, the Stamp Act was extremely long, complicated and controlling. The law set tax rates for more than 50 different types of documents, and hired scores of administrators to ensure that colonists paid the tax.

Other interesting facts:
- Once again, the Stamp Act illustrated Parliament's mercantilist strategy— for by setting high taxes for diplomas and attorneys' licenses, Parliament tried to bar poor colonists from the privileged professional class. To mercantilists, the proper place for a colonist was on a plantation, not in a courtroom or a professional office.
- The Stamp Act was the first **direct tax** on the Colonies— the first in which tax revenue went not into the Colonies' treasuries, but directly into Britain's.

Penny stamp required by the Stamp Act

INTERESTING IDEAS: During the debate in Parliament over the Stamp Act, Member Charles Townshend— whose name would soon appear on the hated Townshend Acts— expressed his indignation that the colonists might resist new taxes:

"will these Americans, children planted by our care, nourished up by our indulgence until they are grown to a degree of strength and opulence, and protected by our arms, will they grudge to contribute their mite to relieve us from heavy weight of the burden which we lie under?"

To this, an admirer of the Colonies named Isaac Barré replied just as indignantly:

"They planted by your care? No! Your oppression planted 'em in America. They fled from your tyranny to a then uncultivated and unhospitable country where they exposed themselves to almost all the hardships to which human nature is liable…

"They nourished by your indulgence? They grew by your neglect of 'em. As soon as you began to care about 'em, that care was exercised in sending persons to rule over 'em…

"They protected by your arms? They have nobly taken up arms in your defense… [these] people I believe are as truly loyal as any subjects the king has, but a people jealous of their liberties and who will vindicate them if ever they should be violated…"

1765: The first Sons of Liberty organization meets to organize protests against the Stamp Act.

DEFINITION: To the Sons of Liberty, a **Loyalist** or **Tory** was any colonist who stubbornly continued to believe that the Colonies should remain loyal to Britain, no matter what unfair laws Parliament passed against them.

FASCINATING FACTS: The Sons of Liberty

The Sons of Liberty was not a single organization, but rather a number of underground organizations formed to protest the Stamp Act and other hated British laws. Every city and colony up and down the Atlantic seacoast had its own Sons of Liberty. Because the Sons of Liberty were underground and anonymous, they had no official members; however, unofficial members included James Otis, Samuel Adams, John Hancock, Paul Revere, Patrick Henry and Benedict Arnold.

For ten years, from 1765 – 1775, the Sons of Liberty organized countless protests against taxation without representation. These protests came in a number of forms, some peaceful, some violent:

1. Some protests were no more than large public meetings to prove how many colonists despised the Stamp Act, and how few Loyalists supported it.

2. Some were sarcastic political cartoons or advertisements filled with longwinded tirades against British unfairness.

3. Some planted **liberty poles**, tall poles often topped with Greek symbols of liberty called **Phrygian Caps**.

4. Some burned in effigy hated Loyalists like Andrew Oliver, the official responsible for enforcing the Stamp Act in Massachusetts. The Sons of Liberty hung Oliver's effigy from the **Liberty Tree**, a beloved elm that stood on Boston Common— until the British cut it down during the Siege of Boston (see below).

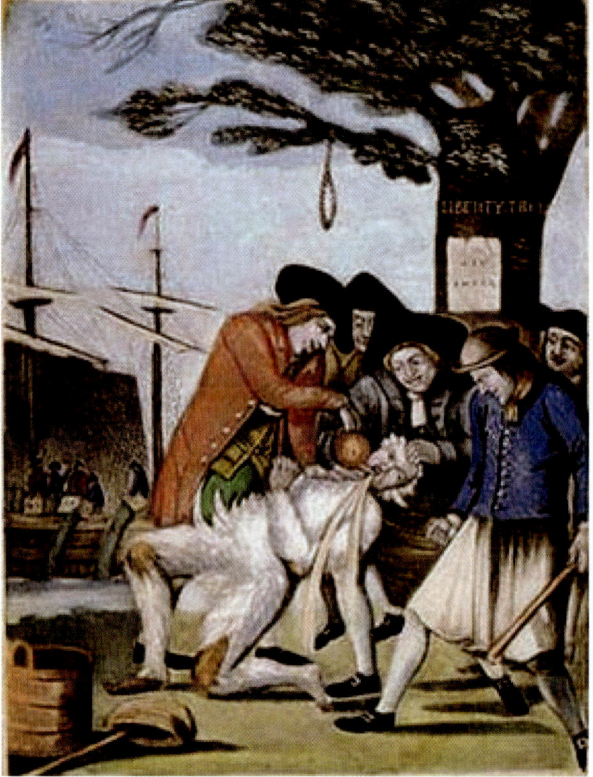

5. Some went so far as to burn down homes— including the home of Thomas Hutchinson, a hated Loyalist and future Governor of Massachusetts.

6. Some were well-organized boycotts of certain British goods, designed to hit British traders where they would feel it most— in their pocketbooks.

Boston's Sons of Liberty tarring, feathering and pouring hot tea down the throat of British customs official John Malcolm, 1774

1765, October: The Stamp Act Congress, a meeting of delegates from nine of the Thirteen Colonies, issues the "Declaration of Rights and Grievances." Three of this declaration's fourteen points are these, which echo the protests of the Sons of Liberty:

1. That colonists are British citizens entitled to the same rights as all Britons.

2. That British law protects citizens from taxation without representation.

3. That because the Thirteen Colonies have no representatives in Parliament, Parliament has no right to levy direct taxes on the Colonies.

1766, March: So badly do the Sons of Liberty's protests and boycotts damage British trade that Parliament reluctantly repeals the Stamp Act. However, Parliament vengefully re-asserts its authority in the **Declaratory Act**— a declaration that the Thirteen Colonies are bound to obey whatever laws Parliament prescribes.

1766: The colonists find a new act to protest: the Quartering Act of 1765.

FASCINATING FACTS: The Quartering Act

As the French and Indian War drew to a close, Britain made the unusual decision to maintain a large standing army in the Colonies— partly because disbanding that army would have meant dismissing its officers. At the time, most officers below the rank of general paid great sums of money for the privileges of rank and position. So long as these officers' units survived, they could recover that money by selling their positions to the next officers who wanted them. If, however, Parliament disbanded their units, then they could only recover that money if Parliament chose to repay it. Having no wish to repay several hundred officers' expensive commissions, Parliament decided that it would be easier and cheaper to maintain its standing army— especially if the Thirteen Colonies bore the expense.

The colonists resented this standing army for several reasons:

- Because now that the war was over, local militias were perfectly capable of defending the Colonies.
- Because Britain's standing army often acted more like an occupying army than a friendly one.
- Because the Quartering Act sometimes forced the Colonies to pay British troops' expensive room and board.

1767, June: Parliament passes the first of several hated laws called the **Townshend Acts**. Unlike the Stamp Act, which was designed to generate revenue, the Townshend Acts are designed to punish the colonists for boycotting British traders and undermining Parliament's authority. The Sons of Liberty decry the punitive Townshend Acts as the worst examples yet of taxation without representation.

1768: One of the Townshend Acts creates three new juryless admiralty courts like the one created under the Sugar Act— one each at Boston, Philadelphia and Charleston. The Sons of Liberty respond to these hated courts with more angry protests, especially in Boston.

1768, May: The 50-gun British warship HMS *Romney* sails into Boston harbor, tasked with keeping the peace. Finding himself shorthanded, *Romney*'s captain sends **press gangs** through the streets of Boston to impress merchant sailors into his crew— further infuriating Boston's Sons of Liberty.

A British press gang kidnapping sailors and impressing them into Royal Navy service

1768, June 10: A Boston mob clashes with *Romney*'s crew over *Liberty*— a trade vessel owned by Boston's wealthiest trader, the popular Son of Liberty John Hancock.

ENLIGHTENING EPISODES: The *Liberty* Affair

Boston, Massachusetts in May – June 1768 was a city in chaos. Under the watchful eyes of HMS *Romney* and her 50 guns, Loyalist customs officials were hauling accused smugglers before Boston's new, juryless admiralty court; press gangs were roaming the harbor, seizing American merchant sailors and impressing them into the Royal Navy; and all the while, Boston's Sons of Liberty were organizing furious protests.

Into the midst of this chaos sailed the trade vessel *Liberty*— whose owner, Son of Liberty John Hancock, customs officials suspected of smuggling. Because smugglers rarely kept records, historians are uncertain whether or not Hancock was actually a smuggler; however, he certainly operated during a time when smuggling thrived in New England. One common smuggler's trick was to sail a shipload of taxable goods into harbor in the evening, too late for customs officials to inspect that day. Overnight, the smuggler would quietly unload about three-fourths of these taxable goods, replacing them with non-taxable goods so that his hold still appeared full. When customs officials boarded the next morning, they counted only the taxable goods that remained— allowing smugglers to avoid three-fourths of the tax, while still appearing to abide by the law.

One evening in early May, *Liberty* sailed into Boston harbor with a load of mixed goods, including wine from the Portuguese islands of Madeira. By now, customs officials had grown wise enough to hire **tide-minders**— guards who boarded late arrivals and watched all night to ensure that no one unloaded taxable goods. Two tide-minders dutifully boarded *Liberty* the evening she arrived. The next morning, customs officials were naturally suspicious to find *Liberty*'s hold only one-fourth full of wine. However, the two tide-minders reported no problems, so the officials let the matter drop.

About a week later, HMS *Romney* arrived in Boston; and a couple of weeks after that, one of *Liberty*'s tide-minders changed his story. Perhaps emboldened by the protection of *Romney*'s guns— or perhaps encouraged by bribes from his bosses— this tide-minder now claimed that Hancock's men had locked him in a cabin below decks while they unloaded most of the wine, and then threatened him to keep him quiet. In light of this new evidence, customs officials decided to seize *Liberty* and haul her owner before Boston's admiralty court.

On June 10, two customs officials defended by two boatloads of sailors from *Romney* arrived at the wharf to seize *Liberty*. The sight of the Royal Navy seizing John Hancock's private property brought a mob of angry Bostonians to the wharf, protesting that customs officials should at least wait for Hancock to arrive before seizing his ship. When *Romney*'s master threatened to fire on them, though, the unarmed Bostonians backed down, leaving the sailors free to tow *Liberty* away.

Portrait of John Hancock from 1765

With the sailors out of the way, the mob turned on the now-defenseless customs officials, chasing them into their office and shattering its windows with stones. Still unsatisfied, the mob seized a lovely pleasure boat that belonged to one of the officials. This they dragged to Boston Common, where they condemned it in a brief ceremony under the Liberty Tree and then burned it to ash. Afraid that the furious mob might return, the customs officials rowed out to the safety of *Romney*, where they sent word to their superiors that the situation in Boston had gotten out of hand.

Other interesting facts:
- The attorney John Hancock hired to defend him before the admiralty court, future President John Adams, eventually convinced the court to drop its smuggling case against Hancock.

1768, July: For the crime of refusing to rescind the **Massachusetts Circular Letter**— a Samuel Adams-authored letter urging Massachusetts' sister colonies to join her protest against the Townshend Acts— Massachusetts' Loyalist governor dissolves his House of Representatives. The dissolution of the House leaves Massachusetts without elected representatives for the first time since the Dominion of New England days (see Chapter 12).

1768, October 1: The first of what will eventually be four regiments of British regular army— about 4,000 red-coated troops, all commanded by General Thomas Gage— sail into Boston Harbor to restore order. Boston essentially becomes a British-occupied city under martial law.

1769: Boston merchants respond to their occupation by organizing a **boycott**— that is, they refuse to buy British goods. By the end of the year, this boycott will spread to every colony except New Hampshire.

1770, March 5 – The Boston Massacre: A squad of redcoats fires into an angry crowd in Boston, killing five.

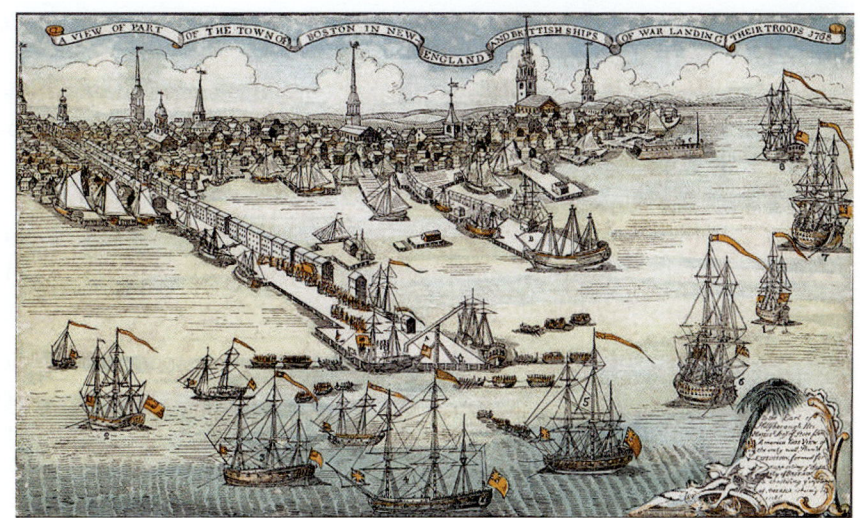

British navy landing troops at Boston Harbor in 1768, engraving by Paul Revere

FASCINATING FACTS: The Boston Massacre

By 1770, 1-1/2 years into its occupation, Boston had learned to hate its British occupiers. Wherever Britain's red-coated soldiers went, they faced rude behavior, insults and taunts from angry Bostonians who wanted them to leave.

One evening in March 1770, redcoat Private Hugh White was standing guard outside Boston's Custom House when a young wig-maker's apprentice started taunting a British officer nearby, accusing him of failing to pay his master for a wig. Feeling that the officer deserved more respect, Private White decided to teach the upstart apprentice a lesson; so he strode up to the boy and dealt him a sharp blow to the head with the butt of his musket. The boy's cries of pain drew a small crowd of protesters, all instantly furious at White's brutality.

As the crowd grew, White sent someone to warn the Officer of the Guard that the situation was getting out of hand. When Captain Thomas Preston arrived with seven additional redcoats, he found as many as 300 – 400 angry Bostonians gathered around White— spitting on him, pelting him with snowballs and threatening him with clubs. Forcing their way to White's side, Preston's men loaded their muskets as their captain ordered the mob to disperse. Instead of dispersing, though, the angry Bostonians only drew in tighter.

Exactly what happened next is uncertain. According to one version of the story, one of the mob's leaders— a runaway slave-turned-sailor named Crispus Attucks— struck British Private Hugh Montgomery with a club, knocking him to the ground and causing him to drop his musket. Now past the limit of his patience, and perhaps in fear for his life, Montgomery took up his dropped musket and fired it at Attucks, killing him instantly. As the crowd closed in on Montgomery and his spent musket, the rest of Preston's squad fired a ragged volley that instantly killed two more men, and wounded

"The Bloody Massacre Perpetrated in King Street Boston on March 5th 1770," engraving by Paul Revere

several more. One of the wounded died hours later, and another two weeks later, bringing the total dead in the brutal Boston Massacre to five.

After the volley, the crowd drew back in horror, but still threatened Preston and his squad. Governor Thomas Hutchinson finally managed to disperse the mob by promising to conduct a full and fair investigation.

Some Results of the Boston Massacre

- The ugly incident convinced the occupying army's commander, General Thomas Gage, that his troops were doing more harm than good in Boston proper; so he withdrew them to Castle Island, a stronghold in Boston Harbor.

- Three weeks after the Boston Massacre, Massachusetts formally indicted Captain Preston and his men on charges of murder. The trial, held months later, hinged on the question of who had ordered the squad to fire. Some said that Montgomery yelled "fire" after Crispus Attucks struck him. Others said that Preston issued the order. Still others said that the angry mob was responsible; for the mob's taunts included mocking dares to "fire."

- Determined to give the British government no further cause to complain about the Colonies' lawlessness, Boston did its best to give Preston and his men fair trials. In the end, the soldiers' able attorneys— including Boston's foremost attorney, future President John Adams— convinced a jury that Preston and all but two of his soldiers were innocent. One of the guilty was Montgomery, convicted of manslaughter in the death of Crispus Attucks. Adams called the Boston Massacre "the strongest proof… of the danger of standing armies."

1770, April: The Colonies' well-organized boycott costs British merchants so much business that Parliament finally agrees to repeal some of the Townshend Acts. With Boston's occupying army mostly out of sight on Castle Island, and the law beginning to go their way, the Colonies' rebellion quiets down for a time. However, the Sons of Liberty still publish pamphlets to ensure that no one forgets the brutal Boston Massacre.

1772, June 9: Outrage over the *Gaspee* Affair helps reignite the Colonies' rebellion.

FASCINATING FACTS: The *Gaspee* Affair

HMS *Gaspee* was a two-masted customs schooner tasked with patrolling Narragansett Bay, Rhode Island for smugglers. *Gaspee*'s commander, Lieutenant William Dudingston, went about his task with such aggressive energy that he soon became Rhode Islanders' most hated enemy. Even after Rhode Island's governor lodged a formal protest against him, the overzealous Dudingston continued to search nearly every ship that entered the bay, whether or not he had a reason to suspect smuggling. What particularly angered Rhode Islanders was that each time Dudingston seized a ship, five percent of the profit from the seizure went directly into his pocket.

Around low tide on June 9, 1772, Dudingston made the mistake of trying to stop a lighter, faster ship named *Hannah*, commanded by Captain Benjamin Lindsey. Determined to teach Dudingston a lesson, Lindsey refused to stop, even after *Gaspee* fired on him. Instead, Lindsey swiftly and cunningly led *Gaspee* to a part of the bay where he knew of a hidden sandbar. *Hannah*'s shallow draft allowed her to sail right over the sandbar; but when *Gaspee* tried the same trick, she ran fast aground. Hopelessly stuck, Dudingston could do little except wait for the incoming tide to lift *Gaspee* off the sandbar in a few hours.

Rhode Islanders didn't give Dudingston those few hours. The moment Lindsey reached Providence, he alerted his friends to Dudingston's embarrassing predicament, and Son of Liberty John Brown organized an expedition against *Gaspee*. Around midnight, eight longboats full of angry Rhode Islanders surrounded *Gaspee* and demanded Dudingston's surrender. When Dudingston refused, the Rhode Islanders boarded *Gaspee*, shot and wounded Dudingston, overwhelmed *Gaspee*'s crew and plundered the ship. The last man aboard set fire to

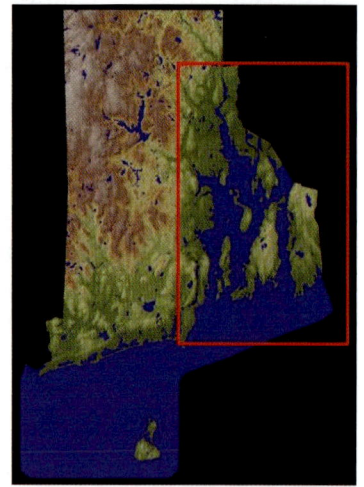

Narragansett Bay boxed in red

Gaspee; and as the Rhode Islanders rowed back to Providence, the fire reached *Gaspee*'s gunpowder magazine, blowing what was left of her sky-high.

The critical element of the *Gaspee* Affair was not the colonists' bold violence, but rather the special court of inquiry that Britain set up to investigate that violence. To its great frustration, this court found not a single colonist who would give evidence about the *Gaspee* Affair— even though scores of them must have known about it. Now convinced that all Rhode Islanders were disloyal to Britain, the court of inquiry announced that it would try any suspects it arrested not in Rhode Island, but in Britain, where it would find jurors sympathetic to Britain's cause.

To Sons of Liberty like Samuel Adams, this announcement was an outrage— the final proof that Britain cared nothing for colonists' right to a fair trial by a jury of their peers. In late 1772, Adams wrote:

"And who among the natives of America, can hear it without emotion? Is there an American, in whose breast there glows the smallest spark of public virtue, but who must be fired with indignation and resentment against a measure so replete with the ruin of our free constitution? To be tried by one's peers, is the greatest privilege a subject can wish for; and so excellent is our constitution, that no subject shall be tried, but by his peers... "

1772, November: At Samuel Adams' urging, Boston establishes a 21-member **Committee of Correspondence** to share Massachusetts' grievances with her sister colonies. Over the year to come, most of Massachusetts' sister colonies will form their own Committees of Correspondence, and the Thirteen Colonies will work together more closely than before.

Rhode Island men burning HMS Gaspee

1773, May: Parliament passes the Tea Act.

FASCINATING FACTS: The Tea Act

The Tea Act of 1773 had two purposes, one more obvious than the other:

1. On its surface, the Tea Act was designed to save the struggling East India Company from collapse. For years, Parliament had been levying high taxes on tea the EIC imported from India, forcing the EIC to charge high prices for its tea. Although customers much preferred the taste of EIC tea, most simply couldn't afford it; so instead, many bought cheaper teas smuggled in from the Dutch East Indies. By 1772, the EIC amassed great quantities of overpriced tea that it couldn't sell anywhere. To pay its bills, the EIC needed to sell its enormous surplus of tea; and to sell its tea, it needed to lower its prices.

Parliament's solution was to let the EIC sell its surplus tea in the Colonies. The Tea Act repealed the heavy tax on tea shipped to the Colonies, allowing the EIC to cut prices on tea sold there— making EIC tea even cheaper than smugglers' tea. To Parliament's way of thinking, everybody won: the Colonies got cheaper tea; the EIC got money to pay its bills; and Parliament got to drive illegal smugglers out of business.

2. Underneath, the Tea Act was designed to re-assert Parliament's right to tax the colonies. Although Parliament had repealed some of the hated Townshend Acts in 1770, it had yet to repeal the Townshend Act tax on tea. If the Colonies wanted the EIC's temptingly-priced tea, then they would have to pay the Townshend Act tax— the very tax the Sons of Liberty had decried as the worst example of taxation without representation.

Colonists also objected to the Tea Act's controlling, mercantilist nature. By putting smugglers out of business, the Tea Act essentially granted the EIC a monopoly on tea in the Colonies. As shrewd businessmen who understood monopolies, the colonists knew that after the EIC eliminated its competition, it would be able to raise tea prices as high as it liked. They also knew that if Parliament got away with creating one monopoly, then it might create more monopolies, driving up prices on other goods as well.

1773, December 16 – The Boston Tea Party: Boston patriots dump three shiploads of East India Company tea into Boston Harbor.

FASCINATING FACTS: The Boston Tea Party (December 16, 1773)

When the Committees of Correspondence got wind of the Tea Act, they all agreed that the Colonies must not buy this EIC tea, however temptingly-priced. The ports of New York, Philadelphia and Charleston all managed to turn away shipments of EIC tea without paying the tax. However, Massachusetts Governor Thomas Hutchinson insisted on allowing Loyalist Boston traders— including two of his sons— to take delivery of the tea.

The standoff between Governor Hutchinson and the Sons of Liberty began on November 29, 1773, when the first of three shiploads of EIC tea arrived in Boston Harbor. By law, Hutchinson's Loyalist traders had 20 days to either pay the tax or send the tea back to Britain. Samuel Adams was determined that no colonist, Loyalist or otherwise, would pay the hated Townshend Act tax; while Hutchinson was just as determined that no EIC tea would leave his harbor. While Adams and Hutchinson argued, the Sons of Liberty posted guards to ensure that no one unloaded those three ships.

On the evening of December 16, the last day before the deadline, about 7,000 – 8,000 Boston patriots gathered at Boston's Old South Meeting House to hear an angry Samuel Adams report Hutchinson's final word: the next day, the governor's Loyalist traders would pay their tax and unload their tea.

Illustration of the Boston Tea Party

Soon after Adams delivered this unwelcome news, about 60 – 100 patriots stood up and strode purposefully out of the meeting. Disguising themselves as Mohawk warriors, these patriots boarded the three ships and, in about three hours:

1. Hoisted the EIC's cased tea out on deck.
2. Chopped holes in the cases to make sure they wouldn't float.
3. Dumped every case into the harbor.

All 342 cases of exotic, expensive tea— some 45 tons of it, a treasure worth somewhere near 750,000

modern-day dollars— dissolved in the harbor. After the Boston Tea Party, the EIC would have to find some other solution to its financial problems, for it would sell none of its surplus tea in the Colonies.

INTERESTING INQUIRIES: Why Mohawk Warriors?

The Boston Tea Party patriots probably chose Mohawk warrior disguises for several reasons:

1. Because they wanted to conceal their identities from British authorities.
2. Because the Mohawk people belonged to the Iroquois Confederacy, which offered a strong example of representative self-government— something the patriots hoped to achieve for Thirteen Colonies.
3. Because Native Americans in general, and the Mohawks in particular, were becoming a symbol of American independence. In songs, pamphlets, posters and political cartoons, Sons of Liberty like Paul Revere often used Mohawk warriors to represent the Thirteen Colonies.

FASCINATING FACTS: Native American Headdresses

War bonnet 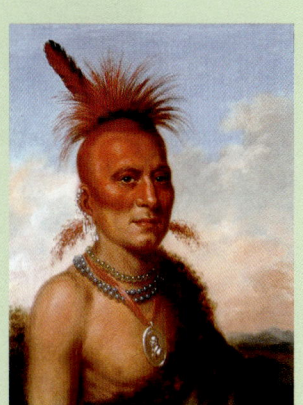 | **Porcupine roach**  | **Feather headband**  | **Buffalo horn headdress**

Different Native American peoples wore different headdresses for different occasions:

- **War bonnets** were elaborate feathered headdresses worn by chiefs and warriors for formal ceremonies, never in battle. Each feather told a story of the warrior's brave deeds in battle.
- **Porcupine roaches** were widely-used battle headdresses made of stiff animal hair— usually the long guard hair of the porcupine— woven into warriors' natural hair.
- **Feather headbands** were bands of leather or fur with decorative feathers tucked into the back or sides. Some wearers also decorated their headbands with beads and/or porcupine quills.
- **Buffalo horn headdresses** were ceremonial helmets worn by the natives of the Great Plains, made of buffalo hide and decorated with feathers and buffalo horns.

1774, March: Infuriated by the patriots' destruction of EIC property, Parliament responds to the Boston Tea Party with a harsh new set of laws called the **Intolerable Acts**— laws that take away every vestige of Massachusetts' self-government.

ILLUMINATING LISTS: The Intolerable Acts, a.k.a the Coercive Acts (1774)

1. The Boston Port Act closed Boston Harbor, driving every Boston trader out of business until Boston could meet three conditions: (1) It must repay the East India Company the full value of the tea destroyed at the Boston Tea Party; (2) It must pay its taxes; and (3) It must demonstrate its submission to the king by restoring order.

2. The Massachusetts Government Act placed Massachusetts under the direct control of King and Parliament. Free elections ceased, as did the town meetings colonists held to discuss elections. Until further notice, the power to choose Massachusetts government officials belonged to the British government alone.

3. The Administration of Justice Act, a.k.a. the Murder Act, allowed Massachusetts' Loyalist governor to try government officials accused of crimes outside his colony— even in Britain, where no colonial witnesses were likely to appear. In other words, a Loyalist official who was guilty of any crime, even murder, could escape justice simply by moving his trial to Britain. What made this act seem particularly unfair was the fact that after the outrageous Boston Massacre, Boston had gone out of its way to give Captain Preston and his soldiers fair trials.

4. The Quartering Act renewed the British army's right to quarter soldiers in colonial buildings at the Colonies' expense (see above). Unlike the first three acts, the Quartering Act applied to all Thirteen Colonies.

5. The Quebec Act expanded the Province of Quebec to include most of the Ohio Country. In colonists' eyes, the Quebec Act of 1774 added insult to the injury of the Royal Proclamation of 1763. The earlier law had forbidden the colonists to claim the prize they had won in the French and Indian War. This new law went even farther, handing over that prize to the very Frenchmen they had defeated— although those Frenchman were now British citizens.

For patriots who demanded their rights as Englishmen, the Intolerable Acts were the last straw— the final proof that King George III and his Parliament cared nothing for their rights, and would stop at nothing to bring the Colonies back under their tyrannical control.

1774, Summer: Charged with containing the rebellion in Massachusetts, General Thomas Gage— who is now military Governor of Massachusetts as well as commander of all British forces in North America— quietly begins removing gunpowder and weapons from forts all along the Massachusetts coast, transferring them to his stronghold at Castle Island, Boston.

1774, September 1 – the Powder Alarm: A rumor spreads among patriots that in the process of confiscating gunpowder from Somerville, Massachusetts, Gage's troops have fired on patriot militia. In response to this rumor, called the **Powder Alarm**, hundreds of patriot militiamen take up arms and march toward Somerville. The patriots back down when the Powder Alarm proves false; nevertheless, the incident shows both sides how close they are to war.

Portrait of General Thomas Gage

1774, September - October: The Thirteen Colonies form Provincial Congresses and Committees of Safety.

FASCINATING FACTS: Committees of Safety

The Powder Alarm drew Massachusetts patriots' attention to what General Gage was doing— quietly collecting powder and arms so that if war broke out, patriots would have no weapons with which to fight. Goaded by the Powder Alarm, the Massachusetts Provincial Assembly— a secret new version of Massachusetts' old elected assembly, the one Gage dissolved— formed a **Committee of Safety** to organize the colony's defense. Soon the other colonies were forming their own Committees of Safety as well, all charged with stockpiling arms and training militia for the war they knew might soon come.

Minuteman statue at Concord, Massachusetts

> DEFINITION: **Minutemen** were elite colonial militiamen trained to be ready for battle at a moment's notice. Massachusetts chose its minutemen not only for their battle skills, but also for their great patriotism and devotion to the cause of liberty. Only about one in four colonial militia units were minutemen units.

1774, September-October – the First Continental Congress: The Colonies unite against the injustice of the Intolerable Acts by assembling the **First Continental Congress**— the first assembly of delegates from all Thirteen Colonies, excepting only Georgia. Among this Congress's 56 delegates are John Hancock, John Adams, Samuel Adams, George Washington, Patrick Henry and Richard Henry Lee. Among other things, the First Continental Congress:

1. Organizes a **colonial boycott** of all British goods, set to begin on December 1, 1774.
2. Issues the **Petition to the King**, a plea to the king which includes these words:

"Had our Creator been pleased to give us existence in a land of slavery, the sense of our condition might have been mitigated by ignorance and habit. But, thanks be to his adorable goodness, we were born the heirs of freedom… The apprehension of being degraded into a state of servitude, from the pre-eminent rank of English freemen, while our minds retain the strongest love of liberty, and clearly foresee the miseries preparing for us and our posterity, excites emotions in our breasts which, though we cannot describe, we should not wish to conceal…"

Carpenter's Hall, the Philadelphia building where the First Continental Congress met

1775, March 23: Patrick Henry, one of the drafters of the Continental Congress's Petition to the King, inspires Virginia patriots to rebel against tyranny with his "Give me liberty or give me death!" speech.

> ILLUMINATING EXCERPTS from Patrick Henry's March 23, 1775 Speech before the Second Virginia Convention
>
> Soon after Parliament announced the Intolerable Acts, Virginia's House of Burgesses called for a colony-wide day of prayer to support the beleaguered patriots of Boston. To punish his burgesses' act of defiance, the Loyalist Governor of Virginia Lord Dunmore dissolved the House of Burgesses.
>
> Forbidden to meet legally, the burgesses nevertheless continued to meet illegally under a new name: the **Virginia Conventions**. The First Virginia Convention chose Virginia's delegates to the First Continental Congress. It was the Second Virginia Convention that heard delegate Patrick Henry deliver his best-known speech, which included words like these:
>
> "Sir, we have done everything that could be done to avert the storm which is now coming on. We have petitioned; we have remonstrated; we have supplicated; we have

Patrick Henry imploring the Virginia Convention to take arms

prostrated ourselves before the throne, and have implored its interposition to arrest the tyrannical hands of the ministry and Parliament… There is no longer any room for hope. If we wish to be free, we must fight! I repeat it, sir, we must fight! An appeal to arms and to the God of hosts is all that is left us…

"It is in vain, sir, to extenuate the matter. Gentlemen may cry, 'Peace, Peace'— but there is no peace. The war is actually begun! The next gale that sweeps from the north will bring to our ears the clash of resounding arms! Our brethren are already in the field! Why stand we here idle? What is it that gentlemen wish? What would they have? Is life so dear, or peace so sweet, as to be purchased at the price of chains and slavery? Forbid it, Almighty God! I know not what course others may take; but as for me, give me liberty or give me death!"

1775, April 18: General Gage quietly dispatches about 700 British troops to seize patriot gunpowder and arms stockpiled at Concord, a town about 20 miles northwest of Boston. As Gage's troops prepare to leave Boston, several patriots embark on a warning mission called the **Midnight Ride**.

FASCINATING FACTS: The Midnight Ride

Ever since the Powder Alarm, Massachusetts' Committee of Safety had been stockpiling gunpowder and arms in preparation for war. To shield those arms from the prying eyes of British spies, patriots stored them at inland towns like Concord, well away from the British-controlled coast. The patriots had little doubt that when General Gage finished collecting arms along the coast, he would come after their arms inland. Therefore they watched Gage closely.

On the night of April 18, 1775, some unknown spy— perhaps General Gage's maid, or even his American-born wife— told Boston patriot/physician/Son of Liberty Joseph Warren that Gage had scheduled an inland mission for the next day. Exactly what Gage's mission was, Warren's spy didn't know. However, Warren did know that Gage was under standing orders to arrest patriot leaders John Hancock and Samuel Adams— both of whom were hiding in Lexington, midway between Boston and Concord. At about 9:30 PM on the night before Gage's mission, Warren dispatched two experienced patriot messengers— silversmith Paul Revere and tanner William Dawes— to warn Hancock and Adams that Gage's redcoats might be coming for them.

Paul Revere

"One if by land, two if by sea"

There were two possible routes the redcoats might take to Lexington: (1) a land route down the Boston Neck, the narrow isthmus that connected Boston to the mainland; and (2) a water route across the Charles River to Charlestown. To better the odds of evading redcoat patrols, Warren sent Dawes by the land route, and Revere by the water route. By the time Revere left Boston, he was fairly sure that the British were taking the water route; so he asked the sexton of the Old North Church to hang two lanterns in the church's belfry— a pre-arranged signal to let the patriots of Charlestown know that the redcoats were coming their way, in case a patrol should capture Revere on his way across the Charles.

Romanticized illustration of Paul Revere's ride

Reaching Charlestown safely at about 10:30 PM, Revere borrowed a fine horse from a patriot friend and raced toward the town of Medford, where he planned to rouse the minutemen. Along the way, two redcoat patrolmen galloped out from behind a tree and gave chase. With one patrolman hot on his heels, Revere swerved off the road and raced for an obstacle he knew, a patch of low, muddy ground called a clay pond. Because Revere knew his way around the clay pond, he was able to keep his horse clear of the mud. Because the patrolman did not, he mired his horse in muddy clay— freeing Revere to slip past the other patrolman and gallop on to Medford. After rousing the minutemen of Medford, Revere stopped to warn several houses along the road to Lexington. By the time Revere and Dawes rendezvoused in Lexington, around midnight, other riders were out warning patriots in all directions.

In Lexington, Revere and Dawes' first task was to warn Hancock and Adams that the redcoats might be coming for them. Next, Revere, Dawes and a third rider— a Lexington patriot-physician named Samuel Prescott— decided to carry the alarm on to Concord. The three patriots were about halfway to Concord, stopping often to warn others along the way, when a mounted redcoat patrol materialized out of the darkness ahead. At this, the three patriots split up:

1. **Prescott** managed to evade his pursuers by jumping his horse over a low stone wall, and went on to raise the alarm in Concord.

2. **Dawes** used a clever ruse to escape. Galloping for the yard of a nearby house, Dawes started shouting at the unseen colonists inside, telling them to get ready for the two redcoats right behind him. Dawes' pursuers, fearing that he was leading them into ambush, gave up the chase. No sooner was Dawes free, though, than his horse threw him, leaving him with only his feet to carry him back to Lexington.

3. **Revere** tried to escape by galloping for a nearby wood; but just as he reached the wood, six more mounted redcoats emerged from it and captured him. Questioned by an officer who threatened to blow out his brains if he didn't tell the truth, Revere cheerfully revealed that he had warned patriots all along the road, and that 500 armed Americans would soon descend upon Lexington to rescue him. As the already-nervous redcoats led Revere back toward Lexington under guard, Lexington's militiamen fired a loud volley that proved the truth of Revere's words. Now terrified of being caught behind enemy lines, the redcoats decided to gallop back to Boston. Because one of their horses was too tired to gallop, they took Revere's excellent horse— leaving Revere free to walk back to Lexington.

William Dawes

ILLUMINATING EXCERPTS from "Paul Revere's Ride" by Henry Wadsworth Longfellow (Published 1861)

"Paul Revere's Ride" is a romanticized version of the Midnight Ride written by poet Henry Wadsworth Longfellow in 1860. For artistic reasons, Longfellow's version of the tale takes several liberties with the facts. For example, Longfellow has Revere waiting in Charlestown for the signal lights from the Old North Church, not asking the sexton to set them before he leaves Boston. Longfellow also has Revere warning Concord at 2 AM— when in fact it was Prescott who warned Concord, as Revere never even reached Concord.

Listen my children and you shall hear / Of the midnight ride of Paul Revere
On the eighteenth of April, in Seventy-five / Hardly a man is now alive
Who remembers that famous day and year.

He said to his friend, "If the British march / By land or sea from the town to-night,
Hang a lantern aloft in the belfry arch / Of the North Church tower as a signal light
One if by land, and two if by sea / And I on the opposite shore will be
Ready to ride and spread the alarm / Through every Middlesex village and farm
For the country folk to be up and to arm."

The Revolutionary War, Part One

1775, April 19: An unknown combatant fires the first shot of the Revolutionary War at the Battle of Lexington.

FASCINATING FACTS: The Battle of Lexington (April 19, 1775)

At 5 AM on April 19th, about 3 hours after Paul Revere's release, some 400 of Gage's 700 redcoats marched into the small town of Lexington on their way to Concord, where they hoped to find great stockpiles of patriot gunpowder and arms— including, according to Gage's spies, some well-concealed cannon. Awaiting the redcoats on Lexington's town common was a formation of 77 trained patriot militiamen, all aroused by Revere's warning. Also waiting were a number of untrained bystanders, some of them armed and hiding behind cover.

The irony of the Battle of Lexington is that neither side wanted to fight that day. General Gage's mission was to prevent a war, not start one. His men had strict orders to fire only if fired upon, and to treat the colonists as fairly and politely as possible— for Gage still hoped to win fence-sitting colonists over to the British side. As for the patriots, their orders ran something like this: "Stand your ground; don't fire unless fired upon, but if they mean to have a war, let it begin here."

Despite these well-meaning orders, every one of the several hundred men who faced off in Lexington early that morning was both tired and tense; and in the midst of that tension, someone fired a shot. Exactly who fired first, none can tell: some witnesses blamed the redcoats, some the patriots, and some the bystanders hiding on the sidelines.

Engraving of British troops firing on Massachusetts militiamen at Lexington

Whoever fired first, the redcoats didn't wait for their officers' orders to respond. Moments after that first shot, long lines of redcoats fired devastating musket volleys, followed immediately by bold bayonet charges. Within seconds, 8 patriot militiamen lay dead, and 10 more wounded; the overwhelmed patriots had suffered nearly 25% casualties at a single blow. While stunned redcoat officers struggled to bring their troops back into line, the surviving patriots broke and ran— many of them without ever firing their muskets.

FASCINATING FACTS: The Battle of Concord

After Lexington, the British moved on to search Concord for gunpowder and arms. Having routed the patriots at Lexington, the battle-proud redcoats expected no more trouble from these backward, cowardly rebels that day; and at first, they had none. By the time the redcoats reached Concord, only about 250 patriot militiamen had gathered there, too few to resist 700 redcoats. Therefore instead of giving battle in Concord, the patriots withdrew across the North Bridge to watch and wait. Gage's officers posted about 100 redcoats to guard the North Bridge before filing into Concord and splitting up to begin their search.

Fortunately, there were few weapons to find in Concord, as patriots had already moved most of them to other towns. However, Gage's men did manage to find three heavy cannon buried near a tavern south of town, as well as some wooden cannon carriages in the town meetinghouse. Determined that the rebels must never use these cannon, Gage's men set fire to these cannon carriages. As the fire spread to the meetinghouse itself, a pillar of smoke rose over the center of town.

Meanwhile, more patriots arrived on the far side of the North Bridge— far more than the number of redcoats tasked with guarding that bridge. When these patriots saw smoke rising over Concord, they decided that the time had come to defend their homeland or die trying. Marching down to the North Bridge, more than 400 patriots lined up against fewer than 100 redcoats, 50 yards away on the Concord side of the river. This time, the alarmed redcoats definitely fired first; and this time the patriots answered, firing a fearsome volley that killed or wounded at least 15 redcoats. Now came the redcoats' turn to break and run, as patriots raced over the bridge and took cover behind a stone wall.

After that first volley, there still remained hundreds of redcoats unfought in Concord. Instead of tackling them in open battle, the patriots decided to set ambushes for them along the road back to Boston. By the time the redcoats finished their search and left Concord, well over 2,000 patriots awaited them, all eager to avenge their fallen comrades. All the way back to Boston, the patriots sniped at the redcoats from behind cover, picking off scores of them one by one. If General Gage hadn't dispatched another 900 redcoats from Boston to rescue his men, then the patriots might have surrounded the survivors and destroyed them all.

Other interesting facts:
- In an 1837 poem titled "Concord Hymn," Concord author Ralph Waldo Emerson described the patriots' answering volley at Concord's North Bridge— the first patriot volley that actually killed British troops— as **"the shot heard 'round the world,"** the shot that marked the true beginning of the Revolutionary War.

Engraving of redcoats filing into Concord

1775, April 19: Immediately after the Battles of Lexington and Concord, Massachusetts patriots lay siege to British-held Boston, cutting it off by land but not by sea. <u>The Siege of Boston begins</u>.

1775, May 10: Benedict Arnold, Ethan Allen and a Vermont militia called the **Green Mountain Boys** seize British-held Fort Ticonderoga, New York without firing a shot. In the process, they capture nearly 200 cannon needed for the Siege of Boston. However, these heavy cannon are many long, hard miles from Boston.

Ethan Allen demanding Fort Ticonderoga's surrender from a surprised night watchman "in the name of the great Jehovah and the Continental Congress"

1775, May 10: The Second Continental Congress convenes at Philadelphia. One of this Congress's acts will be to select George Washington as Commander in Chief of the Continental Army.

1775, June 17: General Gage attacks patriot defenders on Breed's Hill and Bunker Hill, Charlestown Peninsula.

FASCINATING FACTS: The Battle of Bunker Hill

The Battle of Bunker Hill was a struggle for Charlestown Peninsula, which lay just across the Charles River from Boston. On Charlestown Peninsula stood two fair-sized hills, Bunker Hill and Breed's Hill, from which the patriots could easily bombard British troops— if they ever found cannon to set upon those hills. General Gage calculated that if he wanted to hold Boston, then he needed those two hills.

Unfortunately for Gage, the patriots learned of his plan to capture Charlestown Peninsula in advance, and determined to stop him. On the night of June 16, about 1,200 patriots climbed Breed's Hill and quickly dug a small earthen fort there. The next morning, Breed's Hill proved its strategic value— for when British warships in the Charles River fired their cannon at the patriots' new fort, their cannonballs all fell short.

Despite its strengths, the patriots' fort suffered from three major weaknesses: (1) it was nowhere near complete; (2) it was woefully short on supplies; and (3) it was easily cut off from the mainland— for although British warships couldn't bombard Breed's Hill, they could easily bombard Charlestown Neck, the narrow isthmus that connected the peninsula to the mainland.

"Don't fire until you see the whites of their eyes"

That afternoon, Gage sent a total of about 3,000 redcoats to seize the patriots' inconvenient new fort on Breed's Hill. Against Gage's redcoats stood a total of about 2,400 patriots— some inside the fort, and some behind temporary defenses along the fort's flanks. As the redcoats approached, one or more patriot commanders issued the order "Don't fire until you see the whites of their eyes"— a reminder that the patriots' muskets had a maximum range of just 50 yards, and worked far better at about half that distance.

Twice that afternoon the redcoats charged up Breed's Hill; twice the disciplined patriots waited until their enemies were only 100 feet away before firing; and twice the patriots drove the redcoats back down the hill with terrible losses. It was only on the third charge, which came after most of the patriots had run out of ammunition, that the redcoats finally captured Breed's Hill. From there, the patriots retreated to Bunker Hill. Because the patriots had no fort on Bunker Hill, they suffered heavy losses there, and soon abandoned it. Thus Gage won Charlestown Peninsula— but at a staggering cost of over 1,000 casualties, more than one-third of the troops he sent there.

Scene from the Battle of Bunker Hill

Other interesting facts:
- Dr. Joseph Warren, the patriot who dispatched Paul Revere and William Dawes on their Midnight Ride, was one of about 115 patriots who gave their lives for their country at the Battle of Bunker Hill. Although Massachusetts had commissioned Warren a major general, he volunteered to fight as a private on Breed's Hill because he had less command experience than other officers there. The incredibly brave Dr. Warren fought on long after he ran out of ammunition, and died trying to cover his comrades' retreat.

1775, July 3: General George Washington arrives to take command of the Siege of Boston.

1775, July 6: The Second Continental Congress issues the "Declaration of the Causes and Necessity of Taking Up Arms," which includes these words:

- "We are reduced to the alternative of choosing an unconditional submission to the tyranny of irritated ministers, or resistance by force. The latter is our choice. We have counted the cost of this contest, and find nothing so dreadful as voluntary slavery. Honor, justice, and humanity forbid us tamely to surrender that freedom which we received from our gallant ancestors, and which our innocent posterity have a right to receive from us."
- "In our own native land, in defense of the freedom that is our birthright, and which we ever enjoyed till the late violation of it; for the protection of our property, acquired solely by the honest industry of our forefathers and ourselves… we have taken up arms. We shall lay them down when hostilities shall cease on the part of the aggressors, and all danger of their being renewed shall be removed, and not before."

1775, July 8: Two days later, the Continental Congress appeals directly to King George III in the **Olive Branch Petition**, pleading with him to intervene with Parliament on the Colonies' behalf.

1775, August 23: King George III rejects the Olive Branch Petition, and instead issues the **Proclamation of Rebellion**— his declaration that the Colonies are in "open and avowed rebellion" against the Crown.

1775, Winter: Parliament passes the **American Prohibitory Act**, cutting off all trade with the Colonies and declaring all captured colonial ships to be the property of the Crown. In response, the Continental Congress will issue letters of marque granting American privateers legal authority to attack and seize British ships.

1776, January: Thomas Paine unites the Colonies in favor of independence with an anonymously-published pamphlet titled "Common Sense."

POWERFUL PAMPHLETS: "Common Sense" by Thomas Paine

Thomas Paine was an English corset-maker, customs official and shopkeeper who didn't even live in America until late 1774, when he moved to Philadelphia at the suggestion of Benjamin Franklin. Nevertheless, after only one year as an American, Paine published a 15,000-word pamphlet that was to convince thousands of Americans to join the cause of American independence.

Even after the deadly battles of Lexington, Concord and Bunker Hill, the idea of independence was still far from many American minds. Plenty of Americans still hoped to resolve the Colonies' differences with Britain, perhaps by sending colonial representatives to Parliament. Plenty of Americans also still believed in the Divine Right of Kings, and worried that blaming King George III for their troubles was sacrilege. Instead of blaming the king, they wanted to blame Parliament or the king's advisers. By explaining the true origins and purposes of government, much as John Locke did, Thomas Paine gave Americans permission to despise their king's corrupt hereditary monarchy— and to long for a new, less corruptible government of their own choosing. Among Paine's arguments in "Common Sense" were these:

Thomas Paine

- **Whatever the true origins of monarchy were, they were certainly not divine.** *In Paine's words*: "…could we take off the dark covering of antiquity and trace [kings] to their first rise, we should find the first of them nothing better than the principal ruffian of some restless gang…"
- **Although America had once benefited from its connection to Britain, it benefited no longer.** *In Paine's words*: "I challenge the warmest advocate for reconciliation to show a single advantage that this continent can reap by being connected with Great Britain."

- **Britain lay too far away to govern America effectively or fairly.** <u>In Paine's words</u>: "To be always running three or four thousand miles with a tale or a petition, waiting four or five months for an answer, which when obtained requires five or six more to explain it... will in a few years be looked upon as folly and childishness. There was a time when it was proper, and there is a proper time for it to cease."
- **America was far too large to be governed by an island as small as Britain.** <u>In Paine's words</u>: "...there is something very absurd in supposing a continent to be perpetually governed by an island."

John Adams considered "Common Sense" so crucial to the American Revolution that he later wrote, "Without the pen of the author of 'Common Sense,' the sword of Washington would have been raised in vain."

1776, January – The Noble Train of Artillery: After a long, incredibly arduous winter journey over nonexistent roads, former Boston bookshop owner Henry Knox succeeds in delivering 60 tons of heavy cannon from Fort Ticonderoga to General Washington at the Siege of Boston.

1776, March 17: Unable to hold Boston any longer under the threat of Washington's guns, General Gage's replacement, General Howe, loads his occupying army aboard a fleet of British ships and abandons the city. <u>The Siege of Boston ends with an American victory</u>.

1776, June 7 – The Lee Resolution: Virginia delegate Richard Henry Lee introduces to the Continental Congress a resolution from the Fifth Virginia Convention which includes these words:

Henry Knox and crew using ox-drawn sledges to haul cannon through heavy snow from Fort Ticonderoga on Lake Champlain, New York all the way to Boston

"Resolved, that these United Colonies are, and of right ought to be, free and independent states, that they are absolved from all allegiance to the British Crown, and that all political connection between them and the state of Great Britain is, and ought to be, totally dissolved."

1776, June 11: The Continental Congress adjourns for three weeks, but also appoints a **Committee of Five** to draft a Declaration of Independence in case the Lee Resolution should pass.

1776, July 4 – Independence Day: The Continental Congress approves the final text of the Declaration of Independence.

<u>ILLUMINATING EXCERPTS</u>: The Introduction and Preamble of the Declaration of Independence

- "When in the Course of human events, it becomes necessary for one people to dissolve the political bands which have connected them with another, and to assume among the powers of the earth, the separate and equal station to which the Laws of Nature and of Nature's God entitle them, a decent respect to the opinions of mankind requires that they should declare the causes which impel them to the separation."

- "We hold these truths to be self-evident, that all men are created equal, that they are endowed by their Creator with certain unalienable Rights, that among these are Life, Liberty and the pursuit of Happiness. That to secure these rights, Governments are instituted among Men, deriving their just powers from the consent of the governed, That whenever any Form of Government becomes destructive of these ends, it is the Right of the People to alter or to abolish it, and to institute new Government, laying its foundation on such principles and organizing its powers in such form, as to them shall seem most likely to effect their Safety and Happiness. Prudence, indeed, will dictate that Governments long established should not be changed for light and transient causes; and accordingly all experience hath shewn, that mankind are more disposed to suffer, while evils are sufferable, than to right themselves by abolishing the forms to which they are accustomed. But when a long train of abuses and usurpations, pursuing invariably the same Object evinces a design to reduce them under absolute Despotism, it is their right, it is their duty, to throw off such Government, and to provide new Guards for their future security."

Independence Hall in Philadelphia, meeting place of the Continental Congress

FASCINATING FACTS: The Declaration of Independence

- The Committee of Five was a diverse group that included Congressional delegates from all three regions of the Colonies: one from the South, Thomas Jefferson of Virginia; two from New England, John Adams of Massachusetts and Roger Sherman of Connecticut; and two from the Middle Colonies, Benjamin Franklin of Pennsylvania and Robert Livingston of New York.

- The other four members of the committee persuaded the best writer among them, Thomas Jefferson, to draft the Declaration on his own. Jefferson wrote his original drafts at the Philadelphia boarding house where he was staying at the time, which has since been renamed the Declaration House. Jefferson's writing drew on several influences, including John Locke, the Sons of Liberty and George Mason— author of the Virginia Declaration of Rights, which Virginia had just adopted on June 12.

- After completing his first draft, Jefferson consulted with Franklin and Adams, who suggested some minor revisions. Jefferson then produced a "fair copy" of the Declaration to present to Congress.

- On Monday, July 1, Congress reconvened to consider the Lee Resolution. After a long day of speeches, the thirteen delegations voted 9-3 in favor of independence, with New York abstaining. This strong majority was technically enough to adopt the Declaration. However, Franklin and Adams wanted a unanimous vote to unite the colonies, so they took another day to coax their fellow delegates.

- On Tuesday, July 2nd, three colonies' delegations changed their votes: (1) Two fence-sitting Pennsylvania delegates agreed to abstain so that the rest of their delegation could vote 3-2 in favor of independence; (2) delegate Caesar Rodney arrived from Delaware just in time to swing his delegation in favor of independence; and (3) South Carolina reversed its vote in favor of independence. New York's delegation had to abstain again because it hadn't received instructions from the New York Provincial Congress— which was on the run, as the British had invaded New York only days before (see Chapter 22). Thus July 2, not July 4, was the day when Congress actually voted for American independence.

- The Congress spent Wednesday, July 3rd revising Jefferson's "fair copy" of the Declaration of Independence. Among other things, Congress deleted a clause that condemned Britain for introducing the morally despicable slave trade to her colonies— a section that some Northern colonies might have accepted, but no Southern colony would.

- After Congress approved its final version on July 4th, Philadelphia printer John Dunlap spent that night producing the first official copies of the Declaration of Independence: the **Dunlap Broadsides**, large, unsigned copies for distribution all over the colonies. The first signed version of the Declaration, which includes John Hancock's famous signature, may not have appeared until a month later.

- At the signing of the Declaration of Independence, President of the Continental Congress John Hancock pointed out the deadly risk that everyone who set his name to that document was taking, adding that the signers "must all hang together now." Benjamin Franklin replied, "Yes, we must indeed all hang together, or most assuredly we shall all hang separately."

Franklin, Adams and Jefferson consulting on the Declaration

AMAZING AMERICANS: Benjamin Franklin (1706 – 1790)

The First American

The oldest signer of the Declaration of Independence, Benjamin Franklin, is often called the "First American"— the original self-made American, a man who owed his remarkable rise to opportunities found only in America. Had Franklin been born in Europe, where opportunity came mainly through high birth, he might have remained poor all his life. Because he lived in America, where opportunity came through ingenuity, creativity and hard work, there was no limit to what he could achieve.

Benjamin was the 15th of 17 children born to a Boston tallow chandler named Josiah Franklin, a man who earned his living rendering beef fat into candles and soap. Having ten sons, the Puritan Josiah determined to tithe one of them into the ministry; and because Benjamin loved books, Josiah sent him to Boston Latin School at age 8. Unfortunately, schooling his son proved too costly for Josiah's budget. Benjamin spent just one year at America's oldest school, and one more at a less expensive school, before Josiah changed his mind about the ministry and brought Benjamin home to work in the candle shop. Thus the entire formal education of Dr. Benjamin Franklin, a man who was to receive honorary degrees from several universities, lasted just two years.

Quickly bored with the dull work of cutting wicks and dipping candles, Benjamin began to consider an adventurous career that was open to all Boston boys: a career at sea. Having already lost an older son to the sea, Josiah was determined not to lose a second; so he reluctantly agreed to find Benjamin another trade. When Benjamin was just 12 years old, Josiah apprenticed him to his brother James, who had recently returned from London with new equipment to set up his own print shop.

Although the indenture agreement Benjamin signed essentially made him a slave, and subjected him to beatings from his brother for the next several years, it also gave him access to what he loved best: books. Benjamin spent every spare moment at his brother's shop reading, studying and practicing his writing skills.

The Silence Dogood Letters

In need of business for his new print shop, James Franklin launched a newspaper called the *New England Courant*. Benjamin longed to have his work published in the *Courant*, but knew that his brother would never accept anything he wrote; so he started writing anonymous letters to the *Courant* under the pen name Silence Dogood, posing as a witty widow in search of a new husband. One of the Silence Dogood Letters was a mocking criticism of Harvard College, which Franklin might have attended himself had his father been able to afford it. According to Silence Dogood, most Harvard students were "little better than dunces and blockheads"— idle, ignorant men who entered the ministry after college only because Harvard taught them no other way to earn their livings. To Benjamin's delight, James found the Silence Dogood Letters so entertaining that he published 14 of them before he discovered his younger brother's secret.

Unfortunately, James' discovery aggravated the brothers' already-strained relationship, which led to more beatings. Tired of James' abuse, 17-year-old Benjamin broke his indenture agreement and ran away to New York, hoping to find work in a print shop. Finding no work in New York, and in constant danger of being arrested as a runaway indentured servant, Benjamin sailed down the coast to Philadelphia. When he arrived at the city he was to call home for the rest of his life, he had nothing but the wet clothes on his back, some extra clothes stuffed in his pockets and a single Dutch dollar.

One of the first things Benjamin Franklin did in Philadelphia was to attend a Quaker service of waiting worship, one where Quaker believers sat in silence waiting to hear from the Holy Spirit. Hearing nothing in his spirit, and much exhausted from his hard journey, Franklin promptly fell asleep.

Portrait of Benjamin Franklin from around 1785

Franklin in Philadelphia

Because Philadelphia was such a young city at the time— William Penn had founded it in 1682, just 41 years before Franklin's arrival— there were as yet few good printers there. When the acting governor of Pennsylvania heard of young Franklin's excellent printing skills, and read a sample of his clear writing, he promised to help set Franklin up in business. On the governor's instructions, Franklin boarded ship for London, expecting to use a letter of credit from the governor to buy his own printing press and type. Upon reaching London, though, he was dismayed to learn that the governor had neglected to write his letter of credit. Instead of buying a printing press of his own, poor Franklin spent 1-1/2 years working in London print shops before he finally found a way back to Philadelphia, where he learned that his false friend the governor had moved on.

Having honed his craft in the superior print shops of London, Franklin returned to Philadelphia with even greater printing skills than before— including the skill to engrave the copper plates used to print hard-to-counterfeit paper money. This skill won his employer government jobs, which paid well. By 1728, Franklin was part owner of a print shop. By 1729, he was publishing a fine newspaper called *The Pennsylvania Gazette*; and by 1732, he was publishing *Poor Richard's Almanac* under the pen name Richard Saunders. By 1747, when Franklin was still just 41, his printing business made him so wealthy that he no longer needed to work at it every day.

FASCINATING FACTS: *Poor Richard's Almanac* (Published 1732 – 1758)

In some ways, *Poor Richard's Almanac* was a typical almanac— a yearly guidebook loaded with useful data like tide tables, moon cycles, weather predictions and the proper dates for planting various crops. In other ways, *Poor Richard's* was like no other almanac; for it alone contained the wit, wisdom and personality of

Benjamin Franklin. With folksy aphorisms like these, *Poor Richard's Almanac* helped make Benjamin Franklin one of the best-known and most-respected characters in the Thirteen Colonies:

- "To err is human, to repent divine; to persist devilish."
- "A friend in need is a friend indeed."
- "Haste makes waste."
- "Little strokes fell great oaks."
- "He that lieth down with dogs, shall rise up with fleas."
- "Fish and visitors stink after three days."
- "He that falls in love with himself, will have no rivals."
- "Search others for their virtues, thyself for thy vices."
- "Three may keep a secret, if two of them are dead."
- "When the wine enters, out goes the truth."
- "A full belly makes a dull brain."
- "Early to bed and early to rise, makes a man healthy, wealthy, and wise."
- "Don't throw stones at your neighbor's, if your own windows are glass."
- "Tart words make no friends: a spoonful of honey will catch more flies than a gallon of vinegar."
- "For want of a nail the shoe is lost; for want of a shoe the horse is lost; for want of a horse the rider is lost."
- "If you would not be forgotten, as soon as you're dead and rotten, either do things worth the writing, or write things worth the reading."
- "Any society that will give up a little liberty for a little security will deserve neither and lose both."

Public Servant

Long before he retired from printing, Franklin was a public-minded man devoted to improving life in Philadelphia. Franklin helped organize Philadelphia's post office; its first fire department; its first hospital; its first library; and its first college. After retiring from printing, Franklin became a city councilman in 1748, a justice of the peace in 1749 and a representative to the Pennsylvania Assembly in 1751.

Inventor

Franklin was also a gifted scientist and engineer known all over Europe and the Colonies for his experiments with electricity—including the famous Kite Experiment, with which Franklin proved that lightning was a form of electricity. In this extremely dangerous experiment, Franklin tied a key to a wet kite string during a

Political cartoon Benjamin Franklin used to promote unity among the Thirteen Colonies during two wars, the French and Indian War and the Revolutionary War

thunderstorm, and connected the flying key to a type of capacitor called a Leiden jar. The experiment proved that static electricity generated by the storm charged the Leiden jar exactly as other forms of static electricity did.

Franklin's many other inventions included the lightning rod, swim fins, bifocals, a carriage odometer, the hot-burning Franklin Stove, and an eerie-sounding musical instrument called the glass harmonica. After Oxford University presented him with an honorary doctor's degree in 1762, everyone knew him as Doctor Franklin.

Glass harmonica

Life Overseas

Ironically, the First American spent most of his later years overseas. The internationally-respected Benjamin Franklin's arguments helped convince Parliament to repeal the hated Stamp Act in 1766. Franklin returned home in 1775 to help lead the American independence movement, only to return to France in 1776 as the new United States Ambassador to France. The French alliance that helped the U.S. win the Revolutionary War was partly the work of Benjamin Franklin. After representing the U.S. at negotiations for the Treaty of Paris in 1783, Franklin returned home to lend his great authority to the 1787 Constitutional Convention, and to serve as Governor of Pennsylvania.

"Franklin's Return to Philadelphia, 1785" by artist Jean Ferris

CHAPTER 22: The American Revolutionary War

U.S. HISTORY FOCUS: The Revolutionary War, Part Two

> **REFRESHING REMINDERS from Chapter 21:**
> - The Revolutionary War began on April 19, 1775, the day Massachusetts militia clashed with British General Gage's redcoats at the Battles of Lexington and Concord. That same day, the militia laid siege to Gage's main stronghold in America, the port of Boston.
> - Three weeks after Lexington and Concord, Benedict Arnold and Ethan Allen captured Fort Ticonderoga from the British without firing a shot, capturing nearly 200 British cannon in the process.
> - Over the winter of 1775 – 1776, Boston bookshop owner Henry Knox hauled 60 tons of heavy cannon all the way from Fort Ticonderoga to Boston, where General Washington had taken command of the siege.
> - The sight of Washington's cannon convinced Gage's replacement, General Howe, that he could hold Boston no longer; so the Siege of Boston ended with a patriot victory on March 17, 1776.

The Quebec Campaign (1775 – 1776)

Continental Army Commanders: Richard Montgomery, Benedict Arnold	**British Army Commanders:** Guy Carleton

Months before General Washington drove the British out of Boston, Congress asked him to drive the British out of Quebec as well. Congress had two hopes for its invasion of Quebec:

1. It hoped to prevent Britain from using Quebec City as a base from which to invade the Colonies.

2. It hoped to convince the people of Quebec to join the Colonies' revolution. At the time, Quebec had been in British hands for just 12 years, since the end of the French and Indian War in 1763. Because the *Quebecois* were still Frenchmen, and had little love for British rule, Congress hoped that skilled negotiator Benjamin Franklin might be able to pry Quebec out of Britain's clutches.

The U.S. invasion of Quebec was two-pronged:

1. In late August 1775, General Richard Montgomery led about 1,200 colonial troops out of Fort Crown Point, which lay on Lake Champlain 10 miles north of Fort Ticonderoga. Montgomery's route to Quebec City ran north across Lake Champlain, then on down the Richelieu River toward the St. Lawrence.

2. Two weeks later, Colonel Benedict Arnold split off about 1,100 troops from the ongoing Siege of Boston and led them north. Arnold's much longer route lay up the coast to the Kennebec River, then on across the wilderness of Maine to the Chaudiere River and Quebec City.

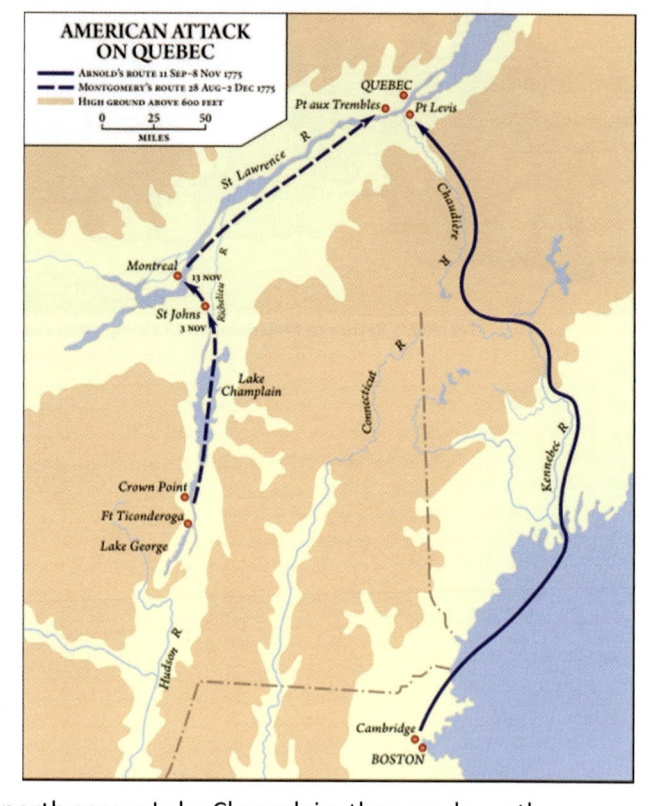

The Battle of Quebec (December 31, 1775)
Both Continental commanders reached Quebec City with only a fraction of their original numbers:

- Colonel Arnold's journey across the wilderness of Maine proved far longer and more difficult than anyone had imagined. The rivers were often impassable, forcing Arnold's men to carry boats and supplies many miles over non-existent roads. Furthermore, Arnold's boats leaked, spoiling both food and gunpowder. Before they were halfway to Quebec City, Arnold's men grew hungry enough to eat shoe leather, tallow candles and at least one pet dog. A deadly combination of hard work, slim rations and sickness carried some 50 troops to early graves, and caused another 450 to give up and go home— leaving Arnold with only about 600 sick, starving troops out of his original 1,100 when he finally reached Quebec.

General Richard Montgomery

- Two factors cut into General Montgomery's troop numbers in Quebec City. First, he had to leave troops behind to guard two forts he captured along the way, Fort Saint-Jean and Montreal. Second, many of his troops' terms of enlistment ran out before he arrived. Even with fresh recruits from local militias, Montgomery reached Quebec City with only about 600 men, bringing the total Continental force to 1,200— against 1,800 defenders inside Quebec's city walls.

Nor were numbers Quebec City's only advantages. As North America's oldest, best-established fortress, upper Quebec City had high, smooth stone walls which were all but impossible to climb under fire. Even lower Quebec City was surrounded by a double row of heavy palisade walls. The city also had plenty of supplies, as well as a wealthy British government to resupply it the following spring— which Montgomery would be unable to prevent, as the Colonies had virtually no navy. Meanwhile, Montgomery was surviving on supplies confiscated from Montreal, and his government had already emptied its pitifully small treasury trying to fund two military campaigns at once.

Despite these advantages, Montgomery was determined to attack before the end of the year, when even more of his troops' terms of enlistment

Modern-day photo of Quebec city showing the lower city below, the upper city above and a steep funicular rail car between, as well as a portion of the upper city's stone wall

would run out. Therefore Montgomery based his battle plan on the one advantage Quebec City didn't have: surprise. On the night of December 30 – 31, under cover of darkness coupled with a blinding snowstorm, Montgomery assaulted Quebec City from four sides at once. Against the upper, walled city, Montgomery sent two feigned attacks, loud demonstrations designed to draw defenders' attention away from the real action— which was against the lower, palisaded city, where Montgomery and Arnold personally led two quieter attacks.

Unfortunately, the British were wide awake and waiting for them. Montgomery and his men had quietly sawed through both palisade walls, and were jogging through the lower city looking for a way to the upper, when they came upon an enemy blockhouse bristling with cannon. With their first burst of cannon fire, the blockhouse's defenders struck brave Montgomery in the head, killing him instantly. Arnold, too, penetrated the lower city, but was forced to withdraw when he took a bullet in the leg. The British later trapped most of Arnold's troops inside several buildings, where they had gone to dry out their damp, useless gunpowder.

Thus the Battle of Quebec ended in disaster for the Continental Army, with scores dead, many more wounded and hundreds taken prisoner.

Difficulties in Montreal

Meanwhile, difficulties in Montreal were destroying all hope of an alliance between the Thirteen Colonies and Quebec. One difficulty was that the soldiers Montgomery had left behind in Montreal needed all sorts of supplies, but had no good money with which to pay for them. Lacking gold or gold-backed currency, the Continentals paid the *Quebecois* in one of two ways:

British regulars and Canadian militia fighting off Benedict Arnold at the Battle of Quebec

1. With **scrip**— hastily-printed paper money that the *Quebecois* considered worthless, with good reason.

2. With IOUs— promises to pay later, after Congress provided real money for its army to spend.

Naturally, few *Quebecois* fancied the idea of trading real goods for paper money and promises. Into the midst of this troubled situation, Congress sent two of its best negotiators.

FASCINATING FACTS: Benjamin Franklin's Mission to Canada

In February 1776, the Continental Congress dispatched two of its members, Benjamin Franklin of Pennsylvania and Samuel Chase of Maryland, to negotiate a treaty of alliance between the Thirteen Colonies and the Province of Quebec. Given the troubles in Montreal, Franklin and Chase had their work cut out for them. To appease the *Quebecois*, Franklin and Chase would have to resolve three major difficulties:

1. The Continentals had come to Quebec as liberators, expecting the *Quebecois* to want the same freedoms the Colonies did. However, Quebec had a different history than the Colonies, and a different idea of which freedoms were most important. Since the end of the French and Indian War, the British had been allowing the *Quebecois* freedoms enjoyed in no other part of the British Empire— freedom to practice their Catholic faith, and to live under the French-style law they preferred. Although the Continentals promised the *Quebecois* those same freedoms, many doubted those promises.

2. The Thirteen Colonies sharply disagreed with Quebec over the Quebec Act— the last of Parliament's Intolerable Acts, the one that made the Ohio Country part of Quebec (see Chapter 21).

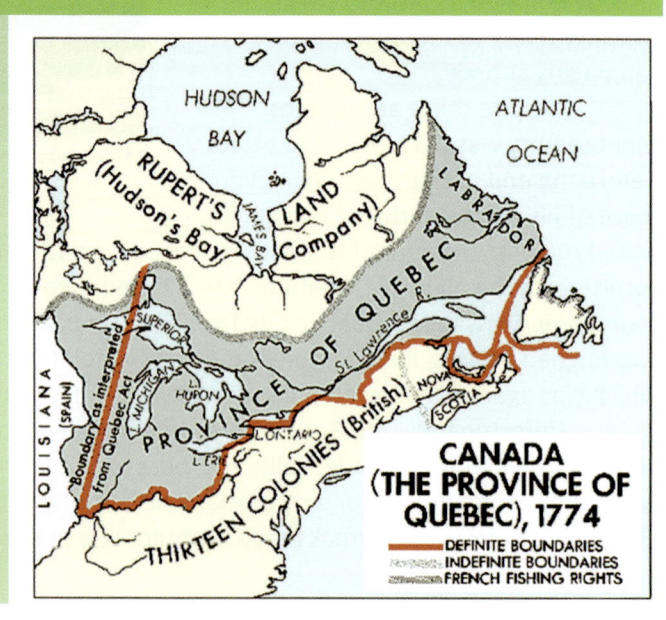

Having fought hard for Ohio in the French and Indian War, the Colonies felt that Ohio properly belonged to them. Now that Ohio belonged to Quebec, though, the *Quebecois* were loath to surrender this precious gift.

3. Congress had spoken out of both sides of its mouth on the issue of Quebec's Catholic faith. On one side, Congress promised to let the *Quebecois* continue as Catholics; but on the other, it criticized Parliament for allowing the same thing. In an open letter of complaint about the Quebec Act, Congress had written, "… we think the legislature of Great Britain is not authorized by the Constitution to establish a religion fraught with sanguinary and impious tenets [i.e., bloody and anti-Christian Catholicism]."

Beset by all these difficulties, Franklin and Chase found it impossible to establish trust with the *Quebecois*. Franklin remained in Montreal for only about two weeks, from late April – early May 1776, before giving up the mission as hopeless.

In the spring of 1776, reinforcements arrived to help British Governor Guy Carleton hold Quebec City. Aided by these reinforcements, Carleton drove the Continentals back up the Richelieu River and across Lake Champlain, all the way to Fort Ticonderoga, by late 1776. Instead of gaining ground with their invasion of Quebec, the Colonies lost ground.

SUCCINCT SUMMARIES: The invasion of Quebec was a disaster that not only cost many patriots their lives, but also destroyed any hope of an alliance with Quebec. However, the invasion did benefit the Colonies in one way: by delaying the Saratoga Campaign, a dangerous British invasion from Quebec City, until the following year.

The New York and New Jersey Campaign (1776)

Continental Commanders:	British Commanders:
George Washington	William Howe
Nathanael Greene	Charles Cornwallis
John Sullivan	Henry Clinton

General Howe, the commander General Washington ejected from Boston, also received reinforcements from Britain during the spring of 1776— including the Revolutionary War's first Hessian troops.

FASCINATING FACTS: Hessians

About one-fourth of the troops Britain sent against the Continental Army belonged not to British regular army units, but to German units hired from Britain's allies in the Holy Roman Empire. Because many of these Germans came from the HRE principality of Hesse-Kassel, patriots called all German troops **Hessians**. Before the Revolutionary War was over, as many as 30,000 Hessian troops would arrive in the Colonies to take up Britain's cause.

Nearly all colonists, whether patriots, fence-sitters or loyalists, despised these German-speaking Hessians. The idea that Britain would send foreign mercenaries against her own Colonies was especially insulting to loyalists, who expected their mother country to treat her Colonies more like disobedient children than foreign enemies. Because the first hated Hessians invaded New York in late June, 1776— just before Congress reconvened to consider the Lee Resolution and the Declaration of Independence (see Chapter 21)— they helped bring fence-sitting Congressmen down on the side of independence.

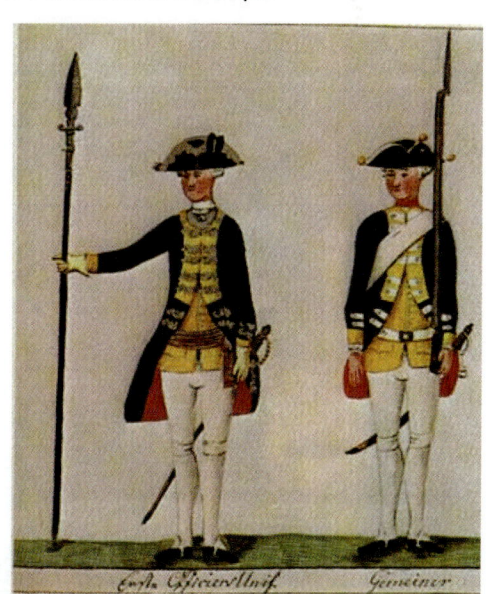

Illustration of blue-coated Hessian troops

The Battle of Long Island (August 22 – 27, 1776)

Howe's reinforcements arrived just in time to join his next campaign, an attack on the centrally-located port of New York City. The first British and Hessian troops landed on defenseless, loyalist-majority Staten Island— just across New York Harbor from Manhattan Island, and just across the Narrows from Long Island— in late June, 1776. Over the next few weeks, some 32,000 British regulars and Hessians amassed on Staten Island.

FASCINATING FACTS: The maneuvering between Generals Howe and Washington began with a fussy standoff over titles. On July 13, Howe sent Washington a letter offering him and his officers official pardons if they would lay down their arms. Washington, however, refused to open Howe's letter—because Howe had addressed it to "George Washington, Esquire," arrogantly ignoring Washington's rank. A second letter addressed to "George Washington, Esq., etc., etc." met the same response. As commander-in-chief of the United States Army, Washington refused to answer unless Howe recognized the United States in his address.

Finally, Washington agreed to meet with Howe's adjutant, who offered him Howe's pardon in person. To this Washington defiantly replied, "Those who have committed no fault want no pardon."

Uncertain which way Howe's immense invasion army might go, General Washington decided to divide his far smaller army of 19,000 troops. Some Washington stationed on Long Island to defend Brooklyn; others on Manhattan Island to defend New York City; and still others in a "flying camp" on the New Jersey side of the Hudson, ready to move quickly in any direction.

Washington got his answer on August 22— the day Howe's second-in-command, General Cornwallis, shipped about 20,000 troops across the Narrows to Long Island. Convinced that he could never hold Long Island against such a large army, Washington laid plans to retreat to Manhattan.

In preparation for his retreat, Washington built a strong defense on **Brooklyn Heights**, a set of low hills just across the East River from Manhattan. Before retreating, though, Washington wanted to inflict as many casualties as he could. Therefore in addition to fortifying Brooklyn Heights, he sent about 2,300 troops to fortify another set of low hills farther south. If all went as planned, then those 2,300 troops would extract a steep price from Cornwallis as he passed through on his way to Brooklyn Heights.

Unfortunately, all did not go as planned— for unknown to Washington, Long Island loyalists told Cornwallis of another road to Brooklyn Heights, one that lay miles to the east. Armed with this intelligence, Cornwallis prepared three attacks, two frontal and one flank. Two small parts of Cornwallis' army would attack by the frontal routes Washington expected, while the main part would circle around to attack from the east. When the action started, Washington's men found themselves beset from three sides at once— leaving them with just one open line of retreat back to Brooklyn Heights.

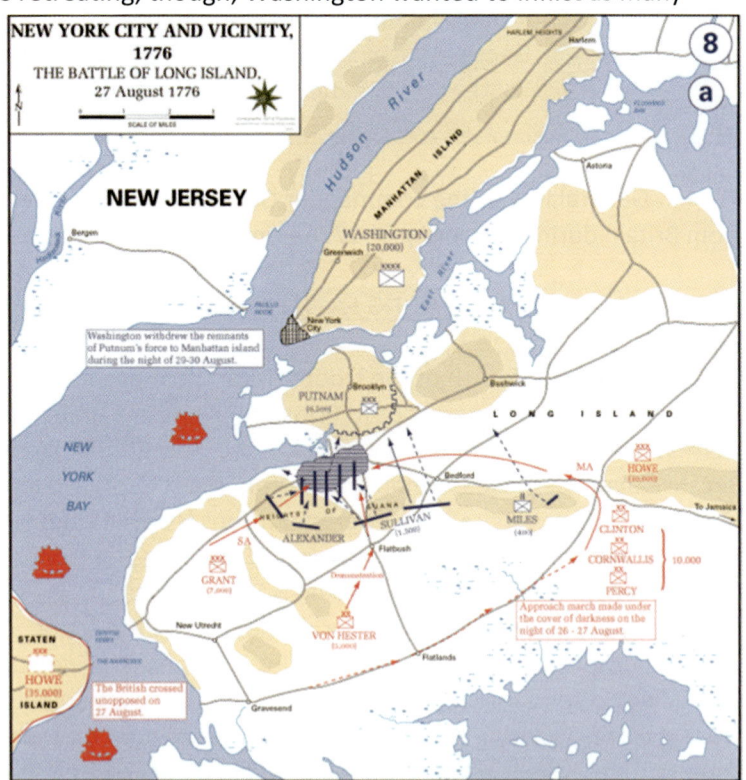

FASCINATING FACTS: The Maryland 400

The unit that covered that last line of retreat was a company of exceptionally brave Maryland men called the **Maryland 400**— although their true numbers were closer to 300, the same number that covered the ancient Spartans' famous retreat at the Battle of Thermopylae (see Year 1). While the rest of Washington's 2,300 retreated, the Maryland 400 went on the attack, launching two doomed frontal assaults against forces that outnumbered them more than ten to one. After their second assault, the dying Maryland 400 tried to retreat as well. Sadly, only about a dozen made it to Brooklyn Heights alive. Watching the Maryland 400's incredibly courageous self-sacrifice, Washington sighed, "Good God, what brave fellows I must this day lose!"

Silent Retreat (August 29 – 30, 1776)

After the retreat to Brooklyn Heights, Cornwallis and Howe might have surrounded Washington and destroyed him; but instead, Howe ordered a halt. Unwilling to spend his troops' lives in a bold frontal assault across the open ground beneath the Heights, Howe decided to cover his advance by digging zigzag trenches across that open ground, much as the Ottomans did at both sieges of Vienna (see Chapter 16).

Howe's decision gave Washington time to plan one of his best maneuvers of the war: a silent retreat across the East River to Manhattan under cover of darkness and fog. On the night of August 29, Washington's troops spoke not a word as they wrapped their horses' hooves in cloth, greased their wagon wheels and silently boarded a fleet of waiting barges. Washington managed the whole affair without alerting the enemy, nor losing a single man. By the morning of August 30, all 9,000 retreating Continentals were safe in Manhattan.

Continental troops boarding a ferry by night for their retreat from Long Island to Manhattan

A Need for Spies

After the Battle of Long Island, Washington desperately needed to know what General Howe was planning next; so he asked for volunteers to slip back to Long Island and spy on the British. Knowing the dreadful fate that awaited any captured spy— a shameful death by hanging— most of Washington's soldiers hesitated to volunteer. They were willing to die honorable deaths in battle, but not to be hanged as traitors. Only one officer stepped forward: Nathan Hale.

AMAZING AMERICANS: Nathan Hale (1755 – 1776)

Nathan Hale was a 21-year-old schoolteacher-turned-soldier from nearby Connecticut. Against the advice of his friends, who warned that he was too honest to make a convincing spy, Hale volunteered to serve his country as Washington asked. On or around September 13, 1776, a boatman quietly deposited Hale on Long Island under cover of darkness, promising to return for him a week later. Disguising himself as an unemployed Dutch schoolteacher in search of work— a character with no reason to love the American Colonies, and every reason to ask a lot of questions— Hale spent the next week on Long Island, blending in with the many loyalists there, learning as much as he could about Howe's plans.

At the last moment, the British somehow discovered that Hale was a spy. Some blame Hale's capture on his loyalist cousin Samuel Hale, who may have recognized him and betrayed him to the British. Others say that a British patrol spotted the light Hale used to signal his boatman in the darkness. If Hale's captors ever doubted he was a spy, they doubted no longer after they found detailed military information hidden in his shoes, all written in a schoolmaster's Latin.

The Great Fire of New York (September 21, 1776)

Hale could not have chosen a worse moment to be captured. During Hale's week as a spy, the British had captured New York City; and on the very night of Hale's capture, September 21, the Great Fire of New York was hungrily burning that city. Hundreds of buildings, important shelters that Howe desperately needed for his military operations, were going up in flames. To his immense frustration, Howe had no way to rouse New York's firefighters— for Washington had ordered the city's church bells removed to keep Howe from re-forging them into cannon.

Having little doubt that some rebel had set fire to New York, Howe wasted no time condemning Nathan Hale to a traitor's death.

British officer John Montresor, who witnessed Hale's hanging, noted the remarkable courage with which Hale faced his ignoble death the next morning. Although Montresor gave Hale pen and paper with which to write last letters to his family and friends, another officer later destroyed these letters— insisting that the rebels must never know of this traitor's incredible bravery, lest they draw inspiration from it. Just before he died, Nathan Hale uttered these famous last words:

"I only regret that I have but one life to lose for my country."

Hale may have been quoting "Cato," a well-known 1712 play about liberty that includes these lines:

"How beautiful is death, when earned by virtue! / Who would not be that youth? What pity is it That we can die but once to serve our country!"

"I only regret that I have but one life to lose for my country"

New York and New Jersey (September – December 1776)

Washington followed his retreat to Manhattan with more retreats, each more desperate than the last.

1. The Battle of Harlem Heights (September 16, 1776): Two weeks after Washington's silent retreat to Manhattan, Howe and Cornwallis followed him there, landing at a convenient site just north of New York City called Kip's Bay. Now in danger of being trapped on Manhattan Island, Washington abandoned New York City and retreated north to Harlem Heights, just south of the Harlem River.

The British captured New York City easily. However, with a small victory at the Battle of Harlem Heights, Washington was able to hold the northwest corner of Manhattan— including Fort Washington, a strong new fort built on the east bank of the Hudson River just before the war.

A LOOK AHEAD: From now until the end of the war, General Howe will make the British army's headquarters in New York City.

General William Howe

2. The Battle of White Plains (October 28, 1776): Howe's next scheme was to trap Washington between three immovable obstacles: (1) Howe's large army on Manhattan, (2) a second large army that Howe landed just north of Manhattan on October 18, and (3) the Hudson River. Wise to Howe's scheme, Washington fled northward across the Harlem River.

About 15 miles north of Manhattan, Washington fought Howe to a draw at the Battle of White Plains. However, as Washington was still badly outnumbered, he decided to turn his back on Howe and flee farther north, finally crossing the Hudson River where it narrowed just north of the Tappan Zee.

3. The Battle of Fort Washington (November 16, 1776): After the Battle of White Plains, Howe turned to attack the Continentals' last stronghold on Manhattan: Fort Washington. Meanwhile, Washington moved down the west bank of the Hudson to Fort Lee, New Jersey, just across the Hudson from Fort Washington.

Three days after he reached Fort Lee, Washington looked on helplessly as the British surrounded Fort Washington and compelled its surrender— taking more than 2,800 Continental soldiers prisoner in the process.

FASCINATING FACTS: Revolutionary War POWS

The 2,800+ prisoners captured at Fort Washington added another item to General Howe's list of difficulties: what to do with prisoners of war? By tradition, the British army usually treated its prisoners decently, partly to ensure that its worthy opponents would treat British prisoners decently. However, Howe did not consider the Continentals worthy opponents; rather, he considered them traitors to the Crown, each one as treacherous as Nathan Hale. Only the fear of stirring up even greater rebellion kept Howe from executing every one of these treasonous wretches on the spot.

American prisoners of war enduring unendurable misery aboard the prison hulk *Jersey*

After the Great Fire of New York (see above), Howe had few decent buildings to use as prisons. Therefore at first, the British confined their prisoners to outbuildings and barns. Guards herded hundreds of prisoners into unheated barns like so many cattle— feeding them maggoty bread or rancid meat that Howe's soldiers had rejected, serving them drinking water in the same buckets they used as toilets. When these unendurable conditions caused their prisoners to sicken and die, the guards buried them in shallow graves that dogs and wolves later dug open.

Next, the British hit upon the idea of confining prisoners aboard **prison hulks**— rotting ships that the Royal Navy no longer wanted, stripped of their masts and anchored near shore to serve as miserable jails. The most notorious hulk was HMS *Jersey*, a huge former warship into which the British stuffed up to 1,200 POWs at a time under the most appalling conditions imaginable. An epidemic of dysentery compounded the filth aboard *Jersey*, leading to smallpox, yellow fever and other infections that claimed American lives by the thousands.

Jersey at anchor near Brooklyn in 1782

Every morning of the four years from 1780 – 1783, when guards awakened *Jersey*'s inmates with the chilling command **"Rebels, turn out your dead,"** American POWs brought forth an average of five fallen comrades.

---

4. The Retreat from Fort Lee (November 19, 1776): Three days after Fort Washington surrendered, General Cornwallis crossed the Hudson with another large army, forcing Washington to abandon Fort Lee as well.

Through November and into December, Cornwallis chased Washington across northern New Jersey. Early in December, Washington had no choice but to surrender New Jersey as he had surrendered New York, retreating across the Delaware River into Pennsylvania.

ILLUMINATING EXCERPTS from *The American Crisis* by Thomas Paine (Published 1776 – 1783)

The months of November – December 1776 were a dark time for the cause of American independence. The loss of nearly 3,000 troops at Fort Washington, followed by humiliating retreats across New Jersey, were convincing arguments that the war was already lost. With their terms of enlistment due to expire at year's end, many Continentals thought of giving up and going home.

Just when it seemed that morale could sink no lower, "Common Sense" author Thomas Paine published these inspiring words about the high cost of freedom:

"These are the times that try men's souls. The summer soldier and the sunshine patriot will, in this crisis, shrink from the service of their country; but he that stands by it now, deserves the love and thanks of man and woman. Tyranny, like hell, is not easily conquered; yet we have this consolation with us, that the harder the conflict, the more glorious the triumph. What we obtain too cheap, we esteem too lightly: it is dearness only that gives everything its value. Heaven knows how to put a proper price upon its goods; and it would be strange indeed if so celestial an article as freedom should not be highly rated."

These were the opening words of *The American Crisis*, a series of 16 pamphlets that Paine published over the years from 1776 – 1783. Paine's inspiring words reminded patriots why they were fighting, and why their cause was worth costly sacrifices like Nathan Hale's. Recognizing the power of these words, George Washington ordered them read aloud to all of his troops on December 23, 1776— three days before the victory that was to turn the tide of the Revolutionary War.

The Battle of Trenton (December 26, 1776)

Each time General Cornwallis advanced across New Jersey, he left behind a garrison to guard his path back to New York. By late December 1776, Cornwallis had garrisons scattered all over northern New Jersey, none of them large enough to resist Washington's army on its own. The scattering of Cornwallis' army created a weakness Washington could exploit.

Washington's target was Trenton, New Jersey, a small town on the east bank of the Delaware about 35 miles northeast of Philadelphia. Since December 14th, Trenton had been hosting about 1,400 Hessians, including some of the same Hessians who had captured Fort Washington. The arrogance of success had convinced these Hessians that they needn't bother building fortifications around their new winter camp, although they did usually post patrols day and night. On the night Washington chose to attack, though, the Hessians posted no patrols at all, for two reasons: (1) because it was Christmas night, a night after a day of celebration; and (2) because the weather that night was so foul that no one was expecting any action at all— much less a war-turning surprise attack.

General Charles Cornwallis

On the frigid, sleety night of December 25 – 26, 1776, George Washington personally led about 2,400 Continentals across the Delaware River from Pennsylvania to New Jersey, landing at what is now **Washington's Crossing**— a ferry site about nine miles upriver from Trenton. Treacherous ice floes delayed Washington's landing until 3 AM, leaving him with just a few hours to march on Trenton before daybreak.

Washington's orders for this march called for absolute silence and secrecy: not a man was to drop out, on pain of death, for fear that man might be a deserter bent on warning the enemy. When an officer complained that the sleet was dampening his troops' gunpowder, Washington replied that they must fight with bayonets if necessary, for he was determined to take Trenton that night.

Washington's surprise attack worked to near-perfection. Three miles outside Trenton, the Continentals divided: Washington approached from the northwest, while General John Sullivan circled around to approach from the northeast. By the time the first stunned Hessian spotted Washington and raised the alarm, he was only a mile outside town. Before the Hessians could organize themselves, Washington seized west Trenton and positioned his cannon to fire down both main streets, making it impossible for Hessian battle formations to stand against him. Finding themselves defeated in the west, the Hessians tried to flee east— only to find another army almost as large as the first blocking their escape route. Trapped between two armies, the Hessians had little choice but surrender.

Washington's triumph cost Cornwallis about 1,000 Hessians— about 20 dead, 80 wounded and an astonishing 900+ captured. An elated Washington reported, "Providence seemed to have smiled upon every part of this enterprise."

"Washington Crossing the Delaware" by artist Emanuel Leutze

"The Capture of the Hessians at Trenton, December 26, 1776" by artist John Trumbull

Pleading with the Troops

On December 30, four days after his brilliant triumph at Trenton, Washington sat astride his horse before a regiment of worn-out, homesick troops whose terms of enlistment were due to expire the next day. The condition of these troops was appalling. After months on the run from Cornwallis, their shoes had disintegrated, to the point where the snow-packed road from Washington's Crossing to Trenton was red with blood from their bare, wretched feet. The strain of the hurried night march to Trenton had left two of the weakest dead beside the road.

Despite all of this, Washington desperately needed this regiment if he wanted to hold Trenton. Therefore he pleaded them to remain for just one more month, promising that Congress would pay each man ten dollars for his sacrifice. Needy as these men were, not one of them stepped forward to volunteer until Washington added this impassioned plea:

"My brave fellows, you have done all I asked you to do, and more than could be reasonably expected; but your country is at stake, your wives, your houses and all that you hold dear. You have worn yourselves out with fatigues and hardships, but we know not how to spare you. If you will consent to stay only one month longer, you will render that service to the cause of liberty and to your country which you probably never can do under any other circumstances."

The Battle of Assunpink Creek (January 2, 1777)

While Washington was struggling to hold his ragtag army together, Cornwallis was assembling a well-seasoned army at Princeton— a college town about 13 miles northeast of Trenton— to deal with the upstart Washington. On the morning of January 2, 1777, Cornwallis detached about 1,200 troops to stand guard around Princeton, and then marched another 6,800 down the road toward Trenton, hoping to trap Washington against the Delaware River and end the war. Along the way, Cornwallis detached another 1,200 guards— still leaving him with more than 5,000 troops for his attack on Trenton, a force roughly equal to Washington's.

Cornwallis would have loved for Washington to come out and face him in open battle; but instead, Washington retreated across the broad obstacle of Assunpink Creek, just south of Trenton. After crossing Assunpink Creek's only bridge, Washington trained several cannon on that bridge and waited for Cornwallis to arrive. At the same time, Washington dispatched snipers to conceal themselves behind every rock, tree and bend in the road between Princeton and Trenton, waiting to fire on Cornwallis' troops. Each time the advancing Cornwallis halted to fight back, Washington's snipers retreated to set up new ambushes.

Washington's tactics so delayed Cornwallis that by the time he finally reached Trenton, night was falling. Three times before dark, Cornwallis' troops tried to charge across the bridge. All three times, the Continentals blasted them with cannon, until the whole bridge was red with British coats and blood.

The Battle of Princeton (January 3, 1777)

That night, Washington pulled another stunt as deceitful and successful as his retreat from Long Island. Under cover of darkness, Washington detached about 500 decoy troops to feed campfires, make digging noises and do all they could to convince Cornwallis that the whole army was still there. With his enemy thus misled, Washington silently led the rest of his army away— but not across the Delaware, as Cornwallis might have expected. Instead, Washington boldly marched on the very town where Cornwallis had lain the previous night, Princeton. The next morning, while Cornwallis was still struggling to get over his surprise, Washington was already blasting away at the British garrison miles away in Princeton.

George Washington rallying his troops at the Battle of Princeton

The Battle of Princeton highlighted the differences between Cornwallis' seasoned troops and Washington's inexperienced militia. Early in the battle, a unit of militiamen who had never even seen a battle before suddenly found themselves in the middle of a deadly one, with shrapnel flying and troops falling on all sides. Terrified at the sight, the entire unit broke and ran. Fortunately, Washington arrived at that very moment with more experienced units, whom he sent to hold off the British while he rallied his fleeing militia with this cry: "Parade with us, my brave fellows! There is but a handful of the enemy, and we shall have them directly!" Recovering their courage, the militiamen rejoined the battle— which the Continentals easily won, as they outnumbered Cornwallis' small Princeton garrison several times over.

The Battles of Trenton, Assunpink Creek and Princeton were turning points in the struggle for New York and New Jersey— for Cornwallis had now suffered three embarrassing defeats in the space of eight days, all at the hands of untrained rebel militiamen whose fighting ability he had only lately ridiculed. In light of these defeats, General Howe decided to pull Cornwallis back to New York while he considered his next moves.

SUCCINCT SUMMARIES: The New York / New Jersey Campaign began badly for the patriots, with most of both colonies falling to their enemies; but it ended in hope, with the patriots recovering most of New Jersey.

The Saratoga Campaign (1777)

Continental Commanders:	British Commanders:
Horatio Gates	John Burgoyne
Benedict Arnold	Barry St. Leger
	Henry Clinton

The Saratoga Campaign began as a British plan to divide the New England colonies, which Britain considered highly rebellious, from the Middle and Southern colonies, which Britain considered less rebellious. In the summer of 1777, three armies were to converge on Albany, New York from three directions: (1) General Burgoyne was to attack from Quebec City; (2) Brevet General Barry St. Leger was to attack from the west, by way of the Mohawk River Valley; and (3) General Clinton was to attack from New York City. If all went according to plan, then by year's end, the British would control every major fort along a north-south line from Montreal to New York City.

The Siege of Fort Ticonderoga (July 2 – 7, 1777)

In mid-June, General Burgoyne led about 7,000 – 8,000 troops southward out of Quebec. Burgoyne's first task was to capture the northernmost fort the Continentals still held, Fort Ticonderoga at the southern end of Lake Champlain.

Strong though Fort Ticonderoga was, it still suffered from the same glaring weakness it had suffered during the French and Indian War, when it was named Fort Carillon (see Chapter 19): it was still vulnerable to cannon attack from higher hills nearby. When the 3,000 Continentals inside Fort Ticonderoga saw British cannon peering at them from nearby Mount

View looking down on Fort Ticonderoga from nearby Mount Defiance, where the British set their cannon on July 4, 1777

Defiance, they knew that they could hold the fort no longer; so they slipped away under cover of darkness, surrendering valuable Fort Ticonderoga to Burgoyne almost without firing a shot.

After this dramatic first success, Burgoyne began to suffer serious difficulties. For one thing, General Howe was too busy with the Philadelphia Campaign (see below) to send Burgoyne any aid from New York City. For another, the Continentals used delaying tactics— burning bridges, felling large trees across roads, carrying off supplies and so on— to slow Burgoyne's advance through New York, giving themselves more time to recruit militia for their defense. The Continentals had far less trouble recruiting militia after one of Burgoyne's Native American allies brutally murdered a defenseless young colonist named Jane McCrea.

TERRIBLE TRAGEDIES: The Jane McCrea Incident (July 27, 1777)

The Revolutionary War was in part a war for the hearts of fence-sitting colonists, with the British trying to turn fence-sitters into loyalists and Continentals trying to turn fence-sitters into patriots. The success of

Burgoyne's Saratoga Campaign depended on winning loyalist support— for if New York's tens of thousands of fence-sitters became patriots, then they might easily overwhelm Burgoyne's small army.

One episode that helped the patriots win over fence-sitters was the sad tragedy of Jane McCrea, a lovely young woman who got caught in the crossfire when the two men in her life chose opposite sides. Jane's fiancé David Jones joined Burgoyne, but her brother John McCrea joined the patriots. When Burgoyne launched the Saratoga Campaign, Jane was living with her brother near Fort Edward, NY, about 40 miles south of Fort Ticonderoga. Three weeks after Burgoyne captured Fort Ticonderoga, his army drew close enough to Fort Edward for David to exchange messages with Jane. Eager to marry Jane, but certain that her brother would never give his consent, David took the risk of inviting Jane to join him on the British side of the battle lines. Just as eager to marry David, Jane donned her wedding dress and set out on a dangerous trek through the woods toward her fiancé.

Unfortunately, Jane crossed paths with some of Burgoyne's allies, a band of Native American warriors who were chasing Continental skirmishers through the woods. When Jane tried to run away, the natives caught up with her and seized her.

Exactly what happened next is uncertain. According to the patriot version of the tale, the natives took to quarreling over Jane's hair— a rare, beautiful red mane that hung almost to her feet— and ended up tomahawking her to death so they could claim her scalp. The natives also stole Jane's valuable wedding dress before they fled, leaving her naked, mutilated remains in the woods for her poor brother to find.

Among colonists who already distrusted Native Americans, Jane McCrea's fate was the final proof of Britain's cruelty. The idea that the British were stirring up the natives to commit savage attacks like the one that killed Jane McCrea brought countless fence-sitting colonists down on the patriot side.

"The Death of Jane McCrea" by artist John Vanderlyn

The Siege of Fort Stanwix (August 2 – 22, 1777)

100 miles to the west, Burgoyne's ally Barry St. Leger was having troubles of his own. Along St. Leger's route to Albany, between Lake Oneida and the headwaters of the Mohawk River, stood a little-used star fort called Fort Stanwix. British intelligence had informed St. Leger that he could expect to find Fort Stanwix abandoned and in poor repair. Instead, St. Leger found the fort well-defended and strong— too strong to bypass without capturing, lest the several hundred Continentals inside come out and attack him from the rear.

When the Continental Army learned that St. Leger had besieged Fort Stanwix, it dispatched two small armies to raise the siege:

1. The first army, commanded by New York militiaman Nicholas Herkimer, fought St. Leger's native allies to a draw at the bloody Battle of Oriskany before retreating with heavy casualties.

2. The second army, commanded by Benedict Arnold, was too small to raise the siege; so instead, Arnold dreamed up a clever ruse involving two loyalist brothers whom the Continentals had taken prisoner. One brother Arnold held hostage, threatening to do him serious bodily harm unless the other brother did what Arnold asked— which was to go to St. Leger's camp and report that Arnold's army was far larger and closer than it really was. Alarmed by this false report, St. Leger and his native allies abandoned the Siege of Fort Stanwix and fled to the west, depriving Burgoyne of much-needed troops.

The Battle of Bennington (August 16, 1777)

Meanwhile, Burgoyne was losing even more troops in battle near what is now Bennington, Vermont. In early August, Burgoyne detached about 800 – 1000 Hessians to raid a patriot supply depot near Bennington, expecting to find the supplies only lightly guarded. Unknown to Burgoyne, the patriots had secretly mustered about twice that many troops to defend Bennington, all under the command of experienced General John Stark.

When the wet weather cleared enough for battle to commence, John Stark gestured across the battlefield and said to his men: "There are your enemies, the Redcoats and the Tories [loyalists]. They are ours, or this night Molly Stark [John Stark's wife] sleeps a widow." Inspired by their leader's do-or-die bravery, Stark's troops surrounded the Hessians and overwhelmed them, killing or wounding about 200 and capturing about 700— more troops Burgoyne could ill afford to lose.

The Battles of Saratoga (September – October 1777)

While Burgoyne's army shrank, the Continentals' swelled. By mid-September, General Horatio Gates had about 10,000 troops under his command, including many who joined the patriots out of fury over the fate of poor Jane McCrea. By the end of September, Gates' command grew to about 15,000, more than twice Burgoyne's numbers. Despite these ever-worsening odds, Burgoyne remained determined to capture Albany that year; so instead of retreating to Fort Ticonderoga, he pressed on down the Hudson.

About 25 miles north of Albany, Burgoyne ran into a stiff obstacle. Between the Hudson and a nearby range of hills called Bemis Heights, Gates had spent more than a week building strong earth-and-timber walls, redoubts and cannon emplacements— all designed by one of the foremost army engineers in the world, a freedom-loving Pole named Thaddeus Kosciusko. Burgoyne's two attempts to outflank these formidable defenses led to two key battles of the Revolutionary War:

1. The First Battle of Saratoga, a.k.a. The Battle of Freeman's Farm (September 19, 1777): Burgoyne's plan for the First Battle of Saratoga was to seize the high ground to Gates' west, beyond his defenses on Bemis Heights. Anticipating Burgoyne's move, Gates sent his most experienced commanders to meet Burgoyne at Freeman's Farm, about a mile north of Bemis Heights. After a long day's battle, Burgoyne finally won Freeman's Farm— but at a terrible cost of 600 casualties, almost one-tenth of his entire army.

2. The Second Battle of Saratoga, a.k.a. the Battle of Bemis Heights (October 7, 1777): After the First Battle of Saratoga, Burgoyne bided his time in the hope that General Clinton might send help from New York City. When it became clear that Clinton wouldn't arrive in time, Burgoyne finally talked his reluctant officers into a second attempt to seize the high ground to Gates' west. This time, the Continentals won the day, costing Burgoyne another 900 troops.

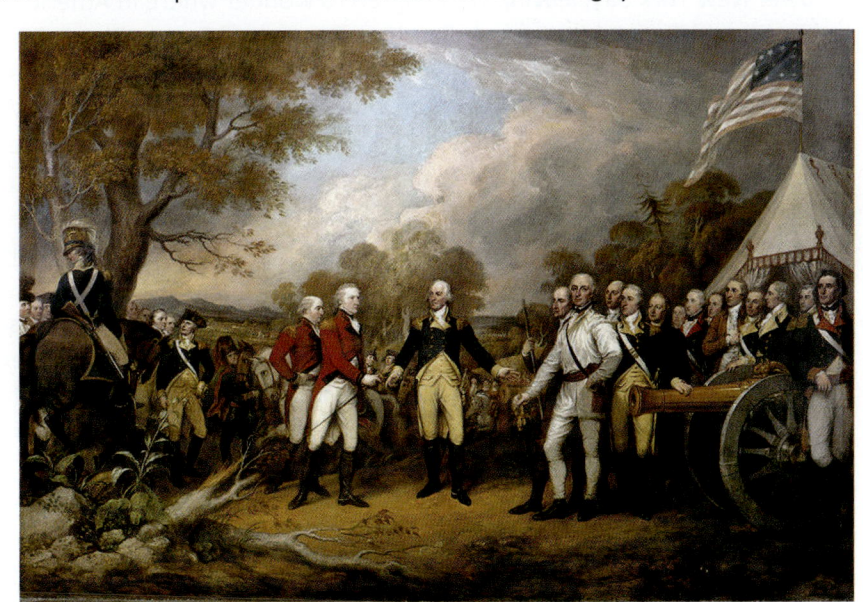

General Burgoyne surrenders to General Horatio Gates

The Second Battle of Saratoga finally convinced Burgoyne that his grand plan to capture Albany had failed, and that he had no other choice but retreat. Ten days after the battle, and about ten miles north of Bemis Heights, Gates caught up with the retreating Burgoyne and surrounded him, forcing him to surrender the nearly 6,000 troops he had left.

Gates' stunning successes at the Battles of Saratoga were the first truly great Continental victories of the Revolutionary War— the first proof that these much-ridiculed patriot militiamen were actually capable of defeating a large army of well-seasoned British regulars and Hessians in open battle. Along with success came greater support for the Revolution— both in the Colonies, where more colonists began to believe that the patriots might actually win; and overseas, where countries like France began to view the young United States as a possible ally against too-powerful Britain.

SUCCINCT SUMMARIES: The Saratoga Campaign began badly for the patriots, with the loss of the important Fort Ticonderoga; but it ended with the patriots' most inspiring victories yet at the Battles of Saratoga.

The Philadelphia Campaign (1777 – 1778)

Continental and Allied Commanders: George Washington Marquis de Lafayette	British Commanders: William Howe Henry Clinton

The Philadelphia Campaign of 1777 was General Howe's second threat to the Continental Congress' seat of government. The first threat came in December 1776, when Cornwallis chased Washington across New Jersey to within 30 miles of Philadelphia (see above). For safety's sake, Congress fled to Baltimore on December 12, 1776, but returned to Philadelphia after Washington's victories at Trenton and Princeton persuaded Cornwallis to retreat to New York for the winter.

Howe chose a different route for his second threat to Philadelphia. Instead of approaching by land— which would have required a difficult Delaware River crossing under Washington's ever-watchful eye— Howe took to the sea. In mid-July 1777, Howe loaded more than 15,000 troops aboard some 260 ships and sailed out of Lower New York Bay, leaving Washington to wonder where in America he was going: north to Quebec City, perhaps to aid General Burgoyne's Saratoga Campaign? East to Rhode Island or Boston? South to Philadelphia— or perhaps to Charleston, which General Clinton had tried and failed to capture a year before? Until his scouts caught sight of Howe again, Washington would have little idea which way to send his own troops.

In the meantime, Washington met a French officer who was to become one of his ablest commanders and closest friends: the Marquis de Lafayette.

FASCINATING FRENCHMEN: Gilbert du Motier, Marquis de Lafayette (1757 – 1834)

The Marquis de Lafayette was a born soldier from one of France's oldest, wealthiest military families. At least one of Lafayette's ancestors had fought in the Crusades, and another had fought for Joan of Arc in the Hundred Years' War. In preparation for his own military career, young Lafayette undertook the finest military education France had to offer— training for the Musketeers of the Guard, a special unit set aside to defend King Louis XVI himself.

Soon after news of the Revolutionary War reached France in mid-1775, the 17-year-old Lafayette attended a special dinner in Metz, France hosted by a well-known French officer who supported the American cause. The guest of honor that evening was King George III's younger brother William Henry, Duke of Gloucester— who, to his brother's dismay, also supported the Americans. As Lafayette listened to Gloucester criticizing his own brother's unfair treatment of the Colonies, his heart swelled with passion for the cause of American liberty. Lafayette would later write of this special evening at the diner de Metz: "The moment I heard of America, I loved her; the moment I knew she was fighting for liberty, I burned with the desire of bleeding for her; and the moment I shall be able of serving her, in any time, or in any part of the world, will be the happiest of my life."

At the moment, however, France had not yet declared war on Britain— which meant that no French officer could join the Colonies' struggle for independence without risking his government's wrath. Determined to join anyway, Lafayette used some of his great wealth to buy a ship and sail for America in secret, arriving at Charleston, South Carolina on June 13, 1777. About a month later, Lafayette knocked on Congress' door in Philadelphia and expectantly offered his services.

To Lafayette's dismay, Congress declined his offer at first— for at the time, Congress was receiving similar offers from a number of French officers, not all of them as selfless as Lafayette. Some were still seeking vengeance against Britain for defeating France in the Seven Years' War; and some were hoping to replace the Colonies' British crown with a French one. Nearly all demanded high rank and pay in recognition of their superior education and experience. It was only when Lafayette offered to serve with no pay at all, and offered several letters of recommendation to vouch for his character— including one from U.S. Ambassador to France Benjamin Franklin— that Congress agreed to commission the now 19-year-old Lafayette as a Major General.

Washington and Lafayette at Valley Forge, Pennsylvania

Even then, Washington wasn't sure what to do with this unknown officer; so at first, he brought Lafayette onto his personal staff as an aide-de-camp. In getting to know Lafayette, Washington realized that this sincere young Frenchman was just as devoted to the cause of American liberty as he himself was. Within just a few months, Lafayette's combination of devotion, courage and skill made him one of Washington's favorite officers— one of the few Washington trusted to care more for the cause than for personal gain.

While Washington and Lafayette were getting acquainted, General Howe was taking the most roundabout route to Philadelphia imaginable. Instead of simply sailing into the Delaware Bay and up the Delaware River, which would have required at most a week, Howe decided to sail all the way around the Delmarva Peninsula—300 miles south to the mouth of the Chesapeake Bay, and then almost 200 miles north back up the bay— to a landing near what is now Elkton, Maryland. Foul weather and contrary winds stretched Howe's journey to four miserable weeks, two more than he had been expecting— which meant that after two weeks, he had to order short rations for both men and horses. When the horses started starving to death, Howe had to drown some in order to save others.

Despite these miscalculations and misfortunes, Howe had little trouble capturing Philadelphia.

The Battle of Brandywine Creek (September 11, 1777)

Washington's plan for defending Philadelphia was to build a defensive line at Brandywine Creek, a broad creek that ran across Howe's path about 25 miles southwest of the city. While Howe marched northeast from Elkton, Washington built a strong set of earth-and-timber walls, redoubts and cannon emplacements on the Philadelphia side

Continental troops in threadbare clothing before the Battle of Brandywine Creek

539

of the Brandywine's main crossing, Chadd's Ford— hoping that Howe would attack him there.

Unfortunately, the Brandywine had other crossings, including two that Washington apparently didn't know about. Instead of attacking Washington head-on at Chadd's Ford, Howe sent only about one-third of his army there as a diversion. The other two-thirds Howe sent miles to the northwest, where they crossed two separate branches of the Brandywine with no interference from Washington at all. Before Washington had any idea what was happening, Howe's main army was attacking his completely defenseless right flank, threatening to destroy him.

The next few hours saw the most desperate retreat of the entire Revolutionary War. If Howe's month-long odyssey around the Delmarva Peninsula hadn't cost him so many horses, then he might have caught up with the fleeing Washington and destroyed him. As it was, some 13,000 Continentals just barely managed to escape to the east.

Occupying Philadelphia (September 26, 1777)

Two weeks after the Battle of Brandywine, Howe outmaneuvered Washington again, crossing the Schuylkill River to march into Philadelphia almost unopposed. Fortunately Congress was safe, having fled the city to establish a temporary capital in York, PA, 100 miles to the west. The British would hold Philadelphia for nearly 9 months, from September 26, 1777 – June 18, 1778.

FASCINATING FACTS: The Battle of Brandywine Creek was the first in which Lafayette proved his worth. After Howe outflanked Washington, Lafayette risked his neck to cover Washington's retreat, receiving for his trouble a bad bullet wound in the leg. Despite his wound, Lafayette went on to save even more American lives by rallying the troops for an orderly retreat.

INTERESTING IDEAS: In a way, Generals Howe's long odyssey around the Delmarva Peninsula doomed his Philadelphia Campaign before it began— for although Howe won Philadelphia, he lost the critical Battles of Saratoga (see above), which he might have won if he hadn't taken 15,000 British troops out of the war for an entire month at the very moment when General Burgoyne needed them most.

A LOOK AHEAD: In April 1778, the British army will replace General Howe with General Clinton— mainly over the Saratoga fiasco.

Washington at Valley Forge (Winter 1777 – Spring 1778)

After a few more fruitless but costly battles, Washington led his discouraged army into winter camp at Valley Forge, Pennsylvania on December 19, 1777. Valley Forge took its name from a blacksmith's forge on Valley Creek, which flowed into the Schuylkill River about 20 miles northwest of Philadelphia. Washington chose Valley Forge partly for the protection the Schuylkill offered, and partly because it lay at a perfect distance from Philadelphia— close enough to keep Howe in check, but far enough away to allow Washington plenty of warning in case Howe decided to attack.

At first, the troops who marched into Valley Forge were in no better shape than the troops who fought the Battles of Trenton and Princeton a year before: they were just as exhausted, just as shoeless and tattered, just as underfed and sick. Lafayette wrote of their condition:

Washington marching his embattled army toward winter quarters at Valley Forge, Pennsylvania

> "The unfortunate soldiers were in want of everything; they had neither coats nor hats, nor shirts, nor shoes. Their feet and their legs froze until they were black, and it was often necessary to amputate them."

Washington added:

> "I feel superabundantly for them, and from my soul pity those miseries, which it is neither in my power to relieve or prevent."

There is no accurate record of how many troops died under these miserable conditions at Valley Forge; but it may have been as many as 1,000 – 3,000.

As the winter of 1777 – 1778 melted into spring, though, Valley Forge began to turn into a place of hope, partly through the efforts of two officers:

1. **General Nathanael Greene**, who reluctantly agreed to become the army's quartermaster— the officer in charge of finding, buying and distributing supplies. Aided by the extra money Washington eventually coaxed out of Congress, the highly competent Greene managed to find what previous quartermasters could not: beef instead of bare flour, boots instead of bare feet, blankets and uniforms instead of bare rags.
2. **Baron Friedrich von Steuben**, a former Prussian army officer trained under Frederick the Great. Like Lafayette, von Steuben volunteered to serve without pay, and arrived in America carrying a personal letter of recommendation from Benjamin Franklin. Von Steuben's monumental task was to transform Washington's ragtag band of green militia into a solid, well-trained army capable of standing against British regulars and Hessians. To accomplish this, von Steuben spent months drilling Washington's men in the skills they needed to survive on the battlefield— skills like loading their muskets quickly, maneuvering as one and fighting with the bayonet.

<u>FASCINATING FACTS</u>: Like modern-day drill instructors, Baron von Steuben often used strong language to correct his trainees' mistakes. Because most Americans couldn't understand his German-language swearing, a frustrated von Steuben often had to order a translator to "Come, swear at him for me!" in English.

The Treaty of Alliance with France (signed February 6, 1778)

The spring of 1778 also brought another reason to hope— for over in France, Benjamin Franklin finally succeeded in negotiating a Treaty of Alliance with Britain's most powerful natural enemy. Franklin owed his success to the Colonies' great victories at the Battles of Saratoga, which completely changed the French way of thinking. Before Saratoga, most Frenchmen believed the Colonies' rebellion was doomed to fail; but after Saratoga, France began to see the Colonies as potential allies against a hated enemy. Eager to take advantage of Britain's misfortune, France agreed, among other things:

Illustration depicting Ambassador Franklin as the toast of fine Parisian ladies

1. To recognize the United States as a sovereign nation, independent of Britain— becoming the first European nation to do so.
2. To fight at the United States' side until she won their independence, never making peace with Britain until the Colonies were safe and secure.

3. That any part of Quebec captured during the war would belong to the United States, not to France— thus overcoming the Colonies' fear that France's real reason for joining the war might be to regain Quebec.

The Treaty of Alliance dramatically altered the war's character. Before the treaty, France offered aid to the United States secretly and in small amounts, mainly in the form of weapons. After the treaty, though, France offered ships, sailors and troops as well. The entry of the French navy altered British strategy in two major ways:

1. It forced Britain to commit more ships and troops to the defense of its colonies in the West Indies— leaving her with too few to hold both New York City and Philadelphia. <u>As a direct result of the Treaty of Alliance, General Clinton reluctantly abandoned Philadelphia on June 18, 1778</u>.
2. Because her troop shortage made it impossible for the British to occupy more rebel territory, they tried to crush the rebellion in another way— through constant harassment and punishment. After abandoning Philadelphia, the British focused not on defeating Washington's armies, but on bombarding ports and raiding coastal towns— doing all they could to make the rebels' lives miserable, in the hope that the Colonies might regret their rebellion and long for the good old days under British rule.

The Battle of Monmouth (June 28, 1778)

Clinton's withdrawal from Philadelphia presented Washington's army— now much improved by the training and supplies received at Valley Forge— with an opportunity. As Clinton retreated across northern New Jersey, Washington shadowed him, hoping for a chance to destroy him before he could reach the safety of New York City. Washington finally caught up with Clinton near Monmouth Courthouse, New Jersey, where the two sides fought the last major battle of the Revolutionary War in the north.

LASTING LEGENDS: Molly Pitcher

The weather on the late June day of the Battle of Monmouth was terribly hot— so hot that troops were nearly as likely to die of heat stroke as they were of battle wounds. To stave off heat stroke, hard-working American cannon crews needed plenty of water; and for water, they relied on water-carrying women of the Revolutionary War nicknamed "Molly Pitcher."

The best-known Molly Pitcher was Mary Ludwig Hays, wife to Pennsylvania artilleryman William Hays. Mary was one of several hundred women who joined their husbands at Valley Forge to handle tasks like tending the sick, cooking meals and carrying water to thirsty troops in training (George Washington's wife Martha was another). Artillerymen like William Hays also had another use for water: they needed it to swab out their cannon between shots, lest a hot spark trapped inside the barrel ignite their gunpowder as they reloaded.

When the Battle of Monmouth broke out, Mary Hays quickly located one or two springs of water— now called the Molly Pitcher Springs— and set to work carrying water for her husband's cannon crew. Midway through the battle, some artilleryman— perhaps Mary's husband, perhaps another— became either too wounded or too heat-exhausted to continue; and so Mary, who had been watching the crew long enough to know exactly how it operated, took over the fallen man's job. According to one report, Mary was reaching for another cartridge when an enemy cannonball passed right between her legs, tearing away the lower part of her skirt. Such a close call might have been enough to frighten any soldier, male or female, into fleeing the

Molly Pitcher filling a fallen artilleryman's place at the Battle of Monmouth

battlefield. Mary's only reaction was to observe dryly "that it was lucky it did not pass a little higher, for in that case it might have carried away something else."

After the two sides battled to a bloody draw at the Battle of Monmouth, General Clinton finished his retreat to New York City. The British continued to hold New York City throughout the war.

The Southern Campaign (1778 – 1781)

Continental and Allied Commanders:	British Commanders:
George Washington	Henry Clinton
Nathanael Greene	Charles Cornwallis
Comte de Rochambeau	Benedict Arnold

As the war progressed, the British began to understand that they might never regain New Englanders' loyalty. However, they still hoped to regain the loyalty of the South. Therefore in 1779, the British turned their attention from north to south— believing that Southern loyalists might join them by the thousands, if they could only defeat the small, bullying rebel minority that had frightened the South's loyalist majority into silence.

The Royal Navy gained Britain's first long-term foothold in the South with a swift capture of Savannah, Georgia on December 29, 1778. Using Savannah as a base, the British built up their southern army until they were ready to tackle the South's biggest port: Charleston, South Carolina.

The Siege of Charleston ended on May 12, 1780, when British General Clinton forced U.S. General Benjamin Lincoln to surrender nearly 5,300 troops at once— a devastating loss that all but collapsed South Carolina resistance for a time, except for guerrilla warriors like Francis Marion.

AMAZING AMERICANS: Francis Marion, the "Swamp Fox" (1732? – 1795)

Francis Marion was a South Carolina army officer who escaped capture at the Siege of Charleston by a curious accident. One evening in March 1780, Marion attended a Charleston dinner party hosted by a heavy drinker who insisted on toasting the American cause time and again. Although Marion heartily approved of the cause, he disapproved of his host's incessant drinking, and longed to leave. Unfortunately, his host had locked all of his doors to seal out loyalist spies. Determined to escape the party without making a fuss, the nearly 50-year-old Marion took the extreme step of leaping out a second-story window— and promptly broke his ankle. Because Marion went back to his estate to nurse his broken ankle, he was absent for the Siege of Charleston.

As one of the few experienced South Carolina officers who wasn't captured at Charleston, Marion became Britain's new worst enemy in the South. Marion and his few volunteers were far too clever to face the overwhelming British in open battle. Instead, they adopted guerrilla tactics— sneaking up on their enemies, striking quickly and then disappearing into South Carolina's swamps. For more than a year, Marion's volunteers lived in swamps, ate in swamps and slept in swamps, using their superior knowledge of the area to stay well ahead of the British. Britain's ablest and cruelest commander in the South, Colonel Banastre Tarleton, remarked after chasing Marion through swamps for seven hours: "… as for this !@#% old fox, the Devil himself could not catch him!"

One of Marion's greatest contributions to the war effort was to keep South Carolina from going loyalist. By constantly embarrassing the British, making them look foolish, Marion inspired South Carolinians' patriotism, and made fence-sitters think twice before joining his enemies.

After the Siege of Charleston came several major battles in the Carolinas— some British victories, some American victories, all bloody:

The Battle of Camden (August 16, 1780): Soon after Charleston fell, Congress assigned General Horatio Gates, hero of the Saratoga Campaign, to defend the Carolinas. Unfortunately, Gates turned out to be less heroic than Congress imagined— for in battle against Cornwallis near Camden, South Carolina, Gates suffered one of the most humiliating patriot losses of the entire war. Moments after the Battle of Camden began, about half of Gates' untrained, untested troops fled the battlefield without even firing their muskets. Instead of rallying his frightened troops as Washington had done at the Battle of Princeton, Gates joined them in their flight. Nightfall would find "Granny Gates" some 60 miles from the battlefield.

Scene from the Battle of Camden

The Battle of Kings Mountain (October 7, 1780): At Kings Mountain, near the border between South Carolina and North Carolina, a small army of patriot militia caught up to a larger army of hated loyalist militia and overwhelmed it, killing nearly 300 loyalists in about an hour. The Battle of Kings Mountain seriously undermined British recruiting, as loyalists realized that their British friends might not be able to protect them.

The Battle of Cowpens (January 17, 1781): Near Cowpens, South Carolina, patriot General Daniel Morgan frustrated the British with an embarrassing victory over Cornwallis' favorite commander, the aggressive Banastre Tarleton.

The Battle of Guilford Courthouse (March 15, 1781): Near Guilford Courthouse, North Carolina, Cornwallis managed to defeat a patriot army led by Gates' replacement, the highly competent Nathanael Greene— but at a terrible cost of over 500 casualties, about one-fourth of Cornwallis' entire force. Even with these terrible losses, Cornwallis failed to capture Greene, leaving him free to fight another day.

Cornwallis Invades Virginia

Soon after the Battle of Guilford Courthouse, Cornwallis made a controversial decision to invade Virginia— reasoning that because General Greene's supplies came through Virginia, Greene would be easier to defeat after Virginia was in British hands. However, invading Virginia also meant leaving Greene behind unbeaten, free to start reclaiming the Carolinas as soon as Cornwallis' back was turned.

In Virginia, Cornwallis joined forces with an unlikely ally: former U.S. General Benedict Arnold.

INTERESTING INDIVIDUALS: Benedict Arnold (1741 – 1801)

Early in the Revolutionary War, Benedict Arnold enjoyed a reputation as one of the patriots' finest officers. Among other things, the highly aggressive Arnold helped seize Fort Ticonderoga from the British in 1775; led part of the Quebec campaign in 1775 – 1776, receiving a musket ball in the leg for his trouble; outfoxed Barry St. Leger at Fort Stanwix in mid-1777; and fought with extraordinary bravery at the Battles of Saratoga in late 1777— receiving more wounds that finally crippled his leg, leaving it two inches shorter and far weaker than the other.

Along with Arnold's remarkable bravery, though, came remarkable ambition and extravagance. Almost from the beginning of the war, Arnold argued with Congress and his fellow officers over two main grievances:

1. **Rank:** Arnold believed that his exceptional performance should entitle him to exceptional rank. Therefore when Congress promoted several less-exceptional officers over his head— usually for political reasons, not military ones— Arnold was deeply insulted.

2. **Accounting:** Arnold sometimes failed to keep proper receipts for the supplies he bought on military campaigns, which led to accusations that he spent the unaccounted-for money on himself. Speaking of these accusations, Arnold wrote his personal friend George Washington:

"Having made every sacrifice of fortune and blood, and become a cripple in the service of my country, I little expected to meet the ungrateful returns I have received from my countrymen."

These grievances against his fellow patriots already weighed heavy on Arnold's mind in June 1778— when the British abandoned Philadelphia, and Washington appointed the still-recovering Arnold as the city's first military governor. More grievances followed, as Philadelphia's city leaders accused Arnold of funneling city money into his own pocket. Adding to Arnold's money troubles was his romance with Philadelphian Peggy Shippen, an extravagant young socialite whose wooing cost Arnold far more than he could afford.

Exactly when and why Arnold chose to act on all these grievances is uncertain. All that is certain is that within a month of his wedding to Peggy Shippen in April 1779, this former American hero turned traitor against his own countrymen.

During the British occupation of Philadelphia, Peggy Shippen had been wooed by Major John André, a British officer who had since been promoted to head of intelligence in the colonies— in other words, Britain's chief spymaster. Even after the British abandoned Philadelphia, the loyalist Shippen remained in touch with André. Through André, Arnold eventually arranged this secret deal with the British:

1. Arnold would exchange his post in Philadelphia for a new post he had been offered as commander of **West Point**— a strong fort on the Hudson River about 50 miles north of New York City. Next, Arnold would do all he could to weaken West Point— providing the British with details about the fort's defenses, reassigning troops elsewhere and selling off supplies. With Arnold's help, West Point would easily fall to the British, giving them exactly what they had sought in the Saratoga Campaign: the ability to cut off the New England colonies from the Middle and Southern colonies.

2. In exchange, the British would (a) pay Arnold the princely sum of 20,000 British pounds, 50 – 100 times as much as he usually earned in a year; and (b) commission him a brigadier general.

At a fateful meeting on September 21, 1780, Arnold committed the irrevocable treachery of handing John André critical details about

Benedict Arnold

The Boot Monument at Saratoga National Historical Park, New York, which honors the leg Arnold sacrificed for his country at the Second Battle of Saratoga, and yet condemns Arnold's treachery by refusing to mention his name

West Point's defenses— details which would virtually guarantee the deaths of his own men, as the British would know exactly where and how Arnold had deployed them.

Unfortunately for Arnold, his treachery backfired on him. Two days after that fateful meeting, an alert patriot patrol stopped John André as he tried to sneak back to New York City, and found Arnold's plans hidden in the spymaster's boot. Only Arnold's position saved him— for as commander of West Point, he received a report of André's capture the next morning, and knew that Washington would soon figure out who had betrayed him. Minutes before Washington's men arrived to arrest him, Arnold made a hurried escape downriver to the waiting British ship *Vulture*, which carried him on to New York City and his new master, General Clinton. As for André, the Americans hanged him to death about a week later, just as the British had hanged Nathan Hale.

After West Point, Arnold perfected his treachery by fighting for the British, turning his detailed knowledge of the patriot army against the very soldiers he had once called comrades. Arnold's attacks on Virginia and Connecticut sealed his reputation as one of the most despicable traitors in U.S. history.

The Battle of the Chesapeake (September 5, 1781)

General Cornwallis' next controversial decision would end up costing Britain the war. In July 1781, Cornwallis received orders from General Clinton to establish a base at some port in Virginia, one capable of receiving oceangoing ships sent from New York. The port Cornwallis chose was Yorktown, which lay on the south bank of the York River about 5 miles from the Chesapeake Bay. Cornwallis could have established other bases as well, inland ones like those the British held in New York and the Carolinas; but instead, Cornwallis chose to concentrate his forces at Yorktown.

The problem with Yorktown was its isolation on the narrow Virginia Peninsula. Before France joined the war, Yorktown's isolation wouldn't have been a problem, as the British could always have escaped by sea if they had trouble on land. Unfortunately for Cornwallis, a powerful French navy commanded by Comte de Grasse was approaching the Chesapeake Bay— raising the possibility that Cornwallis might not be able to escape.

News of this fast-approaching French navy brought rapid responses from both sides:

French and British ships of the line exchanging cannon fire at the Battle of the Chesapeake

- Washington's response was to start marching every troop he could spare toward Virginia.

- Clinton's response was to dispatch a British fleet to answer the French one. Unfortunately for the British, Clinton's fleet proved too small. With a rare victory over the British navy at the September 5, 1781 **Battle of the Chesapeake**, the French navy sealed the Chesapeake Bay against the British— rendering Cornwallis' hoped-for escape by sea impossible.

The Siege of Yorktown (September 28 – October 19, 1781)

By late September, Washington amassed nearly 19,000 troops near Yorktown, including about 8,000 battle-hardened Continentals, 3,100 militiamen and 7,800 Frenchmen. Against this massive army, Cornwallis could set only about 9,000 redcoats and Hessians.

On October 5, Washington began the long, complicated process of moving his cannon within range of Yorktown. Like General Howe at the Battle of Long Island, Washington dug long, zigzag trenches across the open ground around Yorktown to protect his men from enemy fire. When all was ready, Washington personally touched off the first American cannon of the Siege of Yorktown.

After two weeks of near-constant bombardment, Cornwallis finally realized that his troops could hold out no longer, and that no help could possibly reach him in time. Therefore on October 19, 1781, Cornwallis reluctantly surrendered his entire army to Washington. Like General Howe near the outset of the war, Cornwallis peevishly refused to treat Washington as an equal, instead feigning illness so that he could send his second-in-command to surrender in his place.

Redcoats and Hessians surrender to Washington at Yorktown

The Treaty of Paris (1783)

After Cornwallis' humiliating defeat at the Siege of Yorktown, British support for the war collapsed. Although the British still held New York, Charleston and Savannah, they no longer had any reasonable hope of winning the war, as their losses had made it impossible to win fence-sitting colonists over to the loyalist side. The war had cost enough; the time had come to admit defeat and go home. Nearly all fighting ceased by 1782.

The official end of the Revolutionary War came on September 3, 1783, when Britain signed the Treaty of Paris. Among the treasures American negotiators Benjamin Franklin, John Adams and John Jay won in this remarkable treaty were these:

- "His Britannic Majesty" King George III acknowledged the Thirteen Colonies to be "free, sovereign and independent states," relinquishing "all claims to the government, proprietary and territorial rights of the same, and every part thereof."
- All former British territory in North America south of Canada— including the Ohio Country, the Illinois Country and everything else east of the Mississippi, excepting only New Orleans and Spanish Florida— became United States territory.

Consequences and Consequential Characters of the American Revolutionary War

The Demise of the Iroquois Confederacy

The Revolutionary War helped bring about the end of the Iroquois Confederacy, the once-mighty union of tribes that had grown so powerful during the Beaver Wars. When the war broke out, the Great Council couldn't agree on whom the Iroquois should support— their traditional British allies, or

Scene from the Cherry Valley Massacre, one of the incidents that spurred Washington to dispatch the Sullivan Expedition

the upstart Americans. The council's indecision split the Confederacy, bringing the longstanding peace formed by the Great Peacemaker and Hiawatha to a sad end.

Far sadder was the **Sullivan Expedition**— named for General John Sullivan, the same Sullivan who fought beside Washington at the Battle of Trenton and elsewhere. In the summer of 1779, Washington ordered Sullivan north to punish the British-allied Iroquois for atrocities like the murder of Jane McCrea (see above). Sullivan's 3,200 troops sacked scores of Iroquois towns— destroying homes, burning food supplies and making it impossible for the Iroquois to survive the coming winter without help from the British.

The Treaty of Paris granted much of the Iroquois' former territory to the United States. Afterward, many of the surviving Iroquois moved north to Canada.

AMAZING AMERICANS: John Paul Jones (1747 – 1792) and the *Bonhomme Richard*

John Paul was a Scottish sea captain who moved to Virginia in 1773 – 1774, possibly to escape being tried in a British court for the murder of one of his sailors. At around the same time, John Paul added the last name "Jones" to his signature— perhaps to conceal his identity, or perhaps for some unknown reason. When the Revolutionary War began, Jones volunteered his services to the newly-founded United States Navy, becoming one of its first officers.

After spending the first two years of the war harassing British ships along the North American coast, Jones moved on to harass British ships around Europe. For about 18 months, from April 1778 – September 1779, British merchant ships and coast-dwellers lived in constant fear of attack from the American whom they came to regard as the Revolutionary War's most notorious pirate, John Paul Jones.

During those same 18 months, Americans came to regard Jones as their country's first naval hero. Jones' best-known exploit was his capture of HMS *Serapis*, a British warship that considerably outgunned his own *Bonhomme Richard*, at the September 23, 1779

John Paul Jones

Battle of Flamborough Head. Knowing that *Bonhomme Richard* could never stand up to *Serapis*' superior guns, Jones avoided a gun battle, and instead maneuvered close enough for his marines to board his enemy. Midway through the battle, a British sailor taunted Jones, asking him if he was ready to strike *Bonhomme Richard*'s colors yet— to which Jones shouted the famously stubborn reply, "I have not yet begun to fight!" Although Jones finally won *Serapis*, he lost *Bonhomme Richard*, which was so badly damaged in the battle that it sank the next day.

AMAZING AMERICANS: Betsy Ross (1752 – 1836)

Betsy Griscom was a Quaker girl who fell in love with an Anglican boy named John Ross at the Philadelphia upholstery shop where they both worked as apprentices. For eloping with John Ross in 1773, Betsy Ross found herself "read out" of her Quaker meeting house— cut off from her church and family, both emotionally and economically. After their

Betsy Ross presenting the first American flag to George Washington

elopement, the couple attended John's father's church, Christ Church— the same church George Washington attended when he was in Philadelphia.

In the spring of 1776, George Washington approached his church acquaintance and sometimes-seamstress Betsy Ross with a design for the first American flag, one that included 13 six-point stars to represent the Thirteen Colonies. Betsy suggested five-point stars instead, demonstrating how an experienced seamstress could fold cloth in such a way as to cut a perfect five-point star with a single snip of her shears. Impressed with Betsy's skills, Washington and the rest of the flag committee trusted her to produce the first official United States flag, which Congress adopted on the first Flag Day: June 14, 1777.

AMAZING AMERICANS: Deborah Sampson (1760 – 1827)

Deborah Sampson was a Massachusetts woman who disguised herself as a man so that she could serve in the Continental Army. Deborah enlisted under the name Robert Shurtliff— the first two names of her dead brother Robert Shurtliff Sampson— on May 20, 1782.

Although the war was nearly over by 1782, skirmishes were still common. In one of these skirmishes, Deborah received two wounds that required medical attention: a saber cut to the head, and musket wound to the leg. Terrified that her doctor might uncover her secret, Deborah allowed him to treat her head wound, but slipped out of the hospital before he could examine her leg. Then, in a display of warrior toughness equal to any man's, Deborah used a penknife and sewing needle to dig a musket ball out of her own leg.

Later, Deborah caught a fever that left her too weak to avoid hospital care; and while her guard was down, an examining doctor undressed her enough to discover her secret. Instead of revealing her secret, though, the doctor took Deborah home and nursed her back to health. After the Treaty of Paris ended the war, Deborah received an honorable discharge. Years later, Massachusetts awarded Deborah back pay that it had once denied her because she was a woman, explaining that Deborah:

"... exhibited an extraordinary instance of female heroism by discharging the duties of a faithful gallant soldier, and at the same time preserving the virtue and chastity of her gender, unsuspected and unblemished."

U.S. STATE FOCUS

Vermont

FASCINATING FACTS about Vermont:

- State Capital: Montpelier
- State Abbreviation: VT
- Statehood: Vermont became the 14th US state on March 4, 1791.
- Area: About 9,600 square miles (Ranks 45th in size)
- Bordering States: New York, Massachusetts, New Hampshire
- Meaning of Name: "Vermont" comes from *vert mont*, French for "green mountain."
- State Nickname: "Green Mountain State"
- State Bird: Hermit thrush
- State Tree: Sugar maple
- State Flower: Red Clover
- State Song: "These Green Mountains" by Diane Martin and Rita Buglass Gluck
- State Motto: "Freedom and unity"
- Historic Places to Visit: President Calvin Coolidge Homestead, President Chester Arthur Birthplace, Ethan Allen Homestead, Mount Independence, Bennington Battle Monument
- Resources and Industries: Maple syrup, granite, lumber, farming

Ethan Allen demanding Fort Ticonderoga's surrender early in the Revolutionary War

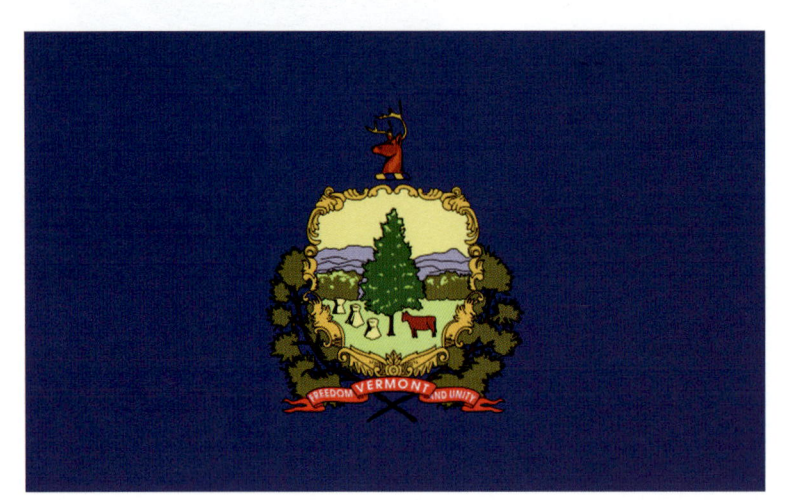

State Flag: Vermont's coat of arms centered on a blue field. The coat of arms is a shield depicting a Vermont landscape with the Green Mountains in the background. In the foreground stand three symbols of Vermont: a cow and three sheaves of wheat to represent Vermont's fine farms, and a pine tree to represent Vermont's abundant forests. The shield's crest is a stag that represents Vermont's wild game. Beneath the shield is wrapped a red banner with the name "Vermont" and the state motto "Freedom and Unity."

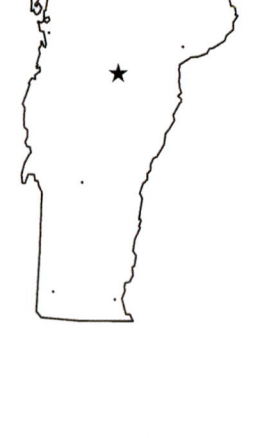

CHAPTER 23: The Constitution of the United States of America

U.S. HISTORY FOCUS

FASCINATING FACTS: The Liberty Bell

- The Liberty Bell began as the tower bell for the Pennsylvania Statehouse, the Philadelphia building later renamed Independence Hall. A London foundry cast the 2,000-pound bell and shipped it to Philadelphia in 1752. Before the city fathers hung their new bell, they struck it to test its tone— at which it immediately cracked. Philadelphia metalworkers John Pass and John Stow had to melt the bell down and recast it twice before it rang true enough to take its place in the Statehouse bell tower.

- After that, the Statehouse bell rang to summon lawmakers into session, as well as on all sorts of special occasions— including, probably, Philadelphia's first public reading of the Declaration of Independence on July 8, 1776.

- During the Revolutionary War, Pennsylvania hid its bell at Allentown to keep the British from recasting it into cannon. After the war, the bell returned to everyday use in Philadelphia for several decades.

- Over time, another crack began to appear. Desperate to save the honored old bell, metalworkers tried filing out the crack and stabilizing it with bolts. Despite their best efforts, though, the crack spread all the way to the top by 1846, rendering the Liberty Bell mute.

- The original bell included two inscriptions: (1) "Proclaim liberty throughout all the land unto all the inhabitants thereof," a reference to Leviticus 25:10; and (2) "By Order of the Assembly of the Province of Pennsylvania for the Statehouse in the City of Philadelphia, MDCCLII [1752]." After recasting, the bell also included the inscription "Pass and Stow, Philadelphia, MDCCLIII [1753]."

The success of the American Revolution created a historic opportunity: for the first time, a European-descended people completely erased their old monarchical government, creating a blank slate upon which to write whatever new form of government they chose. "Common Sense" author Thomas Paine wrote in 1776:

> "We have every opportunity and every encouragement before us, to form the noblest purest constitution on the face of the earth. We have it in our power to begin the world over again. A situation, similar to the present, hath not happened since the days of Noah until now. The birthday of a new world is at hand, and a race of men, perhaps as numerous as all Europe contains, are to receive their portion of freedom… "

The Articles of Confederation

DEFINITIONS:
- A **federation** or **confederation** is a union of semi-independent or independent states.
- A **federal government** is the central government of a federation or confederation.
- The **Articles of Confederation and Perpetual Union** was a constitution that established a weak federal government with very limited powers over the original thirteen states. The newborn United States operated under the Articles of Confederation for about 12 years, from mid-1777 through March 1789.

Earlier Plans of Union

The Articles of Confederation was not the first plan to unite the Thirteen Colonies under some form of federal government. Before the Articles came these four earlier plans, among others:

1. The New England Confederation was a military alliance formed to fight off the Native Americans of New England in early conflicts like the Pequot War and King Philip's War. This confederation dissolved in 1686, the year Governor Edmund Andros replaced all of New England's governments with the single new Dominion of New England (see Chapter 12).

2. The Albany Plan (1754) was a plan of union presented by Benjamin Franklin to the Albany Congress, a convention that met at the outset of the French and Indian War. The purpose of this convention was to plan how the colonies might unite against their common foes, mainly the "Indian nations." The "general government" outlined in the Albany Plan was to have power on behalf of all the colonies:

- To declare war and negotiate peace with Indian nations.
- To raise armies for the colonies' defense.
- To negotiate all land purchases and treaties with Indian nations.
- To govern any new territory purchased from Indian nations until the Crown established a colonial government there.

Franklin envisioned two branches for his general government:

1. A **legislative branch led by a Grand Council**, whose members would be chosen by the colonies' general assemblies.
2. An **executive branch led by a President-General**, who was to be appointed by the Crown. The President-General would have authority to approve or deny any act of the Grand Council.

Delegates to the Albany Congress of 1754

To fund its operation, Franklin's general government was to have power to lay light taxes on the colonies. The nature of these taxes was to be "rather discouraging luxury, than loading industry with unnecessary burdens." In other words, the general government was to tax the luxuries spendthrifts bought, rather than the common goods thrifty citizens bought— for as always, Poor Richard approved of thrift.

Ironically, both the Crown and the Colonies rejected the Albany Plan, but for opposite reasons. The Crown rejected the plan for being too democratic: the king didn't want another troublesome elected council contradicting his every command. The Colonies, on the other hand, rejected the plan for being too monarchical: they didn't want to surrender their authority to a President-General who would forever do the Crown's bidding.

INTERESTING IDEAS: Benjamin Franklin mourned the Albany Plan's demise in his autobiography— even suggesting that if the Crown had accepted the plan, then the Revolutionary War might never have happened:

"The colonies, so united, would have been sufficiently strong to have defended themselves; there would then have been no need of troops from England; of course, the subsequent pretense for taxing America, and the bloody contest it occasioned, would have been avoided. But such mistakes are not new; history is full of the errors of states and princes."

3. The Articles of Association (October 20, 1774) was a temporary plan of union that arose from the Intolerable Acts (see Chapter 21). In response to those hated acts of Parliament, the First Continental Congress decreed a strict boycott on all British goods. To enforce this boycott, the Colonies needed some sort of federal government.

The Articles of Association bound the Thirteen Colonies together "under the sacred ties of virtue, honor and love of our country," making it every citizen's patriotic duty to abide by the boycott. Among other things, the Articles of Association:

The First Continental Congress at prayer, September 1774

- Established committees "in every county, city and town" to enforce the boycott, and to punish any unscrupulous merchant who tried to profit from it.

- Declared that the several colonies would "have no trade, commerce, dealings or intercourse whatsoever with any colony or province in North America" that didn't abide by the boycott— promising to treat that colony "as unworthy of the rights of freemen, and as inimical to the liberties of their country."

A LOOK AHEAD: In his First Inaugural Address on March 4, 1861, incoming President Abraham Lincoln will name the Articles of Association as the document that originally formed the United States of America.

4. The Declaration of Independence (1776) united the Colonies in rebellion against King George III, closing with this pledge of unity: "And for the support of this Declaration, with a firm reliance on the protection of divine Providence, we mutually pledge to each other our Lives, our Fortunes and our sacred Honor."

DEFINITION: To **ratify** a document is to approve and accept it.

The Articles of Confederation and Perpetual Union

Recognizing the need for unity, the Second Continental Congress appointed a constitution committee on June 12, 1776, the day after it appointed the Committee of Five to draft the Declaration of Independence. The constitution committee hammered out the Articles of Confederation over the next year, presenting their work to Congress in the summer of 1777. After a few modifications, Congress approved the Articles for ratification by the states in November 1777— when Congress was meeting at York, as the British had captured Philadelphia (see Chapter 22). From that moment forward, the federal government operated under the Articles of Confederation, even though the last of the Thirteen Colonies would not ratify the Articles until February 1781.

From the beginning of the First Continental Congress, the powers of the federal government had been a sensitive topic. Each delegate to congress was there to serve his own colony's interests, not the interests of all Thirteen Colonies. Furthermore, some colonies grumbled that the trouble with King and Parliament had started in Massachusetts, and should remain there. Even after their growing troubles convinced the Colonies to work together, two concerns remained:

1. All of the Colonies guarded their sovereignty jealously, hesitant to sacrifice their own best interests for the greater good of the new nation.

2. The Southern colonies were particularly cautious because they feared being dominated by the New England and Middle Colonies. Already, differences between North and South were emerging: the North had more bankers and businessmen, while the South had more farmers and slaves. Southerners feared that the North's financial advantages might allow it to dominate the South as easily as Great Britain had.

The Articles of Confederation honored these concerns by setting strict limits on the federal government's power:

- The federal government was to have no executive branch— no president, and no powerful executive agencies.
- The federal government was to have no judicial branch— no courts, and no judges. With neither a judicial branch to adjudge law, nor an executive branch to enforce law, the Confederation Congress's so-called "laws" would actually be little more than suggestions.
- The federal government was to have no power to tax. Instead, the individual states were to tax their citizens, and Congress was to request its money from the states.
- The federal government was to have no power to regulate foreign trade, nor trade between the states. Instead, each state was free to negotiate individual trade agreements with every other state, colony or foreign nation.

Despite these strict limitations, the thirteen Articles of Confederation established some important guidelines for the new nation that Article I named **"The United States of America"**:

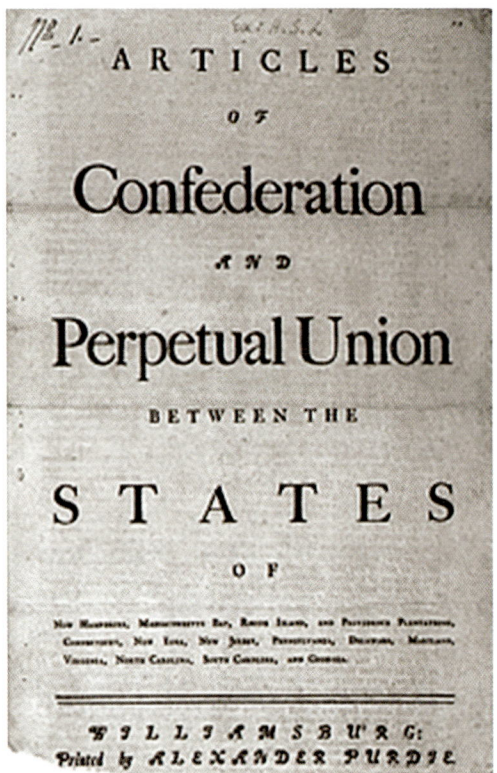

- Article IV bound the United States together by insisting that (1) all citizens were free to travel from state to state; (2) no state could require citizens of other states to pay special taxes and obey special laws; and (3) no criminal could escape justice in one state by fleeing to another. The states were to treat one another as brothers, not as foreigners.
- Articles VI and IX granted Congress exclusive power to negotiate treaties with foreign nations— except "treaties of commerce," which the states were free to negotiate for themselves— and to decide when and how to prosecute war against those nations.
- Article IX also granted Congress power to decide all boundary disputes between the states, as well as to manage all affairs between the United States and the "Indians." It was these two powers that led to the Confederation Congress' greatest achievement: deciding how the United States would govern new territories to the west.

Land Ordinances

The controversy that delayed the ratification of the Articles of Confederation for more than 3 years, from late 1777 – early 1781, was over the original thirteen states' claims to Ohio and territories farther west. Based on their charters, Virginia, Maryland, Pennsylvania, Connecticut and Massachusetts all claimed part or all of Ohio. Some of these claims extended all the way to the Pacific Ocean. It was only after Virginia finally, reluctantly agreed to surrender its claim to Ohio that Maryland finally ratified the Articles of Confederation.

INTERESTING IDEAS: The controversy over Ohio had the potential to tear the newborn United States apart. If Virginia, Maryland and Pennsylvania had decided to fight for Ohio, then their war might have left the United States no more united than the Holy Roman Empire. Fortunately, all three surrendered their claims, agreeing to let the federal government decide how best to manage Ohio.

With that disagreement out of the way, the Confederation Congress was free to plan the United States' westward expansion through two main laws:

1. **The Land Ordinance of 1785** established guidelines for surveying any new territories west of the original thirteen states— mainly so that the cash-starved Confederation Congress could earn money from land sales. Beginning with Ohio, all new territories were to be divided into square townships, their dividing lines oriented precisely north-south by east-west. Each township was to measure 6 miles on a side, and would therefore cover 36 square miles. Each township was then to be subdivided into 36 "sections" of one square mile, or 640 acres each. A quarter section would be 160 acres, an eighth section 80 acres, and a sixteenth section 40 acres. As nearly as possible, the entire United States west of the original thirteen was to be divided in this square, regular fashion.

6	5	4	3	2	1
7	8	9	10	11	12
18	17	16	15	14	13
19	20	21	22	23	24
30	29	28	27	26	25
31	32	33	34	35	36

A township numbering plan adopted by the U.S. General Land Office in 1796, with reserved sections in color. Each township measured 6 miles on a side, while each of a township's 36 sections measured 1 mile on a side.

Not all of a township's sections were for immediate sale. The Land Ordinance of 1785 reserved sections 8, 11, 26 and 29 for the government, setting them aside for future sale or use. It also reserved section 16 "for the maintenance of public schools, within the said township." However, the law didn't necessarily require all townships to locate their public schools on section 16; for a township could also comply with the law by selling section 16, and then using the money to fund public schools elsewhere.

2. **The Northwest Ordinance of 1787** established guidelines for governing the Northwest Territory— basically all territory between the Ohio River, the Mississippi River and the Great Lakes. The vast size of this territory required Congress to strike a balance. If the law allowed too few states there, then those states might grow larger and more powerful than the original thirteen; but if it allowed too many, then those states might hold enough votes in the Senate to outweigh the original thirteen. The Northwest Ordinance compromised by dividing the Northwest Territory into "not less than three nor more than five States."

A LOOK AHEAD: In the end, most of the Northwest Territory will fall into the five states of Ohio, Indiana, Illinois, Michigan and Wisconsin.

Each new sub-territory was to begin under a powerful governor, appointed by Congress to write his territory's law, enforce its law and command its militia. As soon as a territory amassed 5,000 "free male inhabitants of full age," it was to establish a house of representatives consisting of one elected representative for every 500 men. Advised by this house of representatives and its legislative council, the governor would continue to manage the territory until it amassed 60,000 "free inhabitants"— at which time it could join the United States "on an equal footing with the original States in all respects whatever," provided that the state government it designed for itself lived up to all these requirements:

Map of the Northwest Territory (white) showing eventual state boundaries

1. It was to be a republican government with proportional representation for all free male citizens.
2. It was to preserve its citizens' freedom of religion.
3. It was to preserve the legal rights for which the United States had fought in the American Revolution— including property rights, the right of an accused to appear before a judge, the right to a trial by a jury of one's peers, and a ban on "cruel or unusual punishments."

The Northwest Ordinance also included groundbreaking guidelines on three moral issues:

1. **Encouraging public education:** Section 14, Article 3 decreed, "Religion, morality, and knowledge being necessary to good government and the happiness of mankind, schools and the means of education shall forever be encouraged."

2. **Fair dealing with native peoples:** The same article also decreed, "The utmost good faith shall always be observed towards the Indians; their lands and property shall never be taken from them without their consent; and, in their property, rights, and liberty, they shall never be invaded or disturbed, unless in just and lawful wars authorized by Congress; but laws founded in justice and humanity, shall from time to time be made for preventing wrongs being done to them, and for preserving peace and friendship with them."

3. **Forbidding slavery:** Section 14, Article 6 decreed, "There shall be neither slavery nor involuntary servitude in the said territory, otherwise than in the punishment of crimes whereof the party shall have been duly convicted." However, the article also decreed that any runaway slave who fled to the Northwest Territory must be returned; for the Northwest Territory was not to become a legal haven for runaway slaves.

Portrait of Thomas Jefferson, author of the Northwest Ordinance's moral articles

Thus the Northwest Ordinance set the pattern for how new territories would join the United States: not as colonies of the original thirteen states, but as equals, provided they abided by the republican principles of the American Revolution.

INTERESTING IDEAS: Both the Articles of Confederation and the Northwest Ordinance included an important legal idea that the later Constitution of the United States failed to mention specifically: the idea of "Perpetual Union." Both laws required all states to join the United States permanently; no state that later regretted its decision to join was free to withdraw from the United States.

A LOOK AHEAD: The Constitution's failure to mention Perpetual Union will become important in 1860— the year when the anti-slavery candidate Abraham Lincoln will win election as President of the United States, and the slaveholding states of the Deep South will rush to secede from the Union before Lincoln can take office.

FASCINATING FACTS: The Great Seal of the United States (adopted by the Confederation Congress in 1782)

The Front Side, which is also the coat of arms of the United States, features a bald eagle, national bird and symbol of the United States. Defending the eagle is a shield with 7 white and 6 red vertical stripes, symbols of the original 13 states, all under a wide horizontal blue bar to represent the states' union under Congress. The eagle's beak clutches a banner with the motto *E pluribus unum*, Latin for "Out of many, one" — a reminder that the United States is a federation of semi-independent states. One of the eagle's talons clutches 13 arrows, symbols of the nation's power to defend itself; while the other clutches an olive branch with 13 leaves and 13 berries, symbols of peace. To demonstrate the USA's preference for peace, the eagle faces the olive branch. Above all rises a cloud with thirteen stars bursting through, symbolizing a great new nation in the constellation of nations.

The Reverse Side features an incomplete 13-step pyramid, a symbol of permanence and strength, with the Roman numeral year 1776 printed at its base. Atop the pyramid is the eye of God, a symbol of God's over-watching providence. Above the pyramid is the motto *Annuit Coeptis*, Latin for "He has smiled on our undertakings." Below is the motto *Novus Ordo Seclorum*, Latin for "A new order of the ages."

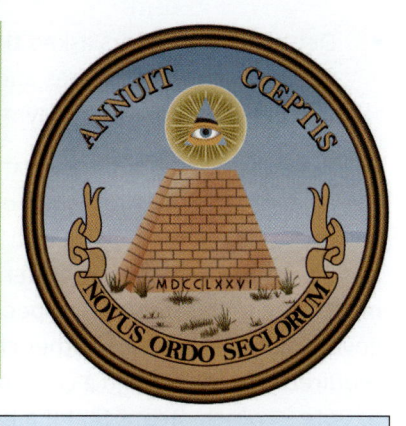

Shays' Rebellion (August 1786 – 1787)

Economic Woes

From the beginning, the weaknesses of the Articles of Confederation made it all but impossible for the federal government to manage its primary task: winning the Revolutionary War. The Continental Army's terrible suffering at Valley Forge sprang directly from Congress's dire lack of money— a lack that Congress couldn't fill through taxes, as the Confederation Congress had no power to tax. Without the option of direct taxes, and with limited money coming in from the states, only two options remained:

1. Borrowing money, which led to a mountain of debt by war's end.
2. Printing paper money, which led to inflation. By war's end, Congress had printed so many paper dollars that each individual dollar was practically worthless— or, as colonists often said, "not worth a Continental."

$3 bill printed by the Continental Congress in 1776

DEFINITION: **Inflation** is an economic difficulty in which the price of goods rises, and therefore the value of money falls. Although inflation can happen for complex reasons, the simplest explanation is this: when a government prints an unlimited number of paper dollars to pay for the same limited number of items, there are more dollars per item; and so each item costs more dollars.

Currency Crisis

The economic situation was even worse later, especially for debt-ridden farmers. After the war, America's trade partners stopped accepting inflated Continental dollars, and started demanding real money— mainly gold and silver, both of which were scarce in America. In turn, American businessmen started demanding gold and silver from customers who owed them money. Poor farmers were used to repaying their debts with money they earned selling grain and livestock raised on their farms. Unfortunately, these goods were hard to sell at the moment— for Britain had closed the British West Indies to American ships, depriving farmers of one of their main markets. Without strong markets for their goods, farmers couldn't raise money to pay their debts.

In desperation, both poor farmers and wealthy businessmen turned to their state governments:

- Debt-ridden farmers asked their state governments to pass laws that favored debtors. Some asked their governments to cut taxes and forgive certain debts. Others asked them to issue paper money, or to force businessmen to accept payment in grain.
- Businessmen asked their state governments to do the opposite— to pass laws that required full payment of all debt agreements in gold or silver.

Unfortunately for farmers, businessmen controlled most state governments— especially Massachusetts' government. Like several other colonies, Massachusetts required citizens to hold a certain amount of property in order to vote— which meant that if a poor farmer didn't hold enough property, then he had no voice in his state government. Wealthy businessmen— who did have voices in government— continued to demand payment of all debts in gold and silver. When farmers couldn't pay, businessmen took them to court.

Massachusetts' courts, which were just as full of wealthy businessmen as its legislature, humiliated the farmers— forcing them to sell their produce at prices far below market value; confiscating their produce to pay their debts; seizing their farms; and even locking them up in debtors' prisons.

Just as vexing to Massachusetts farmers were their state's high taxes. After the war, Massachusetts needed extra money to pay off the war bonds it had sold to finance the war, and to pay its share of the federal government's war debts. To get that money, Massachusetts levied extra-high taxes on poor farmers who were already struggling to pay their bills.

Protesting unfair judgments against farmers outside a Massachusetts courthouse

To add insult to injury, many of these debt-ridden Massachusetts farmers were former soldiers— men who had sacrificed a great deal to buy their country's freedom, only to have their country abandon them when they needed help after the war. Such ill-treatment left former soldiers like Daniel Shays wondering why they had bothered to fight the Revolutionary War, since they were still suffering one of its main causes: taxation without representation.

AMAZING AMERICANS: Daniel Shays (1747? – 1825)

Daniel Shays was a Massachusetts farmer-turned-soldier who served his country honorably at important battles from Bunker Hill to Saratoga, rising from the lowly rank of private to the honored rank of captain. However, Shays' high rank never brought him high pay, as both Massachusetts and the Confederation Congress were forever behind in paying their soldiers. For this reason among others, Shays resigned his captain's commission in 1780, and went home to try to earn money on his farm.

After the war, Shays' debt problem only grew worse. Like other farmers, Shays had trouble selling his goods, and his taxes were terribly high. The irony of Daniel Shays' situation was too much to bear: on the one hand, Massachusetts refused to pay Shays what it owed him for his self-sacrificing service during the war; while on the other hand, Massachusetts threatened to imprison Shays for failing to pay the taxes it said he owed.

Rebellion

In August 1786, Massachusetts farmers like Daniel Shays decided to take action against their state's biased court system. In several communities all around Massachusetts, bands of farmers hundreds strong gathered outside state courthouses and sealed them off— barring them from rendering any more unfair judgments against farmers until the legislature agreed to change its debt laws.

Instead of meeting the farmers' demands, the legislature raised militia to retake its courthouses. By late September, bands of farmers were arriving at courthouses to find militia already there, determined to keep the courts open. These standoffs went on for months, with mobs of angry farmers protesting outside courthouses under the watchful eyes of militia guards. Meanwhile, the courts dispatched more militia to arrest and imprison rebel leaders, by force if necessary. The more rebel leaders the militia arrested, the angrier the rebels grew, and the closer civil war approached.

Shays' Rebellion reached its peak at a federal armory in Springfield, Massachusetts on January 25, 1787. Outside the armory were Shays and about 1,500 of his fellow rebels, determined to arm themselves for the coming civil war by seizing the weapons inside the armory. Against Shays stood about 1,200 militiamen— state troops, not federal ones— determined to keep those weapons out of rebel hands. As Shays' rebels advanced toward the armory, the militiamen fired a cannon over their head in warning. When the rebels continued to advance, the militiamen grimly lowered their cannon and fired directly into the rebel lines, killing 4 rebels and wounding 20.

This brief skirmish at Springfield was all it took to break Shays' poorly-organized rebellion. Stunned that their own countrymen had actually fired on them, the rebels broke and fled. A week later, a 3,000-strong Massachusetts militia commanded by General Benjamin Lincoln— the same Lincoln who had received General Cornwallis' surrender after the Siege of Yorktown— had no trouble defeating and scattering what remained of Shays' army.

Brawling outside a Massachusetts courthouse

The fiasco of Shays' Rebellion highlighted two problems the United States faced after the Revolutionary War:

1. Rebels like Daniel Shays clearly felt that despite all they had sacrificed for the Revolutionary War, they were still living under tyranny. Americans had cast off one tyrant, but had yet to establish firm protections against others— including their own state governments.

2. The federal government established by the Articles of Confederation was weak to the point of uselessness. Although the armory Shays attacked was a federal one, no federal troops defended it; Massachusetts' militia had to defeat Shays' Rebellion all by itself, long before the nonexistent federal army could organize itself.

The Constitution of the United States of America

SUCCINCT SUMMARIES: In 1787, the United States held a Constitutional Convention in Philadelphia, Pennsylvania. The purpose of this Convention was to replace the weak federal government established by the Articles of Confederation with a stronger one.

In all, 55 delegates attended this Constitutional Convention. These delegates came from only 12 of the 13 original states, because Rhode Island refused to send any delegates. The president of the Convention was Virginian George Washington, hero of the Revolutionary War. The oldest delegate was Pennsylvanian Benjamin Franklin, 81 years old at the time. After about four months of debate and compromise, the delegates finally signed the completed Constitution of the United States of America on September 17, 1787.

The next step was for the states to **ratify**— that is, approve and accept— the Constitution; for it would only become law after nine states ratified it. The first state, Delaware, ratified on December 7th, 1787; and the ninth state, New Hampshire, on June 21, 1788. After elections that fall, the 1st United States Congress convened on March 4, 1789, and George Washington became the first President of the United States on April 30, 1789. The last holdout, Rhode Island, waited more than a year after Washington's inauguration before finally ratifying the Constitution.

The Constitution designed the United States as a **republic**— that is, a state in which the people govern themselves through their elected representatives. It also divided the government into three branches:

- A **legislative branch** to write law. This branch was to consist of two houses, a Senate and a House of Representatives.
- An **executive branch** to enforce law. The chief executive, the President, was also to be commander in chief of the armed forces.
- A **judicial branch** of courts and judges to adjudge and interpret law.

The original Constitution consisted of two main parts: (1) A famous preamble that described its purpose ("We the People..."); and (2) seven articles that described the new government's powers, as well as the limits on those powers. Later, the U.S. added several amendments to the Constitution; the first ten are the Bill of Rights.

Shays' Rebellion was only one example of the federal government's pitiful weakness under the Articles of Confederation. The Confederation Congress had so much trouble collecting money from the states that by 1785, it couldn't meet the interest payments on its war debt to its closest ally, France. By 1787, it couldn't meet the principal payments either. The longer the United States failed to make good on its debts, the more likely it became that some foreign power would invade the weak new nation to collect them. Meanwhile, Congress became so irrelevant that some delegates stopped bothering to attend— which led to even more weakness, as Congress couldn't vote on any issue unless a quorum of delegates was present.

As of 1787, a majority of lawmakers agreed that the time had come to revise the Articles of Confederation at least, if not replace them entirely.

The Constitutional Convention (May 25 – September 17, 1787)

Eleven years after the Declaration of Independence, several of America's elder statesmen returned to Philadelphia's Independence Hall to redesign the federal government. The Constitutional Convention unanimously elected George Washington as its president. Benjamin Franklin was there too, although he was by now so old and arthritic that four prisoners from the local jail had to carry him to the hall every day.

Other elder statesmen were conspicuously absent. Patrick Henry refused to attend because, he said, he "smelt a

Constitutional Convention meeting room inside Independence Hall

rat"— by which he meant that any new federal government would undoubtedly take away the individual states' rights that he believed in so strongly. Neither Thomas Jefferson nor John Adams could attend, as both were in Europe serving as ambassadors. In all, 55 delegates would attend the convention at various times over the following four months. Rhode Island alone refused to attend.

INTERESTING IDEAS: Rhode Island's reluctance to join the Convention sprang from more than one cause:

- As the smallest state, Rhode Island had good reason to cling to the Articles of Confederation, under which tiny Rhode Island's power in the federal government matched the powers of giants like New York, Pennsylvania and Virginia. Any new constitution was likely to reduce Rhode Island's power.

- During the currency crisis after the Revolutionary War, poor Rhode Island did what wealthy Massachusetts refused to do: it printed paper money to ease its war veterans' debt burdens, earning for its compassion and poor business sense the derisive nickname "Rogue Island." Rhode Islanders suspected that if the federal government became more powerful, then their neighbors would take away their power to print money.

A LOOK AHEAD: For these reasons among others, Rhode Island will be the last of the original thirteen states to ratify the Constitution.

Secrecy

The first decision the Constitutional Convention made was to conduct itself as secretly as possible: the delegates locked Independence Hall's doors, shuttered its windows, and even poured sand on the cobblestones outside so that the sound of their negotiations wouldn't carry. Furthermore, no delegate was to publish or communicate anything that happened inside Independence Hall without express permission from the convention. Redesigning the government was an explosive business; the delegates didn't want over-eager reporters spreading half-true rumors about their new constitution before they even finished writing it. Thomas Jefferson criticized the convention's obsession with secrecy, writing in a letter to John Adams:

> "I am sorry they began their deliberations by so abominable a precedent as that of tying of the tongues of their members. Nothing can justify this example but the innocence of their intentions and ignorance of the value of public discussions."

The Virginia Plan

No delegate to the Constitutional Convention arrived better prepared than Virginian James Madison. Unlike most delegates, who expected only to amend the Articles of Confederation, Madison expected to scrap them entirely, and replace them with a whole new plan of government. Madison's plan, the Virginia Plan, called for a government with three distinct branches:

- **A legislative branch** with a bicameral Congress— that is, a two-sided Congress with an upper house and a lower house.

- **An executive branch** with a single powerful president, to be chosen by Congress.

- **A judicial branch** with one or more supreme courts and other lesser courts, their judges also to be chosen by Congress.

James Madison, author of the Virginia Plan

Because Madison's Virginia Plan was the most complete and the most popular, it became the starting point for negotiations over the new Constitution. Partly for this reason, historians call James Madison the "Father of the Constitution"— even though the Convention insisted on major changes to his Virginia Plan.

The Legislative Branch: The Congress of the United States

DEFINITION: The **legislative branch** is the branch of government responsible for writing law. The U.S. government's legislative branch is a Congress made up of two houses, the Senate and the House of Representatives, both of which meet at the U.S. Capitol Building in Washington D.C.

The Constitutional Convention needed several weeks to resolve its first major controversy: how to ensure that both small states and large states received their fair shares of power in Congress. Small states felt that all states should have equal power in Congress, as they had under the Articles of Confederation. Large states, on the other hand, felt that each state's power in Congress should be based on its size. The delegates chose sides between two ideas:

1. **Proportional representation**, the idea that the number of representatives each state sent to Congress should be proportional to that state's population: the more people, the more representatives. The Virginia Plan proposed proportional representation— arguing that it was hardly fair for the people of Virginia, who numbered more than 700,000, to have no more representatives than the people of Delaware, who numbered only about 50,000.

2. **Equal representation**, the idea that each state should send an equal number of representatives to Congress. The New Jersey Plan, introduced by delegate William Paterson about two weeks into the Convention, proposed equal representation.

DEFINITION: The final plan, hammered out over weeks of negotiation, called for a **Great Compromise** between these two ideas: there would be proportional representation in Congress's lower house, but equal representation in Congress's upper house.

The Great Compromise was much more than a simple compromise between equal representation and proportional representation. In crafting the Great Compromise, the Constitutional Convention made important decisions that affected the character of each house:

- The lower house, the **House of Representatives**, was to represent average voters— the lower and middle classes. These representatives were to be elected directly by the voters, and stand for re-election every two years— which meant that they would have to pay close attention to their voters, for voters might not forget their representatives' mistakes in such a short time. Furthermore, all tax bills were to originate in the House of Representatives— forever linking taxation to the house most accountable to average voters.

The Liberty Bell on display near Independence Hall, Philadelphia

- The upper house, the **Senate**, was to represent the wealthy voters of the upper class. Senators were to be elected, not directly by the voters, but by their state legislatures. Furthermore, they would stand for re-election every six years, not two. Both conditions called senators to pay less attention to the ever-changing whims of average voters, and more attention to the long-term interests of wealthy businessmen. Thus the Convention designed the Senate as a steadying influence— a body of wise elders to calm the impulsive, easily-swayed youngsters in the House.

The Great Compromise was also a compromise between a **national government**— one which saw the U.S. as a single nation— and a **federal government**, one which saw the U.S. as a federation of semi-independent states. The House of Representatives would act more like a national government, with proportional representation for voters from all over the nation. The Senate would act more like a federal government, with equal representation for all of the states.

The Three-fifths Compromise

A second major controversy arose between North and South. After the Convention accepted the idea of proportional representation in the House, the question arose: how to account for slaves? Should the states include in their population totals both free citizens and slaves, or only free citizens? Naturally, Southern states wanted to include slaves, as this would give them more representatives in the House. Northern states wanted to exclude slaves, for the opposite reason.

The question of counting slaves grew into a debate over a moral issue: should slavery be legal at all, especially in a nation founded on the Enlightenment principle "that all men are created equal"? Northern delegates argued that counting slaves for representation made no sense: if slaves were human beings deserving of representation in Congress, then should they not be free? But if slaves were farm property, no different than oxen, then should not the North be allowed to count its oxen as well? Southern delegates countered that their states' economies could not survive without slaves— and that no Southern state would ratify any Constitution that limited slavery in any way.

The question of how to count slaves had actually come up years before, during an argument over apportioning taxes to different-sized states under the Articles of Confederation. At that time, someone had proposed the idea of counting three-fifths of slaves— based on the idea that each slave contributed about three-fifths as much to a state's economy as each free citizen did. Ironically, the South had taken the opposite position in that

Examining an enslaved man for sale

earlier argument: because more people meant more taxes, the South had argued against counting its slaves at that time. Now, however, the South insisted on counting its slaves. Therefore North and South compromised: for proportional representation, the Constitution would allow all states to count three-fifths of their slaves toward their population totals.

INTERESTING IDEAS: It is true that the Three-fifths Compromise demeaned slaves by counting them as only "three-fifths of a person," as critics of slavery often say. However, the argument at the time was not whether slaves should be free, but whether they should count for proportional representation; and in that argument, critics of slavery argued the opposite: that slaves shouldn't count at all. The purpose of counting only three-fifths of slaves was not to demean slaves, but rather to reduce the slave states' power in Congress.

The Constitution also included two other important compromises on the issue of slavery:

1. Article IV, Section 1 required the return of all runaway slaves who fled across state lines. Like the Northwest Ordinance, the Constitution insisted that the North must not become a legal haven for runaway slaves.
2. Article I, Section 9 forbade Congress to ban the importation of slaves until 1808, twenty years after the Constitution's ratification.

ILLUMINATING LISTS: Among other things, the Constitution granted Congress powers to:

• Levy taxes	• Borrow money
• Regulate trade	• Coin money and punish counterfeiters
• Establish post offices and post roads	• Issue patents to inventors
• Create courts inferior to the Supreme Court	• Punish piracy
• Declare war	• Raise and administer armies and navies
• Directly govern the District of Columbia	• "Make all Laws which shall be necessary… for carrying into Execution the foregoing Powers"

ILLUMINATING EXCERPTS from Benjamin Franklin's Call to Prayer

With 55 delegates working on the Constitution, each with his own state's agenda in mind, arguments were inevitable. After five weeks of little progress, Benjamin Franklin arose to remind the delegates how in that very room, during the darkest days of the war against Great Britain, they had called upon the Father of Lights to guide them:

"To that kind providence we owe this happy opportunity of consulting in peace on the means of establishing our future national felicity. And have we now forgotten that powerful friend? Or do we imagine that we no longer need his assistance? I have lived, sir, a long time, and the longer I live, the more convincing proofs I see of this truth—that God governs in the affairs of men. And if a sparrow cannot fall to the ground without his notice, is it probable that an empire can rise without his aid? We have been assured, sir, in the sacred writings, that "except the lord build the house, they labor in vain that build it." I firmly believe this; and I also believe that without his concurring aid we shall succeed in this political building no better, than the builders of Babel: we shall be divided by our little partial local interests; our projects will be confounded, and we ourselves shall become a reproach and bye word down to future ages. And what is worse, mankind may hereafter from this unfortunate instance, despair of establishing governments by human wisdom and leave it to chance, war and conquest.

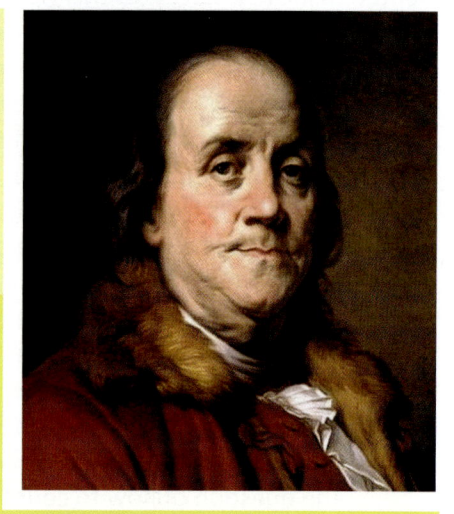

"I therefore beg leave to move that henceforth prayers imploring the assistance of heaven, and its blessings on our deliberations, be held in this assembly every morning before we proceed to business, and that one or more of the clergy of this city be requested to officiate in that service."

The Executive Branch: The President of the United States

DEFINITION: The **executive branch** is the branch of government responsible for enforcing law and commanding the armed forces. The U.S. government's executive branch consists of the President, the Vice President, a cabinet of executive secretaries and a host of executive agencies. The Oval Office of the President of the United States lies in the West Wing of the White House in Washington D.C.

A third major controversy arose over the makeup of the executive branch:

1. Some delegates called for a single, powerful president, one who would be able to react quickly and decisively in times of crisis.
2. Other delegates worried that such a powerful president might become a tyrant, no less oppressive than the king they had just overthrown. To avoid creating a new tyrant, these delegates called for an executive council of three men.

On June 4, a majority of delegates finally agreed that a 3-man executive committee would be like a "general with three heads," and voted to establish a single president.

Having agreed on a single president, the Convention next disagreed on the proper way to choose him. Some proposed to let Congress choose the president. Opponents of this idea, though, argued that allowing Congress to choose would make the president too eager to do Congress's bidding. If the president was to be independent of Congress, then he must not depend on Congress for his office.

Others proposed national elections in which the voters would choose the president directly. The arguments against this idea revolved around communication and politics:

- Given the slow speed with which news traveled, how would voters all over this vast nation learn enough about national candidates to make informed decisions? It was true that the American Revolution had introduced a few nationally-known heroes like George Washington. After those heroes died, though, how would voters choose? Some delegates feared that without well-known national candidates, voters would naturally choose favorites from their own states, which would cause two problems:

    1. Candidates from small states would never win.
    2. No candidate would ever win a national majority— something a president would need if he was to lead the whole country, not just a state or region.

George Washington, President of the Constitutional Convention and first President of the United States

- Most delegates found the idea of campaigning distasteful. In most delegates' opinions, no dignified public servant should have to traipse all over the country begging for votes. A true gentleman did not seek office, but rather allowed the office to seek him— much as the ancient Roman Senate sought the gentleman farmer Cincinnatus to be its consul when no other man would do.

- Most delegates also found the idea of political parties distasteful. In most delegates' opinions, dignified public servants should not have to scheme with their cronies, making unethical political promises in their determination to win election at any cost. Rather, true gentlemen ran on the strength of their character, never compromising their ethics for political advantage.

The Electoral College

To avoid all these problems, the Convention designed a complicated system called the **Electoral College**. Instead of voting for president directly, each state would choose a group of electors to cast its votes for president. Under the system laid out in Article II, Section 1:

- Each state was to choose a number of electors equal to its number of senators— two in all cases— plus its number of representatives, a number proportional to its population. Thus even the smallest states were to choose at least three electors, while larger states would choose more. No senator, representative or other federal officeholder was to be an elector; all were to come from outside the federal government.

- Each elector was to cast two votes for president, including at least one vote for a candidate from outside his state. That way, at least one of every elector's selections wouldn't be an in-state favorite.

- Sealed electors' votes from all over the country were to be opened and counted by the president of the Senate in the presence of the whole U.S. Congress. The candidate with the most votes was to become president, provided he had a majority; while the candidate who came in second was to become vice president.

- If no candidate won a majority in the Electoral College, then the House of Representatives was to choose from among the top 5 vote-winners. For this choice, the House was to act as a federal body, with each state receiving one vote. That way, small states would have the same power as large ones.

- If no candidate won a majority in the House, then the Senate— another federal body— was to choose between the top two candidates.

As for the process of choosing electors, the Constitution left this decision entirely to the individual states. Some states would allow their voters to choose presidential electors directly; while others would allow their state legislatures to choose.

A LOOK AHEAD: The years to come will bring several dramatic changes to federal election law:

1. The Twelfth Amendment to the Constitution, ratified in 1804, will change the Electoral College system by requiring each elector to choose one candidate for president and another for vice president— not two candidates for president, as the Constitution originally required.

2. By about 1850, most states will extend voting rights to all white men, dropping the old requirement that men must own a certain amount of property in order to vote.

3. The Fifteenth Amendment to the Constitution, ratified in 1870, will extend voting rights to men of all races; however, the South will continue to limit black voting rights through racist Jim Crow laws.

4. The Seventeenth Amendment to the Constitution, ratified in 1913, will require U.S. senators to be elected directly by the people of their state— not by their state legislatures, as the Constitution originally required.

5. The Nineteenth Amendment to the Constitution, ratified in 1920, will extend voting rights to women.

6. The Twenty-fourth Amendment to the Constitution, ratified in 1964, will ban the most common type of Jim Crow law: the poll tax.
7. The Civil Rights Act of 1964 and the Voting Rights Act of 1965 will complete the ban on racial discrimination in voting begun by the Fifteenth Amendment.
8. The Twenty-sixth Amendment to the Constitution, ratified in 1971, will extend voting rights to all citizens 18 years of age or older.

ILLUMINATING LISTS: Among other powers, the Constitution granted the President power to:

• Serve as "Commander in Chief of the Army and Navy of the United States"	• Pardon convicted felons, except in impeachment cases
• Make treaties— but only under the "Advice and Consent of the Senate," and "provided two thirds of the Senators present concur"	• Appoint "Ambassadors, other public Ministers and Consuls, Judges of the supreme Court, and all other Officers of the United States"

The Judicial Branch: Federal Courts

DEFINITION: The **judicial branch** is the branch of government responsible for adjudging and interpreting law. The legislative branch of the U.S. government consists of a Supreme Court— housed at the U.S. Supreme Court Building in Washington D.C.— and a system of inferior federal district courts.

Article III of the Constitution entrusted the judicial power of the United States "in one supreme Court, and in such inferior courts as the Congress may from time to time ordain and establish." Among other things, the federal court system was to be the final authority on all (1) disputes involving the federal government; (2) disputes between states; and (3) disputes between citizens of different states.

ILLUMINATING EXCERPTS: The Preamble of the United States Constitution

"We the People of the United States, in Order to form a more perfect Union, establish Justice, insure domestic Tranquility, provide for the common defense, promote the general Welfare, and secure the Blessings of Liberty to ourselves and our Posterity, do ordain and establish this Constitution for the United States of America."

FASCINATING FACTS: Separation of Powers, Checks and Balances in the U.S. Constitution

To keep its new government from going off its rails, the Convention made every effort to keep the three branches of government separate, independent and accountable to one another. Lest any branch usurp powers which rightly belonged to another, the Convention gave each branch power to check, or limit, the other two:

The **executive branch** may check the **legislative branch** by:

• Vetoing new laws passed by Congress	• Breaking tie votes in the Senate— for the Vice President is also President of the Senate, and may vote when the senators split 50-50
• Appointing federal officers without the Senate's approval when the Senate is in recess	

The **executive branch** may check the **judicial branch** by:

• Appointing judges	• Pardoning convicted felons

The **legislative branch** may check the **executive branch** by:

• Impeaching presidents for "high crimes and misdemeanors"	• Overriding presidential vetoes (requires a 2/3 supermajority in both houses of Congress)

The **legislative branch** may check the **judicial branch** by:

• Approving or disapproving federal judges	• Impeaching federal judges for wrongdoing
• Changing the number of Supreme Court justices	• Establishing courts inferior to the Supreme Court

The **judicial branch** may check the **executive branch** by:

• Presiding at presidential impeachment trials	• Judicial Review[1]

The **judicial branch** may check the **legislative branch** by:

• Judging cases involving Congress	• Judicial Review[1]

[1] Judicial Review is the Supreme Court's power to decide whether or not any new law is allowable under the United States Constitution. This power was suggested in the Constitution itself, and confirmed in the 1803 Supreme Court case *Marbury v. Madison*.

Signing the Constitution (September 17, 1787)

When the Constitutional Convention gathered to sign the completed Constitution on September 17, 1787, not a man in the room was pleased with all of the compromises he had been forced to make. Recognizing this, Benjamin Franklin nevertheless pleaded for all of his fellow delegates to sign, emphasizing three points: (1) the near-perfection of the new Constitution; (2) the need to value the opinions of others; and (3) the great benefits of a unanimous signing:

"I confess that there are several parts of this constitution which I do not at present approve, but I am not sure I shall never approve them: For having lived long, I have experienced many instances of being obliged by better information, or fuller consideration, to change opinions even on important subjects, which I once thought right, but found to be otherwise. It is therefore that the older I grow, the more apt I am to doubt my own judgment, and to pay more respect to the judgment of others…

"I doubt too whether any other Convention we can obtain, may be able to make a better Constitution. For when you assemble a number of men to have the advantage of their joint wisdom, you inevitably assemble with those men, all their prejudices, their passions, their errors of opinion, their local interests, and their selfish views. From such an assembly can a perfect production be expected? It therefore astonishes me, Sir, to find this system approaching so near to perfection as it does; and I think it will astonish our enemies, who are waiting with confidence to hear that our councils are confounded like those of the Builders of Babel; and that our States are on the point of separation, only to meet hereafter for the purpose of cutting one another's throats. Thus I consent, Sir, to this Constitution because I expect no better, and because I am not sure, that it is not the best…

> "On the whole, [President Washington], I cannot help expressing a wish that every member of the Convention who may still have objections to it, would with me, on this occasion doubt a little of his own infallibility, and to make manifest our unanimity, put his name to this instrument."

"Scene at the Signing of the Constitution of the United States" by Howard Christy

As president of the Convention, George Washington was first to sign, adding his immeasurably great influence to Dr. Franklin's. Even so, 3 of the 42 delegates who remained in Philadelphia at the time refused to sign— including two from Washington's home state of Virginia, where ratifying the Constitution would prove to be an uphill climb.

Ratifying the Constitution (September 17, 1787 – May 29, 1790)

DEFINITION: Ratifying the Constitution was the process of convincing at least nine states to accept it.

Federalists versus Anti-Federalists

After the signing, the Constitution went first to the Confederation Congress, and then on to the individual states for ratification. A few states ratified the new Constitution almost immediately, near-unanimously and with very little discussion. In other states, especially New York and Virginia, two factions battled over ratification:

- **Federalists** like James Madison and Alexander Hamilton fought for all the advantages the powerful new federal government would provide, including:
  1. A strong national defense.
  2. A settled national government that would be less prone to uprisings like Shays' Rebellion.
  3. A strong national economy that would soon grow to rival any in Europe.
- **Anti-Federalists** like George Mason fought to preserve their rights, both states' rights and individual rights. Defenders of states' rights felt that the best governments were small, local ones whose representatives stayed close to the people, never forgetting the wishes of the voters who elected them. Anti-Federalists considered the new federal government too large, and too remote to respond quickly to the voters' wishes. They also reasoned that because the federal government was so remote, wealthy businessmen would manipulate it easily— leaving poor farmers like Daniel Shays with no voice in their own government.

FASCINATING FACTS: The Federalist Papers

During the nine months New York's general assembly spent debating the new Constitution, three Federalist authors—James Madison, Alexander Hamilton and John Jay, all writing under the Roman pen name

"Publius"— published 85 essays touting the Constitution's many benefits, hoping to persuade New York to ratify. Together with the notes James Madison recorded during the Constitutional Convention, the Federalist Papers are the best surviving windows into the minds of the founding fathers who crafted the Constitution.

ILLUMINATING EXCERPTS from Federalist #1:

"It has been frequently remarked that it seems to have been reserved to the people of this country, by their conduct and example, to decide the important question, whether societies of men are really capable or not of establishing good government from reflection and choice, or whether they are forever destined to depend for their political constitutions on accident and force. If there be any truth in the remark, the crisis at which we are arrived may with propriety be regarded as the era in which that decision is to be made; and a wrong election of the part we shall act may, in this view, deserve to be considered as the general misfortune of mankind."

In other words: If the United States fails to ratify the Constitution, then it will prove to all the world that human beings are incapable of choosing good governments for themselves— and must therefore be forever subject to the whims of tyrants.

Alexander Hamilton, author of several Federalist Papers and first United States Secretary of the Treasury

REFRESHING REMINDERS: A **democracy** is a state in which every citizen may vote on every issue. A **republic** is a state in which the people govern themselves through their elected representatives.

ILLUMINATING EXCERPTS from Federalist #10:

"Those who hold and those who are without property have ever formed distinct interests in society. Those who are creditors, and those who are debtors, fall under a like discrimination. A landed interest, a manufacturing interest, a mercantile interest, a moneyed interest, with many lesser interests, grow up of necessity in civilized nations, and divide them into different classes…

"A pure democracy… can admit of no cure for the mischiefs of faction. A common passion or interest will, in almost every case, be felt by a majority of the whole; a communication and concert result from the form of government itself; and there is nothing to check the inducements to sacrifice the weaker party… Hence it is that such democracies have ever been spectacles of turbulence and contention…"

"A republic, by which I mean a government in which the scheme of representation takes place, opens a different prospect, and promises the cure for which we are seeking."

In other words: In every state, majorities who share common interests may band together to deny minorities their rights. Because average voters are so easily swayed by the passions of the moment, democracies do nothing to protect minorities' rights, and in fact make the problem worse. Republics, however, protect minorities' rights by placing power in the hands of elected representatives— settled, respectable, proven leaders who are less easily swayed than the masses.

ILLUMINATING EXCERPTS from Federalist #14:

"But why is the experiment of an extended republic to be rejected, merely because it may comprise what is new? Is it not the glory of the people of America, that, whilst they have paid a decent regard to the opinions of former times and other nations, they have not suffered a blind veneration for antiquity, for custom, or for names, to overrule the suggestions of their own good sense, the knowledge of their own situation, and the lessons of their own experience? To this manly spirit, posterity will be indebted for the possession, and the world for the example, of the numerous innovations displayed on the American theatre, in favor of private rights and public happiness."

"Happily for America, happily, we trust, for the whole human race, [the leaders of the Revolution] pursued a new and more noble course. They accomplished a revolution which has no parallel in the annals of human society. They reared the fabrics of governments which have no model on the face of the globe. They formed the design of a great Confederacy, which it is incumbent on their successors to improve and perpetuate. If their works betray imperfections, we wonder at the fewness of them."

In other words: The fact that the world has never before seen a federal republic composed of semi-independent states is no reason to doubt that such a republic can succeed. Americans are innovators who have always valued their own opinions over those of distant tyrants; and now, American innovations will show the world how free people should govern themselves.

Portrait of Federalist Papers author John Jay as first Chief Justice of the United States

ILLUMINATING EXCERPTS from Federalist #51:

"But what is government itself, but the greatest of all reflections on human nature? If men were angels, no government would be necessary. If angels were to govern men, neither external nor internal controls on government would be necessary. In framing a government which is to be administered by men over men, the great difficulty lies in this: you must first enable the government to control the governed; and in the next place oblige it to control itself. A dependence on the people is, no doubt, the primary control on the government; but experience has taught mankind the necessity of auxiliary precautions."

"In republican government, the legislative authority necessarily predominates. The remedy for this inconveniency is to divide the legislature into different branches; and to render them, by different modes of election and different principles of action [i.e., checks and balances], as little connected with each other as the nature of their common functions and their common dependence on the society will admit."

In other words: Checks and balances are necessary to keep the government from taking away the very liberties it is supposed to protect.

Four Holdouts

New Hampshire's ratification on June 21, 1788 changed the nature of the ratification debate. According to Article VII, the Constitution was to take effect as soon as nine states ratified it. Therefore after #9 New Hampshire, the question was no longer whether there would be a new federal government, but whether the four holdouts— Virginia, New York, North Carolina and Rhode Island— would take part in that government.

In the end, no state could see any advantage in being left out of the powerful new nation, forced to fend for itself with no help from its former allies. Therefore all four holdouts finally ratified the Constitution— although Rhode Island held out for more than a year after George Washington's inauguration as the first President of the United States, which fell on April 30, 1789.

ILLUMINATING LISTS: Ratification Dates of the Original Thirteen States

Even though all of the original thirteen states already belonged to the United States under the Articles of Confederation, the Constitution represented such a complete change of government that from 1787 forward, each state's official date of statehood became the date when it ratified the new Constitution:

State	Date of Ratification	State	Date of Ratification
#1: Delaware	December 7, 1787	#2: Pennsylvania	December 12, 1787
#3: New Jersey	December 18, 1787	#4: Georgia	January 2, 1788
#5: Connecticut	January 9, 1788	#6: Massachusetts	February 6, 1788
#7: Maryland	April 28, 1788	#8: South Carolina	May 23, 1788
#9: New Hampshire	June 21, 1788	#10: Virginia	June 25, 1788
#11: New York	July 26, 1788	#12: North Carolina	November 21, 1789
#13: Rhode Island	May 29, 1790		

INTERESTING IDEAS: Virginia's reluctant ratification of the Constitution included this proviso: "We the Delegates of the people of Virginia… declare and make known that the powers granted under the Constitution, being derived from the people of the United States, may be resumed by them whensoever the same shall be perverted to their injury or oppression…"

In other words: Virginia reserved the right to withdraw from the United States if Virginians ever decided that the federal government was abusing the powers they had granted it.

A LOOK AHEAD: Virginia's reservation of its right to withdraw will become important in 1861, the year President Lincoln will order Virginia to raise troops for an invasion of the seceded states of the Deep South. Lincoln's order will so anger Virginians that instead of obeying, they will join the Deep South in seceding from the Union.

The Bill of Rights (Passed by Congress September 25, 1789; Ratified December 15, 1791)

SUCCINCT SUMMARIES: The Bill of Rights is a set of 10 amendments added to the Constitution to protect citizens' and states' rights. The 2nd United States Congress adopted all ten amendments together on December 15, 1791, just four years after the Constitutional Convention. Amendments 1 – 4 protect the natural rights of free citizens; amendments 5 – 8 protect the rights of citizens accused or convicted of crimes; and amendments 9 – 10 prevent the federal government from seizing powers not granted to it by the Constitution.

Several of the freedoms Americans cherish above all others are protected by the First Amendment:

- Freedom of religion, along with the freedom to express one's religion.
- Freedom of speech, even if one's speech criticizes the government.
- Freedom of the press, even if the press criticizes the government.
- Freedom to assemble in public, and to ask the government to change unfair policies.

Although the Anti-Federalists failed to prevent the creation of a strong federal government, they succeeded in defending at least some of their rights. The four holdout states' ratification letters all proposed long lists of improvements to the Constitution, corrections to define the limits of the new federal government's power. Four years after the Constitutional Convention, Congress answered these letters with a set of ten amendments to the Constitution, ratified together as the Bill of Rights.

Ironically, the author of the Bill of Rights was no Anti-Federalist, but rather one of the very Federalists who had helped write the Federalist Papers: James Madison. Before ratification, Federalists had argued against adding a Bill of Rights to the Constitution, for three reasons:

1. Because the individual states already protected their citizens' rights.
2. Because the people's rights needed no protection from the new federal government, which was after all a free republic and not a tyrannical monarchy.
3. Because the idea of a bill of rights came late in the Constitutional Convention, when the Constitution was already finished— which caused Federalists to see the addition of a bill of rights as a trick to delay ratification.

After ratification, Madison saw matters differently. When a growing number of Anti-Federalists continued to clamor for their bill of rights, Madison began to fear what they might do if they didn't get one. Instead of only amending the Constitution, they might call for a new constitutional convention— one that might rewrite the Constitution altogether, undoing all the good work the first Convention had done.

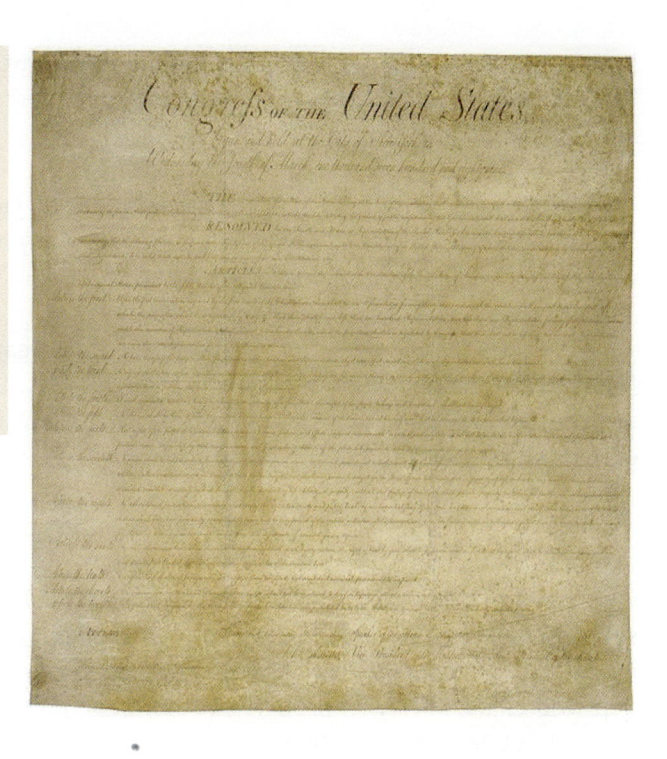

To protect the Constitution that he had worked so hard to ratify, Madison set to work crafting the ten amendments that would become the Bill of Rights. Madison based his amendments partly on the suggestions in the four holdout states' ratification letters; partly on the Enlightenment philosophy of John Locke and others; and partly on the Virginia Declaration of Rights— an earlier bill of rights authored in 1776 by Madison's fellow Virginian George Mason, whose profound work also influenced the Declaration of Independence and the Articles of Confederation.

All ten amendments limit the federal government's power by protecting certain rights:

- Amendments 1 – 4 protect the natural rights of free citizens.
- Amendments 5 – 8 protect the rights of citizens accused or convicted of crimes.
- Amendment 9 protects other rights not specifically listed in the Constitution and the Bill of Rights— in case some tyrant decides that just because a right isn't mentioned, the government can automatically take it away.
- Amendment 10 reserves to either the citizens or their state governments every power not specifically granted to the federal government in the Constitution. This amendment bars the federal government from arrogating to itself powers that the Constitution neglected to mention.

George Mason, author of the Virginia Declaration of Rights

Amendment I: Freedoms of religion, speech, the press, assembly and petition

"Congress shall make no law respecting an establishment of religion, or prohibiting the free exercise thereof; or abridging the freedom of speech, or of the press, or the right of the people peaceably to assemble, and to petition the Government for a redress of grievances."

Amendment II: Right to keep and bear arms
"A well-regulated militia, being necessary to the security of a free State, the right of the people to keep and bear arms, shall not be infringed."

Amendment III: Quartering of soldiers
"No soldier shall, in time of peace be quartered in any house, without the consent of the owner, nor in time of war, but in a manner to be prescribed by law."

Amendment IV: Search, seizure and arrest
"The right of the people to be secure in their persons, houses, papers, and effects, against unreasonable searches and seizures, shall not be violated, and no Warrants shall issue, but upon probable cause, supported by oath or affirmation, and particularly describing the place to be searched, and the persons or things to be seized."

Amendment V: Rights of the accused; property rights
"No person shall be held to answer for a capital, or otherwise infamous crime, unless on a presentment or indictment of a Grand Jury, except in cases arising in the land or naval forces, or in the Militia, when in actual service in time of War or public danger; nor shall any person be subject for the same offense to be twice put in jeopardy of life or limb; nor shall be compelled in any criminal case to be a witness against himself, nor be deprived of life, liberty, or property, without due process of law; nor shall private property be taken for public use without just compensation."

Amendment VI: Right to a fair trial
"In all criminal prosecutions, the accused shall enjoy the right to a speedy and public trial, by an impartial jury of the State and district wherein the crime shall have been committed, which district shall have been previously ascertained by law, and to be informed of the nature and cause of the accusation; to be confronted with the witnesses against him; to have compulsory process for obtaining witnesses in his favor, and to have the assistance of counsel for his defense."

Amendment VII: Rights in civil cases
"In suits at common law, where the value in controversy shall exceed twenty dollars, the right of trial by jury shall be preserved, and no fact tried by a jury shall be otherwise re-examined in any court of the United States, than according to the rules of the common law."

Amendment VIII: Bail, fines and punishments
"Excessive bail shall not be required nor excessive fines imposed, nor cruel and unusual punishments inflicted."

Amendment IX: Rights not listed in the Constitution retained by the people
"The enumeration in the Constitution, of certain rights, shall not be construed to deny or disparage others retained by the people."

Amendment X: Rights not specifically granted to the federal government
"The powers not delegated to the United States by the Constitution, nor prohibited by it to the States, are reserved to the States respectively, or to the people."

FASCINATING FACTS: George Washington's Thanksgiving Proclamation

One early act of the 1st United States Congress called upon President Washington to announce a national day of thanksgiving, a day for all Americans to thank God for the opportunity "peaceably to establish a form of government for their safety and happiness." Especially in light of what was going on in France— where the extremely violent French Revolution had just begun (see Chapter 25)— Congress wanted to remind

Americans that a peaceful change of government was a blessing from God that no one should take for granted. In a Thanksgiving Proclamation issued in October 1789, Washington set aside Thursday, November 26, 1789 as a day:

"... to be devoted by the people of these States to the service of that great and glorious Being who is the beneficent author of all the good that was, that is, or that will be; that we may then all unite in rendering unto Him our sincere and humble thanks for His kind care and protection of the people of this country previous to their becoming a nation; for the signal and manifold mercies and the favor, able interpositions of His providence in the course and conclusion of the late war; for the great degree of tranquility, union, and plenty which we have since enjoyed; for the peaceable and rational manner in which we have been enabled to establish constitutions of government for our safety and happiness, and particularly the national one now lately instituted; for the civil and religious liberty with which we are blessed, and the means we have of acquiring and diffusing useful knowledge; and, in general, for all the great and various favors which He has been pleased to confer upon us."

Washington called upon all Americans to:

"...unite in most humbly offering our prayers and supplications to the great Lord and Ruler of Nations, and beseech Him to pardon our national and other transgressions; to enable us all, whether in public or private stations, to perform our several and relative duties properly and punctually; to render our National Government a blessing to all the people by constantly being a Government of wise, just, and constitutional laws, discreetly and faithfully executed and obeyed; to protect and guide all sovereigns and nations (especially such as have shown kindness to us), and to bless them with good governments, peace, and concord; to promote the knowledge and practice of true religion and virtue, and the increase of science among them and us; and, generally, to grant unto all mankind such a degree of temporal prosperity as He alone knows to be best."

REFRESHING REMINDERS from Chapter 6: In 1863, the middle year of the American Civil War, President Abraham Lincoln called for all Americans to set aside the last Thursday of November as a day of (1) thanksgiving to God; and (2) prayer for all of the orphans, widows and mourners created by that war. Thanksgiving has been an annual U.S. holiday ever since.

U.S. STATE FOCUS

Tennessee

FASCINATING FACTS about Tennessee:

- **State Capital**: Nashville
- **State Abbreviation**: TN
- **Statehood**: Tennessee became the 16th US state on June 1, 1796.
- **Area**: About 42,000 square miles (Ranks 36th in size)
- **Bordering States**: Virginia, Kentucky, Missouri, Arkansas, Mississippi, Alabama, Georgia, North Carolina
- **Meaning of Name**: Tennessee is named for the old Cherokee village of Tanasi, which lay along the Little Tennessee River.
- **State Nickname**: "Volunteer State"
- **State Bird**: Tennessee has two state birds, the Northern Mockingbird and the Bobwhite Quail.
- **State Tree**: Tulip Poplar
- **State Flower**: Tennessee has two state flowers, the Iris and the Purple Passionflower.
- **State Song**: Musical Tennessee has several state songs, including "The Tennessee Waltz," "Rocky Top" and "Smoky Mountain Rain."
- **State Motto**: "Agriculture and Commerce"
- **Historic Places to Visit**: President Andrew Johnson National Historic Site, Chickamauga/Chattanooga National Military Park, Fort Donelson National Battlefield, President James Polk House, Shiloh National Military Park, The Hermitage of President Andrew Jackson
- **Resources and Industries**: Music, hydroelectric power, farming, coal, tourism

Modern-day reconstruction of part of Fort Donelson on Tennessee's Cumberland River

State Flag: Three white stars within a blue circle, all centered on a red field. These three stars represent the three Grand Divisions of Tennessee: mountainous East Tennessee, foothills Middle Tennessee and lowland West Tennessee. A vertical blue bar decorates the fly side of the flag.

CHAPTER 24: Australia and New Zealand

WORLD GEOGRAPHY FOCUS

Australia and New Zealand

Australia is both the world's smallest continent and the world's largest island. With a mainland area of 2.95 million square miles, Australia is only about 25% smaller than the next smallest continent, Europe; but it is more than four times the size of the next largest island, Greenland.

Australia is also the lowest, flattest and one of the driest continents. Nearly one-fifth of Australia's area is dry enough to be considered desert, and about two-thirds is too dry for all but the most determined inhabitants. The overwhelming majority of Australians live in the more hospitable regions— mainly near the eastern and southeastern coasts, in and around cities like Sydney, Canberra and Melbourne.

FASCINATING FACTS about Australia:

- Australia's name comes from the Latin word *australis*, "southern." Years before any European explorer caught sight of Australia, European maps included a hoped-for southern continent called *Terra Australis Incognita*— Latin for "Unknown Southern Land."

- The territory of the modern-day Commonwealth of Australia includes the Australian continent, the large island of Tasmania and many smaller islands.

- Because so much of Australia is uninhabitable, its population density ranks among the lowest on earth— as of 2014, only about 8 people per square mile. By area, Australia is the world's sixth largest country; but by population, it is only about the 50th largest. With about 23 million people as of 2014, Australia has a population roughly equal to that of Taiwan— an island nation of only about 14,000 square miles, less than one-half of one percent of Australia's area.

- Australians have two special names for the vast, little-populated regions of their country: (1) the **bush**, which can mean any territory outside the major cities; and (2) the **Outback**, which usually means the most remote territory.

- The world's largest coral reef system, the 1600-mile-long Great Barrier Reef, lies just off Australia's northeast coast.

- Australia is home to several marsupial species found nowhere else in the world, including kangaroos, wallabies, koalas and Tasmanian devils.

FASCINATING FAUNA: Tasmanian Devils

Tasmanian Devils are meat-eating marsupials that once were found in many parts of Australia, but now are found only on Tasmania. They are also highly aggressive, ill-tempered beasts whose ferocity is limited only by their size— which is no larger than that of small dogs, at most about 30 inches long and 25 pounds weight. When battling one another over mates, or over the choicest parts of animal carcasses, Tasmanian devils behave as if they were truly possessed by devils— baring their teeth, uttering savage growls and shrieking with alarming volume. Oversized heads and powerful jaw muscles give Tasmanian devils more biting force than any other mammals of their size and weight. Devils are also known for the exceedingly foul odor that issues from glands near the bases of their tails; and for storing fat in their tails, as other marsupials do when they find plenty to eat.

ILLUMINATING LISTS: States and Territories of the Commonwealth of Australia

The modern-day Commonwealth of Australia is divided into six states and three territories, not counting some island territories and a claim in Antarctica. Ranked by population, Australia's states and territories are:

States

1. New South Wales	2. Victoria	3. Queensland
4. Western Australia	5. South Australia	6. Tasmania

Territories

1. Australian Capital Territory[1]	2. Northern Territory	3. Jervis Bay Territory[1]

[1] Australia's capital and largest inland city, Canberra, lies within the Australian Capital Territory— a federal territory governed directly by the Commonwealth of Australia, much as the District of Columbia is governed directly by the U.S. Government. To protect the ACT's access to the sea, the Commonwealth also annexed a small coastal territory called Jervis Bay, about 150 miles east of Canberra.

FASCINATING FACTS about New Zealand:

- New Zealand is an island nation located in the southwestern Pacific Ocean. New Zealand's largest city, Auckland, lies about 1,300 miles southeast of Sydney, Australia.

- New Zealand's two main islands, North Island and South Island, comprise nearly 99% of its territory. The rest is divided among scores of smaller islands.

- New Zealand's main islands are so mountainous that barely 2% of their territory is cultivated farmland. South Island is especially mountainous, with 18 peaks over 10,000 feet.

FASCINATING FAUNA: Kiwi

The best-known symbol of New Zealand is the kiwi, a uniquely-shaped flightless bird found nowhere else in the world. Kiwis are long-billed ground burrowers that feed mainly on insects, grubs and worms, which they are able to smell underground through nostrils located at the ends of their bills. Some kiwi grow up to 18 inches height and 9 pounds weight, about the size of chickens.

Because kiwi are so unique, New Zealand military units often use them on their badges as symbols of home. The rest of the world started associating New Zealand with the kiwi after 1906, when an Australian shoe polish maker named his company "Kiwi" in honor of his New Zealander wife. This association became even stronger during WWI— when soldiers from around the world saw kiwi on New Zealanders' unit badges, and started calling all New Zealanders "kiwis."

WORLD HISTORY FOCUS

Australia

Aboriginal Australians

Australia's first people arrived there many centuries ago, long before European explorers found the southern continent. When the first Europeans came to stay in 1788, Australia was home to hundreds of small tribes, each with its own unique language or dialect. Because these dark-skinned people appeared to have lived in Australia always, Europeans labeled them **Aborigines**— from the Latin *ab origine*, "from the beginning."

INTERESTING IDEAS: In modern times, most Australians prefer the terms "Aboriginal Australians" or "Indigenous Australians" to the old "Aborigine." Through decades of discrimination and mistreatment by racist settlers, "Aborigine" became as offensive to some Australians as the misnomer "Indian" is to some Native Americans.

James Cook rowing ashore to meet his first Aboriginal Australians

The arrival of European explorers and settlers was to change Aboriginal Australians' way of life forever.

Early European Explorers

Because the Dutch Empire traded all over the East Indies (see Chapter 15), Dutch explorers were the first Europeans to discover nearby Australia. Early visits to Australia included ones by:

1. **Willem Janszoon**, a Dutch East India Company explorer who crossed over to northern Australia from the East Indies' largest island, New Guinea, in 1606. Aboriginal Australians killed about 10 of Janszoon's crewmen on this first trip— possibly because his crewmen tried to romance Aboriginal women.

2. **Dirk Hartog,** another Dutch East India Company explorer. Hartog happened to strike Australia's west coast in 1616, while searching for a shorter route to the East Indies.

3. **Abel Tasman**, yet another Dutch East India Company explorer. On a long voyage in 1642 – 1643, Tasman became the first European to visit Tasmania and New Zealand, and even caught sight of Fiji. In 1644, Tasman returned to explore and map most of Australia's northwestern coast.

Not one of these explorers, though, found what the Dutch East India Company was searching for: lands bursting with high-value goods like gold or spices, peopled by friendly natives who would be willing to gather these goods for Dutch traders. Finding nothing in either Australia or New Zealand that seemed likely to turn a profit in the near future, Dutch traders instead focused their energies on the already-profitable spice islands of the East Indies.

Australia was to receive few visits from Europeans, and New Zealand none at all, until 1770— the year when the great British explorer James Cook went in search of *Terra Australis Incognita*.

BRILLIANT BRITONS: James Cook (1728 – 1779)

James Cook was an ingenious British navigator, mapmaker and ship's captain whose mission in life was to explore the last unexplored places on earth. Through three great voyages of discovery spanning the years from 1768 – 1779— one to Tahiti, New Zealand and Australia; one to the Antarctic Circle; and one to Hawaii, northwestern North America and the Bering Strait— Cook learned more about the little-known places of the world than any other explorer of his day.

Ironically, this greatest of seafarers was born a landlubber, the son of a Scottish farm laborer who worked in Yorkshire, England. Cook knew little of the sea until 1745, when his father apprenticed his 16-year-old son to a shopkeeper in a seaside fishing village. Given the chance to compare the come-and-go life of a sailor to the stay-at-home life of a shopkeeper, Cook quickly decided which he preferred. After only 18 months as a shopkeeper's apprentice, Cook convinced his master to transfer his apprenticeship to a businessman who owned a small fleet of merchant ships.

Portrait of Captain Cook with his beloved maps

Cook spent the next several years sailing up and down England's east coast, hauling coal from Newcastle on the Tyne to London on the Thames. As drab as coal hauling could be, the experience Cook gained during these years served him well later in life— for the Newcastle coal routes were notoriously stormy, and dotted with enough hidden rocks and shoals to shipwreck all but the wariest of sailors. Cook's years of study in this most dangerous school made him an expert seaman, one who could guide his ships safely through any sea on earth.

With the Seven Years' War threatening in 1755, Cook resigned his merchant job to join Britain's Royal Navy. Cook served as a navigation master at the Siege of Louisbourg, Nova Scotia in 1758— an important victory that cleared the way for General Wolfe's war-winning victory at Quebec City the following year (see Chapter 19). On the way to Quebec City, Cook was one of several cunning masters who probed the tricky St. Lawrence River ahead of the British fleet, safely guiding Wolfe's ships past hidden hazards only French sailors knew.

After the war, Cook applied his great navigational skills to the science of mapmaking. Over the five years from 1763 – 1767, Cook produced the first detailed map of Newfoundland Island, a map so painstakingly accurate that Newfoundland fishermen would continue to use it well into the 1900s.

In 1768, Cook's unexcelled reputation as a navigator and mapmaker made him the obvious choice to guide an important Royal Society of London mission to the South Pacific.

DEFINITION: The **Royal Society of London** was an association of British scientists formed in 1660 to promote discoveries in all sorts of sciences— everything from chemistry, biology and physics to mathematics, astronomy and navigation. Sir Isaac Newton was a fellow of the Royal Society, as were Robert Boyle, Robert Hooke, Benjamin Franklin and many other honored scientists.

Between the Seven Years' War and the Revolutionary War, the excitement of British mercantilists was almost beyond containing (see Chapter 22). Britain's fantastic victories in the Seven Years' War had won her territories around the globe, from Canada and the West Indies to India and the East Indies. With rival France vanquished for the moment, there seemed to be no limit to the number of colonies the British Empire might build, nor to the profits Britons might reap from those colonies.

To control this vast, growing empire, British sailors needed answers to all of these questions:

- What were the best routes for sail-driven vessels to follow from place to place around the empire?
- Were there any undiscovered islands near these routes that might make good stopovers— convenient places for sea-worn ships and sailors to resupply, repair and recuperate?
- Was there really a *terra australis incognita*, an unknown southern continent? If so, then did this continent offer resources that might turn profits for British merchants?

To answer these questions, the Royal Society of London worked to improve two sciences:

1. Navigation science. Navigators had long known how to find latitude— the number of degrees north or south of the equator— by measuring the angle between sun and horizon at high noon. Although the sun's angle changed with the season of the year, it changed slowly enough that a calendar-based chart could always tell a navigator the precise latitude for whatever angle his sextant or quadrant measured.

Unfortunately, measuring longitude— the number of degrees east or west of the prime meridian— was far more difficult. The fact that the earth rotated on its axis one degree every four minutes meant that even a small error could throw off a navigator's longitude calculations by many miles, rendering them all but useless.

2. Cartography (mapmaking): Good navigation also required accurate maps— ones filled not with vague speculation about some *terra australis incognita*, but rather with real, verified measurements that navigators could use to find land when their ships were in trouble. Fortunately, James Cook was an expert mapmaker.

Cook's First Voyage of Exploration	Dates: 1768 – 1771	Vessel: *Endeavour*

Cook in Tahiti

The first mission the Royal Society assigned James Cook was to record the 1769 Transit of Venus.

DEFINITION: A transit of Venus happens when the planet Venus passes directly between the sun and the earth, allowing astronomers to track the black disk of Venus as it travels across the sun.

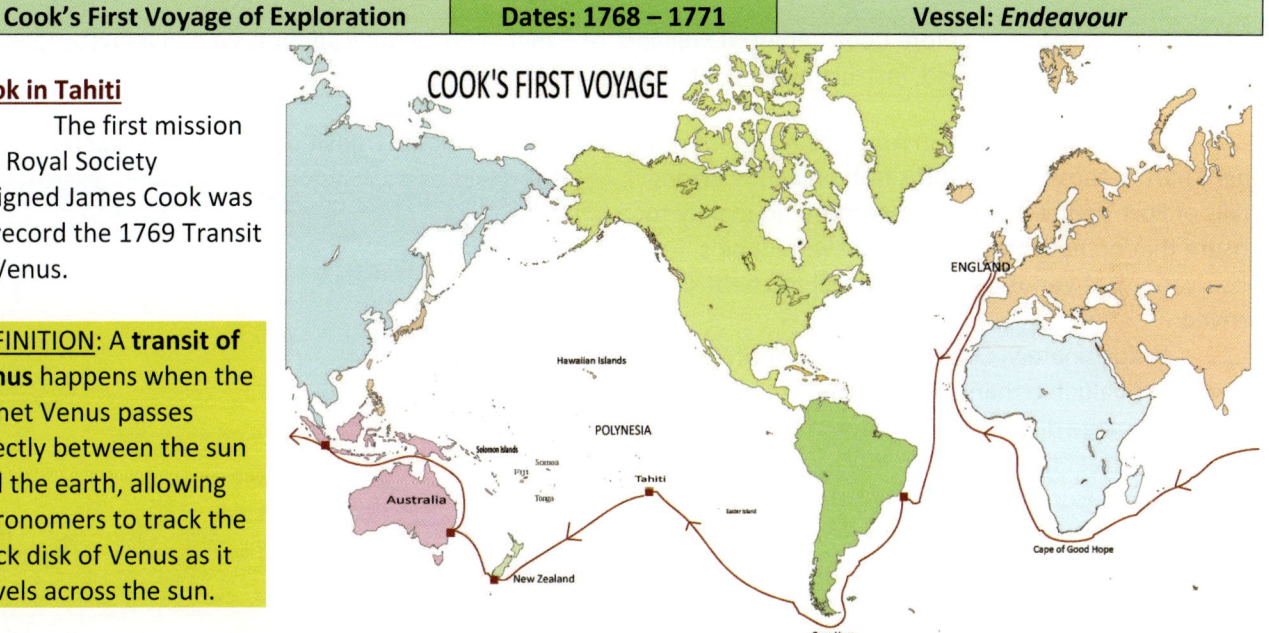

The 1769 transit of Venus was a particularly important astronomical event, for two reasons:

1. Because transits of Venus are so rare. Although the last transit of Venus had fallen in 1761, just 8 years before, the next would not arrive for another 105 years.
2. Because the late, great English astronomer Edmund Halley had outlined a method for using transits of Venus to measure the **astronomical unit**— the average distance between the earth and the sun. Halley's method was to observe the next transit of Venus from at least two places on earth, as widely separated as possible, and then use trigonometry to calculate the astronomical unit. Precise knowledge of the astronomical unit

would allow astronomers to calculate all the other planets' orbits as well, greatly improving their understanding of the solar system.

Cook's first voyage of exploration began in the summer of 1768, when he guided the three-masted bark *Endeavour* out of Plymouth, England. Cook's target was Tahiti, a remote island about 2,500 miles northeast of New Zealand. The Royal Society chose Tahiti for two reasons:

1. Because Tahiti stood on the far side of the world, as far as possible from all other transit of Venus observers— which would improve the accuracy of their calculations.
2. Because Captain Samuel Wallis, who had just discovered Tahiti in 1767, reported making peace with Tahiti's natives after a single battle— a feat no visitor to Australia or New Zealand had yet accomplished.

Captain Wallis using his cannon to persuade the people of Tahiti to make peace

INTERESTING IDEAS: Just before Cook departed England for Tahiti, a Royal Navy admiral slipped a mysterious sealed envelope into his hand, instructing him not to open it until his mission on Tahiti was complete.

Cook reached Tahiti in April 1769, two months before the predicted transit of Venus. The expedition spent part of those two months fashioning the strong walls of **Fort Venus**— a temporary fort built mainly to ensure that no native could interfere with Cook's observations of Venus when the crucial moment arrived.

Unfortunately, Cook's observations of Venus proved less valuable than the Royal Society had hoped; for Venus' image distorted as it entered the sun's orb, making the exact time Venus spent crossing the sun difficult to measure. Even so, scientists used Cook's measurements to determine a value for the astronomical unit that would later prove to be within 1% of the true value.

Fort Venus, Tahiti

New Zealand

Having accomplished his mission in Tahiti, Cook finally broke the wax seal on his admiral's mysterious sealed envelope and read his super-secret orders for his next mission. To Cook's surprise, the letter instructed him to find *Terra Australis Incognita*— the Unknown Southern Land of legend— and claim it for Great Britain before anyone else could do so.

Following these orders, Cook headed south from Tahiti until he reached the latitude of 40° south. He then headed west, searching all the while, until he came to the islands Abel Tasman had discovered back in 1643: the North and South Islands of New Zealand. In addition to claiming New Zealand for Britain, Cook spent six months there:

1. Sailing all the way around the islands, taking careful measurements that allowed him to produce the first detailed map of New Zealand.
2. Proving that these far southern islands weren't connected to any undiscovered southern continent— which meant that if there really was such a continent, then it probably lay too far south to be of much use.

Australia

From New Zealand, Cook moved on to a southern continent that the British were to find quite useful. Cook spent the middle months of 1770 exploring and mapping the most hospitable part of Australia— the as-yet undiscovered east coast, which he named **New South Wales**. In the process, Cook claimed the entire east coast of Australia for Britain.

FASCINATING FACTS: Botany Bay

For his first landing in Australia, Cook chose a shallow bay where his fishermen had been fortunate enough to catch a pair of 600-pound stingrays— leading him to mark the name "Stingray Bay" in his log. This historic landing site lay just south of what is now Sydney, New South Wales.

The welcome Cook received at Stingray Bay was no warmer than the one Willem Janszoon received on Australia's northern coast back in 1606. When two native men tried to warn Cook's longboat off, Cook threw them a bag of beads and iron nails in a gesture of friendship. Although the men seemed pleased with these gifts, they still hurled rocks and darts when Cook came closer. A few blasts of purposely ill-aimed musket fire finally chased the men off, allowing Cook to land safely.

Two botanists aboard *Endeavour*, Sir Joseph Banks and Dr. Daniel Solander, made excellent use of their time in Australia, collecting and describing hundreds of plant species that no European had ever seen— so many species that Cook later renamed the site of his first landing "Botany Bay."

Cook's first landing at Botany Bay

A LOOK AHEAD: In 1771, when the Cook expedition will finally return to England after nearly three years at sea, Banks' and Solander's glowing descriptions of Botany Bay will make adventurous Britons long to experience its wonders with their own eyes.

One reason Cook's expedition was able to remain at sea for so long was that for most of its first two years, it suffered no major mishaps. Cook's extraordinary seamanship through storm and shoal preserved the lone *Endeavour* from mishaps at sea; while his strict attention to his crewmen's diets preserved them from the deadly scourge that killed so many other sailors: scurvy. Confident in their captain's skill and sensibility, Cook's crewmen felt no need to save themselves through mutiny, as Henry Hudson's did (see Chapter 7).

The final year of Cook's long journey, though, contained enough mishaps for all three years.

INTERESTING INCIDENTS: *Endeavour* on the Great Barrier Reef (June 1770)

As *Endeavour* was departing Australia bound for New Guinea, the cautious Cook came across a hazard that even he failed to avoid: the Great Barrier Reef. On the night of June 11, 1770, *Endeavour* was sailing off

Australia's northeastern coast in what seemed like deep, safe water when she suddenly struck hard upon this long, treacherous coral reef.

With water seeping into his hold at an alarming rate, Cook ordered 40 – 50 tons of ballast stones and cannon thrown overboard, trying desperately to lighten *Endeavour* so that his longboat crews could tow her off the reef. To Cook's increasing alarm, these sacrifices gained him nothing. About 25 hours after the accident, a rising tide finally lifted *Endeavour* free— but then, without the reef to block her leaks, water seeped into her hold almost faster than Cook's men could pump it overboard.

Finally, by **fothering** *Endeavour*'s damaged side— that is, by spreading canvas over it to slow its leaks— Cook managed to keep *Endeavour* afloat long enough to sail back to what is now Cooktown, Queensland, where his crew needed several weeks to repair the damage.

Endeavour in peril for her life

Months later, *Endeavour* put in for more repairs at what is now Jakarta, Indonesia; and while she was there, her crewmen picked up a combination of malaria and intestinal illnesses that killed far quicker than scurvy. Before Cook finally reached home in June 1771, more than 30 of his original 94 crewmen succumbed to these illnesses— compared with fewer than 10 losses before Jakarta.

Cook's Second Voyage of Exploration	Dates: 1772 – 1775	Vessels: *Resolution, Adventure*

The Antarctic Circle

Just over a year later, Cook departed on a second search for the unknown southern land. Among Cook's many accomplishments on this second voyage were these:

- In January 1773— six months into his voyage, and about a month into the southern hemisphere's summer— Cook's new sloop *Resolution* became the first ship to pass the line of 60° south latitude, now called the Antarctic Circle. The following January, Cook penetrated the Antarctic region to the frigid latitude of 71°10' south before solid sea ice blocked his way farther south.

- Cook traveled all the way around the world at far southern latitudes— proving once and for all that if an undiscovered southern continent existed, then it was unconnected to any other land, and could only be a frozen wasteland.

- From his observations of icebergs, Cook theorized that there must indeed be a continent farther south.

FASCINATING FACTS: Glaciers and Icebergs

On each of his trips south of the Antarctic Circle, Cook saw hundreds of huge, floating mountains of ice that he called "ice islands." Some of these were low and flat-topped, while others were jagged and taller than *Resolution*'s masts. When Cook tasted water melted from these ice islands, he found to his delight that it was far fresher and sweeter than the drinking water in *Resolution*'s casks.

While other explorers had certainly seen icebergs before, especially around Greenland, Cook was among the first to make these important observations about them:

- Because icebergs contained fresh water, not salt, they could not come from frozen seawater. Instead, they must come from the only source of fresh water available in these frigid latitudes: snow.
- Because some icebergs were so tall and jagged, it seemed unlikely that snow falling on the flat surface of the sea could have formed them, as Cook reported in his journal:

"… for we cannot suppose that snow alone, as it falls, can form on a plain surface, such as the sea, such a variety of high spired peaks and hills as we have seen on many of the ice isles. It is certainly more reasonable to suppose that they are formed on a coast whose surface is something similar to theirs."

From these observations, Cook deduced the most interesting conclusion of his second voyage: that there must be "… a tract of land near the [South] Pole, which is the source of most of the ice which is spread over this vast Southern Ocean." In other words, Cook's icebergs could only have formed on the unseen continent that lay just beyond his reach, Antarctica. Cook's intuition taught him what modern-day scientists have verified: that icebergs like the ones he saw come from glaciers.

Resolution searching for land south of the Antarctic Circle

DEFINITION: **Glaciers** are massive bodies of compressed snow that build up on frozen lands over time, sometimes taking centuries to form. Glaciers that form near a coast eventually spread out over the adjoining sea. When the weight of accumulating snow becomes too great for the glacier's structure to stand, the glacier "calves," breaking off a free-floating iceberg.

Other interesting facts:
- Explorers first sighted Antarctica in 1820, and first landed there in either 1821 or 1840.
- Norwegian explorer Roald Amundsen first reached the South Pole on December 14, 1911— one month ahead of British explorer Robert Scott, who not only lost his race to the South Pole, but also froze to death on his way back.

FASCINATING FACTS: Marine Chronometers

One of the innovations Cook carried with him on his second voyage was a remarkably accurate timepiece called a **marine chronometer**.

Most early timepieces depended on the regular motions of pendulums to keep time, much like grandfather clocks. Unfortunately, the incessant tossing of ships' decks rendered pendulum clocks useless. To solve this problem, the Royal Society of London asked Parliament to offer a large reward to the first inventor who could produce an accurate shipboard clock. Spurred on by this reward money, the clockmakers of the 1770s produced wonderful spring-driven marine chronometers that always kept perfect time, no matter how much a ship tossed.

> **INTERESTING IDEAS**: With his marine chronometer set to the precise time in Greenwich, England— the city through which the Prime Meridian passed— Cook had a fantastic new way to measure *Resolution*'s longitude wherever he went:
>
> - Using a quadrant or sextant, Cook could determine when the sun stood directly overhead. This observation gave him the precise moment of his location's high noon.
>
> - At that same moment, Cook could consult his marine chronometer to learn the precise time in Greenwich. The difference between those two times was the length of time the earth had been rotating since Greenwich's high noon.
>
> - Because the earth rotates at a constant rate of fifteen degrees per hour, Cook could convert this time difference to a degree difference, pinpointing his longitude more precisely than ever before— which made his new maps of the South Pacific more accurate than any the world had ever seen.

Cook's Third Voyage of Exploration	Dates: 1776 – 1779	Vessels: *Resolution, Discovery*

The Hawaiian Islands

Cook's mission on his third voyage was the same as Henry Hudson's on his fourth: to find the elusive Northwest Passage that supposedly, hopefully connected the Atlantic to the Pacific north of Canada. Cook, however, chose a far more roundabout route than Hudson's— south around Africa, and then eastward across the Indian Ocean. Crossing into the South Pacific, Cook revisited his old haunts of New Zealand and Tahiti before moving into the North Pacific, where he made perhaps the most important discovery of his career: Hawaii.

Scene from Cook's first visit to Hawaii

> **INTERESTING IDEAS**: Upon reaching the Hawaiian Islands, Cook found that the natives there spoke a language similar to the one he had learned in Tahiti, more than 2,600 miles away to the south. To his astonishment, Cook realized that the people of Hawaii must share a common origin with the people of Tahiti and other South Pacific islands. Somehow, these supposedly primitive people must have found a way to accomplish something that even Europeans, with all their advanced technology, still found difficult: they must have navigated by the stars, hopping from island to island across unthinkable distances until they finally reached Hawaii.

> **DEFINITIONS**:
> - Modern-day anthropologists mark Hawaii as part of **Polynesia**, a group of Pacific islands whose native peoples all share common origins— origins which appear to be separate from those of most Aboriginal Australians.
>
> - Polynesia consists of more than 1,000 islands, many of them gathered in groups, all scattered over a vast area of the Pacific Ocean called the **Polynesian Triangle**. The Polynesian Triangle's three traditional corners are (1) New Zealand to the southwest; (2) Hawaii to the north; and (3) Easter Island to the southeast.

North America and the Bering Strait

From Hawaii, Cook moved on to take the first detailed measurements of the northwest coast of North America. Striking land on what is now the Oregon coast in March 1778, Cook spent the next seven months exploring and mapping his way northwest— past Canada and Alaska, then through the Aleutian Island chain and on into the Bering Sea. Just north of the Bering Strait— the narrow strait that separates North America from Asia— sea ice once again blocked Cook's way, forcing the expedition to turn back to Hawaii that October.

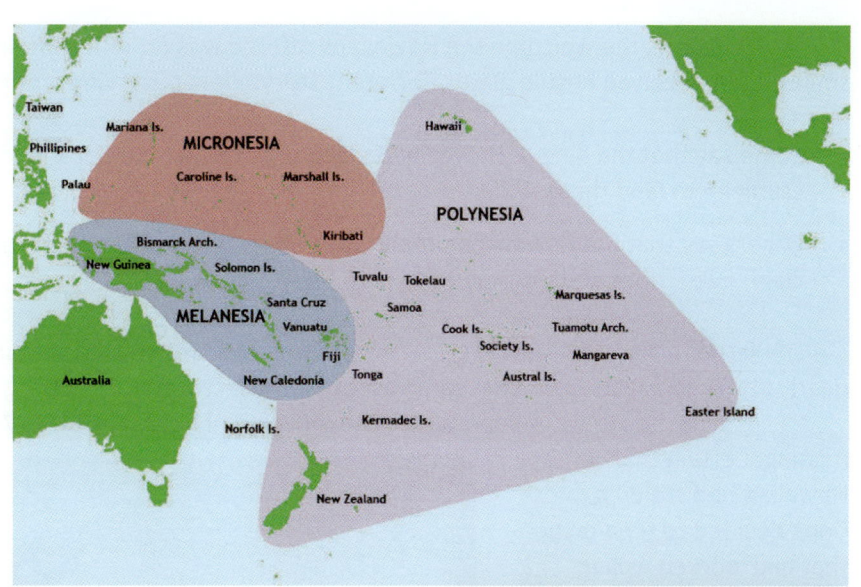

FASCINATING FACTS: Leis

Leis are traditional necklaces that Hawaiians and other Polynesians make by stringing together natural objects— either perishable ones like flowers and leaves, or more permanent ones like shells, feathers, teeth and bones. In former times, Polynesians made and gave leis to mark all sorts of occasions, everything from births and deaths to weddings and treaty signings. In modern times, Hawaiians give leis mainly as signs of welcome, affection and respect.

DEFINITION: A **kahuna** is any elite member of Hawaiian society— a priest, a healer, a chief, a chief's adviser or even a well-respected craftsman.

FASCINATING FATES: Captain Cook's Fate

Fatefully, Cook's second trip to Hawaii fell during a Hawaiian religious festival dedicated to a god-king named Rono or Lono. According to legend, Rono had departed Hawaii in a canoe long ago, promising to return one day bearing trees and livestock to help Hawaii feed its people. For some combination of reasons— perhaps because *Resolution*'s masts resembled trees; perhaps because Cook carried livestock aboard; or perhaps because Cook circled Hawaii for weeks before landing, as Rono had promised to do— Hawaii's priests appeared to accept Cook as an incarnation of Rono. To Cook's amazement, the Hawaiians clothed him in red robes, showered him with gifts and generally treated him and his crewmen as if they were gods.

A few days' acquaintance, though, convinced the Hawaiians that Cook and his crew were no gods, nor even good guests. Instead of providing food, as gods should have done, Cook and his crew demanded an astonishing amount of food to refill their ships' larders— food that could have been saved to feed hungry Hawaiians. After giving Cook and his crew more than they could spare, the Hawaiians started signaling that the festival was over, and it was time for their honored guests to leave.

Cook finally left Hawaii in February 1779, bound northward to resume his search for the Northwest Passage. Unfortunately, a spring gale damaged *Resolution*'s foremast after only a week at sea, forcing Cook to turn back for repairs.

This time, the welcome the Hawaiians offered was far different: instead of bows, gifts and enthusiastic smiles, Cook received hostile glares. Different storytellers offer different reasons for the Hawaiians' change of heart:

- Some say that the King of Hawaii had placed the bay where Cook landed under *kapu* or *taboo*, making it sacrilege to land there.
- Others say that the Hawaiians simply were not pleased to see these unwanted freeloaders returning to claim even more of their islands' limited food.

Either way, the situation grew tense: the Hawaiians started stealing small items from the explorers, and nearly attacked a work crew that came ashore to collect water.

The tension grew unbearable on the morning of February 14, 1779, when one of Cook's longboats went missing. Certain that some Hawaiian had stolen it, Cook decided to try a tactic that had worked well in Tahiti and New Zealand: he would bring a native chief aboard his ship, holding him hostage until the thief returned what he had stolen. Cook would also order his men to fire on any canoe that tried to leave the bay, thus barring the thief from escape.

At first, Cook's plan seemed to be working— for when he rowed ashore with an armed guard, the King of Hawaii seemed just as determined to catch the thief as Cook was, and willingly agreed to come aboard as Cook's hostage. As the king walked down the beach toward Cook's longboat, though, his people pleaded with him not to go. Then, while the king hesitated, someone rushed up to inform him that Cook's crew had just fired on a canoe, killing a Hawaiian sub-chief.

At this news, chaos erupted on the beach: Hawaiians lunged at Britons with spears, and Britons returned scattered musket fire. Cook, too, fired his musket at a spearman who tried to skewer him. Then, as Cook turned to organize his sailors' retreat, the Hawaiians clubbed the great explorer to the ground and stabbed him to death.

Hawaiians attacking Captain Cook

Colonizing Australia

A LOOK ELSEWHERE: The year Captain Cook died on a Hawaiian beach was a middle year of the American Revolutionary War. As of 1779, the United States had allied with France against Britain. The British had retreated from Philadelphia, but had since moved south to capture Savannah, and were soon to capture Charleston.

From the beginning of the Revolutionary War, Britain faced a new and difficult problem: what to do with its thousands of convicted criminals. From the beginning, judges had been using Britain's American colonies as convenient places to punish criminals. For crimes large and small, thousands of convicts had found themselves shipped to the colonies and sold off as indentured servants. With most of America closed to Britain after 1776, the British needed new places to house their convicts— places like the hulks.

FASCINATING FACTS: Prison Hulks

A **prison hulk** was an old, rotting ship that the Royal Navy no longer wanted, stripped of its sailing gear and anchored near shore to serve as a prison ship. From the late 1770s through the mid-1800s, Britain floated as many as 40 prison hulks at a time, some of them housing as many as 500 convicts. Prison hulks were notoriously miserable places to live— overcrowded, filthy, damp, and supplied with barely enough food to keep their inmates alive.

REFRESHING REMINDERS: Conditions aboard the hulks were even worse for prisoners of war. One early prison hulk was HMS *Jersey*, aboard which General Howe confined up to 1,200 Americans at a time during the Revolutionary War. As many as 8,000 American POWs may have died aboard *Jersey* alone, nearly twice the number that died on battlefields.

A long row of prison hulks in Portsmouth Harbor, fitted with roofs to shed water

Penal Colonies in Australia

The idea of using cheap prison labor to build new British colonies in the South Pacific had been around for years, since before James Cook even discovered hospitable ground in eastern Australia. After Britain lost her American colonies, though, the need for new colonies grew more urgent.

ILLUMINATING EXCERPTS from "A Proposal for Establishing a Settlement in New South Wales"

In 1783, the year when the Treaty of Paris ended the Revolutionary War, a former Cook crewman named James Matra wrote these arguments in favor of British colonies in Australia:

- "I am going to offer an object to the consideration of our government that may in time atone for the loss of our American colonies… By the discoveries and enterprise of our officers, many new countries have been found which know no sovereign, and that hold out the most enticing allurements to European adventurers. None are more inviting than New South Wales…

- "In this immense tract of more than 2,000 miles there was every variety of soil, and great parts of it were extremely fertile, peopled only by a few black inhabitants who, in the rudest state of society, knew no other arts than such as were necessary to their mere animal existence… The climate and soil are so happily adapted to produce every various and valuable production of Europe… that with good management, and a few settlers, in twenty or thirty years they might cause a revolution in the whole system of European commerce…"

Aboriginal Australians

> **INTERESTING IDEAS:** Madras' proposal highlights two important ideas about Britain's colonization of Australia:
>
> 1. The British Empire decided to colonize Australia for three reasons: not only because it needed more room to house its convicts, but also because it needed to replace the colonies it had lost in the Americas, and establish a firm foothold in the South Pacific.
>
> 2. Unlike the Polynesian peoples of Hawaii, Tahiti and New Zealand, Aboriginal Australians appeared to have no governments— no kings, and no confederations of tribes. No governments meant that in British eyes, Britain need not bother with buying land or negotiating treaties; it could simply take whatever it wanted.

FASCINATING FACTS: The First Fleet

- The first convicts departed for Australia on May 13, 1787 aboard the **First Fleet**— a fleet of eleven ships, including six convict transports, three supply transports and two Royal Navy escorts.

- The First Fleet carried (1) about 1,030 convicts, including about 800 men and 200 women; (2) about 300 marine soldiers, along with some of their wives; and (3) nearly 300 sailors and Royal Navy officers.

- After a voyage of 252 days, 1,373 living souls arrived in eastern Australia on January 26, 1788— the day modern Australians still commemorate as **Australia Day**.

- Arthur Philip, first Governor of New South Wales, took such good care of his convicts that only about 40 died en route to Australia.

The First Fleet entering Sydney Cove on the first Australia Day, 1788

- Although Sir Joseph Banks had recommended settling near Botany Bay, Governor Philip found Botany Bay too shallow, and the ground around it unsuitable. Instead, Philip moved his landing site a few miles north to **Sydney Cove**— a fine harbor where, Philip said, "a thousand sail of the line may ride in the most perfect security." There Philip established the beginnings of Sydney, New South Wales, which is still Australia's most populous city.

Starving in Sydney

Like all new colonies, New South Wales struggled to feed itself. Governor Philip's food supply problems included some that sprang from Australia itself, and some that sprang from the people he led there:

Arthur Philip, first Governor of New South Wales

1. Although the soil around Sydney was rich enough to grow grass for grazing, it was not rich enough to grow abundant grain— not without fertilizer, of which the colony had very little at first.

2. Most of Philip's convicts were city folk— petty thieves who had grown up poor in England's cities, and had been caught stealing a bite to eat or a much-needed pair of shoes. Having never worked on farms before, most of them had little idea how to raise crops, or keep livestock fed and healthy.

3. Because Philip's convicts owned nothing in Australia, and were essentially working to build their own prison, they had little to gain from extra work. With this in mind, they naturally worked as little as possible.

4. Most of Philip's soldiers were too proud to join in menial tasks— feeling that farm work was for convicts, not military men.

Due to all these problems, Australian farms produced almost no grain in 1788, and very little in 1789. Food soon grew so scarce that Philip took extraordinary measures like (1) placing colonists on half rations; (2) decreeing the death penalty for the crime of stealing food; and (3) sending ships to buy food in Calcutta, India.

Nor did the arrival of the Second Fleet in 1790 stave off famine— for the Second Fleet's managers cared only for profit, and nothing for their passengers' health. Of the 1,026 convicts who boarded the Second Fleet, only about 759 reached Australia alive— a criminally low survival rate of only about 76%. Furthermore, the survivors were so weak from malnourishment and disease that they often burdened the colony more than they benefitted it. The Third Fleet, which arrived in 1791, improved on the second: of the 2,057 convicts who boarded the Third Fleet, 1,875 reached Australia alive, a survival rate of about 91%.

By this time, several improvements were helping New South Wales feed itself:

HMS Neptune, a ship of the Second Fleet

1. Desperate to get more work out of his convicts, Governor Philip started promoting hard-working convicts as farm managers. The benefits that came with these promotions helped more convicts see the value of hard work.

2. When convicts finished their prison terms— which some did within 1-1/2 years of the First Fleet's arrival— they were no longer prisoners, but rather free citizens. Unlike prisoners, free citizens had every reason to hope that New South Wales would succeed; for unless they could somehow afford passage back to Britain, Australia would be their home for the rest of their lives.

3. For producing the colony's first successful wheat crop in 1790, Governor Philip rewarded a former convict named James Ruse with New South Wales' first grant of privately-owned land: 30 acres in Rosehill, Sydney called Experiment Farm. As more and more former prisoners became free landowners, New South Wales became less a penal colony, and more a place to call home.

So helpful were these improvements that by the time Governor Philip returned to Britain in 1792, New South Wales was nearly self-sustaining.

MORE FASCINATING FACTS about Penal Colonies in Australia:

- Over the 80 years from 1788 – 1868, Britain transported more than 160,000 convicts, including about 25,000 women, to various penal colonies in Australia.

- Attracted by the good news of New South Wales' success, the first free settlers started arriving there in 1793, only five years after the First Fleet. Even so, a combination of convicts and former convicts continued to outnumber free settlers in Australia for decades.

- After 1801, good behavior could earn convicts **tickets of leave**— permission to live and work as more or less free citizens, provided they attended church regularly and avoided trouble with the law. However, early governors hesitated to grant too many tickets of leave.
- New South Wales' fifth governor, Lachlan Macquarie, fought to improve conditions for **emancipists**— former convicts who served out their sentences to become free citizens. Some free settlers insisted that former criminals should never be trusted with positions of authority. Macquarie, however, regarded emancipists as some of his best-behaved citizens.

FASCINATING FORGERS: Francis Greenway (1777 – 1837)

Francis Greenway was a Bristol-born English architect who went bankrupt around 1809, and tried to ease his money problems by forging a financial document. For the crime of forgery, an English court sentenced Greenway to 14 years' punishment in the penal colony at New South Wales.

When Governor Macquarie learned that he had an accomplished architect on his hands, he hired Greenway to design and manage a few building projects in Sydney. After Greenway

Portrait of emancipist Francis Greenway on an Australian $10 bill

proved himself both talented and trustworthy, Macquarie first freed him, and then hired him as the colony's first official government architect. One ironic result is that a portrait of Francis Greenway, a convicted forger, wound up where one would hardly expect to find a forger's portrait: on an Australian $10 bill.

FASCINATING FICTIONS: Abel Magwitch

The tale of Abel Magwitch, a character from Charles Dickens' 1861 novel *Great Expectations*, illustrates the bizarre circumstances of British prison life during the early 1800s. Magwitch is a convict who, as the novel begins, escapes from the miserable prison hulk where he is serving out his sentence. After swimming ashore, Magwitch bullies a poor young blacksmith's apprentice named Pip into stealing a metal file, which Magwitch uses to file through his leg irons. Unfortunately for Magwitch, the police later recapture him; and this time, he receives an even harsher sentence. For the crime of escaping, a judge orders him transported to New South Wales.

Unknown to Pip, the boyish innocence he displayed during his brief encounter with Magwitch has a profound effect on the hardened convict. Several years later, a lawyer informs Pip that some unknown benefactor is sending regular gifts of money to pay for his education. Through most of the story, Pip believes his mysterious benefactor to be a strange, secretive

Illustration of Abel Magwitch in leg irons

spinster named Miss Havisham. Near the end, though, Pip's benefactor turns out to be the former convict Abel Magwitch— who is now a free man, and has somehow taken advantage of the boundless opportunities found only in Australia to strike it rich.

The Australian Frontier Wars

Watkin Tench, a British soldier who served as a guard aboard one of the First Fleet's convict transports, published these descriptions of the Aboriginal Australians he met around Sydney Cove in 1788:

- "… they are fond of adorning themselves with scars, which increase their natural hideousness. It is hardly possible to see anything in human shape more ugly, than one of these savages thus scarified, and farther ornamented with a fish bone struck through the gristle of the nose…"

- "Exclusive of their weapons of offence, and a few stone hatchets very rudely fashioned, their ingenuity is confined to manufacturing small nets, in which they put the fish they catch, and to fish-hooks made of bone, neither of which are unskillfully executed. On many of the rocks are also to be found delineations of the figures of men and birds, very poorly cut."

- "Of the use or benefit of clothing, these people appear to have no comprehension, though their sufferings from the climate they live in, strongly point out the necessity of a covering from the rigor of the seasons. Both sexes, and those of all ages, are invariably found naked. But it must not be inferred from this, that custom so inures them to the changes of the elements, as to make them bear with indifference the extremes of heat and cold; for we have had visible and repeated proofs, that the latter affects them severely, when they are seen shivering, and huddling themselves up in heaps in their huts, or the caverns of the rocks, until a fire can be kindled. Than these huts nothing more rude in construction, or deficient in conveniency, can be imagined…"

- "To cultivation of the ground they are utter strangers, and wholly depend for food on the few fruits they gather; the roots they dig up in the swamps; and the fish they pick up along shore, or contrive to strike from their canoes with spears…"

Example of Aboriginal Australian rock art

    Because these Aboriginal Australians were so primitive and disorganized, they could not adapt to the rapid changes that came with British settlement. Unlike their Polynesian neighbors, Aboriginal Australians were slow to acquire muskets and organize armies. Therefore when Aboriginal Australians attacked Britons for encroaching on their hunting grounds, they usually did so in small numbers, and with spears instead of guns. The British responded with overwhelming force, killing at least 20,000 Aboriginal Australians in scattered frontier wars fought off and on for more than a century.

    Even deadlier to Aboriginal Australians were European-borne diseases like smallpox, to which they had no inborn immunity. Like the natives of Mexico, New England and other parts of the New World, Aboriginal Australians fell to the plague of smallpox in uncounted tens of thousands.

The *Bounty* Incident

    The first time James Cook visited Tahiti, he nearly lost two marines to a psychological condition called the **Tahiti Syndrome**. To sailors who were used to lives of harsh discipline, constant danger, little liquor and no women, Tahiti seemed like paradise— a stunningly beautiful, restful place that no sane man would ever want to leave. Unlike European men, Tahitian men did not toil endlessly to fulfill the whims of mad, distant tyrants. Unlike European women, Tahitian women were exotically beautiful, friendly and free with their attentions.

    As Cook prepared to depart for Australia, two Tahiti Syndrome-stricken marines suddenly disappeared to the island's interior with their new Tahitian wives, hoping to build lives of ease in this tropical heaven they had been blessed to find. In the interest of discipline, Cook could not simply leave these men behind— for if he had, then half his crew might have been inclined to join them. To get his marines back, Cook resorted to the same tactic that would later cause so much trouble on Hawaii: he took several chiefs hostage until the Tahitians returned his men, even though the Tahitians weren't responsible for their escape.

Mutiny on HMS *Bounty* (1789)

The tale of HMS *Bounty* is interwoven with Cook's earlier tale. Cook's botanist on his first voyage of exploration, Sir Joseph Banks, noticed a Tahitian tree that provided an astonishing amount of food: the breadfruit tree, a tropical species whose abundant fruit tasted like sweet bread. Banks calculated that if Britain could transplant these trees to its sugar plantations in the West Indies, then slaves there could eat breadfruit as the Tahitians did, and never run out of food.

The Royal Navy's scheme for putting Banks' plan into action was to transform HMS *Bounty*— a 91-foot-long, 220-ton, three-masted former merchant ship— into a floating greenhouse. In December 1787, a 33-year-old lieutenant named William Bligh guided *Bounty* toward Tahiti on a mission to gather healthy breadfruit saplings for transplantation in the West Indies. Bligh was also connected to Cook, having served as sailing master on Cook's third voyage of exploration. With Bligh traveled 45 others, including master's mate Fletcher Christian.

Unfortunately, *Bounty*'s voyage out was not the happiest on record, for a couple of reasons:

- Like many Royal Navy officers, Bligh was in the habit of cursing sailors who didn't live up to his expectations, and flogging ones who showed disrespect. Some storytellers say that Bligh cursed and flogged more than most; while others insist that he was neither stricter nor more lenient than most officers.

Ripe breadfruit

- Misfortune stretched the voyage to a full 10 months, far longer than the usual 6 – 7 months. Bligh had planned to sail around the world west; but when heavy waves south of Cape Horn, South America barred his path, he decided to turn east, nearly doubling the length of his voyage.

After sailing more than 28,000 miles, *Bounty* finally reached Tahiti in October 1788. Over the next five months, as Bligh's botanists collected and loaded more than 1,000 breadfruit trees, Bligh's crewmen enjoyed carefree lives of ease and plenty. Most of the men loved Tahitian women, and master's mate Fletcher Christian loved one enough to marry her.

Therefore it was with a heavy heart that Fletcher Christian boarded *Bounty* for her long-dreaded, breadfruit-tree-laden voyage to the West Indies. The thought of trading his easy life on Tahiti for a brutal life at sea too much for Christian— especially when Bligh, who was determined to restore proper discipline after his crew's months of ease in Tahiti, started cursing and flogging his men more than ever.

Three weeks out and 1,300 miles west of Tahiti, Fletcher Christian finally decided that he would tolerate no more abuse. Before dawn on April 28, 1789, Christian and three others mutineers snuck into the sleeping Bligh's cabin and took him by surprise,

Fletcher Christian and company sending William Bligh and company off in a longboat

binding his hands and threatening to kill him if he uttered a sound. Once Bligh was outside his cabin, the size of the mutiny became clear: eighteen sailors, nearly half his crew, had taken sides with Christian. These stood outside the cabins of officers loyal to Bligh, barring the officers inside. Several other sailors stood by, uncommitted for the moment.

Lowering the ship's boat over the side, the mutineers started ordering Bligh's officers out on deck one at a time. Any who sided with Bligh, the mutineers ordered into the boat. In all, 19 men went over the side for siding with Bligh— including Bligh himself, still clad only in his nightshirt. Out of sympathy, the mutineers also lowered overboard supplies the abandoned men would need to survive: food, water, clothes, ropes, sails, a quadrant and compass, carpenter's tools— and, at the last moment, a meager four cutlasses to defend 19 souls.

After casting Bligh and his loyalists adrift, Fletcher Christian and his mutineers were free to pursue the lives of ease they wanted. Sadly, those carefree lives eluded them:

- Christian first tried to settle on Tubuai, a tiny island about 350 miles south of Tahiti. Unfortunately, serious trouble with the natives there forced him to abandon that plan.

- From Tubuai, Christian reluctantly sailed *Bounty* back to Tahiti, where most of his fellow mutineers longed to stay. Christian viewed this trip to Tahiti as a fool's errand— knowing that if he stayed on such an oft-visited island, then the Royal Navy would certainly hang him to death for mutiny one day. In the end, the group split up: 16 Britons chose to take their chances on Tahiti; while Christian sailed away east with 8 Britons, 6 Tahitian men and an unknown number of Tahitian women.

The Remarkable Voyage of Lieutenant Bligh (1789)

Meanwhile, Lieutenant Bligh and his loyalist crew were living out one of the most remarkable survival stories of all time. In a low ship's boat only 23 feet long, heavily overloaded with 19 men and their gear, Bligh spent the six days after the mutiny sailing 400 miles westward. There Bligh landed on a small island called Tofua, where he tried to gather a few meager supplies.

To Bligh's horror, he soon realized that the natives of Tofua were cannibals gathering for an attack. Had Bligh been without sails, the 200 canoe-borne cannibals who chased him almost certainly would have eaten him. As it was, only one crewman died at Tofua.

Fearing a repeat of Tofua, Bligh approached no more islands for about three weeks. Instead, he and his men survived those weeks on the most meager rations imaginable: one ounce of bread and one quarter pint of water per day, supplemented by tiny scraps of pork, coconut or breadfruit. Above all, Bligh and his men valued the occasional teaspoonful of rum they were able to share from the small supply the mutineers had given them.

William Bligh (1754 – 1817)

For the sake of fairness, Bligh divided all of these rations as evenly as possible on a balance scale made from two coconut shells. For reference weights, Bligh used musket balls. Bligh eventually reduced his men's daily bread ration to 1/25 pound, the weight of a single musket ball.

One month after the mutiny, Bligh passed through a gap in the Great Barrier Reef to the calmer waters on the Australia side— which was a tremendous relief, as the men had often had to bail furiously to keep the sea water that constantly washed into their boat from foundering them. Of even greater relief were the oysters and fruits they found on a small island off the far northern Queensland coast. This island Bligh christened **Restoration Island**, for two reasons: (1) because the island restored him and his crew to life; and (2) because he arrived there on May 29, 1789, the 129th anniversary of the Restoration of the Monarchy (see Chapter 10).

Two weeks later, on June 14— forty-seven days after the mutiny, and more than 3,600 miles west of his starting point— Bligh finally arrived at the Dutch East India Company port of Kupang, Timor, East Indies. From there, Bligh returned to Britain, where he arrived to lay his accusations against Fletcher Christian in March 1790.

FASCINATING FATES: For the remarkable skill and courage he showed in rescuing his men, the oft-maligned William Bligh emerged as the hero of the Bounty incident. Bligh would later serve as the fourth governor of New South Wales, Australia— where, ironically, he would face a second major mutiny.

FASCINATING FATES: Fletcher Christian's Fate

Although the Royal Navy eventually found and hanged some of the mutineers Fletcher Christian left behind on Tahiti, it never found Christian himself. From Tahiti, Christian sailed *Bounty* to the remotest island he could find: tiny, unoccupied, little-known Pitcairn Island, which lay about 1,350 miles southeast of Tahiti. Once there, Christian destroyed all evidence of his passage by first running *Bounty* aground, and then burning her to the waterline.

A few years later, Christian and all of his fellow mutineers save one were dead, along with all of the Tahitian men they had brought to Pitcairn Island with them. According to the wives and children they left behind, these peace-loving men who had hoped to build an island paradise wound up murdering one another.

Other interesting facts:
- As of 2014, some of the mutineers' descendants still live on Pitcairn Island.

Illustration of the idyllic home Fletcher Christian built on Pitcairn Island

- In the 1935 Hollywood film "Mutiny on the Bounty," actor Clark Gable played the role of Fletcher Christian.

New Zealand

The Maori People

The natives of New Zealand, the Maori, were far fiercer than Aboriginal Australians— as the crew of *Adventure* learned to its cost.

Adventure was James Cook's companion ship on his second voyage of exploration. One day in November 1773, *Adventure* dispatched ten lightly-armed crewmen to forage fresh greens from what is now Wharehunga Bay, South Island, New Zealand. To their captain's alarm, his foragers failed to return by day's end as ordered. The next morning, the concerned captain dispatched a rescue team of ten heavily armed men to find his missing crewmen.

After chasing off a few surprised Maori, *Adventure*'s rescue team discovered twenty baskets full of fresh meat. In examining these baskets, the men realized that what they had hoped was dog meat was actually the flesh of their dead comrades— all cooked, carved and ready to serve. A further search revealed dogs feasting on human entrails, along with assorted human heads, limbs and organs— removing all doubt that these particular Maori, at least, were cannibals.

The Musket Wars (early 1800s)

The Maori were also more technologically inclined than Aboriginal Australians, and far more adaptable to change. Within a single generation after the First Fleet reached New South

Illustration of a tattooed Maori chief drawn during James Cook's first voyage of exploration

Wales in 1788, hundreds of Maori bought muskets, and learned precisely how to use them— not only to fire them, but also to clean, oil and repair them, as well as to store gunpowder and mold shot.

The arrival of muskets completely upset the balance of power in New Zealand. The tribes that acquired muskets first gained the ability to wreak terrible vengeance on musket-less tribes, turning minor old feuds into major, genocidal wars. In a long set of **Musket Wars**, fought throughout the first half of the 1800s, musket-armed Maori used their superior technology to kill tens of thousands of musket-less Maori— perhaps as many as half of all the Maori in New Zealand.

CHURCH HISTORY FOCUS

MIGHTY MISSIONARIES: John Williams (1796 – 1839)

John Williams was a London-born metalworker who cared little for spiritual matters until the night of January 30, 1814. As the 17-year-old John stood in the street that Sunday evening waiting for some drinking buddies, a Christian friend stopped by to invite him to evening worship. More out of embarrassment than conviction, John went with his friend to church, where he heard a sermon based on these words of Christ from Matthew 16:24-27:

"Whoever wants to be my disciple must deny themselves and take up their cross and follow me. For whoever wants to save their life will lose it, but whoever loses their life for me will find it. What good will it be for someone to gain the whole world, yet forfeit their soul? Or what can anyone give in exchange for their soul? For the Son of Man is going to come in his Father's glory with his angels, and then he will reward each person according to what they have done."

From that moment forward, John Williams was determined to carry the gospel of Jesus Christ to the last unreached places on earth. In 1816, when he was still just 19 years old, John joined the London Missionary Society, which ordained him as a missionary to the Polynesian islands. The following year, John and his wife Mary Chawner Williams sailed for Tahiti, where earlier missionaries had already begun sharing the gospel.

Portrait of John Williams

What young John Williams lacked in education and experience, he supplied with energy and enthusiasm. Not content to minister on Tahiti alone, John used his metalworking skills to build two ships, *Messenger of Peace* and *Olive Branch*, to carry the gospel from island to island. Over the next 18 years, John ministered on island groups across a wide swath of Polynesia, including:

The Society Islands (largest island: Tahiti)	The Cook Islands (largest island: Raratonga)
The Samoan Islands (largest islands: Tutuila, Savai'i)	The Marquesas Islands (largest island: Nuku Hiva)

Williams' ministry was so successful that by 1834, when he returned to Britain to raise money for a new ship, he was able to report that every known island along a 2,100-mile line from Tahiti to Fiji had received at least some gospel preaching. Even better, many of these islands had thriving Christian churches.

TRAGIC TRUTHS: Infanticide and the *Arioi*

John Williams' close relationships with Polynesians taught him one reason why the Polynesian lifestyle seemed so carefree: because many Polynesians relieved themselves of a heavy burden by killing their own infants. Some of Williams' female converts reported killing 6, 9 or even 16 of their own babies, for all of these reasons:

- Because Polynesia's frequent wars made caring for infants both difficult and dangerous.

- Because some Polynesian men belonged to an elite warrior class called the *Arioi*. By custom, *Arioi* warriors killed every infant they fathered until they passed the age for constant fighting, and were ready to train warrior sons to take their places.

- Because upper-class Polynesian men, driven by a desire to keep their race pure, killed whatever infants they fathered with lower-class women.

- Because nursing and caring for infants made young women less attractive to men.

When John Williams taught these women a Christian understanding of God's nature, they were horrified at what they had done to their own children, and wondered how God could ever forgive them. Williams offered these grieving mothers the comfort of Paul's words in 1 Timothy 1:15:

"The John Williams Missionary Ship, 1845," painting by Australian artist R.B. Spencer

"Here is a trustworthy saying that deserves full acceptance: Christ Jesus came into the world to save sinners— of whom I am the worst."

John Williams saw Polynesian infanticide as an example of this universal truth:

"... in every place, and under all circumstances, men need the Gospel. Whether you find them upon the pinnacle of civilization, or in the vortex of barbarism; inhabiting the densely populated cities of the east, or roaming the wilds of an African wilderness; whether on the wide continent, or the fertile islands of the sea; surrounded by the icy barriers of the poles, or basking beneath a tropical sun; <u>all need the Gospel; and nothing but the Gospel can elevate them from the degradation into which they have been sunk by superstition and sin</u>. You may introduce among them the arts and sciences, and by these means refine their taste, and extend the sphere of their intellectual vision; you may convey to them our unrivalled constitution, modified and adapted to the peculiar circumstances, and thus throw a stronger safeguard around their persons and property, and elevate them from a state of barbarous vassalage, to the dignity and happiness of a free people; but if you withhold the Gospel, you leave them still under the dominion of a demoralizing and sanguinary superstition, aliens from God, and ignorant of the great scheme of redemption through his Son."

After returning from Britain to Polynesia in 1837, John Williams attempted to carry the gospel to a new island group called the New Hebrides, 2,800 miles west of Tahiti. There on the island of Erromango, part of what is now Vanuatu, John Williams paid for his faithfulness with his life. Finding the just-arrived John unarmed and helpless, a band of savage cannibals murdered the great missionary and ate his remains.

U.S. HISTORY FOCUS

Washington, District of Columbia

For the first 17 years after the Revolutionary War, the federal government moved from place to place. Congress' first move came after the **Pennsylvania Mutiny**, an alarming uprising by Continental soldiers who were furious with their government over lack of pay. The Pennsylvania Mutiny sent Congress fleeing from

Philadelphia, PA to Princeton, NJ in June 1783. From there, Congress moved to Annapolis, MD in November 1783; Trenton, NJ in November 1784; and then on to New York City, NY in January 1785.

New York City remained the capital of the United States through the Constitutional Convention, and then on through the ratification process. Federal Hall on Wall Street, NYC was the first U.S. capitol building under the new Constitution, and the site of George Washington's inauguration as first President of the United States on April 30, 1789.

The Compromise of 1790

The Constitution granted Congress the power to govern "such District (not exceeding ten Miles square) as may, by Cession of particular States… become the Seat of the Government of the United States." When the Constitution was ratified, though, no one knew where that district would be. Northerners hoped to keep the capital in the North, where it was; while Southerners hoped to coax the capital to a more central location, away from the corrupting influence of greedy Northern businessmen.

The negotiations that sent the capital south came in 1790, when first Secretary of the Treasury Alexander Hamilton needed votes to pass the Funding Act of 1790— a.k.a. the Assumption Bill. At

The U.S. Capitol under construction during the Civil War

the time, several Northern states still owed a great deal of Revolutionary War debt, and wanted the new federal government to assume that debt— in other words, take over payments on it. Meanwhile, the Southern states had already paid down most of their war debts, and were not at all eager to assume the North's. Because each side had something the other wanted, North and South compromised:

- The South agreed to vote for the Assumption Bill, spreading war costs more evenly across all the states.
- In exchange, the North agreed to vote for the **Residence Act of 1790**— the act that established Washington, D.C. as the permanent capital of the United States.

The Residence Act sent the seat of government to Philadelphia in 1790, where it was to remain until 1800— by which year President Washington was to have the new capital ready.

FASCINATING FACTS: Washington, D.C.

- The name "Washington" honors President Washington; while the name "Columbia" is an affectionate name for America in honor of Christopher Columbus.
- The Residence Act empowered President Washington to select and survey a 10-mile x 10-mile square district astride the Potomac River, on land that Virginia and Maryland promised to cede to the federal government.
- The original capital city was to occupy only a small part of the 100-square-mile District of Columbia. Partly because President Washington owned land on the Virginia side of the Potomac, the law required him to build the capital city on the Maryland side.
- In early 1791, Washington hired French-born architect Pierre Charles L'Enfant to design the capital city. The L'Enfant Plan called for a grid of north-south by east-west-running streets, interrupted by wider, diagonally-running "grand avenues" which met at important sites like the Capitol and the President's House.

- In accordance with the Residence Act, second President of the United States John Adams and his government moved from Philadelphia to Washington, D.C. on the first Monday of December 1800— even though the new capital was as yet nowhere near complete.

- Because the Virginia side of the District of Columbia suffered all the inconvenience of federal rule without any of the benefits of government offices, the people of the Virginia side later asked the federal government to return it to Virginia— which the government did in 1846. Most of the returned portion became Arlington County, VA.

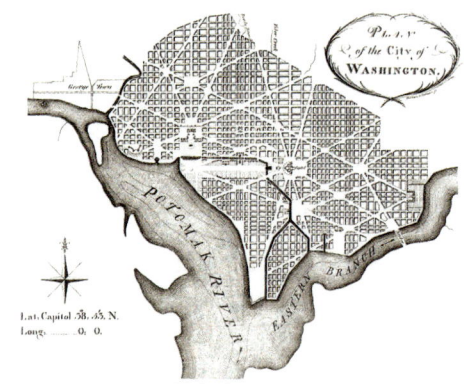

A 1792 version of the L'Enfant Plan

FASCINATING FACTS: The Washington Monument

Original sketch by Robert Mills  — *The unfinished monument in 1860*  — *Modern-day photo courtesy of David Iliff*

- After the Revolutionary War, the Continental Congress paid tribute to its victorious commander-in-chief by authorizing a statue of George Washington on horseback. Pierre L'Enfant's original plan for Washington D.C. included a place for this statue. In reviewing those plans, though, Washington humbly set the statue aside.

- Soon after Washington died in 1799, Congress resolved to build a marble mausoleum for the Father of the United States. For several reasons— including (1) a persistent lack of funds and (2) disagreements over the mausoleum's design— Congress never acted on this resolution.

- Beginning in 1832, the Washington National Monument Society laid plans to memorialize Washington with private funds. Three years later, architect Robert Mills won the Monument Society's design competition. Mills' design featured a 600-foot obelisk surrounded by a Roman-style colonnade, with a statue of Washington driving a chariot over the main entrance.

- Work on the obelisk portion began with a cornerstone-laying ceremony on July 4, 1848, using the same shovel that President Washington had used to begin work the U.S. Capitol. Unfortunately, the Monument Society went bankrupt in 1854, leaving the monument an unfinished eyesore for the next 22 years.

- The monument stood unfinished until 1876, when Congress and President Ulysses Grant authorized federal funds finish the obelisk only— scrapping Mills' colonnade. By this time, builders could find no marble to match the original, which explains why the monument's top two-thirds don't match its bottom one-third.

- Upon completion in 1884, the Washington Monument stood 555 feet tall, and 55 feet square at the base. To reach its top, visitors could either ride a steam-powered elevator or climb a total of 898 stairs.

- Until Paris erected its Eiffel Tower in 1889, the Washington Monument was the tallest building in the world.

PRESIDENTIAL FOCUS

PRESIDENT #1: George Washington (1732 – 1799)	
In Office: April 30, 1789 – March 4, 1797	**Political Party:** None
Birthplace: Virginia	**Nickname:** "Father of his Country"

As the great and humble hero of the Revolutionary War, George Washington was most Americans' first choice to become the first President of the United States. In the first presidential election, held from December 1788 – January 1789, every presidential elector from every state cast one of his two votes for Washington. The same happened in the election of 1792, in which Washington won his second term.

One of Washington's jobs as first president was to establish precedents— a list of dos and don'ts for later presidents to follow. Among the precedents Washington set were these:

- By taking frequent trips to visit all of the states— not just his home state, or the states of his home region, the South— Washington demonstrated that he was president of the whole United States. Holding the new union together was the highest goal of Washington's presidency.

- Washington carefully guarded the authority that the Constitution set aside for the executive branch of government— authority that some in Congress would have liked to seize for the legislative branch.

- By leaving office after two terms, Washington set a precedent that no president should remain in office for more than two terms— a precedent that every other president save one, Franklin Roosevelt, obeyed.

Fun Facts about George Washington:
- Washington was in his 50s when he finally lost all of his teeth save one, possibly due to his bad habit of using them to crack open Brazil nut shells. Dentists crafted Washington more than one set of dentures over the years. The materials they used probably included gold, lead, bone, human teeth, cow's teeth and ivory.
- By crossing male donkeys with female horses on his Mount Vernon farm, Washington produced the United States' first mules.
- Mount Vernon also operated a large distillery that produced whiskey, brandy and vinegar.

Notable Quotes from George Washington:
- "I do not think myself equal to the command I am honored with." — *after the Continental Congress named him overall commander of the new United States Army*
- "I can with truth assure you, I heard bullets whistle and believe me, there was something charming in the sound." — *after his first major battle, the 1754 Battle of Jumonville Glen*
- "In the discharge of this trust, I will only say that I have, with good intentions, contributed towards the organization and administration of the government the best exertions of which a very fallible judgment was capable." — *from his 1796 Farewell Address*

CHAPTER 25: The French Revolution

WORLD HISTORY FOCUS

> DEFINITIONS: The **French Revolution** of 1789 – 1799 was a decade-long upheaval in which France temporarily replaced its old government, the tyrannical *Ancien Régime*, with a republican government called the **First French Republic**. The Revolution's motto was *Liberté, égalité, fraternité*, French for "Liberty, Equality, Brotherhood."

> REFRESHING REMINDERS:
> - A **republic** is a state in which the people govern themselves through their elected representatives.
> - The **Age of Enlightenment** was an era when philosophers like Locke, Montesquieu, Rousseau and Voltaire taught the West new ways of thinking about government, religion and science.

The Age of Enlightenment, Part Two

In some ways, the French Revolution was much like the American Revolution; for both sprang from the changed thinking that came with the Age of Enlightenment. In both revolutions, freedom-loving citizens fought to replace their old, tyrannical monarchies with republican governments founded on the ideas of great thinkers like Montesquieu, Rousseau and Voltaire.

Charles-Louis de Secondat, Baron de Montesquieu, a.k.a. Montesquieu (1689 – 1755)

Montesquieu was a French philosopher who argued convincingly for **Separation of Powers**— the idea that the executive, legislative and judicial branches of any good government must always remain separate. In a 1748 treatise titled "The Spirit of the Laws," Montesquieu explained how power corrupts:

> "...experience shows us that every man invested with power is apt to abuse it, and to carry his authority as far as it will go..."

To limit this corruption, Montesquieu recommended "that power should be a check to power"— in other words, that each branch of government should have the power to restrain the other branches. For example, a fair-minded legislature should have power to block a tyrannical executive from enacting unfair laws. Some of the checks and balances built into the U.S. Constitution (see Chapter 23) come directly from Montesquieu's work.

Portrait of Baron de Montesquieu

Portrait of Rousseau

Jean-Jacques Rousseau (1712 – 1778)

Rousseau was the Geneva-born author of "The Social Contract," a 1762 political treatise that began with these revolution-inspiring words:

> "Man is born free; and everywhere he is in chains."

According to Rousseau, the reason for this sad state of affairs was not "that some are born for slavery, and others for dominion." Rather, it was that "force made the first slaves, and their cowardice perpetuated the condition"; for "slaves lose everything in their chains, even the desire of escaping from them." In other words, tyrants force people into slavery; and once enslaved, people grow too timid to take back their freedom.

Like John Locke, Rousseau insisted that when a government takes more power than its people willingly give, then the people have a right to overthrow that government:

> "Let us then admit that force does not create right, and that we are obliged to obey only legitimate powers."

Voltaire (1694 – 1778)

The French author Francois-Marie Arouet, better known by his pen name Voltaire, was among the most prolific writers ever to hold a pen. As an artist, Voltaire wrote novels, plays and poems; as a scholar, he wrote histories and scientific treatises; and as a correspondent, he wrote more than 20,000 letters. In everything he wrote, Voltaire's tremendous intelligence and humor shone.

Among the Enlightenment principles that Voltaire championed were some that later appeared in the U.S. Bill of Rights, including: (1) freedom of expression; (2) freedom of religion; and (3) separation of church and state.

Voltaire at work

The Dark Side of the Enlightenment

Unfortunately, Voltaire also championed some Enlightenment ideas that helped make the French Revolution much darker and deadlier than the American Revolution:

- **Voltaire was an unapologetic hedonist**, one who openly adopted personal pleasure as his highest goal. Under the tutelage of Voltaire and others, wealthy Frenchmen grew immoral and decadent, living extravagant lifestyles in all-out pursuit of happiness. Sadly, the luxuries of the wealthy came at the expense of the poor, who took terrible vengeance when the French Revolution began.

- **Voltaire was highly irreligious**— an atheist who scoffed at the Bible, and ridiculed the Catholic Church. Unlike Locke, Montesquieu and Rousseau, Voltaire had no use for organized religion, nor for its moral codes of moderation and self-denial. In Voltaire's opinion, reason was the highest authority, far higher than faith; and when he applied his critical reason to Bible and church, he judged both to be unreasonable. When wealthy churchmen failed to take the poor's side in the French Revolution, they confirmed Voltaire's scornful opinion of the church— leading to terrible vengeance against the church as well.

> INTERESTING IDEAS: Even though Montesquieu died nearly 25 years before the French Revolution began, his "Spirit of the Laws" included an explanation of the French Revolution's failures. According to Montesquieu, republicanism rests on the principle of equal opportunity for all. Therefore republican governments may fail for two reasons:
>
> 1. **Because their people stop believing in equal opportunity, and start placing their own personal good ahead of their country's good.** According to Montesquieu, this why the English Civil War failed, and why England restored its monarchy after Oliver Cromwell died: because the English didn't really believe in equality, but instead preferred their old system of aristocratic privilege.
>
> 2. **Because their people believe in equality so strongly that they no longer trust any government institution— not even the delegates they elect to represent them.** When this happens, "the people… want to manage everything themselves— to debate for the senate, to execute for the magistrate, and to decide for the judges." This second failure is the one that was to derail the French Revolution.

The French Revolution

Enlightenment Causes of the Revolution

Ironically, the French government wanted little to do with French thinkers' Enlightenment philosophy. All the while Montesquieu and Voltaire were championing enlightened principles like equal opportunity for all, separation of powers and separation of church and state, France's tyrannical *Ancien Régime* was stubbornly sticking to these principles' exact opposites.

Poor Frenchmen had the opposite reaction. Enlightenment philosophy taught poor Frenchmen to blame their wealthy government for all of these grievances:

- **Famine:** The years leading up to the French Revolution were years of poor harvests, which led to grain shortages, which in turn led to rising bread prices. In the Revolution's first year, 1789, a loaf of bread large enough to feed two people for one day might cost a poor laborer a full day's wages— leaving him with no money to pay for meat, vegetables, clothes or any other luxuries beyond daily bread.

- **Poverty:** Although France was one of the wealthiest nations in Europe, poor Frenchmen owned only a small fraction of that wealth. Roughly 60 percent of all French property belonged to either the royal family, the nobility or the Catholic Church— three institutions whose members added up to only about one percent of France's total population.

- **Callous Nobles:** In order to enjoy their great wealth and property, French nobles had to overlook an astonishing amount of famine and poverty. In the eyes of poor Frenchmen, few nobles cared less for the problems of the poor than Queen Marie Antoinette.

Portrait of King Louis XVI (reigned 1774 – 1792)

CALLOUS QUEENS: Marie Antoinette (1755 – 1793)

Princess Marie Antoinette was born in Vienna, Austria to Queen Maria Theresa of Austria, archenemy to Prussia's Frederick the Great. Because Austria and France were traditional enemies, an arranged marriage between an Austrian princess and the French *Dauphin* might have been unlikely if not for an unusual circumstance: the Diplomatic Revolution of 1756, the dramatic reversal of European alliances that fell just before the Seven Years' War (see Chapter 20). To cement its shaky alliance with Austria, France wedded its *Dauphin* Louis to Marie Antoinette in 1770. Four years later, King Louis XV died, and his grandson the *Dauphin* took his place as King Louis XVI— elevating Marie as his queen.

Both as princess and as queen, Marie had a bad reputation for spending lavish sums on needless luxuries for herself, while spending not a *sou* to ease the plight of starving Frenchmen all around her. Like many European nobles, Marie loved to gamble at cards and on horse races; and like most gamblers, she lost far more than she won.

Marie Antoinette in lavish coronation robes, 1775

Marie also overspent on pet projects at the Palace of Versailles; as well as on festive shopping trips to nearby Paris, where she purchased fantastic numbers of gowns, shoes and accessories for her trend-setting wardrobe.

Ironically, the two episodes for which poor Frenchmen blamed Marie Antoinette most probably weren't her fault.

1. The Diamond Necklace Affair: In 1772, King Louis XV asked a pair of Paris jewelers to craft an exceptional diamond necklace for his mistress. Unfortunately for the jewelers, the king had yet to pay them when he died in 1774, leaving them with a necklace so outrageously expensive that none but a royal could afford it. Naturally, the jewelers offered the necklace to the next queen, Marie Antoinette. For some reason, though, the usually-extravagant Marie wasn't interested— perhaps because the necklace was originally meant for another woman.

Years later, in 1784 – 1785, a wealthy noble and churchman named Cardinal de Rohan was looking for a way to win the queen's favor. Rohan's mistress Jeanne de la Motte, a devious courtier who claimed to be the queen's confidante, offered to help. Jeanne informed Rohan that the queen really wanted the matchless necklace that the late Louis XV had ordered for his mistress, but was afraid to buy such an extravagant gift for herself— for fear that if she did, then poor Frenchmen might despise her even more than they already did. What the queen needed, Jeanne said, was some wealthy courtier to buy the necklace in her place, thus concealing her extravagance from the poor. Jeanne assured Rohan that the man who blessed the queen in this way would earn her eternal gratitude.

To back up her lies, Jeanne produced convincing letters in which the queen supposedly promised to pay for the necklace gradually, over time. These letters all ended with forged signatures which, to Rohan's untrained eye, looked just like the queen's. To Rohan's delight, his con artist mistress even arranged for him to meet the queen herself one dark night. Unknown to Rohan, the well-dressed woman he believed to be the queen was in fact a paid lady of the evening.

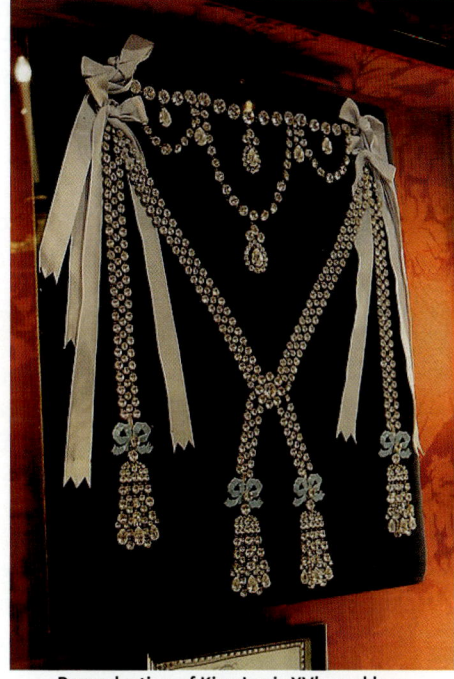

Reproduction of King Louis XV's necklace

Desperate to win the queen's favor, Cardinal Rohan approached the jewelers, who were just as desperate to avoid going bankrupt over the burdensome necklace. Duped by Jeanne's forged letters, the jewelers foolishly gave Rohan the necklace to give to the queen. Later, when the jewelers billed the queen for the unpaid balance on the necklace, the queen replied that she had received no necklace— which was true, as Jeanne's con artist husband had already broken it up and sold off its many diamonds one by one.

The irony of the Diamond Necklace Affair is that while Queen Marie Antoinette apparently bore none of the guilt, she received most of the blame. Even though the queen neither ordered the extravagant necklace nor paid for it, the tawdry episode nourished her reputation as a callous spendthrift who cared nothing for the poor.

2. "Let them eat cake": Upon hearing that many poor Frenchmen had no bread to eat, Marie Antoinette supposedly once responded, *"Qu'ils mangent de la brioche"*— often translated, "Then let them eat cake!" Because brioche is a pastry bread which costs far more than plain bread, such a remark would have meant that the queen neither knew nor cared how much poor Frenchmen struggled to feed themselves.

The irony of "Let them eat cake" is that Marie Antoinette may never have said what her critics claimed. Whether she did or not, though, poor Frenchmen believed she did, and took it as proof that their callous queen cared nothing for their plight.

Other Causes of the Revolution

Beyond famine, poverty and the arrogance of nobles like Marie Antoinette, the French Revolution had at least two more major causes:

1. **The American Revolution:** The fact that the American Revolution would have failed utterly without French aid was not lost on the French. After helping the newborn United States win liberty, equality and republican government, freedom-loving French soldiers like the Marquis de Lafayette longed to bestow these great gifts on their own country as well.

2. **Excessive Debt:** France's last two major wars, the Seven Years' War and the Revolutionary War, had left her deep in debt. A long chain of finance ministers tried to erase that debt by raising taxes on the nobility; but each time, the nobility refused to pay.

The Estates-General of 1789

Unable to pay off his treasury's enormous debts in any other way, King Louis XVI finally summoned an assembly that had not convened for more than 150 years: the Estates-General, a legislature that included representatives from the First, Second and Third Estates.

> DEFINITIONS:
> - Although the medieval era was long over by the 1780s, France still organized its citizens into three medieval-era classes called **Estates of the Realm**. Like other Catholic nations, France ranked these estates according to their distance from God: The **First Estate** represented the clergy; the **Second Estate** represented the nobility; and the **Third Estate** represented all others, from professional lawyers and doctors to the poorest of the poor.
> - The **Estates-General** of France was a legislature composed of representatives from the First, Second and Third Estates. Only the representatives of the Third Estate were elected by the people; all others won their places through either high birth or appointment by the king.

> INTERESTING IDEAS:
> - In theory, French kings needed the Estates-General's permission to raise taxes. In practice, though, the Estates-General was so pitifully weak that no French king had bothered to assemble one since 1614.
> - Since the 1780s, historians have also recognized a **Fourth Estate** that sends no representatives to any legislature, yet still may wield tremendous influence over a legislature's decisions: the press.

Louis XVI's hope in summoning the Estates-General was that this long-silent legislature could accomplish what his finance ministers could not— that it could force the First and Second Estates to shoulder their fair share of France's tax burden.

To the king's dismay, the Estates-General that he summoned in May 1789 behaved just like the Long Parliament that Charles I of

The Estates-General in session at the Palace of Versailles, May 5, 1789

England assembled back in 1640 (see Chapter 8): instead of discussing taxes, the Estates-General wanted to discuss its rights. In particular, the elected representatives of the Third Estate wanted to be sure that the privileged representatives of the First and Second Estates couldn't automatically outvote them on every important issue. The Third Estate's stubbornness on this matter required an immediate decision on how the Estates-General should count its votes:

1. If the Estates-General chose to count votes by the man, then the Third Estate stood an excellent chance of getting its way; for the representatives of the Third Estate numbered about 600, compared to about 300 for each of the other two. Enlightenment-minded Frenchmen considered this the only fair way to count votes.

2. If, on the other hand, the Estates-General chose to count votes by the estate, then the First and Second Estates could automatically win every vote by a two-thirds majority— which meant that the privileged 1 percent of Frenchmen could continue their tyranny over the underprivileged 99 percent, just as if the Enlightenment had never happened.

Until it reached an agreement on this critical voting issue, the Estates-General could accomplish nothing. The First and Second Estates spent most of a month scheming to preserve their extraordinary privileges of wealth, power and freedom from taxation. The Third Estate spent that same month absorbing the passionate arguments of Abbe Sieyes, enlightened author of the political pamphlet "What is the Third Estate?"

ILLUMINATING EXCERPTS from "What is the Third Estate?" by Abbe Sieyes

Abbe Sieyes was a churchman who was born into the First Estate, but whose passionate defense of commoners' rights won him election to the 1789 Estates-General as a representative of the Third Estate. Around election time, Sieyes published a revolutionary pamphlet in which he asked, "What is the Third Estate?" The answer, Sieyes said, was that "the third estate is a complete nation." In other words, the Third Estate did all of the nation's work— even the work of governing— while the lazy, parasitic First and Second Estates reaped all the benefits:

"... who is bold enough to maintain that the Third Estate does not contain within itself everything needful to constitute a complete nation? It is like a strong and robust man with one arm still in chains. If the privileged order were removed, then the nation would not be something less, but rather something more. What then is the Third Estate? All; but an all that is fettered and oppressed. What would it be without the privileged order? It would still be all; but it would also be free and flourishing. Nothing would go well without the Third Estate; everything would go considerably better without the other two."

Cartoon depicting a poor Third Estate laborer carrying a First Estate clergyman and a Second Estate nobleman on his back

Sieyes also asked, "What should have been done [about France's tax difficulties]"? The answer, Sieyes wrote, was that the people should have written a constitution for a new government, just as the Americans did in 1787:

"If we have no constitution, then it must be made, and only the nation [i.e., the Third Estate] has the right to make it."

The National Assembly (June 1789)

After a month's fruitless negotiations with the other two estates, the Third Estate finally took matters into its own hands. In early June, the representatives of the Third Estate declared that the time had come to do the work the king called the Estates-General to do— and that if the other two estates wanted to take part in that work, then they had better join in the Third Estate's meetings. Even though fewer than ten clergymen answered its call at first, the Third Estate plunged ahead with its meetings.

As of mid-June 1789, this mixed body announced that it was no longer the Estates-General. Rather, it was the **National Assembly**— a new national legislature/constitutional convention that represented every Frenchman, regardless of his estate. Although the new National Assembly professed loyalty to King Louis XVI, it issued this bold announcement without the king's approval, just as if France had no king.

A LOOK AHEAD: The National Assembly is only the first of six different assemblies that will govern France over the fifteen years from 1789 – 1804:

Assembly	Dates	Assembly	Dates
1. National Assembly	June – July 1789	2. National Constituent Assembly	July 1789 – Sep 1791
3. Legislative Assembly	Oct 1791 – Sep 1792	4. National Convention	Sep 1792 – Nov 1795
5. French Directory	Nov 1795 – Nov 1799	6. French Consulate	Nov 1799 – May 1804

At the end of those 15 years, First Consul Napoleon Bonaparte will proclaim himself Emperor of France.

FASCINATING FACTS: The Tennis Court Oath (June 20, 1789)

To a firm believer in the Divine Right of Kings like Louis XVI, the proclamation of a National Assembly looked like an assault on his God-given authority. Louis was determined to protect his authority, but also hoped to avoid an ugly confrontation with the already-furious Third Estate; so he decided to attempt a ruse.

When the members of National Assembly arrived for their usual meeting on the morning of June 20, 1789, guards regretfully informed them that there could be no meeting that day— for their usual meeting place, the Hall of State at the Palace of Versailles, was under construction that day. Inside the hall, a carpentry crew was already banging away, hard at work preparing the room for an upcoming speech.

Undeterred by the king's feeble trick, the National Assembly simply reconvened at a nearby indoor tennis court, where its members swore the following **Tennis Court Oath**:

Elected representatives of the Third Estate swearing the Tennis Court Oath

"The National Assembly, regarding itself as called upon to establish the constitution of the kingdom, effect a regeneration of the state and maintain the true principles of monarchy, may not be prevented from continuing its deliberations in whatever place it may be forced to take up its sittings. Maintaining further, that wherever its members are assembled, there is the National Assembly, the assembly decrees that all its members shall immediately take a solemn oath never to separate, and to come together wherever circumstances may dictate until the constitution of the kingdom shall be established and placed upon a firm foundation." *In other words: The National Assembly agreed to meet wherever it had to, never stopping until it accomplished the goal it set for itself: writing a fair, enlightened new constitution for France.*

A few days after the Tennis Court Oath, the king tried the more direct approach of ordering the National Assembly to disperse. In response, Assembly spokesman Honoré Mirabeau defiantly warned the officer who delivered the order:

"Go and tell those who sent you that we are here by the power of the people, and that we are only to be driven out by that of the bayonet!"

Anger in Paris (July 1789)

While all this was going on in Versailles, nearby Paris was launching a revolution of its own. In public houses, gardens and street corners all over the city, angry citizens were gathering to hear speechmakers deliver scathing criticisms of France's old, unfair government, and to discuss the latest news of the new government in Versailles. In particular, Parisians were watching for signs that the king was planning to take Mirabeau's defiant suggestion literally, and drive out the National Assembly at the point of the bayonet.

As June gave way to July, Parisians saw two signs that the king was preparing to do just that:

1. Fearing that his native French troops might be reluctant to attack their own countrymen, the king started positioning foreign mercenary units from Switzerland and Germany near Versailles and Paris.

2. On July 11, the king abruptly dismissed Jacques Necker, a finance minister whom the Third Estate had come to see as its champion in the king's administration.

Upon hearing of Necker's dismissal, a revolutionary pamphleteer named Camille Desmoulins leapt upon a table outside Paris' *Palais Royal* and cried, "Citizens, there is no time to lose! ...this very night all the Swiss and German battalions will... massacre us all! Only one tactic remains: to take arms!"

Inspired by Desmoulins' passionate speech, angry revolutionary mobs started roaming the streets of Paris, gathering arms with which to fight off the king's mercenaries. The French army's reaction to these mobs was mixed: some units scuffled with them, while others joined them.

The Storming of the Bastille (July 14, 1789)

Over the next few days, these mixed revolutionary/military mobs managed to gather plenty of muskets, but little gunpowder. In search of gunpowder, they turned their attention to a stronghold that was sure to be well-stocked with it: the Bastille.

FASCINATING FACTS: The Bastille

The **Bastille** was an 8-towered stone fortress built in the 1300s to guard Paris' eastern gate, the *Porte Saint-Antoine*. For centuries, French kings had also used the Bastille for a second purpose: as a prison for their political enemies, many of whom received lifetime sentences without ever appearing before a judge. One such prisoner was the Man in the Iron Mask, the mysterious enemy of King Louis XIV who died at the Bastille in 1703 (see Chapter 9).

Thus to the revolutionaries who roamed the streets of Paris in July 1789, the Bastille was much more than a fortress well-stocked with arms. It was also a powerful symbol of everything that was wrong with France's government— a miserable dungeon where arrogant nobles could lock up their political enemies forever without trial, as if Frenchmen possessed none of the natural rights that the Enlightenment guaranteed to all.

On the morning of July 14, 1789, a revolutionary mob nearly 1,000 strong gathered outside the Bastille, hoping to break through the old fortress's gates and seize its cache of gunpowder. Standing guard inside were about 100 veteran defenders, well-armed but otherwise ill-prepared for a siege.

Hoping to hold out until more help could arrive, the officers inside the Bastille tried negotiating with the mob; but the mob would accept nothing less than full, unconditional surrender. Meanwhile, the Bastille's defenders started firing on mob members to keep them from breaking in. As the day wore on, the number of dead revolutionaries outside the Bastille climbed to nearly 100.

At around 3:00 in the afternoon, more experienced soldiers arrived to join forces with the furious mob, bringing with them small cannon to break down the Bastille's stout wooden gates. Seeing that the Bastille could not hold out for long, and perhaps hoping for mercy from the mob, the soldiers inside finally lowered a drawbridge and opened a gate— at which the mob instantly flooded inside, seized the Bastille's officers and dragged them outside. Later, the mob executed the officers, cut off their heads and skewered them on pikes— foreshadowing many more beheadings to come.

"The Storming of the Bastille" by artist Jean-Pierre Houël

Other interesting facts:
- Over the months that followed the Storming of the Bastille, revolutionaries completely leveled the old prison, leaving not one stone standing on another to remind them of their oppressive old government.
- Modern-day Frenchmen still celebrate July 14 as **Bastille Day**, the day their ancestors broke the chains of tyranny.

The Great Fear (July – August 1789)

The Storming of the Bastille released a flood of chaos and violence far beyond Paris. All over France, angry mobs plundered manor houses and monasteries, burning and tearing down symbols of the old government that had oppressed them for so long. Most nobles and churchmen responded to the **Great Fear** in one of two ways:

Painting of the Fête de la Fédération, a celebration in honor of France's first Bastille Day

1. When it became clear that the king was powerless, and that the National Assembly was the only power angry mobs would respect, many representatives of the First and Second Estates reluctantly joined the National Assembly.

2. Others fled the country to form *Armée des Émigrés*— **Emigrant Armies** led by angry nobles and churchmen who plotted to re-invade France and take back what they had lost.

The August Decrees (August 11, 1789) and the Declaration of the Rights of Man (August 26, 1789)

Having established itself as France's highest authority, the National Assembly— which, in mid-July, renamed itself the National Constituent Assembly— set about redesigning the nation's government. To reassure angry mobs that their new government would be fairer than the old, the Assembly issued the **August Decrees**, a set of nineteen laws that went a long way toward dismantling the nobility. For example:

- Article One abolished France's old feudal system— which meant, among other things, that the August Decrees immediately freed hundreds of thousands of French serfs from their noble lords.

- Article Eleven declared all citizens to be equally qualified for any government office or military rank— regardless of whether they were born rich or poor, noble or commoner.

Two weeks later, the National Assembly approved the **Declaration of the Rights of Man and Citizen**, an affirmation of basic human rights that was to become as important to France as the Declaration of Independence is to the United States.

ILLUMINATING EXCERPTS from the Declaration of the Rights of Man and Citizen (Approved August 26, 1789)

Like the Declaration of Independence, the Declaration of the Rights of Man begins with a preamble that describes its purpose:

"The representatives of the French people, organized as a National Assembly, believing that the ignorance, neglect, or contempt of the rights of man are the sole cause of public calamities and of the corruption of governments, have determined to set forth in a solemn declaration the natural, unalienable, and sacred rights of man, in order that this declaration, being constantly before all the members of the social body, shall remind them continually of their rights and duties…"

After the preamble, the Declaration lists seventeen of the Enlightenment ideals for which the French were fighting their Revolution, including these:

Article 1: "Men are born and remain free and equal in rights…"

Article 2: "…these rights are liberty, property, security and resistance to oppression."

Article 6: "Law is the expression of the general will. Every citizen has a right to participate personally, or through his representative, in its foundation. It must be the same for all, whether it protects or punishes. All citizens, being equal in the eyes of the law, are equally eligible to all dignities and to all public positions and occupations, according to their abilities, and without distinction except that of their virtues and talents." *In other words*: In choosing people to fill government jobs, the government must base its hiring decisions on a candidate's virtues and talents alone, never on high birth or rank.

Article 10: No one shall be disquieted on account of his opinions, including his religious views, provided their manifestation does not disturb the public order established by law.

Article 11: The free communication of ideas and opinions is one of the most precious of the rights of man. Every citizen may, accordingly, speak, write, and print with freedom, but shall be responsible for such abuses of this freedom as shall be defined by law.

The Women's March on Versailles (October 5 – 6, 1789)

After a string of revolutionary victories from June – August 1789, the French Revolution slowed in September. As the Revolution slowed, some citizens of the Third Estate began to grow suspicious of their new government in Versailles, for a couple of reasons:

- Because in the process of drafting a new constitution for France, the National Constituent Assembly granted the king power to veto new laws. Although the executive veto was one of the checks and balances that Montesquieu had approved, radical revolutionaries like Jean-Paul Marat— author of the influential newspaper *L'Ami du people*, "The Friend of the People"— insisted that no unelected noble should have the power to overrule the people's elected representatives.

- Because as inspiring as the Declaration of the Rights of Man was, it did nothing to lower bread prices. Poor Frenchmen remained just as hungry under the new government as they had been under the old.

On the morning of October 5, 1789, a band of angry Parisian women decided to carry their complaints about the high price of bread to the new government at Versailles. By beating drums, ringing church bells and delivering rousing speeches, these women were able to raise a mixed mob thousands strong within just a few hours. Arming itself first with kitchen knives, then with pikes, swords and even a few cannon, this revolutionary mob marched the twelve miles from Paris to Versailles to demand bread and sympathy from their king.

Scene from the Women's March on Versailles

At first, it appeared that Louis XVI might weather the storm of the Women's March on Versailles unscathed— for the pantries of Versailles were bursting with food, and Louis was a charming fellow. By sharing his food and pretending to believe in the Revolution's ideals, Louis persuaded part of the mob to go back to Paris.

The rest of the mob, though, was not so easily convinced— for some had not forgotten their disdain for the king's spendthrift wife Marie Antoinette. Early the next morning, this skeptical remnant of the Women's March burst into the palace and started hunting for the queen's apartments, curious to know what she thought of their Revolution. Caught by surprise, the alarmed queen fled her apartments and raced through the palace halls barefoot, even as guards behind her sacrificed their lives to save hers.

1860 photo of Tuileries Palace, King Louis XVI's virtual prison from 1789 – 1793

According to some storytellers, the queen pounded on her husband's apartment door for several anxious minutes before the king finally heard her over the din of the mob and let her in.

In the end, the only way the new government could satisfy the angry mob was by moving from Versailles to Paris, where revolutionaries could keep both the royal family and the National Constituent Assembly under their watchful eyes. The royal family moved into Paris' **Tuileries Palace**, an old palace that was connected to the even older Louvre Palace— the same palace that now houses Paris' Louvre Museum.

At the Tuileries, the royals became more or less prisoners. The queen had so little authority in her own home that she couldn't even order male revolutionary guards out of her rooms at night. As for the National Constituent Assembly, it found new accommodations inside the *Salle du Manège*, a former horseback riding school on the Tuileries Palace grounds.

FASCINATING FLAGS: The Tricolor Cockade

The tricolor cockade was a blue, white and red rosette that decorated French revolutionaries' **Phrygian caps**— simple stocking caps that had symbolized liberty since ancient Greek times.

Adopted in the early days of the French Revolution— when most revolutionaries still hoped to remake France as a constitutional monarchy— the tricolor cockade combined the white flag of France's Bourbon kings with the blue-and-red flag of Paris. In 1794, revolutionary France adopted the cockade's colors for its new national flag, the same tricolor flag France flies today.

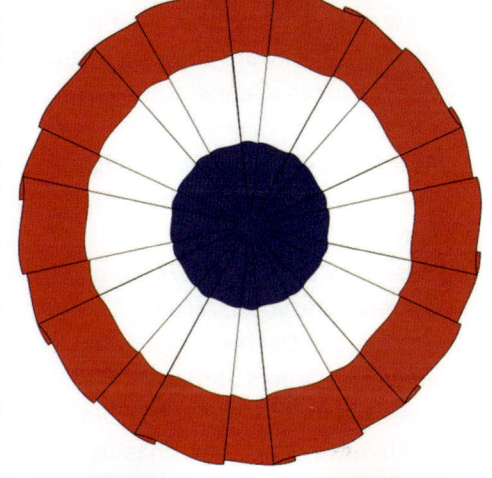

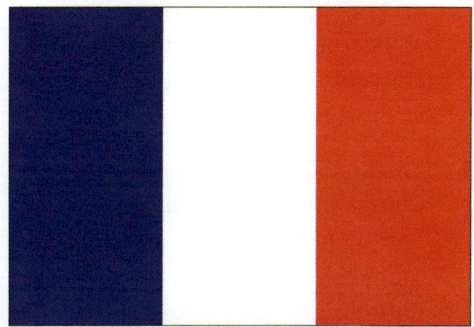

French revolutionaries wearing tricolor cockades on their Phrygian caps

The De-Christianization of France (1789 – 1790)

In the process of tearing down their nobility, French revolutionaries also tore down another too-privileged institution: the French Catholic Church. Although poorer churchmen tended to support the Revolution, wealthier ones had two tempting reasons to support the *Ancien Régime*:

1. Because the regime had made them wealthy.
2. Because the Revolution defied both God and the pope— two authorities that churchmen considered higher than any earthly government.

Notre Dame Cathedral on the *Île de la Cité*, Paris

The Catholic Church's decision to side with the *Ancien Régime* made it one of the French Revolution's biggest enemies.

Before the Revolution, churchmen received their incomes from two main sources: (1) **tithes**, forced donations that the law required all Frenchmen to pay; and (2) **rents** earned from church-owned property. Early in the Revolution, the National Constituent Assembly attacked both of these income sources:

1. To ease the suffering of the poor, the August Decrees (see above) abolished forced tithes.

2. A November 1789 decree seized all Church rental properties for the government. Instead of lining the pockets of wealthy churchmen, rent from these properties went to fund the new government, becoming the basis of a new national currency called the *Assignat*.

As Voltaire's Enlightenment philosophy took hold of France, revolutionaries began to resent the Church in a new way— not only as a parasite whose corrupt bishops fattened themselves off the Third Estate's labor, but also as a backward-thinking institution whose ideals were completely incompatible with the Revolution. With these ideas in mind, the Assembly issued even harsher decrees against the Church:

- **The Decree Suppressing Religious Orders (February 1790):** In October 1789, the Assembly received a report that a nearby convent had forced two women to take nun's vows against their will— a blatant violation of these citizens' liberties. The Assembly's response was to ban all monastic vows. All over France, the Decree Suppressing Religious Orders abruptly released monks and nuns from their vows of poverty, chastity and obedience. This decree also shuttered all monasteries and convents that didn't operate schools or hospitals.

- **The Civil Constitution of the Clergy:** In July 1790, the Assembly took over management of the French Catholic Church— essentially making it an independent state church, much as England had done in creating the Anglican Church 250 years before. The Civil Constitution of the Clergy decreed that the people of France, not the pope, would choose their Church's bishops. Furthermore, it required all churchmen to swear oaths "to be loyal to the nation, the law, and the king, and to support… the constitution decreed by the National Assembly and accepted by the king." In other words, French churchmen were to obey the government of France, not the pope of Rome.

Fanciful illustration of monks and nuns joyously hugging one another after the National Constituent Assembly freed them from their vows of chastity

The *Fête de la Fédération* (July 14, 1790)

Louis XVI's confinement at Tuileries Palace placed the charming king in a difficult situation. To avoid angering the Paris revolutionaries who watched him and his wife day and night, Louis had to pretend to believe in the ideals of the Revolution—Enlightenment ideals like representative government, equal opportunity and equality under the law. At a grand party called the *Fête de la Fédération*— a Celebration of the Union held on the first anniversary of the Storming of the Bastille, July 14, 1790— the king made a fine show of swearing the following oath before a cheering crowd:

"I, King of the French, swear to use the power given to me by the constitutional law of the State, to maintain the Constitution as decided by the National Assembly… and to enforce the laws."

Marie Antoinette won cheers as well by presenting to the crowd her 5-year-old son, the future Louis XVII, and swearing a similar oath: "This is my son, who, like me, joins in the same sentiments."

On the other hand, the king still held out hope that some ally might rescue him from these mad revolutionaries— most of whom, he suspected, were only waiting for the right moment to execute him, just as the English had executed Charles I. Louis' hopes rested on some combination of three possibilities:

1. That the noble Emigrant Army (see above), the one that fled France during the Great Fear, might return to claim its property from upstart revolutionaries.

2. That his queen's home country, Austria, might invade France— perhaps to rescue its daughter Marie Antoinette; perhaps to keep unwanted revolutionary ideas from spreading beyond France; or perhaps to seize French territory.

3. That certain units of France's Royal Army might remain loyal to their king.

The Flight to Varennes (June 20 – 21, 1791)

Acting on the third possibility, Louis XVI made the fateful decision to flee France for the safety of Austria. On the night of June 20 – 21, 1791, Louis disguised his children's governess as a Russian noblewoman traveling home from Paris; his children as the governess' children; his wife and sister as the governess' maids; and himself as the governess' lackey. His disguises complete, Louis loaded his family aboard a horse-drawn coach and headed east for Montmedy, France, where loyalist troops were waiting to help him on to Austria.

Unfortunately for Louis, a revolutionary postmaster recognized him when he stopped to change horses, and rushed ahead to report what he had seen. At the town of Varennes-en-Argonne— about 120 miles northeast of Paris, and only about 30 miles southwest of Montmedy— revolutionaries captured the fleeing royals and escorted them back to the Tuileries.

The king's failed **Flight to Varennes** destroyed what little trust revolutionaries still placed in him. Before the flight, some revolutionaries still believed the glib oath that Louis had sworn at the *Fête de la Fédération*— the one in

The disguised royal family of King Louis XVI captured at Varennes-en-Argonne

which he claimed to support the Revolution. After the flight, though, most revolutionaries understood that Louis despised the Revolution, and had only been waiting for the right moment to betray them.

The Constitution of 1791 and the Legislative Assembly

Meanwhile, the National Constituent Assembly carried on with its main business: negotiating a new constitution for France. Two political parties dominated these negotiations:

1. The **Jacobins**, so named because they met in a former Jacobin (French Dominican) monastery. The Jacobins were the Revolution's strongest supporters, radicals who wanted their new constitution to give France's king little or no power.

2. The **Feuillants**, also named for the former monastery where they met. The Feuillants were more moderate revolutionaries who wanted France to adopt a constitutional monarchy like Britain's.

In September 1791, France finally adopted its first written constitution, the **Constitution of 1791**. To Jacobins' delight, this constitution adopted as its preamble the Declaration of the Rights of Man and Citizen, the affirmation of basic human rights the Assembly had adopted back in August 1789.

To some Jacobins' dismay, though, the Constitution of 1791 also granted France's unelected king a great deal of power over the people's elected representatives. Although the king could not dissolve France's new legislature, which the Constitution named the **Legislative Assembly**, the king did receive power:

- To veto decrees passed by the Legislative Assembly.
- To choose his own department heads, without the bother of consulting the Legislative Assembly.
- To appoint his own military commanders, again without consulting the Legislative Assembly.

In some Jacobins' minds, the Constitution of 1791 gave the king almost as much power as if the Revolution had never happened.

After the Legislative Assembly convened for the first time in October 1791, two sub-groups of the radical Jacobins emerged to vie with one another for power:

Portrait of Montagnard leader Jean-Paul Marat

1. The **Girondists**, named for a region of southwestern France called the Gironde. The Girondists were less-radical Jacobins who were willing to work with the king under the Constitution of 1791.

2. The **Montagnards**, named for the high seats (the "mountain") they occupied in the Assembly's meeting hall. The Montagnards were more-radical Jacobins who wanted to dispense with constitutional monarchy, and instead have a pure republican government with no king at all.

The French Revolutionary Wars, Part One

The Beginning (April 1792)

The more radical the Revolution's ideals grew, the more France's neighbors worried that those ideals might spread beyond France, threatening neighboring monarchies and churches. To prevent this, Austria and Prussia formed the beginnings of the **First Coalition**, a military alliance designed to protect the rest of Europe from revolutionary France. In the **Declaration of Pillnitz**, issued on August 27, 1791, Austria and Prussia called upon all European monarchies to help Louis XVI reclaim his throne, promising to be ready whenever the rest of Europe decided to act.

Instead of waiting for the First Coalition to strike, revolutionary France struck first. In April 1792, France launched the French Revolutionary Wars with an attack on the Austrian Netherlands, a southern region of the Netherlands that Austria had controlled since 1714.

Lacking inspiration for this first attack, the French army failed miserably, with disorganized troops fleeing before their battles even began.

In response to this failed invasion, the First Coalition built a joint Austrian-Prussian army under the command of Charles William Ferdinand, Duke of Brunswick. As he prepared to invade France in July 1792, the Duke of Brunswick issued a public proclamation that would provide all the inspiration the French needed.

ILLUMINATING EXCERPTS from the Brunswick Manifesto (issued July 25, 1792)

The Brunswick Manifesto began by listing the purposes of the Duke's invasion, which included these:

"… to put an end to the anarchy in the interior of France; to check the attacks upon the throne and the altar; to reestablish the legal power; to restore to the king the security and the liberty of which he is now deprived; and to place him in a position to exercise once more the legitimate authority which belongs to him."

Brunswick also declared his certainty that the "sane portion" of the French public would be eager to join him in overthrowing France's "oppressors," the leaders of the French Revolution. To reassure France of his invasion's good intentions, Brunswick promised that Austria and Prussia had "no other aims than the welfare of France, and… no intention of enriching themselves by conquests."

To the great ire of French revolutionaries, the Brunswick Manifesto also included these grave threats against any and all Frenchmen who dared to stand in the First Coalition's way:

Portrait of the Duke of Brunswick

- "… the inhabitants of the towns and villages who may dare to defend themselves… shall be punished immediately according to the most stringent laws of war, and their houses shall be burned or destroyed…"
- "… if the least violence be offered to their Majesties the king, queen, and royal family… they will inflict an ever-memorable vengeance by delivering over the city of Paris to… complete destruction…"

Thanks to these belligerent threats, the Brunswick Manifesto's real results turned out to be the opposites of its intended ones:

1. Instead of frightening the French, the Brunswick Manifesto inspired them to defend their homeland more determinedly than ever before. In response to Brunswick's threats, the king's Girondist defense minister proposed to create a new army of volunteer soldiers from all over France. These volunteers, called **fédérés**, would gather in Paris, where they would receive arms and training before marching out to face Brunswick.
2. Instead of saving Louis XVI, the Brunswick Manifesto inspired French revolutionaries to even greater hatred of their king, who probably hoped that Brunswick's invasion would succeed.

Despite their anger over the Brunswick Manifesto, French revolutionaries did nothing worse to their king than threaten him— that is, until they heard "La Marseillaise" for the first time.

ALARMING ANTHEMS: "La Marseillaise"

With war threatening France in mid-1792, French soldier-composer Claude Rouget de Lisle wrote an anthem that he hoped would inspire his countrymen to resist the invading armies of Prussia and Austria. The bloody lines of Rouget's lyric include some that may be translated:

"Do you hear, in the countryside / The howling of those fearsome soldiers?
They're coming into your arms / To cut the throats of your sons and women!
To arms, citizens! / Form your battalions! / March, march! / Let our enemies' impure blood water our furrows!"

> A LOOK AHEAD: "La Marseillaise" will become so popular that in 1795, the First French Republic will adopt the song as its national anthem. This same song is also the anthem of the Fifth French Republic, which governs France as of 2014.

A-rise, chil-dren of the Fa-ther-land, the day of Glo-ry has ar-rived!

The Revolution of 10 August (August 10, 1792) and the National Convention

"La Marseillaise" reached Paris at a dark time for the French Revolution. In the eleven months after France adopted the Constitution of 1791, revolutionaries amassed a long list of grievances against their new constitutional monarchy, including these:

1. The French Revolutionary Wars were going badly for France— probably, some Frenchmen believed, because their king wanted them to go badly. After the Flight to Varennes, revolutionaries suspected Louis XVI of plotting against them with his foreign allies. As if to confirm their suspicions, the Duke of Brunswick was now invading France with the stated goal of rescuing Louis.

2. The king was making frequent use of a power that many revolutionaries felt he shouldn't even possess: the veto power granted him by the Constitution of 1791. In particular, the king vetoed his defense minister's proposal to create a new army of *fédérés*, leading revolutionaries to wonder— did their king really want to defend France? Or was he secretly, treacherously hoping that Brunswick's invasion would succeed? In the end, the king's reasons didn't matter— for despite his veto, tens of thousands of *fédérés* gathered in Paris to answer his defense minister's call.

In fact, Louis may have had a simpler reason for vetoing his defense minister's proposal: because he suspected that these volunteer *fédérés* might turn against him. On August 10, 1792, the very day they heard "La Marseillaise" for the first time, the *fédérés* did just what the king feared: they marched on Tuileries Palace to overthrow France's year-old constitutional monarchy.

Upon seeing their revolutionary comrades up in arms, most of the regular army troops assigned to

"The Taking of the Tuileries" by French artist Henri-Paul Motte

guard the king abandoned him— leaving fewer than 1,000 Swiss mercenaries to defend the Tuileries against some 20,000 *fédérés*. As Louis fled across the palace grounds toward the protection of the Legislative Assembly, his Swiss Guards fired on the advancing *fédérés*, killing scores of them. Now truly outraged that these foreign mercenaries had dared to kill loyal Frenchmen in their very capital, the *fédérés* stormed the Tuileries, massacring Swiss Guards by the hundreds. About 600 of the Swiss Guards died, and another 200 became prisoners; the rest managed to escape by shedding their uniforms and blending into the crowd.

From the sack of the Tuileries forward, no moderate Feuillants interfered with the radical Jacobins' authority. Within a few weeks after the Revolution of 10 August, the Jacobins and their militant allies, the *fédérés*:

1. Suspended the constitutional monarchy, stripping the king of his powers under the Constitution of 1791.
2. Moved the royal family from the ransacked Tuileries Palace to far harsher accommodations: the **Temple**, a dreary fortress prison similar to the old Bastille.
3. Overthrew the year-old Legislative Assembly, replacing it with a new legislature called the **National Convention**.

The September Massacres of 1792

After the Revolution of 10 August, the *fédérés* who had just stormed the Tuileries prepared to march east against the Duke of Brunswick. Before they left, though, they wanted to ensure that their enemies couldn't seize Paris while they were gone. To prevent this, the *fédérés* started hunting down and slaughtering every Parisian who had ever uttered a negative word against the Revolution, especially those locked inside Paris' prisons. Among the **September Massacres'** hundreds of victims were:

- Feuillants, the moderate politicians who had worked with King Louis XVI under the Constitution of 1791.
- The survivors from the Swiss Guard who had tried to defend the royal family at the Tuileries.
- Churchmen and women who refused to swear loyalty to France under the Civil Constitution of the Clergy.
- Princess Marie Louise of Savoy, a close personal friend of Marie Antoinette's whose only crime was refusing to swear that she hated the king and queen.

DEADLY DEVICES: The Guillotine

Some of the September Massacres' victims lost their heads on the **guillotine**, a beheading device that was soon to become the most-recognized symbol of the French Revolution.

The guillotine took its name from Joseph-Ignace Guillotin, a French physician and member of the National Assembly who actually opposed the death penalty. In October 1789, Guillotin proposed to the Assembly that if France's enlightened new government still found it necessary to execute criminals, then it should at least execute them more mercifully than the oppressive *Ancien Régime* did— for the regime still favored medieval-style torture devices like the breaking wheel. On Guillotin's advice, the National Assembly assembled a committee to develop some simple mechanical device that would render beheadings as quick and painless as possible.

The committee based the design of its guillotine on earlier devices that dropped heavy blades on their victims' necks. Where other devices used straight blades, though, the guillotine used a 45° angled blade. The advantage of the angle was that the blade sliced cleanly as it fell, like a straight sword swiped skillfully across the neck.

Unfortunately for its victims, the guillotine could also be as clumsy as an axe— especially if the executioner allowed his blade to grow dull, or its tracks dirty. During the Reign of Terror (see below), wealthy families often bribed their loved ones' executioners to make sure their guillotines were sharp and clean.

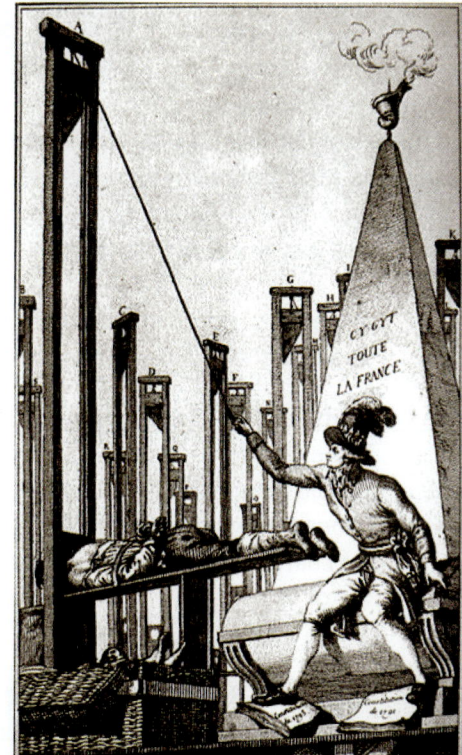

Caricature of Montagnard leader Maximilien de Robespierre overusing France's many guillotines

The Abolition of the Monarchy and the Founding of the First French Republic (September 21, 1792)

Meanwhile, the new National Convention convened for the first time on September 20, 1792. The very next day, the radical Jacobins finally accomplished what they had been trying to do all along: with the **Proclamation of the Abolition of the Monarchy**, the National Convention removed Louis XVI from office, and set to work replacing France's year-old constitutional monarchy with a pure republican government.

INTERESTING IDEAS: The Proclamation of the Abolition of the Monarchy marks the beginning of the **First French Republic**, the first French government without a king.

FASCINATING FATES: The Fate of King Louis XVI (January 21, 1793)

After abolishing the monarchy, the National Convention placed the former King Louis XVI on trial for crimes against France. In most Jacobins' eyes, the Flight to Varennes and the Brunswick Manifesto were more than enough to condemn Louis, regardless of any evidence presented at trial. Therefore on the question of guilt or innocence, the Convention voted unanimously for guilt.

On the question of punishment, though, the Jacobins split: the less-radical Girondists preferred to treat Louis mercifully; while the more-radical Montagnards preferred a traitor's death for Louis. Boosted by the anger that swirled around the Revolution

Illustration of an executioner displaying King Louis XVI's severed head

of 10 August and the Duke of Brunswick's invasion, the Montagnards finally convinced the rest of the Convention to send Louis to the guillotine.

According to Abbe Edgeworth, the priest who accompanied the former king to his death on January 21, 1793, Louis' last words were these:

"I die innocent of all the crimes laid to my charge; I pardon those who have occasioned my death; and I pray to God that the blood you are going to shed may never be visited on France."

The Committee of Public Safety (April 1793)

The execution of France's king placed her in the troublesome position of having no chief executive, no one who could act quickly and decisively against the many threats the country faced. To solve this problem, the National Convention named several of its members to the **Committee of Public Safety**— a powerful executive committee charged with defending France against all enemies, whether from without or within. Among the Committee of Public Safety's members were two radical Montagnards whose power and influence were just then reaching their peak:

1. **Maximilien de Robespierre**, a gifted speaker who famously argued at the end of Louis XVI's trial: "With regret I pronounce this fatal truth: Louis must die so that the nation may live."

2. **Jean-Paul Marat**, author of a popular revolutionary newspaper called "The Friend of the People." As the radicals' boldest spokesman, Marat became the focus of the power struggle between Girondists and Montagnards— a struggle that intensified after Louis XVI's execution.

The creation of the Committee of Public Safety was partly a reaction to a new threat: the **French Counter-Revolution**, a growing rebellion against the National Convention's authority. Although the Revolution was overwhelmingly popular in Paris, it was less popular in certain rural regions, where less-enlightened Frenchmen wondered why their mad government was suddenly murdering their priests. In the Vendee region, the Brittany region and elsewhere, armies of rebel Frenchmen arose to resist the National Convention's unwanted decrees.

The Girondists and the Montagnards reacted to these rebels differently. The Girondists wanted to compromise with the rebels, relaxing some of the Convention's harsher decrees. The Montagnards, however, viewed any compromise whatsoever as an utter betrayal of the Revolution's principles.

The least compromising Montagnard of all was Jean-Paul Marat, who recommended guillotining anyone who betrayed the Revolution in word or deed. Marat added that in order for the Revolution to be secure, as many as 200,000 Frenchmen might have to lose their heads!

The power struggle between Girondist and Montagnard climaxed in two dramatic episodes:

1. In April – May 1793, the Girondists placed Marat on trial for using his popular newspaper to arouse the public against his political opponents. The **Revolutionary Tribunal**, an almighty revolutionary court whose decisions were beyond appeal, acquitted Marat of all charges— thus sealing the Girondists' doom.
2. A month later, on June 2nd, a revolutionary mob burst into the National Convention and arrested its Girondist delegates, jailing them for crimes against the Revolution.

FASCINATING FACTS: Charlotte Corday and the Assassination of Jean-Paul Marat (July 13, 1793)

After the Montagnards jailed their Girondist rivals in the National Convention, a misguided young Girondist named Charlotte Corday thought she knew best how to save France from the guillotine-happy Montagnards. Reasoning that the best way to defeat the Montagnards was to silence their mouthpiece, Corday went to Paris, bought a knife and knocked on the door of the fiery Jean-Paul Marat. Having studied Marat's habits, Corday knew that he sometimes spent entire days in a medicinal bath at home, seeking relief from a miserable skin condition that covered his body with painful sores.

"The Assassination of Marat" by artist Baudry

Twice, Marat's live-in companion turned Corday away. On her third try, though, Corday won the companion's confidence by claiming to have information on some Girondists whom Marat was hoping to guillotine. Admitted at last, Corday took a seat beside Marat's tub and started sharing Girondist names and addresses, all of which Marat wrote down with relish. As Corday finished her list, Marat joyously assured her, "We'll soon have them all guillotined in Paris!"

Having won Marat's trust, Corday waited until he wasn't looking; and when the time was right, she pulled her knife and plunged it deep into his chest. Considering that Corday had never killed a man before, her blow was remarkably accurate: Marat bled so copiously that he died within minutes.

The Reign of Terror (September 1793 – July 1794)

Four days after her assassination of Marat, Charlotte Corday went to the guillotine to pay the ultimate price for her crime. Before she died, Corday made clear why she had assassinated Marat: because she believed that by killing one man, she could save 100,000 others— innocent Frenchmen whom Marat's mad, reckless writings would otherwise drive to the guillotine. Corday also tried to draw all punishment onto herself— bravely insisting that the assassination had been her idea alone, not the fruit of some well-organized Girondist plot.

Unfortunately, Corday accomplished just the opposite of what she intended— for after the assassination, the Montagnards had even better reason to imagine anti-Revolutionaries hiding around every corner. To protect themselves, the Montagnards passed the **Law of Suspects**.

ILLUMINATING EXCERPTS from the Law of Suspects (adopted September 1793)

The Law of Suspects was a harsh law that Committee of Safety leader Maximilien de Robespierre claimed he needed to defend the Revolution. The law began:

"Immediately after the publication of the present decree, all suspects within the territory of the Republic and still at large, shall be placed in custody. The following are deemed suspects:

- "Those who, by their conduct, associations, comments, or writings have shown themselves… enemies of liberty…

- "Those former nobles, together with husbands, wives, fathers, mothers, sons or daughters, brothers or sisters… who have not constantly demonstrated their devotion to the Revolution…"

In other words, the Law of Suspects allowed the Montagnards to jail and execute anyone who wasn't a Montagnard. Also, because the Revolutionary Tribunal's decisions were beyond appeal, the Montagnards could execute anyone they chose, whenever they chose. The slightest suspicion that a person held anti-Revolutionary beliefs was enough to send him or her to the guillotine. In passing such a law, Robespierre ironically violated the very human rights for which he claimed to stand.

Portrait of Maximilien de Robespierre, chief villain behind the Reign of Terror

The passage of the Law of Suspects in September 1793 marked the true beginning of the **Reign of Terror**. Over the ten months that followed, revolutionaries imprisoned as many as 200,000 Frenchmen on charges of conspiring against the Revolution. Throughout those months, the blades of France's guillotines rose and fell without ceasing, cleaving necks by the thousands.

TRAGIC TRUTHS: Most of those necks belonged to men and women who were innocent of any crime, and whose deaths moved the French people not one millimeter closer to liberty. Instead of advancing liberty, the Reign of Terror forever stained the French Revolution's memory with the blood of countless innocents.

The many victims of Robespierre's 10-month Reign of Terror included:

- **Queen Marie Antoinette**, who followed her husband to the guillotine on October 16, 1793.
- **Camille Desmoulins**, the revolutionary whose fiery speech outside the *Palais Royal* had helped spark the Storming of the Bastille. Desmoulins' crime was to criticize Robespierre for executing his political enemies.
- **Imprisoned Girondist delegates to the National Convention**, politicians whose only crime was that their opinions were less radical than the Montagnards'.

- **Madame Roland**, the influential wife of a Girondist leader named Jean-Marie Roland. Before laying her neck on the guillotine, Madame Roland bowed to a statue of the goddess Liberty that stood nearby and exclaimed, "Oh Liberty, what crimes are committed in thy name!"

DEFINITION: A **tumbril** was a two-wheeled farm wagon that the French adapted to a grim use during the French Revolution: hauling Reign of Terror victims from jail to guillotine. From September 1793 – July 1794, the sound of heavy tumbril wheels clattering over cobblestones became a well-known signal that the day's beheadings would soon begin.

Tumbril-load of condemned en route to the guillotine

FASCINATING FACTS: *Les Tricoteuses*, "The Knitting Women"

For a few months during the Reign of Terror, public executions at the guillotine were a popular form of entertainment. Hucksters added to the fun by publishing programs listing the enemies of the state who were to lose their heads that day, along with descriptions of their crimes. Some families brought their children along for the educational experience of watching once-privileged nobles pay the ultimate price for crimes against the Revolution.

Among the most faithful spectators at Reign of Terror executions were **les tricoteuses**— angry "knitting women" who filled the time between beheadings with their usual work of knitting socks, hats, scarves and the like. Among these knitting women were many whose families had starved before the Revolution, and who had taken part in the Women's March on Versailles. These angry revolutionaries now sat near the guillotine, where they could more thoroughly savor their revenge against the wealthy.

FASCINATING FICTIONS: Madame Defarge

The best-known *tricoteuse* was Madame Defarge, a character in Charles Dickens' 1859 novel *A Tale of Two Cities*. Madame Defarge and her husband Ernest were early Jacobins who led secret revolutionary meetings in their Paris wine shop, which stood near the Bastille. Early in the novel, the reader often sees Madame Defarge about her knitting. Later, the reader discovers that Madame's knitting had a revolutionary purpose— that she has used it to encode the names and crimes of arrogant nobles whom she hopes to see beheaded once the French Revolution begins.

Les Tricoteuses enjoying their grim entertainment

INTERESTING INDIVIDUALS: Marie Tussaud, founder of Madame Tussauds Wax Museums (1761 – 1850)

Marie Grosholtz was a French girl whose mother kept house for Philippe Curtius, a Swiss expert in the art of modeling lifelike figures in beeswax. By studying at the feet of her mentor Curtius, whom she came to call "Uncle," young Marie became as expert as he at sculpting lifelike replicas of real people. Before the French Revolution, Marie sculpted Enlightenment heroes like Rousseau and Voltaire. During the Revolution, the French government hired her to mold beeswax death masks from the severed heads of several famous dead, including King Louis XVI, Queen Marie Antoinette and Jean-Paul Marat.

Some of Marie's figures are still on display at the London wax museum she later founded: **Madame Tussauds**, named for Marie after she wedded her second husband Francois Tussaud. Among the historical items on display at Madame Tussauds of London is a guillotine blade that may have severed Marie Antoinette's head.

FASCINATING FACTS: Sans-culottes

One way to identify a French Revolutionary was to look at his pants. In keeping with European fashion before the Revolution, wealthy Frenchmen usually wore *culottes*— stylish pants that came only to the knee, revealing fine silk stockings below the knee. The poor, who couldn't afford such stockings, usually wore plain long trousers. During the French Revolution, when it was fashionable to be poor, rich and poor alike went *sans-culottes*— "without *culottes*"— to mark themselves as devoted revolutionaries. Many sans-culottes also wore red berets, short coats called *carmagnoles* and wooden shoes called *sabot*.

Sans-culotte

FASCINATING FACTS: Political Left, Right and Center

The political terms "left," "right" and "center" began with the National Constituent Assembly, the French legislature that replaced the National Assembly in 1789. The more liberal Assembly delegates, those who wanted to change France's government the most, tended to sit together on the left side of the Versailles Hall of State. To avoid the jibes of these often-caustic liberals, the more conservative delegates— those who wanted less change— sat on the right. Ever since, reporters have called liberals "the left," conservatives "the right" and moderates "the center."

FASCINATING FACTS: A Few French Inventions

The world owes some of its most exciting inventions to French scientists and engineers, including these that appeared near the era of the French Revolution:

1. **Paddle steamers:** French inventor Claude de Jouffroy built the first steam engine-driven paddleboat in 1774.
2. **Hot air balloons and hydrogen balloons:** French brothers Joseph-Michel and Jacques-Etienne Montgolfier floated the first large-scale hot air balloons in 1782 – 1783.

Model of an early French steamboat

Technical description of an early Montgolfier Brothers balloon, the design of which featured King Louis XVI's face as the center of the sun

SUCCINCT SUMMARIES: Some Pivotal Events and Consequences of the French Revolution

Date	Event	Consequence
May 1789	In need of tax money to resolve France's financial crisis, King Louis XVI assembles the Estates General.	The Third Estate vows the Tennis Court Oath and forms the National Convention.
July 1789	The king posts foreign mercenaries to guard Versailles and Paris against possibly violent revolutionaries.	Looking for gunpowder with which to defend themselves, Paris revolutionaries storm the Bastille, and later level it.
October 1789	The bread-starved women of Paris march on Versailles to confront their king.	Both king and National Constituent Assembly are forced to move to Tuileries Palace.
July 1792	The Duke of Brunswick threatens France in his Brunswick Manifesto.	France's defense minister calls for the creation of the *federes*. Thousands answer the call.
August 1792	King Louis XVI vetoes the creation of the *federes*.	The *federes* storm the Tuileries. The king loses his constitutional powers, and winds up imprisoned in the Temple.
September 1792	The National Convention abolishes the monarchy, replacing it with the First French Republic	King Louis XVI goes from the Temple to the guillotine.
July 1793	Girondist Charlotte Corday assassinates Montagnard mouthpiece Jean-Paul Marat.	The Committee of Safety demands passage of the Law of Suspects, thus beginning the Reign of Terror.

U.S. HISTORY FOCUS

AMAZING AMERICANS: Johnny Appleseed (1774 – 1845?)

The future Johnny Appleseed was born John Chapman on a Massachusetts farm in 1774. John's father fought in the Revolutionary War, which began the year after John's birth. In the following year, 1776, John's mother died, leaving him and his elder sister Elizabeth to move in with relatives. After his father remarried in 1780, John welcomed ten more half-siblings.

As a young man, John served as an apprentice to the owner of an apple orchard, who taught him the craft that was to become his life's work: raising apple trees from seed. At age 18, John moved with Elizabeth and his half-brother Nathaniel to Pennsylvania, where he planted his first apple tree nurseries near the Susquehanna River. From Pennsylvania, the trio moved westward to Ohio, planting more nurseries as they went. After his sister and brother left the road to start families, Johnny Appleseed became a lone wanderer, spreading his apple tree nurseries all over the Northwest Territory. All by himself, Johnny Appleseed may have planted enough apple trees to cover about 100,000 square miles. Johnny's apples offered several benefits:

- Cooked apples provided variety for settler's diets.
- The laws Congress passed to draw settlers westward sometimes required them to establish orchards on their new properties, which would have been difficult without Johnny's nurseries.
- Sour apples provided raw material for a strong brandy called applejack.

Settlers all over the growing United States honored Johnny Appleseed as a humble man who cared nothing for material things, and everything for his Christian faith. No matter what happened, Johnny always remembered to thank the Lord for life, health and provision. Johnny charged as little as possible for his seedlings, no more than a few cents per seedling. When settlers couldn't pay in cash, Johnny traded his seedlings for food or clothes. Content to use rough seed bags for his own simple clothing, Johnny often donated any good clothes he received to the needy. He rarely wore shoes in the summer; and if he did, then they might not match. Like St. Francis of Assisi, John cared for animals as well as people: late in life, he ate no meat, and sometimes bought mistreated farm animals so that he could take them to someone who would care for them.

Johnny was also a well-known lover of the Swedenborgian Hymn, a glad, thankful song that many American families still use as a mealtime prayer. The song begins:

Oh, the Lord's been good to me / And so I thank the Lord
For giving me the things I need / The sun, the rain and the apple seed / The Lord's been good to me!

U.S. STATE FOCUS

Ohio

FASCINATING FACTS about Ohio:

- State Capital: Columbus
- State Abbreviation: OH
- Statehood: Ohio became the 17th US state on March 1, 1803.
- Area: About 45,000 square miles (Ranks 34th in size)
- Bordering States: Pennsylvania, Michigan, Indiana, Kentucky, West Virginia
- Meaning of Name: Ohio's name comes from an Iroquois word meaning "Great River."
- State Nickname: "The Buckeye State"
- State Bird: Cardinal
- State Tree: Ohio Buckeye
- State Flower: Scarlet Carnation
- State Song: "Beautiful Ohio" by Ballard MacDonald and *Mary Earl*, a pen name for composer Robert King
- State Motto: "With God, all things are possible"
- Historic Places to Visit: Thomas Edison Birthplace, Fallen Timbers Battlefield, President James Garfield Home, President Warren Harding Home, President Ulysses Grant Boyhood Home, President William McKinley Tomb, Dayton Aviation Heritage National Historical Park
- Resources and Industries: Tires, car and truck parts, coal, oil, natural gas, shipping

Orville Wright in a 1905 flight near Dayton, Ohio

State Flag: Ohio's flag is the only state flag that is swallowtailed, not rectangular, in shape. The white "O" may stand for Ohio. With its red center, though, the "O" may also represent a buckeye, the nut of Ohio's state tree. Seventeen stars around the "O" represent Ohio's position as the seventeenth U.S. state.

CHAPTER 26: The Whiskey Rebellion; Napoleon's Rise

CHURCH HISTORY FOCUS

> REFRESHING REMINDERS from Chapter 22: In the Treaty of Paris, the 1783 treaty that ended the Revolutionary War, King George III acknowledged the United States "to be free sovereign and independent states," and relinquished "all claims to the government, propriety, and territorial rights of the same and every part thereof."

The Treaty of Paris created serious difficulties for American churchmen who had sworn oaths of loyalty to the British Crown— especially American Anglicans and American Methodists.

The Anglican Church in the Thirteen Colonies

From the colonies' beginnings in the early 1600s, Anglicanism was a poor fit for America, for several reasons:

- Because colonies like Massachusetts, Rhode Island, Connecticut, Maryland and Pennsylvania all began as havens for religious dissenters— Puritans, Catholics, Quakers and others who fled England specifically to escape the too-controlling Anglican Church.

- Because independent-minded Americans liked to elect their own church leaders, not have them appointed by some distant archbishop who never even visited the colonies.

- Because Anglican bishops typically raised funds by charging rent on vast tracts of donated land— an idea that was most unwelcome in the colonies, where every American dreamed of owning his own land.

Bruton Parish Church in Williamsburg, Virginia, a former Anglican church built in 1715 and visited by George Washington, Thomas Jefferson, Richard Henry Lee, Patrick Henry and George Mason, among others

For all of these reasons, the Anglican Church in America had yet to receive its first bishop when the Revolutionary War broke out in 1775.

The Revolutionary War made Anglicanism even less popular in the United States— mainly because so many Anglican ministers remained loyal to the Crown. To patriotic Americans, the idea of sitting in church praying loyalist blessings on King and Parliament was at best ridiculous, and at worst treasonous; several states passed laws against such prayers. By war's end, so many Anglican churches had closed their doors that only a few thousand Anglicans remained in all of the United States. Far more lived in eastern Canada, where tens of thousands of loyalists relocated during and after the war.

When the war was over, those few thousand U.S. Anglicans faced a new problem: Apostolic Succession.

> REFRESHING REMINDERS: **Apostolic Succession** is the idea that priests and bishops receive their authority through the laying on of hands of elder bishops, who in turn received their authority from their own elders. Roman Catholics believe that this line of succession extends unbroken all the way back to the Apostle Peter, who received his authority directly from Christ Himself (Matthew 16: 19). Because the Anglican Church broke with the Roman Catholic Church in the 1500s, its line of succession is about 1,500 years shorter; but even so, no Anglican priest or bishop may be consecrated without the laying on of an elder bishop's hands.

The problem American Anglicans faced was that they had no bishop, and thus no way to consecrate new priests.

To solve this problem, at least one American would have to receive the laying on of hands in Britain. However, this raised a second problem. British law required all Anglican bishops to swear oaths of loyalty to Britain's king— which meant that any American Anglican who received the laying on of hands in Britain would automatically become a traitor to the United States.

Over the years from 1785 – 1790, American Anglicans found two ways around this problem:

1. In 1784, Samuel Seabury of Connecticut received the laying on of hands from Anglican bishops in Scotland. At the time, Scottish Anglicans also refused to swear oaths of loyalty to Britain's king— for most Scottish Anglicans were Jacobites, still loyal to the Stuart line of the deposed King James II (see Chapter 12).

2. A few years later, the Anglican Church changed its rules to accommodate foreigners who couldn't swear oaths of loyalty to Britain's king. This change allowed three more Americans— William White of Pennsylvania, Samuel Provost of New York and James Madison of Virginia (not the same James Madison who wrote the Virginia Plan and the Bill of Rights)— to receive the laying on of hands by 1790.

DEFINITION: The **Episcopal Church of the United States** is the U.S. descendant of the Anglican Church, forced to separate from its parent by the change of loyalties that came with the Revolutionary War.

The Methodist Episcopal Church of the United States

The Revolutionary War also forced the founders of the Methodist movement, the Wesley brothers (see Chapter 19), to do some quick thinking. More than four decades after the Great Awakening, both Wesleys were still ordained Anglicans, and still hoped to make their Methodist movement a recognized part of the Anglican Church. The Revolutionary War changed these plans in two important ways:

1. Now that the United States was independent of Britain, it seemed highly unlikely that American Methodists would ever join Britain's Anglican Church.

2. America's lack of Anglican priests left American Methodists with no church-approved way to receive the sacraments of baptism and communion.

Unwilling to leave his beloved American Methodists without their sacraments, John Wesley sent Methodist minister Thomas Coke to America on a slightly unorthodox mission. Like Wesley, Coke was an Anglican priest with full authority to administer the sacraments. Coke did not, however, have authority to consecrate new priests; only Anglican bishops could do that. Nevertheless, this is precisely what Wesley sent Coke to do: ordain American Anglican-Methodist priests, who could then administer the sacraments all over America.

Bishop Francis Asbury receiving the laying on of hands from Bishop Thomas Coke, 1784

To avoid angering British Anglicans, Wesley was careful not to bestow the bishop's title on Coke. American Methodists, however, cared little for the opinions of distant British Anglicans. In 1784, American Methodists conferred the bishop's title upon Thomas Coke and one other beloved Methodist minister, Francis Asbury. Thus Coke and Asbury became the first two bishops of the **Methodist Episcopal Church of the United States**, the largest of several churches that would later unite to form the United Methodist Church.

U.S. HISTORY FOCUS

The Whiskey Rebellion (1791 – 1794)

> DEFINITIONS:
> - A **tariff** is a tax on imports or exports, collected at a country's borders by customs agents.
> - An **excise** is a tax on the manufacture or sale of certain goods, collected inside a country by revenue agents.
> - The **Whiskey Rebellion** was an armed protest against the federal government's first excise, a distilled spirits tax passed in 1791.

The Whiskey Tax (1791)

In its first year, the new federal government created by the U.S. Constitution survived on tariffs. One of the U.S. Congress's first laws was the **Tariff Act of 1789**, which authorized federal customs agents to collect tariffs at all U.S. ports— a task the states had handled under the old Articles of Confederation. Like most early federal tax laws, the Tariff Act was part of a plan developed by the man President Washington trusted to set the new country's finances in order: first U.S. Secretary of the Treasury Alexander Hamilton.

In the following year, 1790, Congress passed the **Assumption Bill**, Hamilton's plan for the federal government to assume the states' Revolutionary War debts (this was the plan that resulted in the Compromise of 1790, see Chapter 24). After the Assumption Bill, Hamilton needed more tax money to fund the federal government's increased debt burden. Therefore in March 1791, Congress passed the United States' first excise tax: the "**whiskey tax**," a tax on alcohols distilled inside the country.

Portrait of Alexander Hamilton

> INTERESTING IDEAS: Although Hamilton was well aware that any new tax was likely to be unpopular, he hoped that a whiskey excise might be less unpopular than most, for two reasons: (1) because whiskey was a luxury, something people generally didn't need to survive; and (2) because his whiskey excise doubled as a "sin tax," a fee to discourage people from drinking too much.

Hamilton's mistake was to overlook the fact that his whiskey excise affected different parts of the country differently. In the east, where long-established distilleries produced whiskey in great quantities, the whiskey excise added only a small fraction to the cost of doing business. On the western frontier, where struggling farmers distilled whiskey in smaller quantities, a host of objections arose:

- The excise rate varied in a way that favored big business. In effect, the more alcohol one produced, the lower the excise rate— which meant that small western distillers always paid more than large eastern ones.
- The law required all distillers to apply for federal licenses, a legal hassle no westerner had ever faced before.
- The law required all legal disputes over federal taxes or licenses to be heard in federal court— which, for western farmers, meant an expensive journey hundreds of miles to the east.
- The law required payment in cash, which was in short supply out west. In fact, cash was so scarce that westerners often used whiskey as cash— which made the whiskey excise a lot like an income tax, a hated tax that took a chunk out of every dollar westerners earned.

Protests

To make matters worse, many of the westerners who so resented the whiskey excise were also veterans of the Revolutionary War— former soldiers who had sacrificed a great deal to win their country's independence, and had received only a fraction of the pay promised them in return. Such veterans felt that repealing the whiskey excise was the least their government could do to honor their sacrifices.

Therefore when the government refused to repeal the excise, these veterans responded with the same cries of outrage they had shouted against the British fifteen years before. All along the Appalachians, western veterans organized loud protests against taxation without representation and unequal treatment under the law.

These protests were especially loud in western Pennsylvania. In counties around Pittsburgh, many Pennsylvanians simply refused to pay the whiskey excise. Some even harassed the revenue agents whom President Washington sent to collect it. In September 1791, six months after Congress approved the whiskey excise, a band of protesters in Washington County, Pennsylvania went so far as to tar and feather a revenue agent named Robert Johnson.

FASCINATING FACTS: Tarring and Feathering

In tarring and feathering a revenue agent, Pennsylvanians were reviving a form of punishment that was already old during the American Revolution, when Boston's Sons of Liberty used it to humiliate British customs officers. The usual method of tarring and feathering was to (1) strip off part or all of the victim's clothes; (2) coat the victim with sticky pine tar— which was always available at waterfronts, where ships' crews used it to keep their vessels watertight— and then (3) coat the tar with pillow feathers, instantly transforming a respectable government agent into a ludicrous spectacle.

A federal tax collector tarred, feathered and forced to ride the rail

Other interesting facts:

- **Riding out of town on a rail:** To complete their victims' humiliation, some mobs mounted them on fence rails and paraded them through the streets before dumping them at the edge of town.

- Historians are of two minds about injuries from tarring and feathering. Some say that the punishment was more humiliating than torturous, as the pine tar probably wasn't hot enough to burn victims' skin. Others say that the tar was sometimes hot enough to burn, and that some victims died ghastly deaths— either from overheating, as the sticky tar prevented victims from cooling themselves through sweat; or from terrible skin infections brought on by burns.

Despite many such angry protests, federal revenue agents stubbornly continued to collect the whiskey excise. One of the stubbornest was Washington's chief revenue agent for western Pennsylvania: General John Neville, a wealthy veteran who lived in a fine fortified house on Bower Hill, just southwest of Pittsburgh.

INTERESTING IDEAS: The fact that both General Neville and President Washington operated large distilleries of their own, and therefore qualified for a lower excise rate, convinced some western veterans that their former Revolutionary War generals had turned against them.

Matters came to a head in mid-1794, when a federal marshal toured the Pittsburgh area serving unwelcome **subpoenas**— summons to appear in court— to dozens of distillers who had refused to pay the whiskey excise. The fact that these subpoenas required the accused to appear at a federal court in Philadelphia, more than 300 hard miles away to the east, made them even less welcome.

The Battle of Bower Hill (July 17, 1794)

As General Neville helpfully guided this subpoena-delivering federal marshal from farm to farm on July 15, he had the ominous experience of hearing shots fired nearby. Therefore the next day, when two dozen or more armed protesters gathered outside Neville's fortified home on Bower Hill, Neville didn't doubt that his life was in danger. To protect himself and his family, Neville fired on the protesters, dealing one of them a wound that would prove fatal later that day.

Recognizing that their numbers were too small to break in and punish Neville right away, the protesters retreated for the night to gather reinforcements. Meanwhile, Neville was able to summon ten U.S. soldiers from nearby Pittsburgh to defend his home. When those soldiers peered outside the next morning, a terrifying sight greeted their eyes: an angry army of 500 – 600 protesters had surrounded Bower Hill, and was threatening to set fire to General Neville's fortifications if he didn't open his gates. Instead of opening his gates, Neville stubbornly opened fire on the protesters.

Midway through the Battle of Bower Hill, the protesters' commander— another Revolutionary War veteran named James McFarlane— either saw or thought he saw a white flag waving from Neville's besieged home. The honorable soldier McFarlane immediately called a ceasefire, raised a white flag of his own, and stepped from behind cover to negotiate— at which one of Neville's soldiers shot McFarlane, dealing him a mortal wound. The protesters, seeing McFarlane's murder under a flag of truce as the worst form of treachery, broke in and set fire to Neville's house, forcing Neville to surrender as his fine home burned to the ground.

Threatening to Secede from the Union

As word of Neville's treachery spread, the Whiskey Rebellion grew stronger than ever. One protest on August 1st, 1794 drew 7,000 angry protesters— including some who threatened to secede from the Union. Infuriated by their government's tyranny, several counties threatened to declare independence from the U.S., just as the U.S. had declared independence from Britain.

The size of this protest, combined with the protesters' threat to secede from the Union, moved President Washington to take decisive action. One week after the August 1 protest, Washington summoned militia to put down the rebellion in western Pennsylvania.

President George Washington reviewing the militia who will confront the Whiskey Rebellion

In response, nearly 13,000 militiamen from several states gathered in the eastern foothills of the Appalachians, some of them reluctantly. Washington reviewed some of these troops in person at Fort Cumberland, Maryland before sending them west under the command of Virginia Governor Lighthorse Harry Lee (who would later become the father of Confederate States of America General Robert E. Lee).

Like Shays' Rebellion (see Chapter 23), the Whiskey Rebellion ended in an anticlimax. Faced with Lee's powerful army, the Whiskey Rebellion abruptly collapsed: Lee encountered no rebel armies, and fought no battles. Federal agents did arrest several rebels, and convicted two of treason. However, President Washington was so grateful for peace that he used his presidential power to pardon both convicts. Pennsylvania's state courts punished other rebels for lesser crimes, such as vandalism.

SUCCINCT SUMMARIES: Some Results of the Whiskey Rebellion

- The Whiskey Rebellion tested the new U.S. Constitution on two important questions: (1) whether the new federal government was strong enough to enforce its laws; and (2) whether the U.S. would go to war to keep rebellious territories in the Union. To both questions, the answer was yes.

- Despite Washington's clear victory, his government still had trouble collecting the unpopular whiskey excise. The Whiskey Rebellion was only the beginning of a long struggle between two enemies: (1) **moonshiners**, illegal whiskey-makers who operated small, secret distilleries in the mountains by moonlight; and (2) **revenuers**, federal agents charged with finding and shutting down illegal stills.

AMAZING AMERICANS: Martha Dandridge Custis Washington (1731 – 1802)

Martha Dandridge was the eldest of eight children born to wealthy Virginia planter John Dandridge and his wife Frances. Like most girls of her day, Martha received little formal education beyond the basics of reading, writing and arithmetic. Instead, young Martha spent part of her time at gardening and needlework, and part at the diversions of the well-to-do— attending parties, riding horses and learning to play a small version of the harpsichord called a spinet.

In 1749, the year she turned 18, Martha married one of Virginia's wealthiest bachelors: Daniel Parke Custis, who was 20 years her senior. That same year, Daniel's father died, leaving him plantations totaling nearly 18,000 acres. Over the next seven years, four pregnancies blessed Martha and Daniel with two surviving children, a son named John ("Jacky," b. 1754) and a daughter named Martha ("Patsy," b. 1756). At the end of those seven years, Daniel died— leaving the entire vast Custis estate, with all of its numerous slaves and properties, to Martha, Jacky and Patsy.

Less than two years later, in January 1759, the wealthy Widow Custis remarried to Colonel George Washington. The new family of four moved into Mount Vernon, a plantation home that George leased from the widow of his late brother Lawrence (George would later inherit Mount Vernon). Sadly, Patsy Custis died of complications from epilepsy at age 17, leaving Martha and George— who never had children together— with only Jacky.

Like countless other American families, the Washingtons suffered mightily during the Revolutionary War. Martha bravely joined George at several rough winter camps, including Valley Forge. As wife to the commander-in-chief, Martha's

George and Martha at Mount Vernon with grandchildren Nelly and Parke Custis

main job was to boost morale in any way she could— mainly by visiting soldiers, writing letters of encouragement and organizing social events.

Meanwhile, Jacky sometimes served as his stepfather's aide-de-camp— including a stint during the war-ending Siege of Yorktown. At Yorktown on November 5, 1781, two weeks after his stepfather's greatest victory, Jacky Custis died of camp fever at age 26. Two of the four young children Jacky left behind, Eleanor "Nelly" Custis and George Washington "Parke" Custis, became adoptive children to Martha and George.

Years later, as the first First Lady of the United States, Martha set important precedents for all first ladies to come. "Lady Washington" proved an excellent hostess, organizing weekly receptions for the public and frequent formal dinners for dignitaries. Martha also set a good example by maintaining a well-run household.

FASCINATING FACTS: Smallpox Inoculations

Before Martha Washington entered winter camp at Valley Forge, her husband required her to receive what his soldiers received as well: an inoculation against smallpox.

Early in the Revolutionary War, an epidemic of smallpox swept through the area around Boston, leading some patriots to accuse the British of deliberately spreading the disease. Fortunately, the medical science of the day offered a way to deal with smallpox. Over the last few decades, Western doctors had learned a technique long known in the Far East: **inoculation**, a.k.a. variolation. To inoculate patients against smallpox, doctors extracted material from the pustules of smallpox victims, and then placed that material in small cuts on their patients' skin— deliberately giving their patients mild cases of smallpox, in the hope that they would develop immunity against more serious cases.

Unfortunately, inoculation was risky— for a small percentage of inoculation patients caught serious cases of smallpox, rather than mild ones. Despite the risks, the forward-thinking George Washington chose inoculation for himself, his wife and his troops. Washington's risk paid off, for few of his troops died of smallpox.

A LOOK AHEAD: In 1798, Doctor Edward Jenner will introduce a new method of preventing smallpox: vaccination, rather than inoculation. The main difference is that vaccine makers weaken the disease before injecting it, all but eliminating the risk that patients will develop serious cases of the disease.

FASCINATING FACTS: The Game of Graces

The Game of Graces was a popular outdoor game designed to teach young ladies like Martha Custis physical grace. The only game pieces required are a pair of sticks for each player and an embroidery hoop, which players sometimes decorate with colorful ribbons. To begin, one player takes a stick in each hand, crosses the sticks and balances the hoop on top. Next, she whips the sticks apart in an upward motion, flinging the hoop to the other player, who tries to catch them on her own sticks. Skilled players may use two hoops at once, throwing and catching at the same time.

The Jay Treaty (1795)

The other great challenge of George Washington's presidency was the chaos generated by the French Revolution. In 1793, Britain joined the **First Coalition**, the alliance of European powers bent on preventing the French Revolution from spreading beyond France (see Chapter 25). As part of its war on France, Parliament instructed Britain's Royal Navy to seize all neutral ships that tried to trade with France— including American ships. Within less than two years, Britain seized more than 250 U.S.-flagged merchant ships.

These ship seizures posed a quandary for President Washington. On the one hand, U.S. merchants clamored for their government to defend their ships on the high seas, as was the duty of all national governments. On the other hand, the young U.S. had no navy capable of contending with Britain's; and even if it had, Washington would have hesitated to use it, for fear of starting a war that his struggling new nation might not win. Short of war, Washington had only two options: (1) he could join an alliance with Denmark and Sweden, two other neutral nations who had already banded together to defend their ships against the aggressive Britain; or (2) he could negotiate with Britain, hopefully arriving at a new peace treaty.

Acting on the second option, Washington sent Chief Justice of the Supreme Court John Jay— who had also been Secretary of Foreign Affairs under the old Articles of Confederation government— to see what sort of agreement the British might sign. Jay's highest priorities were (1) to prevent any more ship seizures, and (2) to seek payment for ships already seized. If possible, Jay was also to address other grievances left over from the Revolutionary War, including these:

- More than 10 years after the Treaty of Paris, British troops still occupied forts in the Northwest Territory, forts that they had promised to abandon. From those forts, Britain still armed its Native American allies for attacks on American settlers.

- Ever since the Revolutionary War, Britain had been denying American merchants something they wanted very much: the privilege of trading with the British West Indies.

- The Royal Navy still sent press gangs to impress Americans into service, as it did in Boston before the war.

In late 1794, John Jay returned to the United States with a signed treaty for the U.S. Senate to consider. Having won most of what Washington asked, Jay might well have expected a hero's welcome.

Instead, Jay quickly became one of the most hated men in the United States. All over the country, protesters burned Jay in effigy for making concessions to their hated enemies, the British. According to Jay, these protests were so numerous that had he wanted to, he could have crossed the country from one end to the other by the light of their bonfires.

Despite abundant protests, President Washington supported the Jay Treaty for one main reason: because it allowed the United States to avoid war with Britain, giving the young country time to grow up a bit before facing such a powerful enemy again. At Washington's urging, the Senate finally ratified the Jay Treaty in June 1795— but only by a vote of 20 – 10, exactly the two-thirds majority required by the Constitution.

The controversy over the Jay Treaty revealed a growing political divide between two types of Americans:

1. **Anti-Jay Treaty Americans who supported the French Revolution**, and wanted their government to do the same. Americans like Thomas Jefferson considered the French Revolution just as worthy as the American Revolution, just as devoted to the Enlightenment principles of liberty, equal rights and republican government. These Americans also remembered how very much France had contributed to the cause of American liberty, and considered it treachery not to return the favor— especially because the Treaty of Alliance between the U.S. and France, which had proved so critical to winning the Revolutionary War, was still in effect.

2. **Pro-Jay Treaty Americans who feared that the French Revolution went too far**— that it placed too much power in the hands of angry mobs, and not enough in the hands of sensible, honorable leaders. Americans like George Washington, Alexander Hamilton and John Adams pointed to the Reign of Terror, which was going on even as Jay negotiated his treaty, as evidence that too much democracy could lead to anarchy.

SUCCINCT SUMMARIES: Some Results of the Jay Treaty

- As agreed in the Jay Treaty, the British finally withdrew from their old forts in the Northwest Territory, making it easier and safer for Americans to settle there.

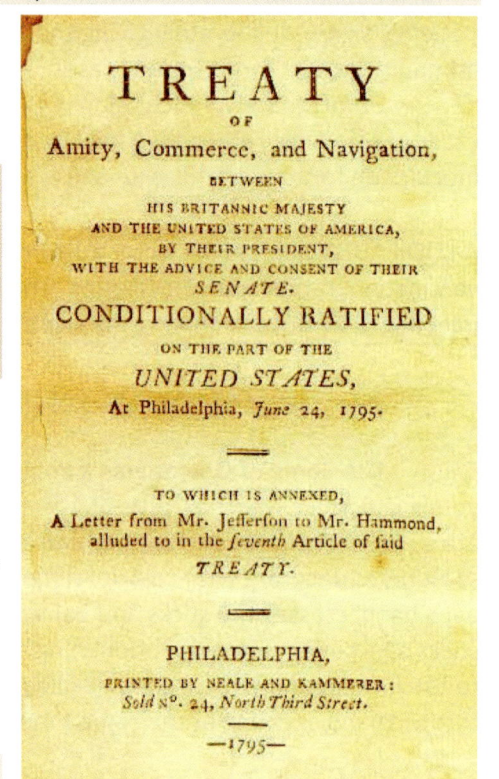

- By avoiding war with Britain, the U.S. drew closer to war with Britain's enemy, France. During John Adams' presidency (1797 – 1801), the U.S. and France fought the **Quasi-War**, an undeclared naval war that only narrowly missed becoming a declared war.

- Public protests over the Jay Treaty helped define the differences between two emerging political parties: Alexander Hamilton's party, the **Federalists**; and Thomas Jefferson's party, the **Democratic-Republicans**.

- Because the Jay Treaty contained no agreement on press gangs, Britain continued pressing American sailors into service— continuing a grievance that was to become a major cause of the War of 1812.

USS *Constellation* battling the French frigate *L'Insurgente* in the Quasi-War

WORLD HISTORY FOCUS

The French Revolutionary Wars, Part Two

MORE REFRESHING REMINDERS: The **Reign of Terror** (Sept 1793 – July 1794) was an ugly period of the French Revolution when Maximilien de Robespierre and his radical Jacobin allies guillotined tens of thousands of Frenchmen, including many whose only crime was to criticize Robespierre.

The Cult of Reason

The eleven months of the Reign of Terror were months when revolutionary ideas reached their peak in France— when the radical Jacobins who controlled the Committee of Safety were determined to destroy every last remnant of their old, tyrannical government, and to crush whatever obstacles stood in their way.

One of those obstacles was an institution that had opposed the Revolution from the beginning: the French Catholic Church. To radical Jacobin minds, it was not enough merely to close down monasteries, as the National Constituent Assembly had done in 1789; nor to guillotine French priests, as revolutionaries had been doing since the September Massacres of 1792. To make their Revolution truly permanent, Jacobins believed, France must completely eradicate her superstitious religion, and replace it with something far better: the enlightened reason of great thinkers like Voltaire. Pushing Voltaire's ideas to their ultimate conclusion, the Committee of Safety and the National Convention attacked the Church in several ways, including these:

- **The Celebration of Reason (November 10, 1793):** Atheist revolutionaries like Jacques Hébert and Antoine-François Momoro tried to replace Christianity with the **Cult of Reason**, a short-lived cult dedicated to perfecting mankind through science. The Cult of Reason reached its peak in November 1793, when cult members transformed Paris' great Notre Dame Cathedral into a Temple of Reason. Dressing Momoro's lovely wife as a Goddess of Reason, the cultists paraded her through the streets of Paris on a litter, and then elevated her to Notre Dame's altar as they sang hymns to her.

- Ever since the Great Fear (see Chapter 25), revolutionaries had been pillaging French churches— often so that they could melt bronze church bells into cannon, or golden communion vessels into coin. Inspired by the Cult of Reason, these attacks took on a more scornful tone: now in addition to pillaging churches, revolutionaries smashed churches' statues, tore out their wall art, danced in their aisles and sang bawdy songs from their altars. Even graveyards were no longer sacred: grave robbers exhumed the dead to steal treasures that had been buried with them, or to melt their coffins' lead linings into bullets. Where the dead had once rested in peace, their dishonored bones now littered the ground.

- A French officer named Joseph Fouché made the Christian symbolism found in church cemeteries his special target. As a firm believer in reason, Fouché

The Celebration of Reason at Paris' Notre Dame Cathedral

insisted that the resurrection was pure superstition, and therefore decreed that no French cemetery gate should bear any inscription but this: "Death is an eternal sleep." To spread his hopeless belief, Fouché went from cemetery to cemetery, smashing crosses, statues and inscriptions from the Bible— every symbol a Christian might have set over a lost loved one as a hopeful reminder of Christ's resurrection.

- **The Cult of the Supreme Being:** Unlike Hébert and Momoro, Robespierre was concerned that a godless France might also be an immoral France. After sending those two to the guillotine, Robespierre tried to establish a less godless state religion called the Cult of the Supreme Being. Robespierre's cult was a version of **Deism**— the Voltaire-approved religion which holds that although the universe obviously had its Creator, that Creator has since gone silent, and no longer has anything to do with his creation.

FASCINATING FACTS: The French Republican Calendar

Another obstacle radical Jacobins sought to crush was the old Gregorian calendar, with its many holidays in honor of Church and king. For about 12 years, from 1793 – 1805, France replaced its familiar old Gregorian calendar with an unfamiliar new **French Republican Calendar**, which included these unique features:

- No longer would France mark its years from Christ's birth, as the old Gregorian calendar did. Instead, the day of the First French Republic's founding— September 22, 1792— became the first day of Year I (One) on the French Republican Calendar.

- No longer would France name its months after old superstitions, so-called gods like Janus and Mars. Instead, the new calendar adopted month names that described the seasons in which they

French Republican clock face marked with two scales: the 10-hour day on the inside, and the old 24-hour day on the outside

fell. For example, a foggy fall month received the name *Brumaire*, French for "fog"; and a hot summer month received the name *Thermidor*, French for "summer heat."

- No longer would France use the complicated old system of 60 minutes per hour, 24 hours per day and so on. Instead, the new calendar adopted a decimal system of 100 seconds per minute; 100 minutes per hour; 10 hours per day; 10 days per week; and 3 weeks per month. One French Republican hour was equal to 2 old hours and 24 old minutes.

Decimal time proved even less popular than the French Republican calendar, lasting only until 1795.

FASCINATING FACTS: The Catacombs of Paris

Some of the human remains Joseph Fouché treated with such scorn probably found their way into the Catacombs of Paris.

Over the centuries, Paris had accumulated astonishing numbers of dead— so many that old cemeteries started digging up the bones of the long-dead to make room for the newly-dead. Around the time of the French Revolution, Paris found a new home for its enormous collection of old bones: inside a network of tunnels beneath the city, abandoned mines from which long-dead builders had once quarried limestone.

Centuries-old bones carefully arranged in the Catacombs of Paris

These Catacombs of Paris, which are still open to the public as of 2014, now preserve the bones of some 6 – 7 million dead Parisians, all arranged in neat stacks. On an archway above the entrance is carved *Arrête, c'est ici l'empire de la mort*— French for "Halt, this is the empire of the dead."

The Thermidorian Reaction (July 1794)

The Reign of Terror transformed once-lovely Paris into a city of unbearable chaos, a place where friendship turned to hatred in an instant. Every night, Parisians went to bed wondering if the allies who had stood beside them that day might guillotine them tomorrow. In the end, this chaos proved just as deadly to Robespierre as it was to King Louis XVI, Camille Desmoulins, Jacques Hébert and countless others.

FASCINATING FATES: The Fate of Maximilien Robespierre (July 28, 1794)

A few months into Robespierre's Reign of Terror, Frenchmen began to have doubts about their leader. Some doubts sprang from unfair laws like the Law of Suspects (see Chapter 25), which clearly violated the very human rights for which Robespierre claimed to stand. Others sprang from the executions of men like Camille Desmoulins and Jacques Hébert— devoted revolutionary leaders who clearly suffered the guillotine not because they deserved it, but because Robespierre desired it.

On July 26, 1794, Robespierre arose before the National Convention

Robespierre sitting in a tumbril awaiting the guillotine

to defend himself against his doubters. In a 2-hour-long speech, Robespierre railed against the many enemies who he claimed were out to get him; yet for some reason, he refused to mention any of those enemies' names.

Robespierre's refusal to name his enemies would prove to be a critical mistake— for no one could feel safe without seeing Robespierre's enemies list. Instead of spending another sleepless night wondering whether or not Robespierre had marked them for the guillotine, several delegates spent that night plotting Robespierre's demise.

The next day, Robespierre's enemies in the Convention arose to accuse him of tyranny and murder. Abandoned by his allies, Robespierre fell prey to the same unfair laws he had used to condemn his own political enemies, and suffered the same fate: a swift beheading at the guillotine on July 28.

Other interesting facts:
- Because the National Convention condemned Maximilien Robespierre on July 27, 1794, a date that corresponds to 9 Thermidor, Year II on the French Republican Calendar, historians named the revolution that overthrew Robespierre the **Thermidorian Reaction**.

The War of the First Coalition (1792 – 1797)

With Robespierre's end came an end to the Reign of Terror, and a slow advance toward freedom of religion for all Frenchmen. Unfortunately, Robespierre's end did nothing to solve the military problems revolutionary France still faced:

- **Invasion Threats:** Although France managed to halt the Duke of Brunswick's invasion in 1792, the First Coalition's armies still stood at France's borders, still determined to block unwanted revolutionary ideas from spreading beyond France. As of 1793, the First Coalition included several enemies, including the one that was to give France more trouble than any other: Great Britain.

- **The French Counter-revolution:** Several cities and regions around France rebelled against the National Convention. These rebels came in two main types:

  1. Some rebels were royalists who still hoped to set a king on France's throne. These included the Emigrant Army nobles who fled France during the Great Fear, and had since joined the First Coalition.

  2. Other rebels were old-fashioned Frenchmen who saw nothing wrong with their Catholic faith, and wondered why their mad government was suddenly murdering their priests, desecrating their churches and smashing the crosses over their lost loved ones' graves.

To solve its military problems, France turned to a soldier who was soon to emerge as one of history's greatest military geniuses: Napoleon Bonaparte.

FASCINATING FRENCHMEN: Napoleon (1769 – 1821)

Napoleone di Buonoparte was born on Corsica, a large, mountainous Mediterranean Sea island that lies about midway between Marseilles, France and Rome, Italy. The Buonapartes were minor nobles who sprang from roots in Tuscany, Italy; and like most Corsicans, they spoke far more Italian than French. One year before Napoleon's birth, the Italian Republic of Genoa sold Corsica to France, making French citizens of the Buonapartes. This explains why Napoleon, who was to become France's greatest general and emperor, spoke French with an Italian accent all his life.

After five years of military school in Brienne, France, the 15-year-old Napoleon moved on to the *École Militaire*, Paris— a fine military academy for young men who showed the potential to become good officers, despite being born to poorer families. There Napoleon first

24-year-old Napoleon laying plans at the Siege of Toulon

showed his military genius. With his exceptional mind and organizational skills, Napoleon was able to complete in one year a difficult artillery officers' training program that required most students two years, and many three.

His schooling complete, the now 16-year-old Napoleon received his commission as a second lieutenant of artillery in 1785, four years before the French Revolution began.

The Siege of Toulon (September – December 1793)

Napoleon's first major contribution to the Revolution came at Toulon, a Mediterranean seaport just east of Marseilles. Toulon was one of several royalist cities that rebelled against the National Convention during the French Counter-revolution. What made Toulon so important was that it was the French navy's main port on the Mediterranean— which meant that if Toulon fell to the royalists, then revolutionary France would have no navy to defend its Mediterranean coast.

To the Convention's horror, Toulon's fall became a certainty in September 1793, when the British navy arrived to reinforce the royalists with thousands of foreign troops. Backed by the British, the royalists were able to seize Toulon, tear down the tricolor flag of the Revolution and raise the fleur-de-lis of France's former kings. With the British navy in control of Toulon, recovering the city would require an aggressive siege.

Ordinarily, an officer as young as Napoleon would have had nothing to do with planning such an important siege. However, Napoleon had advantages over other officers. First, Napoleon was friendly with Augustin Robespierre— brother to the all-powerful Maximilien Robespierre, who was just beginning his Reign of Terror when the royalists seized Toulon. Second, Napoleon had the confidence to take responsibility for the siege— confidence his superiors lacked, for fear that the slightest mistake might send them to Robespierre's guillotine.

The excellence of Napoleon's generalship at Toulon was astounding for such a young officer. His superb organizational skills enabled him to gather hundreds of cannon; and his superior tactics enabled him to drive the British away from the coast, reclaiming Toulon for the National Convention. This first great success of Napoleon's career won him promotion to the high rank of brigadier general at the very young age of 24.

The following year, Napoleon suffered a reversal of fortunes— for that was the year when the Thermidorian Reaction sent scores of Robespierre's friends to prison, including Napoleon. Had not other friends spoken well of him, Napoleon might have gone to the guillotine beside Robespierre.

13 Vendémiaire, Year IV (October 5, 1795)

Napoleon's next major contribution to the Revolution came on October 5, 1795, a date equal to 13 Vendémiaire, Year IV on the French Republican Calendar. On that day, a small army of royalist rebels threatened the National Convention in, of all places, Paris. Having expected no trouble in Revolution-friendly Paris, the Convention had no army in place to defend itself, and was in serious danger of being overrun.

Fortunately, Napoleon was close enough to take charge of the few soldiers the Convention mustered for its defense. Just as fortunately, Napoleon had time before the rebels arrived to find about 40

Napoleon blasting royalist rebels in the streets of Paris on 13 Vendémiaire, Year IV

cannon. These Napoleon hauled into Paris and loaded with grapeshot— cannonball-sized bags of small shot which transform cannon into giant anti-personnel shotguns. When the rebels appeared, Napoleon opened fire, mowing down a royalist army that outnumbered his small band of artillerymen at least six times over.

> **REFRESHING REMINDERS**: Beginning with no constitution under Louis XVI, France progressed through:
>
> 1. The **Constitution of 1791**, the one that transformed France's old *Ancien Régime* government into a constitutional monarchy. This constitution's demise came at the Revolution of 10 August, 1792, which led to the creation of the First French Republic on September 22, 1792.
>
> 2. The **Constitution of 1793**, a constitution that the National Convention approved, but then set aside so that Robespierre could conduct his lawless Reign of Terror.

The Constitution of 1795 and the Directory

Within a month of Napoleon's heroics on 13 Vendémiaire, France adopted its third new constitution within four years.

After the Thermidorian Reaction, no one wanted any constitution that the lawless, merciless Robespierre had approved. Partly for this reason, the National Convention adopted the new **Constitution of 1795**, also called the Constitution of the Year III under the French Republican Calendar.

The Constitution of 1795 brought an end to the National Convention on October 27, 1795. In its place, the constitution set an elected legislature with two houses: (1) a junior house called the **Council of 500**, similar to the U.S. House of Representatives; and (2) a 250-member senior house called the **Council of Ancients**, similar to the U.S. Senate. Because all acts of the Council of 500 required approval from the Council of Ancients, this arrangement would slow down the lawmaking process. Hopefully, this would prevent the new government from suspending law and order like the old one did.

For the new government's executive branch, the Constitution of 1795 created a 5-man executive committee called the **Directory**. In theory, the interplay of five strong personalities would avoid placing too much power in the hands of any one man. In practice, though, the five directors usually divided along party lines, rendering the executive branch of government as chaotic as the legislative.

Napoleon's Campaign in Italy (1796 – 1797)

In a nation that honored its military heroes above all others, Napoleon's heroic victory on 13 Vendémiaire made him instantly popular— but only with the people of France, not with the government. Far from being grateful to Napoleon, the government grew jealous of his popularity, and terrified of how powerful this young general might become. To reduce Napoleon's popularity, the government needed some way to discredit him; but to avoid the public's wrath, the government needed to promote him. In March 1796, the Directory hit upon a tactic that might accomplish both: promoting Napoleon to command of France's worst, most disorganized army, the Army of Italy.

"Napoleon Crossing the Alps," 1800 painting by Jacques-Louis David

Ironically, the plan the Directory intended to discredit Napoleon accomplished just the opposite. Napoleon was such a great military genius— so talented at inspiring soldiers, organizing armies and planning strategy— that when he took charge of the Army of Italy, that army immediately went from worst to best. While France's other, supposedly superior armies were suffering setbacks in Germany, Napoleon was winning dozens of victories over Austria's allies in northern Italy, near cities like Nice, Genoa, Turin, Milan and Mantua.

After Napoleon conquered northern Italy, the atheists on the French Directory wanted him to turn south— hoping that if he conquered Rome as well, then he could cast down the pope once and for all, leaving the Roman Catholic Church disgraced and disorganized. Napoleon disagreed, instead recommending a more practical idea: crossing the Alps to confront France's real enemy, Austria. By winning victory after victory over Austria's armies— victories that brought him within 60 miles of Austria's capital, Vienna— Napoleon forced Austria to negotiate an end to the War of the First Coalition.

> SUCCINCT SUMMARIES: Some Results of the War of the First Coalition
>
> - In the **Treaty of Campo Formio**, signed by Austria and France on October 18, 1797, France won the territory where the French Revolutionary Wars had begun back in 1792: the Austrian Netherlands, most of which now belongs to Belgium. France also won territory along the west bank of the Rhine River, and established republican governments over parts of northern Italy.
> - Napoleon confiscated a great many paintings and sculptures, priceless Renaissance art that departed Italy to fill a Paris art museum founded in 1793: the **Louvre Museum**, housed in the no-longer-royal Louvre Palace.
> - Far from returning from Italy in disgrace, as the Directory had hoped, Napoleon returned to Paris in December 1797 as one of France's greatest heroes.

Napoleon's Campaign in Egypt and Syria (1798 – 1799)

The Directory's next task for Napoleon was to invade France's greatest enemy, Britain. In studying the problem, though, Napoleon determined that the French navy was not yet up to the task of controlling the English Channel— which made any invasion impossible, as Britain's mighty navy would simply sink every troop ship France tried to send across the Channel.

Instead of campaigning in Britain, Napoleon proposed an unexpected campaign in the Middle East— possession of which, Napoleon said, was the key to possessing the riches of the Far East. Ever since the 1600s, Britain's superior navy had dominated the rich markets of the Far East, barring France from becoming a first-rate trading nation. Napoleon envisioned France's navy controlling a new route to the Far East. Instead of sailing around Africa, French traders would cross the Mediterranean Sea to Egypt, where they would unload their ships for a 100-mile trip overland to the Gulf of Suez. From Suez, new ships would carry them on through the Red Sea, the Gulf of Aden and the Arabian Sea to India. Although the land leg of the trip would be inconvenient, Napoleon hoped that it might be more convenient than traveling thousands of miles around Africa.

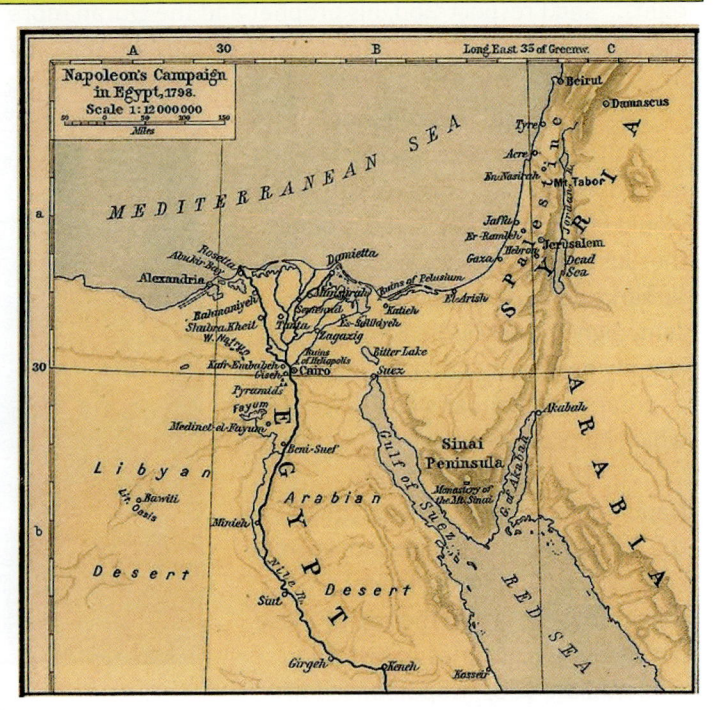

> A LOOK AHEAD: In the long run, Napoleon envisioned a man-made canal to carry his ships from the Mediterranean Sea to the Gulf of Suez. This vision will fail in 1801, when France will lose its grip on Egypt. After that, Napoleon's plan will have to wait until 1869— the year when French engineer Ferdinand de Lesseps and Egyptian leader Ismail Pasha will open the newly-complete **Suez Canal**.

Napoleon's campaign in the Middle East also had a second, related purpose. Once France controlled the Middle East, Napoleon planned to lead troops on to India, where they would join forces with Britain's Indian enemies to drive the British out of India— and hopefully out of the war as well.

On its way to Egypt, Napoleon's fleet stopped at the island of Malta to take on water. When the Knights of Malta— a.k.a. the Knights Hospitaller, who had held Malta since the early 1500s (see Chapter 16)— refused to cooperate, Napoleon seized their island. Thus did the Knights Hospitaller, an order of Crusading knights that had stood since around 1100, lose its last real home to Napoleon of France in 1798.

The Battle of the Pyramids (July 21, 1798)

Although the Ottoman Empire still technically controlled Egypt, Napoleon's real enemies there were the Mamluks— former slaves who had once been the Ottomans' most loyal soldiers, but had since arisen to build Muslim dynasties of their own (see Year 2). Before landing in Alexandria, Egypt, Napoleon issued a proclamation condemning the Mamluks' tyranny over Egypt. To reassure Egyptian Muslims that his invasion was well-intentioned, Napoleon's proclamation administered this dose of Enlightenment wisdom:

"For too long the [Mamluks] who govern Egypt have insulted [France]… The hour of their punishment has come. For too long this horde of slaves, bought in the Caucasus and Georgia, have tyrannized the most beautiful part of the world; but God, on whom all depends, has ordained that their empire shall end. People of Egypt, they have told you that I come to destroy your religion, but do not believe it… I come to restore your rights… and I respect God, his prophet and the Quran more than the Mamluks. Tell [the Mamluks] that all men are equal before God; wisdom, talents, virtues are the only things to make one man different from another…"

Napoleon also reminded his troops that they were landing in a city named for Alexander the Great, and would be treading the same ground that Julius Caesar trod. Such historical remarks pervaded Napoleon's campaign in the Middle East, as if he already dreamed of making his name as great as Alexander's or Caesar's— which he probably did.

The battle with which Napoleon won Egypt, the **Battle of the Pyramids**, also began with such a remark. Exclaiming, "Soldiers! Remember that from the top of these pyramids, 40 centuries of history contemplate you," Napoleon led his troops to a victory that decimated the Mamluks' army— leaving them with no way of defending their capital city, Cairo. Although the Mamluks continued to resist French occupation for a time, Napoleon was master of Cairo— and thus more or less Pharaoh of Egypt— from the Battle of Pyramids forward.

Napoleon at the Battle of the Pyramids

Napoleon was not, however, master of the waters north of Egypt. That honor belonged to Napoleon's worst enemy, British Admiral Horatio Nelson.

BRILLIANT BRITONS: Horatio Nelson (1758 – 1805)

Horatio Nelson was and is the most honored hero in all the long history of Britain's Royal Navy. Like Napoleon, Nelson was a born leader with an exceptional talent for inspiring men to make brave sacrifices for their country. In Nelson's case, part of that inspiration came from the fact that no one was braver, nor sacrificed more, than Nelson himself.

Born a minister's son in Norfolk, England, Nelson lost his mother at age 9. Three years later, Nelson went to sea with his mother's brother, Royal Navy Captain Maurice Suckling, as a 12-year-old midshipman— an officer-in-training. Nelson first saw combat when he was not yet 17; won promotion to lieutenant when he was not yet 19; and commanded his first Royal Navy brig in 1778, at age 20.

Captain Nelson's first encounter with Napoleon came 15 years later, at the Siege of Toulon— the 1793 siege in which Napoleon saved the French navy by driving the British navy, including Nelson, away from France's largest naval port on the Mediterranean.

Frustrated by the loss of Toulon, the Royal Navy moved on to a different target in 1794: Napoleon's home island of Corsica, where Nelson received his first debilitating wound. During an amphibious assault on Corsica, Captain Nelson unloaded his ship's cannon to use on land. Nelson was peering over a wall of sandbags when enemy fire struck the wall, spraying high-velocity sand directly into his right eye. Although Nelson won the battle, thus helping Britain win Corsica, he sacrificed his eye.

Rear Admiral Nelson sacrificed even more at the Battle of Santa Cruz de Tenerife, a losing battle fought in 1797 on the Canary Islands off Morocco's west coast. Here enemy fire shattered the upper bone of Nelson's right arm, damaging it so badly that his ship's surgeon couldn't save it. Despite the shock of amputation, the impossibly tough Nelson was back in command within an hour.

Such tales of toughness and courage made Nelson a living legend in Britain, inspiring other Britons to make the same sacrifices this one-eyed, one-armed Admiral made. Nelson also used his injuries as an excuse to break the rules other officers had to follow. For example, at the 1801 Battle of Copenhagen, Denmark, Nelson clearly saw a superior officer's signal to withdraw. Not wishing to obey, Nelson laughingly held the wrong end of his telescope to his blind eye, pretending that he couldn't see the signal.

Portrait of Horatio Nelson in 1805, with his empty right sleeve pinned out of his way

A LOOK BEHIND: Nelson versus Napoleon en route to Egypt (mid-1798)

In early 1798, the British Navy sent Nelson to the Mediterranean to lie in wait for Napoleon— whom, it had learned, was planning to launch some secret new campaign from Toulon. Nelson arrived off Toulon in May 1798, in time to intercept Napoleon's fleet on its way to Egypt. Much to Nelson's dismay, though, a severe storm scattered his fleet, allowing Napoleon to slip past him.

Having no idea where Napoleon was headed, Nelson spent several fruitless weeks searching for him around southern Italy. Only when Nelson heard of the happenings on Malta did he deduce what Napoleon was really planning, and sail off to search for him around Egypt.

Despite Napoleon's long head start, Nelson bypassed Napoleon's slow troop ships on the way to Africa, and arrived in Alexandria to find no sign of his quarry. Nelson therefore departed on another long, fruitless search, allowing Napoleon time to land his army at Alexandria and win the Battle of the Pyramids.

The Battle of the Nile (August 1, 1798)

While Napoleon battled on land, his idle warships lay at Abu Qir Bay, a wide-open bay just east of Alexandria. To defend the fleet against possible attack from Nelson, French Admiral François-Paul Brueys anchored his thirteen **ships of the line**— large, powerful ships of at least 74 cannon each— close to shore, arranging them in a mighty line of battle that could spew devastating broadsides every few minutes.

Mighty though Brueys' line was, it suffered from two serious weaknesses:

1. **Brueys anchored his line too far from shore**— far enough to allow the returning Nelson's ships to slip between line and shore, and thus attack both sides of the line at once. Because Brueys prepared only his sea-side cannon for battle, shore-side attackers could fire on the line without taking return fire.

2. **Brueys anchored his ships too far apart**, leaving gaps wide enough for Nelson's skilled seamen to slip between them. With Brueys' ships at anchor, Nelson's ships could stand in these gaps and fire on the French without ever exposing themselves to Brueys' devastating broadsides.

Nelson took advantage of Brueys' mistakes to make the **Battle of the Nile** one of the greatest victories of his career. Out of thirteen French ships of the line, Nelson captured nine, and destroyed two more— including Brueys' huge flagship *Orient*, which died in a spectacular explosion when a fire reached its powder magazine. Brueys never knew *Orient*'s fate, having died at his post an hour before. In exchange, Nelson lost 200+ killed and several hundred wounded— but not a single British ship of the line.

Brueys' 118-gun flagship *Orient* on fire at the Battle of the Nile

This devastating loss ruined all of Napoleon's grand plans in the Middle East— for controlling the Middle East meant nothing to Napoleon unless he also controlled the Mediterranean Sea, which he clearly didn't. Furthermore, the loss of the French fleet more or less stranded Napoleon's army in the Middle East. Nevertheless, Napoleon fought on in Syria and Egypt for another year before giving up and moving on.

SUCCINCT SUMMARIES: Some Results of Napoleon's Campaign in Egypt and Syria

- Two years after Napoleon departed the Middle East in August 1799, an alliance of Ottomans, Mamluks and British drove the French out of Egypt for good.

- During the three years when France occupied Egypt (1798 – 1801), French archaeologists made one of the most important historical discoveries of all time: the **Rosetta Stone**, an inscription-carved stone that became scholars' key to understanding ancient Egyptian hieroglyphics. Centuries before, an ancient pharaoh had ordered an important decree carved on the Rosetta Stone in three languages, including ancient Greek and two ancient Egyptian languages. Because scholars already knew Greek, the Rosetta Stone taught them the other two. Unfortunately for the French, the victorious British seized the Rosetta Stone and took it to Britain, where it remains as of 2014.

The Rosetta Stone

The Coup of 18 Brumaire (November 9, 1799) and the Consulate

All the while Napoleon campaigned in the Middle East, he also watched the news from France, which was not good. In Napoleon's absence, Austria and Russia formed a **Second Coalition** to launch the **War of the Second Coalition** against France; and so far, the war wasn't going well for France. Furthermore, France's four-year-old Directory government was in chaos, and might fall at any moment. Eager to be in Paris when the Directory fell, Napoleon quietly shipped out of Egypt in August 1799, and somehow evaded the British navy to arrive back in France that October.

Despite Napoleon's stalled Middle East campaign, the French people greeted him as a hero, the most popular man in France. Napoleon's extraordinary popularity was no accident; for Napoleon was not only a military genius, but also a propaganda genius— a gifted news writer whose glowing, sometimes exaggerated reports of his successes in Italy and Egypt won him millions of fans back home.

One month after arriving back in Paris, Napoleon took advantage of his extraordinary popularity to overthrow the Directory government. It so happened that one of the French Revolution's early heroes— Abbe Sieyes, who had since become a member of the Directory— was already planning to overthrow the Directory. On the morning of November 9, 1799— equal to 18 Brumaire, Year VIII on the French Republican Calendar— Sieyes and two other directors abruptly resigned, leaving the five-man Directory with too few members to render decisions. The next day, Napoleon led soldiers into both councils of France's legislature, the Council of Ancients and the Council of 500, to inform the delegates that their councils were now in recess.

Under threat of force, Napoleon soon convinced what was left of the legislature to name himself, Sieyes and one other as "provisional consuls"— thus creating a temporary three-man **Consulate** with all the powers of a dictator.

Napoleon closing down an angry Council of 500 on 18 Brumaire, Year VIII

The Constitution of the Year VIII (Dec. 1799)

About a month later, Napoleon produced a new constitution that tightened his grip on the French government. The **Constitution of the Year VIII** placed nearly all government powers in the hands of a single, unelected man— the First Consul, whom the Constitution specified was to be "Citizen Bonaparte." Although the Constitution also named Second and Third Consuls, these were no more than advisors to the First Consul. The Constitution allowed them to record their opinions, but insisted that "the decision of the First Consul suffices."

INTERESTING IDEAS: The Coup of 18 Brumaire and the Constitution of the Year VIII mark the end of the French Revolution. The purpose of that Revolution was to win liberty and republican government for the French people. When Napoleon seized power as First Consul, France lost its republican government, and the Revolution ended.

Emperor of the French (1804)

Over the next few years, two more new constitutions further tightened Napoleon's grip:

1. The **Constitution of the Year X**, adopted August 1, 1802. This constitution named Napoleon First Consul for life, not just the 10 years allotted by the Constitution of the Year VIII.

2. The **Constitution of the Year XII**, adopted May 18, 1804. This constitution finally named Napoleon Emperor of the French, and his male descendants heirs to his throne.

INTERESTING IDEAS: Although the Constitution of the Year XII still called France "the French Republic," the government it created was no republic. Rather, it was a tyrannical monarchy much like the *Ancien Régime*. In the fifteen years from 1789 – 1804, the people of France overthrew their government several times, adopting no fewer than six new constitutions— only to arrive back at a monarchy, albeit with a different king.

> **FASCINATING FACTS: Napoleon's Plebiscites**
>
> As a former revolutionary and champion of the Enlightenment, Napoleon always pretended that the people of France still had a voice in their government, even as he stripped their elected representatives of their authority. To accomplish this, Napoleon accompanied each new constitution with a **plebiscite**— a nationwide election in which the people could either accept or reject the proposed constitution, in theory at least.
>
> In practice, Napoleon almost certainly rigged the results of all three plebiscites, one each in 1799, 1802 and 1804. In each case, Napoleon's government reported ridiculous majorities of roughly 3,000,000 to 1,500 in favor of the new constitution— astonishing results which would indicate that only about 1 Frenchman in 2,000 opposed Napoleon's power grabs. Because no free election has ever indicated such a high level of agreement on any issue worthy of a vote, it is safe to assume that Napoleon reported his plebiscites' results as he wanted them to be, not as they really were.

The Napoleonic Code

Even though the rise of Napoleon meant the end of the French Revolution, Napoleon would have been foolish to ignore the Revolution's enlightened principles— for the French had already murdered one tyrant, and wouldn't hesitate to murder another if necessary. Rather than follow in Louis XVI's footsteps, Napoleon governed more like Frederick the Great of Prussia or Catherine the Great of Russia. Like these so-called **enlightened despots**, Napoleon was willing to allow his people all sorts of rights, so long as those rights didn't threaten his supreme authority.

INTERESTING IDEAS: Enlightened despots like Frederick, Catherine and Napoleon were proud to protect freedom of religion and equal treatment under the law. They balked, however, at free speech, freedom of the press and freedom of assembly— rights that might tend to encourage rebellions.

One mark of Napoleon's enlightened despotism was the **Napoleonic Code**, a new code of laws based on Enlightenment principles. Under the old *Ancien Régime*, French law was a confusing mass of overlapping codes written by all sorts of authorities, everyone from kings to

Napoleon receiving his imperial crown from the pope at Notre Dame Cathedral, Paris

bishops to lords of the manor. The Napoleon Code reformed this situation by (1) ensuring that the same laws applied all over the French Empire; and (2) granting Frenchmen the same human rights that citizens of other enlightened countries enjoyed— including the right of the accused to appear before a judge, the right to a fair trial and a ban on cruel and unusual punishments.

Napoleon's other contributions as emperor included these:

1. **The Concordat of 1801:** Unlike the atheist Hebert or the deist Robespierre, Napoleon was willing to negotiate with the Roman Catholic Church. In the Concordat of 1801, Napoleon agreed that because Catholicism was still France's dominant religion, France would pay priests' salaries as it had in the past— provided that priests swore oaths of loyalty to France.

2. **The Metric System of Measurement:** Although the decimal French Republican Calendar faded out of use in 1805, a new decimal system of measurement— the metric system— remained. French scientists led the world in developing the metric system, and still maintain international metric standards in Paris.

FASCINATING FACTS: Re-educating Children through Games

One way French revolutionaries taught their children new ways of thinking was through books and games. Children's stories that had once featured heroic royals could be rewritten to feature heroes of the Revolution. Children's playing cards that had once featured kings and queens could be replaced with ones that featured revolutionary soldiers or Enlightenment philosophers.

One popular board game that faced redesign during the French Revolution was *Jeu de l'oie*, French for **Game of the Goose**. Before the Revolution, the French version of the game had players advancing through pictures of Roman emperors and French kings. After the Revolution, though, such game boards were highly dangerous. Instead, new game boards featured revolutionary heroes like Abbe Sieyes, and events like the storming of the Bastille.

Other interesting facts:
- Europeans and Americans alike enjoyed the Game of Goose. Thomas Jefferson's copy of the game, which he played with his daughters and grandchildren, is still on display at his Monticello home.

The Napoleonic Wars (1803 – 1815)

The rise of Napoleon shifted the war aims of France's neighbors. In the French Revolutionary Wars, France's neighbors fought to block unwanted revolutionary ideas from spreading beyond France. In the wars that followed, the **Napoleonic Wars**, France's neighbors fought to contain the uncontainable ambition of Napoleon Bonaparte— whom, they felt sure, meant never to stop building his empire until it was as great as Alexander's, Caesar's or Charlemagne's.

With Napoleon in charge, France overcame earlier setbacks to win the War of the Second Coalition, and negotiated fragile peace treaties with Austria, Russia and Britain in 1801 – 1802. Despite the promises of peace in these treaties, though, Napoleon's enemies never believed that he was satisfied with the size of his empire. Therefore in 1803 – 1804, a **Third Coalition** of Britain, Austria, Russia and others declared war on France yet again.

A LOOK AHEAD: Although Britain's allies will negotiate separate peace treaties with France by 1806, Britain will remain at war with France without letup until 1814.

From the beginning of this latest war, Napoleon felt confident that he could defeat the British if he could only ship his troops across the English Channel. With this in mind, Napoleon built France's new Army of England— a 200,000-strong invasion force based on the French side of the English Channel, near Boulogne.

Unfortunately, Britain's superior navy still controlled the Channel, rendering any invasion impossible. Immeasurably frustrated at this unacceptable state of affairs, Napoleon howled, "Let us be masters of the Channel for but six hours, and we are masters of the world!" From 1803 – 1805, Napoleon searched constantly for a way to lure the British navy out of the English Channel long enough for his Army of England to board its fleet of barges, cross the Channel and conquer Britain for France.

Once again, it was British Admiral Horatio Nelson who foiled Napoleon's grand plan.

BRILLIANT BATTLES: The Battle of Trafalgar (October 21, 1805)

Like most of his battle plans, Napoleon's plan for luring the British navy out of the English Channel involved a ruse. In March 1805, a Toulon-based French fleet sailed west across the Mediterranean, through the Strait of Gibraltar and out into the Atlantic, apparently bound for targets in the British West Indies. Napoleon hoped that Nelson would sail out in search of this fleet, and would still be searching for it long after it circled around to its true target: the English Channel. Nelson did indeed search the West Indies for this French fleet, but couldn't find it. By August, Nelson was back in Europe, resting and preparing Britain's defenses.

Meanwhile, Napoleon's plan was suffering from a lack of boldness on the part of his fleet's commander, Admiral Pierre-Charles Villeneuve. Upon returning from the West Indies, Villeneuve was supposed to rendezvous with another fleet near Brest, France, just outside the English Channel. On his way to Brest, though, Villeneuve lost two ships to the British in a brief battle off the northwest coast of Spain. At this, Villeneuve apparently took fright, and decided to turn south. While Napoleon was sitting at Boulogne, impatiently waiting for Villeneuve to clear the English Channel, Villeneuve was actually fleeing hundreds of miles to the south— all the way to Cadiz, a Spanish port just west of the Strait of Gibraltar.

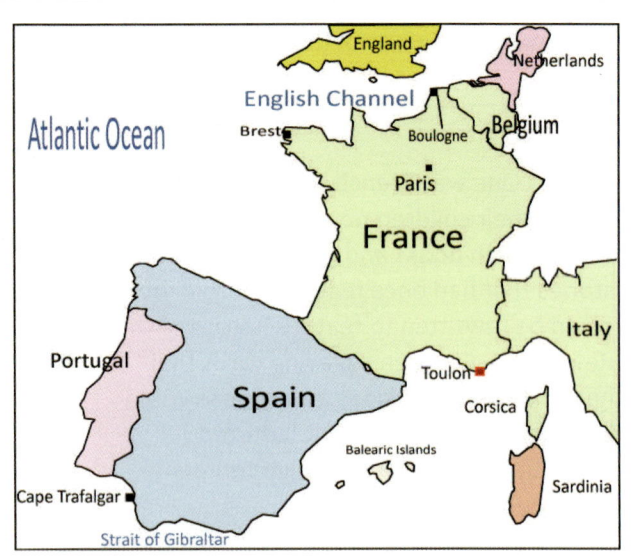

With Third Coalition armies threatening France on all sides, Napoleon couldn't leave his huge Army of England idle forever. Therefore when Villeneuve failed to arrive by late August, Napoleon abandoned his invasion plans for the moment, and led his army east to face other threats.

INTERESTING IDEAS: Thus the major threat of French boots on British soil ended in late August 1805, weeks before the Battle of Trafalgar— although Napoleon stood ready to return if Britain dropped her guard.

Far from dropping her guard, Britain sent a large fleet south to tackle Villeneuve, who was still hiding at Cadiz. In late September, Admiral Nelson arrived near Cadiz to take command of this fleet.

Having no interest in facing Nelson, Villeneuve elected to remain safely in port— that is, until he learned that Napoleon was furious with him, and had promoted a new admiral over his head. In a weak, desperate attempt to save his job, Villeneuve led his fleet out of Cadiz before this new admiral could arrive to take his place. In doing so, Villeneuve exposed his fleet to Britain's most aggressive naval commander, Horatio Nelson.

Nelson caught up with Villeneuve off Cape Trafalgar, a lighthouse midway between Cadiz and the Strait of Gibraltar. Despite being heavily outnumbered— for the French and their Spanish allies had 33 ships of the line and some 30,000 men, compared to 27 ships of the line and 17,000 men for the British— Nelson did not hesitate to attack.

As the British bore down on their enemies, every outnumbered man understood that his country's fate hung on the battle to come. Sensing that his men needed encouragement, the ever-inspiring Nelson sent this message up the masts of his flagship, HMS *Victory*: "England expects that every man will do his duty," encoded in the patterned flags admirals used to issue orders during battle.

To even the odds, Nelson prepared an unusually aggressive plan of attack.

FASCINATING FACTS: Ships of the Line

In Nelson's day, the usual way of conducting major sea battles was for both sides to form their ships into straight lines of battle. This arrangement offered two main advantages: (1) it aimed every ship's greatest strength, its cannon-armed sides, toward the enemy; and (2) it gave ships a way to escape battle— for if they took too much damage, then they could simply veer out of line, and hopefully be far away before their battle-preoccupied enemies could give chase.

One disadvantage of the battle line was that it required extremely heavy, thick-hulled ships that could withstand point-blank cannon fire without suffering too much damage. Any ship heavy enough to take such a pounding was called a **ship of the line**. In Nelson's day, the smallest ships of the line carried 70 cannon, and 74 were preferred. Nelson's flagship, *Victory*, carried 104 cannon. The largest ship at the Battle of Trafalgar, the Spanish giant *Santissima Trinidad*, carried an astounding 140 cannon.

"The Battle of Trafalgar" by artist William Stanfield

Nelson wasn't interested in escaping, nor in leaving his enemies room to escape. Therefore instead of forming a single line alongside his enemy, Nelson divided his fleet into two lines that drove straight at the enemy. The first line, with *Victory* at its head, drove at the middle of the enemy line; while the second line drove at the rear. That way, Nelson could cut the enemy's larger fleet in half, and hopefully defeat the rear before the front could turn around to join battle.

Nelson's plan was a fantastic success. In a long, grim battle on October 21, 1805, the British captured or destroyed more than 20 French and Spanish ships, without losing a single ship of their own. The British also killed or wounded nearly 6,000 enemy sailors and marines, and captured thousands more. In exchange, the British suffered roughly 1,200 wounded and 450 dead— including, to their great grief, their most honored naval hero.

FASCINATING FATES

- **Admiral Nelson's Fate (October 21, 1805):** Nelson's aggressive battle plan brought his ships quite close to his enemies'— so close that ship-to-ship musket fire and hand-to-hand combat became as important as cannon broadsides. At around 1:30 PM, an enemy marine noticed Nelson's highly-decorated uniform jacket moving among the mass of marines on *Victory*'s deck. Seconds later, a well-aimed musket ball struck Nelson high in the back, shattering his spine. Nelson died below decks three hours later. Before Nelson died, though, his loyal officers made sure he knew two important facts: that his tactics had won the day, and that his arch-enemy Napoleon would never lead his armies across the English Channel. Among the heroic Nelson's last prayers were these of thanksgiving: "Thank God I have done my duty… God and my country."

Scene from the deck of Nelson's flagship, HMS *Victory*, during the Battle of Trafalgar

- **Admiral Villeneuve's Fate (April 22, 1806):** Among the captives the British took at Trafalgar was Admiral Villeneuve, who spent several months as a paroled prisoner in Britain before his captors released him back to France. A few months later, Villeneuve's body turned up in a French hotel room, punctured with multiple stab wounds. Although French police recorded Villeneuve's death as a suicide, most Britons believed that Napoleon had sent a hit squad to murder his timid admiral for ruining his grand plan to invade Britain.

MUSICAL MASTERS: Ludwig van Beethoven (1770 – 1827)

The great composer Ludwig van Beethoven was born in Bonn, Germany to a stern music teacher who was determined to make a great musician of his son. According to legend, Beethoven was only four years old when he took up piano and violin; his father made him practice for hours each day, and switched his knuckles when he made mistakes. When young Beethoven began to show signs of genius, his hard-drinking father took to pulling him out of bed in the middle of the night so that he could impress drunken friends with his remarkable skills. To impress even more, his father often led his friends to believe that his genius son was even younger than he actually was.

In 1792, the now 22-year-old Beethoven moved to Vienna, Austria, the city where he was to compose his greatest works. Like other composers of his day, Beethoven survived partly on money earned as a performer, and partly on gifts from patrons of the arts— wealthy Austrian nobles who paid his living expenses so that he could spend more time composing great music for them to enjoy. So exceptional was Beethoven that within a few years, Vienna recognized him as the obvious successor to another musical genius: Beethoven's sometime-teacher Mozart, who died in 1791.

Beethoven's years in Vienna were the years when the French Revolution and the Napoleonic Wars spread chaos all over Europe. As a Viennese composer who depended on noble Austrians for his living, Beethoven could hardly support their enemies' Revolution. Nevertheless as a believer in Enlightenment philosophy, the commoner Beethoven resented the fact that no matter how much genius he displayed, Austrian nobles still considered themselves superior to him by birth. An angry Beethoven once wrote to a proud noble:

> "Prince, what you are you are by accident of birth; what I am I am through myself. There have been and always will be thousands of princes, but there is only one Beethoven."

Beethoven found Napoleon Bonaparte's heroism so inspiring that he wrote one of his first long symphonies— Symphony Number Three, also called *Eroica* or "Heroic"— in Napoleon's honor. However, when Napoleon declared himself Emperor of the French— a clear violation of Enlightenment principles— an enraged Beethoven violently struck Napoleon from the symphony's title page, leaving a hole where his name had been.

Beethoven was around 25 years old when he first began to notice some hearing loss. By age 40, Beethoven was so deaf that he could no longer trust himself to perform in public, and so lost an important source of income. By age 45, he was almost completely deaf. To compensate for his deafness at the piano, Beethoven bolted one end of a metal rod to his piano's soundboard, and gripped the other end with his teeth. The rod transferred the soundboard's vibrations to his skull, helping him perceive the sound without really hearing it. In conversation, Beethoven first resorted to ear trumpets; and when those no longer helped, his friends wrote notes to him in conversation books. Scores of Beethoven's conversation books still survive, filled with interesting details of his later life.

Although Beethoven's deafness deeply saddened him, it did not stop him from composing some of his greatest works late in life. At the premier of one his best-beloved works— his Symphony Number Nine, completed only three years before his death at age 56— Beethoven's friends had to physically turn him around so that the stone-deaf composer could see the audience applauding his work with all its might.

PRESIDENTIAL FOCUS

PRESIDENT #2: John Adams (1735 – 1826)	
In Office: March 4, 1797 – March 4, 1801	**Political Party:** Federalist
Birthplace: Massachusetts	**Nickname:** "Atlas of Independence"

John Adams was a successful Boston attorney who won election to both Continental Congresses, where he became a leading champion of American independence. After serving beside Jefferson and Franklin on the Committee of Five that produced the Declaration of Independence, Adams spent most of the Revolutionary War years overseas, serving as an ambassador to France and the Netherlands. Adams also helped negotiate the 1783 Treaty of Paris, the treaty that ended the Revolutionary War, before becoming the U.S.' first ambassador to Great Britain.

Although his overseas duties forced him to miss the 1787 Constitutional Convention, Adams returned home in 1788 to win election as George Washington's vice president. Eight years later, Adams edged out Thomas Jefferson by three electoral votes to become the second President of the United States. Under the Electoral College rules set forth in the Constitution, Jefferson became Adams' vice president.

The main crisis of Adams' presidency was the international chaos generated by the French Revolution. Four years before Adams took office, Britain joined the First Coalition of European powers united to block revolutionary ideas from spreading beyond France. Britain's war on France led to trouble on the high seas— trouble the U.S. couldn't avoid, as both Britain and France attacked U.S. merchant ships for trading with their enemy. President Washington's solution was the Jay Treaty, a promise of friendship and free commerce between the U.S. and Britain. The problem with the Jay Treaty was that while it prevented war with Britain, it made war with France more likely. Adams spent most of his single term in office striving to avoid war with France, and counted his success in avoiding war as the greatest accomplishment of his presidency.

In the course of avoiding war with France, Adams made the difficult decision to sign the Alien and Sedition Acts— a set of four laws which, among other things, limited Americans' right to free speech. These highly unpopular acts became the main tools Adams' enemies used to defeat him in the election of 1800.

Fun Facts about John Adams:
- Adams was the first president to live in the White House, which was incomplete when he and his beloved wife Abigail moved there in 1800.
- Adams and his son, 6th president John Quincy Adams, form one of only two father-son pairs to serve as presidents. Presidents George H.W. Bush (#41) and George W. Bush (#43) form a second father-son pair.
- Adams died on July 4, 1826, a date that was special for two reasons: (1) because it was the 50th anniversary of the American independence for which Adams fought so hard; and (2) because it was the very same day when Adams' personal friend and political rival Thomas Jefferson died.

Notable Quotes from John Adams:
- "Posterity! You will never know how much it cost the present generation to preserve your freedom! I hope you will make a good use of it. If you do not, I shall repent in heaven that I ever took half the pains to preserve it."

CHAPTER 27: The First Party System; the Louisiana Purchase

U.S. HISTORY FOCUS

ILLUMINATING LISTS: The First Three Presidents of the United States

President #1: George Washington **In office:** 1789 – 1797 (two terms) **Vice President:** John Adams	**President #2:** John Adams **In office:** 1797 – 1801 (one term) **Vice President:** Thomas Jefferson	**President #3:** Thomas Jefferson **In office:** 1801 – 1809 (two terms) **Vice Presidents:** Aaron Burr George Clinton

The First Party System

REFRESHING REMINDERS from Chapter 23: Some of the Constitution's framers, including first U.S. President George Washington, found the ideas of political parties and election campaigns distasteful. Washington felt that dignified public servants shouldn't have to seek office; rather, the office should seek them.

Federalists versus Democratic-Republicans

The most influential member of President Washington's cabinet, Alexander Hamilton, did not share Washington's distaste for political parties. As the first U.S. Secretary of the Treasury, Hamilton wanted Congress to approve his financial program, which included:

- The **Assumption Bill** (see Chapter 24).
- The **whiskey excise** (see Chapter 26).
- A strong new **national bank** called the First Bank of the United States.

Former First Bank of the United States building in Philadelphia

To promote this program, Hamilton founded the USA's first political party: the **Federalist Party**, an organization devoted to building a strong federal government for the newborn United States. The Federalists' first tasks were:

1. To organize representatives in Congress who shared the Federalists' vision, building a strong voting bloc that would always vote together on key issues.
2. To use this strong voting bloc to negotiate give-and-take deals like the Compromise of 1790, in which Hamilton's opponents agreed to pass his Assumption Bill in exchange for moving the U.S. capital from New York City to Washington D.C. (see Chapter 24).

The Federalists' next task was to raise money from Americans all over the country who shared its vision. Armed with this money, the party could:

1. Hire pamphleteers and newspaper writers to present its vision to the voting public in the most appealing, vote-winning ways.
2. Hire political operatives to knock on doors all over the country, encouraging voters who shared the Federalists' vision to vote on election day.

In addition to a strong federal government, the Federalist Party tended to favor:

1. **Big business over small farmers.** Many Federalists were wealthier-than-average northeastern businessmen who would benefit from Hamilton's program, which included: (1) a strong national defense to protect their interests; and (2) a strong national bank to establish stable currency and credit for their businesses.

2. **Rich over poor.** Federalists were leery of too much democracy— that is, of placing too much power in the hands of the poor, whose passion-swept whims might change at any moment. Instead, Federalists wanted to place power in the hands of wealthier, more settled citizens. Among other things, this meant:

    - Allowing state legislatures, not individual voters, to choose senators and presidential electors, as the Constitution originally provided.

    - Requiring citizens to own a certain amount of property before they could vote.

3. **Britain over France.** Federalists favored a strong relationship with the world's greatest sea power, Britain, so that Britain's mighty navy wouldn't interfere with U.S. sea trade. Federalists also distrusted the French Revolution, especially after the lawless Reign of Terror (see Chapter 25).

To oppose Hamilton's aggressive program, Declaration of Independence author Thomas Jefferson and his allies formed the USA's first opposition party: the **Democratic-Republican Party**, which tended to favor:

1. **States' rights over federal power.** Democratic-Republicans were leery of the strong federal government Hamilton was trying to create, fearing that it would seize powers which rightfully belonged to the individual states. Democratic-Republicans felt that the best governments were small, local ones made up of elected representatives who stayed close to the people, never forgetting their voters' wishes.

2. **Voting rights for all.** Democratic-Republicans favored allowing even the poorest of Americans to vote— mainly so that the wealthy couldn't use the government to rob the poor of their God-given rights.

1800 portrait of Thomas Jefferson, founder of the Democratic-Republican Party and third President of the United States

3. **France over Britain.** Democratic-Republicans considered the French Revolution just as worthy as the American Revolution, just as devoted to the Enlightenment principles ofnliberty, equal rights and republican government. They also remembered how much France had contributed to the cause of American liberty, and considered it treachery not to return the favor.

INTERESTING IDEAS: As a U.S. Ambassador to France who lived in Paris for years, Thomas Jefferson loved France, and was one of the French Revolution's biggest American supporters. Two years before that Revolution began, Thomas Jefferson wrote these words in a letter about the far less violent Shays' Rebellion (see Chapter 23):

"God forbid we should ever be 20 years without such a rebellion… And what country can preserve its liberties if their rulers are not warned from time to time that their people preserve the spirit of resistance? …The tree of liberty must be refreshed from time to time with the blood of patriots and tyrants. It is its natural manure [i.e., fertilizer]." *In other words: Unless patriots are willing to defend their liberty with their very lives, power-hungry tyrants will always arise to rob them of that liberty.*

Unlike his Federalist opponents, Jefferson continued to support the French Revolution even after Robespierre's Reign of Terror slaughtered thousands of innocents. Although Jefferson regretted these innocents' deaths, he regretted them no more than the innocents who died fighting the American Revolution. To Jefferson, these innocents were sad casualties in a necessary battle for French liberty.

Later in life, Jefferson described the differences between the first two political parties in this way:

"Men by their constitutions are naturally divided into two parties: (1) those who fear and distrust the people, and wish to draw all powers from them into the hands of the higher classes [i.e., the Federalists]; and (2) those who identify themselves with the people, have confidence in them, cherish and consider them as the most honest and safe— although not the most wise— depositary of the public interests [Democratic-Republicans]."

ILLUMINATING EXCERPTS from "Opposite Sides of a Penny" by Rosemary and Stephen Vincent Benet

In a collection of poems titled *A Book of Americans*, American poets Rosemary and Stephen Vincent Benet wrote this poem to illustrate the differences between Alexander Hamilton and Thomas Jefferson:

Jefferson said, "The many!"
Hamilton said, "The few!"
Like opposite sides of a penny
Were those exalted two.

If Jefferson said, "It's black, sir!"
Hamilton cried, "It's white!"
But, 'twixt the two, our Constitution
Started working right.

Hamilton liked the courtly,
Jefferson liked the plain.
They'd bow for a while, but shortly
The fight would break out again.

President John Adams and the Alien and Sedition Acts

DEFINITION: To commit **sedition** is to say, write or do anything that encourages citizens to rebel against their government.

FASCINATING FACTS: The Alien and Sedition Acts (1798)

The **Alien and Sedition Acts** were a set of four controversial laws passed by the 5th U.S. Congress— a Federalist-dominated congress that met in 1797 – 1798— and signed into law by President John Adams. Basically, these acts gave the federal government two new powers:

1. The power to expel any alien— that is, any non-citizen— whom the government declared "dangerous to the peace and safety of the United States."

2. The power to arrest and prosecute anyone, alien or otherwise, for criticizing the U.S. government.

The driving forces behind the Alien and Sedition Acts were the French Revolution, the Jay Treaty and the Quasi-War (seen Chapter 26). The Federalists claimed that they needed these laws to prevent loud-mouthed agitators, both foreign and domestic, from turning the minor Quasi-War into a major, declared war on France.

Portrait of John Adams, 2nd President of the United States and signer of the Alien and Sedition Acts

The Democratic-Republicans suspected that the Sedition Act, in particular, had more sinister purpose: helping the Federalists silence their political enemies.

From the beginning, America's two political parties didn't always handle their differences in gentlemanly fashion, as the muckraking journalism of James Callender illustrates.

DEFINITION: A **muckraker** was a journalist who published scandalous stories and rumors to embarrass enemy politicians. Muckraking was particularly popular in the United States, where the First Amendment protected journalists against vengeful enemy politicians— that is, until President Adams signed the Sedition Act.

INTERESTING INDIVIDUALS: James Callender (1758 – 1803)

James Callender was a muckraker whose victims included two of America's most successful politicians:

1. Alexander Hamilton: In 1791, Secretary of the Treasury Hamilton— a married father of three small children— began an extramarital affair with a young woman named Maria Reynolds, who was also married. Unfortunately for Hamilton, Mrs. Reynolds' husband discovered the affair. If Mr. Reynolds had been an honorable gentleman of his day, then he might have challenged Hamilton to a duel. Instead, Mr. Reynolds used his knowledge of the affair in a shadier way: he threatened to expose the affair unless Hamilton paid him a great deal of money. To save his reputation, Hamilton paid the blackmail Reynolds demanded.

Despite Hamilton's best efforts to cover up his illicit affair, members of Congress somehow found out about it. Due to Hamilton's lofty position, these members suspected that Mr. Reynolds' blackmail demands might have included something more than money— perhaps something illegal. To prove that he hadn't broken the law, Hamilton took the embarrassing step of handing over to investigators certain love letters that he had exchanged with Mrs. Reynolds. Although these letters badly damaged Hamilton's reputation, they also proved that he was innocent of any crime.

Portrait of Alexander Hamilton

One of those Congressional investigators happened to be a Virginia senator and future president named James Monroe. As a committed Democratic-Republican, Monroe knew that Hamilton's embarrassing love letters might prove quite valuable in the next election; so he forwarded them to his friend and neighbor Thomas Jefferson. Jefferson in turn forwarded the letters to muckraker James Callender, who published some of their juicy details in a collection of essays titled "The History of the United States for 1796."

Partly out of embarrassment over the whole affair, Hamilton resigned as Secretary of the Treasury in 1795. Although Hamilton remained an active Federalist for the rest of his life, he never held public office again.

2. John Adams: The presidential election of 1800 pitted sitting President John Adams against sitting Vice President Thomas Jefferson. Just before the election, Democratic-Republicans hired Callender to write "The Prospect Before Us," a campaign pamphlet that derided Adams in these strong terms:

"[Adams is] one of the most egregious fools upon the continent... a hideous hermaphroditical [i.e., both male and female] character with neither the force and firmness of a man, nor the gentleness and sensibility of a woman."

For their part, Federalist muckrakers disparaged Jefferson as:

"... a mean-spirited, low-lived fellow, the son of a half-breed Indian squaw, sired by a Virginia mulatto [mixed-race] father... raised wholly on hoe-cake, bacon and hominy, with an occasional change of fricasseed bullfrog."

Such attacks played well in the northeast, where urbane New Englanders tended to look down their noses at countrified, slaveholding Virginians.

For publishing such harsh criticisms of President Adams, James Callender became one of only a few Americans ever jailed for political speech. In early 1800, a federal court tried Callender under the Sedition Act, found him guilty and sentenced him to nine months' imprisonment.

The Presidential Election of 1800

The obvious problem with the Sedition Act was that it violated the First Amendment to the United States Constitution— the one that protected all citizens' rights to free speech and freedom of the press. To many Americans, the fact that a Federalist Congress and President passed such a liberty-crushing law confirmed their worst suspicions about Federalists. Thanks to the Alien and Sedition Acts, a large majority of Americans accepted what Democratic-Republicans had been saying about Federalists for years— that they were power-mad monarchists bent on seizing all power for themselves, ignoring the freedoms for which so many Americans had fought and died in the Revolutionary War.

This profound change of public feeling produced dramatic results in the election of 1800:

- Mostly because he had signed the hated Alien and Sedition Acts, the public voted President John Adams out of office, making him the first one-term president.
- In the Senate and the House of Representatives, the election of 1800 brought resounding defeats for many Federalist candidates, and resounding victories for many Democratic-Republican ones— so many that when the victors took office, Democratic-Republicans would control not only the executive branch, but also both houses of the legislative branch.

DEFINITION: The change of public feeling that swept Democratic-Republicans to victory in the election of 1800 was so profound that historians named that election the **Revolution of 1800**— a peaceful revolution that confirmed Americans' love of liberty, and condemned the Federalist Party for attacking that liberty.

A LOOK AHEAD: No Federalist will win the presidency ever again, and the party will disappear by around 1820.

A LOOK BEHIND at the Elections of 1788, 1792 and 1796

The election of 1800 revealed a flaw in the Electoral College system established by Article II, Section 1 of the U.S. Constitution. Under that system, each presidential elector voted for two presidential candidates; the candidate who received the most electoral votes became president, and the second most vice president. This system worked fine in the elections of 1788 and 1792, when every elector cast one of his two votes for the overwhelmingly popular George Washington.

The election of 1796 was the first in which political parties played critical roles. Through the parties' efforts, all Federalist electors cast one vote for Adams, just as all Democratic-Republican electors cast one vote for Jefferson. Thanks to a three-vote Federalist majority, Adams edged out Jefferson to win the presidency.

If all Federalist electors had cast their second votes for the same candidate as well, then their second choice would have won the vice presidency by those same three votes. Instead, the Federalists split their second votes— leaving Jefferson with more votes than any Federalist save Adams. As the candidate with the second-most votes, Jefferson became a Democratic-Republican vice president to a Federalist president— thus producing a divided executive branch, an inconvenience that both parties hoped to avoid in the future.

The Twelfth Amendment (1801 – 1804)

The Electoral College's worst failure came in 1800, by which time both parties were so well organized that all presidential electors voted exactly as their parties told them. On the winning side, all 73 Democratic-Republican electors voted for both of their party's top candidates, Virginian Thomas Jefferson and New Yorker Aaron Burr.

Unfortunately, the Democratic-Republicans' triumph of organization created a sticky problem. Everyone in America knew that the party intended Jefferson to be president, and Burr vice president. What the vote count revealed, though, was a 73 – 73 tie between Jefferson and Burr— with no way to distinguish which candidate was to be which.

Portrait of Aaron Burr

The Constitution provided that in the event of a tie, the House of Representatives was to choose between the top candidates. Because the newly-elected House had yet to convene, the old Federalist-majority House would choose between Jefferson and Burr— which meant trouble for Jefferson, as most Federalists detested him.

Burr could have resolved Jefferson's trouble by simply stepping aside, as Jefferson asked. In light of the Federalists' majority in the old House, though, Burr calculated that his chances of winning were just as good as Jefferson's, if not better. Therefore instead of stepping aside, Burr launched a hard-fought campaign for president against his own former running mate.

Thanks to Burr's stubborn ambition, the House needed 7 days and 36 separate votes before it finally chose the candidate every Democratic-Republican voter had intended to be president, Jefferson. This week-long election ruckus from February 11 – 17, 1801 produced at least three long-term results:

1. It stirred distrust between Jefferson and his vice president, Aaron Burr, whom Jefferson never forgave for refusing to step aside. For the election of 1804, Jefferson would choose a different vice presidential running mate, casting Burr out of national office. Years later, Jefferson would do his best to convict Burr of treason.

2. It stirred greater hatred between Aaron Burr and his fellow New Yorker, Alexander Hamilton. Having battled over New York politics for years, the two were already bitter enemies. During the House vote, Hamilton added to the bitterness by expressing this insulting opinion on the choice between Jefferson and Burr: "I would much rather have someone with the wrong principles [Jefferson] than someone devoid of any [Burr]."

3. It stirred the United States to amend its Constitution.

FASCINATING FACTS: The Twelfth Amendment (Ratified June 15, 1804)

To avoid similar confusion in the future, the United States changed its Electoral College formula months before the election of 1804. Under the **Twelfth Amendment**, each elector submits one vote for president and one for vice president, leaving no doubt which candidate is to be which. By allowing candidates for president and vice president to run together on the same ticket, this new system reduces the likelihood of ties, while increasing the likelihood that the winning president and vice president will belong to the same party.

Marbury v. Madison (1803)

The Midnight Judges Act (February 1801)

The Revolution of 1800 left the badly-beaten Federalists with just one branch of government they might still control, if they acted quickly: the judicial branch.

Between election day and inauguration day, the Federalists remained in power— if only as **lame ducks**, defeated officeholders serving out the ends of their terms. In a desperate attempt to preserve one branch of government for their party, the lame duck Federalist Congress passed, and President Adams signed, the **Midnight Judges Act**— an act that allowed Adams to appoint dozens of new federal judges just before he left office, if not precisely at midnight. Naturally, the judges Adams chose were all Federalists.

AMAZING AMERICANS: John Marshall (1755 – 1835)

It so happened that the 3rd Chief Justice of the Supreme Court, Oliver Ellsworth, was preparing to retire just as Adams left office— a circumstance that might allow President Jefferson to appoint a Democratic-Republican chief justice

Portrait of John Marshall, 4th Chief Justice of the U.S. Supreme Court, appointed by President Adams in 1801

immediately after he took office. To deny Jefferson that opportunity, Adams made another midnight appointment just before leaving office. With the Senate's approval, Adams' Federalist Secretary of State John Marshall became the 4th Chief Justice of the Supreme Court.

A LOOK AHEAD: Despite his midnight appointment, Marshall will become one of the United States' strongest chief justices, the one whose decisions will define permanently the role of the U.S. Supreme Court. Adams will later recall Marshall's appointment as one of his presidency's greatest gifts to the young United States.

Commission Controversy

By law, many of Adams' midnight federal judges had to receive new commissions from the secretary of state before they could take office. Unfortunately for the Federalists, writing and delivering those commissions took more time than President Adams had left in office— which left it up to President Jefferson's new secretary of state, James Madison, to deliver the rest.

As devoted Democratic-Republicans, Jefferson and Madison didn't want Adams' Federalist judges controlling the federal court system for years to come. Therefore on Jefferson's orders, Madison laid the remaining judges' commissions aside, refusing to deliver them. Meanwhile, the new Democratic-Republican congress set to work un-creating some of the judgeships created by the Midnight Judges Act.

Portrait of James Madison as Secretary of State

At least one of Adams' midnight judges, a wealthy Maryland Federalist named William Marbury, was not content to stand meekly by while his enemies denied him his Senate-approved judgeship. In February 1803, Marbury sued Madison in the U.S. Supreme Court, asking the court to force Madison to deliver Marbury's commission.

The suit Marbury filed, *Marbury v. Madison*, was to become one of the most important in American legal history— not because of Marbury's petition, but because the suit gave Chief Justice John Marshall a chance to present his opinion on judicial review.

DEFINITION: **Judicial review** is the legal principle that gives the U.S. Supreme Court authority to approve or disapprove laws passed by Congress and signed by the president. According to Chief Justice John Marshall's opinion in *Marbury v. Madison*, the Supreme Court alone has the authority to decide whether or not a new law is allowable under the supreme law of the land, the Constitution of the United States.

Like many Supreme Court cases, *Marbury v. Madison* was important for reasons that went far beyond its original dispute. In the long run, Marbury's petition mattered little— for although Marshall agreed that Madison was wrong to deny Marbury's commission, he never ordered Madison to deliver the commission, and Marbury never became a federal judge.

The reason for Marshall's refusal was that in his opinion, the Supreme Court had no authority to order the executive branch to do anything. Marshall was well aware that the law that had established the first federal court system, the Judiciary Act of 1789, gave the Supreme Court that authority. However, the Constitution mentioned no such authority; and in Marshall's opinion, the Constitution was the higher law. Marshall ruled that the Judiciary Act of 1789 was in error— for Congress must pass no law that undermined the highest law of the land, the Constitution of the United States.

ILLUMINATING EXCERPTS from Chief Justice John Marshall's Decision in *Marbury v. Madison*

Although Marshall's ruling in *Marbury v. Madison* denied the Supreme Court authority in one area—issuing orders to the executive branch— it also granted the Supreme Court great authority in the area of judicial review. Among the legal principles established by Marshall's opinion in *Marbury v. Madison* are these:

1. **The Constitution of the United States and its duly-ratified amendments are the highest law of the land.** *In Marshall's words*: "… in declaring what shall be the supreme law of the land, the constitution itself is first mentioned; and not the laws of the United States generally, but those only which shall be made in pursuance of the constitution, have that rank."

2. **The U.S. Supreme Court has final authority to decide which new laws are allowable under the Constitution, and which are not.** *In Marshall's words*: "It is emphatically the province and duty of the judicial department to say what the law is. Those who apply the rule to particular cases, must of necessity expound and interpret that rule. If two laws conflict with each other, the courts must decide on the operation of each. So if a law be in opposition to the constitution; if both the law and the constitution apply to a particular case, so that the court must either decide that case conformably to the law, disregarding the constitution; or conformably to the constitution, disregarding the law; the court must determine which of these conflicting rules governs the case. This is of the very essence of judicial duty."

INTERESTING IDEAS: Although the principle of judicial review didn't begin with *Marbury v. Madison*, Chief Justice Marshall's opinion in that case greatly strengthened judicial review in the United States. The Federalists' Sedition Act, which clearly violated the First Amendment, might not have survived had it passed after Marshall asserted the Supreme Court's power of judicial review.

FASCINATING FACTS: The United States Supreme Court Building (built 1932 – 1935)

Despite its great eminence and authority, the U.S. Supreme Court lacked a building of its own for almost 150 years. When Philadelphia served as U.S. capital (1790 – 1800), the court met in Independence Hall or Old City Hall. Later, the court occupied part of the U.S. Capitol Building in Washington D.C.

Convincing Congress to finance a building for the Supreme Court required the influence of a former President of the United States: William Howard Taft. In 1921, President Warren Harding appointed former President Taft as Chief Justice of the Supreme Court, making him the only American in history to hold both top jobs. As Chief Justice, Taft persuaded Congress to fund the building, and then oversaw the project through its planning stages. Sadly, Taft died before masons laid the building's cornerstone in 1932.

1935 photo of the Supreme Court Building

The Thomas Jefferson – Sally Hemings Scandal (1802 – 1804)

The Return of James Callender (1801)

One of Thomas Jefferson's first acts as president was to pardon the few men convicted under the misguided Sedition Act— including the muckraking James Callender, who had just finished his prison term under the now-expired Sedition Act (see above).

Having sacrificed his freedom for Jefferson's sake, Callender expected a far greater reward from his powerful friend than a mere presidential pardon. In addition to his pardon, Callender wanted an appointment to a fine new political post, along with some back pay that he had missed while he was in jail. Even before the election, though, Jefferson had grown uncomfortable with Callender's ungentlemanly language; and now that Jefferson was president, he wanted nothing more to do with Callender. Therefore Jefferson granted Callender no favors beyond his promised pardon.

Infuriated at this snub from Jefferson, Callender started doing for Federalists what he had once done for Democratic-Republicans: digging up mud to smear on their political enemies. This mud on Thomas Jefferson appeared in an 1802 edition of Callender's new Federalist newspaper, the Richmond *Recorder*:

> "It is well known that [Jefferson] keeps, and for many years past has kept, as his concubine, one of his own slaves. Her name is Sally. The name of her eldest son is Tom. His features are said to bear a striking although sable resemblance to those of the president himself. The boy is ten or twelve years of age."

The scandalous rumor Callender spread was that Jefferson had fathered a son with Sally Hemings, an enslaved woman held at his Monticello home. Neither Callender nor anyone else offered any direct evidence that this rumor was true. If it was true, though, then it would mark the widely-revered Jefferson as an immoral hypocrite— for in fathering children with a slave, Jefferson would have been forcing himself on a woman who had no choice in the matter.

Callender no doubt hoped to convince voters that such an immoral president didn't deserve a second term in office. However, by denouncing Callender as a drunken liar, the Democratic-Republicans managed to survive this small scandal, and win re-election for Jefferson in 1804.

Monticello, Thomas Jefferson's home near Charlottesville, Virginia

FASCINATING FATES: James Callender was never to know how his scandalmongering affected the election of 1804; for in 1803, Callender drowned in Richmond's James River. As if to demonstrate the truth of his enemies' ugly claims about his character, Callender drowned in only three feet of water— reportedly because he was too drunk to haul himself out.

As for whether or not Thomas Jefferson truly fathered one or more of Sally Hemings' children, no one can say with certainty— although modern DNA testing has suggested that it is certainly possible, and perhaps probable. As of 2014, the Thomas Jefferson Foundation— the Charlottesville, Virginia foundation that manages Jefferson's historic home, Monticello— considers the idea "highly probable."

The Alexander Hamilton – Aaron Burr Duel (July 11, 1804)

> **INTERESTING IDEAS:** The extraordinary political disagreements of 1800 – 1804 led to a duel between two extraordinary politicians: (1) sitting U.S. Vice President Aaron Burr, and (2) former U.S. Secretary of the Treasury Alexander Hamilton.

American Duelists

America inherited its dueling traditions from medieval Europe, where knights bound by codes of chivalry defended their all-important honor through contests of strength and skill. When one American gentleman felt that another had insulted his honor, his first step toward restoring that honor was to demand an apology. If his enemy refused to apologize, then only two choices remained: the gentleman could either live with a permanent stain upon his honor, or challenge his enemy to face him with deadly weapons upon the field of honor.

FASCINATING FACTS: Dueling in America

- After the challenge, each duelist named a friendly **second** to negotiate with his enemy's second. The seconds' first task was to negotiate apologies, hopefully before any actual dueling began. Failing apologies, the seconds negotiated the duel's time, place and weapons.

- Sometimes the mere act of dueling, of showing the courage to face one's enemy with deadly weapons, was enough to restore one's honor. Therefore not all duelists fought to the death: some agreed to duel only until one of them drew blood, or until one was too wounded to continue.

- Early American duelists fought with swords; while duelists of the 1700s and early 1800s often dueled with flintlock pistols. One way of dueling with flintlocks was to face one's enemy across a set distance, sometimes ten paces. At a signal from one of the seconds, the duelists fired one round each. If both were still able to continue, then they waited for another signal from the second before firing again. Another option was to take turns firing, beginning with the gentleman who received the challenge.

- If both duelists missed, then their seconds encouraged them to forget their differences. Sometimes, the relief of having faced death without actually dying was enough to coax apologies out of stubborn duelists.

- There were several ways to survive duels with flintlocks: (1) a gentlemen could deliberately miss his foe, choosing not to stain his honor with an illegal act of murder; (2) a gentleman could miss despite aiming to hit— for flintlock pistols were notoriously inaccurate; or (3) a gentleman's pistol could misfire— for flintlock pistols were also notoriously unreliable. In most cases, three misses or misfires were enough. No reasonable person doubted the honor of a gentleman who had been brave enough to face death three times.

New Yorkers Alexander Hamilton and Aaron Burr had been political enemies for years, ever since Burr defeated Hamilton's father-in-law in a 1791 election for the U.S. Senate. The ill feelings between the two grew stronger after February 1801, when the Hamilton used his influence with the lame duck Federalist House to ensure that Burr lost the presidency to Thomas Jefferson (see above).

Ill feelings turned to hatred in 1804, the year President Jefferson decided to drop Burr in favor of a new vice presidential running mate. To repair his badly-damaged political career, Burr ran for Governor of New York that year, hoping to use that high office as a springboard for another leap at the presidency. Once again, though, Hamilton used his considerable influence to ensure that Burr lost the governor's race— badly— that April.

Shortly after his election loss, Burr took Hamilton to task for a third-party letter that appeared in an Albany newspaper around election day. In an open letter to Hamilton's father-in-law, a doctor named Charles Cooper wrote of overhearing Hamilton disparaging Burr, calling him "a dangerous man... who ought not be trusted with the reins of government." To Burr's ears, Cooper's next statement was worse: "I could detail to you a still more despicable opinion which General Hamilton has expressed of Mr. Burr." Cooper's letter suggested that some of Hamilton's comments went beyond the usual insults— that instead of merely disparaging Burr's politics, Hamilton had disparaged Burr's honor.

On June 18, Burr wrote Hamilton to demand an apology. Two days later, Hamilton replied that he could hardly apologize for insults that he couldn't remember uttering. When further demands still brought no apology from Hamilton, Burr demanded satisfaction upon the field of honor.

In the early hours of July 11, 1804, the two duelists and their seconds rowed separately across the Hudson River to the shore of Weehawken, New Jersey— a popular dueling ground for New Yorkers, chosen because New Jersey's penalties for the crime of dueling were less severe than New York's. In fact, Hamilton's eldest son Philip had died in a Weehawken duel three years before, gunned down by one of the very dueling pistols that Hamilton now carried to his own deadly contest.

Illustration of the Hamilton-Burr duel

The duelists faced one other across a distance of ten paces, waiting for the designated second to shout "Present!" When the command came, both raised their pistols and fired, probably a few seconds apart.

After this point, the duel's details are uncertain. Hamilton may have fired intending to miss; but if so, then he should have fired far wide of his mark, either into the ground or into the air. Instead, Hamilton appeared to fire directly at his enemy, leaving Burr little reason to doubt that Hamilton intended to kill him. Whatever Hamilton intended, he missed; and seconds later, Burr's answering shot pierced Hamilton's midsection, damaging his liver and spine. Hamilton's seconds ferried him back to Manhattan, where he died the next day.

Other interesting facts:

- Although both New York and New Jersey charged Burr with murder, neither state ever prosecuted him for his crime. After serving out his term as vice president, Burr moved out west in 1805, partly to avoid legal trouble that arose from the duel.

Dueling pistol set used by Hamilton and Burr

- Aaron Burr happened to be a grandson of Jonathan Edwards, hero of the Great Awakening (see Chapter 18).

U.S. GEOGRAPHY FOCUS

North American Continental Divides

DEFINITIONS:
- A **watershed** is an area of land that drains into a particular river, ocean or other body of water. Any excess rainwater that falls in a body of water's watershed runs into that body of water.
- A **continental divide** is a line that divides a continent's major watersheds from one another.

North America has several continental divides, including:

1. The **Great Divide**, which runs along the spine of the Rocky Mountains. West of the Great Divide, all excess rainwater flows into the Pacific— except in the **Great Basin** of Nevada, western Utah and eastern California, where excess rainwater flows into outlet-less lakes like Great Salt Lake.

2. The **Eastern Divide**, which runs along the less lofty spine of the Appalachian Mountains. East of the Eastern Divide, all excess rainwater flows into the Atlantic. Between the Eastern Divide and the Great Divide, all excess rainwater flows into the Gulf of Mexico.

3. Two **Laurentian Divides**, between which all excess rainwater flows into the Gulf of St. Lawrence.

4. An **Arctic Divide**, north of which all excess rainwater flows into the Arctic Ocean.

U.S. HISTORY FOCUS, CONTINUED

The Louisiana Purchase (1803)

Among the successes that helped President Jefferson win re-election in 1804 was a remarkable land deal that his diplomats struck with Emperor Napoleon of France.

REFRESHING REMINDERS:
- In a ceremony held near the mouth of the Mississippi River in 1682, explorer Rene-Robert Cavelier, Lord de La Salle claimed the entire Mississippi River watershed— which he named "Louisiana" after King Louis XIV— for France.
- In the Treaty of Paris, which ended the Seven Years' War / French and Indian War in 1763, France surrendered nearly all of its territory in North America to Britain. Around the same time, France ceded all of Louisiana west of the Mississippi River— along with New Orleans east of the Mississippi— to Spain.

LaSalle claiming Louisiana for France

663

Jefferson versus Napoleon

After the Seven Years' War / French and Indian War, the once-small port of New Orleans began to grow large and important. Before that war, nearly all Americans lived east of the Appalachians, and therefore floated their heavy trade goods to eastern ports like New York City, Philadelphia or Charleston. After that war, though, more Americans settled west of the Appalachians, which meant floating their goods a different way: down North America's largest waterway, the Mississippi River, to New Orleans.

So long as the Spanish controlled New Orleans, as they had since the French and Indian War, Americans had little to fear— for the Spanish Empire had been crumbling since the mid-1600s, and could ill afford to send armies to North America. As of 1801, however, Americans had much to fear— for in that year, President Jefferson learned that struggling Spain had ceded all of Louisiana, including New Orleans, back to France. Now instead of the dying Spanish Empire, Americans had to contend with the most ambitious ruler in Europe: Napoleon Bonaparte, who was already laying plans to retake everything France had lost in North America.

Eager to confine the overambitious Napoleon to Europe, President Jefferson ordered his Minister to France, Robert Livingston, to go and see if Napoleon might sell New Orleans to the United States. At the time, Jefferson had no intention of buying any territory west of the Mississippi; he only wanted New Orleans, along with France's promise to grant Americans free access to the whole course of the Mississippi.

Meanwhile, Napoleon's plans for North America changed. The year Livingston traveled to France, 1802, was the same year Napoleon sent a large army to reconquer Haiti— a.k.a. Saint-Dominic, a French sugar colony just east of Cuba. Since the beginning of the French Revolution, Haiti's many slaves had been demanding their freedom under the Declaration of the Rights of Man (see Chapter 25). For nearly as long, Haiti's slaves had been enjoying partial freedom; but now, the tyrant Napoleon meant to re-enslave them so that he could use their island as a base of operations in North America (see Chapter 29).

Portrait of Robert Livingston, Jefferson's Minister to France

Like Napoleon's other overseas campaigns, the campaign in Haiti went badly— so badly that by the end of 1802, more than three-fourths of the troops he sent to Haiti lay dead or dying, many of them from tropical diseases like malaria and yellow fever. Without Haiti, Napoleon had little hope of reclaiming Louisiana; so he began to think of withdrawing from Haiti, and instead focusing on his invasion of Britain (see Chapter 26).

In the following year, 1803, Jefferson sent future president James Monroe to assist Robert Livingston with his lagging negotiations in France. Monroe arrived in France expecting to find that Livingston had made little progress. Instead, he found that Napoleon had suddenly offered to sell all of Louisiana to the United States.

DEFINITION: The **Louisiana Purchase** was the treaty in which France sold the United States the entire Mississippi River watershed west of the river, plus New Orleans east of the river, for a total of $15 million. With this single treaty, ratified by the U.S. Senate on October 20, 1803, the United States:

- Doubled its size.

- Rid itself of a powerful potential enemy on its western border.

- Gained free navigation of the entire Mississippi River— a critical waterway that every American producer west of the Appalachians needed to carry his goods to market.

FASCINATING FACTS: The Louisiana Purchase (Signed April 30, 1803; ratified October 20, 1803):

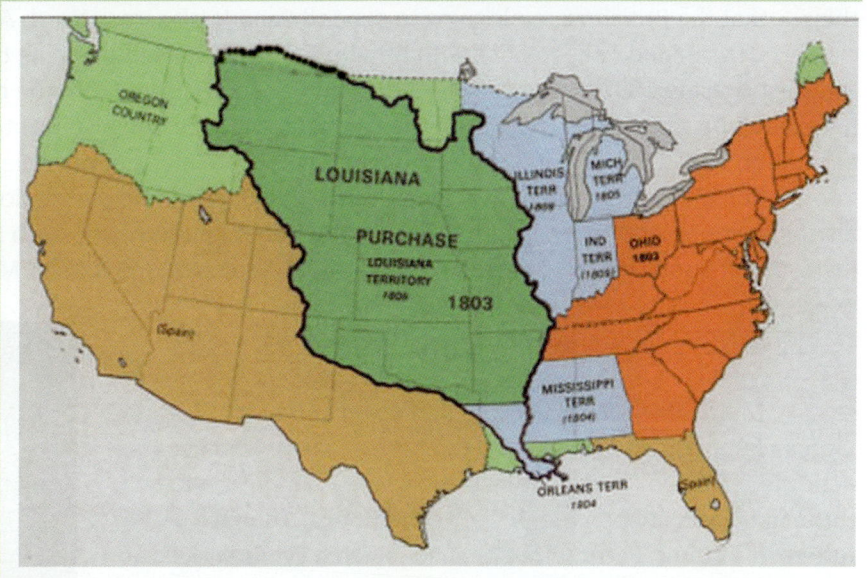

- President Jefferson authorized his diplomats to pay up to $10 million for New Orleans alone. Instead, they brought home one of history's most memorable bargains: for just $5 million more, Livingston and Monroe purchased 530,000,000 acres of territory at the incredibly low price of less than 3 cents per acre.

- The Louisiana Purchase included (1) all of the territory that would belong to Iowa, Missouri, Arkansas, Nebraska, Kansas and Oklahoma; (2) most of the territory that would belong to North Dakota, South Dakota, Montana, Wyoming, Colorado and Louisiana; and (3) part of the territory that would belong to Minnesota, New Mexico and Texas.

- Napoleon used the money from the Louisiana Purchase to fund his planned invasion of Britain— the plan that failed just before Admiral Villeneuve lost the Battle of Trafalgar to Admiral Nelson (see Chapter 26).

INTERESTING IDEAS:

- In Article VI of the Louisiana Purchase treaty, the United States agreed to honor all existing treaties with Louisiana's native peoples. Thus the United States' $15 million purchased only France's claim to Louisiana, not the claims of Louisiana's natives.

- Some felt that the federal government overstepped its authority in arranging the Louisiana Purchase— that because the Constitution made no mention of purchasing new territory, the government had no authority to purchase Louisiana. Others argued that the Constitution did indeed mention purchasing new territory— when it authorized the president to "make Treaties," as it did in Article II, Section 2. Ordinarily, Jefferson might have agreed with those who wanted to limit the federal government's power. In this case, though, the benefits of the Louisiana Purchase were too exciting to ignore.

The Lewis and Clark Expedition (1804 – 1806)

Race to the Pacific

As a renaissance man who loved science far more than he loved politics, Jefferson longed to explore the North American west long before the Louisiana Purchase. What spurred him to action, though, were explorations by the British. In an 1801 book titled *Voyages from Montreal*, British explorer Alexander Mackenzie described a 1793 expedition in which he had traveled overland all the way from Montreal to the Pacific Ocean— becoming the first European explorer to cross the Great Divide north of Mexico. Jefferson also knew of at least two visits the British navy had made to North America's Pacific coast in recent years: one by Captain James Cook in 1789 (see Chapter 24); and a second by Captain George Vancouver in 1793, the

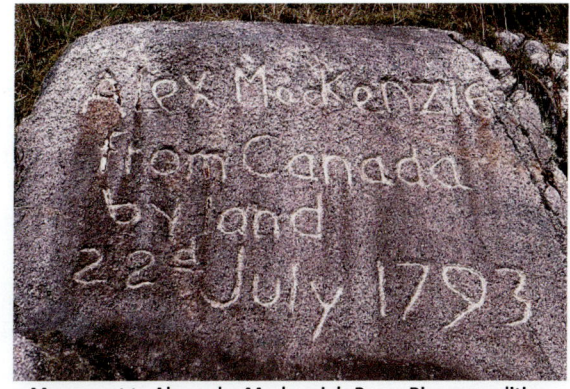

Monument to Alexander Mackenzie's Peace River expedition

same year Mackenzie reached the Pacific overland. Taken together, all these expeditions could mean only one thing— that the British were planning to expand Canada all across North America, from Atlantic to Pacific.

Determined to keep pace with Britain, Jefferson started planning the United States' own expedition to the west coast in 1802, the year before the Louisiana Purchase. From the beginning, though, Jefferson wanted his expedition to do more than claim the Pacific coast. Jefferson also wanted detailed reports on everything his expedition encountered out west— not only (1) accurate maps of possible trade routes, but also (2) political information on the region's native tribes, as well as (3) scientific descriptions of plants, animals, minerals and anything else of interest. In light of all this, Jefferson might have chosen a trained scientist to lead his expedition. Instead, Jefferson chose his personal secretary, 28-year-old army officer Meriwether Lewis.

AMAZING AMERICANS: Meriwether Lewis (1774 – 1809)

Meriwether Lewis was the namesake son of two fine Virginia families, the Lewises and the Meriwethers, who lived near the Jefferson family in Albemarle County, Virginia. All three families had been friendly for generations. Thomas Jefferson's father, Peter Jefferson, had joined a Lewis and a Meriwether as a co-investor in the Loyal Company of Virginia (see Chapter 20).

While on winter leave from Revolutionary War service in 1779, Meriwether Lewis' father William took a shortcut through an icy river in an effort to get home more quickly, and wound up dying of pneumonia. The following year, Meriwether's new stepfather moved the family to the frontier state of Georgia; and it was here that Meriwether learned his extraordinary wilderness skills. According to legend, Meriwether was only 8 years old when he started taking all-night hunting trips through the countryside, accompanied only by his dogs. Meriwether also had his first encounters with a powerful native people, the Cherokee, in Georgia.

Portrait of Meriwether Lewis

Around 1787, the 13-year-old Meriwether returned to Virginia for several years' formal education— including a course of study at Liberty Hall, forerunner of Washington and Lee University. In 1794, the young graduate joined the Virginia militia as an officer. One of Lewis' first missions was in western Pennsylvania, where he helped Virginia Governor Lighthorse Harry Lee end the Whiskey Rebellion (see Chapter 26). The following year, Lewis transferred from the Virginia militia to the U.S. Army— where he remained, mostly guarding the western frontier, until the newly-inaugurated President Jefferson hired him as his personal aide in 1801.

Jefferson's dealings with Lewis convinced him that this promising young captain was the perfect choice to lead his expedition to the Pacific. Unlike most scientists Jefferson might have chosen, Lewis was a skilled outdoorsman with a knack for finding his way where others got lost. Lewis also had command experience, which most scientists lacked; as well as experience dealing with native peoples, which might prove key to the expedition's survival. Although Lewis had less formal schooling than most scientists, his natural interests in zoology, botany and mineralogy supplied what he lacked in classroom hours. During the time he spent as Jefferson's personal assistant, Lewis also had another advantage: access to Jefferson's fine personal library at Monticello, which Jefferson stocked with every known book on the American West.

AMAZING AMERICANS: William Clark (1770 – 1838)

When Meriwether Lewis needed a second officer to help lead his westward expedition, he called upon his old army friend William Clark. Like Lewis, Clark came from a military family: Clark's older brother, George Rogers Clark, was a Revolutionary War general who led Daniel Boone and others to victory in Kentucky and the

Northwest Territory. After the war, George moved the entire Clark family, from his parents to his youngest brother William, to the western frontier; and it was here that William learned his extraordinary wilderness skills.

As soon as William was old enough, he followed his brother into the army. Like Lewis, Clark marched to western Pennsylvania for the Whiskey Rebellion, and spent several years guarding the western frontier. However, eldest brother George needed the family's help with his collapsing finances; so in 1796, Clark resigned his lieutenant's commission. It was during his last few months in the army that William Clark formed a lifelong friendship with one of his junior officers, Meriwether Lewis.

Six years later, Clark received a letter from his old friend inviting him to co-command the most exciting mission imaginable, a journey of discovery across the American West. Just as Jefferson saw strengths in Lewis, so Lewis saw strengths in Clark— practical skills like mapmaking and fort-building, along with an inborn ability to command. Furthermore, Lewis trusted Clark as he trusted no other friend. Even though he outranked Clark, Lewis always treated Clark as a co-commander of equal rank, and called him "Captain" in front of their crew, the **Corps of Discovery**.

Portrait of William Clark

ILLUMINATING EXCERPTS from President Jefferson's Instructions to Meriwether Lewis

- "The object of your mission is to explore the Missouri River, & such principal stream of it, as, by its course and communication with the waters of the Pacific Ocean, whether the Columbia, Oregon, Colorado or any other river may offer the most direct & practicable water communication across this continent for the purposes of commerce." <u>In other words</u>: Lewis' primary mission was to search for what Samuel de Champlain, Henry Hudson and many others had failed to find: a useable water route across North America.

- "The commerce which may be carried on with the people inhabiting the line you will pursue, renders a knowledge of those people important. You will therefore endeavor to make yourself acquainted, as far as a diligent pursuit of your journey shall admit, with the names of the nations and their numbers; the extent and limits of their possessions; their relations with other tribes or nations; their language, traditions, monuments; … and articles of commerce they may need or furnish, and to what extent." <u>In other words</u>: President Jefferson also wanted as much information as possible on the native peoples of the west.

- "In all your intercourse with the natives, treat them in the most friendly and conciliatory manner which their own conduct will admit; allay all jealousies as to the object of your journey; satisfy them of its innocence; make them acquainted with the position, extent, character, peaceable and commercial dispositions of the United States; of our wish to be neighborly, friendly, and useful to them… If a few of their influential chiefs… wish to visit us, arrange such a visit with them… If any of them should wish to have some of their young people brought up with us… we will receive, instruct, and take care of them." <u>In other words</u>: Lewis was to establish friendly relations with as many native peoples as possible.

FASCINATING FACTS: Peace Medals

To impress upon native peoples the United States' desire for peace and friendship, Lewis and Clark carried about 90 **peace medals**— round silver medallions in several sizes, the largest more than four inches in diameter. The fronts of these peace medals bore the name and image of President Jefferson; while their backs bore the motto "Peace and Friendship," along with two symbols of peace: (1) a crossed peace pipe and tomahawk; and (2) two hands clasped in friendship. As the explorers traveled west, they were to bestow a peace medal upon any native chief whom they judged to be a particularly strong leader— a decision-maker capable of choosing peace for his people. In accepting such a medal, a chief promised peace in return.

Despite President Jefferson's talk of peace, the Lewis and Clark expedition also had firm political and military goals, including these:

- The Corps of Discovery was to inform native peoples that the United States, not Spain or France, was master of their territory now.

- The Corps was to overawe the natives with the United States' superior technology, so that they would fear to rebel against their new master. In a standard speech delivered to many tribes, Lewis warned that if the tribes chose rebellion instead of peace, then they risked arousing "the displeasure of your great father [Jefferson], who could consume you as the fire consumes the grass of the plains."

Two sides of the 1801 Jefferson Peace Medal carried by Lewis and Clark

FASCINATING FACTS: The Girandoni Air Rifle

One of the technologies Lewis and Clark used to impress native tribes was one of the world's first repeating rifles. In 1779, an Italian gunsmith named Girandoni or Girardoni designed a revolutionary new type of rifle— one that propelled its shot not with gunpowder, but with compressed air stored in a reservoir behind the firing chamber. This design gave the Girandoni air rifle four remarkable advantages: (1) it produced

Meriwether Lewis' Girandoni air rifle. The butt of the rifle is a reservoir loaded with air at pressures up to 600 – 800 pounds per square inch.

no smoke; (2) it produced very little noise; (3) it could fire 30 – 40 shots before its reservoir ran low on air, and had to be pumped full again; and (4) it required only seconds to reload— for instead of ramming powder and shot down the muzzle after each shot, the rifleman simply pressed a spring-loaded lever, releasing another ball from the rifle's 21-round tube magazine into the firing chamber. Most Girandoni air rifles went to Austria for use in the Napoleonic wars. At least one, however, found its way to the United States, where Meriwether Lewis bought it with his own money before embarking on the Lewis and Clark Expedition.

The Girandoni air rifle played an important role in the grand ceremony Lewis used to impress new tribes. Each time Lewis and Clark encountered a major village, their whole Corps of Discovery marched into that village to the beat of fife and drum, wearing its finest military uniforms and looking as authoritative as possible. Next came a speech in which Lewis explained the great benefits of cooperating with the Great Father Jefferson, and the deadly pitfalls of disobeying him. Finally, Lewis demonstrated a technology that no native had ever seen before— his smokeless, noiseless, deadly accurate air rifle. Many of the natives Lewis met owned muskets or rifles; but none had ever seen any rifle that could fire 20 rounds in less than two minutes. As Lewis intended, his Girandoni air rifle made wary tribes think twice about attacking so well-armed a foe.

A Brief Timeline of the Lewis and Clark Expedition

1803, Spring – Summer: Meriwether Lewis spends several months gathering tools and supplies for the expedition— including a brand-new, specially-designed, 55-foot-long keelboat that will carry the Corps of

Discovery's supplies. After losing several months in Pittsburgh waiting for a drunken shipbuilder to finish his keelboat, Lewis finally sails down the Ohio River on August 31.

1803, October – November: Lewis arrives near Louisville, Kentucky, where he picks up Clark. From Louisville, Lewis and Clark sail down the Ohio to the Mississippi, and then up the Mississippi to St. Louis, near where their target river— the Missouri— flows into the Mississippi.

Artist's conception of Lewis and Clark's keelboat

1803 – 1804, Winter: Having missed the summer travel season, the Corps of Discovery spends its first winter in training at Camp Dubois, a.k.a. Camp Wood— a temporary camp just north of St. Louis.

1804, May 14: Lewis, Clark and their 30-odd-man Corps of Discovery begin the long, difficult task of poling and sailing their way up the Missouri River. For two reasons— because they are traveling against the current, and because they stop so frequently to meet the natives and investigate their surroundings— their progress is often quite slow.

1804, August 20: The expedition's only casualty, Sergeant Charles Floyd, dies of a sudden illness— perhaps acute appendicitis. So far, the expedition has passed through the future sites of three major cities: (1) Kansas City, where the Kansas River joins the Missouri; and (2) Omaha, where the Platte River joins; and (3) Sioux City, where the Sioux River joins.

Missouri River and watershed

1804, September 25: The Corps nearly comes to blows with the Lakota Sioux, a.k.a. the Teton Sioux.

FASCINATING FACTS: Lewis and Clark's Confrontation with the Lakota Sioux (September 25, 1804)

About 1,200 miles upriver from St. Louis, near what is now Pierre, South Dakota— less than halfway to its goal— the Corps of Discovery almost came to a sudden, violent end at the hands of one of the most powerful tribes in America, the Lakota Sioux.

Over the years, some Lakota had grown used to demanding gunpowder, tobacco or whiskey from the European fur traders who traveled their section of the Missouri— more or less charging tolls for the use of their river. Lakota chiefs liked to size up each passing trader, and then demand whatever toll they thought his expedition could afford.

Unfortunately, Lewis and Clark's interpreters spoke no Lakota, and so couldn't explain to the Lakota that the Corps of Discovery was no trade expedition. Given the great size of the Corps' keelboat, the three Lakota chiefs who Lewis and Clark met near Pierre expected great tolls. Given the length of their journey, though, Lewis and Clark didn't dare surrender so many of their limited supplies. Furthermore, Lewis and Clark wanted the Lakota to understand that the Missouri River now belonged to the United States, not the Lakota. Therefore instead of the barrels of gunpowder, tobacco and whiskey the chiefs were expecting, Lewis and Clark handed over just three peace medals and a few trinkets— none of which the chiefs could share with the hundreds of Lakota warriors they led.

When the chiefs started to grumble, Lewis and Clark invited them aboard their keelboat for a drink, hoping that a bit of whiskey might smooth things over. To the two captains' dismay, whiskey only made the chiefs surlier, and their demands larger. Tiring of the chiefs' insulting behavior, Lewis and Clark finally ordered them off the keelboat; and when they refused to leave peacefully, the Corps forced them onto a canoe and back to shore.

Now began the real tension. Set back among hundreds of their own warriors, the emboldened chiefs seized the Corps' canoe, insisting that the Corps would travel no farther until it filled that canoe with the goods they demanded.

At this, Captains Lewis and Clark drew swords and prepared their Corps for battle. For a few tense moments, Lewis stood ready to touch off his keelboat's swivel cannon— which likely would have meant the end of him, as scores of Lakota stood ready to pierce him with arrows. Had Lewis and Clark come to blows with the Lakota, the entire history of the American West might have played out differently:

- In overcoming Lewis and Clark, the Sioux might have not only halted their mission, but also captured its entire stockpile of guns, powder and ammunition— which might have helped the Sioux defend their territory against the next expedition that came their way.

- The United States might have failed to reach North America's west coast for many years— years during which Britain might have staked its claim to the west coast farther south than it did, capturing more of the American northwest for Canada.

Fortunately for everyone present, none of these dire consequences came to pass. Instead, one of the chiefs ordered his men to back down, and everyone slowly relaxed. Lewis and Clark spent a few tense days among the Lakota, ever watchful for signs of treachery, before moving on up the Missouri.

1804, November 4: Near what is now Bismarck, North Dakota, Lewis and Clark hire a French-Canadian trapper named Toussaint Charbonneau— not for his wilderness skills, but because his slave/wife Sacagawea knows the language of an important tribe the Corps will encounter farther west.

AMAZING NATIVE AMERICANS: Sacagawea (1788? – 1812?)

Sacagawea was a Shoshone woman born hundreds of miles west of Bismarck, near the headwaters of the Missouri in the Rocky Mountains. Several years before, an enemy people called the Hidatsa had seized the then 12-year-old Sacagawea and carried her far to the east, forcing her to live among them. About a year later, Toussaint Charbonneau happened to win a rather large wager he made with Sacagawea's Hidatsa masters; and for his prize, Charbonneau took Sacagawea and one other Shoshone woman as slave-wives. Sacagawea was probably about 15 – 16 years old, and about 6 months pregnant, when Lewis and Clark met her in late 1804.

What interested Lewis and Clark most about Sacagawea was that she knew the language of the Shoshone, a people who possessed knowledge that the Corps sorely needed— where and how to cross over the Rocky Mountains. Having narrowly missed disaster among the Lakota for want of a good interpreter, Lewis and Clark were eager to avoid similar misunderstandings farther on.

Lewis, Clark and Sacagawea at Three Forks, Montana

However, communicating through Sacagawea would be no easy matter; for Sacagawea knew only Shoshone and Hidatsa, not French or English. The chain of translation was this: Sacagawea would translate from Shoshone to Hidatsa for Charbonneau; who would translate from Hidatsa to French for an interpreter named Jessaume; who would translate from French to English for Lewis and Clark.

In addition to her language skills, Sacagawea offered the Corps these other advantages:

- Having lived farther west, Sacagawea might recognize some important landmarks there.
- As a native woman carrying an infant, she might make the white men of the Corps appear less threatening.
- She knew which local plants were good to eat.

1804 – 1805, Winter: The Corps of Discovery winters over at Fort Mandan— a temporary fort just north of Bismarck, named for the local Mandan people. One of the Corps' tasks this winter is to build six canoes to replace its keelboat; for this far upstream, the Missouri is growing too shallow for such a large boat.

1805, February 11: While the Corps winters over at Fort Mandan, Sacagawea gives birth to a son. Charbonneau names his son Jean Baptiste, but Clark nicknames the child Pompy.

FASCINATING FACTS: Lewis and Clark's Report from Fort Mandan

Along with their departing keelboat, Lewis and Clark sent home their first official report of their expedition, hundreds of pages filled with descriptions of all they had seen between St. Louis and Bismarck. The two captains also sent (1) 68 mineral samples; (2) 108 plant samples, many of them previously unknown to science; (3) skeletons, horns and stuffed specimens of several previously unknown animal species; and even (4) a few live animals— including a live prairie dog they caught by flooding its underground tunnel with water.

1805, April 7: The Corps resumes its journey up the Missouri River, now headed more west than northwest.

FASCINATING FIGHTS: Lewis versus Grizzly

Lewis and Clark were among the first white Americans to encounter one of the American West's most powerful animals, the grizzly bear. Although his native friends had warned him of the grizzly's incredible toughness, Lewis suspected that he knew why natives had so much trouble with grizzlies: because their weapons were inferior to modern American rifles. The very first grizzly Lewis met corrected his overconfidence— for even with a bullet in it, this half-grown grizzly chased Lewis with frightening speed, and nearly caught him before two more bullets brought it down. In another encounter, two fleeing members of the Corps of Discovery dived off a 20-foot cliff to avoid facing a furious grizzly. Some full-grown grizzlies fought back with six or more bullets in them, howling with a ferocity that frightened even a man as brave as Lewis.

After several such hair-raising confrontations, Lewis wrote in his journal:

"… these bear being so hard to die rather intimidates us all; I must confess that I do not like the gentlemen, and had rather fight two Indians than one bear."

1805, June 16 – July 14: The Corps spends a solid month portaging its supplies and equipment around the impassable Great Falls of the Missouri— a series of five waterfalls spread out over 10 miles of river in central North Dakota. To make wheels for the two wagons they are forced to build, Lewis and Clark saw sections from a 22-inch-diameter cottonwood tree trunk.

1805, July 27: The Corps reaches the Three Forks of the Missouri— the Missouri's headwaters, the point where three smaller rivers flow together to form the Missouri. Three Forks, which lies about 30 miles northwest of what is now Bozeman, Montana, happens to be the very spot where the Hidatsa kidnapped Sacagawea five years before. Lewis and Clark decide to proceed up the westernmost of the three forks, which they name the Jefferson River.

1805, August 12: On an overland mission to find Sacagawea's people, the Shoshone, Lewis crosses the Great Divide for the first time. Lewis' mission among the Shoshone is to buy horses to carry the Corps over the Rocky Mountains.

1805, August 13: Lewis meets his first Shoshone chief, a man named Cameahwait. To Lewis' great dismay, Cameahwait informs him that many miles still lie between him and any passable, westward-flowing river— which means that the long-hoped-for water route across North America does not exist, at least in this part of the country. Nevertheless, Cameahwait does know of a route that a western tribe, the Nez Perce, uses to cross the mountains. Furthermore, Cameahwait is willing to help

View from Lemhi Pass, where Lewis and Clark first crossed the Great Divide

the Corps in exchange for rifles, which Lewis promises that other white Americans will supply in the future. The Shoshone have long suffered from a lack of rifles— for the Hidatsa, Blackfoot and other enemies to the east can buy rifles from Canadian traders, while the mountain-dwelling Shoshone cannot.

> FASCINATING FACTS: Tepees
>
> Tepees were cone-shaped shelters built by the natives of the American West out of long poles and animal skins— often stitched-together buffalo hides. The great advantage of the tepee was its portability: when the tribes decided to move, as they often did, the poles and hides became crude wagons to drag behind their horses. Chimney flaps at tepees' peaks allowed smoke from small fires to escape. In heavy rain, a ceiling flap beneath the chimney flap trapped any rain that fell inside, diverting the water to the low end of the tepee floor.

Tepees in a photo of a Shoshone camp from 1870, 65 years after the Corps of Discovery

1805, August 17: Lewis and Cameahwait cross the Great Divide eastward to find Clark, who has remained behind with Sacagawea and the main body of the Corps. In studying Cameahwait, Sacagawea realizes that he is either her older brother or cousin, someone she has not seen since her kidnapping years before. Despite this heart-touching reunion, Lewis and Clark still have to pay steep prices for some of the worst horses in the Shoshone herd.

1805, September 1 – October 6: Now accompanied by a Shoshone guide named Old Toby, the horse-mounted Corps nearly starves to death during a hard crossing of the **Bitterroot Mountains**— a sub-range of the Rockies that stretches across western Montana and the panhandle of Idaho. Near the western side, the Corps meets some friendly Nez Perce who teach them a faster way to make dugout canoes: by using controlled fire to burn them out.

1805, October 7: The Corps sets off down the Clearwater River in its new dugout canoes, traveling with the current for the first time since it departed St. Louis. From the Clearwater, the Corps passes into the Snake River. In its haste to reach the Pacific, the Corps runs some very dangerous rapids— so dangerous that Old Toby, in fear for his life, abandons the Corps without even waiting for his promised pay.

1805, October 16: The Corps reaches the river that it will follow to the Pacific, the Columbia River.

Columbia River and watershed

1805, November 7: The Corps finally reaches the Pacific Ocean. Clark calculates that the expedition has covered 4,142 miles since departing St. Louis.

1805 – 1806, Winter: The Corps spends a hard winter at Fort Clatsop— a temporary fort near the ocean on the south side of the Columbia River, named for the local Clatsop people.

1806, March: Lewis and Clark begin their homeward journey. Partly thanks to shortcuts they have learned, the journey home will take only one-third as long as their outbound journey. Determined to make their trip home as productive as possible, the two captains split up for further explorations on their way home: Clark explores the Yellowstone River, while Lewis explores far to the north.

1806, September 23: The reunited Corps arrives back in St. Louis after a journey of roughly 2 years, 5 months.

SUCCINCT SUMMARIES: The Corps of Discovery's many successes included these:

- The expedition firmed up the United States' shaky claim to the west coast of North America, between Britain's northern claim and Spain's southern claim.

- The expedition established more or less friendly relationships between the United States and several native peoples, especially the Mandan, the Shoshone, the Nez Perce and the Walla Walla. Sadly, those relationships would soon turn sour.

- The expedition produced beautiful, highly accurate maps that were invaluable to every American who was curious about the West, from traders to scientists to military men.

- The expedition discovered and described some 300 species of plants and animals previously unknown to science.

The expedition's main disappointment was its sad discovery that there could be no easy water route across North America— for the route to the Pacific lay across not one, but several difficult mountain ranges.

FASCINATING FACTS: Appaloosas

The Nez Perce who aided Lewis and Clark west of the Bitterroot Mountains were excellent horsemen. On their return journey, Lewis and Clark lived among the Nez Perce for a few weeks as they waited for the snow on the mountain passes to melt; and while they waited, they joined the Nez Perce in friendly contests of horsemanship and marksmanship. Lewis marveled at Nez Perce warriors' ability to gallop down steep hills at full speed, and to shoot arrows through rolling hoops while their horses galloped beneath them.

To their excellent riding skills, the Nez Perce added excellent breeding skills. Because horses were not native to the Americas, all native peoples acquired their first horses through the Columbian Exchange— the process that brought non-native species from the Old World to the New World and vice versa

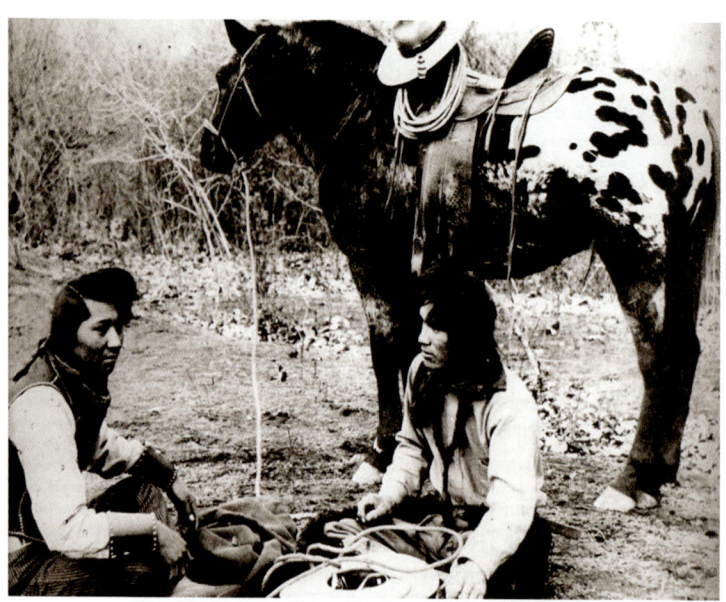

Circa 1895 photo of two Nez Perce with an Appaloosa

(see Chapter 1). More than most other tribes, the Nez Perce taught themselves to breed horses selectively. By choosing only the best horses for breeding stock, the Nez Perce were able to transform common stock into a well-bred, abundant herd of the highest quality. Lewis remarked that a single Nez Perce often owned as many as 50, 60 or even 100 fine horses.

The result was a fine American horse breed called the Appaloosa, best known for its spotted coat. The name "Appaloosa" may be a version of "Palouse," the name of a river that runs through Nez Perce territory.

FASCINATING FACTS: Seaman

While Meriwether Lewis waited in Pittsburgh for his drunken shipbuilder to finish his new keelboat, he spent twenty dollars on a fine black Newfoundland dog whom he named Seaman. Seaman was a strong, useful companion who retrieved game for his hunter master all the way from St. Louis to Fort Clatsop and back— even on the water, for Newfoundlands are excellent swimmers.

On the return trip, while the Corps was still west of the Bitterroot Mountains, three native thieves made the mistake of trying to steal Seaman. Lewis' response was to send three Corps of Discovery members after his dog, with orders to fire on the thieves "if [they] made the least resistance or difficulty in surrendering the dog." Upon discovering three well-armed soldiers in hot pursuit, the thieves set Seaman loose and ran for their lives.

FASCINATING FATES: Meriwether Lewis' Fate (October 11, 1809)

Among the rewards Lewis received for guiding such a successful mission was an appointment as governor of the new Louisiana Territory. Unfortunately, governing required a different set of skills than commanding a wilderness expedition. Lewis was used to making his own decisions, consulting no one except his good friend Clark. As governor, though, Lewis found people of all ranks questioning the wisdom of his decisions. Some questioned the way he spent public money; some questioned his tactics in dealing with the natives; and even his good friend Thomas Jefferson questioned why he took so long to publish the journals of his expedition.

After two years as governor, Lewis decided to travel back to Washington, where he could answer some of these questions in person. Part of Lewis' route from St. Louis to Washington followed the Natchez Trace, an old native trail that led through central Tennessee. On the evening of October 10, 1809, Lewis stopped for the night at Grinder's Stand, an inn just east of what is now Hohenwald, Tennessee.

Sometime before dawn the next morning, gunfire rang out, either from Lewis' room or somewhere outdoors. At dawn, Lewis' servants found him badly injured, bleeding from two or more gunshot wounds. Lewis died of his wounds shortly after dawn, less than two months after his 35th birthday. As to who shot Lewis, there are two leading theories:

1. **That Lewis committed suicide.** In favor of this theory is the fact that Lewis was behaving very strangely just before he died— partly because he was upset by the accusations against him, and partly because he struggled with depression and alcoholism for most of his life.

2. **That some unknown attacker murdered Lewis.** In favor of this theory is the fact that most people who attempt suicide with guns lack the strength to shoot themselves two or more times, as Lewis supposedly did. Against this theory is the fact that Lewis' two best friends in the world, William Clark and Thomas

Jefferson, never doubted that Lewis took his own life in a fit of depression. If they had, then one of these two powerful men surely would have investigated his friend's murder; but neither ever did.

FASCINATING FATES: Sacagawea's Fate

As the Lewis and Clark expedition drew to a close, William Clark offered to help Sacagawea and Charbonneau pay for their infant son Pompy's education back East. Seven years later, in 1813, Clark made good on his promise, taking full custody of Pompy so that the boy could attend school in St. Louis.

Interestingly, the record of this 1813 custody transfer mentions only Pompy's father Charbonneau, not Sacagawea. From this, some historians surmise that Sacagawea died before 1813. However, it is also possible that Sacagawea left Charbonneau to return to her people, and lived on well past 1813.

Other Early Explorations of Louisiana

President Jefferson also sent other expeditions to explore Louisiana, including:

1. **The Red River Expedition (1806)**, which poled its way several hundred miles up the Red River of the South— the river that now forms much of the border between Oklahoma and Texas— before Spanish border guards forced it to turn around.

2. **The Pike Expedition (1806 – 1807)**, in which Captain Zebulun Pike and crew explored the Great Plains of what are now Nebraska, Kansas, Colorado, Oklahoma and New Mexico before the Spanish captured them. Among Pike's discoveries was the mountain that bears his name.

FASCINATING FACTS: Pikes Peak

- Pikes Peak stands about 10 miles west of what is now Colorado Springs, Colorado. At 14,115 feet, Pikes Peak is the highest mountain in the eastern edge of the Rocky Mountains, and the first peak travelers see as they approach the Rockies from the east.

- When Zebulun Pike first saw Pikes Peak in November 1806, he tried to climb it so that he could get a better look at his surroundings. Even though Pike attempted his climb a month before winter, he still found hip-deep snow and sub-zero temperatures well below the summit, forcing him to turn back.

View of Pikes Peak from the east

- The first white American to reach the summit, a scientist named Edwin James, did so in 1820. As of 2014, hardy runners can take part in the annual Pikes Peak Marathon, a grueling marathon whose course follows a rocky trail 13 miles to the summit and back again.

U.S. STATE FOCUS

Louisiana

FASCINATING FACTS about Louisiana:

- <u>State Capital</u>: Baton Rouge
- <u>State Abbreviation</u>: LA
- <u>Statehood</u>: Louisiana became the 18th US state on April 30, 1812.
- <u>Area</u>: About 52,000 square miles (Ranks 31st in size)
- <u>Bordering States</u>: Mississippi, Arkansas, Texas
- <u>Meaning of Name</u>: The French explorer La Salle named Louisiana for King Louis XIV of France.
- <u>State Nickname</u>: "Pelican State"
- <u>State Bird</u>: Brown Pelican
- <u>State Tree</u>: Bald Cypress
- <u>State Flower</u>: Louisiana has two state flowers, the Magnolia and the Louisiana Iris.
- <u>State Song</u>: Louisiana has two state songs, "Give Me Louisiana" and "You Are My Sunshine."
- <u>State Motto</u>: "Union, justice and confidence"
- <u>Historic Places to Visit</u>: Garden District of New Orleans, Natchitoches Historic District, Jean Lafitte National Historical Park, Vicksburg National Military Park, Audubon State Historic Site, Marksville State Historic Site
- <u>Resources and Industries</u>: Oil refining, sugarcane, rice, fishing, lumber, tourism

Native American burial mound at Marksville State Historic Site

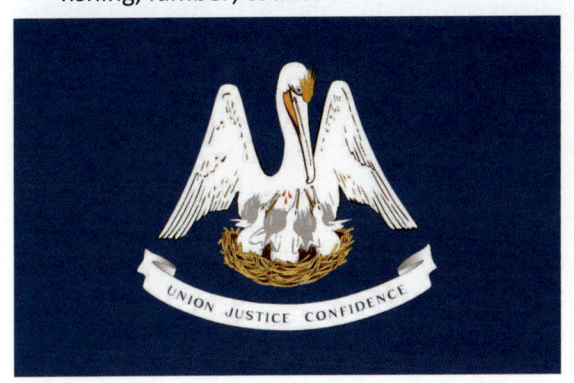

State Flag: A blue field with an image of a Louisiana's state bird, the pelican, sacrificing its own blood to feed three baby pelicans in its nest. Some medieval-era Christians used the self-sacrificing pelican as a symbol of Christ. Beneath the pelicans is wrapped a banner with the state motto "Union, justice, confidence."

PRESIDENTIAL FOCUS

PRESIDENT #3: Thomas Jefferson (1743 – 1826)	
In Office: March 4, 1801 – March 4, 1809	**Political Party:** Democratic-Republican
Birthplace: Virginia	**Nickname:** "Man of the People," "Sage of Monticello"

Thomas Jefferson was a brilliant Virginia attorney whose national political career began with his election to the Second Continental Congress in 1775. The following year, Jefferson became the main author of the Declaration of Independence— a world-changing document that defended as "self-evident" the two principles underlying all United States law: (1) "that all men are created equal"; and (2) "that they are endowed by their Creator with certain unalienable Rights."

From the Continental Congress, Jefferson went on to become a wartime Governor of Virginia from 1779 – 1781; Virginia delegate to the Confederation Congress from 1783 – 1784; U.S. Minister to France from 1785 – 1789; U.S. Secretary of State from 1790 – 1793; and Vice President of the U.S. from 1797 – 1801; before taking office as President in 1801. Jefferson's special place as a "Man of the People"— one who vigilantly defended individuals' and states' rights against the overpowering federal government— made his administration so different from the previous one that some historians call Jefferson's election the "Revolution of 1800."

Jefferson's accomplishments as president included (1) the Louisiana Purchase— a fantastic bargain which not only doubled the United States' territory, but also guaranteed free navigation of the all-important Mississippi River; and (2) a victory in the First Barbary War, a struggle against Berber Muslim pirates who were attacking American merchant ships along the Mediterranean Sea's Barbary Coast.

Jefferson's setbacks as president included the Embargo Act of 1807, passed during the Napoleonic Wars. Jefferson intended this trade embargo to punish Britain and France for seizing neutral American ships. Instead it punished American merchants, who lost fortunes when foreigners took over their business.

Interesting Facts about Thomas Jefferson:
- Jefferson was a fine violinist who romanced his wife Martha, also a fine musician, with his music. Sadly, Martha died in 1782 after only 10 years of marriage. The bereft Thomas never remarried.
- Jefferson was one of the early United States' foremost book collectors. After British troops burned Washington, D.C. during the War of 1812, Jefferson sold the federal government more than 6,000 books from his personal library to replenish the Library of Congress.
- Jefferson was a self-taught architect who designed some of Virginia's best-known buildings, including: (1) his private home, Monticello; (2) the Virginia State Capitol building; and (3) the University of Virginia's Rotunda.
- Jefferson's Monticello gravestone lists the three accomplishments of which he was most proud: (1) writing the Declaration of Independence; (2) writing the Statute of Virginia for Religious Freedom; and (3) founding the University of Virginia. Serving as president didn't make Jefferson's list.

Notable Quotes from Thomas Jefferson:
- "The spirit of resistance to government is so valuable on certain occasions that I wish it to be always kept alive. It will often be exercised when wrong, but better so than not to be exercised at all."
- "When the government fears the people, there is liberty. When the people fear the government, there is tyranny."

CHAPTER 28: The War of 1812; Napoleon's Fall

> DEFINITION: The **War of 1812**, sometimes called the Second War for American Independence, was a deadly struggle between the United States and Britain over the years from 1812 – 1815. This struggle arose from two related struggles: (1) the ongoing Napoleonic wars between Britain and France; and (2) the ongoing war between the United States and the Native American peoples who lived on the frontiers of settlement.

WORLD HISTORY FOCUS

The War of the Third Coalition (1803 – 1806)

> REFRESHING REMINDERS:
> - Napoleon's rise to national office began in 1799 with the Coup of 18 Brumaire, in which he overthrew France's 4-year-old Directory government. In the Directory's place, the Constitution of the Year VIII established a new government called the Consulate, with Napoleon as its all-powerful First Consul.
> - Napoleon completed his rise with two more new constitutions. In August 1802, the Constitution of the Year X named Napoleon First Consul for life. Then in May 1804, the Constitution of the Year XII granted Napoleon the title he had coveted for years: Emperor of the French.
> - One reason Emperor Napoleon sold Louisiana to the United States in 1803 was because he was planning to conquer Britain, and needed money to fund his invasion army.
> - Napoleon's grand scheme for conquering Britain came to nothing on October 21, 1805, the day Admiral Horatio Nelson destroyed a large French/Spanish fleet at the Battle of Trafalgar.

Although Admiral Nelson's self-sacrificing victory at Trafalgar meant safety for the British homeland, it did not mean the end of the War of the Third Coalition; for Britain was not the only neighbor Napoleon was planning to conquer. Just before Trafalgar, Napoleon gave his European neighbors three more reasons to fear him:

1. The Execution of Louis Antoine, Duke of Enghien: The Duke of Enghien was a French noble who fled France during the Great Fear, and fought beside the Duke of Brunswick during his failed invasion of France in 1792 (see Chapter 25). As of 1804, the beaten former duke was living in Baden, a German city just across the Rhine River from France.

In March 1804, French police heard rumors that the Duke of Enghien was plotting to assassinate Napoleon. A more peaceful neighbor would have asked Baden police to investigate the matter. The warlike Napoleon chose a different way: sending French soldiers across the border to kidnap the duke and haul him back to France for trial.

After a brief trial, Napoleon executed the former duke— but not for the assassination plot, as the duke proved innocent of that. Instead, Napoleon executed him for treachery against France, beginning with the Duke of Brunswick's invasion all those years ago. The idea of Napoleon's secret police wandering all over Europe, kidnapping and executing every noble who had ever taken part in a war against France, struck fear in the hearts of nobles from the Netherlands to Russia.

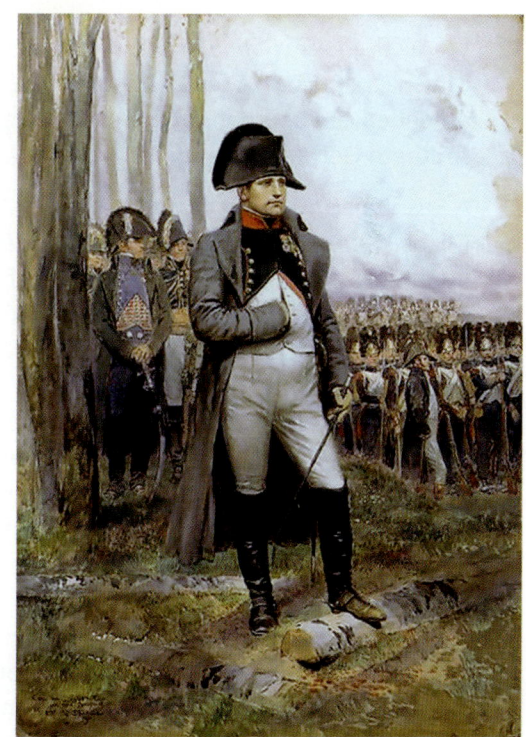

"Napoleon in 1806" by Edouard Detaille

2. Emperor of the French: The title Napoleon claimed for himself in May 1804 was a second cause for concern— for by definition, emperors seek to absorb more kingdoms into their empires.

3. King of Italy: In March 1805, Napoleon claimed this second grand title for himself. Ever since the Italian Campaign of 1797, France had been controlling northern Italy through puppet governments. At first, those governments were Enlightenment-style republican governments. Now, however, Napoleon claimed the kingship, and set his adopted son Eugène de Beauharnais on Italy's throne as his viceroy (sub-king). Napoleon's meddling in northern Italy was particularly troubling to Italy's northern neighbor Austria.

By reminding their European neighbors of the danger Napoleon posed— and by spreading money around Europe— British diplomats added members to their Third Coalition against Napoleon. By mid-1805, Austria, Russia and Sweden all joined Britain's war on France and Spain.

ILLUMINATING UPDATES: As of 1805, Maria Theresa of Austria's grandson Francis II was both Holy Roman Emperor and Emperor of Austria; while Catherine the Great's grandson Alexander I was Emperor of All Russia.

FASCINATING FACTS: The Ulm Campaign (September – October 1805)

Napoleon actually gave up on invading Britain several weeks before the Battle of Trafalgar— in August 1805, when he finally decided that the too-timid Admiral Villeneuve wasn't going to clear the English Channel for him that year (see Chapter 26). Determined to put his vast Army of England to some good use, Napoleon first re-organized it into the Grande Armée of France, and then led his Grand Army east against Austria and Russia. More than 200,000 French troops marched on Napoleon's new target: Austria's capital, Vienna, which lay along the Danube River some 800 miles to the east.
To defend the western approach to Vienna, the Third Coalition prepared two armies:

1. An Austrian army about 40,000 – 60,000 strong, commanded by Marshal Karl Mack. Mack waited for Napoleon near Ulm— a well-defended city about midway between Paris and Vienna, just east of southern Germany's Black Forest region.
2. A Russian army about twice the size of Mack's, commanded by Marshal Mikhail Kutuzov. The problem with this Russian army was that it was hundreds of miles away to the east— which meant that if Napoleon could tackle the Austrians before the Russians arrived, then he would outnumber Mack at least three to one.

The Black Forest's location in yellow on a map of modern-day Germany

As usual, Napoleon's battle plan depended on deception. From his headquarters at Ulm, Mack sent his scouts westward through the Black Forest, expecting Napoleon to approach Vienna by this usual route. To confirm Mack's expectation, Napoleon did indeed send about one-fifth of his army through the Black Forest— beating its drums, blowing its horns and drawing as much attention to itself as possible.
This loud demonstration so mesmerized Mack that he didn't notice what was happening elsewhere. While Mack fixed his eyes on the west, the other four-fifths of Napoleon's Grand Army were racing around the Black Forest to Mack's north and east, moving farther and faster than anyone expected— so fast that before Mack realized what was happening, Napoleon had completely encircled Ulm, cutting off Mack's last retreat. Surrounded by Napoleon's cannon, and running low on supplies, Mack had no choice but to surrender tens of thousands of Austrian troops. Thus Napoleon completely eliminated one of the Third Coalition's largest armies, mainly by outmaneuvering it.

> A LOOK ELSEWHERE: Napoleon's great victory at the Battle of Ulm fell on October 20, 1805, one day before his navy's terrible defeat at the Battle of Trafalgar.

The Fall of Vienna (Nov. 1805)

The elimination of Mack's army left Vienna all but defenseless. Three weeks after the Battle of Ulm, Napoleon accomplished what both Suleiman the Magnificent and Mehmed IV failed to accomplish: he captured Vienna, almost without firing a shot. To reward his Grand Army for this historic victory, Napoleon led it on a grand parade through Vienna, during which the city fathers handed Napoleon the ceremonial keys to the city.

As historic and symbolic as the Fall of Vienna was, it did nothing to solve Napoleon's other problems:

Napoleon receiving the Austrians' surrender at the Battle of Ulm

- The Russian army remained unfought, as did another Austrian army. Joining forces, the Russian-Austrian allies retreated to what is now Olomouc, Czech Republic— a city about 120 miles northeast of Vienna— to consider their next moves.

- Napoleon arrived in Vienna with less than half of his 200,000-man Grand Army— for this far from home, he needed more than half his troops just to guard the long supply line between Vienna and France. As a result, Napoleon's enemies around Vienna now outnumbered him.

1905 photo of the Hofburg, the Habsburg-Lorraine dynasty's imperial palace at Vienna

- Napoleon had no idea what the region's other great power, Prussia, might do. For the moment, Prussia had yet to join the war; but if it decided to join, then another enormous army might suddenly materialize on the side of Napoleon's enemies.

Thus Napoleon's victories left him in a precarious position, one in which he might have to abandon Vienna at any moment. If Napoleon's historic capture of Vienna was to end in anything but a meaningless retreat, then he needed a quick, decisive victory over Russia and Austria.

As a battleground for this planned victory, Napoleon chose a site near Austerlitz— now Slavkov u Brna, Czech Republic, a small town about 90 miles northeast of Vienna.

The Battle of Austerlitz (December 2, 1805)

Once again, Napoleon's battle plan depended on deception. Because time was on his enemies' side, Napoleon needed to tempt them into attacking him; and the best way to tempt them was to appear weaker than he truly was. In arranging his troops around Austerlitz, Napoleon made his right side— the side closest to Vienna— appear especially thin and weak. The temptation of an open road to Vienna, Napoleon hoped, would draw most of his enemies to his right— which would weaken his enemies' center, allowing Napoleon to break through and collapse their lines. Meanwhile, more French troops would fast-march up from Vienna to even the battle on Napoleon's right.

As the sun rose over Austerlitz on the morning of December 2, 1805, a heavy fog lay over the battlefield— which played into Napoleon's hand, as it concealed the strength of his army's center. Sensing no great strength in Napoleon's center, which Napoleon restrained for the moment, more and more enemy units abandoned the center to attack the temptingly weak French right. About 1-1/2 hours into the battle, Napoleon judged his enemies' center weak enough to attack.

Scene from the Battle of Austerlitz

As Napoleon ordered his best units into the fray, the **Sun of Austerlitz** burned through the fog, revealing to his enemies how very wrong they had been to weaken their center. Even so, Napoleon needed several hours of hard-fought battle to push through that center, divide and utterly defeat his enemies.

INTERESTING IDEAS: One circumstance that sweetened Napoleon's victory at Austerlitz was that both enemy rulers— Emperor Alexander I of Russia and Emperor Francis II of Austria and the Holy Roman Empire— commanded their armies in person, allowing Napoleon the privilege of defeating them in person. Alexander would later say of himself and Francis, "We are babies in the hands of a giant."

The Treaty of Pressburg (December 26, 1805)

With his great victory at Austerlitz, Napoleon won the power to dictate terms at the negotiating table. The Treaty of Pressburg, signed three weeks after Austerlitz, cost both of Francis' empires territory. Austria merely ceded some southern territory to Napoleon's Kingdom of Italy; but the Holy Roman Empire disappeared forever.

FASCINATING FACTS: The Demise of the Holy Roman Empire

Throughout the Napoleonic Wars, Napoleon had been rearranging the nation-states of France's eastern neighbor, the Holy Roman Empire— mainly by seizing territory from his enemies and giving it to his allies. After the Peace of Pressburg, Napoleon took his rearranging a step further. On the east bank of the Rhine River, just across the border from France, Napoleon united 16 former states of the Holy Roman Empire into the **Confederation of the Rhine**— a union of German-speaking states allied not with the Holy Roman Empire, but with France. Part of Napoleon's arrangement was that in exchange for France's protection, the Confederation of the Rhine must always supply tens of thousands of troops for France's armies.

With such a large swath of the Holy Roman Empire gone over to France, Francis II could no longer claim to be Holy Roman Emperor. Recognizing this, Francis formally abdicated his Holy Roman Emperor's throne in August 1806, retaining only Austria's throne. Thus did Napoleon's schemes dissolve an empire which had stood, in one form or another, for 844 years— ever since King Otto the Great of Germany became the first Holy Roman Emperor back in 962.

In honor of his world-changing victory at the Battle of Austerlitz, Napoleon commissioned one of Paris' best-known monuments: the *Arc de Triomphe*, French for "Triumphal Arch."

> **FASCINATING FACTS: The *Arc de Triomphe***
>
> - Napoleon's stunningly massive Triumphal Arch measures 164 feet tall, 148 feet wide and 72 feet deep.
>
> - The arch stands at the west end of one of the world's most beautiful streets, the Champs-Élysées in Paris. It also stands at the center of a gigantic intersection, a traffic hub with twelve busy streets as spokes. To reach the arch safely, modern-day visitors pass through one of two underground tunnels.
>
> - Most of the arch's large relief sculptures represent battles from the French Revolutionary and Napoleonic Wars, including Napoleon's great victory at the Battle of Austerlitz. Inside the monument are carved the names of many more such battles, along with the names of the French generals who led them.
>
> - Although builders laid the foundations of the Arc de Triomphe in Napoleon's day, they did not complete it until the 1830s, years after Napoleon's death.

The Arc de Triomphe

Over the four years after Austerlitz, France fought two more brief Napoleonic wars in the east:

1. The War of the Fourth Coalition (1806 – 1807): After the Battle of Austerlitz, Prussia regretted having sat on the sidelines while Napoleon defeated its neighbors Austria and Russia. Prussia's regret deepened after Napoleon established a powerful new French ally, the Confederation of Rhine (see above), so close to Prussia's western border. In fear for its life, Prussia joined Britain, Russia, Sweden and others in a Fourth Coalition against France in 1806. As always, France's arch-enemy Britain provided funds, but few troops for this mainland European ground war.

Unfortunately for the Prussians, their change of heart came too late. With several swift victories— including a crowning victory at the Battle of Jena-Auerstedt on October 14, 1806— the French routed the stunned Prussians, leaving them completely at Napoleon's mercy. Two weeks after Jena, Napoleon paraded his victorious Grand Army through Prussia's capital, Berlin, just as he had paraded through Vienna the year before.

Napoleon celebrating his victory over Prussia by marching his army through one of Berlin's most-recognized symbols, Brandenburg Gate. To humiliate Prussia even further, Napoleon removed the famous gate's crowning sculpture and hauled it back to Paris as a spoil of war.

FASCINATING FACTS:
- During his conquest of Prussia, Napoleon took the opportunity to visit the tomb of a Prussian general whom he admired very much: Frederick the Great, who had died back in 1786. Napoleon ordered his field marshals to doff their hats in Frederick's presence, adding, "If he were alive, then we wouldn't be here today"— by which he meant that France never would have conquered Prussia so easily if Prussia had produced more war-crafty leaders like Frederick the Great.
- Among the dead at the Battle of Jena was the Duke of Brunswick, the Prussian general whose threats had so angered the French at the outset of the French Revolutionary Wars back in 1792 (see Chapter 25).

The following year, 1807, saw Napoleon defeat Russia decisively at the Battle of Friedland.

2. The War of the Fifth Coalition (1809):

Two years later, Austria leapt back into the fight against Napoleon. Although Napoleon clinched Austria's defeat with a victory at the July 5 – 6, 1809 Battle of Wagram, he did so at a terrible cost of nearly 100,000 Grand Army casualties.

SUCCINCT SUMMARIES: Some Results of the Fourth and Fifth Coalition Wars

- As the War of the Fourth Coalition ended, Napoleon forced his enemies to sign two **Treaties of Tilsit**. In the first, Napoleon forced beaten Russia to take France's side in her ongoing war against Britain. In the second, Napoleon forced beaten Prussia to surrender half its territory to his allies— thus cutting Prussia's military might in half as well. Much of Prussia's eastern territory went to the **Duchy of Warsaw**, a puppet state that Napoleon established in the former Poland.

- As the War of the Fifth Coalition ended, Napoleon forced Austria to sign the **Treaty of Schönbrunn**, in which Austria surrendered yet more territory to France's allies.

As this era of the Napoleonic Wars drew to a close in 1809, Napoleon's First French Empire reached its peak in both territory and authority. By this time, Napoleon either controlled, influenced or had some form of alliance with nearly every European power east of Britain.

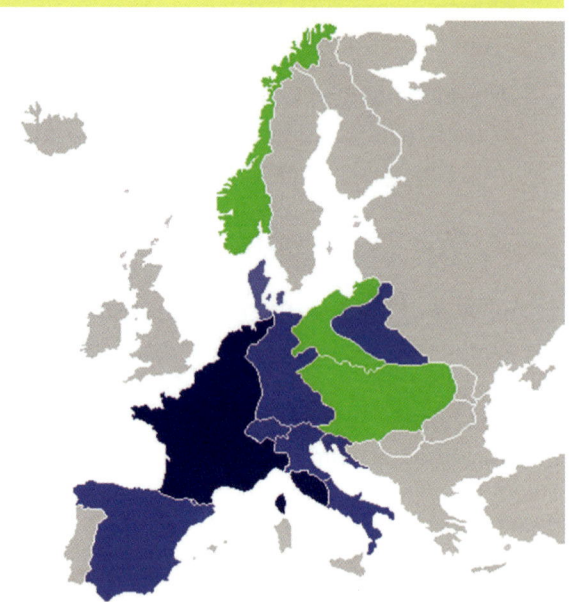

Napoleon's First French Empire at its peak in 1811. Dark blue marks the empire itself; light blue marks French-controlled states; and green marks French-allied states.

FASCINATING FRENCHWOMEN: Napoleon's Wives

In 1809, while Napoleon was in Vienna negotiating the Treaty of Schönbrunn, a German teenager tried to plunge a knife between the French emperor's ribs. Although this would-be assassin never got close enough to harm Napoleon, his attempt had an unexpected effect: it caused Napoleon to reconsider his choice of wives.

During the French Revolution back in 1796, Napoleon had married Joséphine de Beauharnais (1763 – 1814), a breathtakingly beautiful widow whose noble husband lost his head during Robespierre's Reign of Terror. Although Napoleon loved Josephine still, his narrow scrape with his would-be assassin made him doubt the wisdom of remaining married to her, for three reasons:

1. Because his assassin reminded him that he was going to die someday— without the legitimate heir he needed to preserve his legacy. Although Josephine had borne two children for her former husband, she had so far borne none for Napoleon. By 1809, she was in her mid-forties, well past the usual child-bearing age. If Josephine couldn't produce an heir for Napoleon, then he needed a wife who could.

2. Because Josephine lacked royal blood. During the French Revolution, Josephine's non-royal birth hadn't mattered, for the Declaration of the Rights of Man granted no special privileges to royals. Now, however, Napoleon was negotiating with Europe's noblest families, to whom royal birth mattered more than anything. Like other European royals, Napoleon needed a royal marriage to seal an alliance with a major power, and to boost the credentials of his new royal dynasty.

3. Because ever since the Egyptian Campaign back in 1798, Napoleon had doubted Josephine's faithfulness to him. The fact that Napoleon was unfaithful to Josephine as well did nothing to restore his trust in his wife.

For all of these reasons, Napoleon decided to divorce his still-beloved Josephine in favor of a new wife.

Joséphine de Beauharnais, Napoleon's first wife

Among the young European princesses available in 1809, only two likely candidates had fathers who shared Napoleon's emperor rank: (1) Anna of Russia, daughter to the late Emperor Paul I and sister to the current Emperor Alexander I; and (2) Marie Louise of Austria, daughter to Emperor Francis II. Napoleon first offered his hand to Anna; but when the Russians dragged their feet, Napoleon changed his mind and offered it to Marie Louise instead. The French emperor wedded his Austrian princess during the spring of 1810.

One year later, Marie Louise bore Napoleon the son he wanted: Napoléon François Charles Joseph Bonaparte (1811 – 1832), who was to rule France very briefly as Emperor Napoleon II.

Marie Louise of Austria, Napoleon's second wife

The Continental System (1806 – 1814)

Despite his many successes, Napoleon fretted about one nagging failure: his inability to conquer Britain, whose endless money funded so many attacks on France. In speeches delivered to inspire his troops before battle, Napoleon railed against the "malice and gold of England"— gold that made it possible for Britain's "hirelings" Russia, Prussia and Austria to wage war on France. The British were so notorious for fighting the Napoleonic Wars with gold, rather than ground troops, that the British gold received a mocking nickname: the **Golden Cavalry of St. George**, in honor of Britain's patron Saint George.

During the War of the Fourth Coalition, Napoleon proposed a new way of defeating the Golden Cavalry of St. George: by restricting Britain's ability to trade. As a trade-based empire, Britain traded with nearly every country in Europe; and France now either controlled or influenced most of those countries. Napoleon calculated that if his allies stopped trading with Britain, then Britain's trade-based economy would collapse— clearing the way for France to cross the English Channel and conquer Britain at last.

DEFINITION: The **Continental System** was a world-wide trade embargo (an official ban on trade) that Napoleon tried to impose on Britain beginning in late 1806. From that time forward, Napoleon did his best to ensure that neither France nor any of her allies traded with Britain.

A LOOK AHEAD: Napoleon's Continental System will become the wedge that splits asunder everything he has built in Europe.

The difficult thing about the Continental System was that it required Napoleon's allies to sacrifice themselves for Napoleon's benefit— for all of their economies depended on British trade. Not for nothing was Britain the world's largest trade empire; British merchants provided countless tons of cloth, ironwork, tea, spices and other necessities to Napoleon's allies at reasonable prices. If Napoleon managed to enforce his Continental System, then all such goods would immediately become scarce, causing their prices to soar. Although the allies could learn to provide these goods for themselves, doing so would take time. Napoleon's allies feared that long before they learned, they would go hungry and bankrupt.

To save their economies, some of Napoleon's allies resisted his Continental System. Napoleon's worst troubles in enforcing his trade embargo came from two main areas:

1. The Iberian Peninsula, home of **Spain and Portugal**. Through the end of the War of the Fourth Coalition, France and Spain were allies; but in 1807, they became bitter enemies in the Peninsular War (1807 – 1814)— a war that cost Napoleon so much manpower, treasure and grief that he called it his "Spanish Ulcer."
2. **Russia,** which had been relying on British trade ever since the formation of the Muscovy Company in the 1550s.

Napoleon receiving the surrender of Madrid, Spain during the Peninsular War

A LOOK AHEAD: The beginning of Napoleon's end will come in 1812— when, in an attempt to force the Russians to abide by his Continental System, he will launch a doomed invasion of frozen Russia (see below).

The other great problem with the Continental System was Britain, which responded to Napoleon's blockade with its own blockade against France. In need of thousands of experienced sailors to help seal off French ports, Britain took to impressing foreign sailors, forcing them into Royal Navy service against their will.

CAUSE #1 OF THE WAR OF 1812: Many of these impressed sailors came from the neutral United States, whose merchants tried to trade with both sides. When the U.S. complained of these impressments, Britain turned a deaf ear. In this way, Britain's response to the Continental System became a major cause of the War of 1812.

MUSICAL MASTERS: Frédéric Chopin (1810 – 1849)

Frédéric Chopin was a Polish musical prodigy born in the Duchy of Warsaw, the puppet state that Napoleon split off from Prussia after the War of the Fourth Coalition. Chopin's career as a professional piano performer and composer began at the remarkably young age of seven. As a young adult, Chopin won a reputation as one of the finest pianists who ever lived— even though few people heard him in person, as his light touch on the keyboard made his playing too quiet for large performance halls. Unlike Handel or Mozart, Chopin wrote almost exclusively for the instrument he knew best, piano.

Chopin is among the best-known composers of the Romantic period (1820 – 1910), the musical era that followed the Classical Period (1750 – 1830). One characteristic of Romanticism was disdain for Classical-era social norms. In keeping with this disdain, Chopin carried on a well-known affair with Aurore Dupin, a French authoress who wrote under the pen name George Sand. Despite being unmarried, Chopin and Dupin lived together as man and wife for nine years, causing great scandal at the time.

Sadly, Chopin suffered from breathing difficulties and other health problems all his life. He died at age 39, perhaps of tuberculosis.

U.S. HISTORY FOCUS

The Northwest Indian War

REFRESHING REMINDERS:
- In 1774, just before the Revolutionary War, American settlers defeated the Shawnee at the Battle of Point Pleasant, part of Lord Dunmore's War. That war ended with the **Treaty of Camp Charlotte**, in which the Shawnee surrendered all territory south of the Ohio River.
- With help from the British, the Shawnee resumed their territory war against the United States during the Revolutionary War (1775 – 1783).
- The U.S. defined the **Northwest Territory** as basically everything between (1) Pennsylvania to the east, (2) the Mississippi River to the west, (3) the Ohio River to the south, and (4) the Great Lakes to the north.

DEFINITIONS:
- The **Western Confederacy** was an alliance of native tribes that formed after the Revolutionary War to defend the tribes' claims in the Northwest Territory. These tribes included the Shawnee, the Miami, the Kickapoo, the Chippewa, the Lenape, the Potawatomi and the Wyandot, among others. With the Iroquois Confederacy severely weakened by the Revolutionary War, the Western Confederacy became the next great Native American power in the north.

- The **Northwest Indian War** was a twelve-year struggle for control of the Northwest Territory, fought between the U.S. and the Western Confederacy in 1783 – 1795.

Raids and Massacres

The Shawnees' territory war didn't end with the Revolutionary War; nor did the British cease to aid the Shawnee. After the Revolutionary War, the British were supposed to abandon their forts in the Ohio Country. Instead they remained, for two reasons:

1. To pursue the highly-profitable fur trade.
2. To cause as much trouble as possible for the United States, hoping the newborn republic might splinter and collapse.

From the end of the Revolutionary War in 1783 through the signing of the Jay Treaty in 1794 (see Chapter 26), the British supplied the tribes of the Western Confederacy with the weapons they needed to attack American settlers in the Northwest Territory. Hundreds of settlers died in horrible, bloody massacres like the ones that marked Bacon's Rebellion and the French and Indian War.

Scene from the Northwest Indian War

INTERESTING IDEAS: The United States and the Western Confederacy held two very different views about who owned the Northwest Territory:

1. Most Americans believed that the U.S. had won the Northwest Territory in the Revolutionary War. Britain had ceded that territory to the U.S. in the war-ending Treaty of Paris; and the Western Confederacy had fought on the losing side with Britain. Therefore in American eyes, Native Americans no longer had any legitimate claim to the Northwest Territory.
2. The tribes of the Western Confederacy believed that the Treaty of Paris couldn't possibly bind them, for two reasons: (1) because none of its members had signed it; and (2) because no one chief spoke for all the tribes.

In planning his response to the Western Confederacy's massacres, President Washington faced a serious problem. After the Revolutionary War, Congress almost completely disbanded the U.S. Army, arguing that standing armies were against Enlightenment principles. As a result, Washington had only hastily-raised, poorly-trained militia to send against the Western Confederacy. This led to two disasters in 1790 – 1791:

1. Harmar's Defeat (1790): In October 1790, Revolutionary War veteran Josiah Harmar led a disorganized mass of about 1,400 militia through the wilderness toward a large Miami village at what is now Fort Wayne, Indiana. To supply fresh meat, Harmar's clumsy supply train included a herd of lowing cattle, making it impossible for the Miami to miss.

Instead of tackling Harmar head-on, Chief Little Turtle burned Miami villages in Harmar's path, leading him to believe that the Miami were running scared— when in fact, they were only spreading out Harmar's army so that they could destroy it more easily. Playing into Little Turtle's hands, Harmar sent two fast-moving detachments of 250 – 300 men each to chase down the fleeing Miami. Both times, Little Turtle's 1,000+ warriors turned and ambushed the outnumbered Americans, dealing them terrible losses. In all, Harmar's Defeat cost Harmar more than 210 casualties, roughly 15% of his army.

2. St. Clair's Defeat (1791): The next general to face Little Turtle was another Revolutionary War veteran: Arthur St. Clair, who governed the Northwest Territory from his home in what is now Cincinnati, Ohio. That September, St. Clair led another disorganized mass of about 2,000 militia toward the same target Harmar had tried to reach. Early in St. Clair's campaign, heavy rain and other hardships made camp life so miserable that hundreds of troops deserted, leaving St. Clair with fewer than 1,400 when Little Turtle sprang his surprise attack.

The site Little Turtle chose for this attack stood near the headwaters of the Wabash River, about 120 miles north of what is now Cincinnati. Just after dawn on November 4, about 1,100 screaming Miami leapt out of hiding to attack the still-sleeping Americans from all sides at once. Caught by surprise, the Americans struggled to organize their defenses. Over 3 – 4 hours of battle, St. Clair suffered about 900 dead or wounded— a terribly high casualty rate of roughly 65%.

INTERESTING IDEAS: St. Clair's defeat was the costliest defeat U.S. troops ever suffered in any war against native tribes.

Sketch of Little Turtle, who led the Miami to victory over both Josiah Harmar and Arthur St. Clair

Mad Anthony Wayne and the Legion of the United States

For his next general in the northwest, Washington chose a man he knew he could trust, a Revolutionary War veteran who had fought beside Washington from New York to Philadelphia to Yorktown: Anthony Wayne, whose aggressive battlefield tactics earned him the nickname "Mad Anthony." General Wayne spent the winter of 1792 – 1793 training his new army, which he named the **Legion of the United States**, at the U.S. Army's first official basic training camp: Legionville, which stood near Pittsburgh, Pennsylvania.

Wayne's Legion spent its first full year, 1793, building forts deep in the Northwest Territory. About 90 miles north of what is now Cincinnati, Wayne built Fort Greenville, named to honor Revolutionary War general Nathaniel Greene.

To warn the Western Confederacy that the Americans were here to stay, Wayne chose a symbolic site for his second fort: near the headwaters of the Wabash River, the very site where the Confederacy had humiliated St. Clair two years before. To punctuate his symbolism, Wayne named this new outpost Fort Recovery.

General Anthony Wayne

FASCINATING FACTS: The Battle of Fallen Timbers (August 20, 1794)

Wayne's symbolism was not lost on the Western Confederacy's most capable general, Little Turtle. Convinced that his small army could never defeat Wayne's large, well-trained Legion of the United States, Little

Turtle tried to persuade his allies to negotiate with Wayne— arguing that it was better to trade part of their land for peace than to lose all of their land in war.

In light of their crushing victory over St. Clair, though, Little Turtle's overconfident allies saw no reason to surrender any territory north of the Ohio River. Therefore when Little Turtle continued to press for peace, the Confederacy replaced him with less capable generals.

In the summer of 1794, Mad Anthony Wayne led about 3,000 troops out of Fort Recovery on a mission to find and defeat the Western Confederacy army, which was probably about half the size of his own. Knowing that the British still supplied the Confederacy's weapons, Wayne hunted his enemies near one of the last British forts in the area: Fort Miami, which stood near what is now Toledo, Ohio.

After retreating before Wayne for some time, searching for a hiding place from which to ambush him, the Western Confederacy finally chose its battleground: a patch of ground where some storm, perhaps a tornado, had felled scores of trees. The Confederacy planned to wait until Wayne's heavy cannon were thoroughly entangled in these fallen timbers, and then strike him hard before he could pass through.

Unfortunately for the Confederacy, Wayne was too clever to send his heavy cannon among the timbers. Instead, he sent fast-moving infantry. After musket volleys from both sides, the Americans launched a bayonet charge fiercer than any the Confederacy had ever seen, forcing its warriors to retreat. Hoping for protection from the British, the fleeing warriors raced through the woods to nearby Fort Miami— only to watch the British, who had orders to avoid war with the Americans, bar their gates against them.

Mad Anthony Wayne studying the ground at the Battle of Fallen Timbers

Now beaten and abandoned by its former allies, the Western Confederacy scattered.

REFRESHING REMINDERS: 1794, the year of the Battle of Fallen Timbers, was also the year when the U.S. and Britain signed the Jay Treaty (see Chapter 26). Part of this treaty required Britain to abandon its forts in the Northwest Territory.

INTERESTING IDEAS: After the Jay Treaty, the tribes would have to journey all the way to Canada to receive weapons and supplies from their British allies.

The Treaty of Greenville (August 3, 1795)

With its army scattered and leaderless after the Battle of Fallen Timbers,

Scene from the Battle of Fallen Timbers

the Western Confederacy couldn't stop Mad Anthony Wayne from doing the same thing the Sullivan Expedition had done to the Iroquois Confederacy during the Revolutionary War: burning its villages and crops, leaving the survivors with little choice but to move north or west. The Northwest Indian War ended with the **Treaty of (Fort) Greenville**, in which the defeated Western Confederacy ceded to the United States most of what is now Ohio.

Immediately after the Treaty of Greenville, thousands of American settlers flooded into the newly-acquired, newly-safe Ohio Territory— so many settlers that in 1803, the United States admitted Ohio as its 17th state (after #14 Vermont, #15 Kentucky and #16 Tennessee).

FASCINATING FACTS: Dream Catchers

The Chippewa/Ojibwe people taught their children that the night air was filled with dreams, both good and bad. To filter out the bad, the Chippewa fashioned **dream catchers** to hang over their children's beds.

Dream catchers were charm-laced webs that blocked bad dreams, but allowed good dreams to pass through, sliding down the dream catcher's soft feathers to fall on the sleeper below. The first sunrays of the new morning burned off any bad dreams that got caught in the dream catcher overnight.

Tecumseh's War

With Ohio rapidly filling up, the land-hungry United States established another new territory west of Ohio in 1801: the Indiana Territory, under the protection of Governor William Henry Harrison. On President Jefferson's orders, Harrison negotiated treaty after treaty with Indiana's native tribes, buying as much territory as they would sell for as little money as they would accept. Protecting the natives of Indiana from the schemes of William Henry Harrison was the life's work of a gifted Shawnee named Tecumseh.

CAST OF CHARACTERS for Tecumseh's War:

1. Tecumseh ("Crouching Panther," 1768 – 1813)

Tecumseh was the second son of Pucksinwah, a minor Shawnee chief who died at the Battle of Point Pleasant when Tecumseh was only six. Twenty years later, Tecumseh himself narrowly escaped death at the Battle of Fallen Timbers.

Better than any other chief of his day, Tecumseh understood why his people lost Fallen Timbers: not only because Mad Anthony Wayne outfought them, but also because he out-organized them. As much as they needed military strategy, the tribes needed political strategy— a strong alliance to bind them together against their common foe, lest the more-numerous, better-organized Americans always outnumber and defeat them. Tecumseh envisioned a union of tribes stretching from Canada to Florida, and from the Appalachians to the Mississippi and beyond, all bound together by their native blood.

To the task of building such a union, no one was better suited than Tecumseh; for Tecumseh was not only a fine warrior, but also an inspiring speechmaker who touched Native American hearts with elegant words like these:

Portrait of Tecumseh wearing a British uniform jacket during the War of 1812

"Brothers, we all belong to one family; we are all children of the Great Spirit… we must assist each other to bear our burdens. The blood of many of our fathers and brothers has run like water on the ground, to satisfy the avarice of the white men. We ourselves are threatened with a great evil; nothing will pacify them but the destruction of all the red men… The white people came among us feeble; and now that we have made them strong, they wish to kill us, or drive us back, as they would wolves and panthers…

"Brothers, the white men despise and cheat the Indians; they abuse and insult them; they do not think the red men sufficiently good to live. The red men have borne many and great injuries; they ought to suffer them no longer. My people will not; they are determined on vengeance; they have taken up the tomahawk; they will make it fat with blood; they will drink the blood of the white people. Brothers, my people are brave and numerous; but the white people are too strong for them alone. I wish you to take up the tomahawk with them. If we all unite, we will cause the rivers to stain the great waters with their blood. Brothers, if you do not unite with us, they will first destroy us, and then you will fall an easy prey to them."

Along with Tecumseh's vision came this strong opinion on landownership: that because no one tribe owned the land, no tribe could sell its land without all the tribes' consent. Tecumseh was willing to abide by the Treaty of Greenville, which the whole Western Confederacy signed after its disastrous loss at Fallen Timbers. However, he contested any treaty that didn't involve all the tribes.

2. Tenskwatawa ("Open Door," 1775 – 1836)

Tecumseh's younger brother *Lalawethika*, Shawnee for "Noise Maker," was originally Tecumseh's opposite: a poor warrior; a clumsy hunter who accidentally blinded his own right eye on a hunting trip; and a lay-about who didn't mind trading land to the Americans, so long as his end of the bargain included whiskey.

All of that changed one day in April 1805, when Lalawethika fell into a trance so deep that his family thought he had drunk himself to death. To his family's surprise, Lalawethika awoke a new man, forever changed by visions from a Shawnee god called the Master of Life. After these visions, Tecumseh's brother was no longer Lalawethika. Rather, he became *Tenskwatawa*, the "Open Door" through whom the Master of Life revealed his will to the tribes.

The Master of Life's will was that the tribes return to their old ways, rejecting every new thing the white man had brought among them— his whiskey, his weapons, his clothes, his religion and his treaties. Tenskwatawa promised that if the Master's people obeyed him, then the Master would cast out the white man and restore all that the tribes had lost.

At first, the Master's message attracted few followers. Most of the warriors Tenskwatawa tried to persuade were like Little Turtle— convinced that they could never prevail against the Americans' overwhelming numbers, and therefore inclined to remain at peace.

Tenskwatawa, the Shawnee Prophet

Tenskwatawa gained more followers after 1806, when William Henry Harrison made the mistake of challenging the so-called Shawnee Prophet to prove that his visions were real. As a believer in Enlightenment science, Harrison expected Tenskwatawa to humiliate himself with some ridiculous, unfulfilled prophecy. Instead, Tenskwatawa awed new followers by correctly prophesying a solar eclipse— a celestial event that no Native American had ever predicted before.

INTERESTING IDEAS: By the time Tenskwatawa correctly predicted his solar eclipse, European almanacs had been predicting such eclipses for decades. It is possible that Tenskwatawa's brother Tecumseh learned of the coming solar eclipse from some British ally who owned an almanac, and shared the news with his brother in advance. Such a trick might have appealed to Tecumseh for two reasons:

1. Because it would boost Tenskwatawa's reputation and following, in turn boosting Tecumseh's own.
2. Because it would humiliate Governor William Henry Harrison, whom Tecumseh despised.

By 1808, Tenskwatawa's following was large enough to need a home of its own. Near what is now Lafayette, Indiana, Tenskwatawa founded the village of **Prophetstown** as a planned utopia— a place where true believers like Tecumseh could live as the Master of Life commanded, untainted by American influence. Prophetstown lay just downriver from where the Wabash River received a smaller river called the Tippecanoe.

DEFINITION: Prophetstown became the capital of **Tecumseh's Confederacy**, an alliance Tecumseh formed to prevent the United States from spreading any farther west.

3. William Henry Harrison (1773 – 1841)

William Henry Harrison was the youngest son of Benjamin Harrison V, a signer of the Declaration of Independence who also served as Governor of Virginia from 1781 – 1784. Two Harrisons were to become U.S. presidents: (1) William Henry himself, in office for a single month in 1841; and (2) his grandson Benjamin Harrison, in office 1889 – 1893. Long before he was president, William Henry Harrison fought under Mad Anthony Wayne at the Battle of Fallen Timbers, and was among the officers who signed the Treaty of Greenville. When the U.S. established the Indiana Territory in 1801, Harrison became its first governor.

Harrison's vision for the American West was the opposite of Tecumseh's: instead of uniting the tribes, Harrison wanted to divide them. After Fallen Timbers, some beaten Western Confederacy tribes were needy and desperate enough to sell their homelands for a fraction of what they were worth— trading away their entire futures for just enough money and goods to keep them from starving in the here and now. Governor Harrison took advantage of these tribes' neediness, buying land from any tribe that was ready to sell. Harrison's land deals were infuriating to Tecumseh, who believed that no tribe had a right to sell land that belonged to all the tribes.

Portrait of William Henry Harrison

The Confrontation at Vincennes (1810)

Of the several smaller land treaties Harrison negotiated after the huge Treaty of Greenville, the one that angered Tecumseh most was the **Treaty of Fort Wayne**— an 1810 treaty involving more than 3 million acres deep inside Indiana, well north of the old Ohio River line. To Tecumseh, the underhanded tactics that Harrison used to win the Treaty of Fort Wayne were the lowest form of trickery. Aware that certain tribes weren't interested in selling this land, Harrison purposely didn't invite those tribes to his negotiations— calculating that those tribes would sell more easily after learning that their neighbors, the tribes Harrison did invite, had already sold. Sure enough, Harrison convinced several tribes to sign his treaty by the spring of 1810.

In August 1810, an irate Tecumseh appeared at Harrison's home in Vincennes, Indiana to demand that he cancel the Treaty of Fort Wayne. To emphasize Tecumseh's demands, some 400 warriors stood behind him as he explained to Harrison why this piecemeal treaty was so unfair:

"The Indians have resolved to unite to preserve their lands, but you try to prevent this by taking tribes aside and advising them not to join [Tecumseh's] Confederacy. The United States has set us an example by forming a union of their fires. We do not complain. Why, then, should you complain if the Indians do the same thing among their tribes?

"You buy lands from the village chiefs who have no right to sell. If you continue to buy lands from these petty chiefs, there will be trouble, and I cannot foretell the consequences… It is true I am a Shawnee, but I speak for all the Indians— Wyandotte, Miami, Delaware, Kickapoo, Ottawa, Pottawatomie, Winnebago and Shawnees, for the Indians of the Lakes and for those… along the Mississippi, even down to the salt sea…

"What! Sell a country! Why not sell the air, the clouds and the great sea, as well as the earth? Backward have the Americans driven us from the sea, and on towards the setting sun are we being forced… like a galloping horse! …now we will yield no further, but here make our stand."

Harrison had two different reactions to Tecumseh's speech:

1. Politically, Harrison considered the claim that Tecumseh spoke for all the tribes a gross exaggeration— for how could Tecumseh speak for tribes that didn't share his language? Furthermore, if the tribes were as united as Tecumseh claimed, then why had so many signed the Treaty of Fort Wayne?

2. Personally, Harrison considered Tecumseh the most impressive Native American he had ever met— a born leader with more than enough natural talent to unite the tribes, given time. Harrison later wrote of Tecumseh:

Tecumseh challenging William Henry Harrison over the Treaty of Fort Wayne

"The implicit obedience and respect which followers of Tecumseh pay him is really astonishing… [he is] one of those uncommon geniuses which spring up occasionally to produce revolutions and overturn the established order of things. If it were not for the vicinity of the United States, he would perhaps be the founder of an empire that would rival in glory Mexico [the Aztecs] or Peru [the Incas]."

When neither side backed down after Tecumseh's speech, the situation at Vincennes grew tense. For a moment, Tecumseh appeared ready to attack Harrison then and there, and both sides drew weapons to defend themselves. Although no fight broke out that day, both Tecumseh and Harrison knew what the Confrontation at Vincennes meant: that they would almost certainly fight one another, and soon.

FASCINATING FACTS: The Battle of Tippecanoe (November 7, 1811)

With war all but certain after the Confrontation at Vincennes, Tecumseh worked harder than ever to build Tecumseh's Confederacy. Around August 1811, Tecumseh departed on a long tour of the American South, where he used warnings like these to try to persuade the southern tribes to join his cause:

"Where today are the Pequot? Where are the Narragansett, the Mohican, the Pocanet, and other powerful tribes of our people? They have vanished before the avarice and oppression of the white man… Sleep not longer, O Choctaws and Chickasaws... Will not the bones of our dead be plowed up, and their graves turned into plowed fields?"

When Harrison learned of Tecumseh's journey south, he realized that there might never come a better time to confront Tecumseh's Confederacy— for with Tecumseh away, Prophetstown was sure to be in the far less capable hands of his brother Tenskwatawa. Therefore Harrison chose that fall to lead about 1,000 troops to Prophetstown, where he ordered Tenskwatawa to hand over two native warriors he was sheltering— criminals who had been raiding American settlements.

Tenskwatawa's response was more like a prophet's than a warrior's. Playing for time, Tenskwatawa sent messengers to arrange a truce, to which Harrison agreed. As the Americans pitched their tents for the night, Tenskwatawa arranged a surprise attack intended to assassinate Harrison in his sleep. Just before his warriors slipped out of Prophetstown to kill Harrison, the mystical Tenskwatawa promised to cast a spell that would make the white man's bullets fall to earth as harmlessly as raindrops.

Nothing of the sort happened. Instead, Harrison's alert sentries heard Tenskwatawa's surprise attack coming, and raised the alarm— at which Harrison's army awakened to fire very real bullets at its attackers. Without Tecumseh to lead them, the warriors of Prophetstown scattered after about two hours of hard-fought battle, leaving Harrison to burn Prophetstown to the ground behind them.

Scene from Harrison's victory at the Battle of Tippecanoe

CAUSE #2 OF THE WAR OF 1812: Although Governor Harrison won the Battle of Tippecanoe and destroyed Prophetstown, he did so at the high cost of more than 60 dead and 120 wounded. Few Americans doubted that Britain had supplied the weapons Tecumseh's Confederacy used to inflict these grievous losses. Thus American outrage over losses at the Battle of Tippecanoe, and over the Native American raids that led to that battle, became a second major cause of the War of 1812.

The Battle of Tippecanoe also produced another important result. When Tecumseh returned from the South to find Prophetstown in ruins, he joined Britain in declaring all-out war on the United States.

A LOOK AHEAD: Tecumseh's Confederacy will supply a large portion of the troops Britain will use to defend Canada against the United States in the War of 1812.

The War of 1812, Part One

More Causes of the War of 1812

DEFINITION: The **war hawks** were U.S. senators and representatives who pressed Congress to declare war on Britain in June 1812. Most war hawks came from one of two regions: (1) the South, as did South Carolina's war hawk Representative John C. Calhoun; or (2) the West, as did Kentucky's war hawk Representative Henry Clay. One cause these two regions shared was that both stood on the front lines of the ongoing frontier wars between the U.S. and the native tribes— wars the war hawks blamed on Britain.

> **INTERESTING IDEAS**: Few war hawks came from New England. Most New Englanders earned their livings through business and industry— and therefore opposed any war that would disrupt their profitable trade with the world's largest trade empire, Britain.

Underlying the War of 1812's two main causes— British impressment of American sailors, and British support for Tecumseh's War (see Cause #1 and Cause #2 above)— were the war hawks' causes, U.S. independence and national pride. In war hawk eyes, Britain was still treating the U.S. as a second-rate backwater unworthy of nationhood. For example, one way Britain justified impressing American sailors was by claiming that all sailors born in Britain remained British, even if they had since become naturalized U.S. citizens. This was why the war hawks called for a Second War of American Independence— because they believed that if they couldn't defend their sailors' liberty, then an important part of the U.S. still lived under British tyranny.

This same logic led to yet another cause of the War of 1812: the United States' desire to seize Canada from Britain. As the war hawks saw matters, the best way to end the British threat to American independence was to drive the British out of North America forever.

The War in Upper Canada

The War of 1812 began with a struggle for control of Upper Canada, the part that lay up the St. Lawrence River from French-speaking Quebec City and Montreal. Because Lake Ontario, Lake Erie and the Niagara River formed the border between the United States and Upper Canada, those waters became key battlegrounds.

> **A LOOK BEHIND**: Among the prizes the U.S. won in the Treaty of Greenville was Fort Detroit, an important British-held outpost near the western edge of Lake Erie. Unfortunately, Detroit lay deep in native territory, far beyond the Treaty of Greenville line, making Detroit difficult for U.S. troops to reach. Instead of crossing native territory to reach Detroit, the U.S. usually shipped troops and supplies across Lake Erie.

The Siege of Detroit (August 15 – 16, 1812)

Immediately after the U.S. declared war in June, the British used their superior navy to seize control of Lake Erie, making it all but impossible for the U.S. to resupply Fort Detroit. Having cut off the fort, the British laid plans to besiege it and force its surrender.

The Siege of Fort Detroit was one of many battles in which Tecumseh proved his cunning. From American messages intercepted between June and August, Tecumseh knew that Fort Detroit was already running desperately low on supplies. In light of this, Tecumseh calculated that Detroit's commander might surrender without a fight, given the proper push.

The push Tecumseh chose was to parade his native troops past a gap in the forest around Fort Detroit, the only gap through which the Americans inside could see them. As each warrior crossed the gap, Tecumseh sent him back by a route the Americans couldn't see, where he joined the back of the line to continue the parade. Watching this endless parade, Fort Detroit's befuddled American commander began to fear that there was no end to the number of troops he was facing. After surrendering his 2,500 troops without a fight, the commander was stunned to learn that his attackers numbered only about 1,300— roughly half his army's size.

The Battle of Lake Erie (September 10, 1813)

After Detroit's humiliating fall, the U.S. Navy spent about a year building and arming the ships it would need to recapture Lake Erie. At shipyards near Buffalo, New York and Erie, Pennsylvania— cannon-defended ports that British ships dared not approach— the Americans managed to build a fleet that outnumbered the small British fleet on Lake Erie.

After a hard-fought battle near Put-in-Bay, Lake Erie on September 10, 1813, U.S. Navy Master Commandant Oliver Hazard Perry captured his enemy's entire fleet on Lake Erie, bringing the great lake firmly under U.S. Navy control.

U.S. Navy Master Commandant Oliver Hazard Perry transferring his flag from his badly-damaged flagship during the Battle of Lake Erie

INTERESTING IDEAS: After the Battle of Lake Erie, Commandant Perry proudly informed his superiors: "We have met the enemy, and they are ours."

The Battle of the Thames (October 5, 1813)

The fall of 1813 found Tecumseh and his British allies in dire straits, for these reasons among others:

- Because the Americans' capture of Lake Erie gave them two new abilities: (1) the ability to cut off Upper Canada from its usual source of supply, the great lake; and (2) the ability to land troops anywhere along the great lake's northern coast, from Detroit to Buffalo— thus cutting off Detroit by land as well.

- Because after Fort Detroit's befuddled commander surrendered to the British in 1812, the U.S. Army replaced him with a far more capable commander: Tecumseh's old nemesis William Henry Harrison.

Without supplies, Tecumseh's British commander couldn't hope to defend Fort Detroit, nor any other fort so far west. Against Tecumseh's objections, both British and native retreated up the Thames River, a long river that runs roughly parallel to Lake Erie's northwestern shore. As Tecumseh and his allies raced for the safety of the British-held territory around Lake Ontario, Harrison gave chase with about 3,500 troops, more than twice his enemies' numbers.

Tecumseh was less than halfway to Lake Ontario when Harrison caught up with him, forcing the deadly showdown that both had been expecting since their Confrontation at Vincennes.

FASCINATING FATES: Tecumseh's Fate (October 5, 1813)

As Harrison caught up with Tecumseh and his allies on the morning of October 5, Tecumseh's British commander proposed a desperate battle plan. First, his British troops would form a line more or less in the open, directly in Harrison's path. Meanwhile, Tecumseh and his native warriors would conceal themselves in a thick woods that ran beside Harrison's path. As Harrison charged to attack the British, Tecumseh would attack Harrison's unprotected flanks, hopefully knocking him out of the war.

The weakness of this plan was that the British battle line had to block Harrison's charge long enough for Tecumseh to attack Harrison's flanks. Instead, Harrison's charge broke through the British battle line almost immediately. At this, the British commander fled the battlefield, and most of his troops surrendered.

Abandoned by his British allies, brave Tecumseh fought on until Harrison's troops shot him to death. The end of Tecumseh also brought an end to Tecumseh's Confederacy, which dissolved without his leadership. Thus the natives of Indiana lost their greatest protector, and Britain lost a crafty ally.

Tecumseh sacrificing his life for his people at the Battle of the Thames

PRESCIENT PROPHECIES: Tecumseh's Curse, a.k.a. The Curse of Tippecanoe

After Tecumseh gave his life for his people at the Battle of the Thames, someone uttered a prophetic curse against Tecumseh's killer, future president William Henry Harrison. The original author of Tecumseh's Curse is unknown: it may have been Tecumseh's mystical brother Tenskwatawa, or it may have been someone writing decades later, with the benefit of hindsight. Whoever wrote the curse, part of one version reads:

"… A curse shall be upon the Great Chief of the Americans, if they shall ever pick Harrison to lead them. His days in power shall be cut short. And for every twenty winters following, the days in power of the Great Chief which they shall select shall be cut short. Our people shall not be the instrument to shorten their time; either the Great Spirit shall shorten their days, or their own people shall shoot them."

President William Henry Harrison was 67 years old when he won election in 1840. Just as Tecumseh's Curse predicted, Harrison died of pneumonia after holding office for a single month. Also as the curse predicted, there followed a string of early deaths among presidents elected every 20 years after Harrison:

1. President Abraham Lincoln, who won election in 1860, was shot to death in office in 1865.
2. President James Garfield, who won election in 1880, was shot to death in office in 1881.
3. President William McKinley, who won re-election in 1900, was shot to death in office in 1901.
4. President Warren Harding, who won election in 1920, died in office of natural causes in 1923.
5. President Franklin Roosevelt, who won re-election in 1940, died in office of natural causes in 1945.
6. President John Kennedy, who won election in 1960, was shot to death in office in 1963.

The only other president to die in office was Zachary Taylor, who died of natural causes two years after his election in 1848. Interestingly, Taylor also battled Tecumseh during the War of 1812, which means that Tecumseh's Curse may apply to him as well. President Ronald Reagan, who won election in 1980, may have broken Tecumseh's Curse by surviving a would-be assassin's bullet in 1981.

FASCINATING FACTS: Popcorn

The popcorn plant, which is native to the Americas, was among the Spaniards' first discoveries in the New World. Both Christopher Columbus and Hernan Cortes witnessed natives using popcorn for food and decoration. Other interesting facts from the history of popcorn include these:

- According to Native American folklore, tiny spirits live inside each kernel of popcorn. These spirits rest quiet and content until someone heats their houses, at which they angrily burst forth.

- Early French Explorers watched the Iroquois using a popcorn popper made from a pot filled with heated sand. The Iroquois added popcorn to soups.

- The Huron may have eaten their popcorn with maple syrup.

- Some colonial children added sugar and milk to their popcorn and ate it like breakfast cereal.

- In 1948, Harvard graduate students found ancient ears of popcorn in a New Mexico cave, lying among piles of ancient trash. Although the kernels were thousands of years old, they were still fresh enough to pop.

U.S. AND WORLD HISTORY FOCUS

Napoleon's Fall, Part One

REFRESHING REMINDERS from Chapter 20: Over the years from 1772 – 1795, Russia, Prussia and Austria divided Poland among themselves, temporarily wiping Poland off the map.

FASCINATING FACTS: The French Invasion of Russia (June – December 1812)

The month when the United States declared war on Britain, June 1812, was the same month when Napoleon launched his invasion of Russia. Although Napoleon pretended that his invasion's purpose was to liberate Poland, most Europeans understood that the invasion's true purpose was to force Russia to abide by Napoleon's Continental System (see above).

In attacking an empire as vast as Russia's, Napoleon had to choose between three widely-separated target cities: (1) Russia's political capital, St. Petersburg, which Napoleon called its "head"; (2) Russia's food capital, Kiev, which he called its "stomach"; and (3) Russia's spiritual capital, Moscow, which he called its "heart." For his killing strike, Napoleon chose the heart, Moscow.

A LOOK AHEAD: Ironically for this greatest of military leaders, Napoleon's invasion of Russia will become one of the most notorious military failures of all time— an unparalleled disaster that will claim hundreds of thousands of lives, causing immeasurable suffering, without achieving any of Napoleon's war aims.

One factor that should have been a strength, but instead proved to be a weakness, was the immense size of Napoleon's Grand Army—somewhere between 400,000 and 700,000 troops, the population of a large city. To remain in fighting form, such an army required as much food as a large city every day. On earlier campaigns through food-rich Italy, Germany and Austria, Napoleon's armies had little trouble finding food. Now his largest army ever had to forage for food across one of the world's food-stingiest places: vast, frozen Russia.

Napoleon's enemy, Emperor Alexander I of Russia, capitalized on this weakness. When Napoleon led his Grand Army out of Warsaw, Alexander's army was too small to tackle him head-on, and too clever to try. Instead, the Russians retreated toward faraway Moscow, nearly 800 miles northeast of Warsaw. As they went, they either confiscated or burned every scrap of food in Napoleon's path.

The Russians' scorched-earth tactics soon made Napoleon's troops hungry enough to eat things they shouldn't— not only the horses that hauled their equipment, but also spoiled, germ-infested meat and water. Between starvation, disease and deadly battles along the way to Moscow, Napoleon lost an appalling number of troops— perhaps as much as one-half to two-thirds of his entire Grand Army.

The Emperor of the French around 1812

The Battle of Borodino (September 7, 1812)

After Napoleon's losses evened the odds a bit, Emperor Alexander finally decided to stand and fight for Russia's heart. Near the town of Borodino, about 70 miles southwest of Moscow, France and Russia fought one of the Napoleonic Wars' deadliest battles: the September 7, 1812 Battle of Borodino. Napoleon showed none of his usual brilliance at Borodino— no lightning-fast marches, and no encircling maneuvers. Instead, he launched his incredibly brave, devoted troops directly at his enemies' waiting cannon, while the Russians defended their lines just as bravely.

Although Napoleon eventually collapsed the Russian line, he did so at a terrible cost. Each side suffered somewhere near 30,000 – 40,000 casualties or more, for a combined total of 60,000 – 80,000 or more, all on one horrific day.

A few days later, Napoleon celebrated his victory at Borodino with another grand parade through yet another European capital, Moscow. However, two circumstances rendered this victory march less joyous than the ones in Vienna and Berlin:

1. The day after Napoleon's Grand Army paraded into Moscow, a terrible fire destroyed most of the city, perhaps set by fleeing Russians who sought to deny Napoleon Moscow's many benefits. Napoleon had been counting on Moscow's resources to feed, shelter and rebuild his army over the coming winter. After the fire, though, Moscow had few resources left.
2. Unlike the Austrians after Vienna and the Prussians after Berlin, the Russians refused to surrender after Napoleon captured Moscow. Instead, the unbeaten Russians retreated east of Moscow, daring Napoleon to chase them even deeper into Russia.

Retreat in Winter

With a badly-damaged army and a frigid Moscow winter coming on, even Napoleon had to admit that he couldn't possibly force a peace treaty that year. Therefore in mid-October, Napoleon reluctantly ordered a retreat.

Napoleon would have loved to retreat toward the warmer, more food-rich south; but each time he tried, the Russian army forced him west, back over the same war-ravaged track he had followed on his way to Moscow. Having depleted what little food there was to find on their way in, Napoleon's troops found even less on their way out. This time, an early Russian winter added sub-zero temperatures and howling winds to starvation, battle wounds and other unbearable miseries.

The suffering Napoleon's troops endured on this starving, bone-chilling, several-hundred-mile-long westward march is beyond imagining. Tens of thousands of them simply laid their bodies down in the snow and died, unable to march another step. Although the numbers are far from certain, as few as 20,000 – 40,000 of the troops Napoleon led east may have survived to return home. If these are the true numbers, then one of history's greatest military commanders suffered an astonishing casualty rate of about 90 – 95%.

"Napoleon's Retreat from Moscow" by artist Adolph Northen

CRITICAL COMPARISONS: Napoleon's invasion of Russia bore striking similarities to the one Charles XII of Sweden launched against Peter the Great a century before (see Chapter 17). As both Charles and Napoleon learned, Russia is vast and frozen enough to defeat invaders almost by itself, with a little help from its armies.

A LOOK AHEAD: Fuhrer Adolf Hitler of Germany will learn this same lesson when he launches his own invasion of Russia in 1941, during World War II.

FASCINATING FACTS: Russian author Leo Tolstoy (1828 – 1910) set one of the world's longest historical novels, *War and Peace*, during Napoleon's invasion of Russia.

The War of the Sixth Coalition (1812 – 1814)

Sensing weakness after Napoleon's failed invasion of Russia, enemies on all sides— including Russia, Prussia, Austria, Britain, Spain and Portugal, among others— formed yet another coalition against him. The many countries of this Sixth Coalition all shared a single goal: to eliminate the menace of Napoleon from Europe once and for all. The terrible War of the Sixth Coalition saw several battles as large as Borodino, with hundreds of thousands of soldiers leaving tens of thousands of casualties on German battlefields like Lützen, Bautzen and Leipzig.

For all his matchless military talent, not even Napoleon could defeat enormous armies on all sides at once. In March 1814, Paris fell to

Napoleon signing his abdication at Fontainebleau, France on April 4, 1814

the Sixth Coalition. One month later, the usually-silent French senate ordered its absent emperor to abdicate his throne.

Emperor of Elba (April 1814)

After defeating Napoleon, the Sixth Coalition faced the difficult question of what to do with him. Although the idea of executing Napoleon appealed to some, doing so would have set a precedent no royal wanted to set: that executing royals was both legal and acceptable. After the French Revolution, the enlightened despots who still clung to Europe's thrones had more reason than ever to fear execution at hands of their own people.

To avoid setting that precedent, and to avoid angering the still-dangerous French, the Sixth Coalition settled on a different fate for Napoleon.

> **FASCINATING FACTS: Napoleon's First Exile**
>
> In the Mediterranean Sea, between coasts of Italy and Napoleon's native Corsica, lay Elba— an iron-rich island with an area of about 85 square miles and a population of about 10,000 – 12,000. In honor of Napoleon's now-royal blood, the Sixth Coalition gave him Elba to own and rule, hoping that this worthy project would interest the deposed emperor enough to keep him out of mainland Europe's affairs for the rest of his life.

The War of 1812, Part Two

The fall of Napoleon affected the ongoing War of 1812 in two opposite ways:

1. On the one hand, Napoleon's fall freed up more British troops and sailors to wage war on the United States. The harsh blows already struck, and the deadly damage received, made some on both sides more eager for vengeance than ever.

2. On the other hand, Napoleon's fall removed some major causes of the War of 1812. With its war on France won, Britain no longer needed to blockade French ports, seize American ships or impress American sailors into Royal Navy service. Recognizing this, cooler heads were already in Ghent, Netherlands negotiating to end the war when British armies wrought their worst damage on the United States.

The Chesapeake Bay Campaign (August 1814)

A couple of months after France's April surrender, British troops from the now-finished Napoleonic wars started landing on Bermuda, which Britain used as a staging area for the War of 1812. That August, Britain sent several thousand of these troops to a region that had so far seen mostly sailors: the Chesapeake Bay. This unexpected British campaign caught the Americans completely unprepared, with only a few thousand inexperienced militia to set against some 5,000 battle-hardened veterans of the Napoleonic wars.

From the northern end of the Chesapeake Bay, the British might strike either Baltimore or Washington. Not knowing which, the Americans tried to defend both. To keep the Americans guessing, the British sent a small diversionary force up the Potomac River toward Washington; while the main British force bypassed the Potomac to sail up the Chesapeake's next major river, the Patuxent. From their landing point far up the Patuxent, the British still had two options: west toward Washington, or north toward Baltimore.

When the British broke west instead of north, the Americans struggled to defend Washington. After a swift, embarrassing loss at the Battle of Bladensburg, fought on August 24, 1814 about 6 miles northwest of Washington, the American militia scattered— leaving their nation's capital utterly defenseless.

FASCINATING FACTS: The Sack of Washington D.C. (August 24, 1814)

The scene in Washington D.C. after the Battle of Bladensburg was one of utter panic. Every government official in the city, including President James Madison, was rushing to collect his things and escape before the British could capture him. One high priority was to load founding documents like the Declaration of Independence and the Constitution aboard wagons and get them out of the city before the British could destroy them. Another was to clear every government office of military secrets the British might use. Long after most government officials fled, First Lady Dolley Madison remained at the President's House, doing her best to salvage the irreplaceable treasures on display there— including a large portrait of George Washington that required a long time to unscrew from the wall.

The first British soldiers actually entered the city under a flag of truce, hoping to negotiate the city's surrender. However, when a few American patriots fired on them from a house on the city's edge, the British gave up all thought of truce.

Instead, they systematically set fire to nearly every building connected with the government: the Senate, the House of Representatives, the President's House and

The U.S. Capitol Building reduced to a shell by British-set fires

many others. Before setting fire to the President's House, a squad of British soldiers feasted on an abandoned meal that servants had prepared for President Madison himself.

The Battle of Baltimore (September 12 – 15, 1814)

After the Sack of Washington, the British moved on to the far better prepared city of Baltimore. Finding Baltimore's ground troops tougher than the ones they had faced at Bladensburg, the British decided to stake their whole campaign on a day-and-night bombardment of Baltimore's main defense against naval attack: Fort McHenry, which stood on a point of land at the entrance to Baltimore's Inner Harbor.

AMAZING ANTHEMS: The Star - Spangled Banner (September 13 – 14, 1814)

Among the spectators at the Battle of Baltimore was a young attorney from Washington, D.C. named Francis Scott Key. Key had come to Baltimore to plead for the release of William Beanes, a beloved old doctor whom the British had carried off after the Sack of Washington. With help from U.S. Army negotiator John Skinner, Key was able to board an enemy ship and negotiate Dr. Beanes' release on September 13. However, as the British were just beginning their bombardment of Fort McHenry, they refused to release Beanes,

American defenders under fire inside Fort McHenry, Baltimore

Skinner or Key until the battle was over, lest any of them carry valuable military information back to the Americans.

For more than 24 hours, Key waited anxiously as the British lobbed shell after shell at Fort McHenry— some 1,500 – 1,800 long-range rockets and mortar shells in all. Because the British fleet stood out of range of the fort's cannon, the Americans inside the fort could only take cover, watch and wait, ready to bombard any ship that came in range. The waiting was particularly anxious during the overnight hours, when Key could see nothing but British rockets arcing through the air toward Fort McHenry's brave defenders.

When morning arrived at last, Key was moved with pride to see the American flag still waving over Fort McHenry— which could only mean that the fort's defenders were still alive, still standing strong against the British assault. Having failed to reduce Fort McHenry, the British gave up on Baltimore, and soon sailed back down the Chesapeake. Meanwhile, Key wrote a poem about his heart-moving experience. Set to music, this poem became the United States' official national anthem in 1916:

> *Oh, say can you see by the dawn's early light*
> *What so proudly we hailed at the twilight's last gleaming?*
> *Whose broad stripes and bright stars thru the perilous fight,*
> *O'er the ramparts we watched were so gallantly streaming?*
> *And the rockets' red glare, the bombs bursting in air,*
> *Gave proof through the night that our flag was still there*
> *Oh, say does that Star - Spangled Banner yet wave*
> *O'er the land of the free and the home of the brave?*

The Treaty of Ghent (signed December 24, 1814)

After the American victory at Baltimore, the war dragged on for two more months before both sides finally admitted that neither was likely to gain anything. The War of 1812 was supposed to end with the December 24, 1814 Treaty of Ghent, under which no territory whatsoever changed hands. However, news of the treaty took time to cross the Atlantic, allowing battles to continue into January 1815. One of the last was the Battle of New Orleans, an American victory that greatly boosted the reputation of future president Andrew Jackson (see Chapter 30).

FASCINATING FACTS: The U.S. Capitol Building

- The original U.S. Capitol Building— the one the British burned in 1814— consisted of two separate buildings connected by a temporary walkway, with plans for a permanent connecting wing later. The original Senate building was finished in 1800, the year the federal government moved from Philadelphia to Washington. The House of Representatives building remained unfinished until 1811, just three years before the British burned it.

- In the process of rebuilding the Capitol after the War of 1812, builders added a central wing to connect the Senate and House, including a central rotunda capped by a copper-roofed dome.

- Over the next few decades, the U.S. added so many new states that the old Capitol could no longer contain the

The U.S. Capitol as it appeared in 1846, with Senate and House wings less than half their present size and a far smaller central dome

people's representatives. President Millard Fillmore, who held office from 1850 – 1853, presided over the

- first of several major expansions that would more than double the Capitol's size. The current Capitol encloses more than 4 acres of ground.
- Builders completed the Capitol's current, far larger dome during the U.S. Civil War of 1861 – 1865. Framed of cast iron, this dome rises 288 feet above ground level— counting the 20-foot-tall *Statue of Freedom* at its top— and weighs more than 500 tons.

U.S. STATE FOCUS

Indiana

FASCINATING FACTS about Indiana:

- State Capital: Indianapolis
- State Abbreviation: IN
- Statehood: Indiana became the 19th US state on December 11, 1816.
- Area: About 36,000 square miles (Ranks 38th in size)
- Bordering States: Ohio, Michigan, Illinois, Kentucky
- Meaning of Name: "Indiana" means "Land of the Indians."
- State Nickname: "Hoosier State"
- State Bird: Cardinal
- State Tree: Tulip Poplar
- State Flower: Peony
- State Song: "On the Banks of Wabash, Far Away" by Paul Dresser
- State Motto: "The Crossroads of America"
- Historic Places to Visit: Angel Mounds, Levi Coffin House, President Benjamin Harrison Home, Indianapolis Motor Speedway, President Abraham Lincoln Boyhood Home, Tippecanoe Battlefield
- Resources and Industries: Car racing, farming, coal, oil, manufacturing

The Levi Coffin House at Fountain City, Indiana, an important station of the Underground Railroad abolitionist network

State Flag: A golden torch surrounded by nineteen golden stars, all on a blue field. The torch represents liberty and enlightenment, while the nineteen stars represent Indiana's position as the nineteenth state.

PRESIDENTIAL FOCUS

PRESIDENT #4: James Madison (1751 – 1836)	
In Office: March 4, 1809 – March 4, 1817	**Political Party:** Democratic-Republican
Birthplace: Virginia	**Nickname:** "Father of the Constitution"

James Madison was the well-educated, politically-minded son of a wealthy planter from central Virginia. Madison first entered national politics in 1780, when the 29-year-old became the youngest delegate to the Continental Congress.

In 1787, Virginia delegate James Madison arrived at the Constitutional Convention in Philadelphia better prepared than any other delegate. Madison's plan of government, the Virginia Plan, became the starting point from which the Convention compromised its way to the final Constitution of the United States. To help ensure the Constitution's ratification, Madison co-authored a set of pro-federal government articles titled the Federalist Papers. To protect the ratified Constitution against those who wanted to rewrite it, Madison authored its first ten amendments: the Bill of Rights. For all his work on the Constitution, Americans remember Madison as the Father of the Constitution, the Father of the Bill of Rights and the last Founding Father president.

As a Virginia delegate to the U.S. House of Representatives from 1789 – 1797, Madison helped Thomas Jefferson organize the Democratic-Republican Party. When Jefferson defeated the Federalists in the election of 1800, Madison became President Jefferson's highest cabinet officer. Secretary of State Madison served Jefferson for eight years, helping to administer the Louisiana Purchase, before winning the presidency himself in 1808.

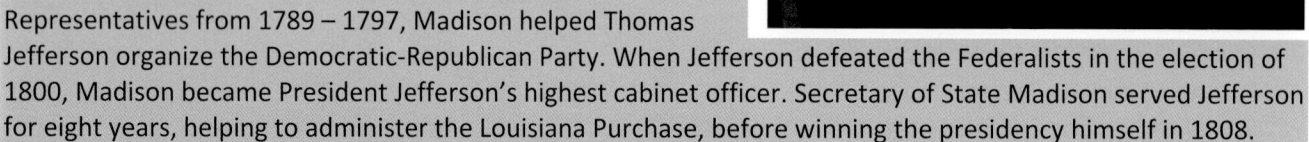

The greatest challenge of Madison's presidency was the War of 1812, which began as he was seeking reelection to his second term. The low point of that war came when the British sacked Washington, forcing Madison to flee the city. The War of 1812 altered some of Madison's opinions about government. Before the war, Madison warned against granting the federal government too much power. After the war, Madison realized that the United States' lack of strong federal institutions— a strong army for national defense, a strong National Bank to issue large loans— had made it all but impossible for the United States to win the war of 1812.

Fun Facts about James Madison:
- At his first inauguration, Madison wore a jacket made from wool produced on his home plantation of Montpelier, which still stands about 3 miles southwest of Orange, Virginia.
- Madison was the first president who ordinarily wore full-length trousers, not the knee breeches and stockings gentlemen usually wore in colonial times.
- Madison was the smallest president, standing about 5'4" tall and weighing only about 100 lbs.
- Because President Jefferson was a widower, Madison's wife Dolley Madison often served as Jefferson's official hostess at White House functions.
- For marrying the Episcopalian James Madison, Quaker-born Dolley Madison found herself read out of her Philadelphia meeting house.

Notable Quotes from James Madison:
- "All men having power ought to be distrusted to a certain degree."
- "I believe there are more instances of the abridgment of the freedom of the people by gradual and silent encroachments of those in power than by violent and sudden usurpations."

CHAPTER 29: The Congress of Vienna; More Atlantic Revolutions

WORLD HISTORY FOCUS

Napoleon's Fall, Part Two

REFRESHING REMINDERS: After the Sixth Coalition defeated Napoleon in 1814, it sent the former Emperor of the French into exile on the small Mediterranean Sea island of Elba.

The Congress of Vienna (1814 – 1815)

Soon after they shipped Napoleon off to Elba, diplomats from Europe's five major powers— victorious **Russia**, **Prussia**, **Austria**, **Britain**, along with defeated **France**— held a congress at Vienna, Austria to discuss how best to clean up the mess Napoleon had made of their continent. After more than two decades of bitter war, the diplomats who met at the **Congress of Vienna** were anxious to find some formula for lasting peace; however, the boundless ambition of Napoleon had taught them that they must always be prepared for war. The best way to resolve these conflicting needs, diplomats decided, was a set of agreements called the Concert of Europe.

DEFINITION: The **Concert of Europe** was a set of peace treaties negotiated by the Congress of Vienna at the end of the Napoleonic Wars. These treaties encouraged peace in three main ways:

1. By satisfying the war aims of the Napoleonic wars' winners— restoring their lost territories, repaying their lost money and protecting their security, mostly at France's expense.

2. By creating a **balance of power**— that is, by rearranging national boundaries so that Europe's five major powers all possessed more or less equal military resources, and therefore had little to gain from attacking one another.

3. By promising to meet and talk with one another often— to negotiate their differences, rather than automatically going to war over them.

Scene from the Congress of Vienna

Each of the Sixth Coalition's four main winners received part of the territory Napoleon disrupted:

1. Among other things, **Prussia** received part of the Duchy of Warsaw, the puppet state that Napoleon set up in the former Poland. Prussia also received part of the Confederation of the Rhine, the French-allied German confederation that Napoleon set up on the western edge of the former Holy Roman Empire. Thus Frederick the Great's legacy survived, as Prussia took a permanent seat at the table of Europe's five major powers.

2. Among other things, **Russia** received part of the Duchy of Warsaw, and retained parts of Poland already claimed in the Partitions of Poland.

3. Among other things, **Austria** received some of the territories that Napoleon seized in northern Italy, along with part of Poland.

4. **Britain** received a number of remote territories and island bases that would help it dominate the seas.

5. As for defeated **France**, it returned to its pre-French Revolution borders— which meant surrendering the territories it had won in Italy, in the southern Netherlands and along the Rhine River.

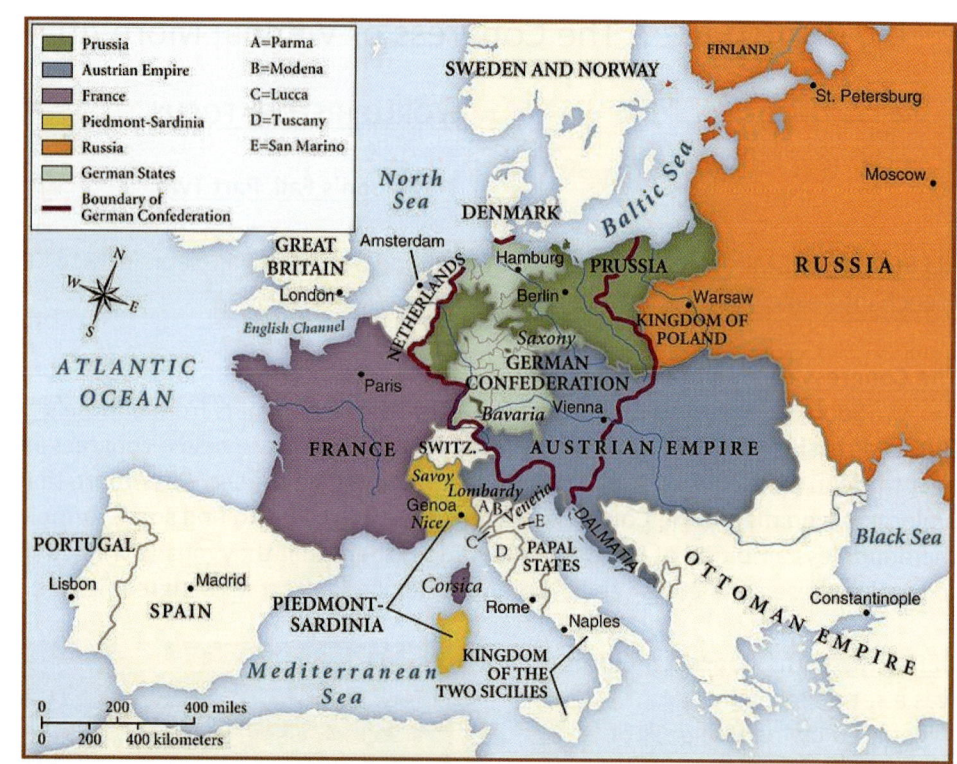

Map of Europe as divided by the Congress of Vienna in 1815

INTERESTING IDEAS: In addition to encouraging peace, the Congress of Vienna had a second major goal: restoring Europe's faith in monarchy. From the American Revolution to the French Revolution, Europe's enlightened despots felt that democracy and republican government had gone too far, depriving too many royals of their rightful territories. At the Congress of Vienna, European diplomats reaffirmed their heartfelt belief that monarchy was the best form of government.

FASCINATING FACTS: The Bourbon Restoration

The best demonstration of this belief came in France, where the Congress of Vienna set the Bourbon King Louis XVIII— brother and heir to the late Louis XVI, the king France executed in 1793— on France's throne. Thus after a quarter century of revolution and strife, the **Bourbon Restoration** brought France full circle, replacing Napoleon with a monarch from the very same Bourbon dynasty the French Revolution overthrew.

Napoleon Senses an Opportunity (April 1814 – February 1815)

While the Congress of Vienna was busy negotiating its treaties, Napoleon was threatening to undo everything the Congress was trying to do. From his exile on Elba, Napoleon eyed the news from the Congress of Vienna with great interest, searching for strategic weaknesses that might help him return to power. Over the eleven months from April 1814 – February 1815, Napoleon developed a strategy based on two weaknesses:

1. Discontent in France: Two powerful groups of Frenchmen grumbled under their restored Bourbon kings:

- **French soldiers** grumbled when Louis XVIII, who needed a fortune to pay France's exorbitant war costs, cut their pay in half. They also mourned France's lost glory, which the Congress of Vienna trampled underfoot when it seized the territory for which their fallen comrades had sacrificed their all. *Napoleon's Response: To both of these complaints, Napoleon considered himself the best answer; for never had the French won more wealth or glory than under Napoleon.*

- **French farmers** grumbled when Louis XVIII restored to his nobles the estates they had lost during the French Revolution. Louis' move required the farmers who had since taken over these estates to either pay for them or return them— neither of which farmers could afford. Farmers also grumbled because after all their sufferings in the French Revolution, the people's representatives wound up with only a little more power than they had enjoyed under Louis XVI. *Napoleon's Response*: *Napoleon calculated that if he offered his people a republican government, then they would gladly take his side against Louis XVIII.*

2. Discontent at the Congress of Vienna: Disagreements over the fairest way to divide Poland, Saxony and other territories almost split the Congress of Vienna, leading to the usual threats of war between Russia, Prussia, Austria and Britain. *Napoleon's Response*: *Napoleon hoped that war would indeed split the Congress— for if it did, then at least one of Europe's great powers would gladly form an alliance with Europe's greatest general, Napoleon of France.*

Portrait of King Louis XVIII in coronation robes

The Hundred Days (March 1 – July 8, 1815)

With all of these strategies in mind, Napoleon quietly slipped out of Elba on the night of February 26, 1815 with a small fleet of troop ships. Aboard Napoleon's fleet sailed about 1,050 troops from his Elban army, many of them loyal French veterans who had been sharing his exile on Elba. Along the way, two warships had opportunity to halt Napoleon's fleet, one British and one French. However, neither captain had any idea what great doings were afoot, so both allowed Napoleon's fleet to pass by unsearched.

The Hundred Days of Napoleon's final rule tentatively began on March 1, when he landed near the southern port of Antibes, France to begin his long march to Paris. Once again, several forces might have blocked Napoleon's march to Paris, were it not for two factors:

1. Napoleon carefully avoided regions of France that tended to support Louis XVIII, royalist regions that might have sent armies to oppose him.
2. Everywhere else he went, Napoleon's natural confidence and magnetic personality drew the French people to him— erasing their memories of the bad old days after his failed invasion of Russia, and elevating their depressed spirits with the hope of better days to come.

The success of Napoleon's return seemed in doubt when one of his former generals, Marshal Michel Ney, led out several thousand troops to confront him near Grenoble, France— a fortified city about 140 miles north of Toulon. Ney had once been Napoleon's bravest, most devoted officer, risking his neck for his emperor countless times. During Napoleon's exile, though, Ney had switched sides, promising to serve Louis XVIII as faithfully as he had served Napoleon. Before departing to confront Napoleon, Ney made Louis XVIII a second promise: that he would carry Napoleon back to Paris for him in an iron cage.

Ney had apparently forgotten Napoleon's matchless ability to inspire soldiers, including his generals. As Ney's army approached, Napoleon boldly stepped out in front of it all alone, baring his chest and crying for all to hear: "If there is among you a soldier who wants to kill his Emperor, then here I am!" Napoleon's reckless bravery so warmed the hearts of Ney's glory-loving Frenchmen that hardly a man thought of firing on him.

Instead, a familiar answering cry rose from a handful of Ney's troops: *Vive l'empereur*, French for "Long live the emperor!" Within minutes, this cry spread through Ney's army— all the way to Ney himself, who couldn't resist risking his neck for Napoleon yet again.

After Grenoble, Napoleon's return was never in doubt. Just before Napoleon reached Paris, Louis XVIII fled to safety in the southern Netherlands, leaving Napoleon to take his place as King of France.

The Seventh Coalition

Much to Napoleon's disappointment, the Congress of Vienna didn't split over the news of his return. Instead, Russia, Prussia, Austria and Britain immediately set aside their differences to form a Seventh Coalition against France, each promising at least 150,000 troops to refight the same war they fought a year before.

Napoleon's return from exile on Elba

Faced once again with enormous armies on all sides, Napoleon saw but one hope: to defeat each army separately, before they could combine into a single army so large that no one could defeat it. This was Napoleon's plan when he led all the offensive troops he could muster against his enemies' two nearest armies:

1. A combined British/Dutch/German army commanded by Briton Arthur Wellesley, Duke of Wellington.
2. A Prussian army commanded by Prussian Field Marshal Gebhard von Blücher.

Both Wellington and Blücher positioned their armies to defend the southern Netherlands— a mostly French-speaking region that had only recently belonged to France, and that Napoleon planned to recapture as soon as possible. Recapturing the southern Netherlands promised several advantages:

- It would win Napoleon important cities like Brussels, Ghent and Antwerp, along with all of their wealth, resources and manpower.
- It would further humiliate Louis XVIII by forcing him to seek a more distant hiding place.
- It might even frighten nearby London, which lay just across the North Sea from Antwerp, into abandoning its war on France.

BRILLIANT BATTLES: The Battle of Waterloo (June 18, 1815)

Having little idea where Napoleon might begin his assault, both Wellington and Blücher spread their armies over wide areas of the southern Netherlands, trying to block as many roads north as possible. Wellington stood to the west, protecting his supply line back to the North Sea; while Blücher stood to the east, protecting his supply line back to Prussia. Thanks to Napoleon's cagy maneuvering, both of his enemies were still scattered when they learned where he was leading his main army. Napoleon was going neither west nor east, but instead due north, hoping to separate his enemies so that they couldn't help each other when the fighting started.

Napoleon's plan almost worked. On June 16th, Napoleon's armies won two key battles:

1. **The Battle of Ligny**, a town about 25 miles south-southeast of Brussels. Here Napoleon defeated part of Blücher's army, forcing him to retreat.

2. **The Battle of Quatre Bras**, a key crossroads several miles northwest of Ligny. When Wellington learned that Napoleon had attacked Blücher at Ligny, he tried to send reinforcements— only to have Napoleon block him at Quatre Bras, forcing Wellington to retreat as well.

One factor that wrecked Napoleon's plan was the direction of each enemy's retreat. Napoleon hoped to force Wellington west, and Blücher east. Instead, both retreated north toward Brussels, remaining close enough to send one another aid. When the retreating Wellington learned where Blücher was, and that he could count on his ally for reinforcements, he chose a place to turn and make his stand: on a ridge near Waterloo, a town about ten miles south of Brussels.

Another factor that wrecked Napoleon's plan was a powerful rainstorm that soaked Waterloo on June 17. This storm delayed Napoleon's attack on Wellington, allowing both Wellington and Blücher more time to arrange their armies. Even on the morning of the battle, June 18, Napoleon delayed his attack for several hours so that his troops could maneuver on drier ground.

Despite this fateful delay, Napoleon's veteran French troops nearly won the day for him. After several hours of hard-fought battle, Wellington was barely clinging to his ridge near Waterloo, praying as his army endured Napoleon's merciless onslaught: "Give me night, or give me Blücher!"

Evening was approaching when the arrival of Blücher finally answered Wellingon's prayer. Bolstered by Blücher's Prussian reinforcements, Wellington drove Napoleon from the field late in the day. Wellington would

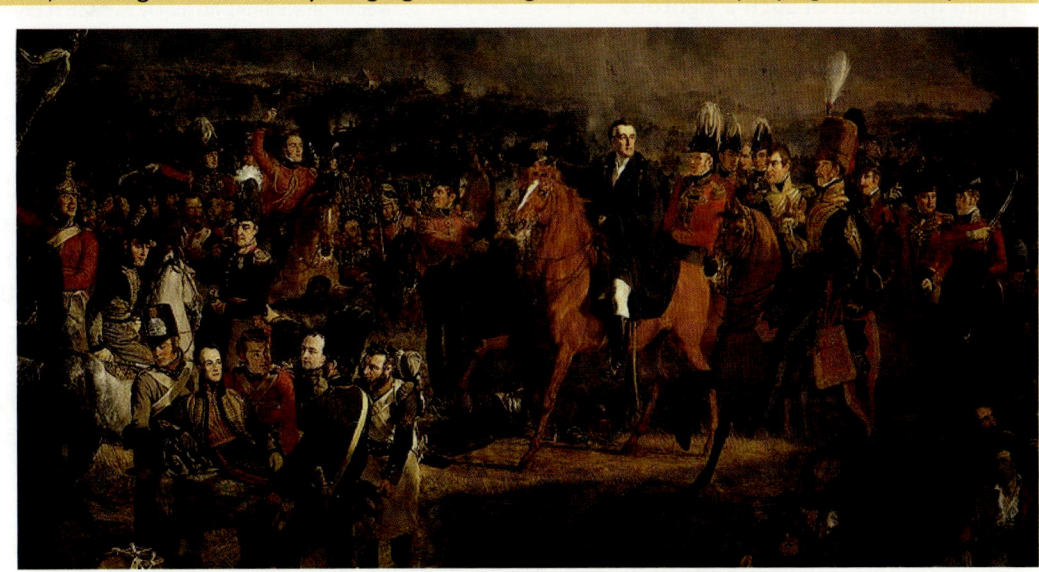

The Duke of Wellington victorious at the Battle of Waterloo

later recall his narrow victory at Waterloo as "the nearest-run thing you ever saw in your life."

Other interesting quotes from the Duke of Wellington:

- After his historic victory at Waterloo, Wellington mourned his losses in a letter: "My heart is broken by the terrible loss I have sustained in my old friends and companions and my poor soldiers. Believe me, nothing except a battle lost can be half so melancholy as a battle won."

- Asked to rank history's great generals, Wellington replied: "In this age, in past ages, in any age, Napoleon!"

The Battle of Waterloo brought the Hundred Days of Napoleon's second reign to a close. Afterward, the Seventh Coalition restored King Louis XVIII to France's throne, and banished Napoleon into his second exile.

FASCINATING FATES

Napoleon's Fate (1821): For this second exile, Napoleon's enemies knew better than to set him on a nearby Mediterranean island. Instead, they imprisoned Napoleon on **Saint Helena**— a tiny, rocky island that stands in the remotest part of the South Atlantic Ocean, nearly 1,200 miles west of Angola, Africa. This time, British authorities kept close watch on Napoleon, restricting him so tightly that he never had a chance to escape. Napoleon endured about 6 years of rough treatment from his worst enemies, the British, before dying on May 5, 1821, months before his 52nd birthday.

From that time to this, Napoleon's supporters have insisted that his British guards must have poisoned him— for how else to explain the death of such a vigorous man at such an early age? At autopsy, though, Napoleon's British doctors offered a less conspiratorial cause of death: stomach cancer.

Napoleon enduring his lonely exile on rocky Saint Helena

Marshal Ney's Fate (1815): Marshal Michel Ney, the French general whose broken promise to Louis XVIII enabled Napoleon's return, suffered a more soldierly fate than Napoleon's. After the Battle of Waterloo, the restored Bourbon government condemned Ney to death for the treason of supporting Napoleon. In honor of the matchless bravery that Ney had displayed in countless battles, the Bourbons allowed him to command the firing squad assigned to execute him. Spurning the usual blindfold, Ney calmly stared death in the face as he issued these final orders:

> "Soldiers, when I give the command to fire, fire straight at my heart. Wait for the order; it will be my last to you. I protest against my condemnation. I have fought a hundred battles for France, and not one against her... Soldiers, fire!"

A LOOK AHEAD: France's restored Bourbon kings will not rest easy on their thrones. Over the next few decades, two more revolutions will bring three more changes of government: (1) the July Revolution of 1830 will replace the Bourbon dynasty with a new dynasty and a new constitutional monarchy; (2) the French Revolution of 1848 will replace this constitutional monarchy with the Second French Republic; and (3) in 1852, Napoleon Bonaparte's nephew will proclaim himself Emperor Napoleon III of the Second French Empire.

ILLUMINATING LISTS: More Results of the Congress of Vienna

- **The German Confederation:** To replace the defunct Holy Roman Empire, the Congress of Vienna formed the German-speaking states into a loose union called German Confederation. Just as under the Holy Roman Empire, the western, German-speaking parts of Prussia and Austria belonged to the German Confederation; while the eastern, non-German-speaking parts did not.

A LOOK AHEAD: Over the years from 1815 – 1871, Prussia and Austria will battle to determine which of these two giants will dominate the German Confederation. After Prussia wins this battle, King Wilhelm I of Prussia and his prime minister, "Iron Chancellor" Otto von Bismarck, will unite most of the German-speaking states into the mighty **German Empire**.

- **Disunity in Italy:** The Congress of Vienna left most of Italy as Napoleon had found it: a disunited collection of several nation-states, many of them heavily influenced by nearby Austria.

A LOOK AHEAD: Over the years from 1848 – 1870, Italy's several nation-states will do for themselves what the Congress of Vienna did not: in a process called the **Risorgimento**, they will form a united Kingdom of Italy, completely independent of Austria.

- **Swiss Neutrality:** As a small crossroads nation surrounded by giants France, Germany, Austria and Italy, Switzerland sought a way to avoid being swept up in its larger neighbors' ceaseless wars. The Congress of Vienna solved this problem by recognizing Switzerland as the world's first permanently neutral nation.

A LOOK AHEAD: In all future wars, Switzerland will declare war on no one, and supply military aid to no one.

- **The Dutch Republic and Belgium:** During the French Revolutionary wars, both the Dutch Republic of the north and the Austrian Netherlands of the south fell to France. After the Napoleonic wars, the Congress of Vienna reunited north and south to form the United Kingdom of the Netherlands. By this time, however, the mostly-Catholic southerners of Wallonia and Flanders wanted nothing to do with their mostly-Protestant Dutch neighbors to the north.

Flag of Switzerland

A LOOK AHEAD: The years from 1830 – 1831 will bring the **Belgian Revolution**, in which the southern Netherlands will separate from the north to form the independent **Kingdom of Belgium**. The north will reorganize as the **Kingdom of the Netherlands**. Both constitutional monarchies survive today.

MUSICAL MASTERS: Robert Schumann (1810 – 1856) and Clara Wieck Schumann (1819 – 1896)

Robert Schumann was a German composer born in 1810, the same year as Frédéric Chopin. Sadly, Robert's father died in 1826. The following year, the 17-year-old Robert enrolled at the University of Leipzig, Saxony to fulfill the terms of his father's will, which required him to finish a three-year course of legal studies there. In Leipzig, Robert rented a room from a piano teacher named Friedrich Wieck, who happened to have a young daughter named Clara. Thus Robert Schumann met the love of his life, the future Clara Wieck Schumann, when she was nine and he nineteen.

When Robert met Clara, she was already well on her way to becoming a great pianist. Robert might have become one as well, had he not injured the middle finger of his right hand, leaving it numb for life. Although the source of this injury is uncertain, it may have come from overusing a mechanical practice tool that supposedly trained the fingers to play more independently. Barred from success as a performer, Robert

Robert Schumann

decided to focus on composing. While Robert struggled at the piano, young Clara blossomed into one of the foremost pianists of her day, delighting audiences all over Europe with her heart-touching style.

As soon as Clara turned 18, she and Robert approached her father asking permission to marry. To the lovers' dismay, Clara's father refused, insisting that his brilliant daughter deserved a better husband than some penniless composer. Determined to marry anyway, Clara and Robert took her stubborn father to court. After nearly three years, their permission-to-marry suit finally succeeded, clearing the way for the couple to wed in 1840.

1840 was the most joyful year of Robert's life, a time when surging feelings inspired him to compose nearly 140 works in just a few months. Schumann's works from this period excelled at the Romantic composer's highest goal: using music to express ideas and emotions usually expressed only in words. Schumann was an expert at composing music that called to mind certain moods, personalities or happenings.

Unfortunately, Robert also suffered dark years of depression and hallucinations— so many that by 1854, Robert feared his mental illness might endanger his family. To prevent this, Robert tried to drown himself by jumping off a bridge. After boatmen fished him out of the Rhine River and took him home, Robert insisted on committing himself to an insane asylum, where he died in 1856. Clara Schumann spent much of her 40-year widowhood playing and popularizing her late husband's work.

Clara Wieck Schumann

The Haitian Revolution (1791 – 1803)

The mighty waves of the French Revolution and Napoleon spread ripples far to the west, into Haiti and South America.

> **WHAT HAS GONE BEFORE: Fascinating Facts about Haiti**

- The modern-day Republic of Haiti occupies the western one-third of Hispaniola, the large West Indian island where Christopher Columbus established Spain's first colony in the New World. Hispaniola lies between Cuba and Puerto Rico.

- After mining out Hispaniola's limited supply of gold in the early 1500s, Spanish colonists turned to filling eastern Hispaniola with sugar plantations. Later, during the 1600s, French colonists filled most of western Hispaniola with sugar plantations.

Map featuring Hispaniola in red

- France and Spain settled their disputed claims to Hispaniola in the Treaty of Ryswick, the treaty that ended the War of the Grand Alliance in 1697:

  1. France claimed Hispaniola's western one-third— which became the French colony of **St. Dominic**, and eventually independent Haiti.

  2. Spain claimed Hispaniola's eastern two-thirds— which became the Spanish colony of Santo Domingo, and eventually the independent Dominican Republic.

> **FASCINATING FACTS:** Just off Haiti's northwestern corner lies the well-known island of **Tortuga**. In the 1600s, Tortuga was a notorious haven for French, Dutch and English pirates who preyed on the Spanish Treasure Fleets.

> **DEFINITION:** The **Haitian Revolution** of 1791 – 1804 was a slave revolt that accomplished something no other slave revolt had yet accomplished: establishing an independent nation led by former slaves.

Slavery in St. Dominic

During the 1700s, St. Dominic grew into one of the West Indies' wealthiest sugar- and coffee-exporting colonies. Sadly, the colony built its wealth on the backs of enslaved Africans, whom plantation owners imported in tremendous numbers. St. Dominic's plantation system divided its people into three main castes, each with different rights:

1. **White Frenchmen:** Colonists born in France, or born in St. Dominic to two French parents, enjoyed the same rights and privileges as all Frenchmen. Before the French Revolution, those rights depended on birth and wealth. Rich white plantation owners, known as *grand blancs*, held the most power. Poor whites, known as *petit blancs*, held the least.

2. ***Gens de couleur libres*, French for "free people of color":** Many, many St. Dominicans were born to white fathers and enslaved African mothers. These mixed-race colonists, known as *gens de couleur*, enjoyed rights somewhere between those of whites and slaves. *Gens de couleur* could attend school, serve in the military, and even own plantations and slaves. However, the law denied *gens de couleur* full French citizenship, barring them from voting or holding high government office.

3. **Enslaved Africans:** African-born slaves and their descendants enjoyed essentially no rights, not even the right to life. Haitian plantation owners treated their slaves so poorly that by the late 1700s, they were importing tens of thousands every year just to replace those who died of overwork, abuse and neglect.

Detail of "Free Women of Color with their Children and Servants in a Landscape" by Agostino Brunias

---

FASCINATING FACTS: The *Code Noir* ("Black Code," first issued 1685)

France's notoriously harsh slave code, the *Code Noir*, was originally the work of France's Sun King Louis XIV (reigned 1643 – 1715). In theory, one of Louis' goals in the *Code Noir* was to protect slaves against too-harsh masters. For example, the law (1) forbade masters to work their slaves on Sundays; (2) required masters to care for their elderly slaves; and (3) forbade masters to break up slave families by selling off a father, a mother and their small children separately.

In practice, most masters ignored these protections to focus on the *Code Noir*'s stronger laws, the ones that protected masters against rebellious slaves. For example, the *Code Noir*:

- Strictly forbade slaves to carry "any offensive weapons or large sticks, at the risk of being whipped…"
- Forbade slaves of different masters to come together for any sort of gathering, not even a wedding or a funeral— for fear they might use such gatherings to organize slave revolts.
- Decreed the death penalty for any slave who struck his master, his mistress or any of their children.

- Decreed harsh punishments for runaway slaves. For the first offense, the runaway was to have his ears cut off, and receive a burning-hot fleur-de-lis brand on one shoulder. For the second, he was to have one of his hamstrings slashed, and receive the same brand on his other shoulder. For the third, the penalty was death.

In publishing such harsh laws, Louis was recognizing the fact that slaves outnumbered their masters— which meant that if he permitted slaves to organize themselves or carry weapons, then their masters would be defenseless against them. This was especially true in St. Dominic, where slaves outnumbered freemen by somewhere near 10 to 1.

The *Code Noir* also included religious requirements for both slaveholders and slaves:

Illustration of an overseer standing by while slaves cut and load sugar cane

- Slaveholders were to arrange for their slaves' training in the Roman Catholic faith within eight days of their purchase, and baptize them as soon as possible.
- Slaves were to forget their native African religions, and practice only Catholicism.

INTERESTING IDEAS: One unexpected side effect of the overly harsh *Code Noir* was that it kept African culture fresh in St. Dominican slaves' minds. In colonies where slaveholders raised replacement slaves from birth, most Africans forgot their native languages and religions within a couple of generations. In St. Dominic, though, slaveholders constantly refreshed their slaves' memories by importing new slaves directly from Africa.

FASCINATING FACTS: Haitian Vodou

- Because St. Dominic's slaves came from several African tribes, the religion they developed came from no one African religion. Instead, St. Dominic developed **Haitian Vodou**— a unique new blend of African religions, native Hispaniolan religions and even a bit of Roman Catholicism. Haitian Vodou believers call themselves **Vodouisants.**

- Vodouisants believe in the one supreme god Bondye, whose name derives from the French *bon dieu*, "good god." Because Bondye is too lofty for humans to approach directly, Vodouisants must approach him through lesser spirits called loa.

- There are scores of loa, all divided into nations and families based on their particular interests and powers. Some believe that during certain rituals, loa possess Vodouisants and speak through them. They also believe that loa have the power to bless Vodouisants who seek them faithfully, and curse those who do not.

Statue of a twelve-eyed Haitian Vodou devil

- Vodouisants call their priests **houngans**, and their priestesses **mambos**. Some houngans and mambos behave as clerics from most other faiths do, encouraging believers to seek god and do good works. Others practice dark magic, claiming the ability to cast curses and wreak havoc on their enemies.

- Even in modern times, some houngans and mambos still sacrifice live animals to feed their loa.

> DEFINITION: In addition to white Frenchmen, *gens de couleur* and enslaved Africans, St. Dominic was home to a class of people called **Maroons**. Most Maroons were slaves who ran away from their masters to join camps of runaways hidden on the fringes of settlement. Other Maroons were descendants of Hispaniola's native Taino people, most of whom the Spaniards had killed or driven out long ago.

HISTORIC HAITIANS: François Mackandal (1728? – 1758)

François Mackandal was a clever African boy whose life changed forever around 1740, the year slave traders kidnapped the 12-year-old and sold him into slavery in St. Dominic. Mackandal never forgave the crime of his enslavement, and never stopped plotting his revenge. Over the next ten years, Mackandal mastered the two skills he would use to launch one of St. Dominic's deadliest slave revolts:

1. The skill to inspire and organize his fellow slaves— partly through his leadership role as a Haitian Vodou houngan.
2. The skill to brew poisons from plants, fungi and other natural substances found in St. Dominic.

Haitian coin bearing an image of a machete-wielding Mackandal

In 1751, Mackandal escaped slavery to join a Maroon camp hidden on the fringes of settlement. The following year, white slaveholders started dying in record numbers. Many died because Mackandal gave their kitchen staffs tasteless poisons to mix with their food. Others died because Mackandal turned trusted household slaves against their masters, coaxing them to slip into their masters' bedrooms by night and slit their throats. Still others died when Mackandal-inspired death squads ambushed them in small groups.

Over the next six years, some 6,000 slaveholders and their family members fell victim to Mackandal's assassins— so many that France feared it might lose its wealthiest sugar colony. Mackandal's massacres continued until late 1757, when French police finally tortured one of his helpers into revealing his hideout. After January 1758, when Mackandal's captors burned him alive at the stake, his slave revolt quickly collapsed.

The French Revolution in St. Dominic

> REFRESHING REMINDERS: The enlightened Declaration of the Rights of Man, first adopted by revolutionary France in 1789, included this principle in Article 1: "Men are born and remain free and equal in rights…"

The French Revolution brought as much turmoil to St. Dominic as it did to France itself. When the *gens de couleur* learned of the Declaration of the Rights of Man, they immediately demanded full French citizenship, including voting rights. Naturally, the colony's all-white government council rejected this idea, which would have meant a drastic loss of power for whites. For the crime of raising a small rebel army to back up his demand for voting rights, a *gens de couleur* named Vincent Oge suffered one of the most excruciating deaths imaginable: being pulled in two on a medieval torture rack.

Despite their disagreement over voting rights, whites and *gens de couleur* still held one firm belief in common: that St. Dominic's wealth-generating plantation system would collapse without its slaves. Very few of St. Dominic's property owners, whether white, *gens de couleur* or even free black, wanted anything to do with liberating slaves. Therefore in 1791, St. Dominic's slaves once again took matters into their own hands.

FASCINATING FACTS: *Bois Caïman*, or the Cayman Wood Ceremony (August 1791)

Exactly what touched off the Haitian Revolution is uncertain: it may have begun as a reaction to the French Revolution, or it may have begun as another slave revolt like François Mackandal's. The following tale represents one version of the revolution's beginnings:

On August 14, 1791, about 200 slave leaders gathered for an illegal secret meeting on a plantation in northern Haiti. Among the foremost slave leaders at this meeting was a very large, very strong Vodou houngan named Dutty Boukman.

When the local slaveholders noticed so many slaves missing at the same time, they realized that something big must be afoot. Therefore when the slaves returned, the slaveholders tortured them to find out what that something might be. Under torture, several slaves revealed that the slaveholders' worst nightmare was about to come true— that St. Dominic's slaves, who outnumbered its slaveholders at least 10 to 1, were about to launch the biggest revolt in the colony's history.

When Dutty Boukman learned that his planned slave revolt was in danger, he called a second illegal meeting on the same plantation, this time at a place called Cayman Wood. Unlike the first meeting, the second was no mere planning session. Instead, it was a dark Haitian Vodou religious ceremony in which Boukman called upon powerful loa to energize his slave revolt. According to legend, *Bois Caïman* included the sacrifice of at least one black pig. Every slave leader present drank some of the pig's still-warm blood, trying to absorb the loa's strength for the coming revolt. Every slave leader also carried some of the pig's bristles with him, believing that these would protect him from slaveholders' bullets.

Some versions of the *Bois Caïman* legend insist that the slaves of St. Dominic sold themselves to the devil that night, trading their very souls for the power to launch history's only successful slave revolt. Some even claim to know the length of time for which the slaves agreed to serve the devil: 200 years. However, it is also possible that *Bois Caïman* was no dark ritual, but only an innocent prayer for a successful Haitian Revolution.

Whether *Bois Caïman* was a satanic ritual or an innocent prayer, it marked the beginning of St. Dominic's longest, most violent slave revolt. Within a couple of months, dozens of once-great sugar and coffee plantations lay in ruins, and hundreds of white plantation

Enslaved Haitians massacring their French oppressors

owners and their family members lay dead. Only within the colony's fortified cities, including Cap-Haitien in the north and Port-au-Prince in the south, could the French colonial government still claim to control St. Dominic.

CAST OF CHARACTERS for the Haitian Revolution:

1. Toussaint Louverture (1743? – 1803): Toussaint Louverture was a full-blooded African slave born to two first-generation slaves on a large sugar plantation in northern Haiti. However, Toussaint's parents were no ordinary slaves; for Toussaint's father may have ruled a small kingdom in West Africa before slave traders captured him.

Probably thanks to his exceptional family, Toussaint received an exceptional education for a slave. Instead of cutting sugar cane, Toussaint probably helped his plantation's overseers organize work schedules and supplies— useful skills for the man who would become the Haitian Revolution's greatest leader. More than a decade before the Revolution, around 1776, Toussaint's owners rewarded him for his excellent service by granting him his freedom.

INTERESTING IDEAS: Toussaint Lourverture's unique background gave him a unique outlook on the Haitian Revolution. Unlike some revolutionaries, Toussaint never despised his former masters, nor wished death upon all whites. When the Revolution broke out, one of Toussaint's first priorities was to escort his former masters to safety on the Spanish side of Hispaniola. Throughout the Revolution, Toussaint frowned on unnecessary violence, preferring disciplined military victories to vengeful massacres. Toussaint also retained his masters' Catholic faith, never adopting Haitian Vodou. Far from despising French culture, Toussaint admired it, and longed for St. Dominic to take part in it— if only blacks could stand on an equal footing with whites.

Soon after the Haitian Revolution broke out in late 1791, the freedom-loving Toussaint Louverture joined a slave army as a medical officer. Toussaint's obvious organizational skills quickly won him a small command of his own, followed by an army of his own. The Revolution's enemies soon learned to see Toussaint as a crafty foe— one whose army covered ground with seemingly impossible speed, appearing out of nowhere to strike where it was least expected. Exactly how Toussaint kept his army fed and supplied, or knew as much as he did about his enemies' plans, remained a mystery throughout the Revolution.

2. Jean-Jacques Dessalines (1758 – 1806): Toussaint's leading lieutenant, Jean-Jacques Dessalines, was another full-blooded African slave. Unlike Toussaint, Dessalines endured slavery in the fields as a youngster, cutting sugarcane for brutal white overseers. Even after his cleverness earned him a place as an overseer's assistant, Dessalines never forgot his hatred of whites.

3. Léger-Félicité Sonthonax (1763 – 1813): Sonthonax was a white governor sent to St. Dominic by the French National Convention in 1792, about a year after the Haitian Revolution broke out. The Convention assigned Sonthonax two tasks: to restore order, and to get his colony back to producing sugar wealth for France.

Toussaint Louverture

The End of the Revolution's First Phase (January 1793)

Sonthonax's job grew easier after St. Dominic started running out of food. Few plantation owners bothered with growing food on St. Dominic; rather, they grew valuable cash crops like sugar and coffee, which they could then trade for food. In wrecking St. Dominic's plantations, the Revolution also wrecked the colony's ability to trade, leading to widespread hunger.

Empty bellies made once-stubborn slaves more willing to negotiate. By meeting just a few of the slaves' demands— promising them shorter working hours and an extra day off per week, along with guaranteed freedom for rebel generals— Sonthonax convinced the slaves to lay down their arms and go back to work.

The French Revolutionary Wars in St. Dominic

All of that changed in February 1793, when news of two important events reached St. Dominic. First, the colonists learned that revolutionary France had just executed King Louis XVI. Next, they learned that both Britain and Spain had joined the First Coalition against France (see Chapter 25). Because Britain controlled the high seas, and Spain controlled the eastern two-thirds of Hispaniola, these two powers' entry into the War of the First Coalition changed everything:

- Instead of sending its own armies against the French in St. Dominic, Spain started supplying St. Dominic's slave armies with food and weapons to help them continue their revolt against the French.

- Sensing an opportunity to capture one of the richest sugar colonies in the West Indies, Britain laid plans to invade St. Dominic. Meanwhile, St. Dominic's wealthy white slaveholders entered negotiations to place their colony under British control— partly to escape France's *exclusif* system.

DEFINITION: The *exclusif* system was a set of mercantilist trade restrictions that France imposed on its colonies. Under the *exclusif*, St. Dominic could buy and sell only from merchants in mainland France— a restriction that placed St. Dominican traders at a great disadvantage.

Like the American traders who so resented British mercantilism (see Chapter 21), St. Dominican traders longed to seek better prices outside France. The British took advantage of St. Dominicans' discontent, promising them freer trade if they would throw their support behind Britain.

Emancipation (August 1793)

Beset by enemies on all sides, and with not the slightest hope of receiving reinforcements from embattled France, Governor Sonthonax could see only one way to keep his colony from slipping through his fingers. Sonthonax would have to call upon the aid of the largest armies in St. Dominic, its slave armies; and to win those armies' aid, he would have to free at least some of St. Dominic's slaves.

FASCINATING FACTS: The Abolition of Slavery in St. Dominic (August 1793)

The abolition of slavery in St. Dominic came in stages:

1. First, Sonthonax liberated about 15,000 slaves whose help he needed to defeat rebellious white slaveholders around his capital, Cap Haitien.

2. Realizing that with the British about to invade St. Dominic, his colony's troubles were only beginning, Sonthonax liberated all of St. Dominic's slaves in August 1793.

3. On February 4, 1794, in the middle of Maximilien Robespierre's Reign of Terror, the French National Convention confirmed Sonthonax's decision by abolishing slavery throughout France and all its colonies.

Portrait of Sonthonax, liberator of St. Dominic's slaves

INTERESTING IDEAS:

- Thus in 1794, France became the first major European power to abolish slavery throughout its empire. The abolition of slavery soon became a point of pride for the liberty-loving French— a demonstration that Frenchmen were more virtuous than their enemies, the still-slaveholding British and Spanish. Revolutionary Frenchmen understood what even many Americans did not: that no government founded on the Enlightenment principles of liberty and equality could possibly justify enslaving its people.

- However, France didn't abolish slavery for purely virtuous reasons— for part of the driving force behind abolishing slavery was the need to save the West Indies' richest sugar colony for France.

The Rise of Toussaint Louverture (1794 – 1801)

After Sonthonax abolished slavery in St. Dominic, but before the National Convention confirmed his decision, Britain made good on its threat to invade St. Dominic. At first, Toussaint Louverture stood on the sidelines, refusing to take France's side against Britain— perhaps because he wasn't sure that France was serious about abolishing slavery.

After the National Convention formally abolished slavery, though, Toussaint threw his support behind the National Convention. From that moment forward, Toussaint was revolutionary France's greatest champion in St. Dominic. For more than four years, from 1794 – 1798, Toussaint harassed the British as he had once harassed the French— restricting them to coastal cities, never allowing them to penetrate the island's interior. By the time the British finally gave up and left in late 1798, Toussaint was the most powerful man in St. Dominic. Two years later, Toussaint expanded his authority even further by capturing Hispaniola's eastern two-thirds from Spain.

In 1801, Toussaint confirmed his authority by issuing a new constitution that:

1. Proclaimed Toussaint Louverture Governor-General for life over St. Dominic, which now included all of Hispaniola.

2. Forever outlawed slavery in St. Dominic.

3. Insisted that St. Dominic was still a loyal colony of France.

Toussaint versus Napoleon

Napoleon Bonaparte, who was then in his second year as First Consul of France, believed that he had good reason to doubt Toussaint's loyalty. For one thing, Toussaint issued his constitution without permission, claiming more authority than Napoleon wanted him to have. For another, Toussaint was already negotiating advantageous new trade arrangements with Britain and the U.S., as if France no longer had the right to *exclusif* trade with its colony.

Napoleon also had another reason for removing Toussaint: because Toussaint stood in the way of Napoleon's plans to expand his empire in the New World.

- The mercantilist Napoleon believed that St. Dominic's highest purpose was to generate money for France. To that end, Napoleon wanted to restore two policies that Toussaint despised: (1) *exclusif* trade between St. Dominic and France; and (2) slavery.

- Napoleon wanted to use St. Dominic as a firm base from which to expand into Louisiana and the British West Indies. To secure that base, Napoleon needed a governor-general he could trust.

The Leclerc Expedition (Dec. 1801 – Dec. 1803)

Determined to reassert his authority over St. Dominic, Napoleon named a new governor-general for St. Dominic, one whose personal loyalties were beyond question: his brother-in-law Charles Leclerc, husband to his sister Pauline. In February 1802, Leclerc arrived in St. Dominic with more than 10,000 French troops and marines, the first of more than 30,000 who would eventually arrive there.

Toussaint's loyalty to France may have clouded his judgment about the Leclerc Expedition. As a loyal subject, Toussaint may have felt that Napoleon had every right to station troops in St. Dominic. Some of Toussaint's subordinates disagreed, suspecting that the true purpose of

Toussaint Louverture proclaiming his new constitution

Charles LeClerc

Leclerc's mission was a sinister one: to revive slavery, undoing everything their Revolution had accomplished over the last ten years. Therefore when Leclerc landed on St. Dominic, part of Toussaint's army resisted him.

All the while Toussaint fought this unwanted war, he searched for some compromise that would lead to peace. After a few months of fighting, Toussaint believed that he had found one. In May 1802, Toussaint agreed that he and his officers would serve in Leclerc's army as loyal Frenchmen; and in exchange, Leclerc promised never to revive slavery in St. Dominic. Part of Toussaint's army accepted this compromise, and joined Toussaint in making peace. However, another part continued to resist Leclerc, still convinced that his true mission was to revive slavery.

FASCINATING FATES: Toussaint Louverture's Fate

Exactly why Leclerc did what he did next is uncertain. Leclerc may have believed that the resistance would never end as long as the highly-honored Toussaint Louverture remained on St. Dominic; or he may have been plotting Toussaint's demise from the beginning.

Whatever Leclerc's reasons, he treacherously invited Toussaint aboard a French ship under false pretenses, and then took him prisoner. As the manacles closed around his wrists, Toussaint warned his captors:

"In overthrowing me you have cut down in St. Dominic only the trunk of the tree of liberty; it will spring up again from the roots, for they are many and they are deep."

When Toussaint reached France, his captors condemned the 60-year-old, warm-climate-accustomed general to captivity in the frigid French Alps. Toussaint endured this rough treatment for less than a year before dying in April 1803, leaving Jean-Jacques Dessalines to take his place as leader of the Haitian Revolution.

The Haitian War for Independence (1802 – 1803)

As word of Leclerc's treachery against the great Toussaint Louverture spread, the Haitian Revolution grew beyond anything Leclerc could hope to contain. Dessalines' army grew by tens of thousands of troops, all bent on vengeance against the hated French. Meanwhile, Leclerc lost tens of thousands— some in battle, and many more to deadly tropical diseases like yellow fever and malaria. Among the many French troops who succumbed to yellow fever was Leclerc himself, who died in November 1802.

Former slaves overrunning France's last stronghold in St. Dominic

With a great victory at the Battle of Vertieres on November 18, 1803, Jean-Jacques Dessalines finally drove the dying French army of occupation out of its last stronghold in St. Dominic.

Six weeks later, on January 1, 1804, Dessalines formally proclaimed St. Dominic's independence from France. To emphasize the former colony's complete separation from France, Dessalines chose a new name that had nothing to do with France's Catholic religion. Instead of St. Dominic, the new country became *Haiti*— which, in the language of Hispaniola's native Taino people, meant "Land of the High Mountains."

> SUCCINCT SUMMARIES: Some Results of the Haitian Revolution
>
> - Through the Haitian Revolution, Haiti became only the second former colony in the New World to win its independence, after the United States. Haiti also became the first and only former colony to win independence through a slave revolt.
>
> - With St. Dominic lost and the War of the Third Coalition threatening in Europe, Napoleon decided to withdraw from the New World for the moment— which is why he agreed to sell Louisiana to the United States in October 1803 (see Chapter 27).

> A LOOK AHEAD: The blessings of independence will by no means bring Haiti's troubles to an end.
>
> - After declaring Haiti's independence, Dessalines will declare an all-out race war on his country's surviving whites. In the vicious **Haiti Massacre of 1804**, Dessalines' people will murder whites by the thousands— men, women and children alike, many of them in the most brutal ways imaginable.
>
> - To restore his country's sugar production, which years of war all but destroyed, the tyrannical Dessalines will force Haiti's former slaves back onto their plantations. Although Dessalines will carefully avoid calling his people "slaves," their rights after fourteen years of revolution will be little better than slaves' rights.

The Spanish American Wars of Independence (1808 – 1833)

> DEFINITION: The **Spanish American Wars of Independence** were a long, complicated set of struggles in which nearly all of Spain's New World colonies gradually won their independence from Spain. These struggles cost the Spanish Empire an astonishing amount of territory. When the Spanish Wars of Independence were over, Spain had lost all of its vast holdings in the New World except two, the islands of Cuba and Puerto Rico.

> A LOOK BEHIND: Just before the Spanish American Wars of Independence, Spain divided its New World colonies in this way:
>
> 1. The **Viceroyalty of New Spain** governed most of Spain's possessions in North America, Central America and the West Indies, including what are now Mexico, Honduras, El Salvador, Nicaragua and Cost Rica.
>
> 2. The **Viceroyalty of New Granada** governed most of northern South America, including what are now Colombia, Ecuador and Panama.
>
> 3. The **Viceroyalty of Peru** governed west central South America, including what are now Peru and part of Chile.
>
> 4. The **Viceroyalty of the Rio de la Plata** governed southern South America, including what are now Argentina, Bolivia, Paraguay and Uruguay.
>
> 5. Smaller sub-governments controlled key territories and islands like Venezuela, Chile, Guatemala, Cuba and Puerto Rico.

> REFRESHING REMINDERS from Chapter 28: The Continental System, a trade embargo that Napoleon tried to impose on Britain beginning in late 1806, was the wedge that split asunder everything Napoleon built in Europe.

The Peninsular War (1807 – 1814)

Through the French Revolution and the Age of Napoleon, Spain's relationship with France changed several times. The two were (1) enemies for the War of the First Coalition (1792 – 1797); (2) allies for the Wars of the Second and Third Coalitions (1798 – 1802 and 1803 – 1806); and finally (3) bitter enemies for the Peninsular War. This last war took its name from Europe's Iberian Peninsula, home to Spain and Portugal.

The Peninsular War arose from Napoleon's burning desire to impose his Continental System all over Europe— even in Portugal, which had traded with Britain off and on since the 1300s. When Portugal refused to abide by the Continental System, Napoleon decided to invade Portugal; and to reach Portugal, he had to cross Spain. Because Spain was France's ally at the time, Napoleon had little trouble arranging for his armies to cross Spanish territory.

Only after Napoleon moved tens of thousands of French troops into Spain did the Spanish royal family realize its mistake. In February 1808, the unstoppably ambitious Napoleon suddenly turned on his ally, ordering his armies to seize key fortresses all over Spain— including Spain's capital, Madrid. That June, Napoleon replaced Spain's royal family with a member of his own family: his elder brother Joseph Bonaparte, who became King of Spain under Napoleon's protection. Both Charles IV of Spain and his heir Ferdinand VII of Spain became Napoleon's prisoners.

French soldiers executing rebellious Spaniards at the outset of the Peninsular War

> DEFINITION: A **junta** is a temporary military government.

The Rise of the Juntas

In the absence of its king— for in the eyes of most Spaniards, Joseph Bonaparte was no legitimate king— Spain needed some new government to organize its Peninsular War against France. To fill this need, officers formed the **Supreme Central Junta**, a military government operating out of Seville, southern Spain. In the minds of most mainland Spaniards, the Supreme Central Junta became the king's regent, with the authority to make decisions in the king's place until he could resume his throne.

Minds were different in Spanish America, where many colonists rejected the Supreme Central Junta's authority. The Peninsular War brought chaos to Spanish America, with colonies splitting in all directions— some supporting the Supreme Central Junta; some supporting smaller juntas of their own; and some seizing the opportunity to declare independence from Spain.

FASCINATING FACTS: Spanish America's *Casta* System

Before the Spanish American Wars of Independence, a Spanish colonist's rights and privileges depended on high or low birth. Spanish America divided its people into race-based categories called *casta*, with most privileges reserved for the uppermost two:

1. A *peninsular* was a white colonist born on the Iberian Peninsula— in other words, in Spain. The law required all colonial governors, generals and other high officials to come from the peninsular casta. Peninsulares tended to be **royalists**, loyal supporters of the Spanish government.

2. A *criollo* or **creole** was a white colonist born in a Spanish colony. Despite their all-white heritage, criollos lived as second-class citizens under the peninsulares. Because of this, criollos tended to support independence from Spain.

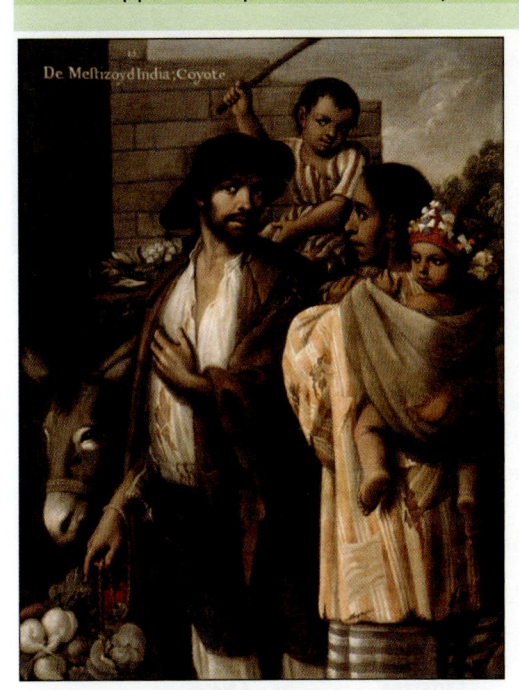

Beneath these privileged all-white *casta* stood a host of less-white, less-privileged ones, including: (1) *Indios*, or Native Americans; (2) *Mestizos*, those with one Spanish and one native parent; (3) *Castizos*, mostly white with a bit of native blood; (4) *Cholos*, mostly native with a bit of white blood; (5) *Negros*, or Africans; (6) *Mulattos*, those of mixed African/white blood; (7) *Zambos*, those of mixed native/African blood; and (8) *Pardos*, those who blended all three races.

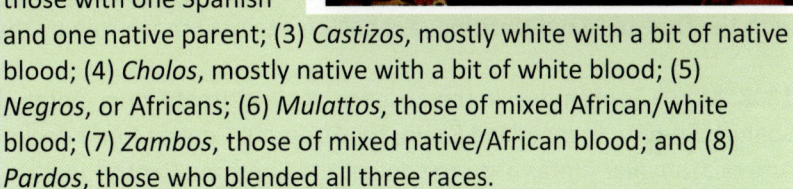

Members of these lower *casta* might be either royalist or independent. Loyalty to king and Church might draw them to the royalists; while promises of liberty and fair treatment might draw them to the independents.

CAST OF CHARACTERS for the Spanish American Wars of Independence

1. **Francisco de Miranda (1750 – 1816):** Miranda was a Venezuela-born criollo army officer who traveled all over Europe and the Americas, fighting in the French Revolution and learning Enlightenment philosophy from the likes of Thomas Paine, James Madison and Thomas Jefferson— all of whom Miranda met in person. Long before the Spanish Wars of Independence broke out, Miranda dreamed of uniting Spain and Portugal's New World colonies into a mighty confederation like the United States.

2. **Simón Bolívar, *el Libertador* ("The Liberator," 1783 – 1830):** Bolivar was another Venezuela-born criollo army officer who loved Enlightenment philosophy, and dreamed of uniting all Spanish America. However, Bolívar was more like Catherine the Great than Thomas Jefferson— more an enlightened despot than a pure republican. In Bolivar's opinion, pure republicanism succeeded in the United States only because so many of its people shared a common heritage. In South America, where people came from so many different heritages, unity would come only at the insistence of a strong emperor— Bolívar himself.

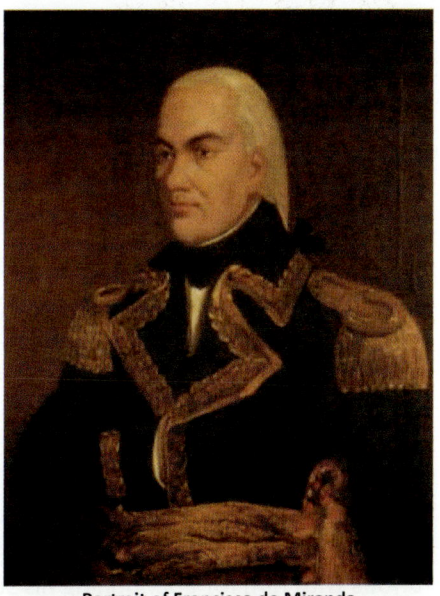

Portrait of Francisco de Miranda

A LOOK AHEAD: Bolívar will become the liberator of the north, from Venezuela and Colombia to Ecuador and Upper Peru.

3. **José de San Martín (1778 – 1850):** San Martín was an Argentina-born criollo army officer. Unlike Bolivar, who thrived on military glory, San Martin was a humble soldier who suffered through the pomp-filled ceremonies his followers intended to honor him.

==A LOOK AHEAD: San Martin will become the liberator of the south, from Argentina and Chile to Bolivia and Lower Peru.==

A Brief Timeline of the Spanish American Wars of Independence

1806: Francisco de Miranda leads a tiny army into Venezuela, hoping to convince his homeland to declare independence. Instead, royalists chase Miranda out of Venezuela within two weeks.

1808, April – May: Napoleon takes King Ferdinand VII of Spain captive and forces him to abdicate his throne. With Ferdinand out of the way, Napoleon's brother Joseph Bonaparte takes his place as King of Spain.

Portrait of Simon Bolivar, el Libertador

1808, May 2 – The Peninsular War: The Peninsular War in Spain begins with the **Dos de Mayo Uprising**, a rebellion against French rule by the Spaniards of Madrid.

1808, May – September: In the absence of a legitimate king, juntas claim authority over various parts of the Spanish Empire. In mainland Spain, the Supreme Central Junta declares itself the king's regent. In Spanish America, smaller juntas arise to contest the Supreme Central Junta's authority.

1810, April: The leaders of Venezuela's capital, Caracas, reject the Supreme Central Junta in favor of a new junta of their own. Francisco de Miranda immediately returns to Venezuela, where both he and Simón Bolívar urge the Caracas junta to declare independence.

1811, July 5 – The First Republic of Venezuela: The Caracas junta establishes the First Republic of Venezuela, making Venezuela the first South American colony to declare independence. However, the Caracas junta controls only some of Venezuela's provinces. Other provinces remain royalist; while even those that support Caracas are reluctant to send troops and supplies to help the junta resist the royalists.

1812, March – July: The Caracas junta promotes Francisco de Miranda as its *generalissimo*, or highest general, hoping that these broad powers will help Miranda preserve Venezuela's independence. However, Miranda believes that with royalists threatening on all sides, independence is already a lost cause. Therefore instead of battling the royalists, Miranda negotiates a secret peace treaty with them. In exchange for Venezuela's peaceful surrender, the royalists promise to let Miranda, Bolívar and other independents leave the country without arresting them. However, Miranda doesn't trust the royalists' promise.

1812, July: Instead of waiting to see whether or not the royalists will live up to their promise, Miranda tries to flee Venezuela before they arrive. By this time, though, Bolívar has learned of Miranda's secret treaty, and is furious with him for abandoning his soldiers. Therefore Bolívar arrests his former generalissimo; and when the royalists arrive, Bolívar hands Miranda over to them. The disgraced Miranda will live out the rest of his days in a Spanish prison.

With the royalists' arrival, Venezuela loses its independence, and the First Republic of Venezuela comes to an end. True to their word, though, the royalists allow Bolívar to leave the country.

1812, October: Simón Bolívar becomes a junior general in the army of what is now Cartagena, Colombia, another city that has just declared independence.

1813, May - August – The Admirable Campaign: Against his superiors' orders, Bolívar leads his small army across the border into Venezuela. Instead of facing the royalist armies that come out to meet him, Bolívar goes around most of them, heading directly for Caracas. Finding little resistance at Caracas, Bolívar declares Venezuela's independence a second time on August 7, 1813, establishing the Second Republic of Venezuela.

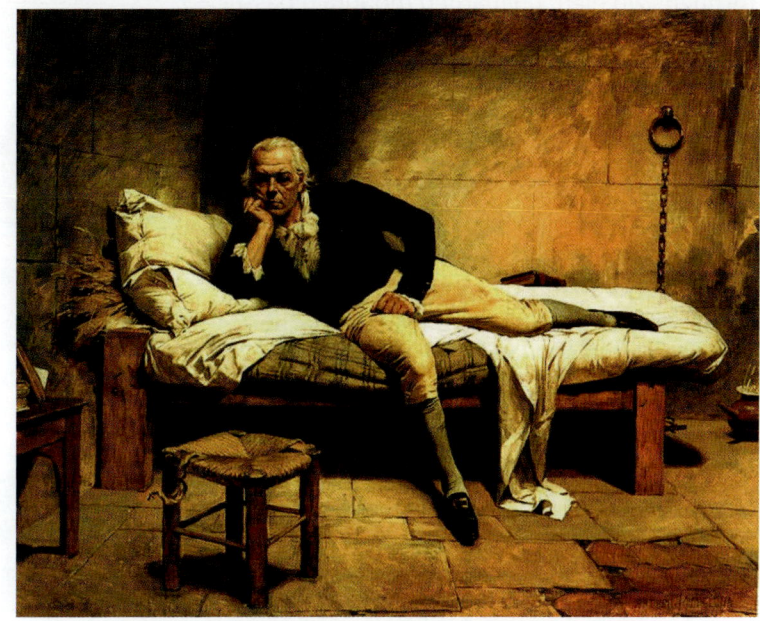

Francisco de Miranda living out his last days in a Spanish prison

1814, July: Royalists drive Bolívar out of Caracas, bringing the Second Republic of Venezuela to an end. This time, Bolívar winds up hiding for a time in British-held Jamaica.

ILLUMINATING EXCERPTS from Simón Bolívar's "Letter from Jamaica" (Published September 1815)

During his exile in Jamaica, Simón Bolívar published an open letter in which he explained why South America's struggle for independence was so difficult. Among other things, Bolívar argued that Spain had controlled South America so strictly for so long that its people had no experience with self-government:

- "The role of the inhabitants of the American hemisphere has for centuries been purely passive... We are still in a position lower than slavery, and therefore it is more difficult for us to rise to the enjoyment of freedom..."

- "We have been harassed by a conduct which has not only deprived us of our rights, but has also kept us in a sort of permanent infancy with regard to public affairs..."

- "Americans... who live within the Spanish system occupy a position in society no better than that of serfs destined for labor, or at best they have no more status than that of mere consumers."

1814: Meanwhile to the south, Argentinian juntas have taken control of the former Viceroyalty of the Rio de la Plata. However, these juntas have been defeated by royalists entrenched in Upper Peru, the mountainous region to their north.

To drive the royalists out of their mountains, Jose de San Martin proposes a new strategy: instead of leading doomed uphill assaults into the mountains of Peru, San Martin will attack Lima, the coastal capital of Lower Peru. To strike at Lima, San Martin will first lead an army across the Andes Mountains into Chile, which has been fighting its own war of independence. A victory over the royalists in Chile's capital, Santiago, will provide San Martin the ships, troops and supplies he needs for his assault on Lima. San Martin spends about two years training a disciplined army for this all-important campaign.

1817, January: San Martin guides a few thousand troops on a dangerous journey through two high, unguarded mountain passes between Argentina and Chile. Despite San Martin's preparations, frigid temperatures and treacherous slopes claim about one-third of his army before he finally reaches the plains near Santiago.

1817, February 12: Having caught Santiago's royalists thoroughly by surprise, San Martin easily defeats them at the **Battle of Chacabuco**, named for a valley outside Santiago. Afterward, San Martin makes a triumphal entry into Santiago to symbolize Chile's newly-won independence.

1819: Back in the north, Simón Bolívar takes a page from San Martin's playbook. Because the war for Venezuelan independence has been going so badly, Bolívar decides to lead his army against a different target: Bogota, capital of the royalist-held Viceroyalty of New Granada. Unfortunately, reaching Bogota will require an Andes mountain crossing even more difficult than San Martin's.

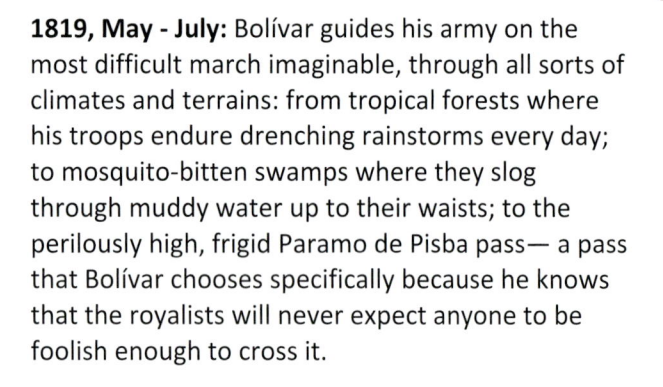

1819, May - July: Bolívar guides his army on the most difficult march imaginable, through all sorts of climates and terrains: from tropical forests where his troops endure drenching rainstorms every day; to mosquito-bitten swamps where they slog through muddy water up to their waists; to the perilously high, frigid Paramo de Pisba pass— a pass that Bolívar chooses specifically because he knows that the royalists will never expect anyone to be foolish enough to cross it.

1819, August 7: Having caught Bogota's royalists thoroughly by surprise, Bolívar wins Colombia's independence with a stunning victory at the **Battle of Boyaca**, named for Colombia's Boyaca region. The Viceroyalty of New Granada falls, to be replaced by Bolívar's new Republic of Gran Colombia.

1821, June 21: With so much of South America independent, the royalists' support begins to collapse. Two years after liberating Colombia, Bolívar liberates Venezuela at last with a great victory at the **Battle of Carabobo**, named for Venezuela's Carabobo region. Bolívar now stands as the undisputed ruler of a liberated north.

Jose de San Martin leading his army over the Andes

FREEDOM IN SOUTH AMERICA

INTERESTING IDEAS: At this point, Bolívar and others have liberated Colombia and Venezuela to the north; while San Martin and others have liberated Argentina and Chile to the south. Meanwhile, the people of the former Viceroyalty of New Spain have been winning their own wars of independence (see Chapter 33). However, royalists still hold Ecuador and the Viceroyalty of Peru, along with Cuba and Puerto Rico.

1821, July 12: Back in the south, San Martin has loaded his army aboard ships for his campaign in Lower Peru. He has also printed thousands of leaflets to explain the need for independence to the people of Lower Peru. The royalists' support collapses, allowing San Martin to march into Lima with little difficulty. San Martin now claims the title "Protector of Peru." However, the royalists still hold Upper Peru, the mountainous inland region that gave Argentina so much trouble earlier in the war.

Scene from the Battle of Carabobo

1822, May 24: Bolívar's second-in-command, General Jose de Sucre, liberates Ecuador with a great victory at the **Battle of Pichincha**, near what is now Quito, Ecuador.

1822, July 26: Bolívar and San Martin meet at Guayaquil, Ecuador to discuss plans for liberating the royalists' last stronghold, Upper Peru.

FASCINATING FACTS: The Guayaquil Conference (July 26, 1822)

In July 1822, Bolívar and San Martin met face-to-face at Guayaquil to discuss two important questions:

1. Even after all of Bolívar and San Martin's victories in north and south, the royalists of Upper Peru maintained enough strength to resist either general by himself— which meant that any final victory over the royalists would require a union between north and south. Which general would lead this union?
2. Which country would claim the important port of Guayaquil— Bolívar's Ecuador? Or San Martin's Peru?

Because no one else was present for this pivotal meeting, no one is certain what the two generals said to one another. The only thing certain is what followed: on the day after the meeting, San

San Martin and Bolivar at the Guayaquil Conference

729

Martin boarded a ship and sailed back to Lower Peru, where he soon retired from public life— leaving Bolívar to lead the battles that drove the last royalists out of South America.

From that day to this, different people have offered different theories about what might have passed between these two heroes at Guayaquil:

- Those who honor Bolívar for his fiery brilliance suggest that in stepping aside, San Martin was merely acknowledging the obvious: that Bolívar was the better general, and therefore the better choice to lead the final struggle against the royalists.

- Those who honor San Martin for his humility suggest that if San Martin had insisted on leading the final struggle, or on possessing Guayaquil, then the conceited Bolívar probably would have responded by invading Lower Peru— leading to a civil war that might have undone everything the two great men had accomplished. By humbling submitting to Bolívar, San Martin proved that he cared only for his people's independence, and nothing for his personal glory.

1824, December 9: Bolivar's brilliant subordinate Sucre liberates upper Peru with a victory at the **Battle of Ayacucho**, named for Upper Peru's Ayacucho region. With this last great victory of the Spanish American Wars of Independence, Spain's former South American colonies are independent from north to south.

1825, August 6: The congress of Upper Peru chooses a new name for its newly-independent nation: "Bolivia," after *el Libertador* Simón Bolívar.

FASCINATING FATES

South America's Fate: When Bolívar returned from his mission in the south, he found his northern Republic of Gran Colombia in chaos: coast-dwellers were arguing with inland-dwellers; *mestizos* were arguing with *criollos*; and everywhere he turned, provinces were threatening to declare independence from Gran Colombia. As Bolívar had predicted in his Letter from Jamaica, South America's inexperience with self-government was making it very difficult for so many races and classes to unite.

In a vain attempt to save his republic from collapse, Bolívar declared himself dictator in August 1828. Instead of uniting around Bolívar, though, his enemies denounced him as a tyrant. Shortly after Bolívar stepped down in 1830, Gran Colombia dissolved into the separate countries of Colombia, Ecuador and Venezuela.

Thus Simon Bolívar's legacy was to leave the countries of South America independent, but not united.

Simon Bolívar's Fate: Upon stepping down as emperor, Bolívar planned to leave South America forever. Before he could depart, though, Bolívar died of tuberculosis at age 47. Bolívar died believing that "all who served the Revolution have plowed the sea"— by which he meant that in failing to unite, South America wasted the sacrifices of the many fine soldiers who suffered and died to win her independence.

MORE FASCINATING FACTS about South America

- The world's longest mountain range, the Andes, runs all along South America's west coast.

- The world's largest river by volume, the Amazon, runs across South America from west to east. The Amazon drains almost 40% of South America's territory. The Amazon rainforest produces 20% of the earth's oxygen.

- The world's largest salt lake, Salar de Uyuni, lies in southwest Bolivia.

- The *Cueva de las Manos*, or Cave of the Hands, is a group of caves in Argentina whose entrances are covered with ancient hand prints. Bone pipes found inside the caves reveal how ancient artists painted some of the hand prints: by placing their left hands on the cave wall, and then blowing paint over them through pipes held in their right hands.

- Neither Spanish nor Portuguese conquistadors ever conquered a cold, far southern region of South America called Patagonia. After Ferdinand Magellan first passed through Patagonia in the 1520s, the legend arose that the people of Patagonia were giants. According to Magellan's chronicler, one Patagonian was *"so tall that we reached only to his waist, and he was well proportioned..."* This giant myth lasted for almost 250 years.

Cueva de las Manos

FASCINATING FACTS: *Ojo de Dios* (God's Eye)

The *ojo de dios*, or "eye of god," is an ancient Middle and South American eye symbol woven in multi-colored yarn. The Aymara people of Bolivia placed god's eyes on their altars as a sign that their gods watched over the faithful, hearing their prayers and protecting them from harm. The Huichol people of Mexico wove god's eyes as gifts to their children: the father wove a central eye when a child was born, and then added another color for every year of the child's life through the age of five.

U.S. HISTORY FOCUS

The Monroe Doctrine

President James Monroe responded to the Spanish American Wars of Independence in his December 2, 1823 State of the Union address to Congress, the speech that introduced the Monroe Doctrine.

DEFINITION: The **Monroe Doctrine** is a long-standing U.S. foreign policy which holds that the western hemisphere is closed to European colonization. President Monroe promised not to interfere with any colonies that European countries already held in the Americas as of 1823. However, if any European country tried to invade the Americas after 1823, then Monroe would go to war to prevent it.

ILLUMINATING EXCERPTS from President Monroe's Seventh State of the Union Address

- "...the American continents, by the free and independent condition which they have assumed and maintain, are henceforth not to be considered as subjects for future colonization by any European powers."

- "It is impossible that [Europe's] allied powers should extend their political system to any portion of either continent without endangering our peace and happiness; nor can anyone believe that our southern brethren, if left to themselves, would adopt it of their own accord. It is equally impossible, therefore, that we should behold such interposition in any form with indifference..."

FASCINATING FACTS about the Monroe Doctrine:

- Simon Bolívar applauded the Monroe Doctrine, welcoming it as a sign of U.S. support for South American independence.

- Long after Monroe stated his doctrine, other presidents used it to justify actions that may have gone beyond what Monroe intended. For example, President William McKinley used it to help justify the Spanish-American War, in which the U.S. helped Cuban rebels drive the Spanish off their island in 1898; and President Theodore Roosevelt used it to justify building the Panama Canal beginning in 1904.

- In light of these later uses, some see the Monroe Doctrine as a mark of U.S. imperialism— the United States' selfish desire to control South America, while rarely bestirring itself to help South America.

U.S. STATE FOCUS

Mississippi

FASCINATING FACTS about Mississippi:

- State Capital: Jackson
- State Abbreviation: MS
- Statehood: Mississippi became the 20th US state on December 10, 1817.
- Area: About 48,000 square miles (Ranks 32nd in size)
- Bordering States: Alabama, Tennessee, Arkansas, Louisiana
- Meaning of Name: "Mississippi" is altered form of an Algonquian word meaning "Great River" or "Father of Waters."
- State Nickname: "Magnolia State"
- State Bird: Mississippi has two state birds, the Northern Mockingbird and the Wood Duck.
- State Tree: Southern Magnolia
- State Flower: Mississippi has two state flowers, the Magnolia and the Tickseed.
- State Song: "Go, Mississippi" by William Davis
- State Motto: *Virtute et armis*, Latin for "By valor and arms"
- Historic Places to Visit: Emerald Mound Site, Natchez National Historical Park, Vicksburg National Military Park, Mississippi Governor's Mansion
- Resources and Industries: Cotton, shrimp, oil, fishing, lumber

Governor's Mansion at Jackson, Mississippi

State Flag: Mississippi's flag uses the Confederate States of America's battle flag as a canton, or corner emblem, because Mississippi belonged to the CSA during the American Civil War years (1861 – 1865). The flag's field is divided into three broad horizontal stripes, one red, one white and one blue.

PRESIDENTIAL FOCUS

PRESIDENT #5: James Monroe (1758 – 1831)	
In Office: March 4, 1817 – March 4, 1825	**Political Party:** Democratic-Republican
Birthplace: Virginia	**Nickname:** "Era of Good Feelings President"

James Monroe was the last U.S. president born early enough to fight in the Revolutionary War, which began when he was a 17-year-old freshman at the College of William and Mary in Williamsburg, Virginia. The following year, Lieutenant Monroe took a bad wound to the shoulder while leading a brave charge against enemy cannon at the Battle of Trenton.

After resigning his officer's commission in 1779, the still-young Monroe prepared himself for a career in politics by studying law under his personal friend and mentor, Thomas Jefferson. Over the next several years, Monroe held all sorts of government offices— everything from Virginia delegate to the Confederation Congress (1783 – 1786); to U.S. Senator from Virginia (1790 – 1794); to U.S. Minister to France (1794 – 1796); to Governor of Virginia (1799 – 1802); to U.S. Minister to Britain (1803 – 1808). Monroe was doubling as President Jefferson's special envoy to France when he helped Robert Livingston negotiate the Louisiana Purchase in late 1803.

When Monroe returned from Britain in 1808, some of his political allies asked him to run against James Madison in the contest to become the Democratic-Republican Party's presidential nominee. Although Monroe lost the nomination, his contest with Madison had a surprising consequence: campaigning against one another built a fast friendship between the two men. Therefore when President Madison needed a new secretary of state during the run-up to the War of 1812, he called upon a friend whose diplomatic experience he trusted: Monroe. Partly because the war ended on a high note for the U.S. — thanks to Andrew Jackson's late victory over the British at the Battle of New Orleans— Monroe easily won the presidential election of 1816.

A Boston journalist dubbed the years of Monroe's presidency the Era of Good Feelings, for two reasons:

1. Because they were years of high spirits and prosperity, brought on by the end of the miserable War of 1812.
2. Because they were years when party politics were less bitter than before. By this time, the Federalist Party had collapsed so thoroughly that it didn't even nominate a presidential candidate in 1820— allowing Monroe to run for reelection to his second term unopposed.

The Monroe years were also the years when Spanish America won its wars of independence. These wars helped Monroe pressure Spain into selling an important possession, Florida, to the United States. The wars also led to the Monroe Doctrine, Monroe's famous insistence that the entire Western Hemisphere would henceforth be closed to European colonization.

Fun Facts about James Monroe:
- In Emanuel Leutze's famous "Washington Crossing the Delaware" painting, Monroe is holding the U.S. flag.

Notable Quotes from James Monroe:
- "Never did a government commence under auspices so favorable, nor ever was success so complete. If we look to the history of other nations, ancient or modern, we find no example of a growth so rapid, so gigantic, of a people so prosperous and happy."

CHAPTER 30: The Indian Removal Act; the Industrial Revolution

U.S. HISTORY FOCUS

The Indian Removal Act

DEFINITIONS: The **Indian Removal Act** was an 1830 law that allowed the United States to resettle all Native American tribes who still lived east of the Mississippi River onto new homes west of the Mississippi. This law led to one of American history's saddest tragedies: the **Trail of Tears**, in which thousands of innocent Native Americans from the Cherokee, Choctaw and other tribes died of exposure, famine and disease on their way to the **Indian Territory** in Oklahoma.

REFRESHING REMINDERS: Europeans and Native Americans clashed from the days of Jamestown and Plymouth Colony. Before the first Virginia Company colonists even reached Jamestown, they skirmished with Algonquians at Cape Henry, Virginia (see Chapter 3). Before the Pilgrims even reached Plymouth, they skirmished with Nauset on Cape Cod (see Chapter 6). Later skirmishes and wars, from the Massacre of 1622 to Bacon's Rebellion to the French and Indian War, only added to the bitterness between the two races.

Throughout the colonial era and into the early American era, many white Europeans believed as Nathaniel Bacon believed: that most Native Americans were savages, and that white Americans would never be safe until they either killed or removed most Native Americans.

Scene from the Massacre of 1622

Far fewer believed what Mary Jemison came to believe when she lived among the Seneca: that native peoples "are naturally kind, tender and peaceable towards their friends, and strictly honest; and that [torture and murder] have been practiced only upon their enemies, according to their idea of justice" (see Chapter 19).

DEFINITION: The **Five Civilized Tribes** were five Native American peoples who lived in the North American southeast in the early 1800s:

1. The **Cherokee** lived in the southern Appalachians, on territory that now belongs to northwest Georgia and northeast Alabama.
2. The **Creek** were the Cherokee's southern neighbors.
3. The **Chickasaw** lived west of the Cherokee, mainly on territory that now belongs to northern Mississippi.
4. The **Choctaw** were the Chickasaw's southern neighbors.
5. The **Seminoles**, who lived in Florida, were a mixed-race tribe composed of several different types of people. Some Seminoles were native Floridians; some were refugees from the Creek, Cherokee and other tribes who fled south to escape the dangers of white settlement; and some were runaway African slaves who fled south seeking freedom.

The Five Civilized Tribes tried a different answer to the problem of constantly-expanding white settlement. Instead of fighting losing battles against the whites' overwhelming numbers, the Five Civilized Tribes traded their old lifestyles as semi-nomadic hunters for new lifestyles as settled farmers— hoping that if they adopted white ways, then whites might stop seeing them as savages, and allow them to stay.

A LOOK BEHIND at "Civilizing the Savages"

The idea of "civilizing the savages" was as old as the colonies. One early believer in the idea of training Native Americans to live as Englishmen was John Eliot, the Puritan missionary who converted some of the Massachusett people into Praying Indians.

REFRESHING REMINDERS from Chapter 11: Sadly, King Philip's War all but destroyed John Eliot's beloved Praying Indians. Soon after that war broke out, the government of Massachusetts tore the Praying Indians from their Praying Villages and confined them to island prisons, convinced that it couldn't trust their loyalties. After the war, the few Praying Indians who didn't starve or freeze to death returned to find their villages in ruins.

President George Washington was the first to make "civilizing the savages" official U.S. policy. One of Washington's first treaties with a native people, the 1790 Treaty of New York, committed the U.S. to train the Creek people in a new way of life:

"That the Creek nation may be led to a greater degree of civilization, and to become herdsmen and cultivators, instead of remaining in a state of hunters, the United States will from time to time furnish gratuitously the said nation with useful domestic animals and implements of husbandry [farming]. And further to assist the said nation in so desirable a pursuit, and at the same time to establish a certain mode of communication, the United States will send such, and so many persons to reside in said nation as they may judge proper, and not exceeding four in number, who shall qualify themselves to act as interpreters…"

Indian agent Benjamin Hawkins training the Creeks to live as farmers

In other words: Thanks to constantly-expanding white settlement, the Creeks could no longer live as hunters, for their territory was no longer large enough to support that lifestyle. Therefore the United States would send the Creeks up to four **Indian agents**, ambassadors who would train them to live as farmers. The U.S. would also provide free livestock, farming tools and other helps "from time to time."

President Thomas Jefferson clarified this policy in his Second Inaugural Address, delivered in 1805:

"The aboriginal inhabitants of these countries I have regarded with the commiseration their history inspires. Endowed with the faculties and the rights of men, breathing an ardent love of liberty and independence, and occupying a country which left them no desire but to be undisturbed, the stream of overflowing population from other regions directed itself on these shores; without power to divert or habits to contend against it, they have been overwhelmed by the current or driven before it; now reduced within limits too narrow for the hunter's state, humanity enjoins us to teach them agriculture and the domestic arts; to encourage them to that industry which alone can enable them to maintain their place in existence and to prepare them in time for that state of society which to bodily comforts adds the improvement of the mind and morals. We have therefore liberally furnished them with the implements of husbandry and household use; we have placed among them instructors in the arts of first necessity, and they are covered with the aegis of the law against aggressors from among ourselves."

In other words: In Jefferson's opinion, the native race was in no way inferior to the white race— neither mentally, physically nor spiritually. However, native civilization was far inferior to white civilization— so inferior that without help from the United States, the natives' "mind and morals" would never improve.

FASCINATING FACTS: Pipe Tomahawks

The pipe tomahawk was a short ax that could serve triple duty as handy tool, deadly weapon and tobacco pipe. Skilled American, Native American and European metalworkers hollowed out the counterweight opposite the traditional tomahawk's blade, fashioning it into a pipe bowl. They then fastened this complex head to a hollow wooden handle that doubled as a pipe stem.

Most pipe tomahawks were more ceremonial than functional. The cutting head symbolized war, while the pipe end served as a peace pipe to smoke at ceremonial treaty signings.

Sequoyah (1770? – 1840?) and the Cherokee Syllabary

One mark of how well the Five Civilized Tribes adapted to their changing circumstances was the work of an ingenious Cherokee named Sequoyah (1770? – 1843?). Through working with white customers as a shopkeeper, silversmith and blacksmith, Sequoyah realized what tremendous advantages the whites' written language offered— how it allowed whites to share knowledge across wide expanses of space and time, with far less fear that their ideas might be lost or misinterpreted. Around 1810, Sequoyah began a quest to claim those advantages for his own people, the Cherokee.

DEFINITION: A **syllabary** is a set of written symbols that represent the syllables of a language's spoken words.

FASCINATING FACTS: The Cherokee Syllabary

Before Sequoyah, no known native people north of Middle America had ever developed a written language of its own. Even in Sequoyah's day, some Native Americans still viewed writing as some form of dark magic, or as a false stunt their white enemies used to deceive them. Sequoyah alone saw matters differently. Sequoyah's quest for a written language is even more impressive because when he began, he knew neither English nor any other written language.

Sequoyah began his quest by trying to create a logographic language— one that used a separate symbol to represent each idea or word, much like Chinese or Japanese. He soon realized, however, that a logographic language would

Sequoyah with his Cherokee syllabary

require a fantastic number of symbols, which would make it extremely difficult for his people to learn.

In search of a better way, Sequoyah hit upon the idea of creating a syllabary. Because Cherokee involved fewer distinct syllables than some other languages, a syllabary turned out to be a perfect fit: Sequoyah was able to represent every syllable with just 85 – 86 symbols. Learning to read Cherokee would actually turn out to be easier than learning to read English— mainly because where English used multiple combinations of letters to represent the same syllables, Cherokee used just one character per syllable.

Sequoyah's written version of Cherokee proved an enormous success. In 1825, his people adopted it as the official language of the Cherokee Nation. By 1828, journalists were using it to publish the first-ever Native American newspaper, the *Cherokee Phoenix*.

The Five Civilized Tribes adapted so well that by 1810, many of their members were behaving exactly as Presidents Washington and Jefferson had hoped they would— living settled lifestyles on farms, sending their children to school every day and attending Christian churches every Sunday. As whites and Native Americans grew used to living side-by-side, some of their loyalties began to shift. Over time, a great many members of the Five Civilized Tribes intermarried with white Americans. Some children of these mixed marriages, having both white and native ancestors, felt as much loyalty to the United States as they did to their native tribes.

Unfortunately, no amount of civilization could solve these two problems:

1. **White Americans' greed:** As white settlement overspread the American southeast, late-coming settlers began to covet the last few territories that the Five Civilized Tribes had managed to set aside for themselves.
2. **Manifest Destiny:** After the Lewis and Clark Expedition, the United States began to envision itself stretching all across North America, from the Atlantic to the Pacific. In that vision, there was no room for native nations— especially ones that might join forces with the U.S.' rivals for North America, Britain and Spain.

The Creek War (1813 – 1814)

INTERESTING IDEAS: The Native American who forged the first link in the chain of events that led to the Indian Removal Act came not from the southeast, but the northwest. Just before the War of 1812, the great Indiana Shawnee Chief Tecumseh embarked on a long tour of the South, urging the Five Civilized Tribes to join him in declaring war on the United States (see Chapter 28).

Tecumseh's tour of the South found the Creek people as divided as the tribes of the northwest. Although some Creeks wanted to fight for their homeland, others felt safer accepting the humiliating peace that whites offered them. Ironically, Tecumseh's inspiring speeches about the brotherhood of all Native Americans sparked a civil war between two groups of Creeks:

1. The **Red Sticks**, warlike Creeks who were determined to raise their red-colored war clubs in support of Tecumseh.
2. Peace-loving Creeks who wanted to accept the livestock, Indian agents and other valuable farm aid offered by the United States.

The Creeks' civil war began with Red Stick attacks on peace-loving Creeks' farms in southern Alabama. The Red Sticks mainly killed livestock and burned crops— trying to force their peace-loving brothers away from farming, and back to hunting. Looking on from the sidelines, white settlers had little doubt that the savage Red Sticks would soon be attacking whites as well.

Illustration of Red Eagle, a Red Stick leader during the Creek war

Soon after Tecumseh returned north, the War of 1812 broke out between the United States, Britain and a less-powerful British ally: Spain, which still held Florida at the time. When the Red Sticks learned that Spain had joined the war against the United States, they immediately sent a small army to Pensacola, Florida to request food, gunpowder and shot from the Spaniards there.

At the time, the nearest U.S. Army troops were stationed at Fort Mims— a frontier fort about 45 miles northwest of Pensacola, and about 20 miles northeast of Mobile, Alabama. By the time the army caught wind of the Red Sticks' supply train, it was already on its way back to Alabama. A small detachment of U.S. troops tried to waylay the Red Sticks along the road; but instead, the Red Sticks defeated the Americans at the brief **Battle of Burnt Corn Creek**, fought near the Alabama-Florida border on July 27, 1813.

Now thoroughly terrified of the rampaging Red Sticks, hundreds of white settlers from all over the area flooded into Fort Mims, seeking protection. By the end of August, more than 500 Americans huddled inside Fort Mims— about half of them soldiers, and the other half settlers and their slaves. Far from saving the Americans, these movements set them up for the Creek War's bloodiest massacre.

MERCILESS MASSACRES: The Fort Mims Massacre (August 30, 1813)

On the night of August 29, two slaves warned the soldiers inside Fort Mims that they'd seen Red Sticks lurking outside. For some reason, perhaps because their commander was drunk, Fort Mims' soldiers did nothing. Ignoring this and other clear warnings, Fort Mims' commander even made the ridiculous mistake of leaving one of his gates open that night— creating a target too tempting for the Red Sticks to ignore.

Around noon on August 30, nearly 1,000 Red Stick warriors descended on Fort Mims. Surging

Scene from the Fort Mims Massacre

through the open gate, the warriors started hacking and slashing at the Americans inside, showing mercy to no one with white skin— not even women and children. When some soldiers retreated to the fort's inner keep, the Red Sticks set fire to the keep, killing these as well. Except for a few whites who escaped, and a few score unarmed black slaves who the Red Sticks captured, all 500+ Americans inside Fort Mims died.

In response to the terrible Fort Mims Massacre, the United States sent the man who was to become the Five Civilized Tribes' worst enemy: Andrew Jackson.

AMAZING AMERICANS: Andrew Jackson (1767 – 1845)

Although James Monroe was the last U.S. president old enough to serve in the Revolutionary War, he was not the last to take part in it— for in 1780, a 13-year-old future president named Andrew Jackson volunteered to serve his local militia as a messenger boy.

Jackson was the third son of first generation Scots-Irish immigrants who lived at Waxhaws, a frontier community on the border between North and South Carolina. Jackson's father died three weeks before his son was born in 1767. The terrible Revolutionary War claimed all of the other Jacksons save one: Andrew's eldest brother Hugh died at the Battle of Stono Ferry in 1779; his elder brother Robert died of an illness caught aboard a British prison hulk; and his mother Elizabeth died, probably of that same illness, while tending sick prisoners. Young Andrew, too, became a prisoner of the British, and received two sword wounds— one on his left hand,

and another on his head— for defying a British army major who ordered him to shine his boots. The scars from these wounds were only two of many scars the hot-headed Andrew Jackson carried through life.

Despite his lack of formal schooling, Jackson managed to become a successful attorney after the war— partly because his new home state, Tennessee, required a different sort of attorney. On the unsettled, often lawless frontier of 1790s Tennessee, prosecuting attorneys doubled as marshals, dragging offenders into court and forcing them to face justice. Enforcing justice on such independent-minded frontiersmen required courage, self-confidence and toughness, all of which Jackson possessed in near-limitless abundance.

Because his temperament so perfectly suited him for the Tennessee frontier, Jackson thrived there. The money he earned practicing law allowed him to build the Hermitage, a large, successful plantation near Nashville where he raised cotton and fine horses. Like most successful Southerners, though, Jackson built his wealth partly on the backs of African slaves.

Currier & Ives illustration of a young Andrew Jackson defying a British officer, Major Coffin, during the Revolutionary War

Rachel Jackson (1767 – 1828)

Soon after he moved to Nashville in 1788, Jackson met and fell in love with a married woman named Rachel Donelson Robards. Rachel's first marriage was such an unhappy one that by 1790, she was no longer living with her husband, and considered her marriage at an end. Believing that her first husband had finalized their divorce, Rachel married Andrew Jackson in 1791. Much to their surprise, the Jacksons later discovered that they had been mistaken, and that Rachel was still technically married to her first husband.

By 1794, Rachel had finalized her divorce and married Jackson again, this time legally. Even so, Jackson's enemies often insulted his wife, denouncing her as an impure woman for having had two husbands at the same time. The quick-to-anger Jackson was never one to take insults against his wife lightly.

DEADLY DUELS: The Andrew Jackson – Charles Dickinson Duel (May 30, 1806)

In 1806, Andrew Jackson's sensitivity about his wife's honor led him into a duel with one of Tennessee's deadliest gunfighters: Charles Dickinson, a fellow plantation owner whose expertly-handled dueling pistol had already killed more than one opponent. The two gentlemen's argument actually began over a wager on a horse race. As the argument escalated, Dickinson made the mistake of impugning Rachel Jackson's honor— at which an infuriated Andrew Jackson demanded satisfaction from Charles Dickinson on the field of honor.

Even if brave Jackson felt no fear of death, he still recognized that he would stand a better chance of surviving his duel if he developed some strategy to offset Dickinson's superior marksmanship. Jackson and his second based their strategy on the rules of the duel. To begin the duel, the duelists were to stand back to back at a distance of ten paces. On a second's command to "fire," each would turn and fire one shot each. Jackson's plan was to hold his fire, allowing Dickinson to fire first— hoping that in his haste to fire quickly, Dickinson would miss, leaving Jackson free to aim his own shot as carefully as he liked.

Although Jackson's strategy may have saved his life, it was not without its sacrifices. True to his reputation, on the command to fire, Dickinson instantly wheeled and shot Jackson directly in the chest. The bullet struck inches from Jackson's heart, breaking some ribs and damaging a lung. Incredibly, Jackson stood as erect as if nothing had happened— leading the stunned Dickinson to exclaim, "My God, did I miss?"

Fighting through what must have been terrible pain, the impossibly tough Jackson leveled his own pistol and pulled the trigger— only to have his pistol's hammer stop at the half-cock position. Poor Dickinson had to stare death in the face as Jackson re-cocked his pistol, aimed and fired, dealing his enemy a chest wound that would kill him a few hours later. Asked how he managed to kill Dickinson despite a bullet in his chest, Jackson replied, "I should have hit him if he had shot me through the brain."

Other interesting facts:
- The doctors who examined Jackson's wound decided not to remove the bullet, for fear that doing so might cause their patient to bleed to death. Dickinson's bullet pained Jackson for the rest of his life, and occasionally caused him to cough up blood.

Andrew Jackson clutching his chest after Charles Dickinson's shot

Despite his fiery temper, Jackson was a likable man who won elections easily. Jackson took part in Tennessee's constitutional convention just before that territory became a U.S. state in 1796. That same year, Jackson became one of Tennessee's first representatives in the U.S. Congress. Then in 1798, Jackson resigned from Congress to take his place as a justice on the Tennessee Supreme Court.

In 1801, five years before his duel with Dickinson, Jackson won election as major general of Tennessee's state militia. It was this office that brought him to Alabama for the Creek War.

The Battle of Horseshoe Bend (March 27, 1814)

In the spring of 1814, Tennessee Major General Andrew Jackson led more than 3,000 troops south to punish the Red Sticks for the Fort Mims Massacre— despite the fact that Jackson was still recovering from wounds suffered as a second in yet another duel. Included in Jackson's army were about 600 warriors from some of the Five Civilized Tribes, all fighting to prove their nations' loyalty to the United States.

Jackson's target was a horseshoe-shaped bend in the Tallapoosa River, several miles north of what is now Dadeville, southern Alabama. Within Horseshoe Bend, the Red Sticks had built a fort surrounded on three sides by water, and on the fourth by a strong log wall some 1,000 feet long— making their position strong and defensible, but also leaving themselves few avenues for retreat.

Jackson's infantry charging the Red Sticks at the Battle of Horseshoe Bend

After pounding the Red Sticks' fort with cannon for hours with little effect, Jackson finally ordered his infantry to attack from all sides. What followed was a massacre even bloodier than Fort Mims. Of the more than

1,000 Red Sticks inside Horseshoe Bend, only about 200 escaped with their lives, and none escaped uninjured. Jackson's great victory at Horseshoe Bend shattered the Red Sticks, bringing their Creek War to an end.

> SUCCINCT SUMMARIES: Some Results of the Creek War
>
> - The Creek War ended with the Treaty of Fort Jackson, in which the United States claimed about 23 million acres of the Five Civilized Tribes' territory— including about three-fifths of what is now Alabama, and the southern one-fifth of what is now Georgia. Some of this territory came not from the Red Sticks, but from the very tribes who helped Jackson defeat the Red Sticks.
> - Jackson's success won him a huge promotion. In May 1814, the former general of Tennessee militia became the U.S. Army Major General in command of the United States' southwestern district.

LAND CEDED BY TREATY OF FORT JACKSON, 1814

> FASCINATING FACTS: Prayer Sticks
>
> A **prayer stick** or medicine stick was a special stick that some Native Americans used to summon spirits for religious rituals— things like giving thanks, blessing warriors before battle, healing the sick and conducting funerals. Native American medicine men selected their prayer sticks carefully, offering thanks to the tree from which they harvested them. They then decorated their prayer sticks with carvings, paintings, feathers, beads, bones and/or rawhide, all chosen to suit the prayer stick's particular purpose.

Thus the Creek War helped transform Andrew Jackson from a Tennessee hero into a national hero. Over the next few years, Jackson boosted his reputation even higher with two more successful campaigns.

The Battle of New Orleans (January 8, 1815)

Late in the War of 1812, Jackson led American troops in a brilliant defense of enemy Britain's last major target: the important port of New Orleans, Louisiana. At first, it seemed that British troops might capture New Orleans as easily as they had captured Washington— for when the still-pitifully-small U.S. Navy tried to bar British troops from landing near New Orleans, Britain's superior navy landed them anyway. No doubt remembering the many family members he had lost to the British as a boy, Andrew Jackson vowed, "By the Eternal! They shall not sleep on our soil!"

Even though more than 10,000 British attackers tried to storm New Orleans, Jackson managed to drive them back with fewer than 5,000 American defenders— costing the British nearly 2,500 casualties, compared to only about 300 for the Americans.

Figurative painting of Andrew Jackson commanding American defenses at New Orleans

REFRESHING REMINDERS: The Battle of New Orleans fell after the U.S. and Britain negotiated peace, but before news of that peace reached New Orleans. Soon after the Battle of New Orleans, the War of 1812 ended with the Treaty of Ghent, in which both sides agreed to return to their pre-war borders.

ILLUMINATING ODES: Years later, when Jackson was running for president, one of his supporters composed a poem to remind the American public of his brilliant leadership at the Battle of New Orleans. One stanza read:

"Our States can of their freedom boast / Although our foes should be a host / We quick can drive them from our coast! Fill up your glass and drink a toast: T' the health of General Jackson! Remember New Orleans, I say / Where Jackson showed them Yankee play / And beat them off and gained the day, And then we heard the people say: Huzza! for General Jackson!"

The First Seminole War

REFRESHING REMINDERS about Florida

- Spain first claimed Florida in 1513, when Juan Ponce de Leon became the first Spaniard to reach it. However, the Spaniards never dominated Florida as completely as they dominated their other New World colonies.
- Florida transferred into British hands for 20 years— from 1763, when Britain won Florida at the end of the Seven Years' War; until 1783, when Spain won Florida back at the end of the American Revolutionary War. One change the British wrought was to divide Florida into two colonies: (1) West Florida, with its capital at Pensacola; and (2) East Florida, with its capital at St. Augustine.

Beginning in the 1700s, Spain's loosely-held colony in Florida became a haven for two types of refugees:

1. **Creek, Cherokee and other tribesmen** who fled their old homelands farther north to escape white settlement. These refugees blended with Florida's natives to form the mixed Seminole people.
2. **Runaway slaves** who fled plantations in Alabama, Georgia, Tennessee and the Carolinas to live as free people in Florida. These former slaves also intermarried with the Seminoles.

Late in the War of 1812, British officers started recruiting these refugees for their campaign in the American South, the same campaign that included the Battle of New Orleans. When the war ended in early 1815, the British abandoned these recruits, along with all of their forts in Florida.

The largest and best-supplied of these forts was the so-called **Negro Fort**, which lay along the Apalachicola River at what is now Fort Gadsden, Florida. With the British out of the way, the refugees took over the Negro Fort, along with its generous cache of military supplies.

In that moment, the Negro Fort became a beacon of freedom for the slaves of the American South— a strong fort just south of the border that promised to defend any slave's freedom, if he could only get there. Whenever slaveholders chased their runaway slaves within range of the Negro Fort's cannon, the refugees inside chased the slaveholders off. Sometimes, the refugees were even bold enough to raid American settlers north of the border, warning them to keep their distance.

Because the Negro Fort stood in Spanish territory, the U.S. asked the governor of Spanish West Florida to handle the

Statue of Andrew Jackson on horseback

problem of its lawless fort. At the time, however, Spain was far too busy fighting the Spanish American Wars of Independence to tackle the Negro Fort.

FASCINATING FATES: The Negro Fort's Fate (July 1816)

Andrew Jackson finally decided that if Spain wouldn't control the Negro Fort, then the U.S. Army would. In July 1816, Jackson sent a pair of heavily-armed gunboats to threaten the fort, daring the refugees to fire on these U.S.-flagged vessels. When the refugees fired their cannon, Jackson's gunboats returned fire with **hot shots**— super-heated cannonballs designed to start fires inside enemy forts.

One of the Americans' hot shots happened to burst inside the Negro Fort's powder magazine, which was well-stocked with tons of gunpowder. Seconds later, a terrific explosion blew the Negro Fort sky-high, instantly killing nearly 300 refugees inside.

The end of the Negro Fort did not mean the end of trouble in Florida. When the refugees' cross-border raids continued, General Jackson invaded Florida a second time— only this time, Jackson didn't bother to consult the Spanish first. Instead, Jackson marched his army to West Florida's capital, Pensacola, and seized the city from the Spanish governor. As of May 1818, West Florida became a temporary U.S. territory under a military governor appointed by Andrew Jackson.

FASCINATING FACTS: The Adams-Onís Treaty (Signed 1819, Ratified 1821)

The ever-expanding United States had first started pressing its claim to West Florida around 1810, soon after the Spanish American Wars of Independence began. Winning Florida from Spain was a pressing foreign policy goal for U.S. Secretary of State John Quincy Adams, who took office under President Monroe in 1817.

Jackson's seizure of West Florida in 1818 affected Adams' negotiations for Florida in two opposite ways. On the one hand, the Spanish were angry over the seizure, and wanted West Florida back. On the other hand, the lawlessness on display in Florida demonstrated that Spain couldn't control the region. Some of Adams' colleagues denounced Jackson for seizing West Florida without official permission. Adams took the opposite view: instead of criticizing Jackson, Adams defended the need to bring law and order to Florida— which, he said, had become "a derelict open to the occupancy of every enemy, civilized or savage, of the United States."

Thus Andrew Jackson's seizure of West Florida helped John Quincy Adams negotiate the **Adams-Onís Treaty**, the treaty in which the United States acquired Florida from Spain. Named for Adams and his counterpart, Spanish foreign minister Luis de Onís, the Adams-Onís Treaty:

- Formally transferred all of Florida, both West and East, from Spain to the United States.

- Clarified the border between United States and the Viceroyalty of New Spain— a border that had been vague ever since the 1803 Louisiana Purchase, which defined Louisiana only as the watershed of the Mississippi River.

- Clarified both countries' claims to Texas and the Oregon Country. The U.S. surrendered its claim to Texas, and Spain surrendered its claim to Oregon.

The Presidential Election of 1824

> **REFRESHING REMINDERS**: Two political disasters for the Federalist Party— a crushing defeat in the election of 1800, and the party's failure to support the War of 1812— so weakened the party that when the Democratic-Republican President James Monroe ran for re-election in 1820, the dying Federalists didn't even bother nominating a candidate.

Andrew Jackson's successful leadership in the Creek War, the War of 1812 and the First Seminole War made him one of the most popular men in the United States— so popular that when President Monroe prepared to retire in 1824, Jackson automatically became a leading candidate to take Monroe's place. However, the Federalist Party's collapse meant that the surviving party, the Democratic-Republican Party, felt less need to unite behind a single candidate. Instead, different regions nominated different Democratic-Republicans for the presidential election of 1824, resulting in these top four electoral vote winners:

- Andrew Jackson of Tennessee, with 38%
- William Crawford of Georgia, with 16%
- John Quincy Adams of Massachusetts, with 32%
- Henry Clay of Kentucky, with 14%

Unfortunately, none of the four won a majority of the electoral vote— which meant that the House of Representatives would have to decide the election of 1824, just as it had decided the election of 1800.

In the general election, where popularity with the people mattered most, Andrew Jackson had the advantage. In the House of Representatives, though, popularity with politicians mattered most— which gave the advantage to the experienced politician John Quincy Adams. By striking a deal with fourth-place finisher Henry Clay, Adams assembled enough votes in the House to become the 6th President of the United States.

Naturally, the fiery Jackson resented being named the loser of an election he had actually won, in the sense that he received more votes than Adams. In Jackson's eyes, Adams' negotiated victory in the House of Representatives was a corrupt bargain— an underhanded trick in which the elites Adams and Clay used their political connections to flout the will of average Americans, who clearly preferred Jackson as their president.

Adams' bargain appeared even more corrupt after the election, when President Adams immediately appointed Henry Clay secretary of state— the very post from which Presidents Madison, Monroe and Adams had all arisen to the presidency. From this, Jackson deduced that Adams must have promised Clay the secretary of state's job before the election, with the understanding that Clay would succeed Adams as president.

FASCINATING FACTS: Jacksonian Democracy

John Quincy Adams

Over the next four years, Jackson developed the political principles he would use to defeat Adams in the next election— a set of principles that historians have since named **Jacksonian Democracy**. Chief among Jackson's principles was this: that it was the will of average Americans, and not the will of privileged elites, that should determine America's course. As the ultimate self-made man— one who began his journey as a penniless prisoner of war defiantly shaking his fist at the British, and was now well on his way to becoming President of the United States— Jackson wanted all Americans to have the same opportunities he had, opportunities found only in America. Within the bounds of the Constitution, Jackson wanted a system as close to pure democracy as possible— one in which all Americans had a voice, regardless of wealth or status.

Beside this chief principle stood two others:

- **One Man, One Vote:** From the colonial era through the early American era, many states allowed only men who owned a certain amount of property to vote. Jackson despised such voting laws, seeing them as symptoms of the same corruption that had allowed John Quincy Adams to steal the election of 1824. Instead, Jackson wanted voting rights for all white males, regardless of their wealth.
- **Manifest Destiny:** Having won his own wealth on America's western frontier, Jackson was a firm believer in Manifest Destiny, the idea that God had foreordained the United States to expand all across North America. Countless poor Americans dreamed of owning a small piece of the abundant land that still lay to the United States' west and south. In these Americans' minds, no one— not Britain, Spain or Mexico, and certainly no sparse native tribe— should bar them from claiming that land.

A LOOK AHEAD: By around 1850, nearly all laws connecting voting rights to ownership of property will be things of the past— although laws denying voting rights to blacks and women will remain as strong as ever.

The Presidential Election of 1828

Armed with these principles, and with help from his New York political ally Martin van Buren, the highly popular Andrew Jackson easily defeated John Quincy Adams in the election of 1828. Adams became only the second president to serve a single 4-year term, behind his father John Adams.

FASCINATING FATES: Rachel Jackson's Fate (1828)

Even though Andrew Jackson had been legally married for 30 years when he first ran for president in 1824, his political enemies still dredged up the same old charge against his wife Rachel— that she was impure because she had married Andrew before finalizing her divorce from her first husband (see above). John Quincy Adams' 1828 campaign was particularly ruthless about Rachel's past, scandalizing her again and again in a desperate attempt to drag down her husband.

Although Andrew was certainly tough enough to handle such criticism, Rachel may not have been— for within weeks of Andrew's victory in the election of 1828, Rachel died of heart failure. For the rest of his life, a deeply aggrieved Andrew Jackson blamed John Quincy Adams for his wife's sad end— for wounding Rachel's tender heart so deeply that it finally stopped in anguish.

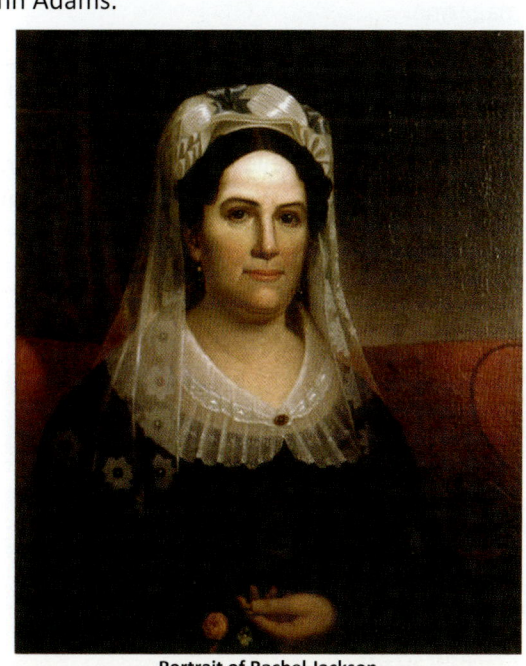

Portrait of Rachel Jackson

DEFINITION: The **Second Party System** was the new two-party system that developed after Jacksonian Democracy turned American politics on its head:

1. Andrew Jackson's party, a new version of the old Democratic-Republican Party, became simply the **Democratic Party**— a party devoted to making sure that all white males had the right to vote, and that privileged elites couldn't use their wealth to trample on poor men's rights.
2. Henry Clay's opposition party became the **Whig Party**, a successor to the Federalist Party. Like the English Whigs who opposed the tyranny of King James II, American Whigs opposed what they saw as the tyranny of Andrew Jackson.

FASCINATING FACTS: The Jackass or Donkey as a Symbol of the Democratic Party

During one of Andrew Jackson's political campaigns, his opponents twisted the name "Jackson" into "jackass"— hoping to convince voters that as president, Jackson would be just as hard to work with as one of these notoriously stubborn, thick-headed animals. Far from being insulted, Jackson adopted the jackass as a symbol of his party—for what his enemies considered stubbornness and stupidity, Jackson considered determination and steady strength, perfect symbols for the stalwart American people his Democratic Party represented.

After Jackson left office in 1837, the jackass symbol died out for a time. The jackass only became a permanent symbol of the Democratic Party after 1870, when political cartoonist Thomas Nast revived it for an issue of *Harper's* magazine.

Political cartoon depicting Martin van Buren (right) preparing to mount the Democratic Party jackass that Andrew Jackson (center) rode into office

FASCINATING FACTS: The Indian Removal Act (Signed May 28, 1830)

True to his belief in Manifest Destiny, Jackson helped push the Indian Removal Act through Congress during his first term in office, and signed it into law on May 28, 1830. Among other things, the Indian Removal Act authorized Jackson to:

1. Set aside unoccupied territories west of the Mississippi River as new homelands for native tribes.
2. Trade those unoccupied territories for the tribes' old homelands east of the Mississippi.
3. Compensate the tribes for any improvements they might have built in their former homelands— homes, barns and so on.
4. Cover all costs of removing the tribes to their new homelands.
5. Cover the tribes' living expenses in their new homeland for the first year, thus easing their transition.

"Jackson Says Go," illustration courtesy of the Five Civilized Tribes Museum

In his annual State of the Union speech to Congress later that year, Jackson predicted all of these advantages arising from Indian removal:

- For the United States, Jackson foresaw that removal would place "a dense and civilized population in large tracts of country now occupied by a few savage hunters… it will incalculably strengthen the southwestern frontier… [enabling that region] to advance rapidly in population, wealth, and power."

- For the Five Civilized Tribes, Jackson foresaw that removal would "enable [the tribes] to pursue happiness in their own way and under their own rude institutions; …retard the progress of decay, which is lessening their numbers, and perhaps cause them gradually, under the protection of the Government and through the influence of good counsels, to cast off their savage habits and become an interesting, civilized, and Christian community."

Jackson also advised Congress:

- "What good man would prefer a country covered with forests and ranged by a few thousand savages to our extensive Republic, studded with cities, towns, and prosperous farms embellished with all the improvements which art can devise or industry execute… and filled with all the blessings of liberty, civilization and religion?" *In other words: Like John Donne before him (see Chapter 4), Jackson argued that North America rightfully belonged to the race that would make the best use of it— the white race.*

- "Can it be cruel in this Government— when by events which it cannot control, the Indian is made discontented in his ancient home— to purchase his lands, to give him a new and extensive territory, to pay the expense of his removal, and support him a year in his new abode? How many thousands of our own people would gladly embrace the opportunity of removing to the West on such conditions! If the offers made to the Indians were extended to [our own people], they would be hailed with gratitude and joy… Rightly considered, the policy of the General Government toward the red man is not only liberal, but generous." *In other words: In Jackson's opinion, the Indian Removal Act was by no means cruel. Rather, it was a benevolence that the United States bestowed upon the tribes at great public expense.*

Negotiations to remove the Five Civilized Tribes began in that same year, 1830. One by one, the U.S. government removed tribe after tribe to the new, thinly-populated **Indian Territory** set aside for them out west, most of which lay in what is now Oklahoma.

Choctaw Removal (1831 – 1833)

Most Choctaws departed peaceably under the Treaty of Dancing Rabbit Creek, ratified in 1831. This treaty required any Choctaw who didn't want to become a U.S. citizen to depart for the Indian Territory by 1833. However, any Choctaw head of household who chose to remain behind was entitled to 640 acres of land in the new state of Mississippi, with extra land for every child in his family— provided that he abandoned his old lifestyle, became a U.S. citizen and abided by U.S. law.

TRAGIC TALES: The Choctaw Trail of Tears (1831 – 1833)

The Indian agents who arranged the Choctaws' move from Mississippi to the Indian Territory could hardly have managed their complicated task any worse. Despite Jackson's promise to cover all costs of removing the tribes— or perhaps because of this promise— government agents provided too little food, too few blankets and too poor lodgings for so many people to move so far safely. Of the 15,000 – 17,500 or more Choctaw who removed to Oklahoma in 1831 – 1833, as many as 2,500 – 5,000 died of disease, hunger and exposure along the way.

"Unending Journey," illustration courtesy of the Five Civilized Tribes Museum

INTERESTING IDEAS: A Choctaw chief was the first to describe his people's westward path as a **"trail of tears and death."**

Chickasaw Removal (1832)

Most Chickasaws removed themselves peaceably under the Treaty of Pontotoc, ratified in 1832. Instead of accepting a government-assigned home, the Chickasaw sold all of their land east of the Mississippi to the government, and then used the money to buy land of their own choosing. The Chickasaw wound up buying part of the Indian Territory land the government assigned their old neighbors, the Choctaw.

Creek Removal (1832)

Some of the Creeks removed themselves peaceably under the Treaty of Cusseta, ratified in 1832. However, many Creek also fled south to Florida, where they swelled the ranks of the Seminoles; while others tried to remain in Alabama as U.S. citizens. White settlers continued to clash with Creeks in Alabama until 1836 – 1837, when the U.S. Army forcibly removed all who would not go quietly.

Seminole Removal (1832 – 1842)

Some of the Seminoles removed themselves peaceably under the Treaty of Payne's Landing, ratified in 1832. However, the Seminoles posed a unique difficulty. Because the Seminoles were a mixed people who included runaway slaves and their descendants, vengeful Southern slaveholders demanded these special provisions in the Treaty of Payne's Landing:

- If the U.S. government ever found proof that the Seminoles had sheltered runaway slaves, then the Seminoles would owe the government a substantial fine.

- Any Seminole with African blood in his veins was forbidden to move to the Indian Territory, but must instead be sold into slavery. Exactly how the government would decide which Seminoles had African blood after all these decades of intermarriage, the treaty did not say.

> **FASCINATING FACTS: The Second Seminole War (1835 – 1842)**
>
> Because some Seminoles signed the Treaty of Payne's Landing, the U.S. government expected all Seminoles to abide by it— which meant that they must all depart for the Indian Territory by 1835. Instead, many Seminoles dragged their feet, arguing that the treaty applied only to those who had actually signed it. As the deadline approached, the government prepared to remove the Seminole by force.

A Seminole village

The Seminole responded to the government's show of force by launching the longest, costliest war the U.S. Army would ever fight against a native tribe: the Second Seminole War. The keys to the Seminole's success against a better-equipped, better-fed foe included these:

- **Florida's geography:** The central Florida region where the Seminoles lived was full of deep, dense swamps that offered plenty of hiding places, making the Seminole all but impossible for their enemies to find. When the U.S. Army tried tracking them with bloodhounds, the Seminoles first befriended the bloodhounds, and then retrained them to track whites.

- **Guerrilla warfare:** Instead of confronting a superior enemy in major battles that they were sure to lose, the Seminoles fought mainly smaller battles, appearing out of nowhere to launch swift surprise attacks before disappearing back into the swamps.

Eventually, the U.S. Army managed to wear the Seminole down, forcing them to retreat farther south— partly through dirty tricks like the one that captured Osceola.

AMAZING NATIVE AMERICANS: Osceola (1804 – 1838)

Osceola was a young Creek whose family joined the Seminoles around 1814, when the loss of the Creek War forced many Red Stick Creeks farther south. Although Osceola was not yet a chief when the Second Seminole War broke out, he quickly won a reputation as the cagiest of the Seminole guerrilla leaders, embarrassing the United States time and again with clever victories like these:

- **The Dade Massacre (December 28, 1835):** The Second Seminole War had hardly begun when Osceola masterminded this deadly surprise attack on a U.S. Army unit led by Major Francis Dade. Of the nearly 110 soldiers in Dade's column, only 2 – 3 survived by pretending to be dead, and even these were sorely wounded. Meanwhile Osceola's 180 Seminoles suffered fewer than 10 casualties.

Portrait of Osceola painted in late 1837, when he was Jesup's prisoner

- A little over a year later, in January 1837, U.S. Quartermaster General Thomas Jesup convinced hundreds of Seminoles to join him near Lake Monroe, central Florida for what he said were peace talks. When Osceola arrived, he quickly realized what Jessup was really planning: to lull the Seminoles to sleep with false promises, and then load them aboard ships and remove them to the Indian Territory. Before that could happen, Osceola whispered some instructions to his followers; and that night, the Seminoles mysteriously vanished from beneath Jesup's very nose.

FASCINATING FATES: Osceola's Fate (1838)

Unable to defeat Osceola in any other way, Jesup decided to trick him— even if doing so meant violating all of the usual laws of war, laws that even so-called savages knew how to honor.

Arrest of Osceola

Despite his January experience with Jesup, Osceola agreed to meet Jesup under a flag of truce that October. The moment Osceola arrived, Jesup treacherously violated his truce agreement and arrested Osceola.

Unfortunately, life in the Florida swamps had already given Osceola a bad case of malaria, leaving his health too fragile to survive the dark, damp prison cells to which Jesup confined him. The 33-year-old Osceola died in one of Jesup's prisons in January 1838.

SUCCINCT SUMMARIES: The Second Seminole War dragged on for more than four years after Osceola's death. Although the Seminoles never really surrendered, nearly 4,000 of them finally moved to the new homeland the government set aside for them in the Indian Territory. A few hundred stubborn holdouts moved farther south, where they built new homes in and around the Florida Everglades.

A Brief Timeline of Cherokee Removal from Georgia

As the most civilized of the Five Civilized Tribes, the one that published newspapers, sent its children to boarding schools and even wrote its own constitution, the Cherokee resisted the Indian Removal Act as any other U.S. citizen might have: in court.

1802 – The Compact of 1802: The state of Georgia agrees to surrender its claims to the west, in what are now Alabama and Mississippi. In exchange, the United States agrees to either purchase or otherwise extinguish all Native American claims to territories within Georgia.

1802 – 1825: The number of white settlers in Georgia multiplies by more than five times, greatly boosting the pressure to remove the Cherokee from Georgia. Although the Cherokee sell much of their homeland, they refuse to sell the part settlers want most: northwestern Georgia, where Georgians are waiting to build an important transportation hub that they will name Atlanta.

1825: The Cherokee Nation establishes a capital called New Echota, near what is now Calhoun, Georgia. Two years later, the Cherokee Nation ratifies a written constitution in which it declares itself to be a sovereign nation, fully independent of the United States.

1828 – The Georgia Gold Rush: The pressure to remove the Cherokee mounts even higher when prospectors discover gold on Cherokee land in northwest Georgia. Ignoring Cherokee rights, squatters and prospectors begin moving onto Cherokee land, panning for gold and digging mines without permission.

1828 is also the year when the Cherokee's worst enemy, Andrew Jackson, wins election as president.

1828 – 1830: Unwilling to wait any longer for the U.S. to fulfill the Compact of 1802, the state of Georgia begins taking over Cherokee territory. Georgia plans to distribute the last of the Cherokee's land as it has distributed other land in the past— through the **Georgia Land Lotteries**, in which white settlers draw lots for sections of Cherokee land.

Georgian settlers drawing lots for Cherokee land

1830 is also the year when Andrew Jackson signs the Indian Removal Act.

1831 – *Cherokee Nation v. Georgia*: The Cherokee Nation tries to block Georgia's land grab by suing Georgia in the U.S. Supreme Court. The Supreme Court rules that the Cherokee Nation is not truly independent, but rather a protectorate of the United States— which means that under the Constitution, the Court has no authority to hear the Cherokee's case.

1832 – *Worcester v. Georgia*: A Cherokee supporter and missionary named Samuel Worcester sues Georgia, arguing that Georgia's state laws cannot possibly bind the independent Cherokee Nation. This time, the Supreme Court agrees— ruling that under the Constitution, the federal government alone has the power to make treaties, including treaties with the Cherokee. However, President Jackson refuses to enforce the court's decision, reportedly insisting: "[Chief Justice] John Marshall has made his decision; now let him enforce it!"

1832 is also the year when the Georgia starts holding land lotteries to distribute some of the Cherokee's last lands.

1835 - 1836 – The Treaty of New Echota: Cherokee Principal Chief John Ross travels to Washington to protest Georgia's continued attacks on Cherokee independence.

While Ross is away, U.S. negotiators sneak into New Echota to meet with about 500 Cherokee who disagree with Ross, and are ready to sell their land and move west. Even though these 500 are not the Cherokee's elected representatives, and have no legal authority to negotiate treaties, they sign the Treaty of New Echota— a treaty that requires all Cherokee to remove to the Indian Territory by 1838. The U.S. Senate later ratifies the underhanded, highly controversial Treaty of New Echota by a single vote.

TRAGIC TRUTHS: The Cherokee Trail of Tears (1836 – 1838)

Like the Choctaw and others before them, the Cherokee walked their 1000-mile-long Trail of Tears from Georgia to the Indian Territory; and like the Choctaw, they suffered terribly along the way. Once again, careless Indian agents provided too little food, blankets and shelter to move so many people safely. Of the nearly 16,000 Cherokee the U.S. government removed from 1836 – 1838, as many as 2,000 – 4,000 died of disease, hunger and exposure along the way.

LASTING LEGENDS: The Cherokee Rose

The Cherokee's suffering along their Trail of Tears was so terrible that some feared it might destroy their people— especially their women, whose strength the Cherokee would need to rebuild their tribe when they reached their new homeland. In desperation, Cherokee chiefs called upon their gods to deliver some sign that might comfort their women and restore their strength.

According to legend, the Cherokee's gods answered this prayer with the Cherokee rose, a beautiful white rose with a golden center. When the weeping Cherokee women looked back along the Trail of Tears, they saw a Cherokee rose growing on each spot where one of their tears had fallen. The rose's pure white petals represented the pure tears of the bereaved Cherokee women; its golden center represented the gold-greed that drove the whites to steal the Cherokee's homeland; and the seven leaves on its stem represented the seven Cherokee clans.

Ironically, the state of Georgia— the very state that worked so hard to evict the Cherokee from their homeland— adopted the Cherokee rose as its state flower in 1916.

FASCINATING FACTS: Chunkey

Chunkey was a popular team game enjoyed by all native peoples of the American southeast. One way to play chunkey was to roll a heavy disc across a smooth, level playing field. Just as the disc ran out of momentum and began to fall, one player from each team hurled a spear at it. The player whose spear landed closest to the disc's final resting place scored a point for his team. Bystanders added to the excitement by gambling on the outcome, sometimes wagering everything they owned.

U.S. AND WORLD HISTORY

Scenes from the Agricultural and Industrial Revolutions

DEFINITIONS:
- The **British Agricultural Revolution** was a revolution in farm technology that boosted British farms' output tremendously over the century from 1750 – 1850.
- The **Industrial Revolution** was a revolution in manufacturing technology that took place during the same century.

Both revolutions transformed lives in countless ways, affecting everything from where people lived and what they owned to what they learned and how they spent their time.

Crop Rotation

Since ancient times, farmers have understood that they cannot always grow the same crops in the same fields. Without necessarily understanding the scientific details, ancient farmers knew that if they replanted the same crops in the same fields year after year, then their yields would begin to suffer, for two reasons: (1) because the soil would eventually run out of the nutrients required by that particular crop; and (2) because the pests and diseases that attacked that crop built up in the soil over time, eventually causing new plants to come in thin and sickly.

To avoid this problem, farmers practiced **crop rotation**— that is, they moved crops from field to field each year, allowing their fields off years in which to recuperate. Unfortunately, early crop rotation schemes placed severe limits on the amount of food farmers could grow:

- Under two-crop rotation systems, farmers sowed half of their fields each year, leaving the other half fallow— which meant that each year, one-half of their land produced absolutely nothing.

Portrait of "Turnip" Townshend

- Under three-crop rotation systems, farmers planted two out of every three fields each year, leaving the third field fallow— which still left one-third of their land out of production each year.

One of the Agricultural Revolution's biggest breakthroughs was the improved four-crop rotation scheme developed by gentleman farmers like Charles Townshend.

> BRILLIANT BRITONS: Charles Townshend, a.k.a. "Turnip Townshend" (1674 – 1738)
>
> Like his grandson Charles Townshend, author of the Townshend Acts (see Chapter 21), Turnip Townshend enjoyed a successful career in Britain's parliament. Unlike his grandson, though, Turnip Townshend retired from politics to spend his last years managing his family's large estate in Norfolk, England.
>
> During those last years, Townshend helped develop a four-crop rotation system that divided fields between four crops: wheat the first year, barley the second, turnips the third and clover the fourth. Townshend's system offered several advantages:
>
> - The introduction of nutrient-restoring crops like clover and turnips allowed farmers to replenish their fields without leaving them fallow— which meant that 100% of their land could produce food every year.
>
> - Both turnips and clover went to feed livestock, not people— which meant more food for livestock. Farmers who stored turnips as winter feed could feed cattle year-round, and thus have meat to eat year-round.

Other improvements that boosted farm output during the Agricultural Revolution included these:

- **Selective Breeding:** By allowing only superior-quality sheep, cattle and horses to breed, gentleman farmers like Robert Bakewell (1725 – 1795) and Thomas Coke (1754 – 1842) developed sheep breeds that produced more wool; cattle breeds that produced more meat and milk; and horse breeds that were stronger and faster.

- **The Enclosure Acts:** Before the Agricultural Revolution, British farms operated under the open-field system— a fenceless system that left most farmland open, for all land technically belonged the Crown. However, detailed operations like four-crop rotation and selective breeding were impossible to manage on open fields. Partly for this reason, the Enclosure Acts transformed open fields into hedged-off private properties closed to all but their owners.

Example of a Lincoln Longwool sheep, a product of Robert Bakewell's selective breeding efforts

- **The development of an improved moldboard plow** allowed farmers to till more ground with less effort.

- **The grain drill** developed by Jethro Tull (1674 – 1741) and others allowed farmers to plant grain quickly and evenly, with less wasted seed.

- **The threshing machine** developed by Andrew Meikle (1719 – 1811) and others allowed farmers to separate wheat from chaff with far less effort.

- **Marling:** The Agricultural Revolution was also the time when farmers began to spread crushed marl on their fields. Because marl contained a high percentage of limestone, it made soil less acidic, and therefore more nourishing for most crops.

Among the many changes that sprang from the Agricultural Revolution were these:

- Improved agriculture provided more-abundant, higher-quality food, allowing Britain's population to grow and thrive as never before.

- Improved agricultural machines left many farmers out of work— leaving them with little choice but to move from farm to city, where they joined in the growing Industrial Revolution.

Water and Steam Power

Before the Industrial Revolution, most people knew of only a few uses for water power. Many water wheels turned the millstones that ground grain into flour. Others turned **trip hammers**— huge, heavy hammers that miners used to crush ore, and blacksmiths used to fashion metal.

During the Industrial Revolution, inventors adapted water power for new uses, especially fabric-making. Engineers rigged water wheels to spin multiple shafts, from floor to floor throughout their large fabric mills. From these spinning shafts, belts transferred power to any number of rotating machines. **Spinning jennies** spun raw cotton or wool into thread; **power looms** wove thread into cloth; and **stocking frames** knitted yarn into socks.

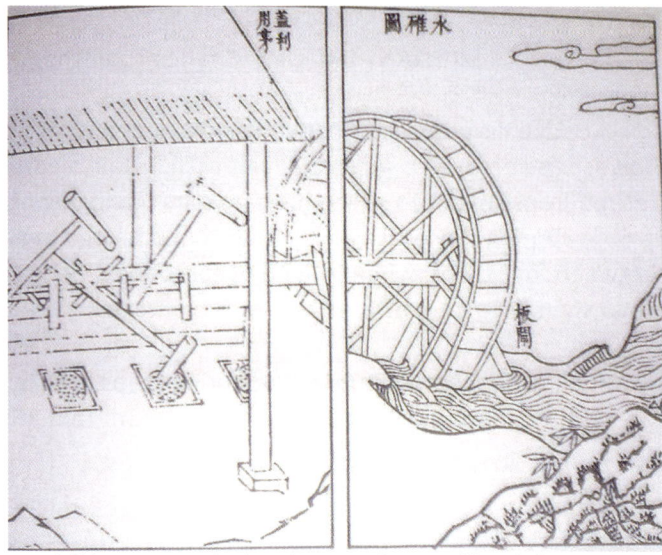

A Chinese water wheel turning a set of ore-crushing trip hammers

The awesome speed of these water-driven machines changed the fabric industry forever. A single factory worker equipped with a power loom could turn out as much fabric as 50 or more workers equipped with old-fashioned hand looms. With high speed and high output came all these drastic changes:

- As the supply of fabric skyrocketed, its price plummeted— which meant that small fabric-makers operating out of home shops disappeared, priced out of the market by stiff competition from the big mills.

- High-output mills produced more fabric with fewer workers— which meant that the faster machines grew, the more fabric workers lost their jobs. As a result, many poor Britons who had already lost their farms due to the Enclosure Acts now lost their factory jobs as well.

- Before the Industrial Revolution, fabric-making was a skilled trade that masters could hand down to their apprentices. After the Industrial Revolution, machines determined the quality of the work, and factory workers needed no skills beyond the ability to tend machines. Naturally, fabric makers wondered what would happen to them when underpaid teenagers could perform work that had once required master fabric-makers, and when they no longer possessed valuable skills to hand down to their children.

- The rise of factories placed the future of the whole fabric industry in the hands of a few wealthy factory owners— many of whom cared only for profit, and not a farthing for their workers' well-being.

FASCINATING FACTS: The Luddite Rebellion (1811 – 1813)

Many times over the years, factory workers attacked greedy factory owners whom they felt were ruining their futures— often by smashing expensive machinery that the owners bought to replace workers. One early machine-smasher was a young factory worker named Ned Ludd or Edward Ludnam. According to legend, Ludd grew so angry over a whipping he received from his overseer that he took a hammer to a pair of expensive sock-knitting machines. Decades after that legendary incident in 1779, factory workers still liked to blame little Ned Ludd whenever machines turned up damaged.

The best-organized attacks on factory machinery came in 1811 – 1813, when protesters who called themselves **Luddites** smashed countless machines all across Nottinghamshire, Yorkshire and Lancashire. Parliament took this Luddite Rebellion so seriously that in 1812, smashing machinery became a death-penalty offense. Britain deployed more troops against the Luddites than it did against Napoleon of France, who chose that year to launch his doomed campaign in Russia (see Chapter 28).

Other interesting ideas:
- In modern times, the word **Luddite** has a slightly different meaning. It usually refers to anyone who resists life-changing technologies like computers and smart phones.

Luddites smashing an overhead-shaft-driven loom

As useful as water power could be, it was useless for any job that couldn't be performed near falling water. Such jobs required a new, more portable kind of power: steam power, which came through the work of engineers like James Watt and Robert Fulton.

INGENIOUS ENGINEERS: James Watt (1736 – 1819)

James Watt was a Scottish engineer who worked for the University of Glasgow, Scotland as an engineer and machinist. The pivotal moment of Watt's career came in 1763, when the university asked Watt to repair its clumsy old steam engine.

Since around 1700, British miners had been using a primitive steam engine called the Newcomen engine to pump water out of deep mines. Unfortunately, the Newcomen engine suffered from two major weaknesses: (1) it consumed a tremendous amount of coal for the tiny bit of work it performed; and (2) it produced only up-and-down motion, not rotating motion. In studying the engine, Watt came to understand why it burned so much coal. Watt spent the next 20-odd years developing and improving the **Watt Engine**— a new steam engine that not only burned far less coal than the Newcomen engine, but also produced a rotating motion like a water wheel's. With rotating motion came the ability to produce power anywhere one could burn coal, even aboard ships and on farms.

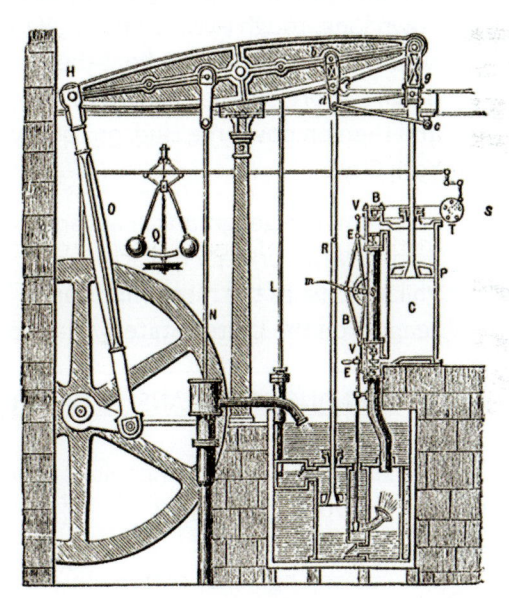

Diagram of a Watt steam engine built to pump water out of mines

AMAZING AMERICANS: Robert Fulton (1765 – 1815)

Robert Fulton was a Pennsylvania-born artist and engineer who built the world's first successful commercial steamboat: the *North River Steamboat*, also called the *Clermont*. In 1807, Fulton's steamboat started ferrying paying passengers up the Hudson River from New York City to Albany. The roughly 150-mile trip required about 30 hours, for an average of about 5 miles per hour against the current.

FASCINATING FACTS: The Erie Canal

- The **Erie Canal** is a manmade waterway that connects Albany, New York in the east to Buffalo, New York in the west. Built over the years from 1817 – 1825, the original Erie Canal was about 40 feet wide, 4 feet deep and 363 miles long. The canal included 36 locks to manage the 550-foot rise in elevation from Albany to Buffalo.

- The Erie Canal took advantage of the only real break in the Appalachian Mountains between Georgia and Maine— the Mohawk River Valley— to connect points west of the Appalachians to points east. In doing so, the canal provided producers west of the Appalachians with a fantastic new option: instead of floating their goods down long, rough rivers all the way to New Orleans, they could float them down a short, serene canal to Albany, and then on down the Hudson to New York City.

- This immense geographical advantage helped New York City replace Philadelphia as the most important seaport on the United States' Atlantic coast.

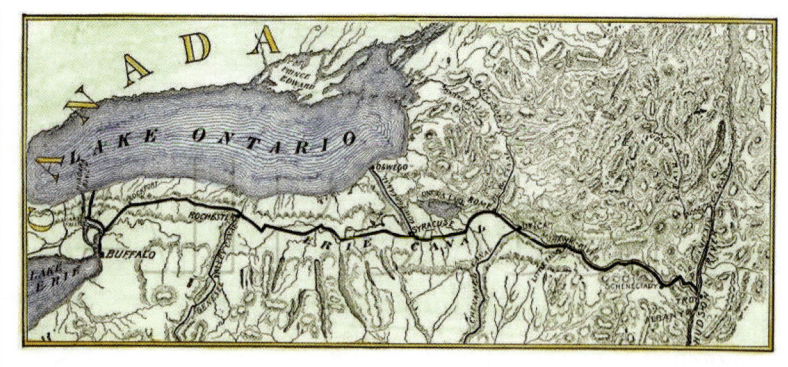

1839 illustration of the Erie Canal by W. H. Bartlett

AMAZING AMERICANS: Eli Whitney (1765 – 1825)

Eli Whitney was an ingenious American engineer best known for two innovations:

1. The cotton engine, or **cotton gin**— a machine for removing seeds from cotton bolls, first patented in 1794. Before the cotton gin, cleaning cotton was so labor-intensive and expensive that cotton was hardly worth growing in the United States. After the cotton gin, cotton became the American South's most valuable cash crop.

2. **Interchangeable parts**, especially for weapons. Before the Industrial Revolution, a flintlock mechanism built in Harpers Ferry, Virginia might not fit a musket built at Brooklyn, New York. Whitney promoted the idea of producing interchangeable parts that would fit any U.S. musket, whatever armory built it— making all muskets far easier to assemble and repair.

Portrait of Eli Whitney

U.S. STATE FOCUS

Illinois

FASCINATING FACTS about Illinois:

- State Capital: Springfield
- State Abbreviation: IL
- Statehood: Illinois became the 21st US state on December 3, 1818.
- Area: About 58,000 square miles (Ranks 25th in size)
- Bordering States: Indiana, Wisconsin, Iowa, Missouri, Kentucky
- Meaning of Name: Uncertain; may come from any of several native words.
- State Nickname: "Prairie State"
- State Bird: Cardinal
- State Tree: White Oak
- State Flower: Violet
- State Song: "Illinois" by Charlie Chamberlin and Archibald Johnston
- State Motto: "State sovereignty, national union"
- Historic Places to Visit: President Abraham Lincoln Log Cabin, Lincoln Tomb, Lincoln Home, President Ulysses Grant Home, John Deere Home and Shop, Hull House
- Resources and Industries: Farming, commodities trading, finance, coal, mining

Abraham Lincoln Home in Springfield, Illinois

State Flag: Illinois' state seal on white field. The seal depicts an American eagle perched on a rock marked with two dates: (1) 1818, the year of Illinois statehood; and (2) 1868, the year Illinois adopted this seal. The eagle's right talon clutches a shield decorated with the stars and stripes of the U.S. flag. The eagle's beak clutches a banner with the motto "State sovereignty, national union."

PRESIDENTIAL FOCUS

PRESIDENT #6: John Quincy Adams (1767 – 1848)	
In Office: March 4, 1825 – March 4, 1829	**Political Party:** Democratic-Republican
Birthplace: Massachusetts	**Nickname:** "Old Man Eloquent"

    John Quincy Adams learned the art of diplomacy under his father, former President John Adams. As a boy, John Quincy accompanied his famous father on several diplomatic assignments, including ones to France, the Netherlands and Britain. As a young man, John Quincy served as President Washington's Minister to the Netherlands, and as his father's Minister to Prussia.

    After his father lost the election of 1800, John Quincy returned home to win election as a U.S. Senator from his home state of Massachusetts. As a Federalist-majority state, Massachusetts expected Adams to support

Federalist causes. Instead, Adams often supported Democratic-Republican ones, partly because he admired Thomas Jefferson so much. After five years, Massachusetts' state legislature grew so frustrated with Adams that it finally chose a loyal Federalist to replace him in 1808— at which point Adams immediately (1) resigned from the Senate, and (2) transferred his membership from the dying Federalist Party to the Democratic-Republican Party. The Democratic-Republican President James Madison appointed Adams as his Minister to Russia, and also sent him to Ghent to negotiate an end to the War of 1812. Madison's successor, President James Monroe, appointed Adams as his highest foreign policy official— secretary of state, the office from which both Madison and Monroe had ascended to the presidency.

Adams found his own ascension more difficult. With the collapse of the Federalists, Democratic-Republicans around the country nominated four candidates for president in 1824. One was the highly popular Andrew Jackson, who won more electoral votes than Adams— but without winning a majority of electoral votes. Because no candidate won a majority, the election went to the House of Representatives, where the more-experienced Adams managed to assemble enough votes to defeat Jackson. Jackson so resented the "corrupt bargain" with which Adams won the election of 1824 that he spent the next four years plotting to unseat Adams— which Jackson did, overwhelmingly, in 1828.

Instead of retiring from politics after he lost the presidency, Adams went on to serve in the U.S. House of Representatives for another 18 years, beginning in 1831. During this time, Adams earned the nickname "Old Man Eloquent" for his fine speeches on the House floor— many of them in support of his favorite issue, the abolition of slavery. Adams was still serving in the House when he collapsed and died there in 1848.

Fun Facts about John Quincy Adams:
- President Adams was a strong swimmer who often removed all his clothes for early-morning dips in the Potomac River. According to legend, a female reporter named Anne Royall took clever advantage of this situation. When Adams repeatedly refused Royall's requests for an interview, she finally strode down to the Potomac one morning and sat on Adams' clothes until he answered her questions.

Notable Quotes from John Quincy Adams:
- "To believe all men honest would be folly. To believe none so is something worse."

PRESIDENT #7: Andrew Jackson (1767 – 1845)	
In Office: March 4, 1829 – March 4, 1837	**Political Party:** Democratic
Birthplace: North Carolina / South Carolina border	**Nickname:** "Old Hickory"

Andrew Jackson was the first American who rose from impoverished roots to the highest office in the land. Jackson's parents were first-generation Scots-Irish immigrants who both died before the end of the Revolutionary War, leaving Jackson a teenaged orphan with little education. From this lowly estate, Jackson rose to become a Tennessee frontier attorney; a Tennessee member of the U.S. House of Representatives; a justice of the Tennessee Supreme Court; a major general of Tennessee's militia; and a major general of the U.S. Army. Jackson's victories in the Creek War, the War of 1812 and the First Seminole War made him one of the most popular generals in the United States, an ideal presidential candidate.

The unusual circumstances of Jackson's rise made him the least educated president so far— one with no college degree, and little knowledge of any arts or sciences beyond those of warfare. Throughout his time in the

White House, Jackson remained as he advertised himself: a common man's president with a common man's education. Key events of Jackson's presidency include:

- **The Indian Removal Act (1830):** Jackson sponsored and enforced the law that resettled all Native American tribes who still lived east of the Mississippi onto new homelands west of the Mississippi. Mismanagement and cruelty along the natives' Trail of Tears brought thousands of innocent native lives to premature ends.

- **The Nullification Crisis (1832):** South Carolina's reaction to a high national tariff that damaged its economy was the Ordinance of Nullification— an 1832 law which said that if South Carolina judged a U.S. law to be unconstitutional, then South Carolina need not abide by that law. The Nullification Crisis might have split the United States 30 years before the Civil War, had not Jackson (1) threatened South Carolina with force, and then (2) reduced the hated tariff to a level South Carolina could abide.

- **The Demise of the Second National Bank (1836):** Jackson despised the Second National Bank of the United States, believing that its policies favored the wealthy over his beloved average Americans. Therefore when Congress passed a bill to renew the bank's 20-year charter, which expired in 1836, Jackson vetoed the bill— destroying the National Bank.

Fun Facts about Andrew Jackson:
- For his 1828 rematch against his rival, sitting President John Quincy Adams, Jackson founded the organization that was to become the modern-day Democratic Party.
- In keeping with his reputation as the common man's president, Jackson opened the White House to all who wanted to attend his first inauguration party. This led to common folk flooding into the White House, fouling its fine furnishings with their rude manners and muddy boots. To lure Jackson' unruly mob outside, the shocked White House staff resorted to serving alcohol out on the lawn, and then locking the doors behind their unwanted guests.
- Jackson was the first president to face an assassination attempt. As Jackson was departing a deceased congressman's funeral at the Capitol Building in January 1835, a madman named Richard Lawrence drew a pistol and tried to fire it at the president— only to have it misfire. Next, the well-prepared Lawrence drew a second pistol— only to have it misfire as well. Because the chances of two consecutive misfires with two different pistols were so low, some praised God for protecting Jackson. Others blamed this bizarre happening on damp weather, which may have fouled Lawrence's gunpowder.
- Jackson was the only president on whose watch the United States ever paid off its national debt in full.

Notable Quotes from Andrew Jackson:
- "It is to be regretted that the rich and powerful too often bend the acts of government to their own selfish purposes."
- "The planter, the farmer, the mechanic, and the laborer... form the great body of the people of the United States. They are the bone and sinew of the country— men who love liberty, and desire nothing but equal rights and equal laws."

CHAPTER 31: The British Empire in India and China

WORLD GEOGRAPHY FOCUS, PART ONE

Important Ports of India

India's coasts along the Arabian Sea, the Indian Ocean and the Bay of Bengal are dotted with port cities. From west to east, some of India's larger ports are:

- **Mumbai**, once called Bombay. Bombay was a former Portuguese trading post that passed to the English in 1662, when King Charles II received it as a dowry for his marriage to Princess Catherine of Braganza, Portugal.

- **Kochi**, also called Cochin or Ernakulum. Kochi is an ancient port where Eastern traders bought and sold spices for centuries before the first Europeans arrived in India. Mumbai and Kochi are two main ports of India's southwestern coast, the **Malabar Coast**.

- **Pondicherry**, capital of French India.

- **Chennai**, once called Madras. Chennai began as a tiny English trading post called Fort St. George, and then grew into one of India's largest cities.

- **Visakhapatnam**, a beautiful natural harbor about midway between Chennai and Kolkata. Visakhapatnam, Pondicherry and Chennai are three main ports of India's southeastern coast, the **Coromandel Coast**.

- **Kolkata**, also called Calcutta. Calcutta became the capital of British India, and the main port of the region where the British East India Company maintained its largest presence: Bengal, northeast India.

WORLD HISTORY FOCUS, PART ONE

The British Empire in India

REFRESHING REMINDERS from Chapter 15:
- India's second great Moghul dynasty emperor, Akbar (reigned 1556 – 1605), discovered the formula that helped Muslim emperors win the allegiance of Hindu Indians: Akbar always respected the Hindu faith, and never insisted on strict Islamic law. The next two Moghul emperors, Akbar's son Jahangir (reigned 1605 – 1627) and grandson Shah Jahan (reigned 1627 – 1658), followed his lenient example.

- Shah Jahan's son Alamgir (a.k.a. Aurangzeb, reigned 1658 – 1707) was Akbar's opposite— a strict Muslim who insisted on destroying Hindu temples and enforcing strict Islamic law. Alamgir further weakened his dynasty by spending the last 27 years of his reign fighting a long, mostly fruitless war in southern India. In all those 27 years, Alamgir never once visited his power base in northern India.

The Decline of the Moghul Empire (1707 – 1857)

Through the mistakes of Alamgir, the once-great Moghul Empire began to crumble. The first 200 years of the Moghul Empire saw just six emperors, five of whom enjoyed long reigns and fantastic wealth. The next

100 years saw ten less-wealthy emperors, several of whom suffered short reigns followed by violent deaths. Three of the ten may have died at the hands of the Syed brothers.

INTERESTING INDIANS: The Syed Brothers, a.k.a. Hassan Ali (1666 – 1722) and Hussain Ali (1668 – 1720)

The Syed brothers were a pair of Indian Muslim generals who became standouts in the service of the last great Moghul emperor, Alamgir. After Alamgir died in 1707, the Syed brothers took advantage of the Moghul dynasty's growing weakness to become emperor-makers, the true power behind the thrones of three weak emperors:

1. Farrukhsiyar (9th Moghul Emperor, reigned 1713 – 1719):
The 8th Moghul emperor, Alamgir's grandson Jahandar Shah, was a notoriously frivolous alcoholic and drug addict who shamed his dynasty by marrying a lowly dancing girl. Sensing opportunity, Jahandar Shah's cousin Farrukhsiyar enlisted the Syed brothers to assassinate his ridiculous cousin, which they did. After taking Jahandar Shah's place, Farrukhsiyar rewarded the Syed brothers with two of the highest offices in his empire.

A few years later, Farrukhsiyar began to question the Syeds' loyalties. Sensing that they meant to overthrow him, Farrukhsiyar launched several secret plots against them, hoping to overthrow them first. Upon learning of their ungrateful emperor's plotting, the Syeds (1) seized and imprisoned Farrukhsiyar; (2) poked needles into his eyes, blinding him; and then later (3) strangled him to death.

The Syed brothers' first victim, Jahandar Shah

2. Rafi ud-Darajat (10th Moghul Emperor, reigned 1719):
The emperor the Syed brothers set on India's throne in Farrukhsiyar's place, Rafi ud-Darajat, reigned for just a few months in 1719 before dying on the throne— perhaps of lung disease, or perhaps because the Syed brothers murdered him for refusing to obey them.

3. Shah Jahan II (11th Moghul Emperor, reigned 1719):
The next emperor the Syed brothers set on India's throne, Shah Jahan II, followed an identical path— a reign of just a few months, followed by a suspicious death in late 1719.

After disposing of their third Moghul emperor within the single year of 1719, the Syed brothers needed yet another replacement. The Moghul heir the Syeds chose, Muhammad Shah, was the emperor who was to preside over the Moghul Empire's utter collapse.

HUMILIATED MOGHULS: Muhammad Shah (12th Moghul Emperor, lived 1702 – 1748, reigned 1719 – 1748)

Muhammad Shah was a grandson of Alamgir born under the name Roshan Akhtar in 1702. As of 1719, when the Syed brothers needed a replacement for Shah Jahan II, Roshan was still just 17 years old. The Syeds elevated Roshan for just this reason, calculating that an inexperienced boy might prove easier to control than his predecessors.

Muhammad Shah's first years on the Moghul throne were optimistic ones, for two reasons:

1. Because early in Muhammad Shah's reign, the Syed brothers' rivals in the Moghul court defeated and killed them— thus freeing the young emperor from the Syeds' controlling influence.

2. Because Muhammad Shah returned to the lenient religious policy that Akbar, Jahangir and Shah Jahan had all followed— a policy of making peace with India's many Hindus, rather than persecuting them.

However, the passage of time revealed two weaknesses that would combine to destroy Muhammad Shah's reign:

1. The too-pampered Muhammad Shah was more interested in fine art, music and dance than he was in managing his empire. While the fine arts flourished under his reign, military arts did not.

2. The Hindus who still dominated the Deccan Plateau region of southern India never forgave the Moghul dynasty for the ravages suffered under Alamgir. When Muhammad Shah allowed his empire's military might to slip, these southern Hindus pressed their advantage, prying more and more territories out of Moghul hands. Lost territory meant lost tax revenue and fewer military resources.

Muhammad Shah and his hunting falcon being carried on a litter

FASCINATING FACTS: Persia versus India (1738 – 1739)

Nineteen years into Muhammad Shah's reign, the Moghul Empire's growing weakness drew the attention of India's western neighbor, Persia. Emperor Nader Shah of Persia was Muhammad Shah's opposite: a military genius who cared only for growing his empire, and nothing for the pleasures of fine art.

Around 1736, Nader Shah invaded a much-contested no man's land that lay between Persia and India: Afghanistan. Over the next two years, Afghan rebels on the run from Nader Shah started seeking safety in India. Because Persia and India were supposedly allies, Nader Shah wrote Muhammad Shah, asking him to control the lawless Afghan rebels who were taking refuge within his borders.

Unfortunately, the weak Muhammad Shah no longer had enough military resources to solve his own problems, much less Nader Shah's; so he denied his neighbor's request. Different historians offer two different explanations for what happened next:

1. Some say that Nader Shah crossed the border into India only because he needed to defend Persia against the rebel Afghans who had taken refuge there.

2. Others say that the aggressive Nader Shah had always intended to invade India, and that the Afghan rebels only provided a convenient excuse to do so.

Nader Shah

Whatever his reasons, Nader Shah invaded India in late 1738; and when Muhammad Shah sent troops to defend his borders, Nader Shah declared war on India. Pressing his attack to the east, Nader Shah threatened the Moghul capital city of Delhi itself.

Fighting on his home ground, aided by armies that often outnumbered his enemy's by two to one or more, Muhammad Shah should have been able to defend his empire. Unfortunately, he was battling an aggressive military genius whom historians have since dubbed the "Napoleon of Persia." With an overwhelming victory at the Battle of Karnal— fought about 75 miles north of Delhi on February 13, 1739— Nader Shah overcame the last of Muhammad Shah's armies, clearing the way for the Persian army to march into Delhi.

Nader Shah crushing Muhammad Shah's army at the Battle of Karnal

TRAGIC TALES: The Sack of Delhi (March 22, 1739)

From the moment the conquering Nader Shah marched into Delhi, tensions between Indians and Persians ran high. All India wondered what the Persians hoped to accomplish in Delhi: Would Nader Shah overthrow the Moghul dynasty? Would he leave Muhammad Shah on his throne as a puppet emperor? Or would he satisfy himself with some of the Moghul dynasty's legendary wealth— priceless treasures from the Taj Mahal and the Peacock Throne?

In the midst of all this tension, a misunderstanding led to a terrible massacre. On the night of March 21, a rumor spread that Muhammad Shah was dead, killed by one of the Persian guards who held him prisoner. Reacting to this rumor, angry Indians started attacking every Persian within reach. Although no one knows how many Persians died in these riots, the number may have been as high as several hundred.

The next morning, March 22nd, Nader Shah rode in full battle armor to old Delhi's most prominent mosque. With a cry and flourish, Nader Shah drew his sword and raised it into the air; and as he did so, his well-armed Persian soldiers started butchering the ill-armed men, women and children of Delhi. The next several hours saw unspeakable violence, horrifying scenes of fire, rape, murder and infanticide too terrible to imagine. When Nader Shah finally sheathed his sword, some 20,000 – 30,000 defenseless Indians lay dead, mutilated or burned. The once-great Moghul Empire lay in ruins, a shattered remnant of its former glory.

An outraged Nader Shah absorbing the horrific sight of his murdered soldiers just before ordering the Sack of Delhi

SUCCINCT SUMMARIES: Some Results of the Battle of Karnal and the Sack of Delhi

In the end, the only way Muhammad Shah could convince Nader Shah to leave Delhi was by opening his treasury to the Persians. Like Tamerlane before him (see Year Two), Nader Shah marched out of Delhi staggering beneath the weight of a fantastic amount of treasure, including:

- A fortune in gems plundered from the Taj Mahal, the elaborate mausoleum/mosque Shah Jahan built for his beloved wife Mumtaz Mahal.
- The Peacock Throne, an incredibly ornate symbol of Moghul wealth and power that may have cost Shah Jahan twice as much as the Taj Mahal.
- The Koh-i-noor, an immense, flawless diamond that was once part of the Peacock Throne.

Muhammad Shah never recovered from his humiliating defeat. Although the Moghul dynasty continued in much-weakened form until 1857, none of its later rulers held more than a tiny fraction of the immense wealth and power that Shah Jahan enjoyed during the Moghul Empire's golden age.

FASCINATING FATES

- **Nader Shah's Fate:** Nine years after Nader Shah departed Delhi, his own Persian army officers surprised him in his sleep and stabbed him to death. After that, the great Persian Empire built by Nader Shah began to break apart.
- **The Peacock Throne's Fate:** The rivals who divided the late Nader Shah's empire apparently also divided the Peacock Throne. Because no one has seen the Peacock Throne since those days, historians assume that Nader Shah's rivals argued over it, and wound up breaking it up so that they could divide its riches. Despite the throne's short run in Persia, the Persians adopted "Peacock Throne" as a name for their imperial throne.

One artist's interpretation of the Peacock Throne

Britain versus India

Muhammad Shah's defeat also led to another important result: it left India more lawless, and thus more dangerous for European traders who counted on law and order to protect their livings. All traders detest lawlessness— for without law, bandits may run wild, plundering traders of a year's profits in minutes. To promote law and order, the British East India Company took steps to defend its trading posts in India— trying to ensure that these would always be safe, no matter what wild happenings went on in the rest of India.

The British also had a second reason for protecting their overseas trading posts: because India became a battleground in international wars like the War of the Austrian Succession and the Seven Years' War. From the moment two European countries declared war on one another, their colonies in India were at war as well— for a victory anywhere in the world, even in distant India, might affect treaty negotiations back home.

The Seven Years' War in India (1756 – 1763)

During the Seven Years' War, the British East India Company took its first bold steps toward Company Raj.

Indian war elephants in action during the War of the Austrian Succession

DEFINITIONS:
- **Company Raj** was a century-long period during which the British East India Company conquered India piece by piece, gradually replacing the Moghul dynasty as the dominant power in India. Under Company Raj, the EIC became less like a trading company, and more like the government of India— complete with powers to enforce law, collect taxes and so on.
- A **nawab** or nabob was an Indian governor in charge of a certain sub-region of India, such as Bengal. After Nader Shah of Persia humiliated the Moghul dynasty, nawabs showed less loyalty to their weak Moghul emperors, and started behaving more like independent kings.

The spring of 1756 brought critical changes in Bengal, a region that was critical to the EIC.

First, the elderly Nawab of Bengal died, to be replaced by his grandson Siraj ud-Daulah. In addition to his lofty post as nawab, Siraj inherited from his grandfather a deep distrust of the British, whom he resented for two main reasons: because they interfered in his affairs, and because they shared with him such a small share of their profits. Siraj also suffered from two serious weaknesses:

EIC ships off Fort William, Calcutta, 1735

1. He was young and inexperienced, being only about 20 years old in 1756.
2. A number of older, more-experienced rivals were jealous of Siraj's good fortune, and longed to be nawab in his place.

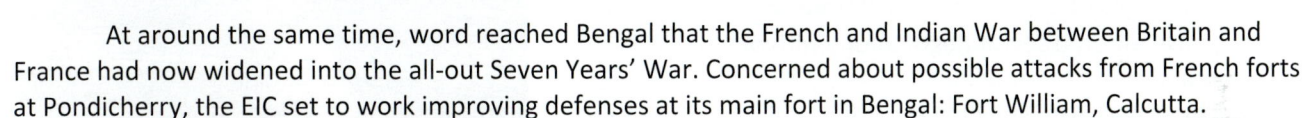

At around the same time, word reached Bengal that the French and Indian War between Britain and France had now widened into the all-out Seven Years' War. Concerned about possible attacks from French forts at Pondicherry, the EIC set to work improving defenses at its main fort in Bengal: Fort William, Calcutta.

At this, Nawab Siraj balked. In Siraj's opinion, improved defenses at Fort William were a step in the wrong direction, one that would allow the EIC to seize an even larger share of Bengal's wealth. Determined to put an end to British arrogance in Bengal once and for all, Siraj ordered the EIC to cease improving its fort.

When the EIC refused, an irate Siraj led an immense army against Fort William. With only about 180 British troops to defend against some 50,000 Bengali troops and 500 war elephants, Fort William quickly fell to Nawab Siraj on June 20, 1756— leading to a notorious incident in the Black Hole of Calcutta.

DEFINITION: The **Black Hole of Calcutta** was a lone, miserable prison cell inside Fort William, Calcutta. At about 18' long by 14'-10" wide— roughly the size of a one-car garage— the Black Hole was the proper size to hold 2 – 3 prisoners overnight, or perhaps as many as 6 – 12 in a pinch.

TRAGIC TALES: The Black Hole of Calcutta Incident (June 20 – 21, 1756)

After the EIC surrendered Fort William, Nawab Siraj needed a way to confine his British prisoners of war. With 50,000 troops at his disposal, Siraj easily could have set a guard around his hundred-odd prisoners. For some reason, though, Siraj or one of his officers chose to lock them all inside the only prison cell available: the Black Hole of Calcutta. Despite the Black Hole's small size, Siraj's guards pushed prisoner after prisoner into it, forcing them against one another until they hardly had room to stand or breathe. To make matters worse, the night of June 20 – 21 was miserably hot and humid, making the air inside the Black Hole all but unbreathable.

Exactly how many prisoners Siraj's men packed into the Black Hole of Calcutta is uncertain. According to John Holwell— an EIC officer who spent that night in the Black Hole with his troops, and later reported his experience to Parliament— the number was no less than 146. However, the Black Hole was so small that it may have held only about half that many, no matter how hard Siraj's guards pushed.

Whatever the number going in, most sources agree that the number who came out alive the next morning was about 20 – 23, including Holwell. All the rest, perhaps as many as 126, died miserable deaths from a combination of heat exhaustion and suffocation.

Just as important as the Black Hole of Calcutta Incident was another incident that followed. After the fall of Calcutta, Siraj allowed his troops to run wild over Fort William, pillaging a tremendous fortune in EIC money and goods.

When news of the Black Hole of Calcutta incident reached Madras/Chennai, the EIC was understandably furious over Siraj's shameful mistreatment of British prisoners of war. Company officers were just as furious over the pillage of Fort William, which threatened the EIC's very existence— for if the EIC was to succeed in India, then its investors back home must be able to trust that their investments were safe. For both of these reasons, the EIC dispatched one of its most experienced army commanders, Robert Clive, to retake Calcutta and punish Nawab Siraj.

FASCINATING FACTS: The Battle of Plassey (June 23, 1757)

To any commander less aggressive than Robert Clive, the task the EIC set him might have seemed impossible. The greatest force Clive could muster stood at about 1,100 Europeans and 2,100 native Indians— a total of only 3,200, a puny force to set against Siraj's tens of thousands.

Painfully aware of his disadvantage in numbers, Clive sought advantages of a different kind. Before confronting Siraj in battle, Clive entered secret negotiations with one of Siraj's sub-commanders, a traitor named Mir Jafar. Mir Jafar was one of the jealous rivals who still hoped to take Siraj's place; and he also happened to command about one-third of Siraj's army. The arrangement Clive proposed was simple: if Mir Jafar would take Clive's side against Siraj, or at least restrain his troops from attacking Clive, then Clive would set Mir Jafar on the nawab's throne in Siraj's place.

Just before Clive confronted Siraj, an unforeseen disaster nearly spoiled Clive's plan. Late in the game, the go-between who negotiated with Mir Jafar on Clive's behalf— a

Sir Robert Clive later in life, standing before an image from his great triumph at the Battle of Plassey

greedy merchant named Umichand— threatened to tell Siraj everything unless Clive promised him a huge sum of money. Desperate to silence Umichand, but having no intention of paying him such a grand sum, Clive adopted the dishonest tactic of preparing two contracts: one for Umichand, in which he promised to pay his exorbitant demand; and another for the EIC's records, in which he promised nothing of the kind.

Unfortunately for Clive, British Admiral Charles Watson— the naval officer who co-commanded his mission in Bengal— was too honest to sign Clive's false contract. The inconvenient scruples of Admiral Watson required Clive to take yet another dishonest step: forging Watson's signature on Umichand's false contract.

Even with cooperation from Mir Jafar and Umichand, Clive still doubted his ability to defeat some 60,000 – 70,000 Indian troops with only about 3,000 of his own. Just before the Battle of Plassey, Clive asked several of his fellow officers to help him decide whether he should attack or retreat. A majority of officers voted for retreat— including Clive himself.

Despite this vote, the power of decision rested with General Clive alone. After another hour's reflection, Clive made the bold, fateful decision to attack Siraj near Plassey, a town about 80 miles north of Calcutta.

Mostly thanks to Siraj's uncertain leadership, Clive won the Battle of Plassey with almost absurd ease. Other keys to Clive's victory included:

1. The assistance of Mir Jafar, who played his traitor's role perfectly— careful not to support Clive outright, just in case Siraj should win; but equally careful not to support Siraj.

2. A rainstorm that blew up during the battle, soaking the Indians' gunpowder. After the storm subsided, some of Siraj's troops tried a bold bayonet charge against Clive, expecting his gunpowder to be as wet as their own. Instead, they found that the British had done an excellent job of keeping their gunpowder dry— allowing Clive's cannon to mow down Indians by the hundreds.

FASCINATING FATES: The humiliating end of the Battle of Plassey found Siraj miles away, collecting a cache of precious gems to fund his escape. A few days later, someone betrayed the fleeing Siraj into the hands of one of Mir Jafar's friends, who swiftly executed him.

Company Raj (1757 – 1858)

Meanwhile, Clive installed Mir Jafar as the new Nawab of Bengal. Unfortunately for the people of Bengal, Mir Jafar was not free to do all he thought best for them— for

Sir Robert Clive greeting Bengal's new nawab, Mir Jafar, after the Battle of Plassey

having won his throne with British help, Mir Jafar had to do as the British commanded. Over the years to come, the EIC assumed ever more control over Bengal, and Bengal's nawabs grew more like puppets in British hands.

Clive's great victory at the Battle of Plassey is only the first of several milestones historians use to mark the beginning of Company Raj over India. Other milestones include:

- **The Battle of Buxar** (1764), in which the EIC further humiliated the Moghul dynasty by dealing 16th Moghul Emperor Shah Alam II a crushing defeat. After the Battle of Buxar, Shah Alam II reluctantly bestowed upon the EIC the *diwan* of Bengal— that is, the authority to collect taxes from Bengal's citizens, just as if the EIC were Bengal's legitimate government.

- **The year 1773**, in which the EIC (1) established Calcutta as its official capital of British India; and (2) promoted Warren Hastings as Bengal's first governor-general— officially setting aside Bengal's nawabs, who became no more than EIC puppets.

- **The Anglo-Mysore Wars** (1766 – 1799), in which the EIC gradually brought most of western India under its control— especially the area around Mumbai.

- **The Anglo-Maratha Wars** (1772 – 1818), in which the EIC gradually brought most of southern India under its control. After 1818, the EIC suffered no serious rivals anywhere in India.

SUCCINCT SUMMARIES:
- During the century of Company Raj (1757 – 1858), and especially after 1818, the British East India Company performed all the functions of India's rightful government: (1) levying and collecting taxes; (2) adjudging and enforcing law; and (3) commanding India's armies.
- The ability to control an entire sub-continent, especially one as rich as India, boosted the British Empire's fortunes immeasurably. Vastly aided by India's wealth, the British Empire grew into one of the largest and wealthiest the world has ever seen.

Company Raj was a disaster for Indian independence. Although the EIC functioned like a government, its true purpose remained what it had been since its founding back in 1600: to generate profit for its investors. What Indians needed was a friendly government to protect their interests— to police them, protect them and promote their well-being. Instead, what Indians received was a selfish trading company that cared only for profits, and nothing for their well-being.

For Indians, the costs of the EIC's selfish mismanagement of India included humiliation, widespread poverty, famine and death. For Britons who cared, the costs were moral and spiritual— the guilt that came from exploiting poor Indians for Britons' benefit.

The East India Company's massive headquarters in London around 1800

A LOOK AHEAD: Company Raj will last until the Sepoy Rebellion of 1857— in which the sepoys, Indian soldiers serving in EIC armies, will rebel against EIC control (see Year Four). The circumstances of the Sepoy Rebellion, along with the EIC's failure to contain it, will destroy the British government's trust in the EIC. In 1858, the India Office of the British government will take control of India for most of another century— a period called **British Raj**. Mohandas Gandhi, Jawaharlal Nehru and other Indian leaders will finally win India's independence from Britain in 1948.

ILLUMINATING EXCERPTS from *The Discovery of India* by Jawaharlal Nehru (published 1944)

In 1944, nearly two centuries after the Battle of Plassey, Jawaharlal Nehru summarized the woeful impacts of Company Raj in a history titled *The Discovery of India*. Nehru was a much-beloved leader of the Indian independence movement who, in 1948, became the first prime minister of a newly-independent India. Nehru's criticisms of British rule included these:

- "Clive, by promoting treason and forgery and with very little fighting... won the Battle of Plassey in 1757... It was an unsavory beginning, and something of that bitter taste has clung to it ever since."

- "Bengal had the first full experience of British rule in India. That rule began with outright plunder... The corruption, venality, nepotism, violence and greed of money of these early generations of British rule in India is something which passes comprehension..."

- "A significant fact which stands out is that those parts of India which have been longest under British ruler are the poorest today..."

FASCINATING FACTS: Holi, a.k.a. the Festival of Colors

Holi is a spring festival celebrated mainly by Hindus. The celebration begins with Holika, a giant bonfire on Holi eve. The next day, Hindus chase one another through the streets, playfully trying to cover one another's faces with brightly-colored powders.

According to legend, Holi began with an unfortunate Hindu god whose face happened to be blue, causing him to worry that a certain female god might not like him. His mother's suggestion was to sneak up on the girl and color her face as well. Hindus have been coloring one another's faces ever since.

FASCINATING FACTS: Christmas Crackers

Christmas crackers are a British tradition that began in 1847, when Briton Tom Smith invented them. The simplest Christmas crackers are small cardboard tubes containing a trace of a mild explosive, along with a cheap gift— often a crown-shaped paper hat that the winner wears for Christmas dinner. To open these gifts, each of two partygoers grabs one end of the cracker and pulls, at which the tube bursts open with a loud crack.

CHURCH HISTORY FOCUS

Early British Missionaries in the Far East

MIGHTY MISSIONARIES: William Carey (1761 – 1834), "Founder of Modern Missions"

Britain's first Protestant missionary to India, William Carey, began his church life as his father did: a contented member of the Anglican Church. William's father Edmund Carey was a weaver who became a village schoolmaster when William was six. The years William spent in his father's schoolhouse constituted his whole formal education.

William was about 16 when his father apprenticed him into the trade he would follow well into adulthood: shoemaking. Oddly enough, it was the shoemaker's shop that turned William away from the Anglican Church— for one of William's fellow apprentices was a dissenter, a member of a smaller church that disagreed with the Anglican Church. Influenced by this apprentice and others, William became first a dissenter; then a devoted Baptist believer; and then finally a Baptist pastor.

As a young Baptist, William became fascinated with the lives of missionaries like John Eliot (see Chapter 11) and David Brainerd (see Chapter 18)— men of God who devoted their careers to sharing Christ's gospel with Native Americans who had never heard it before. The years of William's youth were also inspiring for another reason: because those were the years when Britons learned of the globe-spanning adventures of James Cook (see Chapter 24), and when the East India Company took charge of Bengal.

William Carey

As Carey pondered these world-changing events, the Lord inspired him to share the gospel with all races everywhere, wherever the growing British Empire cleared the way. The first time William tried to share this vision with his elders, one of them rebuked him with these words: "Young man, sit down; when God pleases to convert the heathen, he will do it without your aid and mine."

To convince such reluctant elders, William Carey wrote one of the world's first missionary manuals.

ILLUMINATING EXCERPTS from William Carey's *An Enquiry into the Obligations of Christians to Use Means for the Conversion of the Heathens* (Published 1792)

William Carey's *Enquiry into the Obligations of Christians* was four types of literature wrapped into one. The first section was a persuasive essay in which Carey tried to convince lazy Christians that it was their duty to share the gospel around the world. To bolster this argument, the second section related the history of the Christian missionary movement, from Bible times forward. To demonstrate the size of the task, the third section offered an expansive set of tables estimating the populations of countries around the world, along with how many in each country had yet to hear the gospel.

Explaining why so many Christians resisted sharing the gospel with unbelievers around the world, Carey wrote: "Some think little about it, others are unacquainted with the state of the world, and others love their wealth better than the souls of their fellow-creatures."

The fourth and last section was a manual to explain Carey's missionary strategy. Carey envisioned a legion of dedicated missionaries serving all over the world, supported by strong organizations back home.

Describing the type of missionaries required, Carey wrote: "They must be very careful not to resent injuries which may be offered to them, nor to think highly of themselves, so as to despise the poor heathens, and by those means lay a foundation for their resentment, or rejection of the gospel. They must take every opportunity of doing them good, and laboring, and travelling, night and day, they must instruct, exhort, and rebuke, with all long suffering, and anxious desire for them, and, above all, must be instant in prayer for the effusion of the Holy Spirit upon the people of their charge. Let but missionaries of the above description engage in the work, and we shall see that it is not impracticable."

William Carey in Bengal (1793 – 1834)

Persuaded by Carey's arguments, a group of elder Baptist pastors formed one of Britain's first missionary societies: the Particular Baptist Society for Propagating the Gospel to the Heathen, founded in 1792. This society later became the Baptist Missionary Society, now known as BMS World Mission.

As one of its first two missionaries, BMS chose William Carey himself, who departed for Bengal in 1793. Carey was 32 years old when he arrived in Bengal with his wife and two sons. Persisting through innumerable hardships, Carey served in Bengal for 41 years, until his death at age 73. Carey's many accomplishments in Bengal included these:

- Translating the New Testament into the Bengali language, as well as assisting other missionaries to translate Scripture into somewhere near 40 Eastern languages. Carey also operated a printing press that produced hundreds of thousands of Bibles in Eastern languages— thus opening the Word of God to about one-third of the world's people for the first time.

- Founding India's first missionary school, Serampore College, as a training ground for native Indian pastors.

- Building nearly 20 mission stations in Bengal, and manning many of them with native Indian pastors.

- Persuading the East India Company to ban *sati*— a terrible Hindu practice in which grieving widows cast themselves upon the burning funeral pyres of their dead husbands.

Alexander Duff

> **INTERESTING IDEAS:** William Carey's well-known motto comes from an inspiring sermon that he delivered just before departing for India: "Attempt great things for God; expect great things from God."

> **MIGHTY MISSIONARIES: Alexander Duff (1806 – 1878)**
>
> Just as William Carey was the BMS' first missionary to India, Alexander Duff was the Church of Scotland's. Duff's mission strategy was to offer high-quality English educations to the children of upper-caste Indians— reasoning that if these upper castes adopted Christianity, then their faith might filter down to the lower castes as well. The difficulty was that Hindus loved their culture too much to replace it with a foreign one. Instead, they tried to blend the Christian teaching Duff offered with Hindu ideas of their own. Even so, the colleges and schools that Alexander Duff established contributed mightily to India's education system, providing Indians the schooling they needed to take part in their British-led government.

WORLD GEOGRAPHY FOCUS, PART TWO

Important Ports of China

> **REFRESHING REMINDERS:** Most of China's territory drains into the eastern seas through one of three major river systems: the Yellow River in the north, the Yangtze River in the center and the Pearl River in the south.

China's coasts along the South China Sea, the East China Sea, the Yellow Sea and the Bohai Sea are dotted with port cities. From south to north, some of China's larger ports are:

- **Sanya**, which lies on the large southern island of Hainan.

- **Macau**, an island port on the west side of the Pearl River Delta.

- **Hong Kong**, an island port on the east side of the Pearl River Delta.

- **Guangzhou** (once called Canton), which lies at the mouth of the Pearl River.

- **Hangzhou**, an inland port which lies at the southern end of the Grand Canal.

- **Shanghai**, which lies at the mouth of the Yangtze River. As of 2014, giant Shanghai is home to more people than any other city in the world.

- **Tianjin**, an inland port which lies on the Grand Canal near its northern end at Beijing.

- **Dalian** (once called Port Arthur), which lies at the end of the Liaoning Peninsula in the Bohai Sea.

WORLD HISTORY FOCUS, PART TWO

The British Empire in China

> REFRESHING REMINDERS from Chapter 13: In 1644, the Manchurian Qing dynasty swept down from the north and conquered the Chinese Ming dynasty, forcing China's native Han people under foreign control. To emphasize their dominion over the Han, the Qings issued the Haircutting Command— an imperial decree that required all Han men to wear their hair in the severe Manchu queue hairstyle.

China under the Qing Dynasty (1644 – 1912)

The Qing dynasty spent its first century-and-a-half in China accomplishing three tasks: first, disposing of the last remnants of the Ming dynasty; second, expanding China's borders to the north and west; and third, uniting China's many different cultures into one. Uniting China was mostly the work of two great Qing dynasty emperors, Kangxi and Qianlong.

The Kangxi Emperor, a.k.a. the K'ang-hsi Emperor (lived 1654 – 1722, reigned 1661 – 1722)

The Kangxi Emperor was the fourth Qing dynasty emperor, and the second to reign over China as well as Manchuria. The main events of Kangxi's remarkable 61-year reign include:

1. The Revolt of the Three Feudatories (1673 – 1681): Early in its reign, the Qing dynasty named three special governors to control four far southern provinces of China— provinces that were too remote to control directly from Beijing, which lay in the north. Foremost among these governors was Wu Sangui, the turncoat Ming general who allowed a Qing army through the Great Wall of China at Shanhai Pass in 1644 (see Chapter 13). As a special reward for betraying the Ming, Wu Sangui received two southern provinces instead of one.

To help these three governors control their provinces, the Qing granted them powers far beyond those of ordinary governors. Elated with their powers, and unimpressed by their child emperor Kangxi, these three soon began to see themselves not as Qing dynasty subordinates, but as independent kings.

In 1673, the now 19-year-old Kangxi emperor grew so concerned about these three governors' growing power that he ordered them to retire. Far from retiring, the three governors launched a major rebellion called the Revolt of the Three Feudatories. Despite having betrayed the Ming 29 years before, Wu Sangui was bold enough to adopt this bit of hypocrisy as his rebellion's motto: "Overthrow the Qing, restore the Ming!"

As matters turned out, Wu Sangui and his allies underestimated their opponent— for despite his youth and inexperience, Kangxi managed to defeat all three rebel governors at once, bringing all four of their distant provinces firmly under Qing dynasty rule.

Portrait of the Kangxi Emperor in courtly robes

2. The Conquest of Taiwan (1683): When the three feudatories declared their intention to restore the Ming, the Ming-loving King of Taiwan immediately joined their rebellion. This would prove to be a mistake— for two years after Kangxi defeated the three feudatories, he defeated the King of Taiwan as well, bringing the important island of Taiwan firmly under Qing control.

SUCCINCT SUMMARIES: These two triumphs for Kangxi— the defeat of the Revolt of the Three Feudatories in 1681, and the Conquest of Taiwan in 1683— mark the real end of Ming resistance, and the real beginning of Qing dynasty rule over a united, growing China.

The Qianlong Emperor, a.k.a. the Chien-lung Emperor (lived 1711 – 1799, reigned 1735 – 1796)

Kangxi's grandson, the Qianlong Emperor, was the sixth Qing dynasty emperor, and the fourth to reign over China as well as Manchuria. If Kangxi's greatest accomplishment was to cement the Qing dynasty's hold on China, then Qianlong's was to expand China through conquest:

- To the northeast, Qianlong conquered outer Manchuria, home to more Manchu people and some Russians.
- To the north, Qianlong conquered Inner Mongolia and Outer Mongolia, home to remnants of the Mongol Empire.
- To the northwest, Qianlong conquered the vast Xinjiang region, home to Turkish-speaking Muslim peoples like the Uighurs and the Khazaks.
- To the west, Qianlong conquered Tibet— although Tibet's Buddhist spiritual leader, the Dalai Lama, retained his powerful influence over Tibetans.

Qianlong's successful, extremely expensive program of conquest more or less doubled China's territory, building it into the giant country it is today. However, Qianlong was less successful to the south, where Vietnam and Burma (modern-day Myanmar) managed to resist his armies.

Jeweled helm worn by the Qianlong Emperor

Unifying China

Along with the privilege of conquering so much territory came the responsibility of unifying that territory— of melding several different cultures into a single culture loyal to China. One way Qianlong unified China was by reviving a doctrine developed by earlier emperors: *tianxia*, Chinese for "all under heaven."

DEFINITION: *Tianxia* was a widely-believed Chinese doctrine which held that China was the world's "Inner Kingdom"— the most important country on earth, the pinnacle of earthly culture and heavenly favor. By extension, *tianxia* held that countries outside China were less cultured, and lower in heavenly favor.

INTERESTING IDEAS: One way to understand *tianxia* is to picture a bright, circular heaven floating over a square earth, with the emperor of China at earth's center. The circle of light and favor that heaven's glow casts on earth represents China; and the closer one stands to the emperor, the brighter that heavenly favor shines. Upon earth's square corners, beyond the favored circle of China, heaven shines not at all— which means that nothing important can come from beyond China's borders.
In other words, believers in *tianxia* cared mainly for Eastern, Chinese ideas, and little for Western ones.

To his military interests, Qianlong added deep interests in Chinese literature and art. These, too, Qianlong used to unify China.

FASCINATING FACTS: *Siku Quanshu*, Qianlong's "Complete Library in Four Branches of Literature" (1773 – 1782)

Midway through his 61-year reign, Qianlong commissioned a board of honored Chinese scholars to create what was to become the largest library in the world: the *Siku Quanshu*, a collection of all the greatest

Chinese writings in four categories: (1) classic literature; (2) history and geography; (3) philosophy, science and art; and (4) poetry and prose. Qianlong set three main goals for his *Siku Quanshu*:

1. To collect and preserve all the great literature and art China had accumulated over the centuries— works that defined the Chinese experience, the great privilege of belonging to the world's greatest culture.

2. To unite all Chinese in a common appreciation of these great works.

3. To destroy any literature that suggested, or even seemed to suggest, that the Qing dynasty might not be China's rightful ruling dynasty.

Interesting facts about the Siku Quanshu:
- In its final form, the *Siku Quanshu* consisted of about 36,000 volumes stuffed with more than 2 million pages containing a total of roughly 800 million words— many times larger than any other library on earth.

- Although the Chinese were the first to develop a movable-type printing press, Qianlong used no printing presses for the *Siku Quanshu*. Instead, he hired more than 3,800 artist/scholars to copy every word in beautiful hand calligraphy.

- Qianlong ordered seven copies of the *Siku Quanshu*, four for his imperial palaces and three for the public.

- In the process of creating his library, Qianlong destroyed almost as many books as he preserved— mainly books by authors who expressed a dim view of Manchurian outsiders seizing control of China.

The Qianlong Emperor at his studies

Thus Qianlong became the world's foremost collector, preserver and guardian of his beloved Chinese literature, art and culture.

Falling Behind the West

REFRESHING REMINDERS from Chapter 30: The **Industrial Revolution** was a revolution in Western manufacturing technology that took place from about 1750 – 1850.

In focusing so much on China, Qianlong ignored the Industrial Revolution that was going on in the West— a revolution that was rapidly propelling Western technology far beyond China's. While Britain was developing steam-driven, iron-clad battleships, China was still relying on the same old sail-driven, wooden-hulled junks it had used for centuries.

DEFINITIONS:
- The **Great Divergence** is a historian's term for the profound changes the Industrial Revolution brought to East – West relations during the early 1800s. Because the Industrial Revolution came earlier to the West than to the East, the West quickly bypassed the East in science, technology and economics— a development that allowed the West to dominate and humiliate the East.

- The **Century of Humiliation** was the hundred-plus years when the West took advantage of the Great Divergence to humiliate the once-proud Chinese, forcing them to bow to Western wills. China's humiliation began in 1839, when Britain launched its First Opium War against China (see below); and it lasted until 1949, when Chinese communist Mao Zedong founded the People's Republic of China (see Year Four).

INTERESTING IDEAS: The ironies of the Great Divergence and the Century of Humiliation could hardly have been greater. The Chinese of the Han, Tang and Song dynasty eras were the first to invent all sorts of technologies, including gunpowder, muskets and cannon. During the 1300s, the Italian merchant/author Marco Polo returned from his long stay in China marveling at Eastern wizardry, describing technological wonders that no Westerner had ever dreamed. By the 1800s, though, the Industrial Revolution carried Western technology so far beyond the East's that China was utterly defenseless against Britain.

Important though technology was, the Great Divergence was not the only explanation for China's Century of Humiliation. Late in Qianlong's reign, China began to suffer from other weaknesses, including:

1. The Canton System (est. 1757): Qianlong was a strong opponent of adopting Western technology, for two reasons: because he preferred China's old ways, and because he feared that rebel Chinese warlords might use modern technology to overthrow him. To prevent this, Qianlong set strict limits on contact between China and the West— trying to ensure that no Western technology found its way into Chinese hands.

Part of Qianlong's policy was to allow Chinese merchants to trade with Western merchants at only one port: **Canton**, now Guangzhou. Even at Canton, Qianlong allowed only a small, closely-watched group of merchants to deal directly with Westerners. Furthermore, Qianlong (1) restricted Westerners to a small section of Canton; (2) banished Westerners altogether during the winter months; (3) banned all Chinese from working for Westerners; and (4) banned all but a few Chinese from even speaking to Westerners.

Had Qianlong and his heirs been willing to accept even a few Western ideas, China's technology might have caught up to the West's more quickly. Instead, China fell farther and farther behind.

2. The Corruption of Heshen: Late in his reign, the elderly Qianlong placed his trust in a most untrustworthy bureaucrat: Niohuru Heshen, who would turn out to be one of the most corrupt public officials in history. Every year from 1780 through the end of Qianlong's reign in 1796, Heshen siphoned away a huge portion of the emperor's tax revenue for his own personal fortune. He also (1) stole priceless gifts intended for the emperor, (2) accepted bribes, and (3) granted illegal favors to corrupt businesses he co-owned. So unbelievably corrupt was Heshen that by 1799, he amassed a personal fortune worth some 10 – 15 times the amount Qianlong collected in taxes from all of China in a year.

Nor was Heshen alone in his corruption; for his corrupt example spread throughout the government he led, affecting the mindsets of both rich and poor Chinese:

- Among rich Chinese, Heshen's corruption helped build a sense of entitlement— as if the poor had always existed to serve the rich, and always would. Having no need to work, many rich Chinese grew lazy, weak and demanding, as did many officers of the corrupt Chinese military.

- Among poor Chinese, Heshen's corruption helped build a sense of hopelessness— for they couldn't help noticing how much of their tax money fell into the pockets of the rich, and how little came back to them in their times of need. Poor Chinese grew distrustful of their Qing government, and therefore less willing to make sacrifices for it.

Heshen, one of history's most corrupt public officials

FASCINATING FATES: Heshen's Fate (February 22, 1799)

Qianlong's son and heir, the future Jiaqing Emperor, knew of Heshen's corruption for years, but couldn't convince his father to investigate. Even after Qianlong stepped down as emperor in 1796, he continued to protect Heshen. Only after Qianlong died in 1799 could Jiaqing condemn Heshen to the fate his profound corruption earned him: death by slow slicing (see Chapter 13), later reduced to death by strangulation.

3. Opium Addiction: More money for the rich meant more money for indulging in one of the Chinese people's favorite vices: opium-smoking.

FASCINATING FACTS: Opium Addiction in China

- Opium began as a useful drug extracted from the not-quite-mature seed pods of the opium poppy flower. Since ancient times, doctors have used opium as analgesic (painkiller) to help patients through painful medical procedures— everything from pulling teeth to amputating legs.

- Sometime around the 1300s, some Easterners started using opium in a new way: as a recreational drug, beloved for the fun, long-lasting feelings of ease and well-being it offered its users. There were three main ways to enjoy this sticky drug: one might (1) eat it; (2) mix it with a drink; or (3) heat it until it vaporized, then scoop it into an opium pipe and inhale it.

1902 photograph of two Chinese addicts smoking in an opium den

- Because opium was so expensive, opium-smoking began mainly as a pleasant indulgence for a few rich Chinese. During the 1600s, though, the pleasures of New World tobacco began to spread around the world. Once tobacco reached China, even poor Chinese found a way to enjoy a bit of opium: by mixing it with tobacco to form a smoke-able blend called *madak*.

- The Chinese people's fondness for *madak* was so great, and its effect on them so damaging, that Qianlong's predecessor banned *madak* in 1729. However, he did not ban pure opium. Therefore instead of smoking *madak*, more and more addicts turned to smoking pure opium, which grew cheaper as the supply increased.

- Most of the opium the Chinese enjoyed came to them by way of British traders, who carried it to China from vast poppy fields in British India.

Opium and the British Balance of Trade

The fact that most opium came to China from British India led to a world-changing set of circumstances.

From the days of the ancient Silk Road, Westerners had treasured all sorts of goods from the Far East, especially fine porcelain, silk and tea. On the other hand, *tianxia*-believing Chinese like Qianlong wanted nothing to do with Western goods, however fine. Therefore when British merchants wanted to buy Chinese goods, they had nothing to offer in trade— except silver. As a result, silver began to grow rare and expensive in Britain.

> INTERESTING IDEAS: By offering British merchants tea, porcelain and silk, but accepting nothing but silver in return, China damaged Britain's **balance of trade**— its ability to trade goods from port to port around the world without creating a shortage of silver money. By the early 1800s, so much British silver had passed into Chinese hands that Britain suffered a severe silver shortage, threatening its all-important international trade.

The antidote to its silver shortage, Britain discovered, was opium. The more Chinese grew addicted to opium, the more silver flowed from Chinese hands into British ones; and the more silver flowed, the more opium the British supplied. By the late 1830s, British merchants were selling hundreds of tons of opium to the Chinese every year, which threatened China in two ways:

1. Opium imports reversed the balance of trade, to the point where China began to suffer the same silver shortage that Britain had suffered before.

2. The Chinese people's obsession with opium was ruining them— transforming them from an industrious people capable of mighty deeds into a broken people who cared only for their next opium fix.

When the Qianlong Emperor's successors— first his son the Jiaqing Emperor (reigned 1796 – 1820), and then his grandson the Daoguang Emperor (reigned 1820 – 1850)— understood what opium was doing to their people, they tried to set limits on the amount of opium coming into their country. With so many Chinese addicted to opium, though, British merchants had little trouble finding Chinese smugglers to buy their opium illegally.

COMPETENT COMMISSIONERS: Lin Zexu (1785 – 1850)

When China's opium troubles continued to mount, the Daoguang Emperor handed the problem off to one of his most capable public officials: Lin Zexu, whom Daoguang named Commissioner of Canton in late 1838. Because Canton was the only port where China allowed western merchants, it was the ideal place to attack the illegal opium trade.

Like the emperor, Lin Zexu viewed opium addiction as a moral danger that threatened to tear out the heart of the finest people on earth. Therefore Lin's first tactic was to attack the Chinese demand for opium. Within a few months, Lin Zexu:

1. Decreed the death penalty for any Chinese caught selling or smoking opium in Canton.

2. Closed down hundreds of opium dens, seizing thousands of opium pipes in the process.

3. Arrested hundreds of Chinese opium smugglers in and around Canton.

Lin Zexu

Destroying British Opium (June 3 – June 26, 1839)

Having done all he could to destroy the demand for opium, Lin Zexu set about destroying the supply. In searching Canton's many wharves, Lin discovered an astonishing amount of British and other opium waiting to be sold— some 22,000 cases of it, totaling more than 1,300 tons. Shuddering at the damage so much opium would do to the Chinese people, Lin commanded all foreign merchants to hand over their opium for destruction.

For a time, British opium merchants tried making the same corrupt bargains with Lin that they had once made with Heshen. Their plan was to hand over part of their opium for destruction, enough to convince the emperor that Lin was doing a good job fighting the opium trade. To compensate Lin for his trouble, British merchants were more than happy to pay him hefty bribes.

Much to their dismay, the merchants discovered that Lin was nothing like Heshen. Lin Zexu was no corrupt bureaucrat, but rather a moral paragon on a mission to save the Chinese people.

After Lin refused their bribes, the foreigners finally, reluctantly handed over all of their opium for destruction. Lin's laborers spent more than three weeks:

1. Breaking open all 22,000 cases of opium.
2. Mixing all 1,300 tons of valuable opium with salt and lime, thoroughly destroying it.
3. Dissolving the resulting mess in Canton harbor.

Lin Zexu supervising laborers as they break open opium cases and destroy their contents

CRITICAL COMPARISONS: The value of the 22,000 cases of opium Lin Zexu destroyed was many times that of the 342 cases of tea American patriots destroyed at the 1773 Boston Tea Party. Negotiations at the end of the First Opium War set the wasted opium's value at 6 million silver dollars, more than enough to launch a war.

ILLUMINATING EXCERPTS from Lin Zexu's Open Letter to Queen Victoria of Britain (1839)

Even as Lin Zexu destroyed a fortune in British opium, he composed a letter to Britain's Queen Victoria scolding her for the terrible misdeed her greedy merchants were perpetrating in China— forcing their deadly opium on innocent Chinese. According to Lin's letter to the Queen:

- "…we of the heavenly dynasty nourished and cherished your people from afar… It is merely from these circumstances, that your country— deriving immense advantage from its commercial intercourse with us, which has endured now two hundred years— has become the rich and flourishing kingdom that it is said to be!" *In other words: Britain owes all its prosperity to China, the all-important Inner Kingdom at the center of the world.*

- "Some [British merchants]… by means of introducing opium by stealth, have seduced our Chinese people, and caused every province of the land to overflow with that poison… Without meaning to say that the foreigners harbor such destructive intentions in their hearts, we yet positively assert that from their inordinate thirst after gain, they are perfectly careless about the injuries they inflict upon us! And such being the case, we should like to ask: What has become of that conscience which heaven has implanted in the breasts of all men?" *In other words: Instead of being grateful for the prosperity China has generously allowed them, greedy British smugglers insist on selling opium to the Chinese— even though they know that opium addiction is destroying their customers. Where, Lin asks, are these merchants' consciences?*

- "It is only in sundry parts of your colonial kingdom of Hindustan [India] where the very hills are covered with the opium plant… You, the queen… ought immediately to have the plant in those parts plucked up by the very root! Cause the land there to be hoed up afresh, sow in its stead the five grains, and if any man dare again to plant in these grounds a single poppy, visit his crime with the most severe punishment!" *In other words: Lin asks Queen Victoria to (1) root up every opium poppy in British India; (2) replant former opium fields in wheat, barley or other beneficial grains; and (3) punish opium farming as a serious crime.*

Unfortunately, Lin's letter reached Britain too late to shame young Queen Victoria into calling off the First Opium War.

The First Opium War (1839 – 1842)

Commissioner Lin Zexu's destruction of a fortune in British opium was only one of several incidents that destroyed China's once-friendly relationship with Britain. Other incidents included:

1. The Kowloon Incident (July 7, 1839): One evening in July 1839, several drunken British sailors who were on shore leave at Kowloon— one of Canton's many sub-ports— beat a Chinese man so severely that he died the next day. As Commissioner of Canton, Lin Zexu ordered British officials to hand these soldiers over to him for punishment. The British refused, arguing that they couldn't possibly hand British citizens over to China's justice system— a barbaric system in which Chinese police still tortured suspects into making false confessions.

Lin Zexu was so outraged over this insult to Chinese justice that he took his first hard steps toward driving the British out of Canton. Among other things, Lin: (1) cut off British traders' privileges in Canton; (2) banned all Chinese from selling food to British traders; and (3) posted signs indicating that he had poisoned the water wells British traders used. Lin's message was clear: British traders were no longer welcome in Canton, nor anywhere else in China.

2. The *Thomas Coutts* Incident (October 1839): Between August and October, Lin Zexu offered to restore trade privileges to any British trader who pledged never to sell opium. Official British policy was that no British trader was to sign Lin's pledge. However, not all traders agreed. When the captain of the Quaker-owned British trader *Thomas Coutts* arrived in Canton that October, he immediately signed Lin's pledge— for the morally upright Quakers wanted nothing to do with Britain's filthy opium trade.

Steam-driven British warships destroying old-fashioned Chinese junks

To prevent any more traders from joining the *Thomas Coutts*, the British commander ordered a blockade of the Pearl River. When Chinese warships came out to challenge the blockade, Britain's superior warships sank several of them. Although the two sides had yet to declare war, the sinking of several Chinese warships rendered the First Opium War inevitable.

INTERESTING INQUIRIES into the Causes of the First Opium War

Different historians offer different opinions on the First Opium War's causes:

- Some place all blame for the war squarely on the British, arguing that Britons fought only to preserve their profitable opium trade. Without that trade, Britain would have suffered enormous losses, including (1) its favorable balance of trade with China; (2) the immense profits generated by poppy fields in British India; and (3) the 6 million silver dollars owed to British traders for the opium Lin Zexu destroyed.

- Others place equal blame on the Chinese— arguing that the Chinese could have avoided the war had they been less proud, and more open-minded. If the Chinese had treated the British as equal trade partners, and

==not as upstart barbarians intruding on the affairs of their Chinese superiors, then both sides might have felt less need to defend their international reputations.==

In the war that followed, Britain's greatest advantages were steam-driven, iron-hulled warships like *Nemesis*, the first of several Britain sent to fight the First Opium War. These potent destructors offered numerous benefits:

- They could attack anywhere, anytime, regardless of the wind.
- They could tow Britain's sail-driven ships of the line into attack position anytime, also regardless of the wind.
- Their shallow drafts allowed them to penetrate far up China's many rivers.
- Their sturdy iron hulls were all but impervious to Chinese cannon.

Armed with such superior weapons, the British had little trouble overcoming the primitive Chinese, even on China's very doorstep. By 1841, British troops controlled all of Canton— which meant that they controlled all trade along southern China's main river, the Pearl. By mid-1842, British troops controlled Shanghai as well— which meant that they controlled all trade along middle China's main river, the Yangtze, dividing China south from north. In the process, British troops and sailors killed as many as 20,000 Chinese, while suffering fewer than 70 dead on the British side.

Britain's first iron steam warship, the Nemesis, destroying Chinese war junks

The Treaty of Nanjing (1842)

Faced with such staggering losses, the Daoguang Emperor had little choice but to swallow his pride and negotiate a humiliating peace. Under the terms of the Treaty of Nanjing, signed aboard the British ship of the line *Cornwallis* on August 29, 1842:

- China opened four more ports to British trade, for a total of five "treaty ports": **Canton, Shanghai, Amoy, Fuzhou and Ningbo**. Within those ports, British traders would be free to negotiate with the Chinese as they chose, with little interference from customs officials.
- China offered British traders a low, fixed tariff rate on all goods imported to China— a rate the Chinese could never boost without British permission.
- China agreed to pay the British a tremendous amount of money: 6 million silver dollars for the opium Lin Zexu destroyed, plus another 14-15 million silver dollars to cover war costs and bad debts.
- **China ceded the island of Hong Kong to Britain**, making it a permanent British territory— a well-placed port on China's doorstep where British traders could always be certain of a warm welcome.

==A LOOK AHEAD: Hong Kong will remain a British overseas territory for more than 150 years— until 1997, when Britain will finally return Hong Kong to Chinese control.==

INTERESTING IDEAS: Treaty Ports in China

A **treaty port** was any Chinese port where Western traders enjoyed special privileges under the Treaty of Nanjing or later treaties. The unique features of Chinese-British treaty ports included these:

- **The British Quarter:** Each treaty port contained a "British quarter," a section of the city that operated much like a British colony. Within their quarters, the British built British-style homes, schools and Christian churches; operated exclusive private clubs at which no Chinese were allowed; and generally behaved as if they were living on British soil.

- **Extraterritoriality:** British citizens living in treaty ports obeyed British law, not Chinese law— which meant that British citizens who committed crimes on Chinese soil were tried in British courts, not Chinese ones.

Together, these features had a humiliating effect on China. Although the British never controlled China as they did India, the extraordinary freedom they enjoyed in their treaty ports made it seem as if they did.

Soon after the Treaty of Nanjing, other Western nations signed treaties with China, and built quarters of their own at certain treaty ports. These countries included France, Germany, Austria, Italy, Portugal, Belgium, Russia and the United States. Several decades later, a fast-rising Japan acquired Chinese treaty ports as well.

One of the few concessions the Chinese received in the Treaty of Nanjing was that the rest of China— all non-treaty ports, along with all of China's interior— remained sealed off against unwanted Western influence.

ANOTHER LOOK AHEAD: At the end of the Second Opium War (1856 – 1860), China will lose even the privilege of sealing itself against Western influence. Under the 1858 Treaty of Tianjin, Britain will force China to open 11 more treaty ports to British traders, and to open its whole interior to Westerners— including Christian missionaries like Hudson Taylor, who will penetrate China's interior for the first time.

FASCINATING FACTS: The *I Ching*, or the "Book of Changes"

The *I Ching* is an extremely old work of Chinese philosophy that the Chinese have long used to divine the will of heaven. For example, Ming dynasty founder Zhu Yuanzhang probably used the *I Ching* when he was trying to decide how best to escape the Red Turban Rebellion— and wound up joining it instead (see Chapter 13).

There are many ways to consult the *I Ching*. One common way is to cast a set of three coins six times, all the while concentrating on the question one wants heaven to answer. The diviner then takes the results of these coin tosses to a chart, which reveals one of 64 different answers: good fortune or bad fortune, prosperity or poverty, joy or sorrow, harmony or discord.

FASCINATING FACTS: Fan-Tan

Fan-Tan is a Chinese gambling game that dates back to the Han dynasty, which governed China from 206 BC – 220 AD. According to legend, the Han dynasty government once needed to raise taxes, but feared that doing so might anger its citizens; so instead, it started sponsoring Fan-Tan games all over the city, two every morning and two every evening. Because the government received a portion of the winnings from each round of Fan-Tan, it didn't matter who won— only that the Chinese loved to play, which most of them did.

To play a round of Fan-Tan, the dealer scoops a double handful of "cash"— beans, buttons, beads or other small objects— into a square frame on a flat tabletop. He then covers the cash while players place their bets around the square, gambling on the answer to this question: how many cash will be left over when the pile is divided by four? After all bets are in, the dealer uses a crook-ended stick to count out four cash at a time, until there are no more groups of four left. The number of cash left over determines the winner: if there is one cash left over, then those who placed their bets on side one of the square win, and so on.

FASCINATING FACTS: The Tangram

The tangram is an ancient Chinese puzzle with a unique origin. According to legend, the tangram comes from a time before glass was common in China. When a king demanded glass for a new window, an elderly Chinese sage undertook the task of carrying a precious pane of glass to the palace. With great care, the sage carried his thoroughly-padded glass safely across deserts, rivers, valleys and mountains— only to drop it just when the palace came in view.

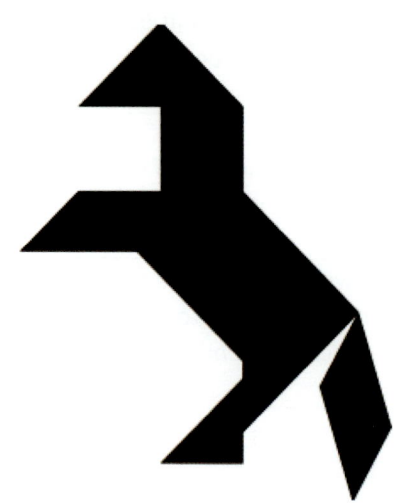

Upon unwrapping the square pane, sage and king discovered to their delight that it had broken into seven regular shapes. By rearranging these shapes, the sage was able to illustrate the tale of his journey for the king. Thus arose the tangram—a puzzle whose object is to rearrange the seven geometric shapes in the picture to fit inside a given silhouette. The silhouette might represent anything at all— a man, a house, a sailboat, a mountain range or anything in between.

Tangram silhouette of a rearing horse

MIGHTY MISSIONARIES: Adoniram Judson (1788 – 1850) and Anne Judson (1789 – 1826)

One of the United States' very first overseas missionaries, Massachusetts-born Adoniram Judson, followed an unusual path to Christian faith. Adoniram's father was a strict New England Congregationalist who sent his son to Rhode Island College, the future Brown University, because he believed this Baptist-founded college to be less infected with liberal ideas than Harvard or Yale. The father's caution failed to protect the son, though. At Rhode Island College, Adoniram soon met a charismatic upperclassman who did precisely as the father feared, persuading Adoniram to become an atheist.

A few years later, Adoniram spent a miserable night at an inn, tortured by desperate moans issuing from a dying man in the next room. All night, Adoniram longed to offer this stranger some sort of comfort; but all night, he remembered that godless men like himself could offer the dying no comfort whatsoever. Sometime that night, the man died. The next morning, Adoniram was horrified to learn that the dead man was no stranger, but in fact his charismatic atheist friend from college! Shaken at the idea of his friend beginning an eternity in hell, Adoniram returned to his father, who soon persuaded him to return to his Christian faith.

Adoniram Judson

In 1812, the now staunchly-Christian, newly-married Adoniram Judson embarked from Salem, Massachusetts to begin one of the most remarkable lives of suffering and persevering for Christ the world has ever seen. Adoniram and his wife Anne wanted to minister in India, but couldn't get permission from the stubbornly anti-missionary East India Company. Instead, they moved across the Bay of Bengal to Burma (modern-day Myanmar). The Judsons made their first home in Rangoon, Burma with Felix Carey, son of William Carey, who wrote to tell his father that the Judsons possessed the perfect temperaments for the hard work of sharing the gospel among the Burmese.

Hard indeed was that work; for the Burmese government detested Christians, and the Burmese language proved far more difficult to learn than Bengali. The Judsons studied Burmese for years, sometimes for 12 hours a day, before they finally grew comfortable enough to start sharing their faith. Adoniram labored for 6 years before he won his first Christian convert, and 10 years before he won more than a dozen or so. Meanwhile, Anne lost their first two children to deadly jungle fevers, and had to go back to the United States to recover her own health.

Not long after Anne returned to Burma in 1823, the Anglo-Burmese War broke out between Burma and the EIC. At once, the Burmese government accused Adoniram of spying for the British. Adoniram spent the next twenty-one months in miserable Burmese prisons, chained, abused and starving. During this impossibly difficult time, Anne proved the most faithful wife imaginable. Instead of giving up on her husband, Anne risked her life traipsing from office to office, begging stone-faced Burmese officials to release Adoniram. Six months into Adoniram's imprisonment, Anne bore the couple's third child. After that, Anne started carrying the infant along with her on prison visits, until both mother and child grew seriously ill.

Anne Judson

Near the end of the Anglo-Burmese War, the Burmese finally realized that they had imprisoned one of the few men in all the world who was capable of negotiating directly with the British on their behalf. Thus the Burmese freed Adoniram to work as their translator, although they still guarded him closely. A few months after Adoniram's release came the worst tragedies of all— for Anne Judson died, and so did their third child.

Apostle to the Karen People (1826 – 1850)

Only after all of this suffering did Adoniram's labor in Burma finally begin to bear fruit. That fruit came mainly among the Karen people— a tribe whose heritage differed from that of other Burmese, most of whom were Buddhists. Karen legends bore striking similarities to stories from the Bible, including a creation story in which God created woman from the rib of man. Another Karen legend held that long ago, God gave each of two brothers— one a dark-skinned Karen, the other white— copies of a precious Book of Gold containing God's plan of salvation. Nearly as long ago, the white brother sailed far away, taking his copy of the Book of Gold with him. Since then, the Karen brother had lost his copy of the book. Therefore when white missionaries appeared from across the sea with a book containing God's plan of salvation, the Karen were more than ready to listen.

Through the Karen, God rewarded Adoniram's persistence with more converts than he had ever dared dream. Upon arriving in Burma in 1813, Adoniram had set a modest goal of eventually founding a single church of 100 members. Instead, Adoniram helped found about 100 churches, with more than 8,000 members.

U.S. STATE FOCUS

Missouri

FASCINATING FACTS about Missouri:

- **State Capital**: Jefferson City
- **State Abbreviation**: MO
- **Statehood**: Missouri became the 24th US state on August 10, 1821.
- **Area**: About 70,000 square miles (Ranks 21st in size)
- **Bordering States**: Iowa, Nebraska, Kansas, Oklahoma, Arkansas, Tennessee, Kentucky, Illinois
- **Meaning of Name**: Missouri takes its name from a Native American people called the Missouria, whose name meant "people of the canoes."
- **State Nickname**: "Show-Me State"
- **State Bird**: Eastern bluebird
- **State Tree**: Flowering dogwood
- **State Flower**: White hawthorn blossom
- **State Song**: "Missouri Waltz" by J. Eppel and J.R. Shannon
- **State Motto**: *Salus populi suprema lex esto*, Latin for "Let the welfare of the people be the highest law"
- **Historic Places to Visit**: Lewis and Clark State Park, Pony Express National Museum, Harry S Truman National Historic Site, Ulysses S. Grant Historic Site, George Washington Carver National Monument, Mark Twain Boyhood Home and Museum, Laura Ingalls Wilder House
- **Resources and Industries**: Agriculture, food processing

Gateway Arch in St. Louis, Missouri

State Flag: Missouri's coat of arms on a red, white and blue field. Twenty-four stars surrounding the coat of arms represent Missouri's admission as the 24th state. The coat of arms contains a shield with the Great Seal of the United States on the right, and two symbols of Missouri on the left: a just-past-new moon to represent great potential, and a grizzly bear to represent strength. Wrapped around these symbols is the motto "United We Stand, Divided We Fall"— which is actually Kentucky's state motto, not Missouri's. Two more grizzlies support the shield. Underneath all is wrapped a banner with Missouri's true state motto, along with the Roman numerals for 1820, the year of the Missouri Compromise.

PRESIDENTIAL FOCUS

PRESIDENT #8: Martin Van Buren (1782 – 1862)	
In Office: March 4, 1837 – March 4, 1841	**Political Party:** Democratic
Birthplace: New York	**Nickname:** "The Little Magician," "Martin Van Ruin"

Like Andrew Jackson before him, Martin Van Buren was a poor man's president, one who rose from common circumstances to the highest office in the land. Van Buren's legal career began at age 15, when his father— a Dutch-American farmer and innkeeper from Kinderhook, New York, about 20 miles south of Albany— found him an apprenticeship in a local law office. By age 30, Van Buren was a highly successful attorney with enough wealth to pursue his greater interests: first New York politics, and then national politics. Van Buren served in the New York State Senate from 1812 – 1820, doubling as New York's Attorney General from 1815 – 1819, before serving in the U.S. Senate from 1820 – 1828.

Van Buren's greatest gift was his natural ability to organize politicians into tight-knit, loyal voting blocs. In a time when the Federalist Party was dying out, Van Buren reminded a divided Democratic-Republican Party of the tremendous power that came with party loyalty— the power to sweep aside a less-organized, less-loyal opposition party, and thus dominate a legislature. When Andrew Jackson needed someone to organize New York voters for the election of 1828, he turned to the noted political bargainer New Yorkers called "the Little Magician." After Jackson won, he rewarded Van Buren with a job as U.S. Secretary of State from 1829 – 1831. Then in the election of 1832, Van Buren easily won election as the popular Jackson's vice president. Thus Martin Van Buren stands beside Andrew Jackson as co-creator of the modern-day Democratic Party.

Van Buren won the presidential election of 1836 mainly by promising to follow in the popular Jackson's footsteps. Unfortunately for Van Buren, the first year of his presidency was also the first year of the Panic of 1837— a deep economic depression that left many Americans poor, hungry and homeless. As a believer in limited powers for the federal government, Van Buren was reluctant to take the strong steps his Whig opponents recommended to relieve the Panic of 1837. Whether or not those steps would have helped, the Whigs succeeded in blaming "Martin van Ruin" for the Panic of 1837, which led to his defeat in the election of 1840.

Fun Facts about Martin Van Buren:
- As a New Yorker of Dutch heritage, van Buren spoke Dutch as his first language, and English as his second.
- Van Buren was the first president born after the Declaration of Independence, and thus the first born a U.S. citizen.
- Van Buren's close friendship with Andrew Jackson made him an enemy of Jackson's enemies, some of whom were deadly duelists like Jackson. To defend himself, Van Buren took to carrying loaded pistols wherever he went— even into the U.S. Senate, which he chaired as Vice President of the United States.
- President Van Buren once received two tiger cubs as gifts from the Sultan of Oman.

Notable Quotes from Martin Van Buren:
- "The less government interferes with private pursuits, the better for general prosperity."
- "As to the presidency, the two happiest days of my life were those of my entrance upon the office and my surrender of it."

CHAPTER 32: The Abolitionist Movement; the Boers in South Africa

U.S. HISTORY FOCUS

The Abolitionist Movement in the United States

DEFINITION: **Abolitionism** was a movement to outlaw slavery. In the Thirteen Colonies/United States, the abolitionist movement began among the Quakers in the 1680s, and ended with the passage of the 13th Amendment to the Constitution— the amendment that permanently banned slavery as of 1865, the last year of the U.S. Civil War.

Before the Revolutionary War, slavery was legal in all Thirteen Colonies, both Southern and Northern. From the beginning, though, Southern colonists bought far more slaves than Northern ones did; for the Southern economy depended on slave labor to raise vast quantities of tobacco, cotton and the like— cash crops that thrived only in the warm, sunny South. Thus the institution of slavery grew strong in the South, but dwindled in the North.

Virginia slaves processing tobacco around 1670

REFRESHING REMINDERS: To protect their investments in slaves, Southern slaveholders wrote ever harsher laws like Virginia's 1705 slave code, part of which read:

"All servants imported and brought into the Country... who were not Christians in their native Country... shall be ... slaves. All Negro, mulatto [half-Negro, half-white] and Indian [Native American] slaves within this dominion... shall be held to be real estate. If any slave resist his master... correcting such slave, and shall happen to be killed in such correction... the master shall be free of all punishment... as if such accident never happened." *In other words*: According to some racist Southern laws, a non-white slave was a piece of property, no different than a barn, plow or horse; and to beat a slave to death was no crime.

Early Quaker Abolitionists

The strictly moral Quakers were among the first to be troubled by the evils of slavery.

The first Quaker farmers in the colonies did as their non-Quaker neighbors did: finding land plentiful, but labor scarce, they bought slaves to perform the endless work of clearing land and tending farms. From the beginning, though, Quakers were uneasy about the un-Christian cruelty that went hand-in-hand with slaveholding. Early Quaker critics of slavery included:

- **George Fox (1624 – 1691):** The founder of the Quaker movement, George Fox, first questioned the morality of slavery during a visit to slaveholding Quaker friends on Barbados in 1671.

- **Francis Pastorius (1651 – 1720?):** Pastorius was the founder of the first permanent German-speaking settlement in the New World: Germantown, Pennsylvania. In 1688, Pastorius promoted the **Germantown Quaker Petition against Slavery**, which argued that any Christian who honored Christ's Golden Rule— "Do to others what you would have them do to you," Matthew 7:12— should be ashamed of holding slaves.

- **John Woolman (1720 – 1772):** Woolman was a young clerk who first considered the evils of slavery when his employer, a Quaker storekeeper, asked him to write a bill of sale for a slave he was selling. Even this minuscule role in the dirty business of slave trading troubled Woolman's conscience enough to change his life. A few years later, Woolman became a wandering preacher with one main mission in life: to persuade the Quakers of the middle colonies (Pennsylvania, Delaware, New Jersey and New York) to liberate their slaves.

Like George Fox, John Woolman drew attention to his beliefs by paying the strictest attention to moral details. In the case of slavery, this meant refusing to benefit from slave labor in any way. For example, if Woolman spent a night in a slaveholder's home, then he insisted on paying the slaves for any services they performed for him, just as if they weren't slaves.

ILLUMINATING EXCERPTS from John Woolman's "Considerations on the Keeping of Negroes" (Published 1754)

In 1754, wandering preacher John Woolman asked some of his fellow Quakers for help publishing "Considerations on the Keeping of Negroes," a 4,000-word essay he wrote on the ills of slavery. Woolman's main arguments in "Considerations" were these:

1. That Africans were Europeans' brothers, not their inferiors. If Africans seemed inferior, it was only because they lacked the education and opportunities available to Europeans.
2. That to subject Africans to the terrible evils of slavery just so Europeans could enjoy more comfortable lifestyles was a grave sin, a sign of extreme arrogance and misplaced pride.
3. That any European who was thoughtless enough to continue in the terrible sin of slavery was likely to face terrible punishment from God in the next life.

Woolman also pleaded with his readers to consider the true costs of slaveholding:

"When trade is carried on productive of much misery, and they who suffer by it are many thousand miles off, the danger is the greater of not laying their sufferings to heart. In procuring slaves on the coast of Africa, many children are stolen privately; wars are encouraged among the Negroes, but all is at a great distance. Many groans arise from dying men which we hear not. Many cries are uttered by widows and fatherless children which reach not our ears. Many cheeks are wet with tears, and faces sad with unutterable grief, which we see not. Cruel tyranny is encouraged. The hands of robbers are strengthened.

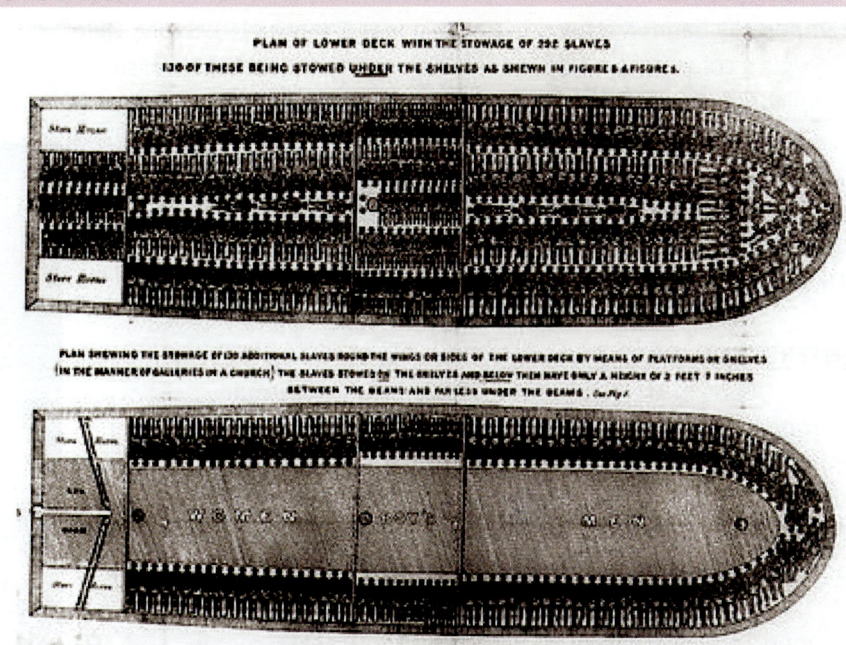

From a plan illustrating how slave traders crowded slaves onto their ships' decks

"Were we, for the term of one year only, to be eyewitnesses of what passeth in getting these slaves; were the blood that is there shed to be sprinkled on our garments; were the poor captives, bound with thongs, and heavily laden with elephants' teeth, to pass before our eyes on their way to the sea; were their bitter lamentations, day after day, to ring in our ears, and their mournful cries in the night to hinder us from sleeping— were we to behold and hear these things, what pious heart would not be deeply affected with sorrow?"

In other words: Most slaveholders are comfortable with slavery only because they don't have to watch the immeasurable suffering that goes with capturing Africans, enslaving them and shipping them to the Americas. If slaveholders took this suffering to heart, then they would all be ashamed to take part in it.

Woolman's abolitionist ministry worked. In 1758, the Philadelphia Yearly Meeting of Quakers became the first to add its voice to Woolman's, officially calling upon all Quakers to liberate their slaves. With that, Quakers in Pennsylvania and other colonies started paying visits to slaveholding Quakers, quietly pressuring them to liberate their slaves. Within a few years, Quaker meetings throughout the middle colonies were refusing membership to slaveholders. By the Revolutionary War years, very few Quakers held slaves.

Abolitionism and the Enlightenment

Besides Christian feeling, the other great driving force behind the abolitionist movement was the Enlightenment— the liberty-loving philosophy of Locke, Montesquieu, Rousseau and Voltaire (see Chapters 21 and 25). For slaveholding patriots of the American Revolution, Enlightenment philosophy raised an uncomfortable contradiction: with one hand, they were fighting for their own liberty; while with the other, they were fighting to deprive their slaves of liberty. This hypocrisy made slaveholding patriots no better than the arrogant king they fought to overthrow, the tyrannical George III.

The Enlightenment also raised a second contradiction: How could any government based on the principles of equality, liberty and human rights justify enslaving people based on the color of their skin? British author Samuel Johnson shamed American patriots when he asked in 1775, "How is it that we hear the loudest yelps for liberty among the drivers of Negroes?"

REFRESHING REMINDERS: One Enlightenment thinker who defended Africans' rights was James Oglethorpe, who temporarily banned slavery in Georgia (see Chapter 19). Sadly, Oglethorpe's slavery ban lasted only a few years. Georgia's colonists protested that their economy couldn't possibly succeed without slave labor— not when their main competitors, South Carolina and the West Indies, used slave labor so freely.

Other Enlightenment thinkers who wrestled with slavery included three of the United States' best-known founding fathers: Benjamin Franklin, George Washington and Thomas Jefferson.

INTERESTING IDEAS: Franklin's Changing Views on Slavery

Early in life, Benjamin Franklin believed as many Europeans and their descendants did: that Africans were an inferior race born to slavery. Franklin himself held slaves, though nowhere near as many as Washington or Jefferson. Franklin also supported slavery by publishing slave traders' advertisements in his newspaper, the Pennsylvania *Gazette*.

By mid-life, Franklin's views on slavery began to change. Around 1760, a group of abolitionists who Franklin met in London asked him to help establish schools for black children in Philadelphia. After a visit to one such school, Franklin reported:

Benjamin Franklin in London, 1767

"[The black children] appeared all to have made considerable progress in reading... I was on the whole much pleased, and from what I then saw, have conceived a higher opinion of the natural capacities of the black race, than I had ever before entertained. Their apprehension seems as quick, their memory as strong, and their docility in every respect equal to that of white children." *In other words:* By the time Franklin entered his 60s, he came to believe that black children could learn as well as white ones, provided they received the same opportunities.

Franklin expressed even stronger abolitionist opinions when he reached his 80s. From 1787 through the last year of his life, 1790, Franklin served as President of the Pennsylvania Society for the Abolition of Slavery. Among the last works Franklin ever published was this society's February, 1790 "Petition to the Senate & House of Representatives of the United States," which called on Congress to devote:

"... serious attention to the subject of slavery, that you will be pleased to countenance the restoration of liberty to those unhappy men [blacks], who alone, in this land of Freedom, are degraded into perpetual bondage, and who, amidst the general Joy of surrounding freemen, are groaning in servile subjection, that you will devise means for removing this inconsistency from the character of the American people..." *In other words:* By the end of his life, Franklin came to believe that slavery was completely inconsistent with America's founding ideals of liberty and equal rights for all. He therefore called on Congress to abolish slavery in the United States.

However, Franklin never believed that the answer was simply to liberate all slaves immediately; for:

"Slavery is such an atrocious debasement of human nature, that its very extirpation, if not performed with solicitous care, may sometimes open a source of serious evils... The unhappy man, who has long been treated as a brute animal, too frequently sinks beneath the common standard of the human species. The galling chains, that bind his body, do also fetter his intellectual faculties, and impair the social affections of his heart... Under such circumstances, freedom may often prove a misfortune to himself, and prejudicial to society." *In other words:* For the good of all, both slave and free, Franklin wanted to educate America's slaves as thoroughly as possible before liberating them— for he feared that their years in bondage had weakened them in both mind and heart, leaving them completely unprepared for the challenges of living as free people.

INTERESTING IDEAS: Washington's Changing Views on Slavery

Like nearly all Virginia farmers, George Washington held slaves for most of his life. When Washington died in 1799, his Mount Vernon plantation was home to more than 300 slaves. About 120 belonged to Washington himself; about 150 belonged to his wife Martha, who inherited them from her late first husband Daniel Custis; and about 40 were rented from other slaveholders.

Like Franklin, Washington came to doubt the morality of slavery later in life— perhaps because the free blacks who served with him in the Revolutionary War taught him a greater respect for the African race. As president, Washington sometimes spoke of abolishing slavery, but never did so— probably because his highest priority was holding the new Union together. Washington probably calculated that the Southern states would rebel at the first sign that the new federal government meant to take away their slaves— especially since that government was operating out of Philadelphia, which was full of abolitionist Quakers.

Only at the end of his life did Washington make his strong abolitionist opinions known. Months before he died in late 1799, Washington abruptly wrote a new will that included a detailed plan for liberating Mount Vernon's slaves. Washington's will explained that he would have liberated his own slaves immediately had they not intermarried with Martha's slaves, whom he had no legal power to liberate. These intermarriages meant that liberating his

Washington with his personal servant/slave Billy Lee

own slaves would break up slave families, a heartache Washington hoped to avoid. Therefore instead of liberating his slaves at his own death, Washington chose to liberate them at Martha's death— hoping that Martha would liberate hers as well, which would hold slave families together.

Washington's will also contained two extraordinary provisions for his slaves:

1. Any slave who was under the age of 25 at Washington's death, and who had no parents to care for him, was to be taught reading, writing and some profitable trade before going out into the world.

2. As if expecting his heirs to deny his wishes, Washington added this forceful paragraph:

"... I do hereby expressly forbid the sale, or transportation out of [Virginia], of any slave I may die possessed of, under any pretense whatsoever. And I do moreover most pointedly, and most solemnly enjoin it upon my executors... to see that this clause respecting slaves... be religiously fulfilled... without evasion, neglect or delay."

FASCINATING FACTS: Jefferson's Views on Slavery

No founding father wrote more on the issue of slavery than Thomas Jefferson, who agonized over it again and again in documents like these:

1. **The Declaration of Independence (1776):** The final version of the Declaration of Independence affirmed "that all men are created equal," and "that they are endowed by their Creator with certain unalienable rights." In Jefferson's mind, those affirmations applied to all people, black or white.

    An earlier version of the Declaration also included this grievance against King George III:

    "He has waged cruel war against human nature itself, violating its most sacred rights of life and liberty in the persons of a distant people who never offended him [Africans]; captivating and carrying them into slavery in another hemisphere, or to incur miserable death in their transportation thither..."

    1800 portrait of Thomas Jefferson

    Against Jefferson's wishes, pro-slavery delegates to the Continental Congress insisted on striking this grievance out of the final version.

2. *Notes on the State of Virginia* **(1781):** In this description of Virginia life and government, Jefferson wrote:

    "There must, doubtless, be an unhappy influence on the manners of our people, produced by the existence of slavery among us. The whole commerce between master and slave is a perpetual exercise of the most boisterous passions— the most unremitting despotism on the one part, and degrading submissions on the other." <u>In other words</u>: *The institution of slavery damages the characters of both races— that is, it makes tyrants of whites, and sorely weakens blacks.*

3. **The Northwest Ordinance (1787)** As a delegate to the Confederation Congress, Jefferson included this line in the law governing the Northwest Territory:

    "There shall be neither slavery nor involuntary servitude in the [Northwest] Territory, otherwise than in the punishment of crimes whereof the party shall have been duly convicted."

By insisting on this crucial line, Jefferson guaranteed that slavery could never advance into the territory that was to become the five states of Ohio, Indiana, Illinois, Michigan and Wisconsin.

Ironically, the founding father who criticized slavery more than any other usually held about 200 slaves on his Monticello plantation. Of these, Jefferson liberated only two during his lifetime, and only five more in his will. Jefferson's reasons for liberating so few slaves probably included these:

1. Like Franklin, Jefferson believed that years of bondage had weakened his slaves' minds and hearts, which meant that they would need years of education before they could survive as free people.

2. Jefferson feared dire consequences if too many slaveholders released their slaves to live in Virginia as free blacks. Like many slaveholders, Jefferson predicted that any slave who lived near free blacks would naturally covet their freedom for himself, leading to slave rebellions and race wars. For this reason, Jefferson recommended sending free blacks elsewhere— perhaps out West, or perhaps to Africa.

3. Between Washington's death in 1799 and Jefferson's in 1826, changes in Virginia law made liberating slaves far more difficult. For example, an 1806 law required all liberated slaves to leave the state within a year, or else return to slavery. Sadly, this meant that liberated slaves would have to leave behind their still-enslaved families, which many slaves were loath to do.

For all his good intentions about abolishing slavery, Jefferson remained unconvinced that blacks were whites' intellectual equals. One black who challenged Jefferson's thinking on this was Benjamin Banneker.

AMAZING AFRICAN AMERICANS: Benjamin Banneker (1731 – 1806)

Benjamin Banneker was a free black born to two black parents near what is now Ellicott City, Maryland, just west of Baltimore. Under colonial law, black children inherited their status from their mothers, either slave or free. Because Benjamin's mother was a free black, Benjamin was as well.

From childhood, Benjamin showed an aptitude for science and engineering that would have been remarkable for anyone, white or black. For example:

- After a friend gave him a clock to examine, Benjamin carved his own working clock entirely out of wood. Benjamin' wooden-geared clock kept excellent time for about 40 years, until a house fire destroyed it on the day of his funeral.

- Benjamin was approaching old age when he taught himself the math-intensive sciences of astronomy and surveying. As an astronomer, Benjamin published a new almanac in which he correctly predicted solar eclipses. As a surveyor, Benjamin assisted Pierre L'Enfant and others in marking out the new city of Washington, D.C. (see Chapter 24).

After ill health forced him to leave the Washington D.C. project in 1791, Benjamin sent Thomas Jefferson a copy of one of his almanacs— hoping that if he offered Jefferson this proof of his intelligence, then Jefferson might agree that black minds were as good as white ones. Benjamin's letter chided Jefferson with these words:

"... how pitiable is it to reflect, that although you were so fully convinced of the benevolence of the Father of mankind, and of his equal and impartial distribution of those rights and privileges which he had conferred upon them, that you should at the same time counteract his mercies, in detaining by fraud and violence so numerous a part of my brethren under groaning captivity and cruel oppression, that you should at the same time be found guilty of that most criminal act, which you professedly detested in others, with respect to yourselves." *In other words: It is sad to think that the man who defended human rights so eloquently in the Declaration of Independence still participates in an institution that robs so many of their God-given rights.*

Near the end of his life, a tired, discouraged Thomas Jefferson wrote that he despaired of abolishing slavery in his lifetime, and had decided to leave the issue in God's hands:

> "We are not in a world ungoverned by the laws and the power of a superior agent. Our efforts are in His hand and directed by it; and He will give them their effect in His own time. Where the disease is most deeply seated, there it will be slowest in eradication. In the Northern states, it was merely superficial and easily corrected. In the Southern, it is incorporated with the whole system and requires time, patience, and perseverance in the curative process."

Abolition in the North

Regarding the "easily corrected" problem of slavery in the North, Thomas Jefferson spoke with the benefit of hindsight; for the Northern states all passed abolition laws before the end of Jefferson's presidency. Quaker-heavy Pennsylvania came first, passing its abolition law in 1780; followed by Massachusetts, Connecticut, Rhode Island, New Hampshire and New York, all by 1799. When Vermont joined the Union as the 14th state in 1791, it did so as a free state. The last to pass its abolition law, New Jersey, did so in 1804.

INTERESTING IDEAS: Despite all these Northern abolition laws, slavery continued in the North long after 1804— for in order to protect slaveholders' investments, most Northern states abolished slavery only gradually.

- Most states liberated only blacks born after the date of the law, not before— which meant that some older slaves remained slaves for life. This was especially true for slaves whose masters sent them to the South to be sold, as many masters did when they understood that slavery was finished in the North.

- Even blacks born after the date of the law often remained slaves into their twenties— which allowed slaveholders to exploit them while they were young and strong.

The Northern states' reasons for liberating slaves went far beyond abolitionists' prodding. Most of these other reasons centered on two circumstances: the Revolutionary War, and the changing economics of slavery.

- Just before the Revolutionary War, the coastal regions of Africa where slave traders found most of their new slaves started running out of young black men to kidnap. The collapsing supply of new slaves cut most New Englanders out of the slave trade, making that trade far less important to the North's economy.

- During the Revolutionary War, the British offered to liberate any slave who would desert his American master and fight for Britain. Because the British army headquartered itself in the Northern cities of New York and Philadelphia, most of the thousands of slaves who answered Britain's call came from the North. Following Britain's lead, some Northern states also offered to liberate slaves in exchange for military service. The result was a dramatic reduction in the number of Northern slaves— which made it far easier for the Northern states to liberate the few who remained after the war.

- Before, during and after the Revolutionary War, many Northern slaves were no common farm laborers, but rather highly skilled workers— blacksmiths, carpenters and so on— hired out by their masters for good wages. After the war, white soldiers who returned home looking for work coveted those slaves' high-wage jobs. The abolition of slavery helped whites take those jobs— for abolition broke employers' contracts with slaveholders, opening their slaves' jobs for whites. Thus some Northerners supported abolition not because it was right, but because it drove slaves out of jobs whites wanted for themselves.

<u>AMAZING AFRICAN AMERICANS: Sojourner Truth (1797? – 1883)</u>

Sojourner Truth was a living illustration of the fact that slavery continued in the North long after the Northern states passed their abolition laws. Sojourner was born under the name Isabella Freebaum around 1797, just two years before her home state of New York passed its *Act for the Gradual Abolition of Slavery*. Had

Isabella been born after 1799, the law would have required her master to liberate her on her 25th birthday; but because she was born before 1799, the law made her more or less a slave for life.

Nearly three decades later, a new law required New York slaveholders to liberate all slaves by 1827, even those born before 1799. However, 1827 was too late for Isabella— for by then she had suffered under too many cruel masters, and decided to take matters into her own hands. One day in 1826, Isabella picked up the only one of her children she could carry, an infant daughter, and walked to the home of some white friends. When Isabella's master came looking for her, her friends paid him twenty dollars for one year of her services— just until 1827, when the law would have liberated her anyway.

A few months after her escape, Isabella learned that her former master had illegally sold one of the children she left behind to an Alabama man. Against all odds, this penniless former slave woman sued to reclaim her five-year-old son— and won, becoming one of the first black women to win a judgment against a white man in a New York court.

Years later, Isabella joined the abolitionist movement as Sojourner Truth, a wandering minister/speaker who fought for abolition and women's rights. Sojourner's great charisma and spell-binding speeches made her one of the best-known abolitionists of her day, alongside her personal friends Frederick Douglass, William Lloyd Garrison and Harriet Beecher Stowe (see Year Four).

Sojourner Truth

FASCINATING FACTS: Pinkster

Pinkster is a spring holiday that came to America with the Dutchmen who settled New York. *Pinksteren* is Dutch for Pentecost, the celebration of the Holy Spirit that falls on the seventh Sunday after Easter each year (Acts 2). Pinkster week was a time for Dutch Christians to gather for special church services like baptisms and confirmations, as well as to visit family members who were taking part in those services.

In keeping with the spirit of Pinkster, Dutch farmers allowed their slaves to celebrate as well. Every year, New York slaves built temporary shelters so that they could invite family members from all over the state to come and join their week-long celebrations. These included food, games, storytelling and much music and dancing. Pinkster was also a time for slaves to poke fun at their masters, playfully mocking them. Over time, the Pinkster holiday became more African-American than Dutch.

Retrenchment in the South

Regarding the "curative process" in the South, Thomas Jefferson would prove to be quite wrong; for instead of abolishing slavery, the South grew ever more determined to preserve its peculiar institution.

DEFINITION: **"Our peculiar institution"** was a Southern euphemism for the institution of

"The Old Plantation," an image of slaves dancing on a South Carolina plantation

slavery— a softening term that Southern slaveholders used so they wouldn't have to utter the distasteful name of "slavery" in polite company. In this context, "peculiar" meant not that slavery was strange, but that it was unique to the Southern states— an institution that Southerners believed was necessary to preserve their plantation economy.

Although the Revolutionary War reduced slave numbers in the North, it increased slave numbers in the South. Before the war, the British Crown sometimes set limits on the Thirteen Colonies' expansion— limits like the Royal Proclamation of 1763, which forbade settlement west of the Appalachians (see Chapter 20). The Revolutionary War put a stop to these annoying limits, freeing the United States to expand as quickly as it could.

SOBERING STATISTICS: In the South, expanding settlement meant expanding slavery. As slavery spread into the new slave states of Kentucky, Tennessee and beyond, the South's slave population started doubling every 20 – 30 years. As of 1790, the South's total slave population stood at around 650,000. By 1810, it stood at around 1.1 million; by 1830, nearly 2 million; and by 1860, nearly 4 million.

FASCINATING FACTS: The Mason-Dixon Line

The Mason-Dixon Line was a survey line that divided Maryland from two of her neighbors, Pennsylvania and Delaware. British surveyors Charles Mason and Jeremiah Dixon spent the years from 1763 – 1767 marking out a 233-mile-long east-west line to divide the southern colony of Maryland from the middle colony of Pennsylvania. The surveyors' starting point, which lay precisely 15 miles due south of Philadelphia, set the Mason-Dixon Line's latitude at 39°43' north.

Because Pennsylvania later became a free state, while Maryland remained a slave state, Americans came to know the Mason-Dixon Line as the boundary between the slaveholding South and the free North— even though Mason and Dixon finished their line in 1767, more than a decade before any colony abolished slavery.

Legal Compromises over Slavery

The hard task of holding the young United States together required a number of compromises between Southern slaveholders and Northern abolitionists.

REFRESHING REMINDERS from Chapter 23: The Constitution of the United States was by no means an abolitionist document— for if it had been, then no Southern state would have ratified it. Instead, the original Constitution contained three important compromises designed to win Southern states' approval:

Slave catchers pursuing runaway slaves

1. Article IV, Section 2 required the return of all runaway slaves who might flee across state lines seeking freedom. Like the Northwest Ordinance before it, the Constitution insisted that the North must never become a legal haven for runaway slaves from the South.

2. Article I, Section 2 contained the Three-fifths Compromise, which assigned each state a number of representatives based on its whole population of free citizens plus three-fifths of its slaves. The Three-fifths Compromise was a double-edged sword; for while it demeaned slaves by counting them as less than whole persons, it also gave the slave-oppressing Southern states less power than they would have held if the Constitution had allowed them to count all of their slaves.

3. Article I, Section 9 forbade Congress to enact any law that banned the international slave trade. However, Section 9 expired in 1808, twenty years after the Constitution's ratification.

FASCINATING FACTS: In 1807 Congress passed, and President Jefferson signed, the slave-importation ban that the Constitution foresaw: **An Act Prohibiting Importation of Slaves,** which took effect in 1808. Abolitionists hoped that this act would eventually end slavery in the South, as slaveholders would be unable to replace lost slaves. By this time, however, Southern slaveholders were already raising enough slave children to grow their slave populations without depending on fresh slaves from overseas.

After the compromises in the Constitution, the next compromises required to hold the U.S. together involved the balance between slave states and free. The more the North threatened to abolish slavery, the more the South needed control of the federal government, which would help the South preserve slavery. Because the North's population was larger, the South could not hope to control the House of Representatives, where representation depended on population. Instead, the South fought to control the Senate, where all states received equal representation.

As of 1804, the year New Jersey began its gradual abolition of slavery, the count of slave states versus free states stood at a slightly unbalanced 8 – 9:

- The eight states of Delaware, Maryland, Virginia, North Carolina, South Carolina, Georgia, Kentucky (admitted 1792) and Tennessee (admitted 1796) were all slave states.
- The nine states of New Hampshire, Massachusetts, Rhode Island, Connecticut, New York, New Jersey, Pennsylvania, Vermont (admitted 1791) and Ohio (admitted 1803) were all free states.

The admission of the 18th state, Louisiana, corrected this unbalance; for Louisiana joined the Union as a slave state in 1812. After that, compromisers in Congress admitted one new slave state for each new free state:

- After #19 Indiana joined the Union as a free state in 1816, #20 Mississippi joined as a slave state in 1817.
- After #21 Illinois joined the Union as a free state in 1818, #22 Alabama joined as a slave state in 1819.

The Tallmadge Amendment (1819)

By 1819, yet another new territory amassed the minimum 60,000 population required for statehood: Missouri. Because most Missourians came from the South, they planned to join the Union as a slave state— which meant that Missouri's admission would tip the Senate balance in the slave states' favor for the first time.

Determined to deny slaveholders this victory, New York Representative James Tallmadge proposed the **Tallmadge Amendment**— an amendment to the Missouri statehood bill which required the new state to abolish slavery over time, as most Northern states had done. What came next demonstrated the value of holding the Senate— for with the Senate equally divided between slave states and free, the slave states were able to defeat the Tallmadge Amendment. However, the amendment's defeat meant that the Missouri statehood bill died in the Senate, leaving Missouri unable to join the Union— for the moment.

The Missouri Compromise (1820)

The following year brought an opportunity for compromise— for 1820 was the year when Maine applied to join the Union, independent of its old master Massachusetts. Because Maine was joining as a free state, it was now possible to admit Missouri as a slave state without upsetting the balance between slave and free.

However, there were two catches:

1. The new statehood bill Missouri proposed was even more racist than the first. This time, Missouri actually tried to ban free blacks from moving to their state.

2. Illinois Senator Jesse Thomas was so outraged at Missourians' racism that he refused to support their statehood without receiving something in return.

DEFINITION: The Missouri Compromise

Senator Thomas' proposal was another amendment to the Missouri statehood bill. Determined to ban slavery in the North at least, if he could not ban it in the South, Thomas proposed an amendment that forever banned slavery in any part of the Louisiana Territory north of Missouri's southern border, which lay at 36°30' north latitude. Under Thomas' **Missouri Compromise**, only Missourians could hold slaves north of 36°30'. The rest of the Louisiana Territory north of that line must remain forever free.

Kentucky Senator Henry Clay, one of the masterminds of the Missouri Compromise

With help from Kentucky Senator Henry Clay, the Missouri Compromise passed both House and Senate. Free Maine joined the Union as the 23rd state; slave Missouri joined the Union as the 24th state; and Congress forever banned slavery in any part of the Louisiana Territory north of 36°30'.

Like many compromises, the Missouri Compromise was difficult for both sides to accept:

1. The slave states resented the compromise because they felt that new states should decide for themselves whether or not to allow slavery. By banning slavery in the Louisiana Territory ahead of time, Congress was taking an important power out of new states' hands— something the Tenth Amendment expressly forbade Congress to do.

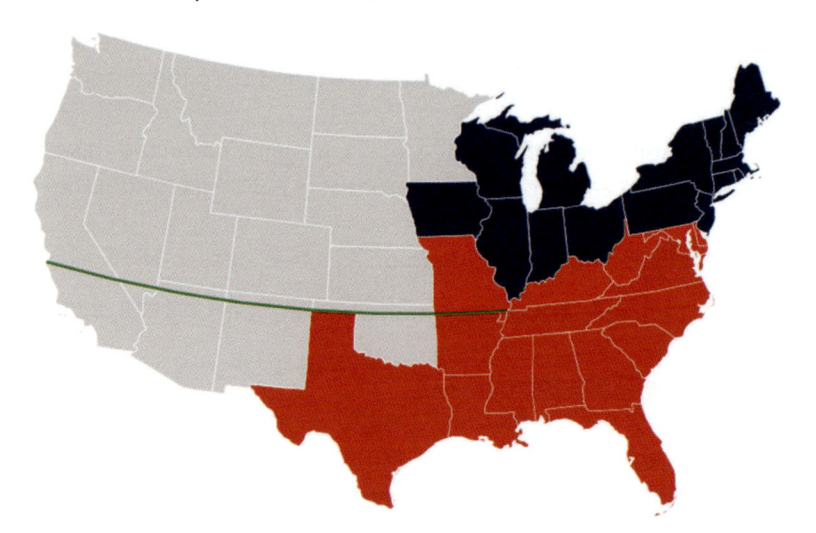

2. The free states resented the compromise because it allowed the stain of slavery to spread throughout the huge new state of Missouri, something they had hoped to prevent.

Slave states (red) vs. Free states (blue) as of 1848, with the Missouri Compromise line in green

Thomas Jefferson feared the Missouri Compromise for a different reason: because it drew a clear line between North and South, slave and free. In an 1820 letter, the aged Jefferson wrote:

"But the coincidence of a marked principle, moral & political with a geographical line, once conceived, I feared would never more be obliterated from the mind; that it would be recurring on every occasion & renewing irritations until it would kindle such mutual & mortal hatred, as to render separation preferable to eternal discord. I have been among the most sanguine in believing that our Union would be of long duration. I now doubt it much, and see the event at no great distance..." *In other words: Jefferson feared that the Missouri Compromise would soon divide the United States forever, North from South.*

TWO LOOKS AHEAD:
- The Missouri Compromise will stand until 1854, when the Kansas-Nebraska Act will replace it with a new compromise: **popular sovereignty**, the idea that the people of each new state should decide for themselves whether or not to allow slavery.
- Jefferson's prediction will come true after the presidential election of 1860, when several Southern states will secede from the Union before President-elect Abraham Lincoln can even take office. From 1861 – 1865, the U.S. will fight a terrible Civil War— partly over the issue of slavery, but also over the issue of federal power versus individual states' rights raised by the Missouri Compromise.

Slave Rebellions and Consequences

Unlike the French and British West Indies, the United States never faced a slave rebellion that involved more than a few hundred slaves. Even so, some of these small U.S. rebellions produced lasting results.

FASCINATING FACTS: Gabriel's Rebellion (August 30, 1800)

Gabriel Prosser was a slave born near Richmond, Virginia in or around 1776. Several qualities set Gabriel apart as a natural leader:

- He was uncommonly large, strong and charismatic, as well as a convincing speaker.
- His work as a blacksmith gave him opportunity to mingle with a great many blacks, both slave and free.
- His ability to read and write kept him well informed about current events.

Gabriel Prosser

Gabriel's study of current events introduced him to the two revolutions that inspired his own: (1) the French Revolution, which produced the Declaration of the Rights of Man in 1789 (see Chapter 25); and (2) the Haitian Revolution, in which Haiti's slaves won their freedom in 1794 (see Chapter 29). Because Napoleon had not yet sent the Leclerc Expedition to re-enslave Haiti, Gabriel still held a high opinion of Frenchmen when he planned his own rebellion in 1800.

Gabriel spent the spring and summer of 1800 quietly organizing slaves, free blacks and even some poor whites for a major assault on Richmond, seat of Virginia's government. Because Gabriel's plans were secret, no one is quite sure what they were. One theory is that Gabriel planned to kidnap Virginia Governor James Monroe, and then trade this valuable hostage for promises of freedom and fair treatment for slaves. Gabriel also ordered his rebels to kill all whites in their path except Quakers, Methodists and Frenchmen— three groups who stood against slavery.

Unfortunately for Gabriel, powerful thunderstorms on the target date of his rebellion— August 30, 1800— forced him to delay his plans until the following day. As his nervous rebels sat through these storms, their restlessness aroused their masters' suspicions. Under pressure from their masters, some of Gabriel's rebels revealed his plans, and the whole affair fell apart before it ever got started. Instead of leading a successful slave rebellion, Gabriel wound up captured, tried and hanged to death, along with about 25 of his fellow rebels.

SUCCINCT SUMMARIES: Some Consequences of Gabriel's Rebellion

Virginia responded to Gabriel's Rebellion with harsh new laws designed to keep slaves in their place:

- Because Gabriel drew inspiration from reading, a new law barred Virginians from teaching their slaves to read— rendering slaves' futures even more hopeless.

- Because Gabriel's position as a skilled blacksmith helped him organize his rebellion, another new law barred Virginians from hiring out slaves for skilled work. This development left many city-dwelling Virginia slaveholders with no better choice than to sell their slaves farther south.

- In an effort to keep free blacks separate from slaves, yet another new law required all slaves liberated by their masters to leave Virginia within one year, or else return to slavery. This was one of the laws that made it difficult for Thomas Jefferson to liberate his slaves in his will, as George Washington had done (see above).

INTERESTING IDEAS: A second consequence of Gabriel's Rebellion was to convince some abolitionists that blacks and whites could never live together in peace, not even if the South abolished slavery. Thomas Jefferson expressed this fear in *Notes on the State of Virginia*, a 1791 treatise in which he wrote that "deep-rooted prejudices entertained by the whites," coupled with "ten thousand recollections, by the blacks, of the injuries they have sustained," would "produce convulsions which will probably never end but in the extermination of the one or the other race."

The solution, Jefferson believed, was to remove liberated slaves to some new home of their own. Many abolitionists agreed— enough that in 1821, an abolitionist group called the American Colonization Society established the colony of Liberia, Africa as a home for liberated slaves. See Year Four for more on Liberia.

FASCINATING FACTS: Nat Turner's Rebellion (August 1831)

Nat Turner was a Virginia slave born about a week before Gabriel Prosser's hanging in 1800. Nat's home was Southampton County, which lies near Virginia's southeastern corner. Like Gabriel, Nat could read and write; but unlike Gabriel, Nat was a deeply religious man who devoted himself to his own special version of Christianity— which included not only prayer, fasting, Bible study and preaching, but also visions in which Nat claimed to receive special instructions from the Lord.

Like many slaveholders, Nat's masters encouraged their slaves' religion, believing that a religious slave was a more contented slave. Nat's last master, Joseph Travis, was unusually kind to him. Among many other freedoms, Travis allowed Nat to leave his plantation frequently so that he could preach to fellow slaves on nearby plantations.

Blinded by Nat's religious devotion, Travis and his neighbors failed to monitor what Nat was really preaching to his fellow slaves, which was this: that "the time was fast approaching when the first should be last and the last should be first." Nat derived this prophecy from Matthew 20:16— a verse he interpreted to mean that the Lord would soon make the slaves masters, and the masters slaves.

From a woodcut depicting scenes from Nat Turner's Rebellion

Nat's Turner's Rebellion began in the early hours of August 22, 1831. Long before sunrise, Nat and four other slaves slipped into the sleeping Joseph Travis' home and hacked him to death, along with his wife and two of his children. After looting the house and moving on, two members of Nat's squad remembered that they had left a third child, an infant, alive in its cradle; so they returned to murder the infant as well. From there, the rebels moved from house to house as quietly as possible, killing the sleepers inside, leaving not one white person alive. In all, Nat's squad killed about 55 whites— all of them near neighbors who had trusted this religious slave, never suspecting that he was capable of such vicious slaughter.

As he ravaged house after house, Nat gathered horses, weapons and more rebel slaves, boosting his squad's size to around forty. Meanwhile, the Southampton County militia gathered in the nearby town of Jerusalem. Around noon on August 22, a few blasts from militia cannon scattered Nat's squad, sending most of the survivors— including Nat— into hiding.

Nat managed to hide in the Great Dismal Swamp of southeastern Virginia for more than two months, until a white hunter happened upon his hiding place. After some interviews and a brief trial, the state of Virginia hanged Nat Turner to death on November 11.

SUCCINCT SUMMARIES: Some Consequences of Nat Turner's Rebellion

- In all, Virginia legally convicted and executed about 55 blacks for joining in Nat Turner's Rebellion, roughly the same as the number of whites the rebels killed.

- Several mobs of slave hunters, both legal and illegal, may have killed up to four times that many blacks. A months-long hunt for Nat's allies ranged far and wide, deep into neighboring North Carolina. Just as the Romans who defeated Spartacus in 72 BC lined the Appian Way with crucified rebel slaves, Virginians and North Carolinians lined their roads with rebel slaves' heads.

- Innocent slaves all over the South suffered for Nat Turner's Rebellion. Slaveholders who had once trusted their slaves enough to grant them a few small freedoms, as Joseph Travis had done, now took away even these— fearful that even the smallest kindness might lead to another deadly slave rebellion like Nat's.

- To prevent any more slave rebellions from starting in churches, a new Virginia law barred slaves from holding religious gatherings without a licensed white minister present.

Nat Turner's capture

ILLUMINATING LISTS: Two well-known books bear the title *The Confessions of Nat Turner*. One is a short account of the rebellion written by Thomas Gray, an attorney who interviewed Nat during the days between his arrest and his hanging. Gray claimed to report the tale exactly as he heard it from Nat. The other is a long historical fiction by Virginia-born author William Styron, who admittedly embellished Nat's tale.

WORLD HISTORY FOCUS

The Abolitionist Movement in Britain

As in the United States, the legal abolition of slavery in Britain began with a ban on the international slave trade. Among the many Britons who devoted their lives to enacting that ban were these:

BRILLIANT BRITONS: James Ramsay (1733 – 1789)

James Ramsay began his professional life as a young ship's surgeon aboard a British warship stationed in the West Indies. In November 1759, in the middle of the Seven Years' War, an overcrowded British slave ship approached Ramsay's ship to ask for help with a medical problem. Dr. Ramsay climbed aboard to see what he could do. The moment Ramsay stepped below decks, unimaginable horrors confronted him— unforgettable scenes of slaves packed back-to-chest, unable to move, caked with their own feces and blood, scores of them dead or dying of dysentery.

Three years later, the now-civilian Ramsay returned to the West Indies as a combination doctor/Anglican minister, determined to ease the terrible suffering he had witnessed. Often, Ramsay's determination meant chiding sugar plantation owners for mistreating slaves. After nearly 15 years of Ramsay's chiding, angry plantation owners grew so tired of him that they finally pressured him into going home.

Back in Britain, Ramsay published one of Britain's first important abolitionist books: "An Essay on the Treatment and Conversion of African Slaves in the British Sugar Colonies." Ramsay's vivid descriptions of life as a British-held slave inspired many Britons to ask themselves for the first time: is our great Christian empire behaving as morally as it should?

ILLUMINATING EXCERPTS from James Ramsay's "An Essay on the Treatment and Conversion of African Slaves in the British Sugar Colonies" (Published 1784)

- "The ordinary punishments of slaves, for the common crimes of neglect, absence from work, eating the sugar cane and theft, are: cart whipping; beating with a stick, sometimes to the breaking of bones; the chain; an iron crook about the neck… In short… shameless profligacy usurps the place of decency, sympathy, morality and religion."

- "There have been instances of slitting of ears; breaking of limbs, so as to make amputation necessary; beating out of eyes; and castration… It is yet true, that the unfeeling application of the ordinary punishments ruins the constitution, and shortens the life of many a poor wretch."

BRILLIANT BRITONS: Josiah Wedgwood (1730 – 1795)

Josiah Wedgwood brought a unique advantage to abolitionist cause: in addition to being a fervent opponent of slavery, Wedgwood was probably the best-known potter who ever lived. The elegant Wedgwood pottery Josiah produced in his factories was among the most elegantly designed and beautifully crafted in all the world. Because Wedgwood was such a successful, respected businessman, Britons took notice of his opinions on slavery.

FASCINATING FACTS: The Kneeling Slave Medallion

The Kneeling Slave Medallion was a small porcelain cameo designed and produced by the Wedgwood Company beginning in 1780. The medallion featured a chained slave kneeling before his masters, beseeching them: "Am I not a Man and a Brother?" Wedgwood produced thousands of these medallions for his fellow abolitionists to wear as brooches, necklaces, bracelets and hair ornaments. Wedgwood's kneeling slave was also the official logo of the abolitionist organization he helped lead, the Society for the Abolition of the Slave Trade.

BRILLIANT BRITONS: Thomas Clarkson (1760 – 1846)

Thomas Clarkson was another Anglican minister whose highest goal in life was to force an end to the British slave trade. One of Clarkson's contributions was to collect visual aids that helped Britons see the horrors of the slave trade with their own eyes. **Clarkson's Box** of visual aids contained iron shackles used to bind slaves during transport; branding irons used to mark and/or punish slaves; and detailed slave ship plans to illustrate the unbearable overcrowding slaves endured on long voyages across the Atlantic. Clarkson's Box also contained beautiful examples of African craftsmanship— fine carvings, cloth and so on— that inspired Britons to ask: by what right does our great Christian empire enslave a people clever enough to create such wonderful things?

For roughly 20 years, off and on, Clarkson wandered all over the British Isles with his box, carrying it from meeting to meeting in a tireless effort to convince Britons that slavery was evil.

GIANTS OF THE FAITH: William Wilberforce (1759 – 1833)

To make their dream of ending slavery a reality, abolitionists needed a strong voice to plead their case in Parliament. The voice they chose belonged to a wealthy young Member of Parliament named William Wilberforce.

Early in his career, Wilberforce seemed an unlikely candidate to become the best-known abolitionist in all of history. Although Wilberforce was charming, well-spoken and well-liked, he was also dissipated— a fun-loving young man who cared little for great causes, preferring to spend his time drinking and gambling. Around 1785, though, a profound change came over Wilberforce. A growing awareness of heaven began to cloud his earthly pleasures, robbing them of their joy:

> "Often while in the full enjoyment of all that this world could bestow, my conscience told me that in the true sense of the word, I was not a Christian. I laughed, I sang, I was apparently gay and happy; but the thought would steal across me— 'What madness is all this, to continue easy in a state in which a sudden call out of the world would consign me to everlasting misery, and that, when eternal happiness is within my grasp!' For I had received into my understanding the great truths of the gospel, and believed that its offers were free and universal; and that God had promised to give his Holy Spirit to them that asked for it. At length such thoughts as these completely occupied my mind, and I began to pray earnestly."

1794 Portrait of Wilberforce

In other words, Wilberforce became a Christian— not a nominal Christian who paid lip service to his faith, but a strong evangelical Christian who followed Christ every day of his life. Instead of staying up late to carouse, Wilberforce rose early to pray; and instead of gambling away his money, he donated it. The more closely Wilberforce followed Christ, the more he regretted the dissipation of his youth:

> "As soon as I reflected seriously upon these subjects, the deep guilt and black ingratitude of my past life forced itself upon me in the strongest colors, and I condemned myself for having wasted my precious time, and opportunities, and talents."

During this critical stage of his life, Wilberforce held his first deep discussions with abolitionists like James Ramsay, Thomas Clarkson and John Newton (see below). Within a couple of years, Wilberforce believed he understood why God had set a dissipated young man like himself in such a high station: because his seat in Parliament was the perfect post from which to champion the abolitionist cause.

> INTERESTING IDEAS: Early on, the Society for the Abolition of the Slave Trade made a strategic decision. Because so much British wealth depended on slave labor, the Society feared that abolishing slavery altogether was too lofty a goal. Instead, it decided to focus on abolishing a more obvious evil: the international slave trade, with its brutal kidnappings and miserably overcrowded slave ships.

William Wilberforce's campaign to outlaw the international slave trade began in May 1789, when he delivered the first of many, many impassioned speeches on the subject before the House of Commons. The main points of Wilberforce's first speech included these:

- **The kidnapping of slaves destroys Africa's peace and prosperity:** "It is a trade in its principle most inevitable calculated to spread disunion among the African princes, to sow the seeds of every mischief, to inspire enmity, to destroy humanity; and it is found in practice, by the most abundant testimony to have had the effect in Africa of carrying misery, devastation and ruin wherever its baneful influence has extended."

- **All Britons should be ashamed of the wretched conditions aboard slave ships:** "Let anyone imagine to himself 600 – 700 of these wretches chained two and two, surrounded with every object that is nauseous and disgusting, diseased, and struggling under every kind of wretchedness! How can we bear to think of such a scene as this?"

The House of Commons in session

- **The abolitionists' cries have grown so loud that Britons can no longer feign ignorance:** "Having heard all of this, you may choose to look the other way; but you can never again say that you did not know."

Unfortunately, this first speech came at precisely the wrong moment— for even as Wilberforce spoke, the French Revolution was breaking out on the far side of the English Channel (see Chapter 25). To Britons who worried that the French Revolution might spread to Britain, Wilberforce's talk of liberating slaves sounded like Jacobin talk, a plot to overthrow the monarchy. This was especially true after 1794, when the National Convention abolished slavery throughout France and her colonies (see Chapter 29). By tying together the ideas of abolitionism and French-ness, the National Convention only made Wilberforce's task more difficult.

For eighteen years— throughout the French Revolutionary Wars, and on into the Napoleonic Wars— Wilberforce never stopped pleading with Parliament to ban the slave trade, and never succeeded.

The Slave Trade Act of 1807

Ironically, the tyrannical Napoleon aided William Wilberforce's liberating cause; for after Napoleon tried to re-enslave the Haitians in 1802, Britons had less reason to associate abolitionism with the French. After that, Wilberforce's persistent speeches began to carry more weight, even as Thomas Clarkson's anti-slavery meetings convinced more and more Britons that the slave trade was wrong.

A full 18 years after Wilberforce's campaign began, Parliament finally rewarded his persistence with the act that banned Britain's international slave trade: the **Slave Trade Act of 1807**. Just before the vote, Solicitor General Samuel Romilly supported the abolitionists' cause in a memorable speech comparing Wilberforce to Napoleon, who was then at the height of his power:

"When I look at the man at the head of the French monarchy [Napoleon]… when I follow him into his closet, or to his bed, and contemplate the anguish with which his solitude must be tortured by the recollection of the blood he has spilt, and the oppressions he has committed… and when I compare with these pangs of remorse the feeling which must accompany my honored friend [Wilberforce] from this House to his home, after the vote of this night shall have accomplished the object of his humane and unceasing labors… how much more enviable [Wilberforce's] lot? …Who will not be proud to concur with my honored friend, in promoting the greatest act of national benefit, and securing to the Africans the greatest blessing which God has ever put it in the power of man to confer on his fellow creatures?" <u>In other words</u>: *All the earthly glory the tyrant Napoleon achieved is as nothing compared to the heavenly glory achieved by the godly William Wilberforce in banning the slave trade.*

William Wiberforce

INTERESTING IDEAS: Parliament voted to ban its international slave trade in the very month the U.S. Congress did the same, March 1807. For the moment, however, neither Britain nor the U.S. banned slavery itself; nor did they ban trading slaves within their countries.

The Slavery Abolition Act of 1833

Actually banning slavery itself in Britain, and not just the international slave trade, required far longer—another 26 years. Throughout that quarter century, hundreds of thousands of slaves continued to suffer harsh treatment on Britain's sugar colonies in the West Indies. One of the events that drove Britain's next great anti-slavery law was an 1831 slave rebellion called the Baptist War.

TRAGIC TALES: The Baptist War (Christmas 1831)

The more abolitionists protested against slavery, the more slaves in Britain's sugar colonies heard of these protests, and yearned for their freedom. On the large British sugar island of Jamaica, a Baptist minister/slave named Samuel Sharpe taught his followers that they were already free, at least in God's eyes—and that as free laborers, they should demand their wages. On Christmas day, 1831, some 30,000 – 60,000 of Sharpe's followers simultaneously laid down their tools, declaring that they would work no more until their masters started paying them. Naturally, their masters refused.

Exactly what happened next is unclear. One possibility is that the slaves launched a riot over their master's refusal to pay. Another is that their overseers tried to force them back to work, and the slaves fought back. However the rioting began, rebel slaves destroyed a great many sugar plantations— provoking those plantations' owners to drastic action.

Over the next 8 – 10 days, well-armed British soldiers killed more than 200 ill-armed rebel slaves, forcing the survivors to surrender and return to work. Afterward, the British accused, tried and hanged hundreds more slaves, from rebel leaders like Samuel Sharpe to innocents who had nothing to do with Sharpe's rebellion.

After decades of abolitionist meetings and literature, Britons' feelings about the Baptist War were the opposite of Jamaican plantation owners' feelings: instead of outrage over the slave riots, Britons felt embarrassment over the owners' brutality. Partly in reaction to the Baptist War, Parliament finally liberated all slaves throughout its empire with the **Slavery Abolition Act of 1833**.

FASCINATING FACTS: As always, the trickiest part of abolishing slavery was paying for it. In liberating its empire's slaves, Britain was depriving their masters of fortunes large enough to ruin some very prominent British families. The Northern United States had solved this problem by abolishing slavery gradually. Britain's solution was quicker, but more costly: instead of abolishing slavery gradually, Parliament set aside 20 million British pounds— the equivalent of about a billion modern-day dollars, or perhaps more— to repay former slaveholders for their liberated slaves.

FASCINATING FATES: Years before 1833, William Wilberforce's health declined to the point where he could no longer lead the fight for abolition. On July 26, 1833, a gravely ill Wilberforce received word that the Slavery Abolition Act was sure to pass— to which he gratefully replied, "Thank God that I've lived to witness the day in which England is willing to give 20 million pounds sterling for the abolition of slavery!" Three days later, Wilberforce died.

GIANTS OF THE FAITH: John Newton, Author of "Amazing Grace" (1725 – 1807)

John Newton's early years offered even fewer clues to his great destiny than William Wilberforce's. Newton was an English merchant captain's son who found himself pressed into Royal Navy service at age 18, during the War of the Austrian Succession. Newton immediately proved to be a troublemaker, an insubordinate wretch so foul-mouthed and irreligious that even sailors sometimes stared at him in shock. When Newton found out how long the Royal Navy expected him to serve, he tried to escape— at which his captain captured him, stripped off his shirt and served him eight dozen lashes of the whip.

Newton sank even lower on his next assignment, which came after his angry captain traded him to a British slave ship operating off West Africa. Even the lesser discipline required of slavers proved too much for young Newton, who continued to make trouble for his new captain— so much trouble that his captain finally sent him ashore as a slave to an African woman. Had Newton's father not sent a friendly merchant captain to search for his son, Newton might never have returned home.

On his return trip to England in 1748, John Newton had his first religious experience. Midway through the trip, a severe storm battered the ship, pouring in so much water that it nearly foundered. Newton and the rest of the crew labored at the pumps to the point of exhaustion, yet still despaired of saving the ship. When Newton could pump no longer, his captain lashed him to the ship's wheel and left him there for eleven hours, striving his utmost to keep the ship from turning across the waves and capsizing. Those eleven hours in the presence of

John Newton

God's awesome power taught the irreligious Newton that when he was facing death, he really did believe in God, whatever he might have believed before.

Somehow, the ship held together long enough to carry him home, where his father helped him find a job on another slave ship. The new, more religious Newton prospered for several years aboard slave ships— for with the abolitionist movement still 30 years away, Newton saw no more problem with slavery than most Britons.

In 1755, health problems forced Newton to leave the sea; so he started studying to become an Anglican minister. Part of Newton's decades-long ministry was to write a large collection of hymns, including the best-known hymn of all time: "Amazing Grace," parts of which describe the rough road Newton followed to faith:

> Amazing grace, how sweet the sound / That sav'd a wretch like me
> I once was lost, but now am found / Was blind, but now I see!
>
> Through many dangers, toils, and snares / I have already come
> Tis grace hath brought me safe thus far / And grace will lead me home

Years later, abolitionist friends taught Newton to look back on his years as a slave trader with horror. By this time, Newton was such a beloved elder pastor that a young, spiritually struggling William Wilberforce approached him to ask what he should do with his new Christian life. Newton advised Wilberforce to remain in Parliament, where he could use his lofty position to fight for abolition.

FASCINATING FACTS: Child Chimney Sweeps

Abolition was only one of many causes William Wilberforce championed. Another was reforming Britain's child labor laws, including the ones that protected child chimney sweeps.

Britain's many chimneys needed regular cleanings to reduce the risk of chimney fires. Because some chimneys were too tall, narrow and winding for adult sweeps to reach, adults often hired child apprentices to clean them— the younger the better. Master sweeps forced poor children and orphans as young as 4 – 6 up cramped, filthy chimneys, armed with scrapers and brushes to scour soot from their flues. The risks were many: a child might (1) inhale noxious fumes that could wreck his lungs; (2) suffer a long fall that could ruin a limb; or (3) become trapped in a chimney, suffering a terrible fright that could scar him for life. There was also the risk that the master sweep might starve his apprentice— for well-fed children outgrew chimneys too quickly for their cruel master sweeps' liking.

A master chimney sweep and his child apprentice

Other interesting facts:
- If a child chimney sweep balked at climbing, then his master sweep might literally "light a fire under him" to force him up the chimney.

GIANTS OF THE FAITH: Elizabeth Fry (1780 – 1845)

Elizabeth Gurney Fry was an English Quaker who took a deep interest in the sufferings of the poor. On a visit to Newgate Prison, a notorious women's prison in London, Elizabeth found the conditions women endured there appalling. First, the building was atrocious, ridden with filth and disease. Second, the inmates' children were running loose in and around the prison, growing up in the worst circumstances imaginable. Third, Elizabeth discovered legal troubles: some of the inmates were awaiting the death penalty, which Elizabeth and all Quakers despised; while other inmates had been imprisoned without trial, which was against British law.

Elizabeth Fry's hands-on solution was to launch one of the world's first prison reform movements:

- To improve the inmates' spiritual lives, Elizabeth organized Bible studies.

- To improve their prospects after prison, Elizabeth organized sewing and other self-improvement classes.

- To improve their children's prospects, Elizabeth arranged schooling.

- To improve their legal prospects, Elizabeth worked tirelessly to commute death sentences and seek fair trials.

Nor was prison ministry Elizabeth's only interest. During the winter of 1819 – 1820, Elizabeth happened to find the body of a homeless child on the streets of London, frozen to death. This sad discovery prompted Elizabeth to add homeless shelters to her other charities, which included schools for the poor, hospital reform and nurse training programs. Queen Victoria herself donated to the much-beloved Elizabeth Fry's many ministries.

Elizabeth Fry

The *Amistad* Incident (1839 – 1841)

La Amistad was a Spanish schooner whose designers never intended her to be a slave ship. Nevertheless in July 1839, *La Amistad* sailed out of Havana, Cuba with a cargo of 53 slaves— freshly-captured West Africans who had arrived in Havana only recently, and were now on their way to a sugar plantation on the far side of Cuba. The fact that *La Amistad* had no slave decks, though, meant that the slaves aboard often stood out on her main deck— which gave them more chances to rebel. Before *La Amistad* could

Engraving of the *Amistad* Incident

reach her destination, the slaves seized the ship, killing her captain and most of her crew in the process. Once the ship was theirs, the escapees commanded two surviving Spaniards to pilot *La Amistad* to Africa.

Unfortunately, the escapees knew nothing of the sea; while their two captive Spaniards were experienced sea hands. Taking advantage of the escapees' ignorance, the Spaniards secretly guided *La Amistad* north instead of east. Before the escapees knew anything was wrong, their false guides sailed *La Amistad* near Long Island, New York, where a heavily-armed U.S. coast guard vessel intercepted her.

Now captured a second time, the poor Amistad escapees went to jail cells in New Haven, Connecticut to await court decisions that would determine their fate. Because there were so many valuable prizes at stake, several parties laid claims in court. Among others:

- The two Spaniards who guided *La Amistad* northward tried to claim both ship and cargo as their legal property.

- The captain of the coast guard vessel that intercepted *La Amistad* tried to claim both ship and cargo as property seized on the high seas, as did two civilian seamen who guided the coast guard to *La Amistad*.
- Meanwhile, the Spanish government urged the U.S. to return the escapees to Cuba, where Spanish courts could punish them for murdering *La Amistad*'s captain and crew. Because Cuba's sugar plantations still depended on slavery, the Spanish could allow no slave rebellion to go unpunished.

The escapees' defense was that they were no one's property but their own— which was true, as by now Britain, Spain and the United States had all outlawed the international slave trade that brought them to Cuba in the first place.

For help, the Spanish invited a powerful party into the case: President Martin Van Buren. As of 1839, Van Buren desperately needed more electoral votes if he was to win the upcoming election of 1840, particularly Southern votes. Mindful of Van Buren's need, the Spanish took advantage of their connections in the slaveholding South. At Spain's suggestion, Southern lawmakers let Van Buren know that if he sent *La Amistad* back to Cuba— thus showing his support for slavery— then Southerners would gratefully reward him with their votes. Buckling under Spanish and Southern pressure, Van Buren ordered Attorney General Felix Grundy to do all he could to send the escapees back to Cuba.

Fortunately for the escapees, another powerful party took an interest in their case: Northern abolitionists, who hired skilled attorneys to defend them. With help from these attorneys, the escapees convinced the U.S. District Court of Connecticut that they had been illegally kidnapped from Africa, and were therefore no one's property. Nearly two years after the Amistad Incident, the U.S. Supreme Court finally agreed: the escapees were no slaves of Spaniards, but rather free people of Africa.

Abolitionist-sponsored portrait of Joseph Cinque, leader of the Amistad escapees

INTERESTING IDEAS: One of the attorneys who argued the escapees' case before the Supreme Court was former President John Quincy Adams, who had since become the U.S. House of Representatives' "Old Man Eloquent." Adams hoped that the Supreme Court would rebuke his old enemy Van Buren for interfering in Judicial Branch affairs. Instead, the only official punishment Van Buren received was losing the election of 1840.

SUCCINCT SUMMARIES: Some Consequences of the *Amistad* Incident

- Only 36 of the original 53 escapees actually returned home to Africa. A few young escapees chose to remain in America, and several older escapees died awaiting the courts' decisions— including at least one homesick African who took his own life in hopes of reuniting with his loved ones in the next life.
- The Supreme Court's anti-slavery decision in the Amistad case did not mean that the court would oppose slavery in all future cases— far from it. Instead, the Supreme Court would often defend Southerners' right to hold slaves, particularly in the 1857 case of *Dred Scott v. Sandford* (see Year Four).

FASCINATING FACTS: The New England Whaling Industry

The 1800s were peak years for the whaling industry. For more than a century, thousands of New England whaling men were always at sea, harvesting whales for the two main resources their bodies provided:

1. **Whale oil,** a clean-burning lamp oil rendered from blubber (whale fat).
2. **Whalebone,** another name for baleen— the tooth-like structures baleen whales use to filter their food from seawater. Among other things, garment makers used whalebone to fashion flexible ribs for ladies' corsets.

Massachusetts was home to two of the biggest whaling ports in the world, Nantucket and New Bedford. Every year, scores of ships and thousands of sailors departed these ports on 2- to 3-year journeys that carried them around the globe in search of whales. All the work of harvesting whale oil happened at sea: from (1) harpooning the whale; to (2) removing the blubber from its carcass, a process called flensing; to (3) boiling the blubber into whale oil, a process called rendering; to (4) storing the valuable oil in casks for the journey home.

The whaling industry's demise began in the mid- to late-1800s, with the development of a lamp oil that was far easier to come by: kerosene, which engineers learned to refine from crude oil.

Other interesting facts:
- Sojourner Truth's son Peter, the one she reclaimed in court (see above), later sailed out of Nantucket on a whaling voyage and never returned.

NOTED NOVELS: Much of Herman Melville's 1851 novel *Moby Dick*, which describes Captain Ahab's ill-fated vendetta against a great white sperm whale, is set aboard a whaling ship launched from Nantucket.

FASCINATING FACTS: Scrimshaw

Scrimshaw is an art form developed by whale hunters whose long journeys around the world left them with a lot of time on their hands. Into whale's teeth, baleen or ivory, scrimshaw artists etched scenes, portraits or geometric designs, creating unique objects of remarkable beauty. Touches of black ink helped set the etchings apart from their ivory-colored bases.

Currier & Ives image of whalers at work

Scrimshaw etching

Boers, Britons and Zulus in South Africa

The Dutch East India Company established the first permanent European outpost in South Africa: Cape Town, built on a cape about 100 miles northwest of Africa's southernmost tip in 1652. Cape Town began as no more than a way station, a stopping point for ships traveling around insignificant South Africa on their way to the all-important markets of the Far East.

One of any way station's critical tasks was to provide fresh food for sailors suffering from scurvy, a disease that was common among ship-bound sailors who ate nothing but dried food for months at a time. To provide fresh food, the Dutch East India Company imported Cape Town's first Boers.

DEFINITION: The **Boers** were Dutch pioneer farmers who first arrived in South Africa during the mid-1600s; *Boer* is Dutch for "farmer."

As the Boers spread out to build farms in the surrounding territory, Cape Town became the capital of a far larger colony named Cape Colony.

Over the century-and-a-half that followed, the hard work of carving out Cape Colony built the Boers into a distinct people, respected around the world for their remarkable toughness and self-reliance. Like most colonists of their day, the Boers built Cape Colony's growing wealth partly on the backs of African slaves.

Dutch governor Jan van Riebeeck landing at Cape Town in April 1652

REFRESHING REMINDERS: The decades after Cape Colony's founding saw the rise of the British Empire, and the decline of the Dutch Empire (see Chapter 12). The Dutch Empire declined even faster during the French Revolutionary Wars (1792 – 1799), when France seized control of the Netherlands (see Chapter 29).

From Dutch Empire to British Empire

To prevent Cape Colony from falling to France as well, Britain seized Cape Town from the Dutch in 1795. After a brief return to Dutch control, Cape Colony became a permanent British possession in 1815, the year when the Congress of Vienna brought the Napoleonic era to a close (see Chapter 29). The Congress of Vienna left the Dutch-descended Boers unwilling subjects of the British Crown.

The Great Trek (1830s and 1840s)

The Boers struggled along under British control until 1833, when important news reached their ears: Britain had just passed its Slavery Abolition Act, and would no longer allow slavery anywhere in its empire (see above). Abolition led to two problems for the Boers:

1. Although the Slavery Abolition Act provided government money for slaveholders who liberated their slaves, the Boers weren't satisfied with the amounts the British offered them, nor with their payment schedules.

2. Furthermore, the Boers resented the moralistic British for forcing them to change their way of life— for the racist Boers saw no reason to be ashamed of slaveholding.

Determined to live as they pleased, the Boers decided to move beyond British control.

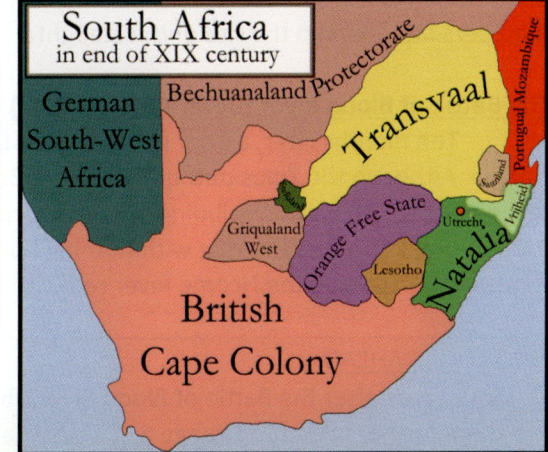

DEFINITION: The **Great Trek** of the 1830s and 1840s was a mass migration in which thousands of Boers abandoned British-held Cape Colony to establish new, independent republics of their own. The three Boer republics were (1) the **Natalia Republic**, a coastal republic just northeast of Cape Colony; (2) the **Orange Free State**, an inland republic west of Natalia; and (3) the **Transvaal Republic**, another inland republic across the Vaal River from Orange.

The Boers' Great Trek led to a clash with one of Africa's most fearsome empires, the Zulu Kingdom.

> ### FASCINATING FACTS: Shaka and the Zulu Kingdom
>
> The Zulu Kingdom was a confederation of South African tribes built by **Shaka** (1787? – 1828), a military genius whose aggressive tactics transformed warfare in his part of the world. Before Shaka, most South African battles were short affairs involving shouted threats and a few hastily-thrown spears, easily deflected; casualties were nearly always light. Under Shaka, those brief battles became long duels to the death with casualties in the thousands.
>
> Shaka's ruthless cunning won him a wide territory, including most of what was to become Natalia, Orange and Transvaal. Sadly, Shaka's ruthlessness also led to one of South Africa's worst tragedies: the **Mfecane**, a deadly horror that sprang from Shaka's ravages. Some Mfecane victims died of hunger or disease after Shaka drove them out of their homes, leaving them with neither food nor shelter. Others died fighting to steal other tribes' homelands as Shaka stole theirs. Shaka's Mfecane may have killed a million or more native South Africans.
>
> Shaka's demise may have come about through excessive grief over the death of his beloved mother in the fall of 1827. To ensure that all Zulus grieved as keenly as he did, Shaka reportedly ordered that no Zulu should plant crops the following spring, nor taste milk— which comes from mothers— for an entire year. To end this madness, two of Shaka's half-brothers assassinated him in 1828.

The Weenen Massacre (February 17, 1838)

The demise of Shaka meant that when the Boers began their Great Trek, Shaka's half-brother Dingane was chief of the Zulu Kingdom.

Dingane's relationship with the Boers began in treachery. According to most storytellers, Dingane signed a treaty in which he agreed to grant the Boers a certain territory. To celebrate the signing, Dingane invited several Boer leaders to join him for a party. Naturally, Dingane told the Boers, there would be no need to carry weapons to such a joyous occasion.

After softening up the Boers with glad entertainment, Dingane and his men suddenly turned on them, slaughtering about 500 Boers, servants and slaves. To commemorate their sorrow over their many lost friends, the Boers later named the site of this slaughter *Weenen*— Dutch for "weeping."

The Battle of Blood River (December 16, 1838)

Ten months later, a Boer general lured Dingane's army into battle on the banks of the Ncome River in Natalia. Although the Zulus outnumbered the Boers by perhaps 10,000 to 500, the Boers brought far superior technology to the battle, including muskets, two cannon and ring of stout wagons for defense. When the Zulus tried to break through this ring with nothing but their short spears, the Boers mowed them down by the thousands— staining the Ncome River red with Zulu blood, and driving the Zulus out of Natalia forever.

> ### TWO LOOKS AHEAD:
> - Four years after the Battle of Blood River, the British will capture Natalia Republic from the Boers, forcing them farther inland to Orange and Transvaal. For the next several decades, the British will hold the coast of South Africa, while the Boers will hold inland South Africa.
>
> - In 1867, a 15-year-old boy will happen upon the huge Eureka Diamond, the first of many diamonds discovered on Boer lands. Diamonds will bring so many Britons to Boer lands that in time, Britons will grow to outnumber Boers there— which will lead to two Boer Wars, one from 1880 – 1881 and a second from 1899 – 1902. At the end of the Second Boer War, Britain will control all of South Africa.

FASCINATING FACTS: Adinkra Cloth

Adinkra cloth is an African-made fabric covered with hand-printed symbols. Adinkra cloth artists first use a special comb dipped in dye to divide their cloth into lined squares. They then stamp each square with adinkra, the special symbols of the Akan people of West Africa. Because each adinkra represents a different idea to the Akan, the adinkra cloth wearer may choose to make a statement through his choice of patterns.

U.S. STATE FOCUS

Florida

FASCINATING FACTS about Florida:

- State Capital: Tallahassee
- State Abbreviation: FL
- Statehood: Florida became the 27th US state on March 3, 1845.
- Area: About 66,000 square miles (Ranks 22nd in size)
- Bordering States: Georgia, Alabama
- Meaning of Name: Spanish explorer Juan Ponce de Leon named Florida for the Easter festival *Pacua Floria*, "Feast of Flowers."
- State Nickname: "Sunshine State"
- State Bird: Northern Mockingbird
- State Tree: Cabbage Palmetto
- State Flower: Florida has two state flowers, the Orange Blossom and the Tickseed.
- State Song: Florida has both a state song, "Swanee River" by Stephen Foster, and a state anthem, "Florida, Where the Sawgrass Meets the Sky" by Jan Hinton.
- State Motto: "In God We Trust"
- Historic Places to Visit: Kennedy Space Center, Colonial Quarter St. Augustine, St. Augustine Pirate & Treasure Museum, Fort Caroline National Memorial, Kingsley Plantation House, National Naval Aviation Museum
- Resources and Industries: Citrus farming, spaceflight, retirement communities, theme parks, tourism

Saturn V rocket at Kennedy Space Center in 1971

State Flag: Florida's state seal centered on a Cross of Burgundy, the battle flag of the Spanish Empire, all on a white field. Most of Florida belonged to the Spanish Empire until 1821, when Spain finally ceded the peninsula to the United States. The state seal depicts a Florida Seminole woman scattering red hibiscus flowers, symbols of Florida's great beauty. The background is a shore scene featuring cabbage palms and steam/sail-driven ships.

PRESIDENTIAL FOCUS

PRESIDENT #9: William Henry Harrison (1773 – 1841)	
In Office: March 4, 1841 – April 4, 1841	**Political Party:** Whig
Birthplace: Virginia	**Nickname:** "Old Tippecanoe"

William Henry Harrison was the seventh and last child of Benjamin Harrison V, a wealthy signer of the Declaration of Independence who also served as Governor of Virginia. Because the late-born William stood to inherit far less than his elder brothers, Benjamin planned to train William for a professional career as a doctor. Sadly, Benjamin died unexpectedly in 1791, leaving the 18-year-old William too poor to pursue his medical studies. Instead, William pursued a career of his own choosing: a military career.

Harrison's first major military assignment was as an aide to Mad Anthony Wayne, hero of the Northwest Indian War (see Chapter 28). Wayne was so pleased with Harrison's brave service— especially at the Battle of Fallen Timbers— that he promoted Harrison rapidly through the ranks. From there, Harrison's respected family name combined with the influence of his wealthy father-in-law to win him two government jobs: first Secretary of the Northwest Territory (1799), and then Governor of the Indiana Territory (1801).

Harrison's primary task as Governor of Indiana was to buy as much native land as possible for as little money as possible. Harrison performed this task better than anyone, taking advantage of the natives' desperate situations after the Northwest Indian War to buy millions of acres for a tiny fraction of their worth. Harrison's often-shady land deals infuriated the great Shawnee chief Tecumseh, who formed Tecumseh's Confederacy in a last, desperate attempt to save Indiana for its natives. Harrison would prove to be Tecumseh's nemesis. With a victory at the 1811 Battle of Tippecanoe, Harrison destroyed Tecumseh's capital at Prophetstown; and with another victory at the 1813 Battle of the Thames, Harrison destroyed Tecumseh himself.

Decades later, Harrison used the popularity he won as a hero of the Indian Wars and the War of 1812 to win election as president. By inauguration day, Harrison was 68 years old, much the oldest president inaugurated so far. To make matters worse, Harrison delivered the longest inaugural speech in history— nearly two solid hours under a cold March rain, protected by neither coat nor hat. Harrison went from the speaker's podium to the sickbed, where he died of pneumonia a month after taking office.

Fun Facts about William Henry Harrison:
- Part of the Whig Party's strategy for winning the election of 1840 involved the first memorable campaign slogan from a U.S. presidential campaign: "Tippecanoe and Tyler Too," derived from (1) Harrison's famous victory at over Tecumseh at Prophetstown and (2) Harrison's running mate John Tyler.
- Harrison was the first president to die in office. At just 32 days in length, Harrison's term in office was shorter than any other president's.
- Harrison and his grandson, 23rd president Benjamin Harrison, form the only grandfather-grandson pair to serve as presidents.

Notable Quotes from William Henry Harrison:
- "There is nothing more corrupting, nothing more destructive of the noblest and finest feelings of our nature, than the exercise of unlimited power."

CHAPTER 33: The Mexican War of Independence; the Mexican-American War

WORLD GEOGRAPHY FOCUS

Four mountain ranges dominate Mexico's geography:

1. The ***Sierra Madre Occidental***, or "Mother Mountains of the West," which run near the west coast.

2. The ***Sierra Madre Oriental***, or "Mother Mountains of the East," which run near the east coast.

3. The ***Eje Volcanico Transversal***, or "Crossing Volcanic Axis," which connects the southern ends of the first two ranges.

4. The ***Sierra Madre del Sur***, or "Mother Mountains of the South," which run near the southwest coast.

Between the first three ranges lies the **Mexican Altiplano**, a huge, high plain that slopes from low average heights in the north to great heights in the south.

Mexico also occupies two major peninsulas:

1. The **Yucatan peninsula**, a southeastern peninsula that divides the Gulf of Mexico to its west and north from the Caribbean Sea to its east. Two of Mexico's neighbors, **Belize** and **Guatemala**, also occupy parts of the Yucatan.

2. The **Baja peninsula**, a long western peninsula that lies across the Gulf of California from mainland Mexico. Baja's largest city, **Tijuana,** stands just across the U.S. border from San Diego, California.

Mexico's major cities include:

- **Mexico City**, Mexico's capital, built on the swampy site of the Aztec Empire's old capital Tenochtitlan. Mexico City's location on the southern Altiplano gives it a remarkably high average elevation of nearly 8,000 feet— about one and one-half times that of the United States' "Mile-High City" of Denver, Colorado.

- **Guadalajara**, which stands in the southern Altiplano about 280 miles west-northwest of Mexico City. Guadalajara's average elevation is nearly as high as Denver's.

- **Veracruz**, Mexico's largest port on the Gulf of Mexico. Veracruz was where Hernan Cortes landed to conquer the Aztecs, and where the U.S. Army and Marines landed to fight the Mexican-American War.

- **Ciudad Juarez**, a northern metropolis that stands just across the U.S. border from El Paso, Texas. Juarez is named for Benito Juarez— a beloved president who stood for Mexican independence during the 1860s, when Emperor Napoleon III tried to absorb Mexico into his Second French Empire (see Year Four).

WORLD HISTORY FOCUS

The Mexican War of Independence (1810 – 1821)

> DEFINITION: The **Mexican War of Independence** was the war in which Mexico won independence from Spain.

> REFRESHING REMINDERS:
> - The **Viceroyalty of New Spain** was the government Spain established to govern its empire in North America. As of the early 1800s, New Spain included not only Mexico and Central America, but also part or all of what are now the U.S. states of Texas, New Mexico, Arizona, California, Nevada, Utah, Colorado and more.
> - Spanish America divided its citizens into race-based categories called *casta*. **Peninsulares**, or whites born on mainland Spain, were the top *casta*; while **criollos**, or whites born in the colonies, stood second.
> - The **Spanish-American Wars of Independence** began shortly after 1807, when Napoleon's Peninsular War upended the government of mainland Spain (see Chapter 29). In the chaos that followed, **juntas** large and small arose to claim various parts of the crumbling Spanish Empire.

Mexico's own Spanish American War of Independence began on September 16, 1810— Mexico's first Independence Day, the day Father Miguel Hidalgo of Dolores, Mexico delivered his *Grito de Dolores* speech. Like the wars Simón Bolívar and José de San Martín fought in South America, Mexico's war was a struggle between two main groups: (1) **royalists** loyal to the Spanish Crown, and (2) **independents** loyal only to Mexico.

CAST OF CHARACTERS for the Mexican War of Independence

1. **Miguel Hidalgo y Costilla (1753 – 1811, Independent):** Miguel Hidalgo was the *criollo* Catholic priest of Dolores, a small town about 170 miles northwest of Mexico City. Two unique qualities set Father Miguel apart from ordinary priests of his day:

   - Where most priests cared about church life, Father Miguel cared about daily life— about helping his beloved Mexican people rise above the poverty that sprang from three centuries of Spanish exploitation. Miguel spent much of his personal fortune planting vineyards for wine, olive groves for oil, mulberry trees for silk— anything that might make Mexico more self-sufficient, less dependent on Spain.

   - Where most priests believed in supporting Pope and Crown, Father Miguel believed in Enlightenment philosophy. Like the French philosophers he loved to read— including Montesquieu, Rousseau and even the atheist Voltaire— Father Miguel believed that when a tyrant oppresses his people, those people have a duty to rebel.

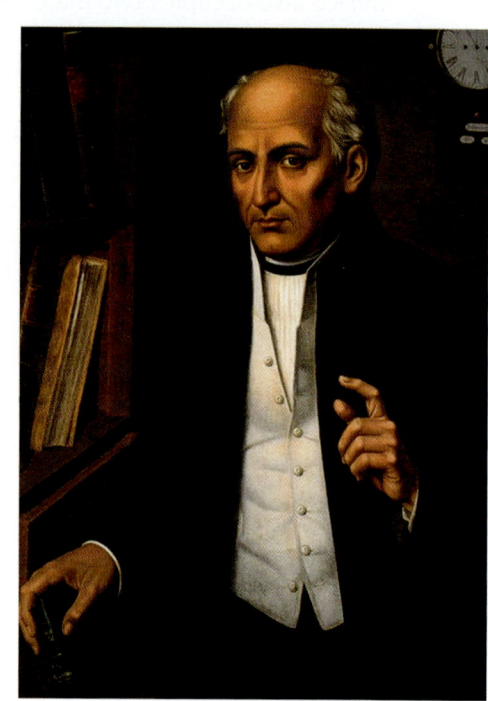

   Father Miguel Hidalgo

2. **Felix Maria Calleja (1753 – 1828, Royalist):** Calleja was a highly skilled, often brutal *peninsulare* army general who won key battles for the royalists early in the war.

3. **Agustin de Iturbide (1783 – 1824, Royalist/Independent):** Iturbide was a *criollo* army general who fought on the royalist side for almost ten years, only to switch loyalties at a critical moment.

Grievances along the Road to Independence

Father Miguel Hidalgo of Dolores wasn't the only *criollo* who read Enlightenment literature. As a member of a large literary club in nearby Queretaro, Father Miguel attended frequent discussions of the latest

Enlightenment philosophy. Through reading and discussion, Miguel and his friends gained a clearer understanding of Spain's cruelty to Mexico:

- Enlightenment philosophy revealed the *casta* system for what it was— a ludicrous injustice that arbitrarily excluded *criollos* from all the best government jobs, even though *criollos* outnumbered *peninsulares* by ten or more to one. From the moment the Enlightenment ideas of equality and representative government took hold in *criollo* minds, the *casta* system was doomed to fall.

- Just as France had its *exclusif* with Haiti (see Chapter 29), so too Spain allowed its colonies to trade only with Spain— a mercantilist policy that made it impossible for Mexican traders to compete with Spanish ones. Like France and Britain, Spain wanted her colonies to enrich the mother country, not compete with her in trade.

- The Spanish government strongly discouraged every attempt to make Mexico more self-sufficient. For example, the government destroyed Father Miguel's Mexican vineyards to keep them from competing with Spanish ones— forcing poor Mexicans to pay high prices for imported Spanish wine.

- As of 1810, Spain stood in desperate need of tax money to fund its expensive Peninsular War against Napoleon. Finding the task of collecting extra taxes from the embattled homeland too difficult, the government instead raised taxes on its colonies. After three hundred years of enriching itself at its colonies' expense, Spain now added insult to injury by setting its highest tax rates on the colonies yet.

The more Father Miguel and his friends discussed these grievances, the angrier they grew— until finally, Miguel's Queretaro literary club grew into a revolutionary organization bent on overthrowing the royalist government of New Spain. Setting December 1810 as their target date for launching their rebellion, Father Miguel and his rebel friends set about gathering the weapons and support they would need.

Unfortunately, someone revealed the rebels' plans to the government long before they were ready. Certain that the royalists would soon arrive to arrest him, a desperate Father Miguel decided to launch his rebellion three months early, through a famous speech called the *Grito de Dolores*.

FASCINATING FACTS: The *Grito de Dolores*, Spanish for "Shout of Dolores" (September 16, 1810)

The Mexican War of Independence began early on the morning of September 16, 1810, shortly after Father Miguel Hidalgo rang Dolores' church bells to gather his people for a hasty town meeting. Although Father Miguel's exact words that day have been forgotten, his Shout of Dolores probably included words like these:

"My friends and countrymen! We have borne this shameful tax, which only suits slaves, for three centuries as a sign of tyranny and servitude— a terrible stain which we shall now wash away with our efforts. The moment of our freedom has arrived, the hour of our liberty has struck; and if you recognize its great value, you will help me defend it from the ambitious grasp of the tyrants! Only a few hours remain before you see me at the head of the men who take pride in being free! The cause is holy, and God will protect it… Long live Mexico, for which we are going to fight! *Viva Mexico*! *Viva la independencia*!"

"Hidalgo," Mexican muralist Jose Orozco's interpretation of Father Miguel delivering the Grito de Dolores

As promised, Father Miguel soon led his rebel army out of Dolores. That army was not well-armed, as most of its soldiers were peasants who owned no guns; nor was it well-organized, as it

had few officers and no training. It was, however, enormous— somewhere between 20,000 – 50,000 strong, many times larger than any royalist army.

The Siege of Guanajuato (September 28, 1810)

Father Miguel's first target was Guanajuato, a wealthy mining town that was also the capital of Guanajuato Province. As Miguel's ragtag army approached, Guanajuato's 400-odd royalist defenders first collected the town's entire supply of gold, silver, guns and ammunition, and then retreated inside a building that was already full of food: the *Alhóndiga de Granaditas*, a large stone granary built like a fort. Thus prepared, the well-armed royalists hoped to hold off Miguel's ill-armed mob long enough for reinforcements to arrive.

At first, the royalists seemed likely to succeed; for Miguel's rebels could come nowhere near the Alhondiga without coming under deadly gunfire from its windows and roof. All of that changed when a hero called *El Pípila* joined the Siege of Guanajuato.

AMAZING MEXICANS: **El Pípila** was the nickname of an unusually strong Mexican rebel who found a way to approach the Alhondiga when no one else could. First, El Pípila strapped to his back a huge, heavy stone broad enough to shield his whole body. Next, he started straining his way toward the Alhondiga's wooden doors, carrying along a bucket of tar and a torch. Royalist bullets struck fragments from the stone on his back, but could do El Pípila himself no harm. Upon reaching the doors, El Pípila smeared them with tar and set them alight, starting a hot fire that the royalists couldn't quench from inside.

El Pípila at the doors of the Alhondiga

MERCILESS MASSACRES: As the Alhondiga's doors burned through, Father Miguel's rebels burst inside. Despite the fact that their leader was a priest, Father Miguel's rebels showed not the slightest mercy to the royalist defenders inside the Alhondiga: all 400 died violent deaths. Afterward, the rebels rampaged through Guanajuato, pillaging and murdering every royalist and *peninsulare* they could find.

INTERESTING IDEAS: The brutal massacre at the end of the Siege of Guanajuato revealed a serious flaw in Father Miguel's leadership: he provided inspiration, but not the discipline required to establish law and order. Instead of guiding Mexico toward better government, Miguel appeared to be guiding it toward anarchy.

The Battle of Monte de las Cruces (October 30, 1810)

From Guanajuato, Father Miguel struck for the greatest prize of all: Mexico City, capital of New Spain's royalist government. The rebels' success at Guanajuato, coupled with the money and arms they seized there, helped boost their numbers to somewhere near 80,000 by the time they reached their next major battlefield: *Monte de las Cruces*, a "Mountain of the Crosses" about twenty miles southwest of Mexico City. This second major battle found the royalists better prepared, but still outnumbered: perhaps 2,000 – 3,000 well-armed royalists stood against Father Miguel's eager, but still ill-armed, rebels.

To make the most of their small numbers, the royalists arranged themselves on a hilltop, forcing the rebels to charge uphill under fire. Twice the rebels charged, and twice the royalists fended them off. After the second charge, though, the rebels managed to surround the royalists, making a rebel victory all but certain.

Hoping to prevent more bloodshed, Father Miguel sent officers to negotiate terms for a royalist surrender. Instead of negotiating, the royalists committed a foul war crime: they murdered Father Miguel's officers under a flag of truce. Now thoroughly enraged, the rebels charged a third time. This time they routed the royalists, driving the survivors off their hill and back to Mexico City.

At this point, Father Miguel made a decision that dramatically altered the course of the war. Having defeated the only royalist army in the area, Miguel almost certainly could have gone on to capture Mexico City; but instead, he chose to retreat. Exactly why is uncertain:

- Father Miguel may have felt guilty over his army's brutal massacre at Guanajuato, and turned away to avoid a similar massacre at Mexico City.

- Father Miguel may have believed that a second, larger royalist army, one led by Felix Calleja, was closer than it really was— close enough to defeat his ill-disciplined rebels before they could capture Mexico City.

- The lack of discipline in Father Miguel's army may have carried away up to half of his troops, leaving him with too few to be certain of capturing Mexico City.

Whatever his reasons, Father Miguel chose to retreat toward Guadalajara— setting in motion a chain of events that plunged all Mexico into chaos.

Warrior priest Miguel Hidalgo

Ten weeks after Father Miguel's retreat, General Calleja dealt him a disastrous defeat at the **Battle of Calderon Bridge**, fought on January 17, 1811 just east of Guadalajara. Although Father's Miguel's rebels still badly outnumbered Calleja's royalists, Calleja caught a lucky break: one of his cannonballs struck the rebels' gunpowder supply, setting off a terrific explosion that scattered the rebel army.

With his rebellion crumbling around him, Father Miguel fled northward, hoping to gather more support. Sadly, Miguel made the mistake of trusting the wrong man, a traitor who betrayed him to the royalists.

FASCINATING FATES: Because Father Miguel was still technically a priest when the royalists captured him, no one dared execute him without the Catholic Church's approval. Fortunately for the royalists, most churchmen were on their side— which meant that the government had little trouble finding a royalist bishop willing to defrock the wayward priest.

Thus in the eyes of the Church, the former Father Miguel was an ordinary citizen when he faced a firing squad on July 30, 1811. After shooting Miguel in the heart, the royalists cut off his head and hung it from a high corner of the Alhondiga, the Guanajuato granary where he had won his first victory— a grim warning to any rebel who might be planning to follow in Father Miguel's footsteps.

FASCINATING FACTS: The Mummies of Guanajuato

Around 1860, Guanajuato's cemeteries started having the same problem Paris' cemeteries had years before: they were running out of space to bury their dead (see Chapter 26). To solve this problem, cemeteries started charging fees to keep families' loved ones buried. If a family failed to pay, then the cemetery removed that family's long-dead loved ones from their tombs to make room for paying customers.

In the process of removing those old remains, cemetery workers happened upon a mystery: instead of finding nothing but bones, they found that scores of Guanajuato's dead had mummified. These mummies were not like Egyptian mummies, which the ancients preserved through a careful drying process. Instead, it is believed, some special combination of climate and soil conditions fast-dried the mummies of Guanajuato, preserving them as thoroughly as the best Egyptian undertakers. Some of these mummies' faces bear expressions of horror, as if they might have been buried alive. As of 2014, dozens are on display at Guanajuato's *Museo de las Momias*.

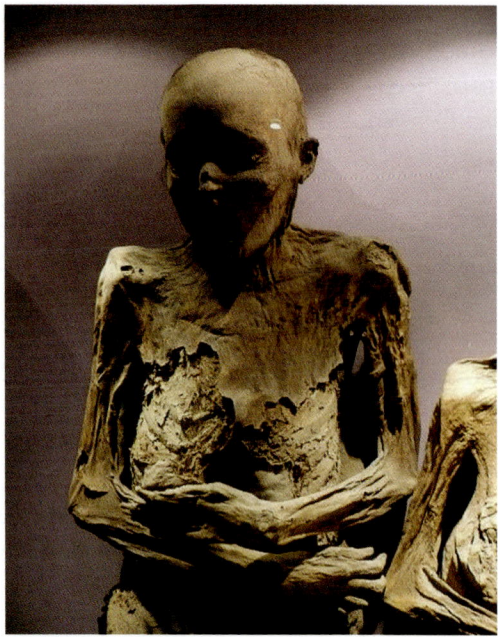

Photo from the Museo de las Momias de Guanajuato

The Rise of Agustin de Iturbide (1811 – 1821)

The next ten years were years of chaos, with Father Miguel-inspired rebellions cropping up all over Mexico. Among the most successful rebel leaders were:

1. **Father José María Morelos**, a fellow priest who took Father Miguel's place after the elder priest's execution in 1811. Morelos won several surprising victories in southern Mexico— but only until 1815, when the royalists captured him and set him before a firing squad.

2. **General Vincente Guerrero**, who took Morelos' place. Guerrero was still leading the rebellion in southern Mexico in 1821, when the royalists made the mistake of sending General Agustin de Iturbide against him.

Before 1815, Iturbide was the royalists' most successful general, and one of their most ruthless. From 1815 – 1820, though, changing circumstances caused Iturbide to rethink his loyalties:

- In 1816, then-Viceroy Felix Calleja demoted Iturbide on charges of cruelty and corruption. Even after the next viceroy reinstated him in 1820, Iturbide remained angry over this stain on his record, and convinced that he knew why Calleja treated him unfairly: because Calleja was a proud *peninsulare*, while Iturbide was only a *criollo*.

- Enlightenment philosophy was causing as much trouble in mainland Spain as it was in Mexico. After Napoleon's first fall in 1814, King Ferdinand VII returned to Spain's throne expecting to resume his full powers as absolute monarch. However, Ferdinand soon proved himself too oppressive a tyrant for enlightened Spaniards to accept. In 1820, these enlightened Spaniards forced Ferdinand to adopt a constitution that set strict limits on his power— remaking Spain's government as a constitutional monarchy.

REFRESHING REMINDERS:
- A **republican government** is one in which the people govern themselves through elected representatives.
- A **constitutional monarchy** is a modified republican government with a legislature made up of the people's elected representatives, and a monarch as head of state. That monarch may be either hereditary or elected.

INTERESTING IDEAS: Spain's transformation from absolute monarchy to constitutional monarchy created an interesting possibility for Mexico. As a royalist, Iturbide fought to defend absolute monarchy in both Spain and Mexico. In light of the successful rebellion in Spain, some royalists feared that Spain might soon become a republic, which would leave King Ferdinand VII without a throne. If that happened, then some Mexican royalists hoped to offer Ferdinand VII a new, more stable throne: Mexico's.

Of course, the royalists could never invite Ferdinand VII to Mexico unless they first ended Vincente Guerrero's rebellion, either by defeating Guerrero or compromising with him. After several clashes in 1820, Iturbide began to think that he might never defeat Guerrero; so he decided to compromise.

FASCINATING FACTS: The Plan of Iguala

Early in 1821, Agustin de Iturbide met Vincente Guerrero at Iguala, a town about 80 miles south of Mexico City, to negotiate a compromise that would end the Mexican War of Independence. The two leaders' negotiations focused on three areas where royalists and independents agreed:

1. **Religion:** At this point in Mexican history, both priest-inspired independents and Church-loving royalists agreed that Mexico must remain a Catholic nation.

2. **Independence:** Now that Spain was a constitutional monarchy, rather than an absolute one, royalists didn't mind declaring independence from Spain. Independents, of course, had been seeking independence all along.

3. **Unity:** Mexico's government must no longer recognize any difference between *peninsulare* and *criollo*.

These three principles formed the basis of the **Plan of Iguala**, a scheme to unite royalists and independents in the common cause of building a strong Mexico. To set their plan in motion, Iturbide and Guerrero combined their forces into a new army: the **Army of the Three Guarantees**, formed to guarantee *Religión, Independencia y Unión* for Mexico.

Portrait of Agustin de Iturbide

Other Interesting Facts:
- Because Guerrero was of mixed race, and therefore Iturbide's inferior under Spanish law, the proud Guerrero refused to sign the Plan of Iguala until Iturbide added these words: "The distinction of castes is abolished... All the inhabitants of the country are citizens, and equal, and the door of advancement is open to virtue and merit." <u>In other words</u>: The Plan of Iguala brought an official end to Mexico's casta system, making all races equal under the law.

<u>Mexican Independence (September 27, 1821)</u>

After his best general joined forces with the rebels, the royalist viceroy had no more hope

Agustin de Iturbide's triumphal entry into Mexico City on September 27, 1821

of victory. The last Viceroy of New Spain stepped down on September 27, 1821, the same day Agustin de Iturbide led his Army of the Three Guarantees on a triumphal entry into Mexico City. Agustin's grand ceremony marked the end of the 11-year Mexican War of Independence.

INTERESTING IDEAS: Iturbide's victory left Mexico with two Independence Days to celebrate. Independents favored September 16th, 1810, the date of Miguel Hidalgo's *Grito de Dolores*. Royalists, on the other hand, favored September 27th, 1821, the date of Iturbide's triumphal entry into Mexico City. Years later, when Mexico finally emerged from its wars as a republic, September 16th emerged as the preferred date.

FASCINATING FACTS: Mexican Independence Day (September 16)

Modern-day Mexico's Independence Day celebration begins with a reminder of how the Mexican War of Independence began. Every year on the night of September 15th, public officials in cities and towns all over Mexico ring church bells to gather their people, just as Father Miguel rang his church bells in 1810. The crowds fall silent as the clocks begin to strike 11 p.m., the traditional hour of the *Grito de Dolores*. At the clocks' last strike, Mexicans all over the country shout "*Viva Mexico! Viva la independencia!*" at the same moment. The celebration continues the next day with fiestas, parades, concerts and bullfights.

Statue of Miguel Hidalgo in front of the church where he delivered the *Grito de Dolores*

FASCINATING FACTS: *Chiles en Nogado*

To honor Agustin de Iturbide as he rode through their town on his way to or from Mexico City, the nuns of Santa Monica convent in Puebla, Mexico prepared a patriotic dish. *Chiles en nogada* are stuffed peppers specially prepared to recall the three colors of the Mexican flag: green, white and red. Chili peppers stuffed with spiced meat provide the green, as does a sprig of parsley. A walnut-based cream sauce provides the white, as well as part of the treat's name; for *nogal* is Spanish for walnut. Pomegranate seeds provide the red.

Troubles after the Plan of Iguala

The happy prospect of winning the war led the independents to overlook some serious weaknesses in the Plan of Iguala. Although the plan promised a new constitution for Mexico, it was silent about what that constitution might contain, saying only that it would be "more suitable to the country." Furthermore, the plan contained no bill of rights, nor even a promise of elected representatives— which meant that after an 11-year struggle, poor Mexicans might emerge no better off than they had been under their old government.

These weaknesses plunged Mexico into another era of chaos, a time when new leaders, governments and constitutions arose every few years.

The First Mexican Empire (1821 – 1823)

Predictably, Spain refused to recognize Mexico's independence. When King Ferdinand VII refused to claim Mexico's throne, Agustin de Iturbide tried to claim it instead, proclaiming himself emperor in 1822.

Unfortunately, Emperor Agustin I of the First Mexican Empire proved to be a terrible tyrant— the sort who (1) automatically jailed his political enemies for speaking out against him; (2) ignored his people's representatives in the new Congress; and finally (3) dissolved Congress altogether. The Mexican people's growing disappointment with Iturbide turned their hearts toward other leaders, including Santa Anna.

> AMAZING MEXICANS: Antonio Lopez de Santa Anna (1794 – 1876)
>
> Antonio Lopez de Santa Anna was a *criollo* from Veracruz who joined the royalist army as a cadet officer in 1810, when he was just 16 years old. Bravery and cleverness quickly propelled Santa Anna upward through the officer ranks.
>
> By 1821, 27-year-old Santa Anna was one of the key officers whose support Agustin de Iturbide needed to overthrow the Viceroy of New Spain. At Iturbide's urging, Santa Anna betrayed the royalists by declaring his support for the Plan of Iguala. In exchange, Iturbide promoted him all the way to general.

> A LOOK AHEAD: Santa Anna's change of loyalties in 1821 was only the first of many. Over the next 35 years, Santa Anna will take office as President of Mexico no fewer than eleven times, nearly always by turning against his predecessors. Despite humiliating losses to come in the Texas Revolution and the Mexican-American War (see below), Santa Anna will remain one of the most popular leaders in Mexico for decades.

Santa Anna

Santa Anna's second switch of loyalties came in 1822, when he turned against the very man who had promoted him only a year before: Agustin de Iturbide. Late that year, Santa Anna joined other generals and politicians in calling for the tyrannical Iturbide to step down— which Iturbide finally did, departing Mexico for European exile in mid-1823.

> FASCINATING FATES: Soon after Iturbide left Mexico, an angry Mexican Congress condemned the fleeing tyrant as a traitor, placing him under a sentence of death should he ever return.
>
> About a year later, Iturbide's supporters convinced him that Mexico was suffering in his absence, and might welcome his strong leadership; so he took the risk of returning. Instead of setting Iturbide on Mexico's throne, one of his enemies set him before a firing squad.

The First Mexican Republic (1824)

With both King Ferdinand VII and Emperor Iturbide out of the way by 1824, Santa Anna and his allies set aside the whole notion of monarchy, and instead adopted Mexico's first republican constitution.

> FASCINATING FACTS: The Federal Constitution of the United Mexican States (Adopted 1824)
>
> Mexico's first constitution had much in common with the Constitution of the United States:
>
> - It recreated Mexico as a republic with three branches of government: executive, legislative and judicial.
> - It established an elected Congress with two houses, the Chamber of Deputies and the Chamber of Senators.
> - It established the elective offices of President and Vice President, each with 4-year terms.
>
> However, there was also one critical difference between the two constitutions. Instead of forbidding the Mexican Congress to establish a state religion— as the First Amendment to the U.S. Constitution did— the Constitution of 1824 established Roman Catholicism as Mexico's state religion, insisting that Mexico would tolerate no other. Thus the new republic became an awkward blend of church and state, with traditional church courts operating side-by-side with new state courts.

A LOOK AHEAD: In years to come, the religious requirements in the Constitution of 1824 will lead to no end of conflict between two types of Mexicans: (1) liberals who believe in separation of church and state; and (2) conservative Catholics who believe that the Church should guide the state. These conflicts will contribute to two terrible wars, the Reform War of 1857 – 1861 and the Mexican Revolution of 1910 – 1929.

FASCINATING FACTS: The Virgin of Guadalupe

The Virgin of Guadalupe is an image of the Virgin Mary that helps explain how Catholicism became so important to the Mexican people— even to descendants of the Aztecs, whose native religion wasn't Catholic at all.

In 1531, about a decade after Hernan Cortes conquered the Aztecs, a poor native Mexican named Juan Diego made a habit of passing by a certain hill on his way to attend Mass at a Franciscan mission station. As Juan passed by his hill one morning, the Virgin Mary suddenly appeared to him with an unusual request: she wanted Juan to ask his bishop to build a church for her on that very hill.

Naturally, Juan's bishop doubted Juan's story, and asked for a miraculous sign as proof. The fourth time Mary appeared to Juan, she provided exactly the sort of sign the bishop wanted. First, she sent Juan to the top of the hill, asking him to gather some flowers for her— special roses that shouldn't have been in season, and yet somehow were. This Juan did, wrapping the flowers inside his cloak. After re-arranging the flowers in the cloak, Mary sent Juan to show them to his bishop. When Juan opened his cloak for the bishop, the flowers fell aside to reveal a perfect image of the Virgin Mary, miraculously imprinted inside Juan's cloak.

The Virgin of Guadalupe as her image appeared on Juan Diego's cloak

That very year, Catholics took their first pilgrimages to Juan's hill so that they could behold the miracle of Juan's cloak with their own eyes. To honor Mary's request, and to house her miraculous image, Juan's bishop built one of Mexico's most important churches: the Basilica of Our Lady of Guadalupe, set on Juan Diego's hill in what is now northern Mexico City. The more Mexicans of all races beheld Mary's miraculous image, the more believed that Mexico held a special place in Mary's heart.

Other interesting facts:
- The battle standard that Miguel Hidalgo carried in 1810 – 1811 bore the Virgin of Guadalupe as a special symbol of the Mexican War of Independence. In addition to *Viva Mexico* and *Viva la independencia*, Miguel's *Grito de Dolores* probably included *Viva Nuestra Senora de Guadalupe*— "Long live Our Lady of Guadalupe!"

The old Basilica of Our Lady of Guadalupe

The Texas Revolution (1835 – 1836)

DEFINITION: The **Texas Revolution** was the war in which the Republic of Texas won independence from Mexico.

Settling East Texas

The first Europeans to make permanent homes in thinly-populated eastern Texas were Spanish Catholic missionaries. Upon arriving near the headwaters of Texas' San Antonio River in the late 1600s, these missionaries established one of the region's oldest cities: San Antonio, home of the Alamo.

FASCINATING FACTS: The Alamo

The Alamo is a walled compound in San Antonio, Texas that began as the headquarters of the early Roman Catholic mission there. Commissioned in 1724, the compound soon grew to include a church, apartments for priests, classrooms for new believers, workshops, barns and more.

Around 1793, the Catholic Church abandoned its then 70-year-old mission compound in favor of newer buildings. Shortly after 1800, the army of New Spain claimed the Alamo for a new purpose: the abandoned mission became a **presidio**, a military outpost charged with defending the frontier of Spanish settlement. Spain's newfound interest in defending Texas sprang partly from the threat of Napoleon, whose 1801 – 1803 invasion of Haiti seemed to indicate greater French ambitions in North America.

Modern-day photo of the Alamo

REFRESHING REMINDERS:
- Whatever Napoleon intended for North America, his ambitions ended when Toussaint Louverture and Jean-Jacques Dessalines defeated the Leclerc Expedition in Haiti. After losing Haiti, Napoleon decided to sell Louisiana to the United States in 1803.
- In 1812, the U.S. admitted Louisiana as the 18th state. Three years later, General Andrew Jackson fought off a British invasion at the Battle of New Orleans, part of the War of 1812 (see Chapter 30).

DEFINITION: A **land speculator** is an investor who tries to earn money by first buying land at a low price, and then selling it at a high price.

After the War of 1812, thousands of American settlers poured into Louisiana, hoping to buy cheap land in the new state. Instead, many settlers found that land speculators had already bought up huge tracts of land all over Louisiana, boosting land prices far beyond what some settlers could afford.

By 1820, some of these frustrated settlers were already shopping for cheaper land farther west, in Texas. To handle these settlers, Mexico negotiated contracts with special land agents called empresarios.

DEFINITION: *Empresario* is Spanish for "entrepreneur" or "businessman." A Texas **empresario** was a land speculator who received special permission from New Spain, and later from independent Mexico, to divide and sell certain large tracts of Texas land. Both parties benefited from the arrangement: (1) the empresario gained a chance to earn money; while (2) New Spain/Mexico gained more settlers for thinly-populated Texas— and therefore more tax money to cover the cost of defending Texas.

AMAZING AMERICANS: Stephen Austin, "Father of Texas" (1793 – 1836)

Texas' most successful empresario, Virginia-born Stephen Austin, inherited his interest in Texas from his father. Moses Austin was an otherwise down-on-his-luck land speculator who, in 1820, somehow won the Governor of Spanish Texas' permission to settle a large tract in eastern Texas. Sadly, Moses died of pneumonia in June 1821, leaving the task of settling east Texas to his son.

Stephen Austin's first task was to travel from Louisiana to San Antonio, where he hoped the governor would renew Moses' contract. Despite the turmoil in Mexico City at the time— for Austin reached San Antonio in August 1821, one month before Agustin de Iturbide's triumphal entry into Mexico City (see above)— the governor granted Austin permission to settle 300 families around the Brazos and Colorado rivers, near what is now Austin, Texas.

From San Antonio, Austin returned to Louisiana to recruit his first settlers. The vastness of Texas, combined with the generous terms of his empresario contract, allowed Austin to offer large riverfront farms at the low price of 12-½ cents per acre— about a tenth of the going rate in Louisiana. Families answered Austin's advertisements by the score, filling his first contract of 300 families by 1825. These became the **Old Three Hundred**, Texas' oldest English-speaking families.

Over the next several years, Austin brought a total of about 8,000 Americans to Texas, most of them from the Southern United States. The hard work of shepherding these settlers— touring farmland with them, surveying their tracts and negotiating with the government of Mexico on their behalf— earned Austin his place as the honorary "Father of Texas."

Stephen Austin

Besides the empresarios' legal settlers, Texas also received two kinds of illegal American settlers:

1. **Squatters** who simply moved onto unclaimed tracts and started farming them, without registering their claims or paying for them.

2. **Filibusters**, former soldiers who hoped to separate Texas from Mexico and join it to the United States. More than one Texas filibuster rebelled against Mexican authority during those early years; however, all such rebellions were minor.

Between empresarios, squatters and filibusters, East Texas received tens of thousands of American-born settlers— several times the number of Mexican-born settlers.

Causes of the Texas Revolution

From the beginning, the Mexican government understood the biggest danger these American-born Texans posed: that they might be more loyal to the United States than they were to Mexico. To guard against this danger, Mexico required all Texans to (1) become citizens of Mexico; (2) obey Mexican law; and (3) make a sincere effort to learn Spanish. Also, because Mexico tolerated no religion but Catholicism, all Texans technically agreed to become Catholics.

Mexico found these requirements hard to enforce. Instead of adopting Mexican culture, most American-born Texans clung to their old culture— the freedom-loving, English-speaking Protestant culture of the American pioneers they were. American-born Texans particularly despised Mexican law, which offered far fewer protections than U.S. law. For example, Mexican authorities could detain accused criminals for as long as they liked, without ever letting them appear before an impartial judge— something no American lawyer would tolerate. Clashes between these two very different cultures and legal systems led to grievances like these:

- By 1830, some Mexicans suspected that Texas' American-born settlers were all filibusters— that they were all plotting to separate Texas from Mexico, and join it to the United States. To prevent this, Mexico abruptly banned all immigration from the United States, hoping to give Texas' Mexican-born minority time to catch up. American-born Texans deeply resented this ban, and longed to see it repealed.

- **The *Siete Leye*, or Seven Laws:** Fifteen years after the Mexican War of Independence, Santa Anna came to believe that the people of Mexico were too undereducated, and too easily influenced by their priests, to govern themselves wisely. Acting on his new belief, Santa Anna replaced the Constitution of 1824 with the Seven Laws of 1835— a liberty-crushing constitution that removed all power from average Mexicans' hands, and placed it in the hands of elite Mexicans like Santa Anna. Having lived under the enlightened U.S. Constitution, American-born Texans wanted nothing to do with Santa Anna's tyrannical Seven Laws.

- Perhaps worst of all, Santa Anna tried to come between Texans and the guns they used to settle the frontier. Acting on the theory that gun-less Texans would be less likely to rebel, Santa Anna first (1) declared that Mexico needed only 1 in 500 Texans to serve in the local militia; and then (2) declared that only militiamen had the right to own guns. All non-militia Texans were to surrender their guns upon Santa Anna's request.

Instead of meekly surrendering their guns to Santa Anna, Texans defied him to come and take them.

CAST OF CHARACTERS for the Texas Revolution:

AMAZING AMERICANS: Sam Houston (1793 – 1863)

Samuel Houston was born in Virginia, but raised in Tennessee, where he spent part of his youth living among the Cherokee. As a young army officer during the Creek War, Houston suffered serious wounds at the Battle of Horseshoe Bend, where his bravery helped Andrew Jackson defeat the Red Stick Creeks (see Chapter 30).

After the war, Houston followed Jackson into Tennessee law and politics. Houston's friendship with the popular Jackson helped send him to the U.S. House of Representatives, where he served from 1823 – 1827; and to the Tennessee governor's office, where he served from 1827 – 1829. In 1829, though, Houston abruptly resigned the governorship— possibly because his 19-year-old wife abandoned him a few weeks into their marriage, humiliating him.

The former governor spent the years from 1829 – 1832 back among his Cherokee friends, who had since moved from Tennessee to the Arkansas Territory. Houston finally drifted to Texas in 1832, just when the Texas Revolution started heating up.

Sam Houston, first commander of the Texan Army

AMAZING AMERICANS: William Barrett Travis (1809 – 1836)

William Barrett Travis was a hotheaded young attorney/newspaperman who ran up so many debts in Alabama that he finally fled to Texas, leaving behind his wife and child, lest his creditors send him to debtor's prison. In 1831, Travis opened a law office in Anahuac, Texas, just across Trinity Bay from what is now Houston.

AMAZING AMERICANS: James Bowie (1796 – 1836)

Jim Bowie was a Kentucky-born, Louisiana-raised adventurer who earned his living as a land speculator, slave trader and treasure hunter, among other things. Before he moved to Texas in 1830, the impossibly tough Bowie was best known for his part in a duel-gone-wrong called the Sandbar Fight.

FASCINATING FACTS: The Sandbar Fight (September 19, 1827)

The famous Sandbar Fight began as a duel between two Louisiana gentlemen named Levi Wells and Thomas Maddox— who, to avoid the laws of their home state, held their contest on a riverside sandbar outside

Natchez, Mississippi. Several onlookers crowded the sandbar in support of each duelist— including Wells supporters Jim Bowie and Samuel Cuny, and Maddox supporter Robert Crain.

Were it not for these onlookers, the duel might have ended peacefully— for after each duelist fired two shots without wounding the other, Wells and Maddox agreed to settle their differences with a handshake. However, several onlookers had quarrels of their own, and were spoiling for a fight. Immediately after the handshake, Cuny mockingly challenged Crain to settle some old score. Crain's irate response was to pull his pistol and fire at Cuny. Unfortunately, Crain missed, and instead struck Jim Bowie in the hip.

Fighting through terrible pain, Bowie drew his knife and lunged at Crain, at which Crain raised his spent pistol and clubbed Bowie to the ground. Immediately, several Maddox supporters descended on Bowie with sword, gun and knife. One attacker thrust a thin sword at Bowie's chest. Although the blade glanced off Bowie's sternum, its point still lodged only inches from his heart. With this sword still jutting from his chest, Bowie seized his attacker and pulled him down on the point of his knife, spilling his heart's blood on the ground— even as another attacker slashed Bowie yet again. Two more attackers fired pistols at Bowie, one striking him in the arm.

Despite two bullet wounds, at least two stab wounds and a hard blow to the head, Bowie remained strong enough to wheel and slice off part of one gunman's arm. Daunted by Bowie's unbelievable toughness, his attackers fled, leaving his friends to patch up his many wounds.

Portrait of Jim Bowie

FASCINATING FACTS: The Bowie Knife

After the Sandbar Fight, Jim Bowie's reputation as the toughest knife fighter in America sold countless **Bowie knives**— long, strong knives like the one Bowie carried, basically hunting knives that doubled as short swords. Most Bowie knives shared these traits in common: (1) broad, stiff blades up to a foot long, with double edges for at least part of their length; (2) sharp points; and (3) sword-style hilts.

AMAZING AMERICANS: Davy Crockett (1786 – 1836)

Like Sam Houston, Davy Crockett was a Tennessee soldier who fought under Andrew Jackson in the Creek War. However, where Sam Houston later supported the popular Jackson, Crockett opposed Jackson. As a member of the House of Representatives from 1827 – 1831, Crockett was the only Tennessee legislator who took the Native Americans' side against Jackson, voting against the Indian Removal Act of 1830 (see Chapter 30). Because the vast majority of Tennessee voters supported the Indian Removal Act, Crockett's principled stand cost him his seat in the House later that year.

Davy Crockett

Crockett returned to the House in 1833, representing a new Tennessee district— only to lose his seat again in the election of 1834. In 1835, a disgusted Davy Crockett departed Washington for the last time, saying:

> "I told the people of my district that I would serve them as faithfully as I had done; but if not, they might go to hell, and I would go to Texas!"

A Brief Timeline of the Texas Revolution

1835, October 2 – The Battle of Gonzales: Acting on Santa Anna's order to relieve Texans of their guns, a small Mexican army orders the militia of Gonzales, Texas to surrender its only cannon. When the Texans refuse, a short fight breaks out. At the end of the fight, the Mexicans retreat— without the cannon.

1835, November 1 – The Consultation of 1835: Delegates from around Texas meet to decide how to answer Santa Anna's growing tyranny, especially the Seven Laws and the Battle of Gonzales. For the moment, the delegates don't declare independence from Mexico; however, they do establish a temporary government for Texas, with the goal of returning Mexico to the Constitution of 1824. They also select the experienced soldier/politician Sam Houston as commander-in-chief of the new Texan Army.

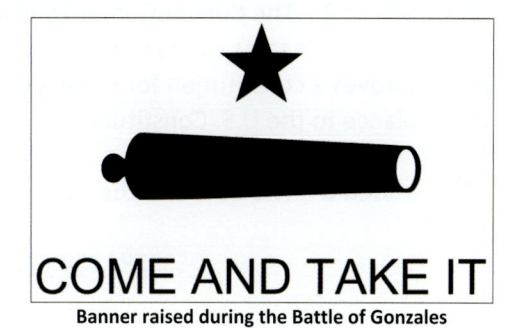

Banner raised during the Battle of Gonzales

Meanwhile, skirmishes break out all over eastern Texas, especially in San Antonio.

1835, December 11 – The Siege of San Antonio de Bejar: After a two-month-long siege involving several brief skirmishes, Texas militiamen drive a small Mexican army out of San Antonio— thus gaining control of San Antonio's presidio, the Alamo. Santa Anna immediately begins plotting his revenge.

1836, January: Former Tennessee Congressman Davy Crockett arrives in Nacogdoches, Texas, where he immediately joins the Texan Army. In exchange, Texas promises Crockett a 4,600-acre ranch. During this same month, Jim Bowie arrives at the Alamo leading a small force of about 30 Texans.

1836, February 3: William Travis arrives at the Alamo, where he and Bowie eventually agree to take joint command of San Antonio's few defenders. Five days later, Crockett arrives to join Travis and Bowie.

1836, February 23 – The Siege of the Alamo: Santa Anna arrives outside the Alamo at the head of at least 1,500 Mexican troops, with thousands more to arrive over the next few days. The Mexicans immediately encircle the decrepit fortress and begin pounding its walls with their cannon. The next day, Travis writes this open letter "To the People of Texas and All Americans in the World":

> "I am besieged by a thousand or more of the Mexicans under Santa Anna… The enemy has demanded a surrender… otherwise, the garrison are to be put to the sword, if the fort is taken. I have answered the demand with a cannon shot, and our flag still waves proudly from the walls. I shall never surrender or retreat.
>
> "Then, I call on you in the name of Liberty, of patriotism & everything dear to

Scene from the Battle of the Alamo

the American character, to come to our aid... The enemy is receiving reinforcements daily and will no doubt increase to three or four thousand in four or five days. If this call is neglected, I am determined to sustain myself as long as possible and die like a soldier who never forgets what is due to his own honor & that of his country. Victory or Death!"

1836, March 2 – The Convention of 1836 and the Texas Declaration of Independence: With the Alamo still under siege, delegates to the Convention of 1836 issue the Texas Declaration of Independence. The Convention also approves a constitution for the newly-independent Republic of Texas— one that bears a strong resemblance to the U.S. Constitution.

1836, March 6 – The Battle of the Alamo: The Alamo's defenders fall victim to a vengeful Santa Anna.

DESPERATE DEFENSES: The Battle of the Alamo (March 6, 1836)

From the beginning, Commander-in-chief Sam Houston doubted his Texans' ability to hold the Alamo against Santa Anna— so much so that in January 1836, Houston recommended abandoning the aged compound. Jim Bowie and William Travis viewed the Alamo differently— not as a military asset, but as an inspiring symbol of Texas independence, something far too valuable to surrender without a fight.

Even after Santa Anna encircled the Alamo, there remained gaps in his lines wide enough for couriers to slip through, allowing Travis to dispatch several pleas for reinforcements. Travis also dispatched scouts, including the wilderness-crafty Davy Crockett, to see when his hoped-for reinforcements might arrive.

Precious few reinforcements answered Travis' pleas. On March 6th, the day Santa Anna launched his attack, only about 180 – 250 Texans defended the Alamo's walls against thousands of besieging Mexicans.

Against such overwhelming odds, and after a 12-day pounding

Davy Crockett swinging his spent rifle as Santa Anna's soldiers pour into the Alamo

from Santa Anna's cannon, the Alamo's fate was never really in doubt. A few hours after Santa Anna ordered his charge, every Texan in the Alamo lay dead— for the vengeful Santa Anna ordered his troops to take no prisoners. Among the first to die was William Travis, struck down by an enemy bullet as he fired from atop the Alamo's walls. Davy Crockett, too, went down— although no one knows where, as Santa Anna burned his victims' bodies immediately after the battle. Among the last to die was Jim Bowie, who had fallen gravely ill several days before. According to legend, the bedridden Bowie died only after emptying his pistols into the Mexican troops who burst into his sickroom.

1836, March 11 – The Runaway Scrape: Desperate to save themselves from Santa Anna's hordes, the women, children and elderly citizens of Texas begin a mad dash toward the safety of the U.S. border. Houston follows them with his badly-outnumbered army, defending their rear even as he searches for an opportunity to attack Santa Anna.

1836, March 19 - 20 – The Battle of Coleto: A large Mexican army surrounds a far smaller Texan one near Goliad, about 80 miles southeast of San Antonio. Based on the Mexican commander's promise to treat them fairly, the Texans agree to surrender without any more fighting. The Mexicans lead nearly three hundred Texans to the Presidio de la Bahia at Goliad, where they join a few dozen more prisoners of war who are awaiting their fates.

1836, March 27 – The Goliad Massacre: Instead of treating the Goliad captives as prisoners of war, Santa Anna treats them as traitors— which means that instead of deporting them, he executes them. Mexican troops march about 350 Texans out of the presidio at Goliad, gun them down, heap their bodies and burn them.

The Presidio de la Bahia, where the Mexican army confined about 350 Texan prisoners of war before the Goliad Massacre

INTERESTING IDEAS:
- To Texans, Santa Anna's grim deeds at the Alamo and Goliad marked him as the most despicable war criminal imaginable, a traitor to all honorable soldiers. Bad enough was the Alamo, where Santa Anna slaughtered every defender, taking not a single prisoner. Even worse was Goliad, where Santa Anna took hundreds of prisoners under a promise of safety, and then treacherously slaughtered them anyway. Had the Texans not surrendered, they could have died honorable deaths on the battlefield, taking who knows how many Mexicans with them. Instead they died traitors' deaths, while the Mexicans stood by in safety.
- To loyal Mexicans, it was the Texans who were traitors. Santa Anna considered his victims not soldiers, but rather treacherous pirates rebelling against Mexico's rightful authority.

1836, mid-April: Convinced that he has the Texans on the run, the overconfident Santa Anna makes the mistake of dividing his army into three parts— leaving himself only about 900 troops, a force roughly equal to Houston's. Sensing opportunity, Houston turns to attack Santa Anna near San Jacinto Bay, just east of what is now Houston.

1836, April 21 – The Battle of San Jacinto: Santa Anna receives about 500 reinforcements— bringing his numbers to about 1,400, half again Houston's roughly 900 Texans. Even so, Houston deals Santa Anna a crushing defeat.

BRILLIANT BATTLES: The Battle of San Jacinto (April 21, 1836)

    The key to Houston's stunning victory at the Battle of San Jacinto was the element of surprise— for although Santa Anna knew that the Texan army was near, he didn't expect an attack, and therefore posted no sentries to raise the alarm. Thanks to this oversight, Houston was able to lead his troops almost under the Mexicans' noses before Santa Anna had any idea what terrible vengeance was upon him.
    Around 3:30 P.M., all 900 Texans charged over the last low rise between the two armies, shouting as they went, "Remember the Alamo! Remember Goliad!" To their amazement, the Texans found about half of their enemies asleep, and the rest woefully unprepared for battle. After this first charge, Houston's main difficulty was to keep his enraged Texans from "taking prisoners like the Mexicans did"— in other words, slaughtering every enemy in sight. Finding themselves trapped between the Texans and San Jacinto Bay, fleeing Mexicans pled with their pursuers, "Me no Alamo! Me no la Bahia [Goliad]!" Despite these pleas, vengeful

Texans slaughtered some 600 Mexicans, and wounded some 200 more, before Houston— who suffered a bad ankle wound during the charge— finally brought his troops under control. All of these casualties the Texans inflicted with fewer than ten dead on their side.

Sometime during the melee, Santa Anna conveniently disappeared. Although different storytellers offer different tales, the usual one is that Santa Anna quietly traded his general's uniform for a common soldier's, and spent the night after the battle hiding in plain sight among several hundred other Mexican prisoners of war. The next day, a Mexican POW who wasn't in on Santa Anna's charade cried out in surprise at seeing him, "El Presidente!"— thus leading Houston directly to his prey. Upon meeting the wounded Houston, the still-proud Santa Anna reportedly congratulated him for having captured the "Napoleon of the West."

Sam Houston leading the charge at the Battle of San Jacinto

SUGGESTIVE SONGS: "The Yellow Rose of Texas"

"The Yellow Rose of Texas" is an old Texas folk song that may explain why Santa Anna was so woefully unprepared for the Battle of San Jacinto. According to legend, the real Yellow Rose was a beautiful young San Jacinto area slave woman named Emily Morgan. The word "yellow" described the lovely color of Emily's skin, blended from some mixture of black and white ancestors. Also according to legend, Santa Anna captured Emily on the morning before the battle began, and was so taken with her that he had no attention to spare for his military duties.

The Treaties of Velasco (Signed May 14, 1836)

The capture of the President of Mexico gave Texans the negotiating power to end the Texas Revolution on their terms. In two Treaties of Velasco, signed three weeks after the Battle of San Jacinto, Santa Anna agreed:

- That he would withdraw all Mexican troops from Texas as soon as possible; and that he would never take up arms against Texas again, nor encourage others to do so.
- That Mexico would officially recognize Texas' independence.
- That Mexico would accept the Rio Grande, the river Mexicans knew as the Rio Bravo del Norte, as the official border between Texas and Mexico.

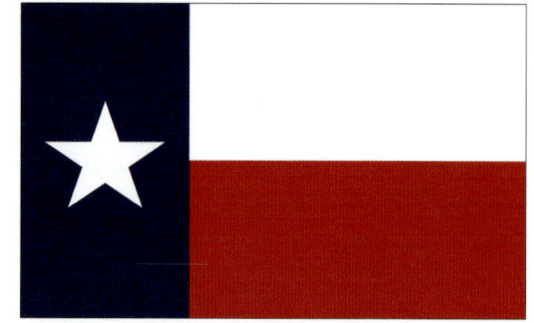

The Lone Star Flag of the Republic of Texas, adopted 1839

CRITICAL CONCEPTS: For just under ten years— from the Texas Declaration of Independence on March 2, 1836 through Texas statehood on December 29, 1845— the Republic of Texas existed as an independent nation situated between two powerful neighbors, Mexico and the United States.

U.S. HISTORY FOCUS

The Mexican-American War (1846 – 1848)

> **DEFINITION:** The **Mexican-American War** was a struggle between the United States and Mexico that ended with Mexico surrendering about half its territory to the United States.

Although the Treaties of Velasco ended the Texas Revolution, they did not end Texas' war with Mexico. Mexico later claimed that Santa Anna had no authority to sign the treaties; while Santa Anna later claimed that he had only signed them under threat of force. For both reasons, Mexico fought on for years, striving to reclaim its lost state.

Texas Statehood (1845)
Seeking protection from Mexico, the Republic of Texas first requested admission as a U.S. state in 1837, the year after it declared independence. However, a great many Americans were leery of annexing Texas, for two main reasons:

1. Because Texas would enter the Union as a slave state, or even several slave states— thus wrecking the delicate balance in the U.S. Senate between slave states and free states (see Chapter 32).
2. Because admitting Texas would mean taking responsibility for Texas' defense— which would almost certainly mean going to war with Mexico.

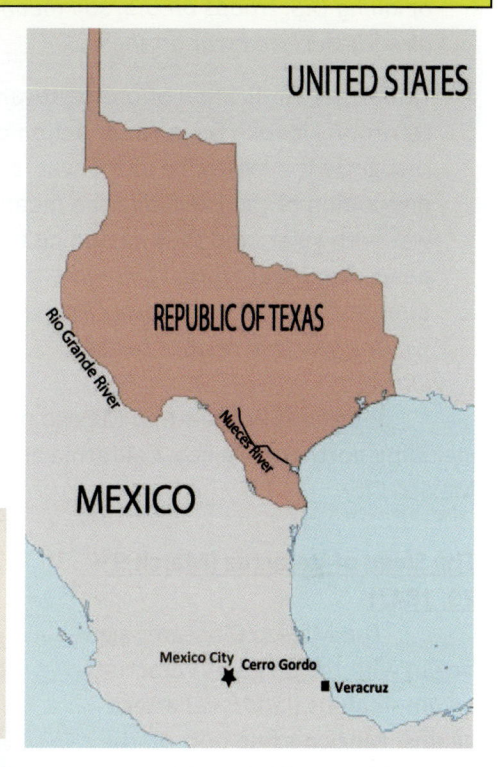

After nearly ten years' wrangling over these and other objections, the U.S. finally admitted Texas as the 28th U.S. state on December 29, 1845. From that day forward, the U.S. and Mexico were headed for war.

The Thornton Affair (April 25, 1846)
The shooting started with a dispute over the **Nueces Strip**— the territory between two Texas rivers, the Rio Grande and the Nueces. According to President James Polk, the Treaties of Velasco set the border between Texas and Mexico at the Rio Grande (see above). Mexico, when it was willing to discuss the matter at all, claimed a border farther north, at the Nueces. Determined to enforce Texans' claims all the way to the Rio Grande, President Polk ordered General Zachary Taylor across the Nueces River in the spring of 1846.

Unfortunately, the Mexican Army already occupied the Nueces Strip, and was waiting for Taylor. On April 25, an American officer named Seth Thornton led 60 – 80 U.S. cavalrymen into an ambush set by some 1,600 Mexicans. Minutes later, 11 of Thornton's troops lay dead.

> ILLUMINATING EXCERPTS from President Polk's Special Address to Congress on May 11, 1846
>
> Three weeks after the Thornton Affair, President Polk appeared before the U.S. Congress to deliver a list of grievances which, in his opinion, left the U.S. with no choice but to declare war on Mexico. Polk's grievances included these:
>
> - "Upon the pretext that Texas, a nation as independent as [Mexico], thought proper to unite its destinies with our own, [Mexico] has affected to believe that we have severed her rightful territory, and... has repeatedly threatened to make war upon us for the purpose of reconquering Texas." *In other words:* If the free people of Texas choose to join the United States, then Mexico has no right to prevent them.

- "The cup of forbearance had been exhausted even before this... But now, after reiterated menaces, Mexico has passed the boundary of the United States, has invaded our territory and shed American blood upon the American soil. She has proclaimed that hostilities have commenced, and that the two nations are now at war." *In other words: The lawless act of killing U.S. troops on U.S. soil means that Mexico has already declared war on the U.S.*

- "In further vindication of our rights and defense of our territory, I invoke the prompt action of Congress to recognize the existence of the war, and to place at the disposition of the Executive the means of prosecuting the war with vigor, and thus hastening the restoration of peace." *In other words: The more money and troops Congress provides, the faster President Polk will be able to win the war and restore peace.*

Portrait of President Polk by photographer Matthew Brady

President Polk battled Mexico on several fronts, including northern Mexico, California and the Pacific coast. The key to Polk's victory, though, was the battle for Mexico City.

The Siege of Veracruz (March 9 – 29, 1847)

The Mexico City campaign began with the Siege of Veracruz, an amphibious (land/sea) attack against Mexico's fine port on the Gulf of Mexico. Without firing a shot on March 9, 1847, General Winfield Scott managed to land several thousand U.S. troops on a beach just south of Veracruz, along with scores of cannon.

Marching north, Scott's army encircled Veracruz from the land side, even as Commodore Matthew Perry's navy encircled it

U.S. troops landing at Veracruz, March 1847

from the sea side. Two weeks later, on March 22, both Scott and Perry started bombarding Veracruz with their cannon. A week after that, Mexico's best port fell to the United States.

The Battle of Cerro Gordo (April 18, 1847)

To reach Mexico City from Veracruz, Scott had to follow the same winding road Hernan Cortes followed more than 300 years before— a road that now led through Santa Anna's homeland, the part of Mexico Scott's enemy knew best. Santa Anna lay in wait for Scott near Xalapa, a town about 60 miles northwest of Veracruz. In a range of hills called Cerro Gordo, Santa Anna and 12,000 Mexican troops— almost half again Scott's 8,500 American troops— prepared strong defenses bristling with cannon, ready to block Scott's path.

Fortunately for Scott, a clever army engineer named Robert E. Lee discovered a weakness in Santa Anna's defenses. Almost in Santa Anna's backyard, Lee somehow found a path Santa Anna had overlooked— a path to the top of a high hill that stood the perfect distance from Cerro Gordo. The difference in heights meant that American cannon set on that hill could rain down scores of cannonballs on Santa Anna's defenses, without fear that a single Mexican cannonball would reach them. When the Mexicans understood their danger, about 3,000 surrendered, and the rest— including Santa Anna himself, the so-called "Napoleon of the West"— fled.

FASCINATING FACTS: Santa Anna's False Leg

Santa Anna never hid the fact that he wore a false leg, having lost his left leg in battle back in 1838. Every Mexican remembered how the flamboyant Santa Anna had celebrated his sacrifice for his country— by burying his amputated leg with full military honors.

Most inconveniently for Santa Anna, the Americans' swift victory at Santo Cerro fell at a moment when he had unstrapped his burdensome false leg. In their haste to escape the onrushing Americans, both Santa Anna and his aides neglected to collect his leg. After the battle, an American soldier happened upon the leg lying beside an abandoned campfire, alongside Santa Anna's uneaten lunch of roast chicken. This soldier carried his trophy home with him to Illinois, where Santa Anna's abandoned prosthetic remains on display as of 2014.

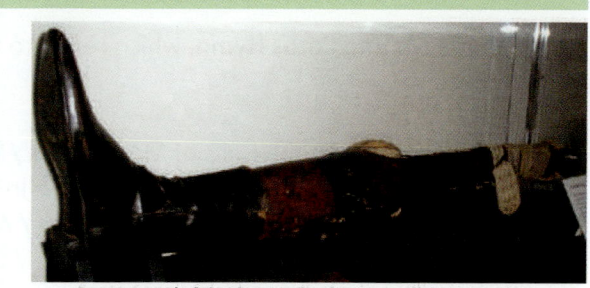

Santa Anna's false leg on display in an Illinois museum

The Battle of Chapultepec (September 12 – 13, 1847)

The key to capturing Mexico City was Chapultepec Castle, a grand old fortress just west of the main city. Two defenses rendered Chapultepec Castle especially formidable: (1) it stood on a steep-sided hill that rose 200 feet above its surroundings; and (2) it was surrounded by smooth, thick stone walls about 12 feet high.

Despite these defenses, General Scott needed less than two days to capture Chapultepec. First, Scott's artillery spent the whole day of September 12th lobbing cannonballs into the fortress, doing all it could to soften the castle's defenses. The next morning, Scott's infantry rushed up the castle's two main causeways, bearing siege ladders to carry them over the walls. Even though some 1,000 Mexicans defended those walls, Scott's unstoppable Americans raised their flag over Chapultepec by 9:30 AM on September 13th.

American troops storming Chapultepec Castle

FASCINATING FACTS: *Los Niños Héroes*, "The Boy Heroes"

As of 1847, the Mexican government was using Chapultepec Castle as a military academy— which meant that when Scott launched his assault, the castle's defenders included cadet officers as young as 13. Among these were **Los Niños Héroes**, six heroic boys who were so determined to hold the castle that they refused to retreat, even after their commander ordered them to. All six of these young heroes died— including one who, according to legend, first wrapped himself in the castle's Mexican flag, and then threw himself off a cliff to keep the precious flag out of enemy hands.

MORE FASCINATING FACTS: The U.S. Marines commemorate the Battle of Chapultepec in two special ways:

- With the **Blood Stripe**, a red stripe that runs down the outer seams of Marine Corps dress trousers in honor of the marines who spent their blood at Chapultepec.

- With the **Marine Corps Hymn**, which refers to Chapultepec Castle as the "Halls of Montezuma":

    From the Halls of Montezuma / To the shores of Tripoli
    We fight our country's battles / In the air, on land, and sea;
    First to fight for right and freedom / And to keep our honor clean;
    We are proud to claim the title / Of United States Marine.

REFRESHING REMINDERS: Montezuma, of course, was the Aztec emperor whom Hernan Cortes overthrew in 1519. Tripoli is the capital of Libya, where marines fought the First Barbary War under President Thomas Jefferson in 1801 – 1805.

The Treaty of Guadalupe Hidalgo (Ratified 1848)

Two days after Chapultepec fell, the rest of Mexico City fell as well. With its capital under U.S. control, the Mexican government had little choice but to accept a humiliating peace. Under the Treaty of Guadalupe Hidalgo, negotiated in Mexico City in 1847 – 1848, Mexico agreed:

- To accept the Rio Grande as the official border between Mexico and Texas.

- To cede to the United States the vast Mexican Cession— in exchange for 15 million dollars, the same amount the U.S. paid France for the Louisiana Purchase. As a further consideration, the United States also agreed to pay up to $3.25 million in debts the Mexican government might owe to American citizens.

DEFINITION: The **Mexican Cession** was the enormous territory ceded to the United States by Mexico under the Treaty of Guadalupe Hidalgo. That territory included most or all of what are now California, Nevada, Utah and Arizona, along with parts of New Mexico, Colorado and Wyoming. In ceding this territory, Mexico lost more or less the northern half of everything it had inherited from New Spain.

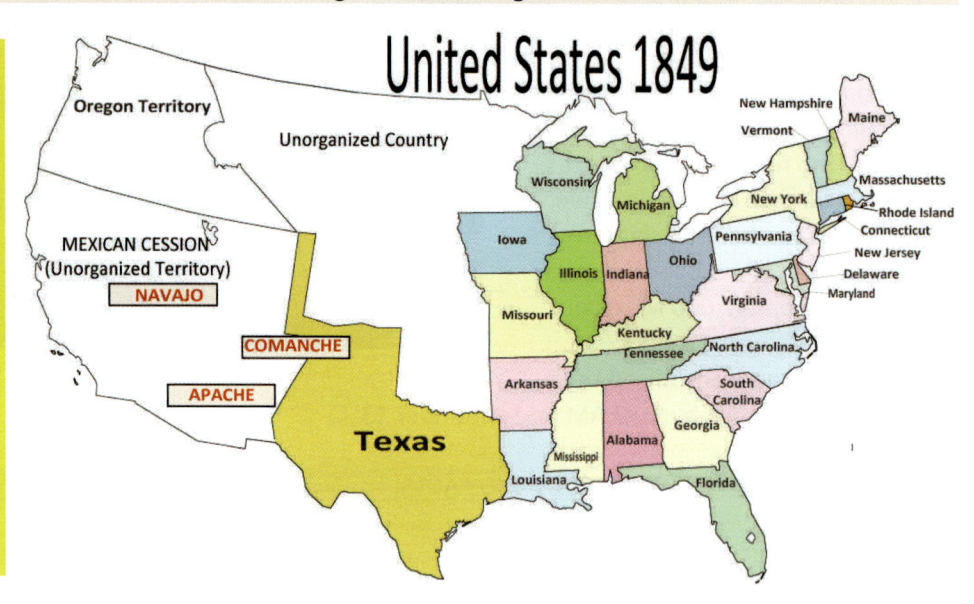

An Unpopular War

The same Americans who opposed annexing Texas also opposed the Mexican-American War, for some of the same reasons. Abolitionists denounced President Polk's war as a battle to extend slavery into a vast new territory, even as Britain and other countries were banning slavery. Others, especially members of the Whig Party, criticized the Democratic President Polk for bullying a weaker neighbor— a desperately poor country that was only beginning to shake off three centuries of Spanish oppression, and still suffered under a government so unstable that it changed presidents every few months.

ILLUMINATING ESSAYS: "Civil Disobedience" by Henry David Thoreau (Published 1849)

Concord, Massachusetts poet/author Henry David Thoreau was a **transcendentalist**— a member of a mid-1800s philosophical movement that stressed high moral standards, among many other things. One of the transcendentalists' standards was that slavery in all its forms was a terrible evil. As a thoroughgoing abolitionist, Thoreau despised the Mexican-American War, and refused to pay any tax that might help fund that war. Thoreau's refusal to pay cost him one night in jail, until an unnamed benefactor paid the tax against his will.

Thoreau's strong feelings about the Mexican-American War helped inspire one of his best-known essays: "Civil Disobedience," in which he argued that people should obey their consciences first, and their government second:

- "A common and natural result of an undue respect for law is, that you may see a file of soldiers... marching in admirable order over hill and dale to the wars, against their wills, ay, against their common sense and consciences..." _In other words_: If Americans had only followed their consciences, rather than blindly following their government, then they might never have fought a war as unjust as the Mexican-American War.

- "How does it become a man to behave toward this American government today? I answer, that he cannot without disgrace be associated with it. I cannot for an instant recognize that political organization as my government which is the slave's government also." _In other words_: Any government that allows slavery is too unjust to be obeyed.

1856 daguerreotype of Henry David Thoreau

In another section of the Treaty of Guadalupe Hidalgo, the U.S. agreed to help Mexico solve its problems with two Native American peoples:

1. The **Apache,** who lived mainly in what are now New Mexico and Arizona. The Apache started battling the Spaniards in the days of Francisco de Coronado (see Chapter 1), and never really stopped.

2. The far more numerous **Comanche**, who lived all over what are now western Texas, Oklahoma and Kansas. Mexico's troubles with the Comanche grew far worse during the 1830s, as more and more American-born ranchers moved into eastern Texas. The ranchers' arrival greatly boosted the demand for horses and cattle. To meet this demand, the Comanche often stole these valuable animals from Mexican farmers— leaving some Mexicans impoverished, and others wounded or dead.

FASCINATING FACTS: Navajo Hogans and Sand Paintings

The Mexican-American War also led to the first meeting between U.S. troops and another Native American people: the **Navajo**, who lived in what is now New Mexico.

Navajo hogan

Most Navajo were sheep- and goat-herders who lived in simple huts called **hogans**— permanent dwellings built of stacked logs or stones, all covered with sun-baked mud.

The Navajo were also known for **sand painting**, an art that sprang from their healing rituals. Navajo medicine men taught that sickness and natural disasters came when the universe fell out of balance. To restore that balance, the Navajo held healing ceremonies that might last up to nine days. On the floors of their hogans, medicine men painted traditional designs in colored sand, praying all the while for healing spirits to come and inhabit their sand paintings. When the painting was finished, the medicine man alternately touched painting and patient, transferring healing spirits from one to the other.

U.S. STATE FOCUS

Texas

FASCINATING FACTS about Texas:

- State Capital: Austin
- State Abbreviation: TX
- Statehood: Texas became the 28th US state on December 29, 1845.
- Area: About 269,000 square miles (Ranks 2nd in size)
- Bordering States: Louisiana, Arkansas, Oklahoma, New Mexico
- Meaning of Name: "Texas" comes from a native word meaning "friends."
- State Nickname: "Lone Star State"
- State Bird: Northern Mockingbird
- State Tree: Pecan
- State Flower: Bluebonnet
- State Song: "Texas, Our Texas" by William Marsh and Gladys Wright
- State Motto: "Friendship"
- Historic Places to Visit: Alamo, Apollo Mission Control Center, Fort Sam Houston, President Lyndon Johnson Boyhood Home, Dealey Plaza Historic District
- Resources and Industries: Oil, oil refining, natural gas, cattle ranching, mining

Photo of the Alamo from the 1860s

State Flag: Texas' flag is divided into three broad stripes in the same red, white and blue as the U.S. flag. The lone white star that decorates the vertical blue stripe recalls the ten years when Texas was an independent republic— after Texas declared independence from Mexico (1836), but before Texas joined the United States (1845).

PRESIDENTIAL FOCUS

PRESIDENT #10: John Tyler (1790 – 1862)		
In Office: April 4, 1841 – March 4, 1845		**Political Party:** Whig
Birthplace: Virginia		**Nickname:** "The Accidental President"

According to legend, John Tyler was on his knees playing marbles with some of his many children when he heard the news that elevated him to the presidency: President William Henry Harrison had just died of pneumonia after only a month in office, leaving Vice President Tyler to take his place.

Because Tyler was the first president to take office in this way, some considered him an "accidental president"— one who lacked the voters' approval, and should therefore bow to the will of Congress until a special election could determine the rightful president. Tyler, however, considered himself just the opposite: a fully legitimate president with all the powers of an elected one. By insisting on taking the oath of office, and assuming all the powers of an elected president, Tyler established an important precedent in U.S. governance— that when a president dies in office, his vice president automatically serves the rest of that president's term, without the chaos of a rushed special election.

Tyler had hardly taken office when his adopted party, the Whig Party, turned against him. Tyler and the Whigs clashed over the National Bank, the institution that Andrew Jackson destroyed back in 1836. Now that Jackson and Van Buren were gone, the Whigs were eager to reinstate the National Bank. Much to the Whigs' dismay, their own Whig President John Tyler vetoed the bank's new charter— arguing that a strong federal bank would rob the individual states of too many powers. Again the Whig-dominated Congress passed a National Bank charter, this time rewording it to make it more acceptable to Tyler; and again Tyler vetoed it. After this second veto, nearly every member of Tyler's cabinet— all Whigs inherited from President Harrison— resigned in anger. A few days later, the Whigs expelled Tyler from their party, leaving him little hope of winning reelection in 1844.

Fun Facts about John Tyler:
- Tyler's first wife, First Lady Letitia Christian Tyler, died in 1842 of complications from a stroke.
- Less than two years later, the 54-year-old President Tyler married his second wife, Julia Gardiner Tyler. At the time, Julia was only 24 years old, 5 years younger than John's eldest daughter.
- Between his two wives, Tyler fathered a total of 15 children, more than any other president.
- First Lady Julia Gardiner Tyler started the tradition of playing "Hail to the Chief" whenever a president appeared in public.
- Sixteen years after he left office, Tyler became the only former president to swear allegiance to the Confederate States of America— thus becoming a sworn enemy of his former country, the United States. Because of Tyler's Confederate loyalties, there was no official mourning in Washington D.C. when Tyler died in 1862, the second year of the U.S. Civil War.

Notable Quotes from John Tyler:
- "If we find ourselves increasing beyond example in numbers, in strength, in wealth, in knowledge, in everything which promotes human and social happiness, let us ever remember our dependence for all these on the protection and merciful dispensations of Divine Providence."

CHAPTER 34: California; the Second Great Awakening

U.S. GEOGRAPHY FOCUS

The Great Basin

DEFINITION: An **endorheic basin** is a region surrounded by higher ground on all sides— which means that the rivers of that region flow only inward, never outward. Any excess rainwater that falls in an endorheic basin winds up not in any ocean, but in saltwater lakes like Great Salt Lake, Utah. Great Salt Lake is salty for the same reason the sea is salty: because the only way water leaves it is through evaporation, which leaves behind the salty minerals that rivers carry into it.

The Great Basin of the American Southwest is an endorheic basin that covers most of Nevada and western Utah, along with parts of eastern California, southern Oregon and southeastern Idaho. High ground surrounds the Great Basin on all sides:

- To the Great Basin's east stand the **Rocky Mountains**.

- To its west stand two mountain ranges, the **Sierra Nevada** in the south and the **Cascades** in the north.

- To its north stands the **Columbia Plateau**, through which the Columbia River flows on its way to Portland, Oregon and the Pacific. The Columbia is the river Lewis and Clark followed to Fort Clatsop, where the Corps of Discovery spent the winter of 1805 – 1806.

- To its southeast stands the **Colorado Plateau**, through which the Colorado River flows on its way to the Grand Canyon and the Gulf of California.

- To its south stands the **Mojave Desert**, which includes North America's hottest place: **Death Valley**.

Two well-known Native American peoples made their homes in the Great Basin:

1. The **Ute people**, from whom the state of Utah takes its name.

2. The **Paiute people**, relatives of the Utes. Both Utes and Paiutes were well-known for using a mind-altering drug called peyote in their religious ceremonies. Peyote buttons come from a cactus that grows in the mostly-arid Great Basin.

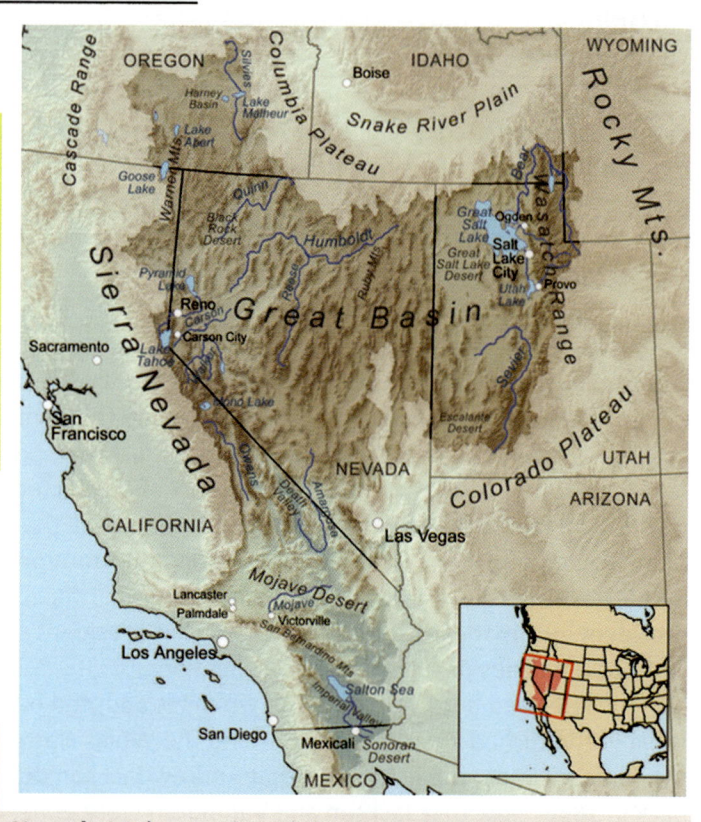

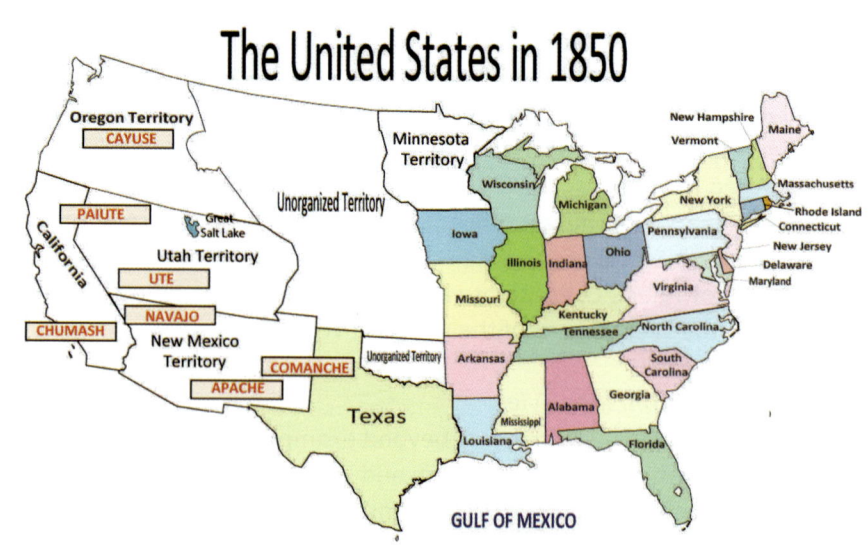

U.S. HISTORY FOCUS

REFRESHING REMINDERS from Chapter 33: In the 1848 Treaty of Guadalupe-Hidalgo, the treaty that ended the Mexican-American War, Mexico ceded the northern half its territory to the United States.

FASCINATING FACTS: The *Peacemaker* Incident (February 28, 1844)

One reason the United States won the Mexican-American War was because its cannon technology was far superior to Mexico's. However, the U.S. paid a high price for its superior cannon.

Peacemaker and *Orator* were two huge cannon mounted aboard USS *Princeton*, a brand-new, state-of-the-art steam frigate built for the U.S. Navy in 1843. When loaded with their maximum charge, 50 pounds of gunpowder, both guns could hurl a 12-inch cannonball up to 5 miles. However, *Peacemaker* suffered a design flaw that *Orator* didn't share: *Orator*'s British builders fitted her with strong, shrunk-fit iron hoops to keep all that gunpowder from bursting her barrel; but *Peacemaker*'s American builders did not.

USS *Princeton*

Heedless of *Peacemaker*'s design flaw, about 400 well-heeled Washingtonians boarded *Princeton* in February 1844 for a demonstration of the big gun's awesome might. At the top of the guest list stood President John Tyler, followed by Secretary of State Abel Upshur, Secretary of the Navy Thomas Gilmer and several other members of the president's cabinet. Among the 200 or so well-dressed ladies in attendance was Julia Gardiner, a vivacious young New Yorker to whom the widower President Tyler had recently proposed marriage. Julia's father David Gardiner was also aboard.

The demonstration began as advertised, with two deafening blasts from *Peacemaker* sending 225-pound cannonballs hurtling miles down the Potomac. After the cheers and applause died down, the much-impressed crowd retired below decks for the afternoon's entertainment, which included a fine meal, champagne toasts and patriotic songs in honor of the Navy's proud accomplishment.

Hours later, several lighthearted guests called for another cannon demonstration; so *Princeton*'s captain climbed out on deck to order a third blast, followed by Upshur, Gilmer, Gardiner and others. President Tyler meant to follow as well, but stopped at the last moment to hear his son-in-law finish singing a song.

Because he stopped, Tyler was still below decks when *Peacemaker* exploded, launching a storm of shrapnel into its crowd of admirers. For several minutes after the blast, a thick cloud of smoke made it impossible for the stunned survivors even to find the wounded, much less aid them. Finally, the smoke cleared to reveal a deck horribly spattered with severed limbs and gore. Among the six who died in the terrible blast were two of

Peacemaker exploding on the deck of USS *Princeton*

the most powerful men in the United States, secretaries Upshur and Gilmer. Upon learning that her father was also among the dead, Julia Gardiner fainted into President Tyler's arms.

Other interesting facts:
- Four months after the *Peacemaker* incident, President Tyler married Julia Gardiner, becoming the first of only three U.S. presidents to wed in office. Out of respect for his late first wife, Tyler didn't hold a glad wedding celebration in the White House, as President Grover Cleveland would later do. Instead, Tyler chose a quieter ceremony, as President Woodrow Wilson would later do.

"Fifty-four Forty or Fight": The Oregon Question

DEFINITION: **Manifest Destiny** was the idea that God foreordained the United States to spread its exceptional form of government all across North America, from the Atlantic to the Pacific.

INTERESTING IDEAS: A journalist named John L. O'Sullivan invented the term "manifest destiny" when he wrote of the United States' claim to Oregon in 1845:

"… that claim is by the right of our manifest destiny to overspread and to possess the whole of the continent which Providence has given us, for the development of the great experiment of liberty and federated self-government entrusted to us."

A LOOK BEHIND at the Election of James K. Polk, the Manifest Destiny President

The presidential election of 1844 looked to be an uphill climb for the Democratic Party. After the Whig Party turned against its own sitting president, John Tyler (see Chapter 33), it nominated a candidate with an even bigger name: Senator Henry Clay of Kentucky, the long-serving, widely-respected author of the Missouri Compromise. Finding no one of Clay's lofty stature to nominate, the Democratic Party settled on a candidate with a much smaller name: Tennessee Governor James K. Polk.

As a lesser-known candidate, a so-called "dark horse," Polk needed some popular issue to draw voters' attention. The issue Polk chose was Manifest Destiny. Like the majority of Americans, Polk was a bold expansionist who argued for annexing the Republic of Texas immediately. Polk also hoped to annex other valuable territories farther west:

- In the southwest, Polk hoped to wrest New Mexico and California from rival Mexico.
- In the northwest, Polk hoped to wrest the Oregon Country from rival Britain.

President Polk and First Lady Sarah Childress Polk

Henry Clay took a more cautious approach toward annexing Texas, for two reasons: because he knew that annexation would bring war with Mexico, and because he feared that bringing Texas into the Union as a slave state might split the nation North from South.

In a country full of pioneers hungry for cheap, abundant land, Polk's boldness proved more popular than Clay's caution. After winning the election of 1844, President Polk set to work fulfilling America's Manifest Destiny— first by annexing Texas; then by settling the Oregon Question; and finally by fighting the Mexican-American War (see Chapter 33).

The Oregon Question

Three treaties from the past set the borders of the disputed territory the U.S. called the Oregon Country, and Britain called the Columbia district:

- The **Adams–Onís Treaty of 1819**, which clarified the border between New Spain and the Louisiana Purchase, set New Spain's northern border at 42° north latitude. Of course, Mexico took over New Spain's claim when Agustin de Iturbide declared Mexican independence in 1821 (see Chapter 33).

- The **Russo-American Treaty of 1824** set the border between the Oregon Country and Russian Alaska at 54°40' north. Britain signed a separate treaty with Russia setting the same border.

- The **Anglo-American Convention of 1818** set the Oregon Country's eastern border at the Great Divide, which runs down the spine of the Rocky Mountains.

FASCINATING FACTS: The Anglo-American Convention of 1818 and the Oregon Question

Shortly after the end of the War of 1812, British and American diplomats met to clarify the border between Canada and the U.S. west of the Great Lakes region. Negotiators divided this territory into two zones:

1. East of the Great Divide, both sides agreed to set their border at 49° north latitude. This same parallel still divides the U.S. states of North Dakota and Montana from the Canadian states of Manitoba, Saskatchewan and Alberta.

2. West of the Great Divide was another matter. The U.S. wanted the border to follow the 49th parallel all the way to the Pacific. Britain, however, pushed for a more southerly border: the Columbia River, which British traders used to carry furs to a fine port near what is now Portland, Oregon. If the U.S. had accepted this border, then most of what is now the state of Washington would belong to Canada, not the U.S.

Unable to agree on a border west of the Great Divide, the two parties compromised: for the moment, the whole Oregon Country would be "free and open" to both Britain and the U.S. This compromise left unanswered the **Oregon Question**— which of the two would finally control the Oregon Country?

Fortunately, the U.S. and Britain were able to settle their Oregon Question without going to war, for two main reasons:

1. Because around 1830, Europeans stopped buying beaver fur hats, and started buying silk ones— a shift in fashion that drastically reduced the demand for beaver fur. Few Britons wanted to risk their lives trying to rescue a fur industry that was already dying of other causes.

2. Because around the same year, American pioneers started widening the **Oregon Trail** that led from Independence, Missouri to Oregon's Willamette Valley (see Year Four). By the time President Polk took office in 1845, Oregon was already home to a few thousand Americans, far more than the few Britons who still pursued the dying fur trade there.

> **INTERESTING IDEAS**: Just as the British had won Canada by outnumbering the French (see Chapter 19), so the Americans now won Oregon by outnumbering the British.

Among the earliest settlers to build permanent homes in Oregon were Protestant missionaries like Jason Lee, Marcus Whitman and Narcissa Whitman.

GIANTS OF THE FAITH: Jason Lee (1803 – 1845)

Sometime in 1832, four Native Americans from the Oregon Country traveled all the way to St. Louis, Missouri looking for something their people heard of in a rumor: the "Book of Heaven," a white man's holy book that taught the only way to heaven. Sadly, no one in all of St. Louis gave these earnest seekers a Bible, nor shared with them the gospel of Jesus Christ. As they prepared to go back to their people, two of these seekers complained to Meriwether Lewis' old friend William Clark, who was now U.S. Superintendent of Indian Affairs:

"Our people sent us to get the white man's Book of Heaven. You took us where they worship the Great Spirit with candles [St. Louis' French Catholic Church], but the Book was not there... You made our feet heavy with burdens of gifts... but the Book is not among them... When we tell [our people] that we did not bring the Book, no word will be spoken by our old men, nor by our young braves. One by one they will rise up and go out in silence. Our people will die in darkness, and they will go on the long path to other hunting grounds. No white man will go with them, and no Book of Heaven to make the way plain."

Jason Lee

A few months later, these seekers' sad speech started appearing in Methodist newspapers all over the United States. The more Methodists read it, the more they believed that God must be preparing a great revival among the natives of the American West. In 1834, two years after the disappointed seekers departed St. Louis, a Methodist missionary named Jason Lee followed the Oregon Trail to a site near what is now Salem, Oregon, where he built the first Protestant mission anywhere near North America's west coast. Soon after Lee arrived, several Native American parents brought him their children to teach.

Sadly, the natives of the West suffered from the same problem as the natives of the East: they had no inborn immunity to measles, smallpox and other deadly diseases that white men brought among them. When students at Lee's mission started dying of measles and smallpox, he lost the natives' trust.

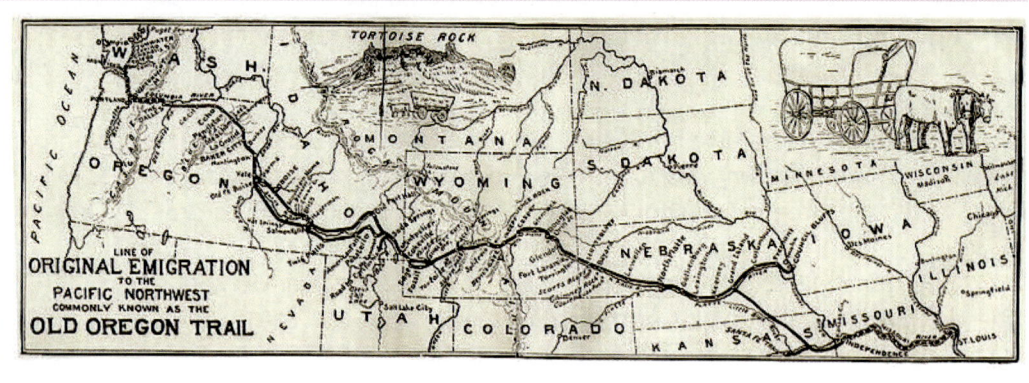

With his spiritual mission failing, Lee turned his attention to secular matters like (1) recruiting more white settlers from back east, and (2) petitioning leaders back east to organize Oregon as a U.S. territory.

GIANTS OF THE FAITH: Marcus Whitman (1802 – 1847) and Narcissa Whitman (1808 – 1847)

Marcus and Narcissa Whitman's mission suffered the same disease problem Jason Lee's did, with far worse consequences.

Marcus Whitman was a doctor/missionary from western New York who made his first Oregon Trail crossing as a bachelor in 1835. Back in New York the following year, Marcus met and married Narcissa Prentiss— a science teacher who had already applied to be a missionary, but had been rejected because she was a woman. Marriage changed all that. Within that same year, 1836, Mrs. Narcissa Whitman became one of the very first white women to follow the Oregon Trail across the Great Divide.

The Whitmans settled on a mission site near what is now Walla Walla, Washington, where they hoped to minister to the native Cayuse people. Like most white missionaries among Native Americans, Marcus and Narcissa tried to teach the Cayuse not only the Christian faith, but also the orderly Puritan way of life. One of their goals was to convince the Cayuse to settle down, trading their old lives as wandering hunters for new lives as settled farmers.

The Whitmans were just getting started in 1837, when Narcissa bore the first white child born in the Oregon Country. Sadly, little Alice Whitman was just two years old when she fell into the Walla Walla River and drowned, to her parents' great grief.

The Sager Orphans

A few years later, the Oregon Trail provided a way for the Whitmans to redeem their grief: by adopting children orphaned by the arduous trail. In 1844, Marcus and Narcissa adopted no fewer than seven orphans from a single trail family— all children of Henry and Naomi Sager, both of whom died along the Oregon Trail just east of the Rockies. In addition to the seven Sager orphans, the Whitmans raised at least four other trail-made orphans as if they were their own.

Marcus Whitman

The Whitman Massacre (November 29, 1847)

The Sager orphans had been living with the Whitmans for about three years when the family's relationship with the Cayuse took an ugly turn. That summer, one of the wagon trains that passed by the Whitman mission on its way farther west left behind a virulent strain of measles. Because most whites had at least a bit of inborn immunity to measles, Dr. Whitman's medical skills allowed him to save some whites. Sadly, those same skills saved almost none of the poor Cayuse, who had no inborn immunity whatsoever.

After scores of Cayuse deaths, one enraged Cayuse spread a false rumor that seemed to explain why so many of his people were dying: because instead of treating the Cayuse, Marcus was secretly poisoning them— exterminating them to make more room for white settlers.

Convinced that this baseless rumor was true, a band of Cayuse attacked the Whitmans' mission on the morning of November 29, 1847. Dr. Whitman died of a tomahawk to the back of the head, as did the eldest of the Sager boys. The self-sacrificing Narcissa Whitman died with a bullet in her chest— spending her last breaths in prayer for the poor Sager orphans, who must now bid farewell to a second set of parents. The Cayuse killed 14 whites in all, and took another 54 prisoner. Several of these prisoners died before the Cayuse finally exchanged the survivors for a supply of guns, blankets and shirts.

Narcissa Whitman

The Oregon Treaty (1846)

At the beginning of his term, President Polk seemed as aggressive about Oregon as he was about Texas. For a time, Polk joined other eager American expansionists in shouting the motto **"Fifty-four Forty or Fight"**— by which they meant that the U.S. should go to war unless Britain surrendered the whole Oregon Country, all the way to its 54°40' border with Alaska.

Polk's aggression faded in 1846, when it became clear that the United States would soon be at war with Mexico over Texas. To avoid fighting two wars at once, Polk agreed to the **Oregon Treaty** of 1846, in which both sides finally accepted the border proposed back in 1818: the 49th parallel.

In the following year, of course, the United States won the Mexican-American War, and with it the Mexican Cession. Thus within a single 4-year term, President Polk added to the U.S. not only Texas, but also the Oregon Country and the huge Mexican Cession— in short, all contiguous U.S. territory west of the Louisiana Purchase, save only the Gadsden Purchase.

FASCINATING FACTS: In 1853, U.S. Ambassador to Mexico James Gadsden arranged to purchase another 30,000 square miles of territory from Mexico— mainly because that territory contained the ideal route for a southerly cross-country railroad. With the addition of the **Gadsden Purchase**, the contiguous territory of the United States was complete as it still stands as of 2014.

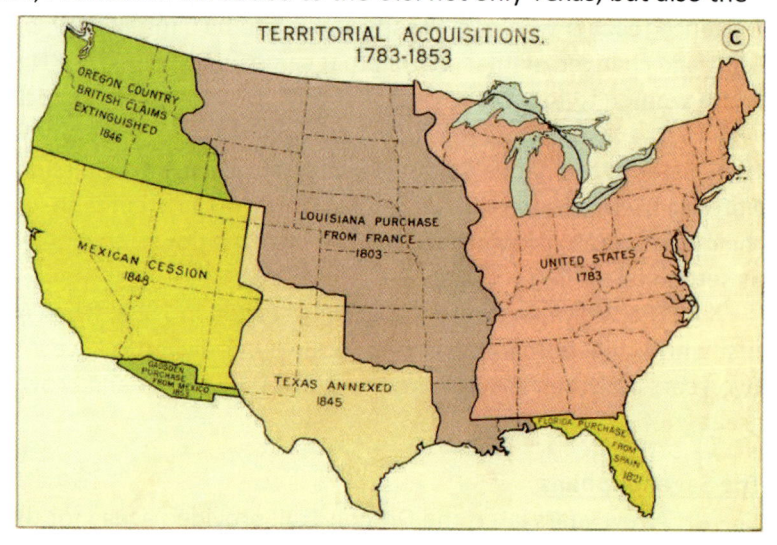

The California Gold Rush

DEFINITIONS:
- The **California Gold Rush** was a gold-mining craze that began with the discovery of gold nuggets at Sutter's Mill, a riverside sawmill about 35 miles northeast of Sacramento, in early 1848. Over the next several years, the prospect of striking it rich brought thousands of hopeful prospectors to California, swiftly transforming Sacramento and San Francisco from sleepy hamlets into bustling boomtowns.
- The **forty-niners** were hopeful prospectors who moved to California in 1849, the single year in which the Gold Rush swelled California's American population from fewer than 1,000 to somewhere near 100,000.

INTERESTING IDEAS: The great irony of the California Gold Rush was that very few of the Californians who struck it rich were actually prospectors. Instead, most of them were shrewd businesspeople who took advantage of naïve prospectors, many of whom squandered their whole lives' savings on ridiculously overpriced tools, food, lodging and land.

A LOOK BEHIND: Fascinating Facts about Early California History
- Long before any European cast eyes on California, the native **Chumash** people rowed their fishing boats up and down the California coast. The Chumash are well-known for their cave paintings, which include some of finest ancient rock art in all of North America.

- The Spanish Empire first claimed California during the 1500s, soon after Hernan Cortes conquered the Aztecs. However, very few Spaniards moved to remote California at first.

- During the 1700s – early 1800s, Spanish Catholics built a chain of 21 mission stations up the California coast. The long list of modern-day California cities that began as Catholic missions includes San Francisco, San Jose, Santa Cruz, San Luis Obispo, Santa Barbara and San Diego.

- California became a Mexican possession in 1821, the year Mexico won its independence from Spain.

The Bear Flag Revolt (June 14 – July 9, 1846)
Like Texas, California was once an independent republic— but only for a few weeks.

In 1845, the same year President Polk sent General Zachary Taylor to claim Texas' Nueces Strip (see Chapter 33), he also sent Captain John Fremont to California. Officially, Fremont's mission was to explore and map the best routes to California. Unofficially, Fremont also undertook a second mission. Possibly acting on secret orders from President Polk, Fremont encouraged American-born Californians to declare their independence from distant, struggling Mexico City. This the Californians did, establishing the California Republic on June 14, 1846.

Less than three weeks later, a U.S. Navy squadron arrived in California with news that the Mexican-American War had begun. The same squadron also delivered military orders for Captain Fremont, instructing him to seize California for the United States. Because most Californians were already eager to join the United States, the California Republic gladly lowered its Bear Flag on July 9, and raised the U.S. flag in its place.

REFRESHING REMINDERS from Chapter 33: At the end of the Mexican-American War, of course, Mexico ceded California to the United States along with the rest of the Mexican Cession.

Bear Flag of the short-lived California Republic

A LOOK BEHIND at Sutter's Fort

John Sutter was a German-born Swiss who fled Switzerland in 1834 to escape bad debts. After wandering the American West for five years, Sutter finally arrived in Mexican California, where he applied for Mexican citizenship so that he would be eligible for a land grant. Two years later, in 1841, Mexico granted Sutter nearly 50,000 acres of land in the **Sacramento Valley**— the northern half of the fertile **Central California Valley**, which lies between the Sierra Nevada and the California Coast Ranges. Although he hardly knew it yet, Sutter had chosen his land well— for his large tract of land would later become Sacramento, capital of California.

Over the next few years, some of the Oregon Trail pioneers started branching off to other destinations besides Oregon. One of those destinations was the Sacramento Valley; and many of those pioneers spent time and money at a convenient stopover: Sutter's Fort, a small fort John Sutter built to defend his land.

As the unofficial western end of the California Trail, thriving Sutter's Fort earned its owner enough wealth to launch several businesses, including a sawmill operation called Sutter's Mill.

Sutter's Fort

Gold at Sutter's Mill

In 1847, Sutter entered a partnership with a carpenter/millwright named James W. Marshall, who agreed to build and operate Sutter's Mill in exchange for a share of the profits. The site Marshall selected for Sutter's Mill stood about 35 miles northeast of Sutter's Fort, where the South Fork of the American River provided water power to spin the mill.

Part of building Sutter's Mill was building its **millrace**— a manmade channel to carry water to and from the mill's waterwheel. On the morning of January 24, 1848, Marshall was checking the progress of his **tailrace**— the part of the millrace below the water wheel— when a glint of gold caught his eye. To the few small nuggets James Marshall pulled from the tailrace, he and John Sutter applied some tests:

1. Marshall tested his nuggets with hammer and anvil, expecting them to shatter like fool's gold. Instead, they proved as malleable as true gold.

2. Sutter consulted an *Encyclopedia Americana* to learn the test chemists used for gold. This test turned out to involve nitric acid— a corrosive that dissolves most metals, but not gold. To both men's amazement, Sutter's **acid test** confirmed that Marshall's nuggets were almost pure gold.

At first, Sutter and Marshall had no idea how important their discovery would become. More concerned with finishing their sawmill than finding gold, the two kept their discovery as quiet as possible. However, Marshall did allow his sawmill crew to hunt for gold during off hours— a mistake that brought his discovery under the keen business eye of Sam Brannan.

From an 1850 daguerreotype of James Marshall standing in front of Sutter's Mill

INTERESTING INDIVIDUALS: Samuel Brannan (1819 – 1889)

California's first millionaire, Sam Brannan, is the foremost example of the sort of businessman who took advantage of naïve prospectors during the California Gold Rush.

As of 1845, Sam Brannan was a Mormon leader in search of a western site for the New Jerusalem following the murder of Joseph Smith (see below). Instead of following the Oregon Trail, Brannan traveled to California by sea— a choice that allowed him to carry a flour mill, a printing press and other useful tools for settlers. Brannan reached the excellent port of San Francisco in July 1846, hoping to find no one in charge. Instead, he found that the U.S. Navy had arrived ahead of him, and that John Fremont had already raised the U.S. flag over California. According to legend, Brannan met this unwelcome news with curses: "By !@#$, there is that !@#$ American flag!"

Despite his disappointment, Brannan still hoped that Brigham Young might lead the main body of Mormon pioneers to the Sacramento Valley the following year (which Young did not, see below). In the meantime, he used his equipment to build several businesses, including (1) San Francisco's first all-English-language newspaper, the *California Star*; and (2) S. Brannan's General Store at Sutter's Fort.

After James Marshall's discovery in early 1848, Brannan couldn't help but notice that some of his customers were paying for their purchases with raw gold. Months before anyone else, Brannan realized what such a discovery might mean for California businesses— especially with a bit of help from his *California Star*, which published its first gold stories in mid-March. Most Californians greeted this news skeptically, waiting for proof; and while they waited, Brannan quietly bought up the area's entire supply of mining tools.

Sam Brannan

The California Gold Rush Begins (May 12, 1848)

According to eyewitnesses, the California Gold Rush began on May 12, 1848— the day Sam Brannan strode through the streets of San Francisco waving a clear vial full of gold dust from Sutter's Mill, crying at the top of his lungs: "Gold! Gold! Gold from the American River!" The sight of real gold sent almost every able-bodied man in San Francisco scurrying for Sutter's Mill, half expecting to find riverbeds lined with flakes of gold. In the months that followed, forty-niners from around the world started pouring into San Francisco on their way to the gold-laden hills of the Sierra Nevada and Northern California.

The forty-niners soon learned that the only general store in all the long miles between San Francisco and the gold fields was S. Brannan's— and that Brannan's prices weren't cheap. A mining pan that sold for 20 cents before the Gold Rush now cost 15 dollars. Food, clothing and lodging were also ridiculously overpriced. In an era when most general stores counted their monthly earnings in hundreds of dollars, S. Brannan's raked in tens of thousands, up to $150,000 per month.

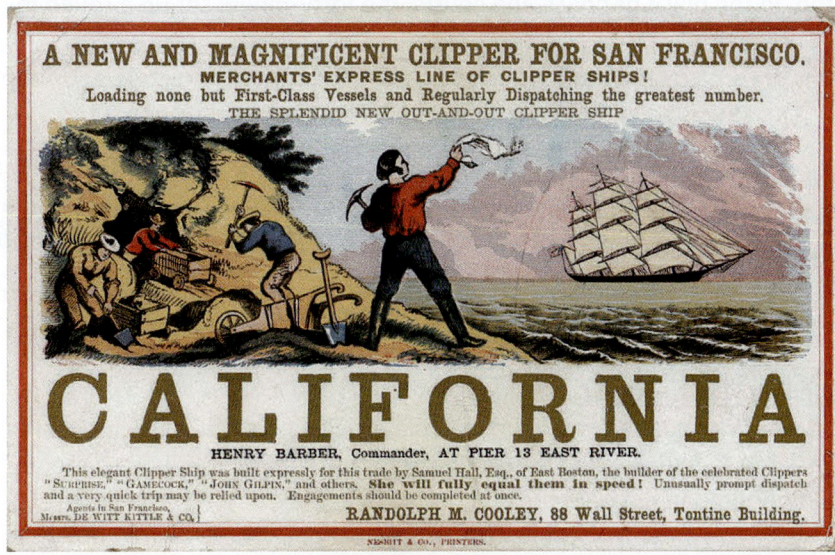

Advertisement for the new clipper ship *California*, built to carry California Gold Rush hopefuls from New York City to San Francisco

INTERESTING IDEAS: Samuel Brannan's growing fortune soon came between him and the Mormon Church. When Brigham Young sent a messenger from Salt Lake City to request a tithe of Brannan's vast income, the once-devoted Brannan reportedly replied: "You go back and tell Brigham that I'll give up the Lord's money when he sends me a receipt signed by the Lord!"

FASCINATING FACTS: Gold Panning

The gold nuggets James Marshall discovered in the American River were only traces of much, much larger lodes to be found upriver, hidden in the mineral-rich Sierra Nevada. Rushing water carried those loose traces down from the mountains, where patient prospectors could find them if they knew where to look— mainly at bends and wide spots, where the water slowed enough to let heavy gold settle down to the riverbed.

The process of gold panning also depended on gold's unusual heaviness. To pan for gold, a prospector (1) dug sediment from a riverbed; (2) placed the sediment in a riffled mining pan; (3) lowered pan into river; and then (4) carefully swirled. As the lighter minerals on top washed away, the prospector searched the pan's bottom for flecks of heavy gold. Five to eight tiny flecks of gold dust per pan were enough to keep most prospectors panning in the same spot. Any less sent them searching for better spots higher in the hills.

Prospectors panning for gold at a sluice outlet

The Miner's Code

The gold-greed of the forty-niners led to no end of trouble over property rights. In the Treaty of Guadalupe Hidalgo— the 1848 Mexican-American War-ending treaty that transferred California to the United States— the U.S. agreed to protect the property rights of former Mexican citizens like John Sutter. However, suing trespassers took time, especially because California's courts were just getting started. In the meantime, the forty-niners unanimously declared that all gold belonged to whoever found it, regardless of who owned the land. In the place of police and courts, the forty-niners set up a rough miner's code with rules like these:

- Any prospector could claim a stretch of riverbed or tract of land simply by **staking a claim**— that is, by marking his claim with wooden stakes bearing his name.

- However, no prospector could claim more than one tract at a time; and furthermore, his claim quickly expired unless he actually worked it. If any prospector left his claim unguarded for more than a few days, long enough for a trip to S. Brannan's and back, then other prospectors were free to remove his stakes.

- To steal another prospector's hard-won gold was a terrible crime. However, with so few police to protect so many prospectors, countless thieves went unpunished.

The End (1852 – 1855)

With so many new prospectors arriving every day, the forty-niners soon harvested most of the gold that was easy to find. Finding the hidden gold that remained required money and organization, resources only big mining companies could provide.

While the forty-niners were busy panning flecks of gold downstream, mining companies were digging mines upstream, at the gold's source. After the panning frenzy died down, many former prospectors found themselves swinging picks for mining companies— often for lower wages than they had earned back home.

FASCINATING FATES:

- With nearly every able-bodied man in California out prospecting for gold, **James W. Marshall** couldn't find enough laborers to finish Sutter's Mill; nor did the forty-niners pay him a share of the gold he had discovered for them. Marshall died penniless in 1885.

- The marauding forty-niners devastated **John Sutter**'s property, eating his crops, slaughtering his livestock and squatting on his land. Sutter's main occupation in later life was suing the federal government, trying to recover the fortune that the Gold Rush cost him— only to die disappointed and bankrupt in 1880.

- **Sam Brannan** squandered most of his vast wealth on two misguided ventures: (1) an expensive resort project in northern California's Napa Valley that never caught on; and (2) an ugly divorce in which an angry ex-wife walked away with half his fortune. Brannan, too, died penniless in 1889.

AMAZING AMERICANS: Kit Carson (1809 – 1868)

Kit Carson was a living legend of the American West, a hero so famous that dime store authors starting writing him into their adventure novels decades before he died. Everything a Western hero could do, Kit Carson did— from unerringly guiding soldiers across unthinkable distances; to rescuing lost, luckless pioneers along the Western trails; to surviving some very narrow scrapes against enemies both Native American and Mexican.

Christopher "Kit" Carson was the eleventh of fifteen children born to a father who died when Kit was young, leaving Kit and his brothers to support the family. With no time for school, Kit never learned to read or write. However, he did learn to fire a rifle with incredible accuracy, a skill that was to save his life time and again. Kit left his Missouri home for good at age 16, when he signed on to tend horses for a wagon train bound for Santa Fe, New Mexico. Life in New Mexico taught Kit Spanish, another skill that was to prove highly useful.

Kit Carson

New Mexico was also where Kit met the fur-trapping mountain men who taught him his fantastic wilderness skills. Kit spent the 12 years from 1829 – 1841 trapping beaver all over the West, from New Mexico to Colorado, California, Oregon, Montana and everywhere between. He fought his first Native Americans on his very first trapping expedition. However, he also made many native friends, including the two women he married at different times. Kit's first wife was an Arapaho who bore him two daughters before dying of a fever; and his second was a Cheyenne who soon left him to remain with her people. Partly through his wives, Kit learned Arapaho and Cheyenne, along with Navajo, Apache and other native languages.

Around 1840, the declining demand for beaver pelts (see above) forced the mountain men to find new jobs. In 1842, Kit signed on as a guide for John Fremont, the same Fremont who would seize California from Mexico four years later. At the time, Fremont was preparing to lead the first of four U.S. Army mapping expeditions through the West, and had great need of a guide with Kit's experience and language skills. Kit's hair-raising adventures as a U.S. Army scout were the tales that made him a living legend.

1. Fremont's Second Expedition (1844): As Kit guided Fremont's second expedition through the Mojave Desert, he met two Mexicans who told him a tale of woe. The two men had been traveling with four others, including two women, when a band of thirty Native American horse thieves ambushed them. Although these two managed to escape, they had no idea what had happened to the other four, nor to their horses.

Unwilling to let these horse thieves and possible murderers escape unpunished, Kit and his partner Alex Godey tracked the natives through the desert for a day and a night, until they found them feasting on horse steaks the following morning. Even though they were only two men against thirty, Kit and Alex burst into the camp with guns blazing and instantly killed two horse thieves. The rest scattered— probably thinking that no two men would be foolish enough to attack thirty unless help was close behind. Sadly, Kit and Alex rescued only the horses, as the murderers had already mutilated all four of their Mexican captives. John Fremont's report of this daring deed included this praise:

Kit Carson featured in a dime adventure novel

"The time, place, object, and numbers considered, this expedition of Carson and Godey may be considered among the boldest and most disinterested which the annals of western adventure, so full of daring deeds, can present. Two men, in a savage desert, pursue day and night an unknown body of Indians into the defiles of an unknown mountain— attack them on sight, without counting numbers— and defeat them in an instant— and for what? To punish the robbers of the desert, and to avenge the wrongs of Mexicans whom they did not know."

2. The Battle of San Pasqual: General Steven Kearny commanded Kit Carson at the Battle of San Pasqual, a battle of the Mexican-American War fought about 25 miles northeast of San Diego, California. Finding himself surrounded by a superior Mexican force and running out of ammunition, a desperate Kearny ordered Kit and two other scouts to sneak through Mexican lines and bring reinforcements from San Diego. Unfortunately, the route to San Diego lay across the waterless Mojave Desert, and the need for absolute silence allowed Kit to carry no clanking, sloshing canteen. Despite these and other hardships, Kit returned two days later with 200 U.S. cavalrymen to save the day.

CHURCH HISTORY FOCUS

"A Wall of Separation between Church and State"

> REFRESHING REMINDERS:
> - Most of the original Thirteen Colonies established state churches— government-approved churches run by tax-supported ministers. Three New England colonies established Congregational churches modelled after John Cotton's (see Chapter 9); while several Southern colonies established Anglican churches under mother England's. After the Revolutionary War, American Anglican churches became Episcopalian.
> - Every colony that established a state church required any citizen who wished to vote or hold public office to be a member in good standing of that state church.
> - Most of the few colonies that didn't have state churches were the ones founded as havens of religious freedom by dissenters like Roger Williams (Rhode Island) and William Penn (Pennsylvania and Delaware).

In 1777, the year after he drafted the United States' Declaration of Independence from Britain, Enlightenment scholar Thomas Jefferson drafted a declaration of religious independence for his home state of Virginia. In the **Virginia Statute for Religious Freedom**, Jefferson argued that freedom of religion is a God-given right just like life, liberty and the pursuit of happiness; and that no good comes from governments trying to force unwanted state churches on people who don't agree with them.

> ILLUMINATING EXCERPTS from the Virginia Statute for Religious Freedom (Drafted 1777, Adopted 1786)
>
> - "Whereas Almighty God hath created the mind free; that all attempts to influence it by temporal punishments… tend only to beget habits of hypocrisy and meanness…" *In other words: Because God created His people with the ability to reason and decide for themselves, it is ridiculous for governments to try to force people to believe a certain way.*
>
> - "… that to compel a man to furnish contributions of money for the propagation of opinions which he disbelieves and abhors, is sinful and tyrannical…" *In other words: It is tyranny for governments to force people who don't believe in their state churches to donate money to those churches.*
>
> - "… that our civil rights have no dependence on our religious opinions, any more than our opinions in physics or geometry…" *In other words: All people should enjoy the same rights, regardless of their religious beliefs.*

1788 Portrait of Thomas Jefferson

The Enlightenment philosophy of Jefferson's Virginia Statute contributed to two lasting changes:

1. It helped convince most of the Southern states to **disestablish** their Episcopalian churches. In other words:
   - The Southern states all stopped forcing citizens to pay tithes in support of the Episcopalian church.
   - The Southern states also stopped barring Baptists, Quakers and other non-Episcopalians from public office.

2. It helped inspire the First Amendment to the U.S. Constitution, which begins: "Congress shall make no law respecting an establishment of religion, or prohibiting the free exercise thereof…"

Thomas Jefferson's Letter to the Danbury Baptists (1801)

Although the First Amendment forbade the federal government to write religious laws, it set no limits on state religious laws— which left the New England states free to retain their state churches. Ten years after Congress ratified the First Amendment, a group of Baptists from Danbury, Connecticut wrote the recently-inaugurated President Thomas Jefferson to complain that their state was still collecting tithes to pay Congregationalist ministers, and still barring Baptists from voting or holding public office:

- "Our sentiments are uniformly on the side of religious liberty: that religion is at all times and places a matter between God and individuals, that no man ought to suffer in name, person, or effects on account of his religious opinions, [and] that the legitimate power of civil government extends no further than to punish the man who works ill to his neighbor." *In other words: The Danbury Baptists believe as Jefferson believes, that no government has the right to punish its people for refusing to join a state church.*

- "Sir, we are sensible that the President of the United States is not the national legislator and also sensible that the national government cannot destroy the laws of each state, but our hopes are strong that the sentiments of our beloved President, which have had such genial effect already, like the radiant beams of the sun, will shine and prevail through all these States— and all the world— until hierarchy and tyranny be destroyed from the earth." *In other words: Although the Danbury Baptists realize that Jefferson has no power to rewrite state laws, they still hope that the election of a liberty-loving president like Jefferson means that Connecticut's religious tyranny will soon end.*

A few months later, Jefferson penned this carefully-considered response to the Danbury Baptists:

"… I contemplate with sovereign reverence that act of the whole American people which declared that their legislature would 'make no law respecting an establishment of religion, or prohibiting the free exercise thereof,' thus building **a wall of separation between Church and State**. Adhering to this expression of the supreme will of the nation in behalf of the rights of conscience, I shall see with sincere satisfaction the progress of those sentiments which tend to restore to man all his natural rights…" *In other words: Jefferson regards the First Amendment as a "wall of separation" that bars the government from interfering in church matters; and he hopes that all governments, even state ones, will eventually disestablish their state churches.*

Over the next few decades, Jefferson's wall of separation helped persuade the last two U.S. states to disestablish their state churches. Connecticut disestablished in 1818; and the last of all, Massachusetts, disestablished in 1833.

A LOOK AHEAD at Incorporation of the Bill of Rights

The years to come will bring profound changes in the way U.S. courts interpret Thomas Jefferson's "wall of separation of church and state."

Before the Civil War, the Supreme Court will apply the First Amendment only to the federal government, as written. Just after the U.S. Civil War, though, Congress will adopt the Fourteenth Amendment— a Reconstruction amendment which will require that "no <u>state</u> shall… deprive any person of life, liberty or property without due process of law, nor deny to any person… equal protection of the laws." In light of the Fourteenth Amendment, the Court will begin to apply the First Amendment to the states as well— a process lawyers will call **Incorporation of the Bill of Rights**.

Decades later, lawyers will carry Incorporation of the Bill of Rights far beyond anything Jefferson imagined or intended. In the 1950s, a Supreme Court led by Chief Justice Earl Warren will interpret Jefferson's "wall of separation between church and state" to mean that no public school may offer any religious instruction whatsoever, nor any sort of public prayer.

The Second Great Awakening

> REFRESHING REMINDERS from Chapters 18 and 19: The **Great Awakening** was a heart-changing Protestant revival that swept through the Thirteen Colonies and Britain during the 1730s and 1740s. Great Awakening figures like Jonathan Edwards, George Whitefield and John Wesley challenged churchgoers to take a second look at their faith, asking themselves: Am I a true follower of Christ— one whose heart the Holy Spirit has truly changed? Or am I a "sleeping soul," one who attends his state church only because law and habit demand it?

> DEFINITION: The **Second Great Awakening** was another major revival that swept through the United States from about 1790 – 1840. Sparked partly by broadening religious freedom in America, this second revival affected different believers in different ways. Some drew closer to traditional Protestant beliefs; while others abandoned traditional beliefs altogether, forming new churches that other Christians denounced as cults.

Revival on the Western Frontier

After the Revolutionary War, the frontiers of Kentucky and western Pennsylvania were hardly known for their high moral standards— quite the opposite. Western churches suffered from several problems:

1. As the first territory open to new settlers after the Revolutionary War, Kentucky drew all sorts of heavy-drinking, church-avoiding souls, including (a) greedy land speculators hoping to take advantage of simple-minded settlers; (b) criminals hoping to escape lawmen back east; and (c) debtors hoping to escape creditors back east.

2. Even honest Kentuckians suffered from the same difficulty other Southerners faced: their revolutionary outrage at all things British had destroyed their faith in Britain's Anglican/Episcopalian Church, leaving them less interested in church than before.

3. Too few well-educated, well-heeled ministers were willing to leave their comfortable homes back east to serve in the wild, unsettled west.

All of that began to change when revivalists James McGready and Barton Stone moved to Kentucky.

GIANTS OF THE FAITH: James McGready (1763 – 1817)

James McGready was a Presbyterian preacher who began his ministry back east, in his home state of North Carolina. From the beginning, McGready was a revivalist who longed to awaken sleeping souls to energetic faith. Sadly, the souls of Orange County, NC found McGready's sermons too challenging for their taste. To get rid of him, they wrote a threatening letter ordering him out of their county— using blood as ink.

Finding himself unwelcome in the east, McGready sought new pulpits in the west, where the scant supply of ministers forced churches to be less choosy. In 1796, McGready took on three churches in Logan County, Kentucky: one at Muddy River, one at Red River and one at Gasper River, all just west of Bowling Green.

Scene from a Methodist camp meeting

McGready began his ministry in the West by calling upon his new churches' few members to join him in this strong commitment to prayer:

> "... we bind ourselves to observe the third Saturday of each month, for one year, as a day of fasting and prayer for the conversion of sinners in Logan County, and throughout the world. We also engage to spend one half hour every Saturday evening, beginning at the setting of the sun, and one half hour every Sabbath morning, from the rising of the sun, pleading with God to revive his work."

Four years later, the Lord answered these persistent prayers in a mighty way. In June 1800, McGready's Red River church invited guests to a four-day revival meeting in preparation for Holy Communion. For the first three days, nothing out of the ordinary happened; most of McGready's 400 – 500 guests merely listened politely as he and others spoke. On the fourth day, though, McGready's guests rose to his challenge in ways he had never seen. Convicted of their sin, and terrified of God's judgment, guilt-ridden Kentuckians started moaning, writhing and/or falling senseless to the ground, "slain in the Spirit."

The excitement at Red River drew even more listeners to McGready's next revival, held a month later at his Gasper River church. This time, some 8,000 Kentuckians came from miles around to witness the supernatural movement of the Holy Spirit; and this time, that movement was even more dramatic, with countless sinners slain in the Spirit or crying out for salvation.

GIANTS OF THE FAITH: Barton Stone (1772 – 1844)

In his eagerness to witness McGready's revival at Gasper River, Presbyterian minister Barton Stone traveled more than 150 miles— all the way from his church at Cane Ridge, Kentucky, about 20 miles northeast of Lexington. Stone arrived at Gasper River a skeptic, half expecting to uncover a sham. After the remarkable things he witnessed there, Stone departed Gasper River a believer— convinced that the Holy Spirit was doing a mighty work in Kentucky, and determined to invite that same Spirit to Cane Ridge.

In the next year, 1801, Stone hosted the biggest revival yet: the Cane Ridge revival, which attracted some 20,000 seekers from all over Kentucky. Cane Ridge was also the most dramatic revival yet, with thousands of convicted sinners writhing, convulsing and confessing. Skeptics and scoffers who attended Cane Ridge to poke fun found themselves slain in the Spirit, unable to utter a word.

Barton Stone

The Restoration Movement

Two years after the Cane Ridge revival, Barton Stone left the Presbyterian Church forever to help found the Restoration Movement.

> **DEFINITION:** The **Restoration movement** was a church reform movement that sprang from the frontier revivals of the early 1800s, and from the work of founders like Barton Stone, Thomas Campbell and Alexander Campbell. The restorationists' idea was to restore the New Testament church— to remake the Christian church as it was in New Testament times, without the human traditions and inventions that had polluted it since then. Modern-day American churches with roots in the Restoration movement include **Churches of Christ** and the **Christian Church (Disciples of Christ)**.

Among the beliefs that set Restoration movement believers apart from Methodist, Baptist and other Protestant believers were these:

- **Non-denominationalism:** Like the frontier revivals from which they sprang, restorationist churches recognized no differences between denominations. The movement's founders stressed unity, not division, believing that the Scriptures strictly forbade divisions in the body of Christ (I Corinthians 1:11-13).
- **Bible Names:** To emphasize the idea that denominations were mere human inventions, restorationists refused to attach human names like "Presbyterian" or "Methodist" to their churches. Instead, they used names found in the Bible, such as "Christian" and "Disciples of Christ."
- **Anti-creedalism:** Restorationist churches also frowned on another class of human inventions: church-approved statements of faith like the Nicene Creed and the Westminster Confession of Faith. Restorationists felt that the Bible could speak for itself, with no need for humans to condense it into creeds. Furthermore, fighting over creeds led to no end of divisions in the church, which restorationists detested.
- **Believer baptism:** Unlike Calvinists, who believed in infant baptism, restorationists never baptized until believers were old enough to understand what their baptisms meant. Restorationists also insisted on baptizing by immersion, never by sprinkling.

The Revival in Western New York

The most ambitious engineering project of the early 1800s, the Erie Canal (see Chapter 30), brought a great many people to western New York State. The Second Great Awakening reached this thriving region just as the canal opened in 1825, the same year Charles Finney started preaching there.

REFRESHING REMINDERS from Chapter 9:
- **Calvinist Christians** believe that humans are so totally depraved, so utterly sinful, that they are incapable of choosing to accept the salvation God offers in Jesus Christ. Sinners receive saving faith not because they choose to accept it, but because God bestows it as a free gift.
- **Arminian Christians** believe that humans are not so utterly sinful that they have lost all ability to make good choices. Sinners may choose to accept or reject the salvation God offers.

INTERESTING INDIVIDUALS: Charles Finney (1792 – 1875)

Charles Finney was one of the Second Great Awakening's most controversial revivalists. On the one hand, admirers praised Finney's revolutionary style of evangelism— clever, persistent new tactics that helped lead thousands of lost souls to Christian faith. On the other hand, critics denounced Finney's theology, questioning whether the faith he taught was really Christian at all.

One common complaint against Finney was his lack of religious education; for unlike most ministers, he attended neither church, college nor seminary as a youth. Instead, Finney was a self-taught lawyer's apprentice when a Calvinist pastor helped spark his interest in spiritual matters. Finney searched and discussed the Scriptures for about three years, from age 26 – 29, before he suddenly "received a mighty baptism of the Holy Ghost," as he later wrote in his *Memoirs*:

Portrait of Charles Finney

"Without any expectation of it, without ever having the thought in my mind that there was any such thing for me, without any recollection that I had ever heard the thing mentioned by any person in the world, the Holy Spirit descended upon me in a manner that seemed to go through me, body and soul. I could feel the impression, like a wave of electricity, going through and through me. Indeed it seemed to come in waves and waves of liquid love… I can recollect distinctly that it seemed to fan me, like immense wings. No words can express the wonderful love that was shed abroad in my heart."

The next morning, lawyer Finney abruptly informed his first client of the day, "I have a retainer from the Lord Jesus Christ to plead his cause, and I cannot plead yours." Finney started preaching the gospel that very day, and won the first of his many converts that same day.

From the beginning, though, the gospel Finney preached was quite different from his Calvinist pastor's. Finney rejected all five points of Calvinism: Total Depravity, Unconditional Election, Limited Atonement, Irresistible Grace and the Perseverance of the Saints (see Chapter 9). In some cases, Finney merely replaced Calvinist ideas with more lenient Arminian ones. In other cases, he replaced them with ideas that Calvinists considered outright heresy. For example, Finney's *Systematic Theology* argued that Christ's death on the cross did not pay the penalty for believers' sins.

Despite Finney's unorthodox ideas, the Presbyterian Church ordained him in 1824, clearing the way for a missionary society to send him to western New York the following year. Right away, Finney started challenging his listeners with tactics far bolder than any other minister of his day:

- **Altar calls:** Instead of leaving his listeners comfortably in their seats, Finney commanded them to stand up, walk down front and profess their faith in public— warning that if they disowned Christ before others, then Christ would disown them before the angels (Luke 12:8-9).

- **Anxious Seats:** If Finney knew that someone was hesitating over a decision to follow Christ, then he invited that person to sit on an "anxious seat" down front, where ministers and friends could gather around and pray for him by name— pressing him to make an immediate decision for Christ.

- **Long Meetings:** If the hesitation continued, then Finney stretched his meetings to three hours, or even four— whatever it took to get the decisions he wanted.

Finney's tactics worked. From fast-growing Erie Canal towns like Rochester and Utica, all the way to the big city of New York, Finney drew enormous crowds and won thousands of converts. After years of revivals, Finney dubbed western New York the **Burned-over District**— by which he meant that he had won so many converts in that district that there were few more to be found.

The Burned-over District of western New York was also the birthplace of two other major movements: Adventism and the Latter-day Saint movement.

Adventism

DEFINITION: **Adventism** was a Christian movement focused on the second coming of Jesus Christ, which early Adventists predicted to the year, month and day. The largest church to spring from Adventism was the Seventh-day Adventist Church.

Adventism began with the calculations of William Miller (1782 – 1849), a Baptist farmer from Hampton, New York who loved to study the prophetic books of the Bible. In Daniel 8:13-14, Miller read that "two thousand three hundred days" must pass between two pivotal times: (1) the time of "the transgression of desolation," and (2) the time when "shall the sanctuary be cleansed" (KJV). Miller attached a special interpretation to each of these phrases:

William Miller

- The transgression of desolation he interpreted as the rebuilding of Jerusalem that began in 457 BC, according to a decree from King Artaxerxes I of Persia (Ezra 7:13-25).

- The cleansing of the sanctuary he interpreted as the second coming of Jesus Christ.

- The 2,300 days he interpreted as 2,300 years.

Putting these interpretations together, Miller calculated the precise year when Christ's followers could expect His second coming: 2,300 – 457 = 1,843. At least three separate calculations based on different Bible passages led to the same conclusion. Allowing for differences between the Gregorian calendar and the Hebrew Rabbinic calendar, Miller predicted that Christ must surely return sometime between March 21, 1843 and March 21, 1844.

Miller first published this stunning prediction in 1832, giving the world eleven years to prepare for its fast-approaching end. Intrigued readers clamored for more of Miller's teaching— which he published in newspapers and books, writing long articles that grew ever more popular as the fateful year approached. By 1843, Miller had followers in several countries. Some of these **Millerite** followers were so sure of their beliefs that they gave away everything they owned, confident that all earthly possessions would be utterly meaningless after Christ's return.

Much to the Millerites' dismay, Miller's predicted doomsday of March 21, 1844 came and went like any other day, leaving them scrambling to explain his mistake. By hastily switching to a different Hebrew calendar, Millerites were able to predict a new doomsday for April 18. After this second prediction failed, many gave up in defeat. Even more Millerites gave up after a third predicted doomsday— October 22, 1844, the date on which they set their last hopes— came and went without a sign of Christ's return. This was the **Great Disappointment**, the day when the much-mocked Millerites finally had to admit that they had no more idea when Christ might return than anyone else.

Millerite poster illustrating several Biblical ways of arriving at 1843

A LOOK AHEAD: Among the many Millerites who suffered the Great Disappointment that October was 17-year-old Ellen G. Harmon, who was soon to take her married name Ellen G. White. Over the decades to come, Ellen G. White will become one of the most-published religious writers of all time. White's writings will unite former Millerites and others into a major international denomination called the **Seventh-day Adventist Church**.

INTERESTING IDEAS: The adjective "Seventh-day" means that Seventh-day Adventists celebrate their Sabbath on the seventh day of the week, Saturday, as the Fourth Commandment instructs (Exodus 20: 8-10). Most Christian denominations celebrate the first day of the week, Sunday, in honor of Christ's Sunday resurrection.

The Latter-day Saint Movement

DEFINITION: The **Latter-day Saint movement** was a movement based partly on the Bible, and partly on the prophecies of a western New York visionary named Joseph Smith. The largest church to spring from Smith's movement was the **Church of Jesus Christ of Latter-day Saints**, also called the Mormon Church.

Joseph Smith (1805 – 1844) was another of the Second Great Awakening's most controversial figures. Mormons revered Smith as a latter-day prophet of God; while others denounced him as one of the most dangerous heretics in all of history. Smith was 24 years old when he published his prophetic Book of Mormon, which came from a mysterious bound set of Golden Plates.

FASCINATING FACTS: The Golden Plates

Before he became a prophet, Joseph Smith worked as a **scryer**— a mystic who studied the earth through special lenses called "seeing stones," searching for buried objects no one else could find. In Smith's day, frontiersmen often hired scryers to search newly-settled lands for hidden treasures, especially valuable grave goods concealed in Native American burial mounds. Smith may or may not have used his scrying talents to find the Golden Plates, and to translate the strange language he found on them.

In September 1823, according to Smith, an angel named Moroni appeared to him with an earth-shattering message. Inside a stone box buried near his Palmyra, New York home, Smith would find a book of Golden Plates inscribed with the true history of ancient North America. To help him translate the foreign language on the plates, Smith would find two seeing stones mounted like a pair of eyeglasses. He would also find other ancient artifacts, including a breastplate like an ancient Hebrew priest's.

For various reasons, four years passed before Smith finally uncovered Moroni's box and brought plates, stones and breastplate home with him. Smith spent two more years translating the plates, dictating his English version to friends and relatives who served as his scribes. Exactly how Smith produced his translation, no one knows— for he always worked in secret, allowing no one but himself to study the plates. His translation complete, Smith returned the plates to Moroni in 1829, and no one has seen them since.

All of this secrecy convinced doubters that the Golden Plates were a lie— a self-serving fiction intended to give Smith's Book of Mormon more authority than it deserved. To answer such doubters, the book begins with testimonies from a total of eleven witness, all claiming to have seen the plates before Smith returned them to Moroni. However, all eleven witnesses were either relatives or close friends of Smith's, people who had every reason to lie. Thus from the day Smith published his Book of Mormon in 1830, skeptics accused Smith and his friends of inventing the whole story of the Golden Plates, along with the book itself. One leading skeptics' theory is that Smith stole at least part of the Book of Mormon from a retired minister/author named Solomon Spalding.

Joseph Smith receiving the Golden Plates from Moroni, along with the urim and thummim

Other interesting facts:
- Smith named the two seeing stones he found in Moroni's box *urim* and *thummim*, the names of two mysterious Biblical objects Hebrew priests carried in their breastplates (Exodus 28:30). Consulting *urim* and *thummim* was one way Hebrew priests determined the will of God (I Samuel 28:6).

FASCINATING FACTS: The Book of Mormon (Published 1830)

- The Book of Mormon claims to be a historical record of four ancient North American peoples: the Jaredites, the Nephites, the Lamanites and the Mulekites.

- The most ancient, the Jaredites, were one of the peoples God scattered around the globe after confusing their languages at the Tower of Babel (Genesis 11:1-9). The other three were all Hebrew peoples who moved to North America from Jerusalem around 600 B.C., when the Babylonian Empire was about to conquer the Hebrews' Southern Kingdom of Judah (II Kings 25).

- The book begins with the story of Lehi, a Hebrew prophet who warned the people of Jerusalem to change their sinful ways, lest God allow Babylon to overtake them. Instead of changing their ways, angry Hebrews drove Lehi from his home. With nowhere else to go, Lehi and his followers finally built a ship and sailed across the "large waters" to North America.

- For guidance on his long journey, Lehi followed the **Liahona**, a small globe that miraculously appeared outside his tent one morning. The Liahona guided Lehi in two ways: through a compass-like needle that always pointed him in the right direction; and through a hollow center in which he sometimes found written instructions from God Himself. Joseph Smith listed the Liahona among the objects he found inside Moroni's box with the Golden Plates.

- After reaching North America, Lehi's followers divided into two main peoples. The more righteous were the **Nephites**, named for Lehi's son Nephi; while the more idolatrous were the **Lamanites**, named for Lehi's son Laman. Much of the Book of Mormon describes an off-and-on, centuries-long war between the Nephites and the Lamanites.

- The high point of the Nephites' story comes in the book of III Nephi, when the resurrected Jesus Christ appears before a gathering of about 2,500 Nephites somewhere in North America. Just as He did in the Holy Land, Christ (1) delivers the Sermon on the Mount and other passages from the New Testament; (2) heals the sick; (3) appoints twelve disciples to carry on His ministry; and (4) allows the Nephites to touch His crucifixion wounds, proving that He has truly risen from the dead.

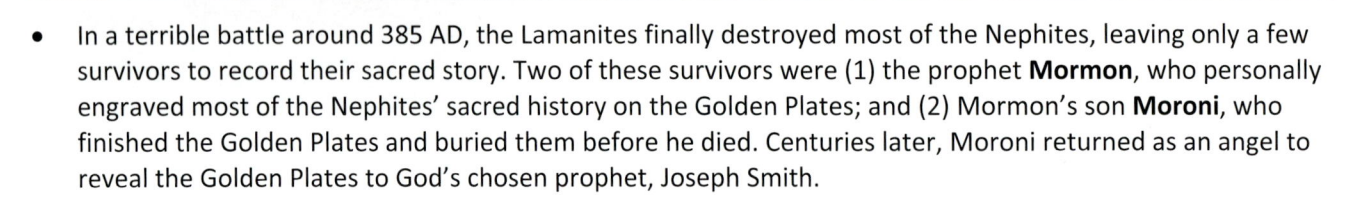

1842 portrait of Joseph Smith, author of the Book of Mormon

- In a terrible battle around 385 AD, the Lamanites finally destroyed most of the Nephites, leaving only a few survivors to record their sacred story. Two of these survivors were (1) the prophet **Mormon**, who personally engraved most of the Nephites' sacred history on the Golden Plates; and (2) Mormon's son **Moroni**, who finished the Golden Plates and buried them before he died. Centuries later, Moroni returned as an angel to reveal the Golden Plates to God's chosen prophet, Joseph Smith.

- From the moment of its publication in March 1830, Joseph Smith and his followers treated the Book of Mormon as if it were God-breathed Scripture with the same authority as the Holy Bible.

Building the New Jerusalem

To all who believed Joseph Smith, the reemergence of the Golden Plates during their lifetimes was a miraculous sign. The book of III Nephi revealed the meaning of that sign: that God had chosen Smith and his followers to build the New Jerusalem, the place where Christ's most faithful disciples were to reestablish His kingdom in North America.

A few months after publishing the Book of Mormon, Smith sent his first scouts westward to search for the ideal place to build the New Jerusalem. Over the next fourteen years, Smith's fast-growing band of followers tried several sites— including (1) Kirtland, just northeast of Cleveland, Ohio; (2) Independence, just east of Kansas City, Missouri; and (3) the brand-new, all-Mormon city of Nauvoo, Illinois, where Smith served as mayor, chief justice and captain of the local militia.

Wherever they settled, the Mormons and their non-Mormon neighbors were soon at each other's throats over conflicts like these:

- Because the Mormons' vision for the New Jerusalem allowed no room for non-Mormons, Mormon leaders often spoke of "inheriting" all non-Mormon property in the area. Such talk left their non-Mormon neighbors with three options: they could (1) convert to Mormonism; (2) sell their property to the Mormons and move away; or (3) drive the Mormons out, by law or by force.

- Each time the Mormons relocated, hundreds of them rushed to the latest New Jerusalem at once, flooding the voting rolls with Mormon voters. Because Mormons always voted for Mormons, they could easily take over local governments— leaving non-Mormons powerless.

- To non-Mormons who revered the Bible, Joseph Smith was no prophet, but rather an arrogant heretic who dared to substitute his own false words for the holy Word of God.

- Although Smith was quick to scold non-Mormons for their immoral behavior, he apparently approved of a practice non-Mormons found shockingly immoral: **polygamy**, or marrying multiple wives.

The Murder of Joseph Smith (June 27, 1844)

Even in all-Mormon Nauvoo, there lived some who considered Joseph Smith a heretic— including William Law, a former Mormon who broke with Smith over polygamy and other issues. In June 1844, Law dared to publish his complaints against Smith in the first edition of his brand-new anti-Mormon newspaper, the *Nauvoo Expositor*.

The first edition of the *Expositor* was to be its only edition. Determined to silence Law, the vengeful Smith ordered a Mormon mob to destroy Law's printing press. This ugly incident led to two charges against Smith:

1. Non-Mormons from all around Nauvoo denounced Smith as an unbearable tyrant for assaulting one of America's most cherished liberties, freedom of the press.

2. The state of Illinois charged Smith with inciting mob violence, and ordered him jailed in nearby Carthage, Illinois to await trial.

Sadly, Smith never got a chance to plead his case— for on his second night in jail, an anti-Mormon mob burst into his second-floor cell at Carthage Prison and shot him to death.

Joseph Smith plummeting from a second-floor window of a Carthage jail cell after being shot to death

The Mormon Exodus (1847 – 1869)

The sad end of their founding prophet convinced the Mormons that if they were ever to build the New Jerusalem, then they would have to do so far from Mormon-haters like the ones around Nauvoo. In 1847, new leader Brigham Young led the first Mormon pioneers to a new home far to the west, hundreds of miles from any other white settlement. On the shores of the Great Basin's Great Salt Lake, Brigham Young and his followers set about building the Church of Jesus Christ of Latter-day Saints in what is now Salt Lake City, Utah.

Mormon wagon train arriving in Salt Lake Valley

INTERESTING IDEAS: The term "Latter-day saint" simply means "modern-day Christian." Like the members of the Restorationist movement, Smith and his followers believed that they were restoring the true Church of Jesus Christ, the way it was before misguided leaders corrupted it with false teaching.

WORLD HISTORY FOCUS

The South Sea Islands

REFRESHING REMINDERS from Chapter 24: The arrival of British muskets completely upset the balance of power in New Zealand. Because some Maori tribes acquired muskets before others, musket-armed tribes were able to wreak terrible vengeance on musket-less tribes, turning minor old feuds into major genocidal wars. The Maori-on-Maori **Musket Wars** of the early 1800s killed off tens of thousands of native New Zealanders.

FASCINATING FACTS: The Treaty of Waitingi (first signed February 6, 1840)

The **Treaty of Waitingi** was the treaty that established British sovereignty over New Zealand— or, if one asks certain New Zealanders, the treaty with which the British stole New Zealand from its natives.

During the chaotic Musket War years, certain Maori chiefs decided that New Zealand might fare better under British protection. In the Treaty of Waitingi— named for a bay settlement on North Island's northeast coast, and first signed by several Maori chiefs on February 6, 1840— Queen Victoria agreed that if the Maori would accept her authority, then she would extend British laws and protection over New Zealand.

The Treaty of Waitingi's main sticking point was a clause that allowed the Maori to sell their land only to the British Crown. This clause worked well enough at first, when many Maori were eager to sell their land. However, it led to trouble later, when British settlers started demanding more land than the Maori wanted to sell. Under pressure from— or perhaps bribed by— these settlers, corrupt British land agents worked land deals as shady as the ones William Henry Harrison worked with the natives of Indiana (see Chapter 28). These deals always favored white Britons, never the Maori. The more land the Maori lost, the more they regretted signing the Treaty of Waitingi.

A LOOK AHEAD: Over the years from 1845 – 1872, Britain will battle the Maori in a long string of **New Zealand Wars**, in which the victorious British will claim even more Maori land.

GIANTS OF THE FAITH: John Paton (1824 – 1907)

John Paton was a Scottish missionary who bravely answered God's call to the New Hebrides, a South Pacific island group now named Vanuatu. What made the New Hebrides particularly frightening was that it was the same island group where cannibals had killed and eaten the valiant John Williams in 1839 (see Chapter 24). When an elderly churchman named Dickson learned that Paton was going to the same islands where Williams died, he exclaimed in horror:

"The cannibals! You will be eaten by cannibals!"

Paton's answer was this serene statement of faith:

"Mr. Dickson, you are advanced in years now, and your own prospect is soon to be laid in the grave, there to be eaten by worms. I confess to you, that if I can but live and die serving and honoring the Lord Jesus, it will make no difference to me whether I am eaten by Cannibals or by worms; and in the Great Day my Resurrection body will rise as fair as yours in the likeness of our risen Redeemer."

Nineteen years after John Williams' grim end, John Paton and his pregnant wife Mary arrived on Tanna, New Hebrides to share the gospel in one of the most dangerous places on earth. Four months later, both Mary and her newborn son lay in their graves, dead of tropical fevers. To be certain that the cannibals wouldn't dig up his wife and child's remains and eat them, Paton guarded their graves for three days and nights, until he was sure their flesh would be too spoiled to eat. Long afterward, Paton was still receiving death threats almost every day— still sleeping in his clothes, listening day and night for warning barks from his faithful dog.

Years later, John Paton's long suffering and self-sacrifice finally began to bear fruit. When Paton retired after 35 years of ministry, not one cannibal remained on the island where he ministered longest, Aniwa. Instead, nearly every Aniwan was a Christian, and most of the New Hebrides had Christian churches.

U.S. STATE FOCUS

California

FASCINATING FACTS about California:

- State Capital: Sacramento
- State Abbreviation: CA
- Statehood: California became the 31st US state on September 9, 1850.
- Area: About 164,000 square miles (Ranks 3rd in size)
- Bordering States: Arizona, Nevada, Oregon
- Meaning of Name: California was the name of a mythical island populated entirely by black women. Spanish author Garci Rodriguez de Montalvo invented this island for his popular novel *The Adventures of Esplandian*.
- State Nickname: "Golden State"
- State Bird: California Quail
- State Tree: California has two state trees, the Coast Redwood and the Giant Sequoia.
- State Flower: California poppy
- State Song: "I Love You, California" by Francis Silverwood and Alfred Frankenstein
- State Motto: *Eureka*, Greek for "I have found it"
- Historic Places to Visit: Alcatraz Island, Sutter's Fort, Donner Camp, Drakes Bay Historic District, President Richard Nixon Birthplace, Pony Express Terminal, Old Sacramento State Historic Park, Presidio of San Francisco, Leland Stanford House
- Resources and Industries: Entertainment, fruit farming, wine, information technology

The Golden Gate Bridge between San Francisco and Marin County, California

State Flag: A grizzly bear prowling a swath of grass over the words "California Republic," with a red stripe beneath and a red star overhead, all on a white field. The bear was the symbol of the California Republic, a short-lived republic that declared independence from Mexico in June 1846. The flag's lone star recalls the lone star on Texas' flag, which also declared independence from Mexico.

PRESIDENTIAL FOCUS

PRESIDENT #11: James K. Polk (1795 – 1849)	
In Office: March 4, 1845 – March 4, 1849	**Political Party:** Democratic
Birthplace: North Carolina	**Nickname:** "Young Hickory"

Like Andrew Jackson, James Polk was born in the Carolinas, but launched his political career from Tennessee. Polk served as a U.S. Representative from Tennessee for fourteen years, from 1825 – 1839, doubling as Speaker of the House from 1835 – 1839. Polk's strong support for President Jackson during those years earned him the nickname "Young Hickory," protégé to "Old Hickory" Jackson. Polk also served as Governor of Tennessee from 1839 – 1841 before the Whig Party turned against its own sitting president, John Tyler— clearing the way for the Democratic Party nominee, Polk, to win the presidential election of 1844.

The main goal of Polk's presidency was to fulfill Manifest Destiny, the belief that God intended the United States to expand all across North America. Polk fulfilled that destiny through three main achievements:

1. **The annexation of Texas** (1845), in which Polk brought vast Texas into the union as the 28th state.
2. **The Oregon Treaty** (1846), which set the 49th parallel as the official border between the U.S. and Canada all the way from the Great Lakes to the Pacific Ocean. In settling the long-standing dispute over the Oregon Territory, Polk firmed up U.S. claims to most or all of what are now Washington, Oregon and Idaho.
3. **A victory in the Mexican-American War** (1846 – 1848), in which the U.S. acquired an immense territory that formerly belonged to Mexico— including most or all of what are now California, Nevada, Utah, Arizona and New Mexico.

Polk's main weakness as president was that he worked too hard, taking on himself too many arduous tasks that other presidents entrusted to their cabinets. Polk was so exhausted when he left office that he soon took ill, and died just 3 months later.

Fun Facts about James K. Polk:
- Polk was the only former Speaker of the U.S. House of Representatives ever to become president.
- To appease his rivals for the Democratic Party's presidential nomination in 1844, Polk promised to serve only one term in office— thus allowing his rivals to seek the presidency for themselves in 4 years, rather than 8. Polk kept his promise, becoming the first president to retire after a single term.

Notable Quotes from James K. Polk:
- "Although in our country the Chief Magistrate must almost of necessity be chosen by a party and stand pledged to its principles and measures, yet in his official action he should not be the President of a party only, but of the whole people of the United States."
- "The world has nothing to fear from military ambition in our Government. While the Chief Magistrate and the popular branch of Congress are elected for short terms by the suffrages of those millions who must in their own persons bear all the burdens and miseries of war, our Government cannot be otherwise than pacific."

IMAGE CREDITS

All images are in the public domain except as follows:

Creative Commons Attribution-Share Alike 3.0 Unported

Chapter 0:
1. Bronze relief of Merovius' victory over Attila the Hun at the 451 Battle of the Catalaunian Plains

Chapter 1:
1. "The route of the first voyage of Columbus"
2. Treaty of Tordesillas lines
3. Cabral's voyage of discovery to Brazil
4. Pizarro statue in Trujillo, Spain
5. The Ransom Room
6. Olive snail shells
7. Chief Tuscaloosa
8. "Fray Bartolomé de las Casas" by Felix Parra

Chapter 2:
1. Grave Creek Mound in Moundsville, West Virginia
2. Modern-day Cherokee loading a dart into a blowgun
3. Hagelslag

Chapter 3:
1. Tudor Rose and Scottish Thistle
2. Guy Fawkes mask
3. Pages from a Geneva Bible
4. Great Falls of the Potomac River
5. Modern-day replica of *Susan Constant*
6. Deer
7. Captain John Smith

Chapter 4:
1. Ripe tobacco leaf
2. Saw pit
3. Water bottle gourd

Chapter 5:
1. Grand Banks Map
2. Pamlico Sound Map
3. Cartier Second Voyage Map
4. Monument to Samuel de Champlain in Quebec City
5. Hiawatha wampum belt
6. Wampum belt
7. Five Nations expansion map
8. New France Map

Chapter 6:
1. Stained glass of Archbishop of Canterbury John Whitgift praying beside Queen Elizabeth's deathbed, photo by Richard Croft
2. All Saints' Church in Babworth, Nottinghamshire, photo by Richard Croft
3. Windmill at Leiden, Holland, the Netherlands
4. Mayflower II, a modern-day replica of the original Mayflower
5. Cape Cod map

Chapter 7:
1. Northeast Appalachians Map
2. NYC Boroughs Map
3. A view of the Catskills
4. Modern Manhattan
5. Holy Roman Emperor Rudolf II's imperial crown
6. Holy Roman Empire map
7. Semla

Chapter 8:
1. Corn shuck doll
2. Hornbook

Chapter 9:
1. Barrel churn
2. Palace of Versailles Hall of Mirrors
3. Bernini bust of Louis XIV

Chapter 10:
1. New Hampshire map
2. Monument at Rye, NH
3. Ruins at Ferryland
4. Maryland map
5. Delaware River Map
6. Log cabin at Valley Forge
7. Descendant of the Royal Oak
8. Copy of St. Edward's Crown

Chapter 11:
1. Bronze statue of Massasoit near Plymouth Rock
2. 6-digit Pascaline

Chapter 12:
1. Statue of Mary Dyer outside Massachusetts Statehouse, Photo courtesy Wally Gobetz
2. Elizabeth Castle on Jersey Island
3. A 37-foot-tall statue of William Penn atop Philadelphia's City Hall

Chapter 13:
1. Qutang Gorge
2. Mooncake
3. Forbidden City at sunset
4. Pagoda in the Forbidden City's Imperial Garden
5. Great Wall guard tower and wall section, photo courtesy Fabien Dany
6. Ming Vase
7. Pair of two-handled Ming vases
8. Guilty Chinese Scholar Tree
9. Eastern end of the Great Wall of China, where it runs into the Bohai Sea near Shanhai Pass
10. Illustration of a Manchu or Qing queue
11. Japanese White Pine bonsai on display at the U.S. National Arboretum

Chapter 14:
1. 1600s-era samurai armor
2. Onigiri

Chapter 15:
1. Humayun's tomb
2. Taj Mahal
3. Tombs of Shah Jahan and Mumtaz Mahal
4. Gold recovered from Whydah Gally

Chapter 16:
1. Dome of the Rock
2. Danube River map
3. Peregrine falcon
4. Coffee beans
5. Triangle Trade map
6. Basket weaving

Chapter 17:
1. Statue of Vladimir the Great
2. Monomakh's Cap

3. Bronze of Peter the Great
4. Lacquer box
5. Swedish Empire map
6. St. Petersburg churches
7. Mississippi River watershed map
8. North American territories claimed by France, Spain and England as of 1700 map
9. La Belle's sunken remains lying off the Texas coast

Chapter 18:
1. St. Nicholas Church at Lanark, Scotland, photo courtesy M22RDY
2. Schultute

Chapter 19:
1. Rum barrels
2. Fort Necessity
3. Acadia Map
4. Gumbo
5. Egg pocking
6. Red Easter eggs, photo courtesay Tony Esopi

Chapter 20:
1. Beaded moccasins
2. Rifling inside a modern-day gun barrel

Chapter 21:
1. Plains people war bonnet, photo courtesy of Children's Museum of Indianapolis

Chapter 22:
1. Modern-day Quebec City
2. Fort Ticonderoga
3. Boot Monument at Saratoga National Battlefield

Chapter 23:
1. Liberty Bell
2. Northwest Territory Map
3. Branches of government chart
4. Constitutional Convention meeting room inside Independence Hall
5. Liberty Bell on display near Independence Hall, Philadelphia

Chapter 24:
1. Australia map
2. Tasmanian devil
3. New Zealand map
4. Marine chronometer
5. Aboriginal rock art
6. Washington Monument, photo courtesy David Iliff

Chapter 25:
1. Tricolor cockade
2. Notre Dame Cathedral
3. Steamship model

Chapter 27:
1. Monticello
2. Continental divides map
3. Monument to Alexander Mackenzie's Peace River expedition
4. Missouri River watershed map
5. Columbia River watershed map
6. View of Pikes Peak from the east

Chapter 28:
1. Black Forest map
2. Arc de Triomphe
3. First French Empire map
4. Dreamcatcher
5. War of 1812 map
6. Popcorn cobs

Chapter 29:
1. Hispaniola map
2. Haitian Vodou devil
3. Cueva de las Manos
4. God's eye

Chapter 30:
1. Adams-Onis Treaty map

Chapter 31:
1. Powdered colors in a Holi shop
2. Jeweled helm worn by the Qianlong Emperor

Chapter 32:
1. Adinkra cloth artist at work

Chapter 33:
1. "Hidalgo" mural
2. Statue of Miguel Hidalgo
3. Chile en nogada
4. Basilica of Our Lady of San Guadalupe
5. Republic of Texas outline map
6. Navajo Hogan, photo courtesy PRA

Chapter 34:
1. Oregon Country Map

GNU Free Documentation License

Chapter 2:
1. Koekhappen

Chapter 6:
1. Plymouth Rock

Chapter 15:
1. Taj Mahal at sunset, photo courtesy Muhammad Mahdi Karim

Chapter 17:
1. Russian Federation on the globe

BIBLIOGRAPHY

Ambrose, Stephen. Undaunted Courage: Meriwether Lewis, Thomas Jefferson and the Opening of the American West. New York: Simon and Schuster, 1996.

Aron, Paul. Unsolved Mysteries of American History. Pleasantville: Readers Digest, 2005.

Ayers, Edward L. American Anthem. Orlando: Holt, Rinehart and Winston, n.d.

Ayers, Edward. American Passages. Tomson and Wadsworth, 2006.

Bagley, Will. "Latter-Day Scoundrel Sam Brannon." Historynet.Weider History, 2014. Web. 8 July 2014.<http://www.historynet.com/latter-day-scoundrel-sam-brannan.htm>.

Barton, David. "George Washington, Thomas Jefferson, Slavery in Virginia." Wall Builders. 2001. Web. 20 Nov. 2013. <http://www.wallbuilders.com/libissuesarticles.asp?id=99>.

Bauer, Susan Wise. The Story of the World: History for the Classical Child, Volume 3: Early Modern Times. Charles City: Book Masters Inc., 2004.

Beard, Charles and James Harvey Robinson. "The Text of the Holy Alliance, 1815." Excerpted from Readings in Modern European History eds. vol. 2. Boston: Ginn and Company, 1908: pp. 354-355. <http://www.shsu.edu/~his_ncp/Alliance.html>.

Bennet, William J. The Spirit of America. New York: Simon and Schuster, 1997.

Bower, Bert. History Alive! America's Past. History Alive, 2001.

Boydston, Jeanne. Making a Nation: The United States and Its People. Upper Saddle River: Pearson Education, 2002.

Brinkley, Alan. American History: A Survey. n.d.

Brown, William Garrott. Andrew Jackson. Project Gutenburg, n.d. Web. 24 Nov. 2013. <http://www.gutenberg.org/ebooks/31068?msg=welcome_stranger>.

Bulliet, Richard, et al. Volume II: Since 1500; The Earth and Its Peoples: A Global History. Boston: Wadsworth Publishing, October 2006.

Bumberg, Rhoda. The Incredible Journey of Lewis and Clark. New York, 1995.

Butler, Steven R. ed. A Documentary History of the Mexican War (Richardson, Texas: Descendants of Mexican War Veterans, 1995), pp. 67-71. "James K. Polk, President of the United States at Washington, D.C., to the Congress of the United States. A special message calling for a declaration of war against Mexico."http://www.dmwv.org/mexwar/documents/polk.htm.

Cannistrato, Philip V. The Western Perspective. Harcourt Brace College Publishers, 1999.

Carey, John. Eyewitness to History. New York: Avon Books, 1990.

Carey, William. An Enquiry into the Obligations of Christians, to Use Means for the Conversion of the Heathens. N.p., n.d.Web. 2 Nov. 2013. <http://www.wmcarey.edu/carey/enquiry/anenquiry.pdf>.

Cavendish, Richard. "The Black Hole of Calcutta."History Today, Volume: 56 Issue: 6 2006 . 2012. Web. 17 ApriL 2014.<http://www.historytoday.com/richard-cavendish /black-hole-calcutta>.

Chadwick, Owen. A History of Christianity. Great Britain: Barnes and Nobles Books, 2005.

Christophe, Marc A. "Ulrick Jean-Pierre's Cayman Wood Ceremony." Journal of Haitian Studies, Vol. 10, No.2 (Fall 2004): pp. 52-55. Center for Black Studies Research, 2004. Web. 30 Oct. 2013.<http://www.jstor.org/discover/10.2307/41715258?uid =3739936& uid= 2&uid=4&uid= 3739256&sid=21104274099467>.

Commager, Henry Steele. The American Destiny. The Danbury Press, 1976.

Cook, Jean, Ann Kramer, Theodore Rowland-Entwistle, and Fay Franklin, Ed. History's Timeline Revised and Updated: a 40,000 Year Chronicle of Civilization. New York: Barnes and Nobles Books, 1981.

Corbett, Bob. "The Haitian Revolution of 1791-1803." Webster. N.p. n.d. Web. 3 March 2014. <http://www2.webster.edu/~corbetre/haiti/history/revolution/revolution1.htm>.

Daniel, Clifton. Chronicle of America. J&L International Publishing, n.d.

Davis, William C. Three Roads to the Alamo: The Lives and Fortunes of David Crockett, James Bowie, and William Barret. New York:1999.

Dickinson, Terri. "The Plan de Iguala."Historical Text Archive. Donald J. Mahbry, n.d. Web. 18 Jan. 2014.<http://historicaltextarchive.com/sections.php?action=read&artid=538>.

Doherty, Kieran. Sea Adventure. New York: St. Martin's Griffin, 2007.

Dugdale-Pointon, T. "Francois Mackandal (Macandal/Makandal) (?-1758)." History of War. N.p. 22 Sept. 2008. Web. 2 Jan. 2013. <http://www.historyofwar.org/articles/people_ mackandal_francois.html>.

Duiker, William J, and Jackson J. Spielvogel. World History: Volume II. U.S., Wadsworth Cengage Learning, 2007.

Eckert, Allan W. Wilderness Empire. Ashland: Jesse Stuart Foundation, 2001.

Faragher, John Mack. Out of Many: A History of the American People Vol. II. Prentice Hall Inc., 1994.

Fischer, David Hackett. Washington's Crossing. Oxford University Press, 2004.

Flexner, James Thomas. Washington: The Indispensable Man. Boston: Back Bay Books, 1994.

Fruchtman,Jr., Jack. Atlantic Cousins. New York: Thunder's Mouth Press, n.d.

George Brown Tindall, David E. Shi. America: A Narrative History (Eighth Edition) (Vol. 1). New York: Norton and Company, 2009.

GNU Operating System. 18 June 2011 http://www.gnu.org/licenses/fdl.html.

Gonzalez, Justo L. The Story of Christianity: Volume 2: The Reformation to the Present Day. NY: Harper One, 2010.

Gray, Thomas R. The Confessions of Nat Turner (1831). Baltimore: Lucas and Deaver, 1831. Digital Commons. University of Nebraska—Lincoln, n.d. Web. 11 May 2014. <http://digitalcommons.unl.edu/cgi/viewcontent.cgi?article=1014&context=etas>.

Green, John Richard. Short History of the English People. London: Macmillan and Company, 1896.

Grenville, J.A.S. A History of the World in the Twentieth Century. Cambridge: Harvard University Press, 1994.

Grun, Bernard. The Timetables of History: A Horizontal Linkage of People and Events. New York: Simon and Schuster, n.d.

Hakim, Joy. From Colonies to Countries. A History of US Book 3. New York: Oxford University Press, 2005.

Hakim, Joy. Liberty for All?. A History of US Book 5. New York: Oxford University Press, 2005.

Hakim, Joy. Making Thirteen Colonies. A History of US Book 2. New York: Oxford University Press, 2005.

Hakim, Joy. The New Nation. A History of US Book 4. New York: Oxford University Press, 2006.

Hall, Brian. I Should Be Extremely Happy in Your Company. New York: Penguin Books, 2003.

Hall, Verna M. The Christian History of the Constitution of the United States of America Volume I: Christian Self-Government . San Francisco, 2006.

Hannula, Richard M. Trial and Triumph: Stories from Church History. Moscow, Idaho: Cannon Press, 1999.

Hartshorne, Thomas L., Mark T. Tebeau, and Robert A. Wheeler. Social Fabric, The, Volume 2 11 edition. Upper Saddle River, New Jersey: Prentice Hall, 24 August 2008.

Hecht, Richard D., and Ninian Smart, Ed. Sacred Texts of the World: A Universal Anthology. NY: The Crossroad Publishing Company, 2002.

Hobar, Linda Lacour, The Mystery of History Vol III. Dover, Delaware: Bright Ideas Press, 2 July 2008.

Hogan, Maggie, and Cindy Wiggers. Ultimate Geography And Timeline Guide. Dover, Delaware: GeoCreations Ltd., 2000.

Holt. American Nation. Rinehart and Winston, 2003.

Hurst, J.F. A Short History of the Christan Church. NY: Fleming H. Revell Company, 1902.

Ireland: past and present. New york: Barnes and Noble, 2005.

Jefferson, Thomas. The Writings of Thomas Jefferson, Albert E. Bergh, ed. (Washington, D. C.: The Thomas Jefferson Memorial Association of the United States, 1904), Vol. XVI, pp. 281-282. "Letters Between the Danbury Baptists and Thomas Jefferson."Wall Builders.Texas Limited Liability Corporation, n.d. Web. 7 Nov. 2013.<http://www.wall builders.com/libissuesarticles.asp?id=65>.

Jennings, Francis. The Creation of America: Through Revolution to Empire. Cambridge University Press, 2000.

Johnke, William. Benjamin Franklin's View of the Negro. N.p., n.d. Latin American Studies. N.p., n.d. Web. 2 Dec. 2013.<http://www.latinamericanstudies.org/slavery/PH-1974.pdf>.

Johnson, Clifton H. "The Amistad Case and Its Consequences in U.S. History." Amistad Research Center.N.p., n.d. Web. 5 Nov. 2013.<http://www.amistadresearchcenter .org/Docs/Johnson%20-%20The%20Amistad%20Case%20and%20Its% 20Consequences.pdf>.

Jones, June English. Thomas. Encyclopedia of the United States at War. New York: Scholastic Inc., 1998.

Kappler, Charles J., Ed. "Treaty With the Creeks : 1790." The Avalon Project. Compiled from Indian Affairs : Laws and Treaties Vol II (Treaties). Lillian Goldman Law Library, 2008. Web. 3 Feb. 2014.<http://avalon.law.yale.edu/18th_century /cre1790.asp>.

King, David. Children's Encyclopedia of American History. New York: Roundtable Press Book, 2003.

Knappert, Jan. Kings, Gods and Spirits from African Mythology. New York: Peter Bedrick Books, n.d.

Krull, Kathleen. Lives of the Musicians: Good Times, Bad Times and What the Neighbors Thought.New York: Harcourt Brace and Co., 1993.

Kuiper, B. K. The Church in History. Grand Rapids, Michigan: Wm. B. Eerdsmans Publishing Co., 1 June 1988.

Lancaster, Bruce. The American Revolution. New York: Garden City Books, 1957.

Link, Arthur. the american people. AHM Publishing Corporation, 1981.

Loewen, James W. Lies my Teacher told me. New York: The New Press, 1995.

Lopez, Angelo. "Benjamin Franklin and His Fight to Abolish Slavery." Everyday Citizen. 6 June 2010. Web. 22 August2013.<http://www.everydaycitizen.com/2010/06/Benjamin _franklin _and_his_figh.html>.

Marshall, Peter. The Light and the Glory. Old Tappan: Fleming H. Revell Company, 1977.

Martin, Goldsmith. Islam and Christian Witness. Illinois: Intervarsity Press, 1982.

McCullough, David. 1776. New York: Simon and Schuster, 2005.

McKinney, Kevin. Everyday Geography of the World: A Concise Entertaining Review of Essential Information with over 80 Maps and Illustrations. Garden City, NY: Doubleday Direct Inc., 1993.

Minister, Christopher."Mexican Independence - The Siege of Guanajuato." Latin American History. About.com, n.d. Web. 25 Nov. 2013.<http://latinamericanhistory.about.com /od/latinamericaindepende>.

Moes, Gary, Eric Bristley. Streams of Civilization Vol 2: Cultures in Conflict Since the Reformation. Christian Liberty Press, 1995.

Montgomery, June, Maurice Hison. Meet the Great Composers Book 1. San Diego, 1995.

Morgan, Edmund S. The Puritan Dilemma. Longman, 1999.

Morris, Benjamin F. The Christian Life and Character of the Civil Institutions of the United States. Powder Springs: American Vision, 2007.

New International Bible. Colorado Springs, CO: International Bible Society, 1984.

New Living Translation. Wheaton, IL: Tyndale House Publishing, 1996.

Osborn, William M. The Wild Frontier: Atrocities During the American-Indian War from Jamestown Colony to Wounded Knee. New York: Random House, 9 January 2001.

Perdue, Peter C. "The First Opium War—The Anglo Chinese War of 1839-1842. Open Course Ware. MIT, 2011.Web.5 Sept. 2013.<http://ocw.mit.edu/ans7870/21f/21f.027/opium_ wars_01/ow1_essay02.html>.

Press, Fall River. The Truth About History. Fall River Press, n.d.

Ragosta, John. "Virginia Statue for Establishing Religious Freedom (1786)." Encyclopedia Virginia. Virginia Foundation for the Humanities, 2 July 2014. Web. 9 July 2014. <http://www.encyclopediavirginia.org/Virginia_Statute_for_Establishing_Religious_Freedom_1786#start_entry>.

Ridpath, John Clark. 1-490 Egypt Babylonia, Ancient World Greece Vol. I. Cincinnati, OH: History of the World Ridpath Historical Society, 1941.

---. 2903-3380 Minor American States, Oriental Nations, The Twentieth Century, Vol VII. Cincinnati, OH: History of the World Ridpath Historical Society, 1941.

---. 490-970 Greece, Macedonia, Rome Vol. II. Cincinnati, OH: History of the World Ridpath Historical Society, 1941.

—. American Passages: A History of the United States. Thomson and Wadsworth, n.d.

---.1441-1912 New World and Reformation, The English Revolution, Vol. IV. Cincinnati, OH: History of the World Ridpath Historical Society, 1941.

---.1913-2410 Frederick the Great, The Age of Revolution, United States, Vol V. Cincinnati, OH: History of the World Ridpath Historical Society, 1941.

---.2411-2902 Europe in the 19 Century, Vol. VI. Cincinnati, OH: History of the World Ridpath Historical Society, 1941.

---.971-1440 The Barbarian and Mohammedan Ascendency, Charlemagne, Feudalism, Crusades, Vol. III. Cincinnati, OH: History of the World Ridpath Historical Society, 1941.

Robert A. Wheeler, Thomas L. Hartshorne. Social Fabric, Volume I. Prentice Hill Press, 2009.

Roberts, Cokie. Founding Mothers: The Women who raised Our Nation. New York: HarperCollins Publishers, 2005.

Robertson, James I., Jr. Soldiers Blue and Gray (Studies in American Military History). South Carolina: University of South Carolina Press, 1 September1998.

Robinson, Fay. "Hidalgo." Mexico and Her Military Chieftains. N.p., 1847. Texas A&M University. Sons of Dewitt Colony Texas, 2009. Web. 23 March 2014.<http://www. tamu.edu/faculty/ccbn /dewitt/hidalgofayrob.htm>.

Rose, J. Holland. The Life of Napoleon I. Project Gutenburg, n.d. Web. 8 June 2014. <http: // www. gutenberg.org/ebooks/14300?msg=welcome_stranger>.

Royer, Galen B. Christian Heroism in Heathen Landsby. Elgin, Ill.: Brethren Publishing House, 1915. "William Carey: The Father of Modern Missions." Wholesome Words.Worldwide Missions, 2014.Web. 17 Dec. 2013. <http://www.wholesomewords.org/missions/ bcarey3.html>.

Sager, Matilda. A Survivor's Recollections of the Whitman Massacre."The Project Gutenberg eBook, A Survivor's Recollections of the Whitman Massacre, by Matilda Sager." Project Gutenburg. Gutenburg, n.d. Web. 20 Sept. 2013. < http://www.gutenberg.org /files/41912/41912-h/41912-h.htm>.

Schulz, Ernst. Essentials of American History. WoodBury: Barron's Education Series, 1975.

Simidor, Daniel. "The Bois Caiman Ceremony: Fact or Myth." Webster. N.p 2002 March. Web. 12 Dec. 2013. <http://www2.webster.edu/~corbetre/haiti/history/revolution/caiman.htm>.

Smith], Robert H. The First Americans. Alexandria: Time Life Books, n.d.

Stearns, Peter N. World History in Brief. Upper Saddle River, NJ: Pearson Education, 2007.

Stratton, Joanna L. Pioneer Women: Voices from the Kansas Frontier. New York: Simon and Schuster, 1981.

Tebbel, John. The Compact History of the Indian Wars. New York: Hawthorn Books, 1966.

Tuck, Jim. "Miguel Hidalgo: the Father who fathered a country (1753–1811)." Mexconnect, 2014. Web. 25 May 2014. <http://www.mexconnect.com/articles/291-miguel -hidalgo-the-father-who-fathered-a-country-1753%E2%80%931811>.

Tucker, Spencer C. Rise and Fight Again: The Life of Nathanael Greene. Wilmington: ISI Books, 2009.

Van Loon, Hendrik Willem. The Story of Mankind. USA: Liveright Publishing, 1951.

Viola, Herman j. North American Indians. New York: Viola Research Associates, 1996.

Walton, Robert C. Chronological and Background Charts of Church History. Grand Rapids, Michigan: Zondervan, 13 Sept. 2005.

Wernecke, Dantan. "My God! Have I missed him?" Teaching American History. Ashbrook Center, 27 May 2012. Web. 15 Sept. 2014.<http://teachingamericanhistory.org/past programs/hfotw/120528-2/>.

Whitelaw, Mark. "Texas Legends: In Search of the Yellow Rose of Texas." Texas A&M University. Sons of Dewitt Colony Texas, n.d. Web. 23 March 2014. <http://www.tamu.edu/faculty/ccbn/dewitt/adp/archives/yellowrose/yelrose.html>.

Whiting, Edward. Atlas of European History. Ed. Fox. New York: Oxford University Press, 1957.

Wiencek, Henry. An Imperfect God: George Washington, His Slaves and the Creation of America. New York: fsgbooks, 2003.

Wikimedia Commons. 2012 <http://commons.wikimedia.org/wiki/Main_Page>.

Wikipedia. 2011 <http://en.wikipedia.org >.

Willison, George F. Saints and Sinners. New York: Reynal and Hitchcock, 1945.

Woolman, John. The Journal of John Woolman. Christian Classics Ethereal Library, n.d. Web. 26 Dec. 2013.<http://www.ccel.org/ccel/woolman/journal.pdf>.

Zacks, Richard. The Pirate Coast. New York: Hyperion, 2005.

Zinn, Howard. A People's History of the United States. New York: Harper and Row, 1980.

WEB RESOURCES

"1709: the year that Europe froze." 2009. http://dropout50394.yuku.com/topic/1016#.UinQ1ja1HuM. 2014.

1996. "Louisiana: European Explorations and the Louisiana Purchase." n.d. *The Library of Congress.* http://memory.loc.gov/ammem/collections/maps/lapurchase/essay3.html.

"A Grant of the Province of Maine to Sir Ferdinando Gorges and John Mason, esq., 10th of August." 2008. *Yale Law School.* http://avalon.law.yale.edu/17th_century/me01.asp. 2014.

A Proclamation Declaring Mr Richard Cameron, and others, Rebels and Traitors. 2013. http://www.thereformation.info/proclamation.htm. 2014.

A Treasury of Primary Documents. n.d. http://www.constitution.org/primarysources/primarysources.html#16. 2014.

AAANativeArts.com. 1999. http://www.aaanativearts.com/tribes_by_region.htm. 2014.

Abbot, Jacob. *History of Peter the Great*. New York, 1869. https://play.google.com/books/reader?id=o6UwAQAAMAAJ&printsec=frontcover&output=reader&authuser=0&hl=en&pg=GBS.PA169.

Abbot, John S. C. *Daniel Boone: The Pioneer of Kentucky*. New York: Dodd and Mead, 2007. http://www.gutenberg.org/files/23798/23798-h/23798-h.htm#CHAPTER_IV.

Abijuration Act 1662. n.d. http://www.thereformation.info/abjurationOath.htm. 2014.

"About the Siege of Vienna." 2014. *CBN.com*. http://www.cbn.com/700club/features/churchhistory/siegeofvienna/About_Siege_of_Vienna.aspx. 2014.

Act of Abjuration, 1581 Dutch Declaration of Independence. 1907. http://www.age-of-the-sage.org/history/dutch_independence_1581.html. 2014.

"Africans in America." n.d. *PBS.org*. http://www.pbs.org/wgbh/aia/part1/index.html. 2014.

"Albany Plan of Union 1754." 2008. *Yale Law School: Lillian goldman Law Library.* http://avalon.law.yale.edu/18th_century/albany.asp. 2014.

"Archbishop Sharp." 2010. *Reformation History.* http://reformationhistory.org/archbishopsharp.html. 2014.

Arminian Responses to Calvinist Arguments. n.d. http://evangelicalarminians.org/files/Arminian%20Answers%20to%20Logical%20Arguments%20for%20Perseverance%20of%20the%20Saints.pdf. 2014.

Arnade, Peter. *Beggars, Iconoclasts, and Civic Patriots: The Political Culture of the Dutch Revolt*. Cornell University, 2008. http://books.google.com/books?id=bm_uS_K_jaEC&pg=PA202&lpg=PA202&dq=beggars+leather+pouch+dutch+revolt&source=bl&ots=fxoXxjMsfL&sig=2OPy5Je5NXYdjTRVj9JZy6c5Cho&hl=en#v=onepage&q=beggars%20leather%20pouch%20dutch%20revolt&f=false.

"Bacon's Rebellion." 2014. *National Park Service.* http://www.nps.gov/jame/historyculture/bacons-rebellion.htm. 2014.

Bartoleme de Las Casas, Brief Account of the Devastation of the Indies. n.d. http://www.swarthmore.edu/SocSci/bdorsey1/41docs/02-las.html. 2014.

Beaglehole, J.C. *The Life of Captain James Cook*. Stanford: Standford University Press, 1974. http://books.google.com/books?id=mIk8x6lsusQC&pg=PA40&lpg=PA40&dq=james+cook+battle+of+quebec&source=bl&ots=wSlUKr3kSw&sig=voBXTKcxEwLlmVDAsooYnEgkz74&hl=en&sa=X&ei=46WsUsywC_OksQSpoYDQDw&ved=0CE8Q6AEwAw#v=onepage&q=james%20cook%20battle%20of%20quebec&f=f.

Beardsley, John. *A Model of Christian Charity*. n.d. http://religiousfreedom.lib.virginia.edu/sacred/charity.html. 2014.

Beck, Matt. *The Harem*. 2010. http://mvilleottomanhistory.wikifoundry.com/page/The+Harem?t=anon. 2014.

Behling, Sam. *Mary Barrett Dyer*. n.d. http://www.rootsweb.ancestry.com/~nwa/dyer.html. 2014.

Berry, Jeff. "Mollowitz 1741." 2013. *Obscure Battles.* http://obscurebattles.blogspot.com/2013/02/mollwitz-1741.html. 2014.

Betros, Gemma. "The French Revolution and the Catholic Church." 2010. *HistoryToday.* http://www.historytoday.com/gemma-betros/french-revolution-and-catholic-church. 2014.

"Biography of George Washington." 2014. *George Washington's: Mount Vernon.* http://www.mountvernon.org/georgewashington. 2014.

Bok, Hilary. "Baron de Montesquieu, Charles-Louis de Secondat." 2014. *Stanford Encyclopedia of Philosophy.* http://plato.stanford.edu/entries/montesquieu/. 2003.

British History Online. 2013. http://www.british-history.ac.uk/report.aspx?compid=56306&strquery=1263. 2014.

Brzezinski, Richard. "Lutzen 1632." n.d. http://books.google.com/books?id=sWQzetlC5X0C&pg=PA74&lpg=PA74&dq=jacob+fabricius+chaplain&source=bl&ots=mQRq3ruCHL&sig=vCR2WTn5EfaPYZ_fNn4yeagh_7s&hl=en&sa=X&ei=6ThtUbAf6eHSAcymgOAP&ved=0CFIQ6AEwBQ#v=onepage&q=jacob%20fabricius%20chaplain&f=false. 2014.

Caldwell, Samuel L. *The Bloudy Tenent of Persecution*. 1644. https://play.google.com/books/reader?id=IL8MAAAAIAAJ&printsec=frontcover&output=reader&authuser=0&hl=en&pg=GBS.PA9.

"Cannibalism and other experiences among the Maori." 2008. *Blogger*. http://excerptsandextracts.blogspot.com/2008/06/cannibalism-and-other-experiences-among.html. 2014.

"Captain John Smith is Saved by Pocahontas." 2003. *EyeWitness to History*. http://www.eyewitnesstohistory.com/johnsmith.htm. 2014.

Captain John Smith, The Generall Historie of Virginia, New England & the Summer Isles. n.d. http://www.swarthmore.edu/SocSci/bdorsey1/41docs/10-smi.html. 2014.

"Captain Nathan Hale." 1996. *THE CONNECTICUT SOCIETY OF THE Sons of the American Revolution*. http://www.connecticutsar.org/patriots/hale_nathan.htm. 2014.

Cardinal Richelieu. 2014. http://www.nndb.com/people/894/000092618/. 2014.

Carter, Linda. *Bacon's Rebellion and the Defeat of the Saponi Tribes at Occoneechee Island*. n.d. http://www.greattradingpath.com/native-american-indian-history/index.htm. 2014.

Cavendish, Richard. "The End of the Holy Roman Empire." 2006. *HistoryToday*. http://www.historytoday.com/richard-cavendish/end-holy-roman-empire. 2014.

—. "The Hampton Court Conference." 2004. *HistoryToday*. http://www.historytoday.com/richard-cavendish/hampton-court-conference. 2014.

Chaplain, Jacob Fabricius. *The Hymns and Hymn Writers of the Church: An Annotated Ed. of the Methodist...* New York: Methodist Episcopla Church, 1911. http://books.google.com/books?id=wZ0NAQAAMAAJ&pg=PA234&lpg=PA234&dq=jacob+fabricius+chaplain&source=bl&ots=dkuWxe534O&sig=a3HMItwZ6C2JSFgQuR7i9fnl9yY&hl=en&sa=X&ei=6ThtUbAf6eHSAcymgOAP&ved=0CE8Q6AEwBA#v=onepage&q=jacob%20fabricius%20chaplain&f=false.

"Charter of Carolina." 2008. *Yale Law School*. http://avalon.law.yale.edu/17th_century/nc01.asp. 2014.

Charter of Massachusetts Bay 1629. 1994. http://www.let.rug.nl/usa/documents/1600-1650/charter-of-massachusetts-bay-1629.php. 2014.

"Charter of Virginia." 2013. *WikiSource*. http://en.wikisource.org/wiki/Charter_of_Virginia,_1606. 2014.

City Archives. 2014. http://www.providenceri.com/archives/375th-essays-roger-williams-champion-of-religious. 2014.

Cline, David A. *Squanto*. 2001. http://www.rootsweb.ancestry.com/~mosmd/squanto.htm. 2014.

Cohen, Jennie. "Did Jamestown's Settlers Drink Themselves to Death?" 2011. *History*. http://www.history.com/news/did-jamestowns-settlers-drink-themselves-to-death. 2014.

"Colonial Settlement 1600's-1763." n.d. *Library of Congress*. http://www.loc.gov/teachers/classroommaterials/presentationsandactivities/presentations/timeline/colonial/virginia/. 2014.

"Colonial Settlement, 1600's- 1763." n.d. *Library of Congress*. http://www.loc.gov/teachers/classroommaterials/presentationsandactivities/presentations/timeline/colonial/georgia/. 2014.

"Colonial Settlement, 1600's-1763." n.d. *Library of Congress*. http://www.loc.gov/teachers/classroommaterials/presentationsandactivities/presentations/timeline/colonial/georgia/. 2014.

"Constitution of the Year XII." 1996. *Research Subjects: Government and Politics*. http://www.napoleon-series.org/research/government/legislation/c_constitution12.html. 2014.

Cook, Captain James. *Captain Cook's Journal During His First Voyage Round the World*. London: Captain W.J.L Wharton, 1768. http://www.gutenberg.org/files/8106/8106-h/8106-h.htm.

Cook, James. *Captain Cook's Journal: First Voyage*. 2005. http://www.gutenberg.org/files/8106/8106-h/8106-h.htm.

Cooks. "Charter of Georgia: 1732." 2008. *Yale Law School: Lillian Goldman Law Library*. http://avalon.law.yale.edu/18th_century/ga01.asp. 2014.

Cotton, Lee Pelham. "Silk Production in the Seventeenth Century." 2014. *National Park Service*. http://www.nps.gov/jame/historyculture/silk-production-in-the-seventeenth-century.htm. 2014.

"Covenant Ladies." n.d. *Apples of Gold*. http://www.applesofgold.co.uk/the_two_margarets.htm. 2014.

"Covenanter Stories – No 15, The Solway Martyrs." 2013. *Semper Reformata*. http://semper-reformata.com/2013/06/14/covenanter-stories-the-solway-martyrs/. 2014.

Crawford, Amy. "The Swamp Fox." 2007. *Smithsonian.com*. http://www.smithsonianmag.com/biography/the-swamp-fox-157330429/. 2014.

Curran, Nancy. *A Brief Outline of the History of New Netherland*. n.d. http://www.coins.nd.edu/ColCoin/ColCoinIntros/NNHistory.html. 2014.

"Cyprus." 2007. *Sovereign Order of Saint John of Jerusalem*. http://www.kmfap.net/index.php?topic_id=17. 2014.

Daniel Shays. 2008. http://shaysrebellion.stcc.edu/shaysapp/person.do?shortName=daniel_shays. 2014.

Deans, Bob. *Captain John Smith*. 2007. http://content.time.com/time/magazine/article/0,9171,1615180-2,00.html. 2014.

"Declaration of Independence." 2014. *the Charters of Freedom.* http://www.archives.gov/exhibits/charters/declaration_history.html. 2014.

"Declaration of the Rights of Man." 1789. *Yale Law School: Lillian Goldman Law Library.* http://avalon.law.yale.edu/18th_century/rightsof.asp. 2014.

Deetz, Patricia Scott. *The Plymouth Colony Archive Project*. 2000. http://www.histarch.illinois.edu/plymouth/mourt1.html. 2014.

Delbridge, J. Andy. *The Sea Adventure*. 2007. http://www.delbridge.net/seaventure.

Dinwiddie, Robert. *To George Washington from Robert Dinwiddie*. Williamsburg: Founders Online, 1754. http://founders.archives.gov/documents/Washington/02-01-02-0031.

Documenting the American South. 2006. http://docsouth.unc.edu/southlit/beverley/beverley.html. 2014.

Documenting the American South. 2004. http://docsouth.unc.edu/southlit/smith/smith.html. 2014.

Donne, John. "Meditation XVII." 2012. *WikiSource.* http://en.wikisource.org/wiki/Meditation_XVII. 2014.

Dope, Straight. "What's the origin of bury the hatchet." 2004. *The Straight Dope.* http://www.straightdope.com/columns/read/2161/whats-the-origin-of-bury-the-hatchet. 2014.

"Duel at Dawn." 2000. *Eyewitness to History.* http://www.eyewitnesstohistory.com/duel.htm. 2014.

Dutch New York. 2009. http://www.thirteen.org/dutchny/interactives/manhattan-island/. 2014.

Duvergier, Jean Baptiste. *The Law of Suspects*. 1834. http://chnm.gmu.edu/revolution/d/417/. 2014.

Easton, John. "Metacom Relates Indian Complaints about the English Settlers." n.d. *History Matters.* http://historymatters.gmu.edu/d/6226. 2014.

Edwards, Jonathan. *Many Mansions*. 1904. http://www.ccel.org/ccel/edwards/sermons.mansions.html. 2014.

"Elizabethan England- The Age of Treason." n.d. *Gunpowder Plot Society.* http://www.gunpowder-plot.org/plot.asp. 2014.

Encyclopedia Virginia. 2013. http://encyclopediavirginia.org/Treaty_Ending_the_Third_Anglo-Powhatan_War_1646. 2014.

England, King James I of. *A Counterblaste to Tobacco*. n.d. http://www.laits.utexas.edu/poltheory/james/blaste/blaste.html. 2014.

Evenari, Gail. "Wayfinders: A Pacific Odyssey." 1986. *PBS.* http://www.pbs.org/wayfinders/polynesian3.html. 2014.

Facts about Chateau de Versailles. 2014. http://lifestyle.iloveindia.com/lounge/facts-about-chateau-de-versailles-3325.html. 2014.

Farley, William P. *Jonathan Edwards and the Great Awakening*. 2014. http://enrichmentjournal.ag.org/200201/200201_104_johnathan.cfm. 2014.

Farmer, Bill. "Daniel Boone and the History of Fort Boonesborough." 2006. *Fort Boonesborough Living History.* http://www.fortboonesboroughlivinghistory.org/html/daniel_boone.html. 2014.

Fausz, J. Frederick. "Dictionary of Virginia Biography." 2010. *Encyclopedia Virginia.* http://encyclopediavirginia.org/Chauco_fl_1622-1623. 2014.

Feathers, Cynthia. *Franklin and the Iroquois Foundations of the Constitution*. 2007. http://www.upenn.edu/gazette/0107/gaz09.html. 2014.

Feinstein, Stephen. *Captain Cook: Great Explorer of the Pacific*. Easlow Publishers, 2010. http://books.google.com/books?id=BV0uRh7bWTYC&pg=PA63&lpg=PA63&dq=measure+latitude+south+of+the+equator+captain+cook&source=bl&ots=aVp0B5NEBY&sig=FPlXREwKvzP43ynahdQfWbrQn7E&hl=en&sa=X&ei=vSqvUrjuAsrlsAS0-oHIAw&ved=0CDIQ6AEwAQ#v=onepage&q=measure%20latitu.

Fouin, Christophe. "A Timeless Journey." n.d. *Catacombes: Histoire de Paris.* http://www.catacombes.paris.fr/en/catacombs/more-2000-years-history. 2014.

Francis, Graeme. *European Cultural Appropriation of Percussion Instruments from the Ottoman Empire* . Lecture Recital Research Paper, 2008. http://www.music.utexas.edu/getFile/pdf.aspx?id=2216.

Franklin, Benjamin. *The Autobiography of Benjamin Franklin*. New York: P F Collier and Son Company, 1909. http://www.gutenberg.org/cache/epub/148/pg148.txt.

French Constitution of 1791. 2008. https://web.duke.edu/secmod/primarytexts/FrenchConstitution1791.pdf. 2014.

Fritz, Der Alte. *Campaigns in Germania*. 2009. http://campaignsingermania.blogspot.com/2009/02/parchwitz-address.html. 2014.

Gee, Henry. *The Act Against Puritans*. 1998. http://history.hanover.edu/texts/engref/er86.html. 2014.

Gottlieb, Matthew S. "House of Burgesses." 2012. *Encyclopedia Virginia.* http://encyclopediavirginia.org/House_of_Burgesses. 2014.

Great, Frederick the. *Frederick 3rd: First King of Prussia*. n.d. http://memoirs-ftg.tripod.com/index.html.

—. *Memoirs of the House of Brandenburg*. 2009. http://memoirs-ftg.tripod.com/hob12.html.

Grout, Lonny L. "Austerlitz: Napoleon Makes His Own Luck." 2007. *MilitaryHistoryOnline.com.* http://www.militaryhistoryonline.com/19thcentury/articles/austerlitz.aspx. 2014.

Guerber, H.A. *The Story of Modern France*. New York: American Book Company, n.d. http://www.heritage-history.com/?c=read&author=guerber&book=modfrance&story=varennes.

Haisall, Paul. "Modern History Sourcebook: Abbe Sieyes: What is the Third Estate." 1997. *Fordham University: The Jesuit University of New York.* http://www.fordham.edu/halsall/mod/sieyes.asp. 2014.

Hakluyt, Richard. *The Principla Navigations, Voyages, Traffiques and Discoveries of the English Nation*. 2008. http://www.gutenberg.org/ebooks/25645?msg=welcome_stranger.

Halsall, Paul. "Modern History Sourcebook: Peter the Great and the Rise of Russia." 1998. *Fordham University*. http://www.fordham.edu/halsall/mod/petergreat.asp. 2014.

—. "Samuel de Champlain: The foundation of Quebec." 1998. *Fordham University*. http://www.fordham.edu/halsall/mod/1608champlain.asp. 2014.

Harper, Douglas. *Slavery in New York*. 2003. http://slavenorth.com/newyork.htm. 2014.

—. *Slavery in the North*. 2003. http://slavenorth.com/slavenorth.htm. 2014.

Hart, Benjamin. *Faith and Freedom*. Christian Defense Fund, 1988. http://www.leaderu.com/orgs/cdf/ff/chap07.html.

Hartley, Cecil B. *Life and Times of Colonel Daniel Boone*. 2004. http://www.gutenberg.org/ebooks/14023?msg=welcome_stranger.

Hartwell, John J. *Li Zicheng: The Dashing Prince*. n.d. http://hauburn.tripod.com/lizicheng.html. 2014.

Hawthorne In Salem. n.d. http://www.hawthorneinsalem.org/Literature/NativeAmericans&Blacks/HannahDuston/MMD2169.html. 2014.

Henry Hudson. 2007. http://www.ianchadwick.com/hudson/hudson_00.htm. 2014.

Herdman, H.F.P. "SOME NOTES ON SEA ICE OBSERVED BY Captain James Cook, R.N., During His Circumnavigation of Antartica." *Early Discoveries* (1772): 530-540. http://www.igsoc.org:8080/journal/3/26/igs_journal_vol03_issue026_pg534-541.pdf.

Hickman, Kennedy. "Thirty Years' War: Battle of Breitenfeld." 2014. *About.com*. http://militaryhistory.about.com/od/battleswars16011800/p/Thirty-Years-War-Battle-Of-Breitenfeld.htm. 2014.

—. "Thirty Years War: Battle of Lutzen." n.d. *About.com*. http://militaryhistory.about.com/od/battleswars16011800/p/lutzen.htm. 2014.

History. 2002. http://www.allabouthistory.org/mayflower-compact.htm. 2014.

History of Bonsai. n.d. http://www.celestialbonsai.com/history.html. 2014.

"History of Classical Music." 2014. *Naxos*. http://www.naxos.com/education/brief_history.asp. 2014.

"History of Prussia." n.d. *History World*. http://www.historyworld.net/wrldhis/PlainTextHistories.asp?historyid=aa54. 2014.

Hoover, Michael. "The Whiskey Rebellion." 2012. *TTB.gov*. http://www.ttb.gov/public_info/whisky_rebellion.shtml. 2014.

Hutton, J.E. "The Letter of Majesty." n.d. *BibleHub*. http://biblehub.com/library/hutton/history_of_the_moravian_church/chapter_xiii_the_letter_of.htm. 2014.

Institute, Combat Studies. *Studies in Battle Command*. Fort Leavenworth: U.S. Army Command and General Staff College, n.d. http://books.google.com/books?id=ZVoWQNIH73cC&pg=PR2&lpg=PR2&dq=parchwitz+address&source=bl&ots=-C_TdQGIiL&sig=ND9x9iW24Jxhp_ivIFpc4KQL68o&hl=en&sa=X&ei=kheKUujoDrLa4AO8toGIBQ&ved=0CEgQ6AEwBA#v=onepage&q=parchwitz%20address&f=false.

"Institutes of the Christian Religon ." n.d. *Bible Explore.com*. http://www.godrules.net/library/calvin/calvin_iv_iv_v.htm. 2014.

"Instructions from the Virginia Company of London to the First Settlers." 2012. *Encyclopedia Virginia*. http://encyclopediavirginia.org/Instructions_from_the_Virginia_Company_of_London_to_the_First_Settlers_1606. 2014.

"Ivan the Terrible." 2014. *bio*. http://www.biography.com/people/ivan-the-terrible-9350679?page=2. 2014.

Ivan the Terrible. 2014. http://www.nndb.com/people/933/000092657/. 2014.

Jefferson, Thomas. *Thomas Jefferson on the French Revolution*. 1793. http://chnm.gmu.edu/revolution/d/592/. 2014.

Jemison, Mary. "Captured by Indians: Mary Jemison Becomes an Indian." n.d. *History Matters*. http://historymatters.gmu.edu/d/5794/. 2014.

John Eliot. 1997. http://www.greatsite.com/timeline-english-bible-history/john-eliot.html. 2014.

John Eliot. 2008. http://www.christianitytoday.com/ch/131christians/missionaries/johneliot.html. 2014.

John Hancock and his Liberty ship. n.d. http://www.publicbookshelf.com/public_html/Our_Country_vol_2/johnhanco_bd.html. 2014.

"John Knox." 2008. *ChristianityToday*. http://www.christianitytoday.com/ch/131christians/denominationalfounders/knox.html. 2014.

John Knox. 1996. http://www.luminarium.org/encyclopedia/knox.htm. 2014.

Johnston, Henry P. *The Campaign of 1776 around New York and Brooklyn*. 2007. http://www.munseys.com/diskfive/cams.htm#1_0_7. 2014.

Jonathan Edwards. 2008. http://www.christianitytoday.com/ch/131christians/theologians/edwards.html?start=2. 2014.

"Journals of the Coninental Congress - The Articles of Association; October 20, 1774." 2008. *Yale Law School: Lillian Goldman Law Library*. http://avalon.law.yale.edu/18th_century/contcong_10-20-74.asp. 2014.

JS Bach: Musical Offering. 2014. http://www.baroquemusic.org/barjsb7980.html. 2014.

King William's War. 2001. http://www.usahistory.info/colonial-wars/King-Williams-War.html. 2014.

Knecht, Robert. "France's Fiasco in Brazil." 2008. *HistoryToday.* http://www.historytoday.com/robert-knecht/france%E2%80%99s-fiasco-brazil. 2014.

Koeller, David W. *Frederick II of Prussia: Political Testament*. 2005. http://www.thenagain.info/classes/sources/frederick%20the%20great.html. 2014.

"La Belle." 2008. *Texas Beyond History.* http://www.texasbeyondhistory.net/belle/. 2014.

Lafayette. *Memoirs of General Lafayette*. Stan Goodman, 2005. http://www.gutenberg.org/files/7449/7449-h/7449-h.htm.

Lee, Richard H. "Land Ordinance of 1785." n.d. *IN.gov.* http://www.in.gov/history/2478.htm. 2014.

Leip, David. *The Electoral College*. 2008. http://uselectionatlas.org/INFORMATION/INFORMATION/electcollege_history.php. 2014.

Leopold, Frederick William. "Declaration of Pillnitz." 2013. *WikiSource.* http://en.wikisource.org/wiki/Declaration_of_Pillnitz. 2014.

"Letter from President Thomas Jefferson." n.d. *Montana Rojoma.* http://rojomoexpedition.com/lewis-and-clark/jeffersons-letter/. 2014.

Letter, March 24, 1832, about the Battle of Princeton. 1832. http://www.fofweb.com/History/MainPrintPage.asp?iPin=EAWd0058&DataType=AmericanHistory&WinType=Free. 2014.

"Lewis's Air Rifle." 2011. *Lewis ad Clark History.* http://lewisandclarktrail.com/lewisairgun.htm. 2014.

Linder, Douglas. *The Story of the Court-Martial of the Bounty Mutineers*. 2004. http://law2.umkc.edu/faculty/projects/ftrials/Bounty/bountyaccount.html. 2014.

Locke, John. *A Letter Concerning Toleration*. Constitution Society, 1998. http://www.constitution.org/jl/tolerati.htm.

—. *Second Treatise of Government*. Dave Gowan, 2005. http://www.gutenberg.org/cache/epub/7370/pg7370.txt.

Loewen, James W. *The Truth about the First Thanksgiving*. 2002. http://www.trinicenter.com/historicalviews/thanksgiving.htm. 2014.

"Louisiana." n.d. *The Library of Congress.* http://memory.loc.gov/ammem/collections/maps/lapurchase/essay3.html. 2014.

Marsden, George M. "Soul on Fire." 2003. *The New York Times.* http://www.nytimes.com/2003/07/06/books/soul-on-fire.html?pagewanted=all&src=pm. 2014.

"Maryland Toleration Act." n.d. *Yale Law School.* http://avalon.law.yale.edu/18th_century/maryland_toleration.asp. 2008.

Mayflower History.com. 1994. http://mayflowerhistory.com/. 2014.

Miller, John. "Indian Peace Medals." 2008. *LewisandClarkTrail.com.* http://www.lewisandclarktrail.com/legacy/peacemedals.htm. 2014.

Ming History English Translation Project. 2013. http://chinesestudies.ucsd.edu/mingstudies/. 2014.

Montgomery, Dennis. *Captain John Smith*. 2014. http://www.history.org/foundation/journal/smith.cfm. 2014.

More, David A. *Drunken Sailor or Imprisoned Writer*. 1996. http://www.marlovian.com/essays/penry.html. 2014.

"Mustafa I of Turkey." 2011. *Royalty in History.* http://madmonarchs.guusbeltman.nl/madmonarchs/mustafa1/mustafa1_bio.htm. 2014.

"Navigation Acts." 2014. *WikiSource.* http://en.wikisource.org/wiki/Navigation_Acts. 2014.

New Netherland. 2003. http://www.sonofthesouth.net/revolutionary-war/colonies/new-netherland.htm. 2014.

"New Perspectives on the West." 2001. *PBS.com.* http://www.pbs.org/weta/thewest/resources/archives/. 2014.

Nicol, George. *William Bligh's Narrative of the Mutiny on the Bounty*. London, 1790. http://law2.umkc.edu/faculty/projects/ftrials/Bounty/blighnarrative.html.

"Nieuw Nederland- New Netherland." 1994. *American History.* http://www.let.rug.nl/usa/essays/general/the-united-states-of-america-and-the-netherlands/nieuw-nederland---new-netherland.php. 2014.

Ozmore, Susan. *The Sultanate of Women*. 2013. http://saintssistersandsluts.com/the-sultanate-of-women/. 2014.

Parkman, Francis. "Letter from Virginia's Governor Dinwiddie to the French Commander in the Ohio Country, October, 1753. ." 1753. *ExplorePAhistory.com.* http://explorepahistory.com/odocument.php?docId=1-4-1A. 2014.

"Peter the Great Biography." 2014. *Bio.* http://www.biography.com/people/peter-the-great-9542228?page=1. 2014.

Pinckney, C.C. *Population Estimates Used at the Philadelphia Convention in 1787*. n.d. http://www.dcte.udel.edu/hlp/resources/newnation/pdfs/PopEstim.pdf. 2014.

Piper, John. " Will Not Be a Velvet-Mouthed Preacher." 2009. *desiringGod.* http://www.desiringgod.org/biographies/i-will-not-be-a-velvet-mouthed-preacher. 2014.

—. *David Brainerd*. Minneapolis: Desiring God Foundation, 2012. http://dwynrhh6bluza.cloudfront.net/resources/documents/5458/DavidBrainerd_final_singlepages.pdf?1341869390.

—. "You Will Be Eaten by Cannibals! Lessons from the Life of John G. Paton." 2014. *desiringGod.* http://www.desiringgod.org/biographies/you-will-be-eaten-by-cannibals-lessons-from-the-life-of-john-g-paton. 2014.

Plakkaat van Verlatinghe. 1994. http://www.let.rug.nl/usa/documents/before-1600/plakkaat-van-verlatinghe-1581-july-26.php. 2014.

Plant, David. "Oliver Cromwell." 2012. *BCWProject.* http://bcw-project.org/biography/oliver-cromwell. 2014.

Proclamation of 1763. 1999. http://www.ushistory.org/declaration/related/proc63.htm. 2014.

Prominent Russians: Ivan IV the Terrible. 2005. http://russiapedia.rt.com/prominent-russians/the-ryurikovich-dynasty/ivan-iv-the-terrible/. 2014.

Prominent Russians: Ivan Susanin. 2005. http://russiapedia.rt.com/prominent-russians/history-and-mythology/ivan-susanin/. 2014.

Prout, Ebenezer. *Memoirs of the life of the Rev. John Williams*. New York: M.W. Dodd, 1843. https://archive.org/stream/memoirsoflifeofrlond00prou#page/n7/mode/2up.

R. *A Covnter Blaste to Tobacco*. London, 1604. http://www.luminarium.org/renascence-editions/james1.html.

Rastatter, Paul J. "Rebel Prisoners Detained in North America." 1995. *Archiving early america*. http://www.earlyamerica.com/review/2002_summer_fall/pows.htm. 2014.

Records of the Parliament. 2011. http://www.rps.ac.uk/search.php?action=fetch_jump&filename=charlesii_ms&jump=charlesii_t1670_7_11_d7_trans&type=ms&fragment=m1670_7_11_d7_ms. 2014.

Reed, Kevin. *A Vindication of the Doctrine*. 1995. http://www.swrb.com/newslett/actualNLs/vindicat.htm. 2014.

"Research Subjects: Government and Politics." n.d. *c*.

Rev. Thomas Hooker. 1996. http://josfamilyhistory.com/stories/hooker.htm. 2014.

Revere, Paul. "Letter from Paul Revere to Jeremy Belknap." 1798. *MHS Collections Online*. http://www.masshist.org/database/viewer.php?item_id=99&img_step=1&mode=transcript#page1. 2014.

Rickard, J. *Napoleon's Campaign in Italy*. 2009. http://www.historyofwar.org/articles/campaign_napoleon_italy_1796.html#1. 2014.

"Robert Browne on Religious Liberty." 2014. *Christian History Institute*. https://www.christianhistoryinstitute.org/study/module/browne/. 2014.

Robinson, Bruce. "The Gunpowder Plot." 2011. *BBC History*. http://www.bbc.co.uk/history/british/civil_war_revolution/gunpowder_robinson_01.shtml. 2014.

Robinson, J.H. *The Civil Constitution of the Clergy*. Boston: Hanover Historical Texts Project, 1790. http://history.hanover.edu/texts/civilcon.html.

—. *The Proclamation of the Duke of Brunswick*. Boston: Hanover Historical Texts Prject, 1792. http://history.hanover.edu/texts/bruns.html.

Robinson, James Harvey. "The Tennis Court Oath." n.d. *Internet Archive*. http://archive.org/stream/jstor-2139955/2139955_djvu.txt. 2014.

Roger Williams and Rhode Island. 2002. http://www.publicbookshelf.com/public_html/The_Great_Republic_By_the_Master_Historians_Vol_I/rogerwill_cg.html. 2014.

Roger Williams Biography. 1983. http://sos.ri.gov/library/history/famous/rogerwilliams/. 2014.

"Roger Williams: Founding Providence." n.d. *National Park Service*. http://www.nps.gov/rowi/historyculture/foundingprovidence.htm. 2014.

Roland, Jon. *The Fundamental Orders*. 1997. http://www.constitution.org/bcp/fo_1639.htm. 2014.

Rothbard, Murray N. "Bacon's Rebellion." 2012. *LewRockwell.com*. http://archive.lewrockwell.com/rothbard/rothbard286.html. 2014.

—. "Pennsylvania's Anarchist Experiment." n.d. *LewRockwell.com*. http://archive.lewrockwell.com/rothbard/rothbard81.html. 2014.

Rountree, Helen C. "Opechancanough." 2014. *Encyclopedia Virginia*. http://encyclopediavirginia.org/Opechancanough_d_1646. 2014.

Rousseau, Jean Jacques. THE SOCIAL CONTRACT. 1762. http://www.constitution.org/jjr/socon.htm. 2014.

"Sally Hemings Acussation." 1818. *PBS*. http://www.pbs.org/jefferson/archives/documents/ih195822.htm. 2014.

"Samuel de Champlain Voyages." 1994. *American History*. http://www.let.rug.nl/usa/documents/1600-1650/samuel-de-champlain-voyages-1604.php. 2014.

Seaver, James. *A Narrative of the Life of Mrs. Mary Jemison*. Robert Connal, 2004. http://www.gutenberg.org/cache/epub/6960/pg6960.txt.

Sedition Act. 1798. http://www.constitution.org/rf/sedition_1798.htm. 2014.

sermonindex.net. 2002. http://www.sermonindex.net/modules/articles/index.php?view=article&aid=2515. 2014.

Severance, Diane. "Susanna Wesley: Christian Mother." 2014. *Christianity.com*. http://www.christianity.com/church/church-history/timeline/1701-1800/susanna-wesley-christian-mother-11630240.html. 2014.

Sieyes, Emmanuel Joseph. *Sieyes: What is the Third Estate*. 1789. http://faculty.smu.edu/rkemper/cf_3333/Sieyes_What_is_the_Third_Estate.pdf. 2014.

Smith, Richard Norton. "The Surprising George Washington." 1994. *About.com*. http://usgovinfo.about.com/gi/o.htm?zi=1/XJ&zTi=1&sdn=usgovinfo&cdn=newsissues&tm=1454&f=10&su=p284.13.342.ip_&tt=2&bt=4&bts=4&zu=http%3A//www.archives.gov/publications/prologue/1994/spring/george-washington-1.html. 2014.

Solomon, Steve. *of the Butter and Cheese Dairy*. 2010. http://www.soilandhealth.org/03sov/0302hsted/030205ellis/030205butter.cheese.html. 2014.

Sommerville, J.P. *Prussian in the late 17th Century*. n.d. http://faculty.history.wisc.edu/sommerville/351/351-151.htm. 2014.

Stanard, Mary Newton. *The Story of Bacon's Rebellion*. New York: The Neale Publishing Company, 1907. https://play.google.com/books/reader?id=MOiTajatRgcC&printsec=frontcover&output=reader&authuser=0&hl=en&pg=GBS.PA3.

"States and Capitals." 2014. *50 States.com.* http://www.50states.com/. 2014.

Stewart, John Hall. *Constitution of the Year III*. 1795. http://chnm.gmu.edu/revolution/d/450/. 2014.

Strong, Josiah. *Our Country*. 1800. http://www.publicbookshelf.com/public_html/Our_Country_Vol_1/sirgeorge_ej.html.

Sultzman, Lee. *Massachusetts History*. n.d. http://www.dickshovel.com/massa.html. 2014.

Susquehannock History. n.d. http://www.dickshovel.com/susque.html. 2014.

Swint, Kerwin. "Founding Fathers dirty campaign." 2008. *CNN.com.* http://www.cnn.com/2008/LIVING/wayoflife/08/22/mf.campaign.slurs.slogans/. 2014.

"Tasmanian Devil." 1996. *National Geographic.* http://animals.nationalgeographic.com/animals/mammals/tasmanian-devil/?rptregcta=reg_free_np&rptregcampaign=20131016_rw_membership_n1p_us_se_c1#close-modal. 2014.

"Tecumseh's Speech, of August 11, 1810, To Governer William Harrison." 2013. *WikiSource.* http://en.wikisource.org/wiki/Tecumseh's_Speech,_of_August_11,_1810,_To_Governer_William_Harrison. 2014.

Tench, Watkin. *A Complete Account of the Settlement at Port Jackson*. Project Gutenburg Australia, n.d. http://gutenberg.net.au/ebooks/e00084.txt.

—. *A Narrative of the Expedition to Botany Bay*. Project Gutenburg Australia, 1788. http://gutenberg.net.au/ebooks/e00083.txt.

Tennent, Gilbert. *An Analysis of His Evangelistic Ministry, Methods and Message during the Great Awakening*. Lynchburg: Cheryl Ann Rickards, 2003. http://digitalcommons.liberty.edu/cgi/viewcontent.cgi?article=1302&context=doctoral.

"Tenskwatwa." 1996. *Ohio History Central.* http://www.ohiohistorycentral.org/w/Tenskwatawa?rec=312. 2014.

"The Adventures of Daniel Boone." 1995. http://www.earlyamerica.com/lives/boone/chapt1/. 2014.

The Anglo Powhatan Wars. n.d. http://www.virginiaplaces.org/nativeamerican/anglopowhatan.html. 2014.

The Battle of Fort Washington. n.d. http://www.theamericanrevolution.org/battledetail.aspx?battle=13. 2014.

"The Battle of Rossbach." 2002. *BritishBattles.com.* http://www.britishbattles.com/frederick/battle-rossbach.htm. 2014.

"The Battle of Rossbach." 2002. *BritishBattles.com.* http://www.britishbattles.com/frederick/battle-rossbach.htm. 2014.

"The Beggars of Holland." 2013. *Heritage History.* http://www.heritage-history.com/?c=read&author=lansing&book=patriots&story=beggars. 2014.

The Beginning of the Fur Trade. n.d. http://www.canadiana.ca/hbc/hist/hist1_e.html. 2014.

"The British Burn Washington, DC." 2003. *Eyewitness to History.com.* http://www.eyewitnesstohistory.com/washingtonsack.htm. 2014.

"The Charter of Maryland." 2008. *http://avalon.law.yale.edu/17th_century/ma01.asp.* http://avalon.law.yale.edu/17th_century/ma01.asp. 2014.

the covenanters. 2013. http://www.thereformation.info/covenanters%20Index.htm. 2014.

The Dutch and English in New Netherland. 1999. http://www.rootsweb.ancestry.com/~nycoloni/dahist.html. 2014.

The Early Seventeenth Century. 2010. http://www.wwnorton.com/college/english/nael/17century/topic_4/donne.htm. 2014.

THE GREAT BINDING LAW, GAYANASHAGOWA. n.d. http://magic.education2020.com/Websites/Literature/Constitution_of_the_Iroquois_Nations.htm. 2014.

"The Great Siege-1565." n.d. *visitMalta.com.* http://www.visitmalta.com/en/great-siege-1565. 2014.

The Half-Way Covenant. n.d. http://www.kingsacademy.com/mhodges/08_Classics-Library/renaiss-reform/colonial-america/half-way-covenant.htm. 2014.

The History of Petanque. 2008. http://rocketcitypetanqueclub.homestead.com/History.html. 2014.

The History of the Russian Navy. Alexander PRINT, n.d. http://www.neva.ru/EXPO96/book/chap1-4.html.

"The Instructions of Catherine II to the Legislative Commission of 1767." 2009. *Documents in Russian History.* http://academic.shu.edu/russianhistory/index.php/Catherine_the_Great%27s_Instructions_to_the_Legislative_Commission%2C_1767. 2014.

"The Liberty Affair." 2014. *The Life of John Hancock.* http://www.john-hancock-heritage.com/the-liberty-affair/. 2014.

The Library of Congress. 1784. http://memory.loc.gov/cgi-bin/query/r?ammem/bdsdcc:@field(DOCID+@lit(bdsdcc13401)). 2014.

"The Making of a Congregationalist." 1999. *The Reformed Reader.* http://www.reformedreader.org/history/shakespeare/bacpch02.htm. 2014.

The Millenary Petition. 2013. http://www.thereformation.info/millenarypetition.htm. 2014.

The Norton Anthology of English Literature. 2014. http://www.wwnorton.com/college/english/nael/17century/topic_3/truelaw.htm. 2010.

"The Pennsylvania Magazine." 2014. *JSTOR.* http://www.jstor.org/discover/10.2307/20086534?uid=3739256&uid=2&uid=4&sid=21104281401377. 1924.

"The Pequot War." 2011. *The Society of Colonial Wars in the State of Connecticut.* http://www.colonialwarsct.org/1637.htm. 2014.

The Petition of Right. 1628. http://www.constitution.org/eng/petright.htm. 2014.

"The Powhatan Confederacy." n.d. *United States History.* http://www.u-s-history.com/pages/h1155.html. 2014.

"The Revolt of the Spanish Netherlands." 2013. *History Learning Site.* http://www.historylearningsite.co.uk/revolt_of_spanish_netherlands.htm. 2014.

The Scottish Confession of Faith. 1993. http://www.swrb.com/newslett/actualNLs/ScotConf.htm. 2014.

"The second Charter of Virginia." n.d. *Primary Sources.* http://www.learner.org/workshops/primarysources/virginia/docs/svc.html. 2014.

The Society of Colonial Wars in the State of Connecticut. 2001. http://colonialwarsct.org/1636.htm. 2014.

"The Third Virginia Charter." 1994. *American History.* http://www.let.rug.nl/usa/documents/1600-1650/the-third-virginia-charter-1612.php. 2014.

The Thirty Years War. 2005. http://www.pipeline.com/~cwa/TYWHome.htm. 2014.

"The tree of liberty." 1987. *The Jefferson: Monticello.* http://www.monticello.org/site/jefferson/tree-liberty-quotation. 2014.

The Triennial Act. 2014. http://www.constitution.org/eng/conpur027.htm. 2014.

"The Virginia Plan." 2014. *U.S. Constitution.* http://www.usconstitution.net/plan_va.html. 2014.

Thorn, John Coutant. *Early Quaker History.* 2002. http://thorn.pair.com/earlyq.htm. 2014.

Towle, Sarah. "Charlotte Corday and the Bathtub Assassination of Jean-Paul Marat." n.d. *France Revisited.* http://francerevisited.com/2012/07/charlotte-corday-and-the-bathtub-assassination-of-jean-paul-marat/.

Transcript of Louisiana Purchase Treaty. 1803. http://www.ourdocuments.gov/doc.php?flash=true&doc=18&page=transcript. 2014.

Transcript of Marbury v. Madison. 1803. http://www.ourdocuments.gov/doc.php?flash=true&doc=19&page=transcript. 2014.

Trial and Interrogatin of Anne Hutchinson. n.d. http://www.swarthmore.edu/SocSci/bdorsey1/41docs/30-hut.html. 2014.

Trueman, Chris. "Economy under Philip III." 2000. *History Learning Site.* http://www.historylearningsite.co.uk/P3econ.htm. 2014.

—. "The Consequences of the Hampton Court Conference." 2000. *History Learning Site.* http://www.historylearningsite.co.uk/Hampton-Court-Conference-consequences.htm. 2014.

—. "Thomas Percy." 2000. *History Learning Site.* http://www.historylearningsite.co.uk/Thomas-Percy.htm. 2014.

Unger, Harlow Giles. *Lafayette.* John Wiley and Sons, 2003. http://www.amazon.com/Lafayette-Harlow-Giles-Unger/dp/0471468851.

Vance, Laurence M. "The Hampton Court Conference." 2004. *LewRockwell.com.* http://www.historytoday.com/richard-cavendish/hampton-court-conference. 2014.

"Virginia State Flower." 2014. *50 States.com.* http://www.50states.com/flower/virginia.htm#.U77puPldUXl. 2014.

Voltaire. *The History of Peter the Great, Emperor of Russia.* 2013. http://www.gutenberg.org/files/42540/42540-h/42540-h.htm#CHAP_XXII.

Wakeley, J.B. *Susanna Wesley and the Unauthorized Meetings.* 2012. http://gbgm-umc.org/umw/wesley/susannawesley.stm. 2014.

Walenta, Craig. "Constitutional Topic: Checks and Balances." 1995. *U.S. Constitution.* http://www.usconstitution.net/consttop_cnb.html. 2014.

Wampum History and Background. 1994. http://www.nativetech.org/wampum/wamphist.htm. 2014.

"War of Independence Timeline: Military Dates." n.d. *United States History.* http://www.u-s-history.com/pages/h1197.html. 2014.

Warner, charles Dudley. *Captain John Smith.* 2006. http://www.gutenberg.org/files/3130/3130-h/3130-h.htm#link2H_4_0017. 2014.

Washington, George. *The Journal of Major George Washington.* Paul Royster, 1754. http://digitalcommons.unl.edu/cgi/viewcontent.cgi?article=1033&context=etas.

"Washington's Thanksgiving Proclamation." 1789. *The Heritage Foundation.* http://www.heritage.org/initiatives/first-principles/primary-sources/washingtons-thanksgiving-proclamation. 2014.

West, Jessamyn. *Marytrdom of Mary Dyer.* 2000. http://www2.gol.com/users/quakers/martyrdom_of_mary_dyer.htm. 2014.

"Westminister passes the Alien Act 1705." n.d. *www.parliament.uk.* http://www.parliament.uk/about/living-heritage/evolutionofparliament/legislativescrutiny/act-of-union-1707/overview/westminster-passes-the-alien-act-1705/. 2014.

"What Happened During the Massacre of Jane McCrea." 2014. *independencetrail.org.* http://www.independencetrail.org/vacation/stories-Massacre-of-Jane-McCrea.html. 2014.

"Who served here?: Baron von Steuben." 1998. *Historic Valley Forge.* http://www.ushistory.org/valleyforge/served/steuben.html. 2014.

wiggs, evan. *Moravian Revival.* n.d. http://www.evanwiggs.com/revival/history/moravian.html.

Williams, John. *A Narrative of Missionary Enterprises.* London: Paternoster Row, 1837. https://archive.org/stream/anarrativemissi00willgoog#page/n8/mode/2up.

—. *A Narrative of Missionary Enterprises.* London: Paternoster Row, 1837. https://archive.org/stream/anarrativemissi00willgoog#page/n8/mode/2up.

Wilson, D. *"The life of Jane McCrea : with an account of Burgoyne's expedition in 1777".* New York: Library of Congress, 1853. http://archive.org/stream/lifeofjanemccrea01wils/lifeofjanemccrea01wils_djvu.txt. 2014.

Winthrop, Robert C. *Life and Letters of John Winthrop*. Boston, 1630. https://play.google.com/books/reader?id=hvsdAZMEtb0C&printsec=frontcover&output=reader&authuser=0&hl=en&pg=GBS.PR2.

Wolfe, Brendan. *First Anglo-Powhatan War*. 2011. http://encyclopediavirginia.org/First_Anglo-Powhatan_War_1609-1614#start_entry. 2014.

Wolverton, Joe. "Secrecy and the States' Rights: The Constitutional Convention of 1787 Begins." 2013. *the New American*. http://www.thenewamerican.com/culture/history/item/15546-secrecy-and-states-rights-the-constitutional-convention-of-1787-begins. 2014.

Zoltvany, Yves F. *LAUMET, de Lamothe Cadillac, ANTOINE*. 1969. http://www.biographi.ca/en/bio/laumet_antoine_2E.html. 2014.

—. *Laumet, de Lamothe, Cadillac, Antoine*. 1969. http://www.biographi.ca/en/bio/laumet_antoine_2E.html. 2014.

"1758: Francois Macandal, Forgotten Black Messiah." Executed Today. Word Press, 20 Jan. 2009. Web. 29 Nov. 2013.<http://www.executedtoday.com/2009/01/20/1758-francois-macandal-black-messiah/>.

"1st millionaire dies broke." California Gold Rush. N.p., n.d. Web. 3 Feb. 2014.<http://www.cal goldrush.com/profiles/pro_brannan.html>.

"A Survivor's Recollections of the Whitman Massacre by Matilda Sager." Project Gutenberg.N.p., n.d.Web. 19 Oct. 2013, <http://www.gutenberg.org/ebooks/41912?msg=welcome_stranger>.

"Abolition of the Slave Trade." The Speeches of Sir Samuel Romilly in the House of Commons. Google Play. Google, n.d. Web. 1 Jan. 2014.<https://play.google.com/books/reader ?id =5AM-AAAAcAAJ&printsec=frontcover&output=reader&authuser= 0&hl=en&pg=GBS.PA15>.

"Address by Thomas Jefferson, 1805." 57th Presidential Inauguration. Joint Congressional Committee, Inaugural Ceremonies, 21 Jan. 2013. Web. 14 June 2013. <http://www.inaugural.senate.gov/swearing-in/address/address-by-thomas-jefferson-1805>.

"Antonio Lopez de Santa Anna." Texas A&M University. Sons of Dewitt Colony Texas, 2010. Web. 23 March 2014. <http://www.tamu.edu/faculty/ccbn/dewitt/santaanna.htm>.

"Considerations on the Keeping-of Negroes Recommended to the Professors of Christianity of Every Denomination." Archive. 1754. Web. 7 Oct. 2013.<http://archive.org/stream/ considerationson00wool/considerationson00wool_djvu.txt>.

"Discovery of India." Archive. N.p., n.d. Web. 4 Nov. 2014.<https://archive.org/stream/ DiscoveryOfIndia/TheDiscoveryOfIndia-jawaharlalNehru#page/n293/mode/2up>.

"Emancipation in New York." Slavery in the North. N.p., 2003. Web. 2 Feb. 2014. <http://slavenorth.com/nyemancip.htm>.

"Fatal Cruise of the Princton." Military.US Naval Institute, 2005. Web. 4 Dec.2013. <http://www . military.com/NewContent/0,13190,NH_0905_Cruise-P2,00.html>.

"Foundations." Teaching the Middle East, A Resource for Educators. 31 May 2011 < http://teachmiddleeast.lib.uchicago.edu/index.html>.

"Gabriel's Conspiracy (1799-1800)." PBS. Africans in America, n.d. Web. 2 July 2013.<http://www.pbs.org/wgbh/aia/part3/3p1576.html>.

"Huzza! For General Jackson." American Memory. Library of Congress, n.d. Web. 23 August 2013.<http://memory.loc.gov/cgi\bin/query/r?ammem/amss:@field%28DOCID+@lit%28as 105670%29%29>.

"James Ramsay (1733-1789): The Ship's Doctor & Preacher." The Abolition Project. E2Bn-East of England Broadband Network and MLA East of England, 2009. Web. 28 Dec. 2013. <http://abolition.e2bn.org/people_28.html>.

"Mexican Independence." Texas A&M University. Sons of Dewitt Colony Texas, 2012. Web. 23 March 2014. <http://www.tamu.edu/faculty/ccbn/dewitt/mexicanrev.htm>.

"Missionary history of the Pacific Northwest: containing the wonderful story of Jason Lee, with sketches of many of his co-laborers, all illustrating life of the plains and in the mountains in pioneer days." Archive. N.p., n.d.Web. 3 Dec. 2013. <https://archive.org/stream/cihm_15235/cihm_15235_djvu.txt>.

"Modern History Sourcebook: Commissioner Lin: Letter to Queen Victoria, 1839." Fordham University. Paul Halsam,Oct. 1998. Web. 7 May 2014.<http://www.fordham.edu /halsall/mod/1839lin2.asp>.

"Monarchs of Britain." Britannia Encyclopedia. 2011 ed. Britannia. 3 Feb. 2012.

"Napoleon Exiled to St. Helena, 1815." Eye Witness to History. Ibis Communications, Inc.n.d.Web.25 May 2014.<http://www.eyewitnesstohistory.com/napoleon.htm>.

"Nat Turner's Rebellion." PBS. Africans in America, n.d. Web. 2 July 2013.<http:// www.pbs. org/ wgbh/aia/part3/3p1576.html>.

"Opinions of the Early Presidents, and of the Fathers of the Republic, upon Slavery and upon Negroes as Men and Soldiers." The University Dayton School of Law. Vernellia R. Randal, 24 April 2012. Web. 29 Nov. 2013.<http://academic.udayton.edu/race/02rights/slave05.htm#Jefferson>.

"People's and Events—Gabriel's Conspiracy (1799-1800)." PBS. Africans in America, n.d. Web. 2 July 2013.<http://www.pbs.org/wgbh/aia/part3/3p1576.html>.

"Petition from the Pennsylvania Society for the Abolition of Slavery."US History. Independence Hall Association, 2013. Web. 16 July 2013.<http://www.ushistory.org/documents /antislavery.htm>.

"Plan of Iguala." Texas A&M University. Sons of Dewitt Colony Texas, 2003. Web. 23 March 2014. <http://www.tamu.edu/faculty/ccbn/dewitt/iguala.htm>.

"Sam Brannon." Sierra Foothill Magazine. N.p., n.d. Web. 6 July 2014. <http://www.sierrafoot   hillmagazine.com/brannan.html>.

"Simon Bolivar's Jamaica Letter." Excerpt Analysis, Indepth Info. W.J. Rament, 2014. Web. 12 April 2014.<http://excerpts.indepthinfo.com/simon-bolivars-jamaica-letter>.

"Slaveholder's Promise." Digital Library. N.p., n.d. Web. 22 Feb. 2014.<http://digital.library.up enn.edu/women/truth/1850/1850.html#14>.

"Statistics on Slavery."Weber. N.p., n.d. Web. 30 Nov. 2013. <http://faculty.weber.edu/kmack ay/statistics_on_slavery.html>.

"The Code Noir (The Black Code)." Edit du Roi, Touchant la Police des isles de lÁmericque Francaise (Paris, 1687): 28-58. Liberty, Equality, Fraternity, Exploring the French Revolution, n.d. Web. 15 April 2014. <http://chnm.gmu.edu/revolution/d/335/>.

"The Congress of Vienna 1814-1815." The Map as History. N.p. n.d. Web. 2 June 2014. <http:// www.the-map-as-history.com/demos/tome01/index.php>.

"The Legend of the Cherokee Rose." Powersource. Cherokees of California, n.d. Web. 28 June 2014. <http://www.powersource.com/cocinc/articles/rose.htm>.

"The Life of William Willberforce." Archive. N.p., n.d. Web. 7 Oct. 2013. <https://archive.org /stream/ lifewilliamwilb11wilbgoog/lifewilliamwilb11wilbgoog_djvu.txt >.

"The Removal Act, 28 May 1830." Mount Holyoke College. Vincent Ferraro, Feb. 2010. Web. 2 July <https://www.mtholyoke.edu/acad/intrel/removal.htm>.

"The Return of the Spirit: The Second Great Awakening." Christian History Institute. N.p., n.d. Web. 30 Nov. 2013. https://www.christianhistoryinstitute.org/magazine/article/return-of-the-spirit-second-great-awakening/.

"Thomas Jefferson Papers." The Library of Congress—American Memory. Library of Congress, n.d. Web. 17 Aug. 2013. <http://memory.loc.gov/cgi-bin/query/r?ammem/mtj:@ field(DOCID+@lit(ws03101))>.

"Transcript of President Andrew Jackson's Message to Congress 'On Indian Removal' (1830)." Our Documents. N.p., n.d. Web. 4 Dec. 2014. <http.//www.ourdocuments.gov/doc.php?flash=true&doc=25&page=transcript>.

"William Carey." Theopedia, an Encyclopedia of Biblical Christianity. N.p., n.d. Web. 3 August 2013. <http://www.theopedia.com/William_Carey>.

Index

A

a general history of the pirates, 365
a proposal for establishing a settlement in new south wales, 589
aaron burr, 652, 656-657, 661-662
abbe sieyes, 607, 645, 647
abel magwitch, 592
abel tasman, 579, 582
abel upshur, 839
abenaki, 425
abigail williams, 343
abolition, 620, 720, 758, 789, 792-793, 795, 799-800, 802-805, 809
abolition of the monarchy, 620
aborigine, 579
abul jazal, 352-353, 359
acadia, 112-114, 140-141, 426, 456, 460-461, 464, 864
acid test, 846
act abolishing the house of lords, 237
act abolishing the office of king, 237
act against puritans, 128
act declaring england to be a commonwealth, 237
act for the gradual abolition of slavery, 792
act of abjuration, 55-56, 249
act of security, 419
act of settlement, 418-419
act of uniformity, 246
act prohibiting importation of slaves, 795
acts of union, 62, 419-420
adams-onís treaty, 841
adinkra, 811, 864
adirondacks, 150
admirable campaign, 727
admiral ribault, 109-110
admiralty court, 500, 503-504
adobe, 26
adolf hitler, 402, 701
adoniram judson, 782-783
adriaen block, 154, 252
adventism, 855
age of enlightenment, 496, 602
agra, 353, 355-358, 362

agricultural revolution, 752-753
agustin de iturbide, 814, 818-821, 824, 841
ahmed i, 383-384
ahone, 75
akbar, 350-353, 358-359, 361, 760, 762
alamgir, 351, 357-360, 362-364, 368, 760-762
alamo, 822-823, 827-829, 836
albany, 150, 153, 155, 231, 250-251, 277, 426, 535-537, 552, 662, 755-756, 785
albany plan, 552
albemarle sound, 104, 256
aldersgate experience, 450
alexander duff, 770-771
alexander hamilton, 569-570, 599, 629, 634-635, 652, 654-655, 657, 661
alexander i, 680, 682, 685, 700
alexander mackenzie, 665, 864
alexander spotswood, 369
alexandre dumas, 223-224
alexis i, 402
algeria, 378
algonquian, 74-76, 78-80, 82-84, 88-89, 94-98, 115, 139, 207, 226, 253-254, 257, 265, 732
algonquin, 115, 119
alhondiga, 816-817
alien and sedition acts, 651, 654, 656
aliens bill, 420
alvarado, 30
amaterasu, 327
amazing grace, 804-805
amazon, 81, 731
american prohibitory act, 517
amistad, 806-807
amsterdam, 49, 133-134, 152-153, 155, 218, 232, 234-235, 250-251, 410
an enquiry into the obligations of christians, 770
anarkali, 352
anatolia, 371
ancien régime, 602, 604, 613, 619, 640, 645-646

ancient brethren, 133-134
andrea doria, 379-380
andrew jackson, 417, 576, 704, 733-734, 738-746, 750, 758-759, 785, 823, 825-826, 837, 862
anglican, 42, 62, 65, 67-68, 93, 97, 126-130, 132-136, 148, 177, 180-181, 188-191, 196, 200, 204, 210, 213-214, 228, 235, 237-238, 240, 245-246, 249, 255, 287-288, 295-296, 319-320, 420, 437, 440, 450-451, 548, 614, 627-628, 769, 800-801, 805, 850, 852
anglo-american convention of 1818, 841
anglo-dutch war, 249-250, 287, 498
anglo-maratha wars, 767
anglo-mysore wars, 767
anglo-powhatan war, 87, 89, 91-96, 98, 253-255
ann austin, 282, 342
ann bonny, 370
anna putnam, 344
anne boleyn, 48, 59
anne hutchinson, 214-217, 234, 265, 282-283
anne judson, 782-783
anne of denmark, 61, 176, 341
antarctica, 34, 578, 585
anthony johnson, 392
antinomian, 214-215, 265
antoine laumet, lord de cadillac, 417
antoine-françois momoro, 635-636
anxious seat, 855
apache, 38, 835, 849
apostolic succession, 627
appalachian, 39, 69, 71, 75, 150, 415, 456, 488, 491, 663, 756
appaloosa, 29, 674-675
aragon, 11-14, 377
arbella, 183-184
arc de triomphe, 683, 864
archaic period, 36
arctic circle, 35, 151-152, 167
argall, 92-93
argentina, 723, 726, 728-729, 731

arioi, 597-598
arminian, 210-211, 854-855
army of the three guarantees, 819-820
arthur dimmesdale, 188
arthur philip, 590
articles of association, 553
articles of confederation, 551-554, 556-557, 559-563, 572-573, 629, 634
aruba, 233
aruj, 377-378
asaf khan, 354-355
ashikaga, 328-329
asia minor, 291, 360, 371, 377, 380
asiento, 452
assumption bill, 599, 629, 652
atahualpa, 23-25, 27, 31, 338, 362
atchafalaya, 414
atlantic revolutions, 496, 707
august decrees, 611, 614
augustus the strong, 409, 411, 413
auld alliance, 41, 44-45, 60
aurangzeb, 357-359, 760
australia, 34, 577-580, 582-584, 588-593, 595-596, 864
avalon peninsula, 229
aviles, 30, 109-110
azov, 404, 412
aztec, 20-23, 25, 30, 36-37, 813, 834

B

babur, 349-351, 358-359
bach, 435
bacon's laws, 262-263
bacon's rebellion, 253, 256-259, 262-264, 392, 688, 734
baffin island, 153
baghdad, 376-377, 385, 387
bahamas, 16, 35
baja peninsula, 813
balance of trade, 776-777, 779
balkan peninsula, 371, 373, 375, 387

bangladesh, 349
baptism of kiev, 395
baptist war, 803-804
barbarossa, 374, 377-381, 404
barbary coast, 377-378, 678
barbary pirates, 377-378, 381-383, 389-390
barebone's parliament, 240-241
barry st. leger, 535-536, 544
bartolome de las casas, 31-33, 392
bartolomeu dias, 11, 18-19
barton stone, 852-853
bastille, 609-610, 614, 619, 622-623, 625, 647
bastion, 76
battle of assunpink creek, 534
battle of austerlitz, 681-683
battle of ayacucho, 730
battle of bemis heights, 537
battle of bennington, 536
battle of blood river, 810
battle of borodino, 700
battle of bothwell bridge, 322-323
battle of bower hill, 631
battle of boyaca, 728
battle of brandywine creek, 539-540
battle of breitenfeld, 169-170, 172, 174
battle of bunker hill, 516
battle of burnt corn creek, 738
battle of buxar, 767
battle of calderon bridge, 817
battle of camden, 544
battle of carabobo, 728-729
battle of carillon, 463
battle of cartagena de indias, 453-454
battle of cerro gordo, 832
battle of chacabuco, 728
battle of chapultepec, 833-834
battle of chotusitz, 433
battle of coleto, 829
battle of concord, 514
battle of cowpens, 544
battle of dunbar, 238-239, 244
battle of fallen timbers, 689-691, 693, 812
battle of flamborough head, 548
battle of fort frontenac, 464
battle of fort necessity, 460, 466
battle of fort washington, 531

battle of freeman's farm, 537
battle of gonzales, 827
battle of guilford courthouse, 544
battle of harlem heights, 530
battle of horseshoe bend, 740, 825
battle of jena-auerstedt, 683-684
battle of jumonville glen, 459, 601
battle of karnal, 763
battle of kings mountain, 544
battle of kolin, 474, 478
battle of kunersdorf, 477-478
battle of lake erie, 697
battle of langport, 195
battle of lepanto, 382-383
battle of leuthen, 476
battle of lexington, 514
battle of ligny, 711
battle of lobositz, 473
battle of long island, 528-529, 546
battle of lützen, 171, 174
battle of marston moor, 194
battle of mohács, 158, 374
battle of mollwitz, 433, 474
battle of monmouth, 542-543
battle of monte de las cruces, 816
battle of narva, 408
battle of naseby, 192, 195-196
battle of new orleans, 704, 733, 741-742, 823
battle of nördlingen, 172-174, 218
battle of oneida/onondaga lake, 121, 125
battle of pichincha, 729
battle of plassey, 766-768
battle of point pleasant, 491, 687, 691
battle of poltava, 411-412
battle of port royal, 426
battle of prague, 474
battle of preveza, 379-380
battle of princeton, 534, 544
battle of quatre bras, 711
battle of quebec, 426-427, 525-526
battle of rossbach, 475-476
battle of rullion green, 321-322
battle of samugarh, 357-358
battle of san jacinto, 829-830
battle of sekigahara, 335-336
battle of shanhai pass, 317
battle of soor, 434

battle of the alamo, 827-828
battle of the chesapeake, 546
battle of the monongahela, 462, 489
battle of the nile, 643-644
battle of the plains of abraham, 464
battle of the pyramids, 642-643
battle of the river lech, 170, 174
battle of the thames, 697-698, 812
battle of the white mountain, 162-164, 176
battle of ticonderoga, 120, 153, 464
battle of tippecanoe, 694-695, 812
battle of trafalgar, 648-649, 665, 679-681
battle of trenton, 532, 548, 733
battle of ulm, 681
battle of vertieres, 722
battle of vienna, 387-389, 405, 409, 423
battle of waterloo, 710-712
battle of white plains, 530-531
battle of worcester, 239-240
battle of yamazaki, 332
battles of saratoga, 537-538, 540-541, 544
bavaria, 161, 163, 166, 170, 172, 220, 432-434
bear-baiting, 242, 245
beaver wars, 121-122, 207, 257, 259, 290, 425, 547
beeldenstorm, 53-54, 220
beethoven, 453, 455, 650
beggars' pouch, 53
beijing, 303, 309, 311, 314-318, 771-772
belgian revolution, 713
belgium, 9, 49, 155, 641, 713, 781
bellum se ipsum alet, 164-165
benedict arnold, 502, 515, 524, 526, 535-536, 543-545
bengal, 349, 361-363, 760, 765-770, 783
benjamin banneker, 791
benjamin church, 268, 270-271
benjamin franklin, 440, 517, 519-524, 526, 539, 541, 547, 552, 559-560, 564, 568, 580, 788
benjamin harrison, 693, 705, 812
benjamin hornigold, 365, 368
bering strait, 36, 580, 587

bermuda, 86-87, 90, 92, 702
betsy ross, 548-549
betty parris, 343
bill of rights, 142, 300, 418, 496, 498, 560, 572-573, 603, 628, 706, 820, 851
birch bark manuscript, 487
birchbark canoe, 123-124
bishops' bible, 68
bishops' dragnet, 321
bitterroot mountains, 673-675
black forest, 680, 864
black hole of calcutta, 765-766
black legend, 33, 338, 391
blackbeard, 365-369, 430
blackstone river, 179
blaise pascal, 274-275
blood stripe, 834
bloody mary, 43, 46, 51, 62, 67, 126-127, 300
blunderbuss, 143-144
boer, 809-810
bohemia, 157-164, 170-172, 176, 419, 433-434, 448, 471, 473-475
bohemian revolt, 156, 159, 161-164, 173, 176, 218-219, 448
bois caïman, 717-718
bolivia, 723, 726, 730-731
bombay, 362-364, 760
bonaire, 233
bonfire night, 64-65
bonhomme richard, 548
bonsai, 318, 863
book of mormon, 857-858
boone expedition, 491
boonesborough, 492-495
boston, 139, 179, 183-185, 187-189, 199-201, 203-204, 208, 214-215, 265-266, 269, 271, 282-285, 291, 295-296, 301, 342, 344, 443, 500-513, 515-516, 518, 520, 524, 527, 538, 630, 633-634, 651, 733, 778
boston latin school, 188, 520
boston martyrs, 284-285
boston massacre, 505-506, 510
boston neck, 512
boston tea party, 508-509, 778
botany bay, 583, 590
boules, 224
bourbon restoration, 708
bowery, 234
bowie knife, 826
boye, 193-194
boyle's law, 275
braddock, 460, 462-463, 489
brandenburg, 157, 220,

422-424, 435, 477-479, 683
brazil, 17-19, 109-110, 360, 601, 863
breaking wheel, 409, 619
breed's hill, 515-516
brief account of the devastation of the indies, 32-33
brielle, 55
british empire, 526, 580, 590, 760, 768-769, 772, 809
british raj, 768
broadway, 234
bronx, 150, 217-218
brooklyn, 104-105, 150, 156, 234, 528-529, 531, 756
brown bess, 494
brownist, 131
brunswick manifesto, 617, 620, 625
buda, 374-375
buffalo horn headdress, 509
burial mound, 37, 677, 857
burned-over district, 855
burying the hatchet, 465
bushido, 328
buzzards bay, 139

C

cabot strait, 102
cabral, 18-19, 863
cajamarca, 24, 27
cajun, 468-469
calcutta, 362, 591, 760, 765-767
calico jack, 365-366, 370, 430
california, 38-39, 70, 663, 813-814, 832, 834, 838, 840, 844-849, 861-862
california gold rush, 844, 846-847
california star, 846
california trail, 845
calvinist, 161, 185, 210-213, 220, 273, 437, 451, 854-855
cambridge, 65, 128, 131, 133, 179, 181-182, 185, 193, 201-202, 259, 265, 278
cambridge agreement, 182
cameahwait, 672-673
camille desmoulins, 609, 622, 637
canada, 15, 35, 39, 70, 102, 104-107, 111-114, 121-125, 180, 303, 414, 427, 456-457, 460, 463, 465, 479, 526, 547-548, 580, 586-587, 627, 666, 670, 690-691, 695-697, 841-842, 862
canadian martyrs, 125
canary islands, 16, 73, 77, 643
candle, 233, 520
cane ridge revival, 853
cangue, 318
cannibal, 861
canonicus, 205, 207
canons of dort, 212
canton system, 775
cape breton island, 102, 460, 464
cape charles, 73
cape cod, 114, 138-139, 141-142, 144, 148-149, 301, 366, 734, 863
cape fear, 104
cape henlopen, 231
cape henry, 73-75, 734
cape may, 231
cape verde, 17-18
captain john smith, 69, 76-80, 82-85, 87-89, 98, 131, 135-136, 140, 143-144, 153, 863
cardinal beaton, 42-43
cardinal mazarin, 220-221
cardinal richelieu, 218-220, 223
carib, 105
caroline era, 176
carthage, 859
cascades, 39, 838
casta system, 724, 815, 819
castile, 11-14, 33, 377
castle island, 155, 231, 506, 510
catacombs of paris, 637
catherine the great, 471, 480-481, 486, 646, 680, 725
catholic league, 161-164, 166, 173
catskills, 150, 155, 231, 277, 863
cavalier, 193
cayuga, 37, 116-118
cecilius calvert, 230, 448
celebration of reason, 635-636
century of humiliation, 774-775
chadd's ford, 540
chain of justice, 353
champlain, 104, 112-116, 119-123, 125, 151, 153, 414-415, 426-427, 460, 463, 518, 524, 527, 535, 667, 863
chanco, 96
charivari, 469
charles cornwallis, 527, 532, 543
charles eden, 368
charles finney, 854
charles i, 12-14, 23, 33, 50-51, 157, 176-181, 188-189, 192, 197-198, 200, 204, 213, 228-230, 235-237, 240, 242-245, 247-248, 250, 255, 258, 277, 292, 319-320, 370, 373, 417-419, 428, 444, 448, 496, 606, 615
charles i of spain, 12-14, 23, 33, 50, 157, 373
charles ii, 177, 213, 236-240, 244-247, 249-250, 255, 257-258, 263, 277, 285-290, 292, 294-296, 299, 319-320, 322-325, 363, 392, 418, 420, 428-429, 437, 448, 760
charles ii of spain, 428
charles mason, 794
charles of austria, 429-430
charles perrault, 225
charles river, 179, 184, 201, 512, 516
charles wesley, 439, 448, 450-451
charles xii of sweden, 402, 407, 412, 701
charlesfort, 109
charlestown neck, 516
charlotte corday, 621, 625
charter oak, 226, 296-297
charter of liberty, 289
charter of maryland, 229-230, 292
charter of virginia, 71-72, 85, 87, 98, 182
checks and balances, 567, 571, 602, 612
chen yuanyuan, 316-317
chennai, 362, 760, 766
cherokee, 38, 470, 489, 491-492, 576, 666, 734, 736-737, 742, 750-752, 825, 863
cherokee nation v. georgia, 751
cherokee phoenix, 737
cherokee rose, 470, 751-752
cherokee syllabary, 736
cherokee trail of tears, 751
chesapeake bay, 69, 73, 76, 79, 82-83, 87, 90-92, 102, 104, 110, 230, 255-256, 539, 546, 702
chesapeake bay campaign, 702
chiaroscuro, 58
chickasaw, 38, 734, 748
child's war, 363-364
chile, 19, 30, 723, 726-729, 864
chiles en nogado, 820
chimney sweep, 805
china, 15-17, 35, 106, 303-307, 311-314, 316-319, 327, 333, 335-337, 339, 349, 360-361, 760, 771-782, 863
chinese new year, 303-304
choctaw, 38, 734, 747-748, 751
choctaw trail of tears, 747
christian church (disciples of christ), 853
christian iv of denmark, 164-165, 168, 219
christmas cracker, 769
christopher gist, 458
christopher newport, 72, 82, 86
chumash, 38, 844
chunkey, 752
church building controversy, 159-160
churches of christ, 853
churn, 863
cibola, 25-27
city of brotherly love, 291
civil constitution of the clergy, 614, 619
civil disobedience, 835
clan, 39-40, 116-119, 331
clara wieck schumann, 713-714
clarendon code, 245-246, 255, 319-320, 437
clark island, 144, 269-270
clarkson's box, 801
claude de jouffroy, 624
clermont, 755
clink, 445
clovis point, 36
code noir, 715-716
coffee, 384, 389, 469, 715, 718-719, 863
colombia, 453, 723, 725, 727-730
columbia plateau, 838
columbia river, 673-674, 838, 841, 864
columbian exchange, 29, 674
columbus, 11, 15-20, 29-31, 34-35, 37, 70, 599, 626, 699, 714, 863
comanche, 27, 38, 835
committee of correspondence, 507
committee of five, 498, 518-519, 553, 651
committee of public safety, 620
committees of safety, 510
common sense, 57, 264, 517-518, 532, 551, 835
commonwealth, 176, 216, 237, 240-241, 244, 248, 258, 495, 577-578
compact of 1802, 750
company raj, 764-765, 767-768
compromise of 1790, 599, 629, 652
comte de grasse, 546
concert of europe, 707
concession and agreement of the lords proprietor of new jersey, 286
concordat of 1801, 646
confederation of the rhine, 682, 707

confessions of nat turner, 799
confrontation at vincennes, 693-694, 697
congregational, 45, 273, 850
congregationalist, 45, 189, 201, 273, 438, 782, 851
congress, 292, 394, 494, 502, 511, 515-520, 524, 526-527, 533, 538-541, 544-545, 549, 552-558, 560-569, 572-574, 598-601, 625, 629-630, 652, 654-655, 657-659, 678, 688, 695, 706-710, 712-713, 730-731, 733, 740, 746-747, 759, 789-790, 795-796, 803, 809, 821, 831-832, 837, 850-851, 862
congress of vienna, 707-710, 712-713, 809
connecticut, 179-180, 189, 199, 201-203, 205, 207-208, 226-227, 250, 252, 265, 277, 285, 295-297, 301, 437-438, 442-443, 448, 519, 529, 546, 554, 572, 627-628, 792, 795, 806-807, 851
connecticut river, 179, 202, 208, 438
conquest of new netherland, 249, 251
considerations on the keeping of negroes, 787
constantinople, 10, 371, 375-376, 380, 386, 395-396, 404, 486
constitution, 117, 142, 199, 203, 226, 241, 243, 470, 496-497, 507, 527, 551, 553, 556, 559-564, 566-574, 598-599, 601-602, 607-609, 612, 614-616, 618-619, 629, 632, 634, 640, 645-646, 651-659, 665, 679, 703, 706, 721, 744, 750-751, 786, 794-795, 800, 818, 820-822, 825, 827-828, 850
constitution of 1791, 615-616, 618-619, 640
constitution of 1793, 640
constitution of 1795, 640
constitution of 1824, 821-822, 825, 827
constitution of the year viii, 645, 679
constitution of the year x, 645, 679
constitution of the year xii, 645, 679
constitutional convention, 292, 523, 559-562, 568, 570, 572-573,
599, 608, 651, 706, 740, 864
consultation of 1835, 827
continental congress, 292, 394, 511, 515-520, 526, 538, 553, 557, 600-601, 678, 706, 790
continental divide, 663
continental system, 685-686, 699, 724
conventicle, 320-322
convention of 1836, 828
corbitant, 147-148
coromandel coast, 760
coronado, 25-29, 835
corporation act, 246
corps of discovery, 667-674, 838
cortes, 21-25, 28-30, 338, 699, 813, 822, 832, 834, 844
cotton gin, 756
cotton mather, 201, 342-343, 346-348, 437
council of 500, 640, 645
council of ancients, 640, 645
council of troubles, 54-55
counter-reformation, 125, 159, 166, 173, 220, 333
country party, 445-446
coureurs de bois, 123
court dwarf, 191, 198
court of high commission, 321-322
court of oyer and terminer, 340, 344-347, 426
covenanter, 196, 303, 319-325
creek, 37-38, 238, 444, 457, 534, 539-540, 734-735, 737-738, 740-742, 744, 747-749, 758, 825-826, 863
creek war, 737-738, 740-741, 744, 749, 758, 825-826
crimean khanate, 399, 486
crimean peninsula, 399, 486
criollo, 725-726, 814-815, 818-819, 821
crispus attucks, 505-506
crop rotation, 752-753
cross of burgundy, 14, 811
crown jewels, 247, 358
crusade, 10-11, 200, 374, 377, 380, 382, 421
cuba, 16-17, 28-29, 32, 35, 72, 664, 714, 723, 729, 806-807
cueva de las manos, 731, 864
cult of reason, 635
cult of the supreme being, 636
cumberland gap, 488, 490-492
cuper's cove, 103, 227, 229
curacao, 233
curse of tippecanoe, 698

cyprus, 380, 383
czech, 157, 161-163, 433-434, 448, 473-474, 681

D

dade massacre, 749
daimyo, 329-330, 333, 335-336
daniel boone, 489-495, 666
daniel defoe, 365, 420
daniel shays, 558-559, 569
danube, 9, 170, 373-375, 455, 680, 863
danvers, 340
daoguang, 777, 780
dara, 357-358
dauphin louis, 429-430, 604
david brainerd, 441-442, 769
david gardiner, 839
david rizzio, 47
david thompson, 227
davy crockett, 826-828
day of blood, 162
de mons, 113-114
de soto, 27-29, 414-415
de villegagnon, 108-109
death by a thousand cuts, 308
death valley, 838
deborah sampson, 549
deccan plateau, 349, 355, 359-360, 762
declaration of breda, 244-245
declaration of independence, 56, 142, 262, 444, 456, 496, 518-520, 527, 551, 553, 560, 573, 611, 651, 653, 678, 693, 703, 785, 790-791, 812, 828, 830, 850
declaration of pillnitz, 616
declaration of rights and grievances, 502
declaration of the causes and necessity of taking up arms, 516
declaration of the hague, 299, 424
declaration of the rights of man, 611-612, 616, 664, 685, 717, 797
declaratory act, 498, 502
decree suppressing religious orders, 614
deer island, 269-270
defenestration of prague, 156, 160, 163-164, 448
deganawida, 117
deism, 636
delaware bay, 104, 231-232, 292, 539
delaware river, 122,

231-232, 235, 288, 290-293, 532, 534, 538-539, 863
delhi sultanate, 350-351, 358
delmarva peninsula, 69, 84, 539-540
democratic party, 745-746, 759, 785, 840, 862
democratic-republican, 635, 652-658, 660, 678, 706, 733, 744-745, 757-758
denmark, 61, 156, 164-165, 168, 176, 218-219, 341, 399, 407-408, 411, 633, 643
description of new england, 135-136
dessalines, 719, 722-723, 823
detroit, 103, 125, 415, 417, 696-697
detroit river, 103
devil's island, 87
devshirme, 371
diamond necklace affair, 605
diner de metz, 538
diplomatic revolution of 1756, 471, 604
directory, 213, 608, 640-641, 644-645, 679
dirk hartog, 579
disestablish, 850-851
divine right of kings, 55, 178-179, 192, 197, 222, 237, 243, 248, 295, 420, 496, 517, 608
doeg, 257, 259
dolley madison, 703, 706
dome of the rock, 372-373, 863
dominion of new england, 295-296, 301, 344, 425, 504, 552
don river, 404
donnacona, 105, 107, 114
dorothy bradford, 143
dream catcher, 691
drought, 85, 313
du pont, 112, 114
duchy of prussia, 422-423
duel, 198, 655, 661-662, 739-740, 825-826
duke of alba, 51-52, 54-56
duke of albany, 251
duke of brunswick, 616-620, 625, 638, 679, 684
duke of enghien, 679
duke of wellington, 710-711
duke of york, 250-251, 277, 285, 287-288, 292, 294, 324
dunlap broadsides, 520
dutch, 35, 48-58, 63, 71, 95, 119, 122, 133, 135-136, 140-141, 150, 152-156, 159, 161,

INDEX | 4

163-164, 183, 202, 207-208, 210-211, 218, 220, 231-235, 249-251, 285, 287, 290-292, 294-295, 298-299, 301, 338-339, 361-362, 391, 405, 410, 418, 423-424, 428, 431, 442, 448, 498-499, 507, 521, 529, 579, 595, 710, 713-714, 785, 793, 808-810
dutch east india company, 152-154, 338, 361, 579, 595, 808-809
dutch golden age, 57-58, 155, 301
dutch india, 361
dutch revolt, 35, 49, 51-53, 55-57, 63, 133, 135, 155, 159, 161, 164, 220, 298, 338, 361, 428
dutch west india company, 155, 232-234, 251
dutty boukman, 718

E

earl of bothwell, 47, 60
east india company, 152-154, 338, 358, 361-363, 507-509, 579, 595, 760, 764-765, 768-770, 783, 808-809
east river, 150, 156, 234, 528-529
eastern shore, 69, 379
eastern woodland culture, 36
ecuador, 723, 725, 729-730
edict of expulsion, 334, 339
edict of fontainebleau, 223
edict of nantes, 108, 223, 297
edict of restitution, 166, 168, 173, 180
edict of sakoku, 313, 339
edict on changing status, 333
edmund andros, 296, 301, 425, 552
edo, 335-336
edward i, 40-41, 62
edward vernon, 453-454
edward vi, 40, 43
egg pocking, 469, 864
eic, 153-154, 362-364, 507-509, 765-768, 783
eje volcanico transversal, 813
el pípila, 816
elba, 702, 707-710
electoral college, 566, 651, 656-657
elizabeth, 40-41, 44, 46-48, 52, 55, 59-63, 70-71, 81, 91, 126, 128-129, 131, 139, 161, 176-177, 193, 228, 242-243, 261, 286, 294, 338, 344, 362, 419, 433, 472, 479-484, 486, 625, 738, 805-806, 863
elizabeth castle, 286, 863
elizabeth fry, 294, 805-806
elizabeth hubbard, 344
elizabeth stuart, 161, 176, 419
elizabethan religious settlement, 59, 62-63
emancipist, 592
embargo act of 1807, 678
emperor of all russia, 412, 480-481, 483, 680
empresario, 823-824
empress elizabeth of russia, 433, 472, 481
enclosure acts, 753-754
encomendero, 31
encomienda, 30-31, 33
endeavour, 581-584
endicott and the red cross, 204
endorheic basin, 838
engagement, 196-197, 235, 240
english bill of rights, 300, 418
english civil war, 176, 189-196, 198, 202, 213, 230, 235-240, 242-245, 247-250, 255, 258, 285, 287, 294-295, 297, 299, 319, 341, 418, 496, 603
english east india company, 153, 362
english india, 361
english reformation, 41-42, 48, 62, 67
enlightened despot, 725
episcopal, 45, 68, 127, 136, 190, 320, 628
episcopal church of the united states, 628
erie canal, 150, 277, 756, 854-855
essay on the treatment and conversion of african slaves, 800
estates-general, 56, 211, 606-608, 625
ethan allen, 515, 524, 550
excise, 629-632, 652
exclusif, 720-721, 815
exclusion bill, 294
executive branch, 497, 552, 554, 560-561, 564-565, 567-568, 601, 640, 656, 658-659
exeter, 216
expulsion of the acadians, 461
expulsion of the ministers, 320
extermination to the third degree, 309

F

fall line, 69-70, 75, 78, 87, 92
fall of vienna, 681
fan-tan, 781-782
fang xiaoru, 310
farrukhsiyar, 761
fatehpur sikri, 350
father joseph le caron, 125
feather headband, 509
federal constitution of the united mexican states, 821
federal government, 81, 370, 551-554, 557-561, 563, 566-567, 569, 571-574, 598-600, 629, 632, 652-654, 665, 678, 704, 706, 751, 785, 789, 795, 848, 851
federalist, 569-572, 651-658, 660-661, 706, 733, 744-745, 757-758, 785
federalist papers, 569-572, 706
fédérés, 617-619
felix maria calleja, 814
fellowship of merchant adventurers, 151
feodor iii, 402
feodor the bell-ringer, 400
ferdinand i, 157, 373
ferdinand ii, 12, 157, 159-165, 168, 170, 173-174, 176-177, 180, 218, 373
ferryland, 229, 863
fête de la fédération, 610, 614-615
feuillant, 615, 619
fifth coalition, 684
fifty-four forty or fight, 840, 843
filial piety, 309
filibuster, 824
fire fishing, 264
firman, 362
first bank of the united states, 652
first barbary war, 678, 834
first bishops' war, 190
first church, 200-201, 203-204, 215-216, 265, 437
first coalition, 616, 633, 638, 641, 651, 719, 724
first continental congress, 511, 553
first english civil war, 192, 195-196, 235, 238-239, 258, 319
first estate, 606-607
first fleet, 590-592, 596
first french republic, 602, 618, 620, 636, 640
first mexican empire, 820
first mexican republic, 821
first opium war, 775, 778-780
first party system, 652
first seminole war, 742, 744, 758
first supply, 83
fishing weir, 264
five articles of remonstrance, 211
five civilized tribes, 734-738, 740-741, 746-747, 750
five mile act, 246
flanders, 49-50, 713
fleet prison, 445
flemish, 49-50
fletcher christian, 594-596
flight to varennes, 615, 618, 620
florida, 27-28, 30, 38, 104, 109-111, 255, 431, 454, 470, 547, 691, 733-734, 737-738, 742-743, 748-750, 811
flotilla, 121, 404
flower war, 21
folsom point, 36
fool's gold, 83, 107, 845
forbes expedition, 464
forbidden city, 311, 316, 863
fort beausejour, 460-461
fort caroline, 109-110, 811
fort casimir, 235
fort christina, 232, 235
fort clatsop, 674-675, 838
fort detroit, 696-697
fort duquesne, 459-460, 462, 464, 467
fort le boeuf, 457-458
fort machault, 457
fort mandan, 671
fort mims massacre, 738, 740
fort moultrie, 417
fort nassau, 155, 231, 235
fort niagara, 460
fort presque isle, 457
fort st. frederick, 460
fort st. george, 362, 760
fort ticonderoga, 277, 463-464, 515, 518, 524, 527, 535-538, 544, 550, 864
fort venus, 582
forty-niners, 844, 847-848
fourth coalition, 683-686
fourth estate, 606
fox tossing, 412
foxe's book of martyrs, 67, 126-127
frame of government, 289-290
france, 9-10, 14, 40-42, 44-46, 48-49, 52, 60, 71, 90, 102, 104-109, 111-115, 121, 123-125, 142, 155-156, 163-165, 168, 172, 174, 177-178, 180, 192, 218-224, 239, 245, 277, 295, 299, 379, 414-417, 420-421,

423-431, 433-434, 452, 456, 460-461, 463-465, 468, 471-474, 479, 496, 523, 538-539, 541-542, 546, 560, 574, 580, 588, 602, 604, 606-622, 624-625, 633-636, 638-642, 644-648, 650-651, 653-654, 663-665, 668, 677-686, 700-702, 707-715, 717, 719-722, 724, 733, 755, 757, 765, 781, 802, 809, 815, 834, 863-864
france antarctique, 108-109
francis asbury, 628
francis bacon, 65-66, 275, 496
francis drake, 59, 70, 72
francis greenway, 592
francis ii, 44, 46, 680, 682, 685
francis lightfoot lee, 456
francis marion, 543
francis pastorius, 786
francis scott key, 370, 703
francis walsingham, 48, 62
francis xavier, 333-334
francisco de miranda, 725-727
françois mackandal, 717
françois-paul brueys, 643-644
frédéric chopin, 686, 713
frederick i, 161, 163, 176, 374, 419, 424, 431
frederick the great, 431-435, 471-472, 474-476, 478-480, 483-484, 541, 604, 646, 684, 707
frederick v, 161
frederick william i, 422-423, 431
french and indian war, 124, 416, 421, 445, 448, 452, 456, 458-461, 464-468, 471-472, 479, 488-490, 498, 500, 503, 510, 522, 524, 526-527, 535, 552, 663-664, 688, 734, 765
french consulate, 608
french counter-revolution, 620, 638-639
french directory, 608, 640
french republican calendar, 636, 638-640, 645, 647
french revolution, 222, 574, 602-604, 606, 612-613, 617-619, 622-625, 633-635, 637, 639, 645-647, 650-651, 653-654, 664, 684-685, 702, 708-709, 712, 714-715, 717, 724-725, 797, 802
french revolutionary wars, 616, 618, 635, 641, 647, 684, 713, 719, 802, 809
french wars of religion, 108-109, 111-112, 114, 218, 223
friedrich von steuben, 541
fronde, 220-221
fundamental orders of connecticut, 202-203, 205
fur, 111-113, 115, 121-125, 136, 140, 146, 154, 207, 256-257, 260-261, 396, 415, 431, 456, 488, 509, 670, 688, 841, 849

G

gabriel's rebellion, 797-798
gadsden purchase, 844
galleon, 34
gallows hill, 346
game of graces, 633
game of the goose, 647
ganges river, 349
ganj-i-sawai, 364
gaspard de coligny, 108-109
gaspee affair, 506-507
gauntlet, 427
gebhard von blücher, 710
geneva bible, 67-68, 134, 863
genghis khan, 305, 350, 395
gens de couleur, 715, 717
george burroughs, 346-348
george calvert, 228-230, 370
george carteret, 256, 285-286, 448
george fox, 278-283, 288, 293, 438, 786-787
george ii, 420, 431, 436, 446, 448, 456-457, 470, 499
george iii, 420, 465, 488, 498-500, 510, 517, 538, 547, 553, 627, 788, 790
george mason, 519, 569, 573, 627
george monck, 238-239, 244, 255-256
george percy, 88, 98
george somers, 86
george vancouver, 665
george washington, 81, 259, 326, 454, 456-460, 463-464, 466, 489, 511, 515-516, 527-528, 532, 534, 538, 542-543, 545, 548-549, 559-560, 565, 569, 571, 574, 599-601, 627, 631-634, 651-652, 656, 703, 735, 784, 788-789, 798
george whitefield, 439-443, 450-451, 852
george wishart, 42-43
georgia, 27-28, 417, 445-448, 450, 452, 454, 470, 511, 543, 572, 576, 642, 666, 734, 741-742, 744, 750-752, 756, 788, 795, 811
georgia gold rush, 750
georgia land lotteries, 750
georgian bay, 116, 121-122, 125
german confederation, 707, 712-713
german empire, 713
germantown quaker petition against slavery, 786
gilbert tennent, 437-438, 441
giles corey, 345-346
girandoni air rifle, 668
girondist, 617, 621-623, 625
glass, 27, 84, 101, 128, 143, 222, 225, 233, 343, 369, 376, 522-523, 742, 782, 863
glass harmonica, 523
glorious revolution, 278, 294, 299-301, 325, 392, 418-419, 424, 496, 498
go, 22, 25, 32, 64, 68, 87-88, 95, 112, 126-127, 129, 136, 141, 163, 198, 214, 217, 240, 260, 272, 278, 296, 310, 325, 328, 337, 357, 368, 372, 375, 411-412, 419, 439, 450, 454, 476, 499-500, 506, 525, 528, 536, 547, 580, 588, 602, 607, 609, 612, 618, 632, 648, 664, 686, 719, 731-732, 746, 748, 766, 783, 807, 827, 842-843, 847, 854, 858
godspeed, 72-73, 77, 82
gold, 11, 15, 17, 19, 22-31, 71, 75, 83-84, 106-107, 109-111, 182, 230, 247, 276, 357, 359, 362, 364, 366, 370, 410, 421, 444, 453, 470, 472, 477, 495, 526, 557-558, 579, 601, 685, 714, 750, 752, 783, 816, 844-848, 863
golden age of piracy, 349, 365, 430
golden cage, 383-386
golden cavalry of st. george, 685
golden horde, 395-396
golden plates, 857-858
goliad massacre, 829
good old cause, 243, 245
gourd, 101, 863
grand banks, 70, 103, 863
grand canal, 303, 305, 311, 771
grand dauphin louis, 429-430
grand embassy, 404-407
grand remonstrance, 191, 193
grandees, 240-241
great apostasy, 206
great awakening, 418, 437, 441-445, 448, 628, 662, 838, 852, 854, 857
great barrier reef, 577, 583, 595
great basin, 38-39, 663, 838, 859
great bible, 67-68, 282
great compromise, 562-563
great council, 117-118, 465, 547
great disappointment, 856
great divergence, 774-775
great divide, 663, 665, 672-673, 841, 843
great elector, 421-424
great fear, 610, 615, 635, 638, 679
great fire of london, 246, 291
great fire of new york, 530-531
great lakes, 102-103, 112, 121, 414-415, 555, 687, 841, 862
great miseries of war, 174
great northern war, 407-408, 411-412
great peacemaker, 117-119, 122, 465, 548
great plague of london, 246, 291, 388
great plague of the 1610s, 140-141, 145-146, 184
great seal of the united states, 556, 784
great swamp massacre, 270
great sword hunt, 333
great trek, 809-810
great wall of china, 311-312, 317, 772, 863
greater antilles, 17
green mountain boys, 515
greenland, 15, 152-153, 577, 584
grenoble, 709-710
grito de dolores, 814-815, 820, 822
grizzly, 672, 784, 861
grog, 454
groundnut, 273
guadalajara, 813, 817
guangzhou, 771, 775
guayaquil, 729-730
guillotine, 619-625,

635-639
guilty chinese scholar tree, 315, 863
gulf of mexico, 29, 413-417, 457, 663, 813, 832
gulf of st. lawrence, 102-103, 105, 113, 115, 464, 663
gunpowder plot, 62-64, 88
gustav ii of sweden, 166-168, 170-171, 174, 219
guy carleton, 524, 527
guy fawkes, 63-65, 247, 863

H

habsburg, 13-14, 33, 50, 157-159, 161-165, 177, 219, 373-375, 423, 428-429, 432-434, 448-449, 681
hacienda, 30-32
hagia sophia, 371
haircutting command, 317-318, 772
haiti, 125, 664, 714, 718, 722-723, 797, 815, 823
haiti massacre of 1804, 723
haitian revolution, 714-715, 717-719, 722-723
haitian vodou, 716-719, 864
haitian war for independence, 722
half freedom, 234-235
half moon, 152-153
halfway covenant, 273
hall of mirrors, 222, 863
hamilton-burr duel, 661-662
hampton court conference, 68, 129-130, 132
han dynasty, 304, 781
handel, 435-436, 453, 455, 687
hangzhou, 303, 771
hannah dustin, 427
hara-kiri, 328-329, 332, 337
harem, 352, 383-385, 387, 389
harlem river, 150, 530-531
harmar's defeat, 688-689
hartford, 179, 201-202, 208-209, 226, 296-297
harvard, 185, 188, 199, 268, 442, 521, 699, 782
hathney, 32
haudenosaunee, 116-118, 465
hawaii, 580, 586-588, 590, 594
haydn, 455, 480
headright, 99-100, 257
heishi, 27

hemlock, 97, 302
henrietta maria, 177, 181, 191, 198, 228, 230, 247, 297, 370
henry avery, 362-366, 368
henry clay, 495, 695, 744-745, 796, 840
henry clinton, 527, 535, 538, 543
henry hudson, 150-154, 231, 250, 397, 415, 583, 586, 667
henry ii, 41, 44-45, 52, 108
henry knox, 518, 524
henry stuart, 46, 60, 176
henry the navigator, 360
henry vii, 11, 40, 70
henry viii, 13, 40-42, 46, 48, 51, 59, 67, 242
herrnhut, 449
heshen, 775-778
hessian, 527-528, 533
hester prynne, 187
hex sign, 291
hiawatha, 117-119, 122, 465, 548, 863
hidatsa, 671-673
hideyoshi, 313-314, 329-339, 361
himalayas, 303, 349
hispaniola, 16-17, 20, 30-32, 35, 86, 714, 717, 719, 721-722, 864
hms bounty, 594
hms romney, 503-504
hobomok, 147
hochelaga, 106, 114-115
hofburg, 681
hogan, 835, 864
hohenzollern, 422-423, 432, 479
hokkaido, 327
holi, 769, 864
holland, 49, 57-58, 134-135, 137, 149, 210-211, 863
holstein, 164-165, 408, 482
holy club, 439-440, 450
holy discipline, 134, 146, 148
holy league, 378-379, 381-383, 404-405
holy roman emperor charles vi, 430, 432, 471
hong kong, 771, 780
hongwu, 306-307
honshu, 327, 329-330, 333
hopewell, 152
horatio gates, 535, 537, 544
horatio nelson, 642-643, 647-648, 679
hornbook, 188, 863
hospitallers, 380-382
hot shot, 743
houngan, 717-718
house of burgesses, 98-99, 101, 118, 142, 258, 262, 511

house of good hope, 202
house of hanover, 419-420, 472
house of representatives, 504, 555, 560, 562-563, 566, 640, 656-657, 703-704, 706, 744, 758, 789, 795, 807, 825-826, 862
house of stuart, 39-40, 418-420
huascar, 23
huayna capac, 23
hudibras, 247
hudson bay, 102, 124, 153-154, 431
hudson river, 122, 135, 140, 150, 153-156, 218, 231, 277, 530-531, 545, 662, 755
hudson strait, 153
hugh montgomery, 505
hugh white, 505
huguenot, 108-110, 223
humble petition and advice, 243
humphrey gilbert, 70
hundred days, 709, 711, 855
hungary, 158, 172-173, 373-375, 382, 387-388, 424, 471, 473
huron, 103, 115-116, 119-122, 125, 153, 256-257, 259, 468, 493, 699
hurricane, 86-87, 110
hussite wars, 158, 162

I

iberian peninsula, 9, 12, 377, 686, 724-725
ice fishing, 264
idabat khana, 350-351, 361
ieyasu, 329, 335-339, 361
immortal seven, 298-299
impasto, 58, 487
imperial city, 311
imperial dynasty, 327
inabayama castle, 330-331
inca, 23-25, 27, 31, 36, 107
incident at hono-ji, 331
incorporation of the bill of rights, 851
increase mather, 201, 301, 342, 346-347
indemnity and oblivion act, 245
indentured servant, 100-101, 257, 392, 521
independence day, 518, 814, 820
independent, 40, 42, 45, 51, 67, 123, 127, 130, 135, 158, 196-197, 203, 217, 219-220,

240, 249, 256, 260, 286, 295-296, 329, 345, 378, 419, 443, 486, 497, 518, 541, 547, 551, 556, 563, 565, 567, 571, 614, 627-628, 713-715, 725, 728, 730-731, 739, 750-751, 765, 768, 772, 795, 809, 814, 819, 823, 828, 830-831, 836, 844
india, 18-19, 35, 57, 152-155, 232-234, 251, 333-334, 338, 349-352, 358-364, 471, 507-509, 579-580, 591, 595, 641, 760-771, 776, 778-779, 781, 783, 808-809
indian agent, 735
indian removal act, 734, 737, 746-747, 750, 759, 826
indiana territory, 691, 693, 812
indus river, 349
industrial revolution, 734, 752, 754, 756, 774-775
inoculation, 633
instrument of government, 241
intolerable acts, 498, 509-511, 526, 553
ironsides, 193-194
iroquois, 37, 99, 102, 115-122, 125, 153, 207, 256-257, 259, 271, 415, 425-426, 430, 456, 465, 489, 491, 509, 547-548, 626, 687, 690, 699
isaac newton, 276, 496, 580
isabella, 11-13, 16-17, 30, 33, 792-793
ivan ivanovich, 399-400
ivan susanin, 401-402
ivan the great, 396-397
ivan the terrible, 151, 308, 396-400, 403-405, 407, 485-486
ivan v, 402, 480, 484
ivan vi, 480, 484-485

J

jacksonian democracy, 744-745
jacksonville, 109
jacobean era, 62, 65, 176
jacobin, 615, 635, 802
jacobites, 301
jacobus arminius, 210-211
jacques cartier, 102, 105, 107, 111-114, 151, 415
jacques hébert, 635, 637
jacques marquette, 414
jahangir, 351-355, 358-359, 362-363, 386,

760, 762
jamaica, 17, 727, 730, 803
james bowie, 825
james callender, 654-655, 660
james cook, 579-581, 589, 593, 596, 665, 769
james fennimore cooper, 468, 493
james fort, 76, 83, 89-91
james i, 40, 61, 91, 112, 126, 161-162, 227-229, 336, 341, 362, 418-419, 448, 456, 496
james ii, 277, 288, 294-301, 319, 324-325, 418, 424, 496, 745
james madison, 561-562, 569-570, 572, 628, 658, 703, 706, 725, 733, 758
james marshall, 845-847
james mcfarlane, 631
james mcgready, 852
james monroe, 655, 664, 731, 733, 738, 744, 758, 797
james oglethorpe, 445-446, 448, 450, 454, 788
james otis, 500-502
james ramsay, 800-801
james stuart, 60, 250-251
james vi, 47, 60-62, 68, 129, 176, 250, 341, 419
james watt, 755
james wolfe, 464
jamestown, 59, 62, 70, 72, 74-92, 96, 98-99, 101, 104, 110, 113, 115, 131, 135, 139, 144-145, 153, 176, 182-183, 186, 254, 261, 263, 734
jamestown fire, 83, 263
jan hus, 157-159, 448
jane mccrea, 535-537, 548
janissaries, 371-372, 383, 385-386, 389
japan, 15-16, 287, 313, 327-330, 333-339, 360-361, 781
japazaws, 92-93
jason lee, 842
jawaharlal nehru, 768
jay treaty, 633-635, 651, 654, 688, 690
jean de brebeuf, 125
jean-paul marat, 612, 616, 620-621, 623, 625
jemima boone, 492-493
jenny geddes, 189-190
jeremiah dixon, 794
jesuit, 159, 195, 329, 333, 350, 414
jianwen campaign, 309
jinyiwei, 308-310, 398
jizya, 351, 359
joanna the mad, 12-14, 33
johann georg i of saxony, 161
johann patkul, 409

john adams, 188, 199, 500, 504, 506, 511, 518-519, 547, 561, 600, 634-635, 651-652, 654-656, 745, 757
john alderman, 271
john andré, 545
john berkeley, 256, 285-286, 448
john bunyan, 249
john burgoyne, 535
john cabot, 70, 102-103, 151, 250, 456
john calvin, 43, 45, 67-68, 180, 201, 210-211
john carver, 143, 145-146, 266
john casor, 392
john cotton, 188-189, 200-201, 203, 214-216, 342, 437, 850
john donne, 65, 97, 747
john eliot, 207, 265-266, 268, 270, 735, 769
john endicott, 184, 204, 207-208, 282
john fremont, 844, 846, 849
john guy, 103
john hancock, 502-504, 511-512, 520
john holwell, 766
john jay, 277, 547, 569, 571, 634
john knox, 42-46, 54, 60, 68, 129, 180, 189, 319, 438
john locke, 496, 517, 519, 573, 603
john marshall, 657-659, 751
john mason, 208, 227, 394, 448
john milton, 248
john neville, 630
john newton, 801, 804
john oldham, 202, 207-208
john paton, 860-861
john paul jones, 394, 548
john potts, 97, 254
john robinson, 133-134, 149
john rolfe, 86-87, 91-93, 100-101, 112, 391-392
john sassamon, 267-270
john stewart, 490
john stone, 208
john sutter, 845, 847-848
john tyler, 812, 837, 839-840, 862
john washington, 259, 457
john wesley, 448, 450-451, 628, 852
john wheelwright, 214-216
john whitgift, 127-128, 863
john williams, 597-598, 860-861
john wilson, 215, 283
john winthrop, 181-184, 189, 193, 215, 273, 282-283, 437

john woolman, 294, 787
john wycliffe, 67
johnny appleseed, 625-626
jolly roger, 366
jonathan edwards, 438, 440-442, 662, 852
josé de san martín, 726, 814
jose de sucre, 729
josé maría morelos, 818
joseph cinque, 807
joseph fouché, 636-637
joseph smith, 846, 856-859
joseph travis, 798-799
joseph warren, 512, 516
joséphine de beauharnais, 684-685
josiah wedgwood, 800
journal of major george washington, 458
joyous entry, 49
juarez, 813
judicial branch, 497, 554, 560-561, 567-568, 657, 807
judicial review, 568, 658-659
julia gardiner, 837, 839-840
jumping the broom, 468
junta, 724, 726

K

kahuna, 588
kamakura, 328-329
kangxi, 772-773
karen people, 783
karl mack, 680
kecoughtan, 78-79, 85, 369
kennebec river, 72, 180, 227, 425, 524
kentucky, 81, 122, 455, 488-492, 494-495, 576, 626, 666, 669, 691, 695, 705, 744, 757, 784, 794-796, 825, 840, 852-853
khizr, 377-378
khurram, 352-354, 359
khusrau, 352-353
kieft's war, 234
kiev, 395, 699
kievan rus, 395-396, 398, 410
killing time, 319, 324-325
king francis i, 104-105
king george's war, 421, 452, 454, 471
king james bible, 62, 66, 68, 129
king over the water, 301
king philip's war, 253, 266, 268-272, 425, 552, 735
king william's war, 421, 425, 427-428, 452, 471

king's daughters, 124
king's malady, 420-421
kirkpinar, 372
kit carson, 848-849
kite experiment, 522
kiwi, 578-579
kneeling slave medallion, 800
knights hospitaller, 380, 382, 421, 642
kochi, 760
koh-i-noor, 358, 764
koprulu, 387, 389
kosem sultan, 384-386
kowloon incident, 779
kubb, 175
kublai khan, 305, 395
kyoto, 331-332, 335
kyushu, 327, 333-334

L

l'enfant plan, 599-600
la belle, 225, 416, 864
la marseillaise, 617-618
la navidad, 16-17
la noche triste, 22-23, 30
la salle, 414-416, 425-426, 456, 663, 677
labrador, 102-103, 153
lachine massacre, 426
lachine rapids, 103, 106, 113
lachlan macquarie, 592
lake champlain, 112, 119-121, 460, 463, 518, 524, 527, 535
lake erie, 103, 116, 150, 456-457, 696-697
lake huron, 103, 116, 121, 125
lake michigan, 415
lake ontario, 103, 116, 121, 415, 460, 464, 696-697
lake st. clair, 103
lake superior, 103, 417
lakota sioux, 38, 669
lame duck, 657, 661
lan yu, 308-310
land of the blacks, 235
land ordinance of 1785, 555
lard, 233
last of the mohicans, 468, 493
latter-day saint, 855-856, 859-860
laurentian mountains, 115
law of suspects, 622, 625, 637
lawrence washington, 454, 456, 458
laws divine, moral and martial, 98
leclerc expedition, 721, 797, 823
lee resolution, 518-519, 527

legion of the united states, 689
legislative assembly, 608, 615-616, 618-619
legislative branch, 497, 552, 560-562, 567-568, 601, 656
lei, 587
leiden, 58, 134-136, 138, 147, 149, 210, 523, 863
leif ericson, 15
leo tolstoy, 701
leonard calvert, 230
leopold von daun, 474
les tricoteuses, 623
lesser antilles, 17
let them eat cake, 605
letter from jamaica, 727, 730
letter of majesty, 158-160, 162
letter to the danbury baptists, 851
levelers, 240
lewis and clark, 665, 667-674, 676, 737, 784, 838
lexington, 512-515, 517, 524, 853
li zicheng, 314-317
liahona, 858
liberty affair, 503
liberty bell, 551, 562, 864
liberty pole, 502
liberty tree, 502, 504
libya, 378, 834
lighthorse harry lee, 631, 666
lin zexu, 777-780
little ice age, 313
livonian war, 399-400
loa, 716, 718
log cabin, 233, 757, 863
london company, 72, 76-77, 83-87, 90, 92, 94, 97-100
long island, 150, 179, 528-529, 534, 546, 806
long parliament, 189, 191-192, 194-197, 213, 235-236, 238, 240, 319, 606
longfellow, 117, 149, 346, 461, 513
longhouse, 39, 116, 118
longhunter, 489-490, 493-494
lord baltimore, 228-230, 292, 370, 448
lord darnley, 46-48, 60, 64
lord delaware, 85-86, 90-91, 326
lord dunmore's war, 491-492, 687
lords of the congregation, 43-44
lords proprietor of carolina, 255, 285, 448
los niños héroes, 833
louis ii of hungary, 158, 374

louis joliet, 414
louis xiii, 177, 218, 220-221, 223, 225
louis xiv, 124, 218, 220-225, 239, 245, 295, 297, 336, 415-416, 423-424, 429-430, 609, 663, 677, 715, 863
louis xv, 218, 429-430, 433, 472, 604-605
louis xvi, 218, 538, 604, 606, 608, 612, 614-618, 620, 623-625, 637, 640, 646, 708-709, 719
louis xviii, 708-712
louis-joseph de montcalm, 463-464, 466
louisiana, 27, 29, 125, 413-415, 652, 663-666, 675-679, 706, 721, 723, 732-733, 741, 743, 795-796, 823-825, 834, 836, 841, 844
louisiana purchase, 652, 663-666, 678, 706, 733, 743, 834, 841, 844
louvre, 221, 613, 641
low countries, 41, 49-55, 57, 76, 159
loyal company of virginia, 488, 666
loyalist, 501-504, 508, 510-511, 528-529, 536, 543-545, 547, 595, 615, 627
lozhki, 487
luddite rebellion, 754-755
lutheran, 14, 41, 45, 156, 158, 161, 166-168, 170-171, 173, 220, 435, 449, 481

M

mabila, 28-29
macau, 771
mad anthony wayne, 689-691, 693, 812
madame defarge, 623
madame pompadour, 472
madame roland, 623
madras, 362, 590, 760, 766
madre de deus, 361-362, 364
magyars, 373
maine, 72, 102, 113, 145, 150, 180, 227, 347, 394, 425, 448, 524-525, 756, 795-796
malabar coast, 760
malleus maleficarum, 341, 343
malta, 380-382, 642-643
maltese falcon, 381
mambo, 716
mamluks, 642, 644

man in the iron mask, 224, 609
manchu queue, 317-318, 772
manchuria, 311, 313-314, 316, 772-773
mandate of heaven, 314-315
manhattan, 105, 150, 155-156, 231-232, 234-235, 528-531, 662, 863
manifest destiny, 737, 745-746, 840, 862
maori, 596-597, 860
maquahuitl, 20
marbury v. madison, 568, 657-659
marco polo, 15, 775
marcus whitman, 842-843
margaret maclachlan, 324-325
margaret of parma, 51-54, 56
margaret tudor, 40, 46, 48
margaret wilson, 324-325
maria theresa of austria, 432, 471, 480, 604, 680
marian exile, 126
marian martyr, 126
marie antoinette, 604-606, 612, 615, 619, 622-624
marie louise of austria, 685
marie louise of savoy, 619
marie tussaud, 623
marine chronometer, 585-586, 864
marine corps hymn, 834
marmaduke stephenson, 284-285
maroon, 717
marquis de lafayette, 538, 606
marshalsea, 445-446
martha corey, 345-346
martha washington, 633
martha's vineyard, 114, 139
martin marprelate, 127-128
martin van buren, 745-746, 785, 807
mary dyer, 282-285, 288, 863
mary fisher, 282, 342
mary i, 12, 40, 43-44, 46, 48, 51-52, 127
mary ii, 299-300, 418, 424
mary jemison, 465, 467, 734
mary of guise, 41, 44-46
mary read, 370
mary rowlandson, 271-273
mary walcott, 344
mary, queen of scots, 41-48, 60, 63, 131
maryland, 69, 81, 113, 122, 228-231, 257, 259, 288, 292, 295, 302, 326, 370, 448, 456, 526, 528-529, 539, 554, 572, 599, 627, 631, 658, 791, 794-795, 863
maryland 400, 528-529
maryland toleration act, 230-231
mason-dixon line, 794
massachusetts, 38, 114, 122, 126, 130, 138-140, 149, 175, 179-189, 199-208, 214-218, 226-227, 242, 252, 258, 265-266, 269, 272, 277, 281-285, 291, 295, 301, 340, 342, 344, 347, 365-366, 380, 393-394, 427-428, 438, 441-442, 448, 492, 500, 502-504, 506-512, 514-516, 519, 524, 549-550, 553-554, 558-559, 561, 572, 625, 627, 651, 735, 744, 757-758, 782-783, 792, 795, 808, 835, 851, 863
massachusetts bay company, 181-182, 184, 186
massachusetts circular letter, 504
massacre at drogheda, 236-237
massacre at matanzas inlet, 109-111
massacre of 1622, 79, 82, 95-97, 101, 253-254, 734
massacre of novgorod, 398-399
massasoit, 139, 141, 145-148, 205, 266-268, 270, 863
matagorda bay, 416
matanzas, 109-111
matchlock, 120, 261, 286, 330, 350, 367
matryoshka, 413
matthew hopkins, 341
matthew perry, 339, 832
maximilian i of bavaria, 161, 163, 170
maximilien de robespierre, 620, 622, 635
mayflower, 136-138, 141-145, 184, 199, 296, 301, 863
mayflower compact, 141-143, 296, 301
maypole, 175
mecklenburg, 168, 174, 218, 444
medicine shield, 469
mediterranean, 12, 15, 373, 377-378, 380-383, 387, 404, 638-639, 641, 643-644, 648, 678, 702, 707, 712
mehmed ii, 371
mehmed iv, 387, 681

mehrunisa, 353-354
memorable providences relating to witchcrafts and possessions, 342
mercantilism, 498, 720
mercy lewis, 344
meriwether lewis, 488, 666-668, 675, 842
merrimack river, 179, 216
messiah, 436
metacomet, 266-271, 273
methodist, 45, 439, 451, 628, 842, 852-854
methodist episcopal church of the united states, 628
metric system, 647
mexica, 21
mexican altiplano, 813
mexican cession, 834, 844-845
mexican independence day, 820
mexican war of independence, 813-815, 819-820, 822, 824
mexican-american war, 813, 821, 831, 834-835, 839-840, 844-845, 847, 849, 862
mexico, 21, 23, 25-27, 29, 37, 39, 391, 413-417, 457, 593, 663, 665, 676, 694, 699, 723, 731, 745, 813-825, 827, 829-836, 839-841, 843-845, 848-849, 861-862
mexico city, 23, 813-814, 816-817, 819-820, 822-824, 832-834, 845
mfecane, 810
michael i, 402
michael romanov, 401
michel ney, 709, 712
micmac, 38, 461, 465
middle peninsula, 70
middle plantation, 254
midnight judges act, 657-658
midnight ride, 512-513, 516
midwife baptism, 127
miguel hidalgo, 814-815, 817, 820, 822, 864
miles standish, 137, 143-144, 147-149
millenary petition, 129
millerite, 856
millrace, 845
miner's code, 847-848
ming dynasty, 304-307, 309-315, 317, 398, 772, 781
mingshi, 306-307
minnehaha, 117
minutemen, 511, 513
mir jafar, 766-767
miracle of the house of brandenburg, 478-479
mississippi, 27-29, 36, 125, 413-417, 425-426, 455-457, 465, 547, 555, 576, 663-664, 669, 677-678, 687, 691, 694, 732, 734, 743, 746-748, 750, 759, 795, 826, 864
missouri, 125, 413, 415, 495, 576, 665, 667, 669-672, 757, 784, 795-797, 840-842, 848, 858, 864
missouri compromise, 784, 795-797, 840
missouri river, 413, 667, 669-671, 864
mitsuhide, 331-333
model of christian charity, 183, 186, 273
moghul empire, 350-351, 354, 356, 359-360, 362-364, 760-764
mohawk, 38, 116-118, 120, 150, 155, 251, 508-509, 535-536, 756
mohawk river, 150, 535-536, 756
mohegan, 207-209
mojave desert, 838, 849
molasses act, 498-500
moll davis, 245
molly pitcher, 542
mongol, 305-307, 312, 318, 350, 395-396, 773
mongol empire, 350, 395-396, 773
monomakh's cap, 396, 863
monroe doctrine, 731-733
montagnais, 115, 119
montagnard, 616, 619, 621-622, 625
montesquieu, 496, 602-604, 612, 788, 814
montezuma, 22, 25, 30, 338, 834
montgolfier, 624
montreal, 102-103, 106, 113-115, 119, 121, 123, 125, 415, 426, 464, 525-527, 535, 665, 696
mooncakes, 307-308
moonshiners, 632
moravia, 157, 162, 448-449
moravian brethren, 158, 448-450, 452
moravian pentecost, 449-450
mormon exodus, 859
morocco, 16, 378, 643
moroni, 857-858
moscow, 151, 396-400, 402-403, 405-406, 409-411, 481, 699-701
moscow print yard, 397
moscow uprising of 1682, 402-403
mount fuji, 327
mount vernon, 81, 454, 458, 601, 632, 789
mourning wars, 122, 467
mourt's relation, 142, 148
mozart, 455, 480, 650, 687
muckraker, 654-655
muhammad shah, 761-764
mumbai, 362, 760, 767
mummies of guanajuato, 817-818
mumtaz mahal, 351, 354-356, 764, 863
muneharu, 332
murad, 357-358, 385-387, 389
muscovy company, 151-152, 397, 686
musical offering, 434-435
musket, 24, 78-79, 85, 95, 120, 143, 194, 286, 333, 433, 458, 494, 505, 514, 544, 549, 583, 588, 595-597, 649, 690, 756, 860
musket wars, 596-597, 860
mustafa the mad, 384-385
myles coverdale, 67
mystic massacre, 209
mystic river, 208

N

nader shah, 762-765
nakaz, 485-486
nanjing, 307, 309-311, 780-781
nantucket, 139, 808
nantucket sound, 139
napoleon, 111, 156, 377, 402, 608, 627, 638-650, 663-665, 679-686, 699-702, 707-714, 721, 723-724, 726, 755, 763, 797, 802-803, 813-815, 818, 823, 830, 833
napoleonic code, 646
napoleonic wars, 647, 650, 668, 678-679, 682-685, 700, 702, 707, 713, 802
narcissa whitman, 842-843
narragansett, 38, 139, 146, 179-180, 205, 207-209, 217-218, 252, 270-271, 506, 694
narragansett bay, 139, 179-180, 205, 252, 506
narrative of the life of mrs. mary jemison, 465
narva, 408-409, 411
nat turner's rebellion, 798-799
natalia, 809-810
nathan hale, 226, 529-532, 546
nathanael greene, 252, 527, 541, 543-544
nathaniel bacon, 258-263, 273, 734
nathaniel hawthorne, 187, 204
national assembly, 608-611, 614, 619, 624
national constituent assembly, 608, 611-615, 624-625, 635
national convention, 608, 618-622, 625, 635, 637-640, 720-721, 802
national covenant, 190, 319-321, 323
nauset, 139-141, 143-145, 734
nauvoo, 858-859
navajo, 38, 835-836, 849, 864
navigation acts, 249-250, 295-296, 498-499
negro fort, 742-743
nell gwynn, 245
nemasket, 147-148
nemattanew, 95
nero, 178-179, 206
netherlands, 9, 14, 33, 49, 51, 55-56, 131, 133, 135, 137, 152, 155, 164-165, 181, 211-212, 233, 244, 251, 290, 323, 361, 391, 405, 408, 423, 430, 472, 616, 641, 651, 679, 702, 708, 710, 713, 757, 809, 863
neva river, 409-410
new amsterdam, 218, 232, 234-235, 250-251
new brunswick, 102, 113, 180, 437, 460
new echota, 750-751
new england, 88, 123, 126, 131, 135-138, 140-141, 145, 147, 155, 179-185, 200-201, 204, 206-208, 214, 227, 229, 236, 250, 265-268, 270-271, 273, 283, 288, 295-297, 301, 342, 344, 365, 425-426, 437, 499-500, 504, 519, 521, 535, 545, 552-553, 593, 696, 782, 807, 850-851
new england confederation, 552
new hampshire, 102, 179-180, 199, 216, 227, 394, 426, 448, 505, 550, 560, 571-572, 792, 795, 863
new haven, 226, 437, 806
new jersey, 105, 156, 230-232, 277, 285-288, 290, 295-296, 302, 326, 348, 437, 442, 448, 527-528, 530-532, 534-535, 538, 542, 562, 572, 662, 787, 792, 795
new jersey plan, 562
new lights, 441-442
new model army, 194-197, 235-240,

242-244, 279
new netherland, 57, 141, 150-151, 154-155, 218, 231-235, 249-251, 256, 285, 292, 448
new south wales, 578, 583, 589-592, 596
new sweden, 231-233, 235, 256, 285, 292, 448
new york, 72, 102, 104-105, 112, 116, 120-122, 150, 153, 156, 199, 218, 226, 231-232, 234, 251, 256, 277, 285, 290, 295-296, 302, 348, 415, 426, 448, 468, 508, 515, 518-519, 521, 527-528, 530-532, 534-538, 542-543, 545-547, 550, 561, 569-572, 599, 628, 652, 657, 661-662, 664, 689, 697, 735, 745, 755-756, 785, 787, 792-793, 795, 806, 843, 847, 854-856
new york and new jersey campaign, 527
new zealand, 577-580, 582-583, 586, 588, 590, 596-597, 860, 864
newcomen engine, 755
newfoundland, 15, 70, 74, 90, 102-105, 124, 140, 227, 229, 431, 456, 580, 675
niagara falls, 103
niagara river, 103, 415, 696
nicolaus zinzendorf, 448
nina, 16, 34
nine familial exterminations, 309-310
noble train of artillery, 518
nobunaga, 329-334, 336
nominated assembly, 240-241
north berwick witch trials, 341
north island, 578, 860
north pole, 17, 151-152
north river steamboat, 755
northeast passage, 151-153, 397
northern neck, 70, 257, 457-458
northern passage, 151-152
northwest indian war, 687-688, 690, 812
northwest ordinance, 555-556, 564, 790, 794
northwest passage, 151-154, 586-587
notes on the state of virginia, 790, 798
nova scotia, 102, 113-114, 124, 153, 431, 460-461, 465, 500, 580
novgorod, 395, 398-399
nueces strip, 831, 844
nur jahan, 353-355, 386

O

oath of abjuration, 319-320, 324-325
occoneechee massacre, 261-262
oda nobunaga, 329-330, 332, 334
ohio country, 416, 456-460, 464, 466, 500, 510, 526, 547, 688
ohio river, 413, 455-457, 467, 488, 491, 555, 669, 687, 690, 693
oiled paper, 233, 294
ojo de dios, 731
old lights, 441-442
old north church, 512-513
old three hundred, 824
olive branch petition, 517
oliver cromwell, 176, 192-197, 202, 235-236, 238-245, 247-249, 258, 270-271, 279, 287, 319, 496, 603
oliver hazard perry, 697
one man, one vote, 745
oneida, 38, 116-118, 121, 125, 536
onigiri, 339, 863
onondaga, 38, 116-118, 121, 125
opechancanough, 78-80, 82, 88, 95-96, 98, 254-255, 261
open decree of predestination, 211
open letter to queen victoria of britain, 778
opitchapam, 95
opium, 351, 354, 387, 775-781
oprichniki, 308, 397-400
orange free state, 809
orator, 839
oregon question, 840-841
oregon trail, 841-843, 845-846
oregon treaty, 843, 862
orinoco tobacco, 92, 100-101, 112, 392
osceola, 749-750
osman i, 350, 371, 386, 389
osman ii, 385
ostsiedlung, 422
otedama, 339
ottoman empire, 14, 57, 76, 158, 282, 350-351, 371-374, 377-378, 380, 382, 386, 389, 396, 399, 404-405, 412, 434, 479, 486, 642
ousamequin, 139
outback, 577
outer banks, 104, 153, 255, 368-369, 444

P

paiute, 38, 838
pakistan, 349, 352
palace of versailles, 221-222, 225, 336, 605-606, 608, 863
palatine war, 163, 219
paleo-indian, 36
palisade, 70, 76-77, 110, 121, 254-255, 460, 525
palisade wall, 70, 76, 121, 254-255
pamlico sound, 104, 863
pamunkey, 78-79, 254, 261, 263
panama, 27, 112, 453, 723, 732
panama canal, 112, 732
panic of 1837, 785
pannaway plantation, 227
paradise lost, 248
paramount chief, 78-80, 95, 139, 253-254
parchwitz address, 476
paris garden, 242
parliament, 40, 42, 45, 60, 63-65, 142, 162, 176, 179, 181, 186, 188-198, 213, 228, 235-238, 240-248, 294, 297, 299-300, 319-321, 364, 403, 418-420, 445, 453, 463, 465, 498-503, 506-512, 517, 523, 526-527, 553, 585, 606, 627, 633, 753, 755, 766, 801-805
parliamentarian, 193-194, 236, 239, 242, 244
parris island, 109
partitions of poland, 486, 707
pascal's triangle, 274
pascal's wager, 274-275
pascaline, 274, 863
pasha, 371, 378, 641
patagonia, 731
patience, 27, 87, 90, 213, 329, 342, 449, 505, 792
patrick henry, 502, 511, 560, 627
patuxent, 69, 702
patuxet, 140-141, 144-145
paul revere, 267, 502, 505, 509, 512-514, 516
paul revere's ride, 512-513
peace medal, 668
peace of massasoit, 266
peace of pocahontas, 82, 93-94, 253
peace of prague, 173-174, 218-219
peace of tokugawa, 337
peace of westphalia, 156, 174, 200, 219-221
peacemaker, 117-119, 122, 141, 465, 548, 839-840
peacock throne, 356-358, 763-764
pearl, 187, 303, 319, 771, 779-780
peculiar institution, 793
pedro menendez de aviles, 30, 109-110
peggy shippen, 545
peine forte et dure, 346
peninsular, 686, 724-726, 814-815
peninsular war, 686, 724, 726, 814-815
pennsylvania, 122, 230-233, 255-256, 277, 285, 287-293, 295, 302, 326, 348, 370, 393, 437, 442, 448, 455-456, 460, 465-466, 489, 519, 521-523, 526, 532, 539-540, 542, 551, 554, 559, 561, 572, 598, 625-628, 630-632, 666-667, 687, 689, 697, 755, 786-789, 792, 794-795, 850, 852
pennsylvania dutch, 290-291
pennsylvania mutiny, 598
penobscot river, 180
pequot, 202, 207-209, 227, 552, 694
pequot war, 207-209, 227, 552
persia, 371, 376, 385, 387, 762-764, 856
personal rule, 179, 181, 189-191, 193
peru, 24-25, 694, 723, 726-727, 729-730
peter i, 402, 480
peter iii, 479-485
peter stuyvesant, 233-234, 251, 285
peter the great, 403-405, 407, 409-412, 433, 472, 480-482, 484-486, 701, 864
petition to the king, 511
petroglyph, 26
peyote, 838
philadelphia, 231, 235, 290-292, 302, 440-441, 465, 503, 508, 511, 515, 517, 519-523, 532, 535, 538-540, 542, 545, 548-549, 551, 553, 559-560, 562, 569, 588, 599-600, 631, 652, 659, 664, 689, 704, 706, 756, 788-789, 792, 794, 863-864
philadelphia campaign, 535, 538, 540
philip ii, 12, 50-57, 59, 63, 109-110, 133, 157, 159, 177, 228, 266, 428
philip iii, 177, 428
philip the handsome, 12-14
philip v, 429-430

phrygian cap, 277
pictogram, 26, 265
piedmont, 69, 75, 78, 458
pierre de chauvin, 112
pierre l'enfant, 600, 791
pierre le moyne, lord
    d'iberville, 417
pierre-charles villeneuve,
    648, 650, 665, 680
pietist, 449
pike expedition, 676
pikes peak, 676, 864
pilgrim, 128, 131-132,
    134-136, 140-149, 249,
    266, 270
pilgrim press, 136
pilgrim's progress, 249
pillory, 98, 187, 189, 281
pinkster, 793
pinta, 16, 34
pipe tomahawk, 736
pirna, 473-474
piscataqua, 227
pitcairn island, 596
pizarro, 23-25, 27-28, 30,
    107, 338, 362, 863
plan of iguala, 819-821
plebiscite, 646
plymouth, 62, 71-72, 114,
    126, 128, 130-132,
    135-136, 138-140,
    143-149, 175, 182-184,
    186, 199, 202,
    204-205, 207, 227,
    266-271, 295, 301,
    448, 582, 734, 863-864
plymouth rock, 145, 149,
    199, 266, 863-864
pocahontas, 79-80, 82-83,
    88, 92-96, 253
poison, 38, 97, 254, 267,
    468, 479, 778
polk, 444, 576, 831-832,
    834, 840-841, 843-845,
    862
polygamy, 859
polynesia, 586, 597-598
polynesian triangle, 586
pomerania, 168, 174, 218,
    475
pomlazka, 163
pondicherry, 760, 765
poor richard's almanac,
    521-522
popcorn, 699, 864
pope alexander vi, 16-17
pope pius v, 62
popham colony, 72, 227
popular sovereignty, 797
porcupine roach, 509
port royal, 113-114, 426,
    428, 431, 461
portsmouth compact, 217
portugal, 9, 11-12, 16-18,
    104, 109, 338-339,
    360-361, 377, 390-391,
    686, 701, 724-725,
    760, 781
portuguese india, 18, 360
post-archaic period, 36-37
potemkin village, 486

potomac, 69-70, 81, 92,
    229-230, 257, 259-260,
    457-458, 599, 702,
    758, 839, 863
pottery, 26, 36, 253, 372,
    800
powder alarm, 510, 512
powhatan, 38, 78-80,
    82-85, 88-89, 91-96,
    98, 253-255, 257, 267
pragmatic sanction, 50,
    432
prague, 156-160,
    162-164, 170, 172-174,
    176, 218-219, 433,
    448, 474-475
prayer stick, 741
praying indian, 267-268,
    271, 735
praying village, 266, 268
preamble, 518, 560, 567,
    611, 616
presbyterian, 45-46, 68,
    127, 129-130, 136,
    190, 196-197, 213,
    236-237, 247, 319-320,
    325, 437, 441, 852-855
presidio, 823, 827, 829,
    861
pretender, 298-299, 301,
    419, 424
pride's purge, 197, 236
priest hole, 239
prince edward island, 102,
    113, 460
prince rupert, 193-195,
    235
prince salim, 352-353
prince-elector, 14, 157,
    161, 163, 166,
    170-171, 173, 423-424,
    436
princess sophia, 481
prison hulk, 531, 589,
    592, 738
proclamation for
    suppressing of pirates,
    368
proclamation of rebellion,
    517
prophetstown, 693, 695,
    812
proportional
    representation, 555,
    562-563
protectorate, 241-242,
    244, 248, 258, 751
protestant union, 161-162
providence, 65, 179-180,
    185, 205-206, 217,
    252, 272, 351, 450,
    506-507, 533, 553,
    557, 564, 575, 837, 840
province of carolina,
    255-256
proxy wedding, 61
prussia, 418, 421-425,
    431-434, 471-479,
    481-483, 486, 604,
    616-617, 646, 681,
    683-686, 699, 701,

707, 709-710, 712-713,
    757
pueblo, 26-27, 38
puerto rico, 17, 86, 714,
    723, 729
pulpit war, 215-216
punjab, 349
puritan, 127-133, 136,
    176, 179-182, 185,
    187-189, 192-193,
    195-196, 200-205, 208,
    210, 213-214, 223,
    230, 235-236, 240,
    242, 244-246, 248-249,
    256, 258, 265-266,
    278, 282-283, 288,
    296, 343, 393, 427,
    437, 449, 520, 735, 843
puritan migration, 176,
    179-180, 182, 185,
    188-189, 200-202, 210,
    223, 236, 256, 265

Q

qianlong, 772-777, 864
qin dynasty, 304
qing dynasty, 313-314,
    317-319, 772-774
quaker, 278-289,
    293-294, 302, 342,
    393, 438, 489, 521,
    548, 706, 779,
    786-788, 792, 805
quartering act, 502-503,
    510
quasi-war, 635, 654
quebec, 102, 104-105,
    112-115, 119, 121-125,
    145, 426-427, 431,
    464, 488, 492, 510,
    524-527, 535, 538,
    542, 544, 580, 696,
    863-864
quebec act, 510, 526-527
quebec campaign, 524,
    544
quebec city, 102, 105,
    113-115, 119, 125,
    145, 427, 464,
    524-525, 527, 535,
    538, 580, 696, 863-864
quebecois, 524, 526-527
queen anne, 94, 367-368,
    418, 420-421, 430-431,
    452, 460-461, 471
queen anne's revenge,
    367-368
queen anne's war, 421,
    430-431, 452, 460-461,
    471
queens, 12, 150, 192,
    604, 647
queretaro, 814-815
quinto real, 19
quit-rents, 286, 296
quivira, 27

R

rachel jackson, 739, 745
raid on dover, 426
raleigh, 60, 70, 91, 104,
    394, 444
ralph waldo emerson, 515
ranger, 271, 369
ransom room, 24-25, 27,
    362, 863
rappahannock, 69-70, 78,
    257, 457
ratcliffe, 77-78, 84, 88-89,
    98
reconquista, 11-12,
    377-378
red river expedition, 676
red stick, 737-738, 749,
    825
red turban rebellion, 306,
    781
redcoat, 505, 512-514
reformation, 13-14, 35,
    41-46, 48, 50-51, 60,
    62, 66-68, 108, 125,
    130-131, 156, 158,
    189, 206, 220, 279, 376
reformation parliament,
    42, 45
reformed presbyterian
    church of scotland, 325
regensburg, 166, 172
regnans in excelsis, 62
reign of terror, 398, 619,
    621-623, 625, 634-635,
    637-640, 653, 684, 720
rembrandt, 58, 353, 487
republic of texas, 822,
    828, 830-831, 840, 864
republican, 237, 555-556,
    571, 602-603, 606,
    616, 620, 634, 636,
    638-641, 645, 647,
    653, 655-658, 678,
    680, 706, 708-709,
    725, 733, 744-745,
    757-758, 785, 818, 821
residence act of 1790, 599
restoration colonies, 255
restoration movement, 853
restoration of the
    monarchy, 227, 235,
    239, 244-245, 250,
    255, 258, 263, 274,
    287, 319-320, 418,
    437, 595
retreat from fort lee, 531
revenuers, 632
revolt of the three
    feudatories, 772-773
revolution of 10 august,
    618-620, 640
revolution of 1800,
    656-657, 678
revolutionary tribunal,
    621-622
rhode island, 139,
    179-180, 189, 199,
    203, 205, 207-208,
    217, 226, 230, 252,

269-271, 282-283, 286, 295, 301, 442, 448, 506-507, 538, 559-561, 571-572, 627, 782, 792, 795, 850
rhodes, 252, 380-381
richard cameron, 323-324
richard clyfton, 132-133
richard cromwell, 244
richard henry lee, 456, 511, 518, 627
richard montgomery, 524-525
richard nicolls, 251
richard pace, 96
richelieu river, 119, 463, 524, 527
riga, 408, 411
rio grande, 26, 830-831, 834
rise of prussia, 418, 421-424, 431
risorgimento, 379, 713
robert boyle, 275-276, 580
robert browne, 130-131
robert castell, 445-446
robert catesby, 63
robert clive, 766-767
robert dinwiddie, 456-459
robert e. lee, 631, 832
robert fulton, 755
robert jenkins, 452-453
robert livingston, 519, 664, 733
robert maynard, 369
robert peary, 151
robert schumann, 713
robespierre, 619-620, 622, 635-640, 646, 653, 684, 720
rocky mountains, 663, 671-672, 676, 838, 841
roger sherman, 519
roger williams, 189, 203-207, 230, 270, 282-283, 448, 850
romanov, 401-403
rosetta stone, 644
roundhead, 192, 231
rousseau, 496, 602-603, 623, 788, 814
royal african company, 392
royal oak, 239, 863
royal proclamation of 1763, 488-489, 498, 500, 510, 794
royal prussia, 422
royal society of london, 276, 580-581, 585
royal touch, 420-421
royalist, 192-195, 236, 238-239, 243-244, 258, 286, 296, 639, 709, 725-728, 814-819, 821
rule of the major generals, 241-242, 244
rule, britannia, 453
rum, 30, 390, 447, 454, 499, 595, 864
rump parliament, 197-198, 236-238, 240-241, 247

runaway scrape, 828
rurik the viking, 395, 400
rurikid, 400-401
rus, 395-396, 398, 410
russia, 151, 303, 395-413, 433-434, 471-472, 474-475, 478-487, 644, 646-647, 679-686, 699-701, 707, 709-710, 755, 758, 781, 841
russian ballet, 486-487
russian empire, 412
russian enlightenment, 485
russian lacquer box, 406-407
russo-american treaty, 841
russo-turkish war, 486

S

sacagawea, 670-673, 676
sack of beijing, 316
sack of delhi, 763
sack of magdeburg, 168-170, 173
sack of washington, 703
sacramento, 844-846, 861
sacramento valley, 845-846
sager orphans, 843
saguenay, 106-107, 112
saint bartholomew's day massacre, 108
saint helena, 712
sakoku, 313, 339
salar de uyuni, 731
salem, 184, 199, 201, 204-205, 208, 284, 287, 327, 340, 342-347, 426, 437, 444, 783, 842
salem village, 340, 342-345, 347
salem witch trials, 201, 327, 340, 342-343, 345-347, 426, 437
salim chisti, 350
sally hemings, 660
salt lake city, 847, 859
sam houston, 825-828, 830, 836
samoset, 145
samuel adams, 502, 504, 507-508, 511-512
samuel bellamy, 365-367, 430, 437
samuel brannan, 846-847
samuel butler, 247
samuel de champlain, 104, 112-115, 119-120, 123, 125, 151, 153, 414-415, 426, 463, 667, 863
samuel prescott, 513
samuel seabury, 628
samurai, 328-333, 336-338, 863
sand painting, 836
sandbar fight, 825-826

sanquhar declaration, 323-324
sans-culottes, 624
santa anna, 821, 824-825, 827-833
santa maria, 16, 34
sapper, 375
saratoga campaign, 527, 535-536, 538, 544-545
sardinia, 12
sassacus, 207-208
saw pit, 101, 863
saxony, 157, 161, 163, 166, 169-173, 220, 411, 433, 449, 472-473, 475, 479, 709, 713
saybrook, 202, 208, 226
scarlet letter, 187
schenectady massacre, 426
schultute, 436, 864
scientific revolution, 274
scotland, 39-48, 54, 60-62, 68, 129, 136, 142, 176, 178, 189-191, 196, 211, 213, 235, 237-239, 241-242, 244, 251, 294, 301, 319-325, 341, 419-421, 424, 431, 628, 755, 771, 864
scottish reformation, 35, 41-46, 60, 68, 189
scottish wars of independence, 40
scrimshaw, 808
scrofula, 421
scrooby, 131-133
scryer, 857
scurvy, 106, 114-115, 154, 186, 454, 583-584, 809
sea beggars, 55
sea venture, 86-87, 89, 92
seaman, 151, 580, 675
second bishops' war, 190, 258
second charter of virginia, 85, 87, 98
second coalition, 644, 647
second continental congress, 515-516, 553, 678
second defense of the english people, 248
second english civil war, 196, 236, 240, 319
second estate, 606-607
second great awakening, 838, 852, 854, 857
second opium war, 781
second party system, 745
second seminole war, 748-750
second supply, 84-85
second treatise on government, 496-498
sedition, 205, 216, 651, 654-656, 659-660
seekonk river, 180, 205

selim ii, 383
seminole, 38, 742, 744, 748-750, 758, 811
semla, 167, 863
senate, 555, 560, 562-563, 565-567, 603, 634, 640, 656, 658, 661, 664, 702-704, 751, 758, 785, 789, 795-796, 831
seneca, 38, 116-118, 467, 734
sengoku, 328-329
separatist, 131, 135-137, 203-204, 206, 295
sepoy rebellion, 768
sequoyah, 736-737
serampore college, 770
serapis, 548
seven laws, 824-825, 827
seven years' war, 111, 124, 421, 431, 452, 464-465, 471-473, 477-479, 482-483, 498, 539, 580, 604, 606, 663-664, 742, 764-765, 800
seventh coalition, 710-711
seventh-day adventist church, 855-856
shah jahan, 351-352, 354-359, 362-363, 760-762, 764, 863
shah jahan ii, 761
shah shuja, 357-358
shahryar, 352, 354-355
shaka, 810
shallop, 79, 143-144, 148, 154
shanghai, 303, 771, 780
shanhai pass, 316-317, 772, 863
shariah, 359, 372
shawnee, 38, 456, 465-467, 489-494, 687-688, 691-692, 694, 737, 812
shays' rebellion, 557, 559-560, 569, 631, 653
shikoku, 327, 333
ship of the line, 644, 649, 780
shogun, 328-329, 336-337
shogunate, 328-329, 336-337, 339
short parliament, 179, 190-191
shoshone, 38, 671-674
shot heard 'round the world, 515
siberia, 36, 399, 402, 487
sicily, 12, 379-380, 382
siege of belgrade, 373
siege of boston, 502, 515-516, 518, 524
siege of constantinople, 396
siege of detroit, 696
siege of fort stanwix, 536
siege of guanajuato, 816
siege of kolberg, 478

siege of louisbourg, 464, 580
siege of malta, 381-382
siege of montreal, 464
siege of osaka castle, 336-337
siege of san antonio de bejar, 827
siege of the alamo, 827
siege of toulon, 638-639, 643
siege of veracruz, 832
siege of vienna, 374-376, 381, 387-388
siege of yorktown, 546-547, 559, 632
sierra madre del sur, 813
sierra madre occidental, 813
sierra madre oriental, 813
sierra nevada, 39, 838, 845, 847
siku quanshu, 773-774
silence dogood, 521
silesia, 157, 162, 433-434, 448, 471-473, 476-477, 479
silesian wars, 432
silk, 11, 101, 360-361, 389, 406, 624, 776-777, 814, 841
silk road, 360, 406, 776
simón bolívar, 725-728, 730, 814
sinners in the hands of an angry god, 438
siraj ud-daulah, 765-767
sixth coalition, 701-702, 707
slave trade act of 1807, 802-803
slavery, 31, 77, 81, 100, 140, 209, 234, 264, 294, 338, 371, 377, 381, 389-392, 443, 511-512, 517, 556, 563-564, 603, 715, 717, 719-722, 727, 748, 758, 786-805, 807, 809, 834-835
slavery abolition act of 1833, 803-804
slow match, 64, 120, 369, 376
slow slicing, 308, 776
smallpox, 21, 29, 140, 185, 208, 268, 418, 429, 446, 482, 531, 593, 633, 842
smolensk, 411
smolny institute, 485
soap, 84, 101, 520
sobieski, 388, 409
sojourner truth, 792-793, 808
sola scriptura, 66
solemn league and covenant, 194, 213, 319-320
song dynasty, 305, 775
sons of liberty, 501-503, 506-509, 519, 630
sonthonax, 719-720
soo locks, 103
sophia alexievna, 402, 406
sophia of hanover, 419-420
soubise, 475-476
south america, 17-19, 21, 23-25, 27, 34, 36-37, 57, 70-71, 91-92, 107-109, 135, 343, 360, 452-453, 496, 594, 714, 723, 725, 727-728, 730-732, 814
south carolina, 109, 150, 255-256, 367, 417, 441, 444, 447-448, 470, 495, 519, 538, 543-544, 572, 695, 738, 758-759, 788, 793, 795
south island, 578, 596
southampton county, 798-799
southern campaign, 543
spanish american wars of independence, 33, 723-726, 730-731, 743
spanish empire, 12, 14, 19, 33, 50-51, 55, 59, 71, 109, 111, 157, 168, 428, 430, 664, 723, 726, 811, 814, 844
spanish florida, 30, 104, 111, 255, 431, 454, 547
spanish match, 176-177, 228
spanish reconquista, 11-12, 377
spanish requirement of 1513, 19-20, 24
spanish ulcer, 686
spectral evidence, 345-347
speedwell, 137-138
split rock, 218
squanto, 140-141, 143-149, 184
squatters, 750, 824
squire boone, 489-490
sri lanka, 349
st. augustine, 30, 110-111, 454, 742, 811
st. clair river, 103
st. clair's defeat, 689
st. croix, 113-114, 180
st. croix river, 113, 180
st. dominic, 714-723
st. giles, 46, 189
st. john's, 103, 229
st. lawrence iroquoians, 114-115
st. lawrence river, 102-103, 105-106, 112-116, 119, 415, 463-464, 580, 696
st. lawrence seaway, 103
st. mary's, 230
st. petersburg, 410-411, 485-486, 699, 864
st. pierre and miquelon, 124, 456
stadacona, 105-107, 112, 114-115
stadtholder, 56-57, 298, 418, 424
stamp act, 498, 501-503, 523
stamp act congress, 502
star - spangled banner, 370, 703-704
starving time, 82, 89, 91, 98, 101, 186, 253
state opening of parliament, 63, 247
staten island, 104-105, 150, 528
stephen austin, 823-824
stocks, 98, 185, 187, 318
storming of the bastille, 609-610, 614, 622, 647
strait of belle isle, 102, 105
strait of canso, 102
strait of kerch, 404
strangers, 137, 141, 143-145, 149, 200, 398, 593
streltsy uprising, 405, 481
suez canal, 641
sugar act, 498, 500, 503
sugarcane, 29-31, 677, 719
suleiman, 158, 372-378, 380-383, 385, 387, 389, 399, 681
sullivan expedition, 547-548, 690
sultanate of women, 383
sun king, 218, 220-223, 225, 423-424, 715
sun of austerlitz, 682
supreme central junta, 724, 726
supreme court, 564, 567-568, 634, 657-659, 740, 751, 758, 807, 851
susan constant, 72-73, 77, 82-83, 131, 230, 863
susanna wesley, 451
susquehanna, 69, 256, 625
susquehannock, 122, 256-257, 259-261, 457
sutter's fort, 845-846, 861
sutter's mill, 844-848
swamp fox, 543
sweden, 156, 164, 166-168, 170-174, 218-219, 223, 231-233, 235, 256, 285, 292, 399, 401-402, 407-409, 411-412, 448, 471, 474-475, 479, 633, 680, 683, 701
switzerland, 41, 43, 46, 67, 201, 609, 713, 845
sydney, 577-578, 583, 590-592
syed brothers, 761
synod of dort, 211-212

T

taconics, 150
tadoussac, 112, 114
tahiti, 580-582, 586, 588, 590, 593-598
tahiti syndrome, 593
taino, 17, 20, 31, 717, 722
taiwan, 577, 772-773
taj mahal, 351, 355-358, 763-764, 863-864
takamatsu castle, 331-332
tales of mother goose, 225
tallmadge amendment, 795
tallow, 233, 520, 525
tamerlane, 350, 763
tang dynasty, 304-305, 315
tangram, 782
tappan zee, 150, 153, 531
tariff, 362, 629, 759, 780
tariff act of 1789, 629
tarring and feathering, 630
tasmanian devil, 864
tatar, 395-397, 399
taxation without representation, 498, 501-503, 507, 558, 630
tchaikovsky, 487
tea act, 498, 507-508
tecumseh, 691-698, 737, 812
tecumseh's confederacy, 693-695, 698, 812
temple, 21, 279, 306-307, 309, 331-332, 373, 400, 619, 625, 635
temple name, 306-307, 309
templo mayor, 21-22, 30
tennessee, 27-29, 81, 444, 470, 488, 490-491, 495, 576, 675, 691, 732, 739-742, 744, 758, 784, 794-795, 825-827, 840, 862
tennis court oath, 608-609, 625
tenochtitlan, 21-23, 30, 37, 813
tenskwatawa, 692-693, 695, 698
tepee, 38, 469, 673
tercio, 20, 167
teutonic knights, 421-422
texas, 25, 27, 38-39, 416, 665, 676-677, 743, 813-814, 821-825, 827-828, 830-831, 834-836, 840, 843-844, 861-862, 864
texas declaration of independence, 828, 830
texas revolution, 821-822, 824-825, 827, 830-831
thaddeus kosciusko, 537
thanksgiving, 148-149, 574-575, 649
the american crisis, 532
the devil in new england, 342
the discovery of india, 768

the discovery of witches, 341, 343-344
the war feeds itself, 164-165
thermidorian reaction, 637-640
third coalition, 647-648, 679-680, 723
third english civil war, 237, 240, 258, 294, 319
third estate, 606-609, 612, 614, 625
third supply, 85-88, 176
thirty years' war, 51, 56, 150, 156-157, 159-161, 163-166, 168, 170-171, 173-174, 177, 179-180, 218-220, 223, 232-233, 235, 373, 387, 392, 401, 407-408, 419, 422, 428, 433, 448, 472
thomas clarkson, 801-802
thomas coke, 628, 753
thomas coutts incident, 779
thomas dale, 98-99
thomas dermer, 141
thomas gage, 504, 506, 510
thomas gates, 86, 89-90
thomas gilmer, 839
thomas hooker, 189, 201-203, 265, 448
thomas hunt, 140, 145
thomas jefferson, 56, 488, 496, 519, 556, 561, 627, 634-635, 647, 651-656, 660-661, 666, 675, 678, 706, 725, 733, 735, 758, 788, 790-793, 796, 798, 834, 850-851
thomas jesup, 749
thomas paine, 264, 277, 517, 532, 551, 725
thomas percy, 63-64
thomas preston, 505
thomas roe, 362
thomas rolfe, 94
thomas west, 85-86, 90, 326
thomas, lord fairfax, 458
thoreau, 835
thornton affair, 831
three great unifiers of japan, 329
three musketeers, 223
three sacred treasures, 327
three-fifths compromise, 563, 795
tiananmen, 311
tianxia, 773, 776
tijuana, 813
tilly, 164-166, 168-171, 173-174, 435
time of troubles, 400-402
tituba, 343-344
to the people of texas and all americans in the world, 827

tobacco, 29, 81, 86-87, 91-94, 99-101, 112, 187, 246, 250, 253, 256-257, 278, 295, 391-393, 495, 670, 736, 776, 786, 863
tokugawa, 328-329, 335-339
tokugawa iemitsu, 339
tokugawa ieyasu, 329, 335-336, 338
tokyo, 327, 335
tomocomo, 94
tortuga, 714
tory, 501
touch piece, 421
toussaint charbonneau, 670-671
toussaint louverture, 718-722, 823
townshend acts, 498, 501, 503-504, 506-507, 753
toyotomi hideyoshi, 313, 329-330, 334-335
trail of tears, 734, 747, 751, 759
transcendentalist, 835
transit of venus, 581-582
transvaal, 809-810
transylvania, 374, 491-492, 494
transylvania purchase, 491-492, 494
treaties of tilsit, 684
treaties of velasco, 830-831
treatise of reformation without tarrying for any, 130-131
treaty of 1646, 255, 267
treaty of aix-la-chapelle, 431, 452
treaty of alliance with france, 541
treaty of berwick, 60
treaty of camp charlotte, 687
treaty of campo formio, 641
treaty of easton, 464
treaty of fort stanwix, 489-491
treaty of fort wayne, 693-694
treaty of ghent, 704, 742
treaty of greenville, 690, 692-693, 696
treaty of hubertusburg, 479
treaty of nanjing, 780-781
treaty of new echota, 751
treaty of paris, 456, 465, 523, 547-549, 589, 627, 634, 651, 663, 688
treaty of pressburg, 682
treaty of ryswick, 423-425, 428, 714
treaty of schönbrunn, 684
treaty of shackamaxon, 290

treaty of sycamore shoals, 491-492
treaty of tordesillas, 16-18, 109, 360, 863
treaty of utrecht, 124, 365, 428, 430, 452
treaty of waitingi, 860
treaty port, 781
tree of great peace, 118, 465
triangle trade, 390, 863
tricolor cockade, 613, 864
trifle, 249
tripolitania, 378
true history of the captivity & restoration of mrs. mary rowlandson, 272
tuckahoe, 273
tuileries palace, 612-614, 618-619, 625
tulip, 57, 212, 495, 576, 705
tulipomania, 57
tumbril, 623, 637
tunisia, 378
turkestan, 371, 395
turkish oil-wrestling, 372
turnip townshend, 753
tuscaloosa, 28, 863
twelfth amendment, 566, 656-657
twenty-six martyrs of japan, 334
tzompantli, 21

U

u.s. capitol building, 80, 562, 599, 659, 703-704
umichand, 766
uncas, 207
union of arras, 55
union of the crowns, 59, 61-62, 419
union of the parliaments, 62, 418, 420
union of utrecht, 55-56
urim and thummim, 857
uss princeton, 839
ute, 38, 838
uttamatomakkin, 94-95, 97

V

vaccination, 633
valdivia, 19, 30
valiant sixty, 282
valide sultan, 384-385
valladolid debate, 33
valley forge, 233, 302, 539-542, 557, 632-633, 863
varangian-byzantine trade route, 395, 409
vasco de gama, 18, 360
venezuela, 92, 233, 723,

725-730
venus glass, 343
veracruz, 813, 821, 832
vermont, 102, 112, 179, 199, 277, 394, 448, 515, 536, 550, 691, 792, 795
verrazano, 104-105, 113, 150, 252
verrazano-narrows bridge, 104
versailles, 221-223, 225, 336, 472, 605-606, 608-609, 612-613, 623-625, 863
viceroyalty of new granada, 723, 728
viceroyalty of new spain, 23, 723, 729, 743, 814
viceroyalty of peru, 25, 723, 729
viceroyalty of the rio de la plata, 723, 727
village green, 185
vincente guerrero, 818-819
vineyard sound, 114, 139
virgin of guadalupe, 822
virginia, 36-37, 39, 60, 69-92, 94-101, 104, 110, 112-113, 115, 118, 122-123, 135-136, 141-142, 153, 155, 182, 187, 208, 227, 229, 236, 250, 253-265, 273, 288, 295, 302, 326, 369-370, 391-393, 444, 448, 454-460, 463, 488-489, 491, 494-495, 511, 518-519, 544, 546, 548, 554, 561-562, 569, 571-573, 576, 599-601, 626-628, 631-632, 655, 660, 666, 678, 693, 706, 733-734, 756, 786, 789-791, 795, 797-799, 812, 823, 825, 837, 850, 863
virginia company of london, 70-72, 82, 135, 141, 448
virginia company of plymouth, 71, 135-136, 182, 227
virginia convention, 511, 518
virginia peninsula, 70, 253-255, 546
virginia plan, 561-562, 628, 706
visakhapatnam, 760
vision quest, 469
vladimir the great, 395, 863
vodouisant, 716
voltaire, 290, 485, 496, 602-604, 614, 623, 635-636, 788, 814
von thurn, 160
voyageurs, 123-124
vulgate, 66-67

W

wabanaki confederacy, 425-427, 430, 456
wahunsonacock, 78-79, 253
waiting worship, 280, 282, 521
walking purchase, 292-293
wall of separation between church and state, 850-851
wall street, 234, 599
wallenstein, 164-166, 168, 170-172, 174, 180, 219
wallonia, 49, 155, 713
walloon, 155
walter raleigh, 60, 70, 91, 104
wampanoag, 38, 139-141, 145-148, 204-205, 207, 266-269, 271
wampum, 117, 119, 290, 863
wamsutta, 266-267
war bonnet, 509, 864
war hawk, 695-696
war of 1812, 370, 635, 678-679, 686, 691, 695-696, 698, 702, 704, 706, 733, 737, 741-742, 744, 758, 812, 823, 841, 864
war of jenkins' ear, 421, 452-454, 457, 471
war of the austrian succession, 421, 431, 434, 436, 452, 454, 471-472, 764, 804
war of the first coalition, 638, 641, 719, 724
war of the grand alliance, 301, 421, 423-425, 452, 471, 714
war of the second coalition, 644, 647
war of the spanish succession, 124, 301, 405, 421, 428-430, 436-437, 452, 471
war of twenty-seven years, 359-360, 363-364
washington d.c., 69, 562, 564, 567, 600, 652, 659, 703, 791, 837
washington's crossing, 348, 532-533
watt engine, 755
weenen massacre, 810
weighing ceremony, 359
weigi, 337
welland canal, 103
werowocomoco, 79-80, 82, 84
west point, 545-546
western confederacy, 687-690, 692-693
westminster assembly of divines, 213
westminster catechism, 265
wethersfield, 202, 226
wetu, 38
whale oil, 135, 808
whalebone, 808
what is the third estate?, 607
whiskey rebellion, 627, 629, 631-632, 666-667
whitman massacre, 843
whuppity scoorie, 421
whydah gally, 365-367, 863
wickiup, 38
wig, 225, 505
wigwam, 38
wilderness road, 492
willem janszoon, 579, 583
william adams, 338-339
william and mary, 299-301, 325, 733
william berkeley, 254, 256, 258-260
william bligh, 594-596
william bradford, 132, 141, 143, 146, 175
william brewster, 128, 131-133, 136, 143
william carey, 769-771, 783
william clark, 666-667, 675-676, 842
william davison, 131
william dawes, 512-513, 516
william dudingston, 506
william fairfax, 458
william henry harrison, 691-694, 697-698, 812, 837, 860
william howe, 527, 530, 538
william iii, 254, 298, 300, 325, 418, 420, 424
william kieft, 234
william laud, 181, 188-189, 195-196, 200-201
william leddra, 285
william miller, 855
william of gloucester, 418
william penn, 287-293, 302, 448, 521, 850, 863
william phipps, 344, 426
william pitt, 463-464
william robinson, 284-285
william the silent, 51-52, 54-57, 161, 298
william travis, 827-828
william tyndale, 67-68
william wilberforce, 801-805
williamsburg, 81, 156, 254, 627, 733
windsor, 202, 226, 230, 242
winfield scott, 832
wingfield, 77-78, 98-99, 131
winthrop fleet, 183-186, 188, 200, 203, 215, 273, 301
witch pins, 344-345
witch's cake, 343
witch's mark, 344-345
women's march on versailles, 612, 623
worcester v. georgia, 751
writ of assistance, 500
wu sangui, 316-317, 772

Y

yangtze, 303, 307, 771, 780
yellow river, 303, 771
yellow rose of texas, 830
yongle, 309
yuan dynasty, 305-307
yucatan peninsula, 813

Z

zakat, 359
zhu di, 309-313
zhu yuanzhang, 305-309, 311, 313, 781
zulu kingdom, 810